Inheritance Tax in Scotland 2016/17

Inheritance Tax in Scotland 2016/17

Fiona McDonald MA (Hons), LLB, Dip LP, ATT (Fellow), NP, Solicitor

Scottish Core Tax Annuals

Series Editor: **Donald Drysdale** CA, CTA (Fellow), TEP, MBCS CITP

Bloomsbury Professional

Bloomsbury Professional

An imprint of Bloomsbury Publishing Plc

Bloomsbury Professional Ltd
9–10 St Andrew Square
Edinburgh
EH2 2AF
UK

Bloomsbury Professional Ltd
41–43 Boltro Road
Haywards Heath
RH16 1BJ
UK

www.bloomsbury.com

BLOOMSBURY and the Diana logo are trademarks of Bloomsbury Publishing Plc

British Library Cataloguing-in-Publication Data

A catalogue record for this book is available from the British Library.

ISBN: PB: 9781 78451 188 3
ePDF: 9781 78451 350 4
ePub: 9781 78451 349 8

Typeset by Phoenix Photosetting, Chatham, Kent
Printed and bound in the United Kingdom by CPI Group (UK) Ltd, Croydon, CR0 4YY

Preface

There have been recent exciting changes and developments relating to inheritance tax and succession in Scotland and these are covered in this book which forms part of the Core Tax Annuals series from Bloomsbury Professional. This book explains how inheritance tax (IHT) operates in Scotland, and provides practical answers. It is designed to assist lawyers, accountants, other professionals and readers with an interest in IHT to comply with ever-increasing compliance challenges at a time when even innocent errors may bring retribution from either or both HMRC and disgruntled clients. This is why the first main chapter is an Overview of Scottish Issues for IHT, with comments on the law of Scotland and its impact on tax practice north of the border, and some pitfalls. Readers should understand that a short chapter of this kind cannot be comprehensive, and that it is able to provide only a summary of relevant pointers. However, it is hoped that the Overview is a useful alert both to Scottish practitioners and readers, and to practitioners and readers from other jurisdictions who need an understanding of Scottish principles. The law of IHT is covered in detail, with examples including charges, exemptions and reliefs, and the technicalities of the IHT trust regime, and, although it is not actually IHT, the pre-owned assets charge. Each client's circumstances are unique and specific advice should be sought to ensure that the law is interpreted correctly.

This book draws heavily on *Inheritance Tax 2016/17* published by Bloomsbury Professional, and ably written by Mark McLaughlin, Chris Erwood and Iris Wünschmann-Lyall, which annually provides an excellent guide to inheritance tax and its application across the UK, in particular as it applies in England and Wales. Those parts of the text where the Scottish position is identical have not been re-written, and indeed much of the original text has been retained. This book follows previous editions which were co-authored by Fiona McDonald and Bill Pagan.

Many thanks to Paula O'Connell of Bloomsbury Professional for her continued help and patience.

Fiona McDonald, October 2016

Contents

Table of examples

[*All references are to paragraph numbers*]

Chapter 6 Compliance

Chapter 7 Trusts: interest in possession

Chapter 8 Relevant property trusts

Table of statutes

[All references are to paragraph numbers]

Table of statutory instruments

[All references are to paragraph numbers]

Table of cases

[All references are to paragraph numbers]

D

E

F

G

H

T

U

V

W

List of abbreviations

A&M	accumulation and maintenance trust
ADS	additional dwelling supplement
AIM	alternative investment market
APR	agricultural property relief
ATED	annual tax on enveloped dwellings
BMT	bereaved minors trust
BPR	business property relief
CA	Court of Appeal
CGT	capital gains tax
CIOT	Chartered Institute of Taxation
CLT	capital lifetime transfer
CTT	capital transfer tax
DPI	Disabled Person's Interest Trust
FA	Finance Act
FSMA 2000	Financial Services and Markets Act 2000
GAAR	General anti-abuse rule
GWR	gift with reservation
HMRC	Her Majesty's Revenue and Customs
ICTA 1988	Income and Corporation Taxes Act 1988
IHT	Inheritance tax
IHTA 1984	Inheritance Tax Act 1984
IHTM	Inheritance Tax Manual
IPDI	immediate post-death interest
IRA	Inland Revenue Affidavit
IRC	Inland Revenue Commissioners
ITA 2007	Income Tax Act 2007
ITEPA 2003	Income Tax (Earnings and Pensions) Act 2003
ITTOIA 2005	Income Tax (Trading and Other Income) Act 2005
LBTT	Land & Buildings Transaction Tax
NNP	non-natural person
PET	potentially exempt transfer
POAT	pre-owned asset tax
QSR	quick succession relief
reg	Regulation
s	Section
Sch	Schedule
SDLT	stamp duty land tax
SLfT	Scottish landfill tax
SI	Statutory Instrument
SP	HMRC Statement of Practice
SRT	statutory residence test
SSCBA	Social Security Contributions and Benefits Act 1992

STEP	Society of Trust and Estate Practitioners
TA 1925	Taxes Act 1925
TCGA 1992	Taxation of Chargeable Gains Act 1992
TLATA 1996	Trusts of Land and Appointment of Trustees Act 1996
TSI	transitional serial interest

Inheritance Tax in Scotland 2016/17

A. OVERVIEW OF SCOTTISH ISSUES FOR IHT

A1 Introduction

A1.1 General Recent years have seen many developments in the field of tax for Scotland. The *Succession (Scotland) Act 2016* was eagerly awaited and it is anticipated that further provisions will follow which affect succession issues in Scotland and impact Inheritance Tax treatment and assessment.

Scotland's tax position continues to change with the political landscape. The No vote in the 2014 Independence vote led to the Smith Commission, and *The Scotland Act 2016*, which received Royal Assent on 23 March 2016, introduced the ability for a Scottish basic rate, higher rate, additional rate and rate bands for income tax purposes (*ss 13–15*). All other income tax aspects are reserved to the UK Parliament. Consideration now must be given to the question of who is a Scottish taxpayer.

UK-wide IHT has continued to be part of the wider political debate across the UK, while attitudes to tax planning have continued to harden, both in Government and in public opinion. The morality of tax planning remains an issue of public debate, with some newspapers continuing to equate 'avoidance', wrongly in law, with 'evasion'. High profile press exposure has become the risk to be assessed when considering legal options. Already in place are the UK's General Anti Abuse Rule ('GAAR') and the Disclosure of Tax Avoidance Schemes regime ('DOTAS'), extended to include IHT. Additionally the *Criminal Finances Bill*, which was introduced to the House of Commons in October 2016, proposes to introduce a new corporate criminal offence of failing to prevent the facilitation of tax evasion by a person associated with a body corporate or partnership. It is expected to come into force some time in 2017, imposing heavy administrative burdens on businesses, especially banks and trust companies.

A1.2 Recent Developments in Scotland The *Succession (Scotland) Act 2016* has brought in major changes, which impact succession planning and assessment and IHT. The changes are discussed throughout this book. They include divorce terminating the entitlement of a former spouse (apart from guardianship provisions), rectification of a Will which fails to accurately express a testator's wishes, treatment of legacies in relation to issue when the legacy fails to vest, vesting treatment for liferent trusts and presumptions of survivorship. There were many matters which had previously been recommended by the Scottish Law Commission (such as changes to the treatment of intestate estates) that were not dealt with in the Act, and it is anticipated that further consultation may take place.

The taxing powers of the Scottish Parliament were expanded by the (Westminster) *Scotland Act 2012*, following the Calman Commission and its resulting report. The Scottish Parliament's *Land and Buildings Transaction Tax (Scotland) Act 2013* (introducing 'LBTT') was the first taxing statute passed in Scotland since 1707. The *Landfill Tax (Scotland) Act 2014* introduced 'SLfT'. Despite the fact that the Annual Tax on Enveloped Dwellings ('ATED') was, at its introduction, justified as a measure to counter the avoidance of UK Stamp Duty Land Tax ('SDLT'), it continues to apply in Scotland despite LBTT having replaced SDLT in Scotland from 1 April 2015. The *Land and Buildings Transaction Tax (Amendment) (Scotland) Act 2016,* introducing the Additional Dwelling Supplement (ADS), came into force on 1 April 2016. It is a new LBTT supplement of 3% on purchases of additional residential properties in Scotland (such as buy-to-let properties and second homes) of £40,000 or more. The knock on effect of ADS means that testators need to carefully consider the impact of their succession wishes for beneficiaries who may purchase additional property at a later date.

A1.3 Scottish Tax Administration The framework for Scottish tax administration is in Holyrood's *Revenue Scotland and Tax Powers Act 2014*, the Scottish equivalent of the UK's *Taxes Management Act 1970.* This Act established Scotland's equivalent of HMRC, 'Revenue Scotland', a non-ministerial department which reports to the Scottish Parliament. It has created a comprehensive structure for Scotland's future tax system, whether devolved or independent. It includes a Scottish General Anti-Avoidance Rule, nicknamed 'McGAAR', which is wider and stricter than the UK-wide GAAR. The GAAR is Anti-*Abuse*, while McGAAR is Anti-*Avoidance*. The Law Society of Scotland argued that the McGAAR regime should have included a formal Advisory Panel, with expert members, and a requirement for Revenue Scotland to publish guidance on their interpretation and practice. At the strategic level it is welcome that the Scottish Government, in part following suggestions from the Law Society of Scotland, has adopted administrative streamlining, by giving Registers of Scotland and the Scottish Environment Protection Agency certain responsibilities for LBTT and SLfT respectively, while leaving Revenue Scotland with the overall responsibility for the administration and collection of Scottish taxes. It is hard to disagree with the four tax principles which were contained in the Independence White Paper, namely simplicity, neutrality, stability, and flexibility, the 21st century's equivalents of Adam

Smith's four maxims: certainty, convenience, efficiency and proportionality (the ability to pay). Scottish taxpayers will hope that these principles will be followed whatever the future of the continuing debate on Fiscal Autonomy – or even Independence.

Revenue Scotland and Tax Powers Act 2014 (Pt 4 and *Sch 2)* also introduced Scottish Tax Tribunals, with the First-tier Tax Tribunal for Scotland and the Upper Tax Tribunal for Scotland to exercise functions in relation to devolved taxes such as LBTT and SLfT. The UK tax tribunals continue to sit in Scotland in relation to all UK taxes.

A1.4 Implications of Independence Had there been a Yes vote in 2014 (or if there is one in the future) there would have been wide-ranging implications, not least on issues such as Domicile and Residence for Tax purposes in the context of existing UK Tax and UK Tax reliefs. For example, reliefs such as Conditional Exemption from IHT require the items to be retained in a part of the UK. It is not clear how an owner of such assets would have been treated if the owner was domiciled in the remainder of the UK ('rUK') but the assets are physically held by him, or on his behalf – perhaps on public display – in an independent Scotland.

A1.5 Scots Law Principles This book is needed because of differences between some general rules of Scots Law and practice and their English, Welsh and Northern Irish equivalents, most of these differences arising from Scotland's distinct legal history rather than detailed enactments. For taxes, the constitutional and jurisprudential background starts with the principle that UK tax law should be applied on both sides of the border in an equivalent way to equivalent circumstances. Tax is itself law and it can be applied only to the legal situation. An example is in the different land laws, so where, in colloquial language, a client could truthfully say on the same day 'I have today bought a farm in England' and 'I have today bought a farm in Scotland' the IHT treatment of his two purchases would not be the same. The summaries of general Scots Law provided in this book are there solely to alert Scottish readers to the possibilities of tax differences or traps, and other readers to relevant points of difference in Scots Law. They are not to be relied on as definitive statements of Scots Law.

A1.6 The Wider View Practitioners are required to think strategically, and, ever more frequently, to look outside their own specific jurisdictions in order to give proper advice to their clients. Assets are found across the globe – for example the right to a 'Digital Asset' (assuming it is an asset at all) may be governed by the laws of a foreign state, despite the owner having dealt with a *dot.uk* site for the 'purchase'. The US State of Delaware was the first US state to grant deceased residents' executors the right to take over the deceased's digital assets – such as email, social media accounts, downloads and online bank accounts. For UK IHT there will be questions over the valuation of digital assets wherever those assets may be legally or practically based.

A1.7 Changes The new *EU Succession Regulation (EU/650/2012)* enabling testators to determine the law to apply to the succession of their estates is now in force. Although the UK has not opted in there can be implications for UK domiciled clients owning properties in other EU Member States, and practitioners will need to be alert to the Succession rules and thus the Tax implications, and continue to watch for other possible changes. For example, in the purely UK context, it is, on the one hand, not that long since the UK government was promising such high IHT thresholds as to make IHT payable by only the highly privileged very few, yet it is on the other hand, not that long since there was speculation that the spouse exemption might be doomed. In fact, IHT is now payable by many more citizens' estates and the threshold has been frozen – but by contrast both spouses' exemptions have been preserved. Practitioners should never assume continuity.

The new residence nil rate band (see **Chapter 14**) being introduced from 6 April 2017 brings changes that impact IHT and requires testators to consider the implications for their estates and indeed their lifetime choices with the detail behind the legislation.

A1.8 Scottish Government and Succession The Scottish Government has given attention to succession over recent years including consultation papers on reviewing the financial limits of prior rights (which led to the uprating in thresholds – see **Table 3.1a**) and reviewing succession following the Scottish Law Commission's Report on the Law of Succession 2009 which was partially implemented in the Succession (Scotland) Act 2016. A further consultation on the Scottish Law Commission's proposals for a new scheme for intestacy, protection from disinheritance under a will and extended rights for cohabitants was published in 2015, the results of which have not yet been released.

The Scottish Government worked with the Ministry of Justice to develop a joined up UK position in relation to the EU Succession Regulation proposals (see **A1.7**) and jointly chose not to opt in to the Regulation.

A1.9 Existing Impact of Devolution Holyrood has no power over UK tax legislation, but has had the power, under the *Scotland Act 2012*, to set the Scottish Rate of Income Tax ('SRIT') since April 2016. The *Scotland Act 2016* (*ss 13–15*) provide for there to be a Scottish income tax rates and bands but allowances and the base for income to be charged may not be altered from the UK amounts. Individuals are assessed against the definition of a Scottish taxpayer and trusts are treated as not being Scottish taxpayers (although their beneficiaries may be). HMRC have helpful guidance and illustrations for employers, agents and taxpayers. Care should be taken in applying the definition as the main residence test differs from the CGT test of main residence.

A1.10 A Continuing Example – Charities There are continuing issues in the law of charities in Scotland, and their tax treatment. The 15 specific charitable purposes spelt out in the *Charities & Trustee Investment (Scotland) Act 2005* are not identical to either the previous or the charitable purposes in England and Wales. The tax exemptions for charities stem principally from *ss 505* and *506* of the *Income and Corporation Taxes Act 1988* (*ICTA*), where the definitions of charitable purposes are those which are recognised in England and Wales. Scottish charities are not guaranteed UK tax exemption, and the Office of the Scottish Charity Regulator ('OSCR') has no control over the UK tax treatment of the charities in its stable. OSCR will not automatically accept as charitable a trust established in Scotland whose purposes are to support causes which qualify for UK charitable tax exemption, and at least one charity failed this test during one of OSCR's earliest Rolling Reviews. The corollary is that the family of a testator who has left a substantial proportion of his estate to a Scottish charity, or on charitable trusts set up by his will and qualifying as charitable in OSCR's eyes, would not be best pleased to find that the IHT exemption did not apply because HMRC did not recognise the purposes as charitable. It is not an anomaly which one would have expected to follow from Devolution: the constitutional principle – that UK taxes should be applied in an equivalent way to equivalent legal situations north and south of the border – has not changed. Specifically on the charity issue, the House of Lords in *IRC v Glasgow Police Athletic Association* held that 'charity' should have the same meaning in Scotland as in the rest of the UK – in other words that the English definition should apply. Logically, this should now change since Scotland has its own Charity Code. HMRC have developed the practice of requiring an application to OSCR (whether or not successful) before they will consider an application for tax exemption, which is an inconvenience for those seeking only tax exemption. See **A7** for further discussion on charities, and **A7.2** in particular for the position following the joint OSCR and HMRC statement of 19 February 2008. Note that Scottish charities (registered with OSCR) do qualify for reliefs from Rates, and, under Schedule 13 of *Land and Buildings Transaction Tax (Scotland) Act 2013*, from LBTT on purchases, since these are Scottish taxes.

A2 Terminology, Administration and Enforcement

A2.1 Definitions UK legislation tends to be drafted with English terminology; for example, the general definitions section, *s 272* of the *Inheritance Tax Act 1984 (IHTA)*, contains provisions such as 'Barrister' including a member of the Scottish Faculty of Advocates, that 'mortgage' includes a heritable security, and specifically states that 'charity' has the same meaning as in the Income Tax Acts. Care is needed to check the Scottish position.

A2.2 Scottish Forms Similarly *Section 261 IHTA* provides that for *Inventories in Scotland* references to an account are construed as under the *Probate and Legacy Duties Act 1808*. The forms for Scottish estates (see **6.2**) differ to those for individuals domiciled in England and Wales and again care is needed.

A2.3 Valuation Principles The main principles of valuation for IHT purposes are the same in Scotland as south of the border. HMRC consider 'wrong' valuations as a major risk to the correct collection of IHT. While this will commonly be in the context of heritable property which is being transferred rather than sold, in the eyes of HMRC it is increasingly an issue for moveables, including works of art. Some auction houses have responded by separating their valuation arms from their selling arms.

Official Valuers argue that in Scotland the 10–15% discount for common ownership of property should not be available, because Scottish common owners have the right to apply to Court for an Action of Division and Sale, by which the Court will, unless there are compelling reasons not to, order that the entire property is sold. See **A6.6** for further discussion on common property. In practice, HMRC's starting point has been a flat £4,000 deduction, deemed to represent the costs of an action for Division & Sale. While £4,000 may be acceptable in cases of less valuable common property, there will be cases where taxpayers will wish to argue strongly for a percentage. The Law Society of Scotland has suggested to HMRC that the discount for common property in Scotland should be 10%. Valuation is, in HMRC's view, the duty of the District Valuer, who should allow what he or she considers to be an appropriate discount in the circumstances, and so HMRC say that they should then not allow any further discount – see IHTM15072. This moves the legal debate from HMRC, with whom it should take place, into the office of a valuer.

There are also valuation differences for joint bank accounts governed by Scots Law in considering the ownership of the funds (IHTM15054) (see **4.21**).

A2.3.1 Practical Valuation Issues Delays in valuation can cause serious problems if the taxpayer seeks to acquire replacement property, for example a farm as a successor property for Agricultural Property Relief. There is no problem if the first property has been sold in the market, but where it has been compulsorily acquired it may take many years before the compensation has been agreed with the District Valuer. This is an issue which similarly frequently affects Capital Gains Tax liabilities and reliefs. The *Community Empowerment (Scotland) Act 2015* includes extended communities' rights to buy, at prices fixed by valuation, so this creates other occasions for concern in this area. The Act envisages that the vehicle for purchase may be a Scottish Charitable Incorporated Organisation ('SCIO'). The *Land Reform (Scotland) Act 2016* is intended to provide greater transparency and engagement also creates equivalent valuation concerns. The Scottish Government has indicated that it intends to take a phased approach to the implementation of the Act as significant parts require further regulation. The Act has also proposed succession and assignation changes to agricultural holdings which will affect entitlements and subsequently IHT.

A2.4 Enforcement *Finance Act 2007, s 23* imported into Scotland a code equivalent to that in England and Wales so that, in practice, enforcement operates in an almost identical way on both sides of the border. *Section 128 Finance Act 2008* strengthened HMRC's powers under Summary Warrant procedure.

A3 Wills and Succession

A3.1 Format of Wills In Scotland, the normal signing of a will is by the testator on every page (including every page of any Schedules attached) before a single witness who signs on the last page of the will itself only. Witnesses in Scotland must be over 16, and should not be close relatives, or executors or beneficiaries named in the will. While a will can be formally valid if signed on only the last page, the Deed cannot be 'self proving' under *s 3* of the *Requirements of Writing (Scotland) Act 1995* and proof of execution would have to be led before a Court on the balance of probabilities (this can create delays, expense and difficulties such as in the recent case of *Hamilton Petitioner* 2015 SCEDIN45, 2015 GWD 20-354, 2015 SLT (Sh Ct) 176). While it is not a legal requirement, many Scots solicitors still use two witnesses on Wills which are going to be seen by English authorities or English professionals. It is common to insert in a will that the domicile of the testator is Scottish, and that the will is to be interpreted and given effect according to the law of Scotland, although this is not conclusive for either general law or tax law.

The English *Wills Act 1837* which creates privileged wills for those on military service, merchant seamen and the like, does not apply in Scotland. The Roman Law *testamentum militare* probably does however still apply in Scotland – *Stuart v Stuart 1942*. Since Military Law for the Armed Forces of the United Kingdom is English law, and will forms are issued to service men and women, many Scots will assume that these provisions apply to them – which for purposes of creating the will they usually will. Such a will cannot however deprive spouses, civil partners and children or their legal entitlements – see **A3.6**, **A3.7** and **A3.8** below – and the IHT consequences will be determined by those entitlements, unless they are competently renounced or varied.

A3.2 Treatment of Divorce, Annulment or Dissolution in relation to Wills and Special Destinations The *Succession (Scotland) Act 2016, s 1* introduced that if a marriage is terminated by divorce or annulment, or a civil partnership is terminated in the event of dissolution or annulment, then the former spouse/civil partner is treated as having died before the testator for the purposes of a will other than any appointment as a guardian. Prior to this none of divorce, annulment nor dissolving a civil partnership revoked a will.

In Scotland, wills are not automatically revoked by the birth of children – but see **A3.6** below. Spouses, civil partners and children have rights in Scots law – see **A3.6** and **A3.8** – as may those who have been cohabiting without the formality of marriage or civil partnership – see **A3.7**. However, if an individual dies after their marriage is terminated by divorce or annulment, or their civil partnership is terminated by dissolution or annulment, and title to heritable property they own with their former spouse or civil partner contains a Special Destinations then *s 2* of the *Succession (Scotland) Act 2016,* treats the former spouse as having predeceased.

A3.3 Ages of Competence, Capacity and Majority A Scot from age 12 onwards can competently make a will. Age 16 is the age of Legal Capacity, but since contracts and equivalent entered into between the 16th and 18th birthdays can be challenged by the child until he reaches 21, great care is needed in dealing with those aged between 16 and 18 – for example Disclaimers and the signing of Instruments of Variation may be challenged by the child until the end of that period. For most practical purposes, the age of majority in Scotland is 18, the only exception being that in children's trusts the period of minority may end at 21 for a child already born at the date of the deed or the relevant death – making it possible to accumulate income until such a child reaches age 21. This was a useful period in Accumulation & Maintenance settlements for Scottish children before *Finance Act 2006, Sch 20*, and may still be helpful in 18-to-25 Trusts as introduced by that Act. If a child was aged four or over at the relevant time, a 21 year period of accumulation will last until at least age 25.

A3.4 Presumption of Death The *Succession (Scotland) Act 2016, ss 9–11* and the *Presumption of Death (Scotland) Act 1977* deal with presumption of death matters. The rules are important for establishing who is entitled to inherit and subsequently the IHT treatment.

Where two people die simultaneously or in circumstances in which it is uncertain who survived whom, each is treated as having failed to survive the other for all purposes affecting title or succession to property.

Where property is to pass or be transferred to the estate of whichever member of a group of persons dies first (or the estates of whichever members die first), whichever member of a group of persons survives the other members or the members of a group of persons equally or the survivor (or survivors) of them and two (or more) of the members of the group die simultaneously or in circumstances in which the order of death is uncertain, the property is to be divided equally among the estates of the members of the group who die simultaneously.

Many wills, in Scotland as elsewhere, require a minimum period of survivance before benefit can be taken under them. *Section 11* of the *Succession (Scotland) Act 2016* provides that if the beneficiary survives the testator but dies in circumstances in which it remains uncertain whether the person survived for the specified period, the person is to be treated as having failed to have survived the testator for the specified period.

Where an individual has not been known to be alive for at least seven years, a Court Action can be raised for a declaration that the person is deemed to have died on the seventh anniversary of the date on which he was last known to be alive.

A3.5 Children and their Status Adopted children are treated as natural children, and the status of illegitimacy has been abolished, except for some purposes of Domicile.

Children who have been adopted do not have the right to claim legal rights (see **A3.8** and **Chapter 3**) in their birth parents' estates. However, for the purposes of the residence nil rate band adopted children are treated as lineal descendants of their birth parents.

A3.6 Presumption in Favour of After-born Children and issue If a will makes no provision for children, but a child or children are subsequently born, Scots law has protected them by the *conditio si testator sine liberis decesserit.* This provides a rebuttable presumption that the will should be revoked on the assumption that the testator would not have intended to fail to make provision for his children. The presumption can be rebutted if there is evidence that he did intend to exclude the child (possibly for example if the will was prepared while he was aware that there was a child *in utero*). The *conditio* is not automatically applicable, and revocation occurs only when the will is challenged by the child. Before making such a challenge, which would lead to intestacy, the child will have to consider the rights of the other parent if surviving, since the intestacy rules may benefit the surviving spouse to the exclusion of the child, including the child's *legitim* claim – see **A3.8**.

Section 6 of the new *Succession (Scotland) Act 2016* provides that where the testator by a will bequeaths a legacy to a direct descendant (or more than one person all of whom are direct descendants) and that beneficiary (or one of the beneficiaries) is alive when the will is executed but fails to survive the date of vesting of the legacy then any issue of the deceased beneficiary alive when the legacy would have vested is entitled to receive the legacy unless it is clear from the terms of the will that the testator intended otherwise.

A3.7 Cohabitants The *Family Law (Scotland) Act 2006* provides important rights, both on death and on separation, for those who have been cohabiting. Death claims may be made only where the cohabitant died intestate. Where the conditions are met, an individual may cohabit for these purposes while still married – or even cohabit with more than one cohabitant while still married (or in civil partnership). Claims of cohabitants, which are within the discretion of the Court and at most will be equivalent to Legal Rights, must be made within six months of the death, and until that period has passed neither the Executors nor HMRC Inheritance Tax should assume the estate distribution (or the assumed Legal Rights claims of a spouse or children) will be implemented as expected. The rights of cohabitants are deferred to Prior and Legal Rights. The rights can be claimed only against the estate of someone domiciled in Scotland, and, in the case of heritable or real property, only against such property if it is in Scotland – *Kerr v Mangan* [2014] CSIH 69, 2014 SLT 866.

A3.8 Legal Rights and Legitim Where there is a will, Legal Rights are available only against Moveable (Personal) property.

Where there is a surviving spouse or civil partner and a child or children, the net Moveable estate after payment of debts is divisible one third to the spouse or civil partner, one third among the children (and representatives of predeceasing children) and one third to the testator's selected beneficiaries (or if there is no will in accordance with the laws of intestacy).

If there is only a spouse or only a child or children then the split is a half to that surviving spouse/child or among the children.

Accordingly, a will which leaves everything to a surviving spouse will not, where there are children, necessarily achieve that, and the children's claims – known as *legitim* – may bring the estate into IHT, as may claims of cohabitants. Where a child has died, his descendants take in his place. Note that partnership property is moveable in succession and therefore susceptible to Legal Rights (see the recent case of *Miller v Pollock* [2016] ScotCS CSOH 30). This is a trap for those dealing with family businesses, particularly farms where banks are often keen to see the farm introduced to the Balance Sheet. Before the changes to IHT on Trusts in 2006, settlor-interested trusts were commonly used by testators to avoid these rules. See **A5.7.**

Prior Rights apply only in intestacy and provide spouses and civil partners with specific rights over the estate which have priority over Legal Rights.

In April 2009 the Scottish Law Commission published their Report on Succession recommending reform aimed at simplifying the Scottish Succession rules accounting for modern day family structures. The proposed changes included the abolition of the distinction between heritable and moveable property, with the consequential amendment of inheritance entitlements. The current testate and intestate rules for Scottish domiciled individual's estates and the application of Prior Rights and Legal Rights, along with details of the proposed reform are outlined in more detail in **Chapter 3**. The ending of the distinction between heritable and moveable property was recommended also by the Land Reform Review Group. The recommendations were not included in the *Succession (Scotland) Act 2016* and further consultation is anticipated.

A3.9 Disclaimers and Renunciations Partial Disclaimers and Partial Renunciations are competent in Scotland. A Disclaimer is competent only before the interest is taken up, while a Renunciation is of an interest already being enjoyed. Disclaimers are exempted by *s 93* of *IHTA* where the interest is created on a death, while a Renunciation is a gift (in practice most likely to be a Potentially Exempt Transfer ('PET') because in most cases the property renounced will pass to an individual or individuals). It will be exempt if the property renounced falls to a Charity, but chargeable if it passes to any Trust other than a Disabled Trust. Wills commonly provide that interests in possession to surviving spouses may be disclaimed in whole or in part or renounced in whole or in part and from time to time – meaning that a series of partial Disclaimers and Renunciations will be competent. Disclaimers and Renunciations will usually be Potentially Exempt Transfers subject to the Gifts With Reservation rules and, up to 5 October 2008, may have created one or more Transitional Serial Interests.

A3.10 Instruments of Variation (IOVs) and Vesting Issues The concept of varying a testator's will after his death was new to Scotland in 1974, with the arrival of Capital Transfer Tax and the need for testators and their advisers to have time to make tax-efficient wills in the new circumstances. Only those whose interests have vested (whether they are immediately payable or are deferred) can competently vary those interests. Normally, HMRC will challenge only in cases where potential beneficiaries whose rights are being reduced are not parties to the deed or lack capacity to sign it, for example where the rights to be reduced are of children under 16. A will which leaves half the estate to the surviving spouse and half to the children, made at a time when it was assumed IHT would not be an issue, may bring the estate into IHT. HMRC will not accept an IOV signed by a child younger than 16 (or children younger than 16 of a predeceasing child) where the child's interests are reduced, but may accept an IOV signed by a parent or guardian. Strictly, the correct – and safe – procedure is an application to Court. HMRC would in any event question carefully what the surviving spouse then did with his or her increased share of the estate, and if the increase was re-directed back to the children by a PET (as in *Executor of Werner Lau Deceased v HMRC* [2009] WTLR 627), HMRC might claim tax on the basis of the will as originally drafted, treating the IOV as a sham, or an Associated Operation as defined in *s 268 IHTA* or amounting to consideration. Such claims should be resisted.

Deeds of variation are considered to be potentially under threat from future legislative changes; however, in December 2015 HMRC stated in their *Review of Deeds of Variation for Tax Purposes* that 'the Government would not introduce new restrictions on how deeds of variation can be used for tax purposes but would continue to monitor their use'.

A3.11 Nil Rate Band Debt Arrangements For IHT the principles behind Nil Rate Band Discretionary Trusts in Wills are the same in Scotland as in England, as are the principles of the debt or IOU arrangements. For the debt to be validly constituted, it must be enforceable, meaning that it must include calculation of the amount due, state when it is due and payable, and to whom it is payable. The duty of Scottish spouses to aliment each other may help arguments with HMRC over levels of contribution by each spouse if it becomes necessary to consider whether transfers have been made from one spouse to another making a debt non-deductible under *s 103 Finance Act 1986*. The *Phizackerly* decision may not be the major problem in Scotland that it was initially at least perceived to be in England.

A4 The Elderly and Disabled in Scotland

A4.1 Powers of Attorney Scotland has had, since 2001, the sorts of protection for those granting Powers of Attorney which were introduced in England in October 2007. In Scotland, Powers of Attorney granted after 1 January 1991 have been able to confer continuing power on the Attorney even if the granter becomes *incapax*. A Power granted before that date is ineffective if the grantor becomes *incapax* – the old principle being one of Agency, under which the grantor has to be in a position to ratify the actings of his agent. By contrast, those granted on or after 2 April 2001 continue in effect after the grantor's incapacity, but only if the requirements of the *Adults with Incapacity (Scotland) Act 2000* are complied with, including registration with the Office of the Public Guardian (Scotland). For a time it was thought that registration would not cure defects in the deed, because of the decision of Sheriff Baird in the case of *NW* (see AW39/14 [2014] SC GLA 1). The position was clarified by the Inner House in a Special Case referred by the Office of the Public Guardian (*Special Case between Great Stuart Trustees Ltd and the Public Guardian* [2014] CSIH 114), in which the recommended wording was held to be appropriate.

An attorney is not able to give will instructions nor sign a will, even if there is a purported power to do so within the Power of Attorney document itself. This is the situation in Scotland no matter what date the Power of Attorney has been signed or whether it is continuing or not. In the case of *T Applicant* 2005 SLT (Sh Ct) 97 the Sheriff authorised the use of an Intervention Order, as defined by *s 53* of the *Adults with Incapacity (Scotland) Act 2000*, allowing the solicitor of an adult to execute a codicil to her will in circumstances where the necessity to correct a difficulty created by the wording of the original testamentary provision had arisen. In the 2009 case of *Application in respect of JG* 2009 SLT (Sh Ct) 122 (see also http://www.scotcourts.gov.uk/opinions/AW259.html) the Sheriff authorised the complete re-writing of a will, based on the known intentions of the testator, imperfectly expressed. These are relatively recent developments and it will be interesting to see how this area develops in Scotland. In addition to recording the adult's wishes there will be IHT planning reasons for making testamentary changes.

A4.2 Gifts by Attorneys For the tax planner, the rules in Scotland are conveniently more flexible, allowing Attorneys, without any form of Court or equivalent authority, to make gifts for tax planning purposes, provided that specific power is included in the Power of Attorney itself. If that is the case, the Attorney may therefore make gifts of capital and not only routine small gifts which the grantor may have been in the habit of making at Christmas or birthdays or equivalent. The Attorney may establish a new course of Normal & Reasonable Gifts out of Income. The importance of having adequate power specified by the grantor is emphasised by *McDowall's Executors v IRC [2004] STC (SCD) 22.*

A4.3 Care Costs and Alienation of Assets The Scottish Government offers elements of free personal and nursing care to those who have been assessed as requiring such. Whilst this assistance has taken some of the pressure off the scrutiny of gifts made by the elderly to see whether they amount to alienation of assets done to avoid assessment for care costs, local authorities have strict financial assessment criteria. While tax planning may save up to 40%, care may cost almost 100% – and tax planning is not always considered by the authorities in Scotland as an adequate reason for alienation.

Turner v Turner [2012] CSOH 41 has provided clarity on how the sale of a property by an Attorney during an Adult's lifetime is dealt with in the administration of the Adult's estate on death which in turn determines the IHT position. If it is necessary for the heritage to be sold during lifetime in order to fund the care of the Adult then ademption will apply on death to the legacy in the will of the property and the bequest of the property will fall. However if the sale during lifetime was not necessary and the Attorney simply sold the property for ease of administration and not out of financial necessity then the funds realised from the sale of the property are in effect ring-fenced to form the legacy on death (unless of course the funds are required at a later stage to provide care).

A4.4 Definitions of Physical and Mental Disability Holyrood enacted the *Adult Support and Protection (Scotland) Act 2007*. The rules for physical disability, for both tax and benefit purposes, are broadly the same in both Scotland and England. For tax purposes, the new *ss 89, 89A* and *89B* of *IHTA* are intended to operate in the same way in both Scotland and England.

A4.5 Personal Injury Trusts Apart from the implications of the Scottish legislation on Mental Incapacity, and doubts over the use of Bare Trusts, the rules for Personal Injury Trusts are thought to be much the same in both Scotland and England. A major purpose of a well established Personal Injury Trust is to preserve benefits rather than mitigate tax, though the tax issues must be considered from the outset.

A5 Trusts in Scotland

A5.1 Definition of 'Settlement' The terms 'Settlement' and 'Settled Property' do not in Scotland have the technical meanings it is understood that they do in England. *Section 43(4) IHTA* contains an extended definition of 'settlement' for Scotland, to include entails (abolished with effect from 28 November 1994 by the *Abolition of Feudal Tenure (Scotland) Act 2000*), a deed charging an annuity on property, and a deed creating a Proper Liferent, with 'deed' – not such a term of art as in English law – stated to include any disposition, arrangement, contract, resolution, instrument or writing. Since *s 43(4)* states what is deemed to be included in relation to Scotland, the remainder of *s 43* also applies, including a lease for life – an important factor in Scotland where leases of domestic property for terms of more than 20 years are prohibited by the *Land Tenure Reform (Scotland) Act 1974* and the *Abolition of Feudal Tenure (Scotland) Act 2000*. While some ancient leases of domestic property for longer than 20 years still survive in specific areas, the Scottish Law Commission, in December 2006, published proposals – including draft legislation – for such tenants' rights to be converted into rights of ownership.

A Scottish Trust requires the full transfer of ownership of the Trust assets to the Trustees against whom the beneficiaries have only personal rights, but those personal rights take priority over creditors of the Trustees. A beneficiary's interest in the capital of a Scottish Trust may be any one of:

A5.1.1 Absolute, but not yet actually paid over – for example a liferenter may have died, with the result that the capital beneficiaries who have survived to the due date are entitled but the Trust is still being administered.

A5.1.2 Vested but not yet payable – for example where under a will the children who survive the testator are to take capital but that entitlement is deferred during the lifetime of their mother who has a liferent.

A5.1.3 Contingent and not yet vested – for example where a capital beneficiary has to survive a liferenter in order to become entitled to the capital, and the liferenter is still alive.

For IHT purposes, the tests are whether the capital is aggregable with the liferenter's estate (a pre-22 March 2006 liferent, a Transitional Serial Interest, an Immediate Post Death Interest, or a liferented Disabled Trust) or whether the Trust assets are in the Relevant Property Regime, liable to ten year charges and not treated as in the estate of any Trust beneficiary.

Section 7 of the *Succession (Scotland) Act 2016* provides that where a liferent terminates other than on the death of the liferenter, if the fee has not vested in the fiar by the date of termination of the liferent, the fee vests in the fiar on that date unless the document creating the liferent expressly provides otherwise or there is an obligation providing otherwise.

The Scottish Law Commission has undertaken a wide-ranging review of Scottish Trust Law examining the Law relating to trustees and the Law governing Trusts themselves. Their report was published in August 2014 covering the majority of the topics which had been consulted on, and contains a draft Trusts (Scotland) Bill.

A5.2 Majority of Trustees a Quorum Though Scottish and English Trusts are not approached historically from the same origins, and have separate statutory codes, for tax purposes Trusts operate in much the same way in both Scotland and England. One important distinction in practice is that, under *s 3* of the *Trusts (Scotland) Act 1921*, a majority of Trustees is a quorum with full power to act. All Trustees must be consulted, and it is insufficient for a majority of Trustees to act without consultation on the basis that they know they can outvote the others. Under *s 7*, a deed signed by a quorum cannot be challenged, unless there is bad faith. Some Trusts contain specific provision for a trustee or trustees to be trustees *sine qua non*, meaning that those specified must be party to any decision. This used to be not uncommon in the case of widows in Testamentary Trusts, but is less frequent in modern practice. HMRC occasionally have to be reminded of the quorum rule when presented with a Resolution of Trustees which has not been signed by all of them. In addition, it is competent for Scottish Trustees to execute a Power of Attorney in favour of a small number of them – or even only one of them – for the purposes of signing Deeds. Such a Power of Attorney cannot of course be used to delegate the exercise of Trustees' decision-making or exercise of discretions, but the use of such a Power simplifies implementation of Trustees' decisions, and makes it easier to achieve action in time to meet tax deadlines. In any event, execution of deeds on behalf of Trustees is sufficient if a quorum has signed, and no challenge is then competent on grounds of lack of consultation with the minority. The exception to that general rule is that the grantee must not be one of the quorum of trustees unless it can be shown that he gave full value in good faith – but that in turn may raise questions of *auctor in rem suam*. This very strict rule requires a trustee in that position to surrender to the Trust the benefit he has received, even in circumstances where the Trust has also benefited from his actions or involvement. The wording of the Trust may make express provision mitigating the effect of the rule, but at present the Scottish Courts do not treat themselves as bound by the terms of such clauses: see *Sarris v Clark* [1994] SCLR 927.

A5.3 The Nature of a Beneficiary's Interest Scottish Trustees have absolute control over Trust assets, subject to directions in the Trust Deed. Even where there is an Interest in Possession, the assets and their income are held by the Trustees in terms of the Trust, and the Trustees are not a mere postbox. However, given the impact of *Pearson v IRC* [1981] AC 753 and the statutory definition of an Interest in Possession in Scotland (*s 46 IHTA*), the requirements for tax planning purposes are much the same. A Scottish liferent interest, equivalent to an English life tenancy, covers both an interest in income generated by an asset, and the use of the asset itself, such as a house. The principle, which goes back to the Roman Law of *Usufruct*, does not in practice cause difficulties of tax interpretation.

A5.4 Treatment of Dividends due to Liferenters Because of the nature of a Scottish liferenter's interest, and the inter-position of Trustees between him and the source of the income, it was necessary to legislate in *Finance Act 1993 s118* to give tax treatment equivalent to 'an equitable right in possession … notwithstanding that no such right is conferred according to the law of Scotland'. This allowed Scottish liferenters to be treated for Income Tax purposes in the same way as English life tenants, and, while not directly relevant to IHT, it encapsulates the distinction between the two jurisdictions on this matter.

A5.5 Registration of Deeds In Scotland there is no public register of private Trusts or Wills register. It is the practice however for Trust Deeds and important Trust Resolutions and documents to be registered in the Books of Council & Session – a public Register, but one which is almost impossible to search unless the date of and parties to a deed are already known.

A5.6 Errors in Distribution *The Succession (Scotland) Act 2016, s 23* provides that a trustee shall not be personally liable for any error in the distribution of any property or the income of property if the error was caused by the trustee not knowing (either or both) of the existence, or non-existence, of a person or of a person's relationship, or lack of, to another person. The distribution has to have taken place in good faith and after reasonable and prudent enquiries.

A5.7 Impact of IHT on Trusts Generally The 2006 trust changes have had a deterrent effect. The number of full self-assessment returns filed by UK family trusts and estates fell to 163,000 in the 2011–12 tax year, 20% below the 2006–07 number. HMRC believes the sharp decline is due to the penal trust taxation regime that began with the introduction of IHT charges in 2006, despite previous ministerial commitments to be tax neutral towards trusts. Since the 2006 changes, Scots domiciled testators have faced IHT entry charges if they wish to create a settlor-interested trust to shelter their assets from the entitlements of spouse and issue, a point which the Law Society of Scotland have made to HMRC on many occasions.

A6 Issues of Scottish Heritable (Real) Property

A6.1 The Concept of 'Ownership' The fundamental rule for the ownership of land in Scotland is very different to that in England. Despite the reference in *s 272 IHTA* to a 'heritable security' meaning a security capable to being constituted 'over any interest in land' in Scotland, there is in Scottish land law no concept of 'interest in land' nor of leasehold tenure. Land in Scotland is owned, though it may be burdened with obligations, title conditions, servitudes or securities for debt or other obligations. There is in Scotland no concept of divided or equitable ownership, though co-ownership is competent, and common.

A6.2 Requirements of Recording or Registration The test of real rights of ownership is registration of title in the Land Register for Scotland (or recording of title in the Register of Sasines, which has been replaced by registration for all transactions where there is monetary consideration). Paragraph 14883 of HMRC's IHT Manual treats the date of transfer of heritable property in Scotland for inheritance tax purposes as the date when the disposition is delivered by the donor to the donee following the *Marquess of Linlithgow and another v HM Revenue and Customs* [2010] STC 1563. The court rejected HMRC's contention that the date of transfer was the date the disposition is recorded in the Register of Sasines or Land Register, which had been based on the advice of HMRC counsel. The qualifying period for business or agricultural property relief starts on registration of recording, not on the conclusion of the binding contract for purchase but the tax relief ends on the conclusion of the binding contract for sale, as it does in England and Wales.

Delivery is used in the ordinary sense and means when the donee receives the signed deed from the donor either by taking possession of it by hand or by post or it being delivered to an agent on the donee's behalf.

This has IHT implications for example, the qualifying period for Business or Agricultural Property Relief on land in Scotland starts on delivery of the deed. But the tax relief ends on conclusion of a binding contract for sale (conclusion of missives in Scotland) as it does in England (sections 113 and 124 respectively).

A6.3 Offers and Binding Acceptances In Scotland, the conclusion of binding missives, after which a purchaser has a personal right to sue for the property but not yet a real right in it, is a key stage in property transactions, in both property law and tax law, which may be achieved months – or years –

before the price is paid and the transaction settled (completed). From October 2007 Automated Registration of Titles to Land (ARTL) has speeded up the process in straight forward transactions. As mentioned in **A6.2**, it is the binding missive of sale which removes the qualification of Business or Agricultural Property Relief, and for Capital Gains Tax ('CGT') purposes it is the binding missive which determines the date of purchase or disposal. However, because real rights in heritable property being transferred to a company require registration this may be necessary before HMRC will agree CGT hold-over on incorporation or gift (*ss 162* and *165 TCGA 1992* respectively).

A6.4 Constraints on Leases of Domestic Property The Scottish legal system also differs from the rest of the UK in relation to various aspects of property law. Since 1974, it has been incompetent to grant a lease of more than 20 years over domestic property in Scotland. Lenders cannot take a fixed charge over a lease of less than 20 years. This combination means that fixed securities cannot be granted over residential leases in Scotland. The restriction on the length of residential leases has been relaxed for registered social landlords and may be relaxed for other types of bodies prescribed by the Scottish ministers. The Scottish Government is considering extending this relaxation to student accommodation and a wider relaxation of the 20-year rule for all residential properties to encourage and assist investment in the private rented sector.

While a lease of agricultural property under what is now the *Agricultural Holdings (Scotland) Act 1991* may give indefinite right to occupy a farm including its farmhouse, long leasehold tenure of property in Scotland was never the norm, and even in the few areas where it was practised it is now obsolete. The *Land Reform (Scotland) Act 2016* proposes changes to agricultural tenancies and the succession and assignation of them which have not yet been implemented.

From a tax point of view, the constraint on leases of domestic property can cause difficulties in planning gifts of the family home: a donor who wants to take a lease back for a period long enough to cover his lifetime may consider that 20 years is too short. Before 22 March 2006, making it a lease for life would have created a liferent in his favour (*s 43(3) IHTA*) and thus undo the tax planning. In the Relevant Property Regime, this is no longer an issue (except for any TSIs created before 6 October 2008), even where, as between the trustees and the beneficiary, a liferent may be created.

A6.5 Securities over Heritable Property To be valid and enforceable against the property, a security over heritable property in Scotland has to be either registered or recorded. *Section 272 IHTA* defines 'Heritable Security' as 'any security capable of being constituted over any interest in land .... and of being recorded [or registered]', and for purposes of IHT generally the English term 'incumbrance' includes any Heritable Security or other debt or payment secured on heritage. Because of this difference, the Inland Revenue Charge, which appears to float above English real property, would be unenforceable against heritable property in Scotland, so *s 237(4) IHTA* states that no heritable property situated in Scotland is subject to the Charge, although HMRC may seek to trace its sale proceeds in order to recover the tax from a beneficiary. In Scots Law, from the point of view of the debtor, a security over heritable property is heritable. From the point of view of the creditor, such a security is moveable – except for the purposes of Legal Rights (see **A3.8**).

A6.6 Common Property In Scotland, co-ownership may be of one of two kinds: joint ownership where survivorship operates, and common property where each co-owner has a severable share. In will planning, it is necessary to check the title of property owned by more than one person, including spouses, since survivorship is often not the desirable result. Although, at present, HMRC generally accept that a survivorship destination can be evacuated by an Instrument of Variation after a death, in strict law that is effective for tax purposes only, and does not affect the true legal situation which is that the survivor will have taken purely by survivance – which by definition must have occurred before the Instrument of Variation. Before an Instrument of Variation is entered into it is sensible to consider the contributions made by each party to the purchase price of the property (to address whether it would have been competent for the deceased to have evacuated the survivorship destination in a *mortis causa* deed – see *Perrett's Trustees v Perrett* which addresses the evacuation issue) and ensure that *s 30* of the *Succession (Scotland) Act 1964* is complied with. For the change in title to also be effective from a property law perspective the survivor should also grant a conveyance in favour of the person named in the Instrument of Variation.

There is a useful article on survivorship destinations and *s 142 IHTA* by Craig Anderson in SLT, 2 November 2007.

The *Family Law (Scotland) Act 2006* (*s 19*) provides that survivorship destinations contained in title of joint property owned by husband and wife or civil partners are automatically revoked on divorce/dissolution of the marriage/ civil partnership and *s 2* of the *Succession (Scotland) Act 2016* treats the former spouse as having predeceased in the event of death after divorce or annulment of a marriage or dissolution or annulment of a civil partnership where the title contained a special destination.

Common owners have the right to an Action of Division and Sale to ensure that the property is sold for full value and not at a discount – but this process can be lengthy and costly, and for tax purposes, a percentage discount should be applied as in England – see **A2.3**.

A7 Scottish Charities

A7.1 The Scottish Legislation See **A1.10** above for general comments on the impact of Devolution on the tax exemptions for Scottish charities. The *Charities and Trustee Investment (Scotland) Act 2005* lists 15 charitable purposes, plus a 16th, namely purposes analogous to the previous 15. Scotland's 15 do, broadly, equate to 15 of the charitable purposes in England's new legislation, although the detailed wording is different. In both jurisdictions, there is a 'Public Benefit' requirement. In England and Wales, there is a 16th specific purpose, namely support to the armed forces, the emergency services and the like, which is not a specific charitable purpose in Scotland. Accordingly, for example, support for the objectives of the Royal Regiment of Scotland was originally thought not to be a charitable purpose in Scotland, though it would be in England. Support for former soldiers of the Royal Regiment of Scotland who have fallen on hard times, or who are disabled, would always have been charitable in both jurisdictions as benevolence. OSCR decided that support for the armed forces etc. is sufficiently analogous to certain of the 15 Scottish objects that it qualifies in Scotland.

A7.2 Position under *ss 505* and *506 ICTA 1988* The specific differences are but a detail. There is a jurisprudential disconnect between recognition as a Scottish Charity and acceptance as a charity for UK tax purposes. 'Charity' is not defined in *ICTA 1988* – presumably because it was understood following the 1552 Act and English judicial precedent. By contrast, the Scots Law definition of 'charity' had developed piecemeal, and is now superseded by the 2005 Act. The joint statement by OSCR and HMRC on 19 February 2008 contains example definition clauses which create a double requirement for a Scottish charity – OSCR registration to operate as a charity in Scotland plus compliance with, in effect, English charity definitions in order to qualify for tax relief. However, even with a different definition of charitable purposes for tax purposes in the *Charities Act (England and Wales) 2006* it is possible that an organisation refused registration by a charity regulator outside England and Wales may still be able to satisfy the conditions in the Taxes Acts and be recognised as a charity for tax purposes. The UK is bound to recognise charitable status across the EU for tax purposes. On 27 January 2009, the ECJ gave its judgement in the case of *Hein Persche v Finanzamt Ludenscheid* which determined that member states could not impose a territorial restriction on a charity exemption. Previously, the UK exemption was restricted to charities established in the UK.

A7.3 Investments The *Charities and Trustee Investment (Scotland) Act, ss 93–95* sets out the powers of investment of trustees and associated duties.

Trustees are entitled to make any kind of investment of the trust estate, including a wider power to acquire stocks and shares. However, these powers are subject to restrictions and exclusions and do not extend to certain categories of trustees.

A7.4 Business Rates Since the levying of Business Rates and equivalent property taxes is delegated to Holyrood, charitable relief from Rates depends upon the Scottish definition of charity, not the tax definition. Accordingly, it has been relevant for the Scottish Parliament to discuss the impact on private education of the removal of rates relief only. Given the financial implications of private schools having to pay rates, some may prefer to ensure continuing OSCR registration even if there is the risk of losing Section 505 relief. OSCR's Rolling Reviews have found that some private schools do provide sufficient 'public benefit' as required under the 2005 Act, while others do not and have been required to amend their policies and practices in order to remain on the OSCR register. The Law Society of Scotland held discussions with both Scottish Ministers and HMRC on the whole issue of charitable recognition under the Law of Scotland and under UK tax legislation, without managing to remove the double requirement.

A7.5 *IRC v Glasgow Police Athletic Association* This was the leading case on tax relief for Scottish Charities, and it provides a gloss on the *CIR v Pemsel* case which deals with the general impact of UK taxes in Scotland. The general principle established by *Pemsel* was that UK tax legislation should be applied on both sides of the border in an equivalent way to equivalent legal situations. On that principle, a Scottish charity would qualify for UK tax relief by virtue of being a Scottish charity. However, the *Glasgow Police Athletic Association* case decided – at a time when Scotland had no detailed charity code of its own – that for tax purposes the charitable test in the UK had to be consistent, and that the English definition was to be followed. The joint statement by OSCR and HMRC of 19 February 2008 follows the case but not the *ratio* of the decision.

A7.6 English Charities Active in Scotland Under the *Scottish 2005 Act*, an English charity operating in Scotland has to register with OSCR. OSCR takes the view that only those English charities which would qualify to be registered in Scotland if they were Scottish charities will be registered as cross-border charities. OSCR is therefore insisting that English charities change their constitutions and objects in order to comply, such changes in practice commonly being needed only to their winding up provisions. Although the Charity Commission has helpfully provided model clauses, the charities which they regulate are finding that the clauses are not always appropriate to their needs. With tax relief at stake, some English charities may feel it appropriate to review the support they give north of the border, so that they do not risk losing their tax status.

A8 Scottish Political Parties

A8.1 The Westminster Requirements The present IHT test of a qualifying political party is that it has two members of the Westminster

Parliament or one member of that Parliament plus a total of 150,000 votes in a Westminster election. This sits uncomfortably in the era of Devolution, although in the short term there may be no practical difficulties. Care should be taken to check whether parties chosen as beneficiaries as part of succession planning qualify, and if the bequest is written in a will their status should continue to be monitored to check if IHT exemption would apply.

Chapter 1

Inheritance tax: introduction

SIGNPOSTS

- **Scope** – Inheritance tax (IHT) broadly applies to lifetime chargeable transfers, the value of an individual's death estate, and on certain chargeable events relating to settled property. Liability to IHT depends on a person's domicile, and on the situs of property (see **1.1**).
- **Who is liable to IHT?** – Domicile is an important factor in the determination of a person's liability to IHT. A person's domicile is a matter of general law. However, 'deemed' and 'elective' domicile in the UK may apply for IHT purposes in certain circumstances, notwithstanding the person's non-UK domicile under general law (see **1.2–1.8**).
- **Calculation and rates** – IHT is a cumulative tax (at rates of 20% or 40%), based on lifetime chargeable transfers within the previous seven years, and on the value of an individual's estate on death, subject to the IHT threshold ('nil rate band'). A reduction in the IHT 'death rate' from 40% to 36% may apply (from 6 April 2012) in certain circumstances where charitable legacies are involved (see **1.13–1.17**).
- **Transfers of value** – These may be potentially exempt transfers (PETs), or immediately chargeable. However, transfers of certain property ('excluded property') are outside the scope of IHT (see **1.18–1.23**).
- **Reliefs and exemptions** – Certain transfers of value are exempt. IHT on chargeable transfers may be subject to relief in certain circumstances (eg taper relief, quick succession relief, double tax relief) (see **1.24–1.30**).
- **Close companies** – IHT charges can arise on transfers of value by close companies, and on certain changes in their capital (see **1.31–1.33**).

BACKGROUND

1.1 Inheritance tax (IHT) replaced the previous regime of capital transfer tax (CTT) in *Finance Act 1986*, with effect from 18 March 1986. CTT in turn replaced estate duty, which was originally introduced in *Finance Act 1894* and applied to deaths occurring up to and including 12 March 1975, prior to its abolition in *Finance Act 1975*.

The IHT regime continued the basic framework and administrative provisions of CTT, whilst following the estate duty principle of only charging tax on lifetime gifts made within seven years of the donor's death. The primary IHT legislation is contained in the *Inheritance Tax Act 1984* (*IHTA 1984*), as amended by subsequent Finance Acts.

IHT is a tax on chargeable transfers (*IHTA 1984, s 1*). It applies to chargeable transfers made by an individual during lifetime, and to the value of his estate on death, subject to various exemptions, exclusions and reliefs. IHT also applies to certain chargeable events relating to settled property.

This chapter provides a brief introduction to the IHT system, the main principles of which are expanded upon in subsequent chapters. Unless otherwise stated, all statutory references are to *IHTA 1984*.

WHO IS LIABLE?

1.2 Individuals domiciled in Scotland (or any other country in the UK) are liable to IHT on chargeable worldwide property. Non-UK domiciled individuals are also liable to IHT, but only on chargeable UK property (*s 6(1)*).

The UK government intends legislating (in *Finance Bill 2017*) to ensure that, from April 2017, IHT is payable on all UK residential property owned by non-UK domiciliaries with a view to blocking what HMRC describes as 'enveloping' (ie holding property indirectly through offshore structures).

DOMICILE

Introduction

1.3 As a general rule, an individual is domiciled in the country (or state) considered to be his permanent home. There are three different types of domicile: domicile of origin, domicile of dependence and domicile of choice. It should be noted that both a domicile of origin and a domicile of dependence are acquired by operation of law rather than by choice. There is no statutory definition of domicile for UK tax purposes. Domicile is a matter of private international law.

In addition to the general law concerning domicile, there is also a 'deemed domicile' rule for IHT purposes (*s 267*). Domicile is also of relevance in considering Prior Rights and Legal Rights (see **3.1**). Domicile is to be distinguished from residence but residence can be a factor determining domicile, especially deemed domicile, so knowledge of the rules as on residence becomes important.

Historically, it did not help taxpayers (or tax practitioners) that very little statutory guidance on residence existed, resulting in extensive case law. This uncertainty over residence status also often resulted in reliance being placed on non-statutory HMRC guidance such as in HMRC6 ('Residence, domicile and the remittance basis'), which replaced booklet IR20. HMRC also state that guidance on domicile in the Residence, Domicile and Remittance Basis manual should enable most trust settlors to decide for themselves whether or not they are UK domiciled, where appropriate. HMRC will only consider opening an enquiry where domicile could be an issue, or making a determination of IHT (under *s 221*), where there is a 'significant risk of loss of UK tax', although no guidance is given on what amount is considered to be 'significant' in this regard (IHTM13034).

It should be noted that a person who is a member of the House of Commons or the House of Lords for any part of a tax year is generally to be treated as resident and domiciled in the UK for IHT (and income tax and capital gains tax) purposes, by virtue of the *Constitutional Reform and Governance Act 2010, ss 41, 42*. 'Ordinary residence' was also a factor, but this status was generally removed for tax purposes by *Finance Act 2013*, with effect from 2013/14.

A statutory residence test (SRT) was introduced in *Finance Act 2013*, generally with effect for 2013/14 and subsequent tax years. The SRT was introduced with the aim of enabling individuals to determine whether they are resident or not resident in the UK with certainty. However, the legislation is long and potentially complex, resulting in the publication of lengthy (and non-statutory) HMRC guidance (RDR3: 'Guidance Note: Statutory Residence Test (SRT)') which is available from the gov.uk website (www.gov.uk/government/publications/rdr3-statutory-residence-test-srt).

The SRT is outside the scope of this publication. Readers are instead referred to the latest edition of *Booth and Schwarz: Residence, Domicile and UK Taxation*, published by Bloomsbury Professional.

Legislative changes affecting non-domiciled individuals were introduced in *Finance Act 2012*. However, those reforms apply for income tax and capital gains tax purposes, and do not change the concept of domicile.

Provisions were introduced in *Finance Act 2013* increasing the IHT spouse exemption for transfers from a UK domiciled individual to a non-UK domiciled spouse or civil partner from £55,000 to the prevailing nil rate band (£325,000 for 2016/17). This is subject to an election facility for the non-UK domiciled spouse or civil partner to be treated as UK domiciled for IHT purposes. The election broadly has the effect of removing the above restriction in the spouse exemption, but bringing the individual's worldwide estate within the scope of IHT. Both measures apply to transfers of value (including on death) on or after 6 April 2013 (see **1.20**).

HMRC guidance on the common law principles of domicile and its application of those rules in practice is contained in the Residence, Domicile and Remittance Basis Manual at RDRM20000 and following.

Domicile of origin

1.4 A person's domicile of origin is first acquired at birth. In Scotland, for children under 16 *s 22* of the *Family Law (Scotland) Act 2006* provides that the child shall be domiciled in the same country as its parents if the parents are domiciled in the same country and the child has a home with one/both of them. Otherwise for children under 16 their domicile shall be the country which, for the time being, the child has the closest connection. This remains the person's domicile until it is replaced by a domicile of dependence or a domicile or choice.

HMRC guidance states that a domicile of origin at birth can subsequently be altered only by adoption (RDRM22010). A domicile of origin remains the person's domicile until it is replaced by a domicile of dependence (eg during minority) or a domicile of choice. A domicile of origin can revive when a domicile of choice is lost (see, for example, *Barlow Clowes International Ltd (in liquidation) and others v Henwood* [2008] EWCA 577).

In some cases, it may be necessary to determine a person's domicile of choice in order to decide the person's domicile in later years, such as where it is claimed that a domicile of choice (see **1.5**) has been abandoned and the person's domicile of origin has revived (*Wrottesley v Revenue & Customs* [2015] UKUT 637 (TCC)).

A domicile of origin will only be displaced if a person acquires a domicile of choice or a domicile of dependence. It will revive if, for example, a domicile of choice is abandoned, unless immediately replaced by a new domicile of choice (*Udny v Udny* (1869) LR 1 Sc & Div 441, HL).

HMRC consider that 'a domicile of origin can be placed into abeyance (that is "temporarily suspended") by the acquisition of a domicile of dependency or a domicile of choice, but it remains in the background to fill any gap that would otherwise arise' (RDRM22100). This is on the basis that an individual must always have one (and only one) domicile.

Domicile of choice

1.5 A domicile of choice is acquired by both physical prescence in another country, and the settled intention to voluntarily reside there permanently, or for an unlimited time (*Re Fuld's Estate (No 3)* [1968] P 675), and actual physical presence. Thus, a domicile of choice will not be acquired if the intention is conditional, or by going to work in another country unless there is a definite intention to remain permanently or indefinitely when the work has ceased.

A domicile of choice can be lost by leaving the country without any definite intention of returning. A new domicile of choice will be acquired if a person moves to another country with the intention of settling there permanently or indefinitely. However, the mere intention to abandon a previous domicile may be insufficient in itself; active steps may be required to acquire a new domicile elsewhere (eg see *Re Foote Estate*, 2009 ABQB 654, a Canadian case reported in *Trusts and Estates Law and Tax Journal*, December 2012).

If a domicile of choice is lost and a new one is not acquired, the person's domicile of origin will revive.

HMRC consider that 'a domicile of choice can only be acquired where the individual is both resident in a territory subject to a distinctive system or "municipal law"...and intends to reside there indefinitely' (RDRM22300). A person seeking to establish that a domicile of origin has been lost and a domicile of choice acquired, or that a domicile of choice has been replaced, must establish the change with very clear proof. HMRC consider that statements of intention by individuals must be considered in the context of all relevant evidence, and states: 'Mere statements are generally less important than actual conduct and may carry little weight if the statement does not correlate with actions taken' (RDRM22320).

Case law has underlined the potential difficulties faced by those wishing to shed a domicile of origin in favour of a domicile of choice (eg see *Re Clore (No 2)* [1984] STC 609, and subsequently *Agulian v Cyganik* [2006] EWCA Civ 129) and *Holliday v Musa* [2010] EWCA Civ 335).

In addition, HMRC consider that the loss of a domicile of choice requires cessation of both residence and intention. An intention subject to a contingency may be insufficient to result in a domicile of choice (*IRC v Bullock* [1976] 1 WLR 1178). The same applies if an intention is too vague to form a definite aspiration (*Furse v IRC* [1980] 3 All ER 838).

Domicile is essentially a concept of private international law rather than tax law, and a detailed consideration of the principles involved and relevant case law are outside the scope of this book.

Domicile of dependence

1.6 The domicile of a minor initially follows that of the person on whom he is dependent. A domicile of dependence only affects children (under 16 for Scotland, England, Wales and Northern Ireland) and persons of unsound mind. The separate Scottish statutory basis for determining the domicile of origin of any individual under the age of 16 (see **1.4**) also applies for determining domicile of dependence (see RDRM22120).

Prior to 1 January 1974, a married woman acquired her husband's domicile on marriage, and her domicile changed with his (ie she acquired a domicile of dependence from her husband). This rule was abolished by the *Domicile and Matrimonial Proceedings Act 1973*. For women who were married before 1 January 1974, their domicile of dependence was effectively reclassified as a domicile of choice on 1 January 1974 (ie capable of being changed by the acquisition or revival of another domicile, in the same way as any other domicile of choice).

However, the above rule has no relevance to women married on or after 1 January 1974, and a woman can therefore have a different domicile than that of her husband.

For transfers between spouses (or civil partners), it is important to know the domicile of both spouses. If the transferor spouse is domiciled in the UK but their spouse is domiciled abroad, the spouse exemption is limited to the prevailing nil rate band (£325,000 for 2016/17). The statutory limit was increased from £55,000, following changes introduced in *Finance Act 2013*, with effect in relation to transfers of value made on or after 6 April 2013 *(IHTA 1984, s 18(2), (2A))* (see **1.20**).

Care is needed where the domicile of a parent (upon which a child's domicile is dependent) changed from a domicile of origin to a domicile of choice before the child reaches the age of 16. For example, if the child's father had a domicile of origin abroad but subsequently acquired a domicile of choice in the UK when the child was under the age of 16, the child will also become UK domiciled. The child's UK domicile would be retained throughout adulthood, unless replaced by a domicile of choice.

Interestingly, HMRC guidance states (in the context of legitimate children): 'This principle is generally accepted, but it should be noted that it has not been applied in every case' (RDRM22210).

Election to be treated as domiciled in the UK

Further changes introduced in *Finance Act 2013* make available the facility for non-UK domiciled individuals with a UK domiciled spouse or civil partner to elect in writing to HMRC to be treated as UK domiciled for IHT purposes (*IHTA 1984, ss 267ZA, 267ZB*).

If no election is made to be treated as UK domiciled, the overseas assets of the non-UK domiciled spouse or civil partner generally continue to be excluded property for IHT purposes, but transfers from their spouse or civil partner are subject to the 'capped' exemption limit.

The effect of the above election is that transfers from a UK domiciled spouse (or civil partner) are exempt from IHT without limit. However, the electing spouse's worldwide estate becomes liable to IHT.

An election may be made if:

- the non-UK domiciled spouse had a UK domiciled spouse at any time on or after 6 April 2013 and within the seven-year period before the election is made (a 'lifetime election'); or
- for deaths on or after 6 April 2013, the deceased was (within seven years before death) UK domiciled and the spouse of the person who would (by virtue of the election) be treated as UK domiciled (a 'death election').

The above provisions effectively allow for a retrospective election following a change of domicile status, in the circumstances outlined. They also allow individuals whose marriage has ended to retrospectively elect to cover the period when they were married to a UK domiciled person.

Those spouses making a lifetime or death election may choose the date from which it applies, up to a maximum of seven years previously. However, the earliest date that may be specified is 6 April 2013 (*s 267ZB(4)(a)*). A lifetime election can be made at any time (but see below), whereas elections following a death must be made within two years of the death, or such longer period as HMRC may allow. The personal representatives of non-domiciled individuals may make death elections on their behalf.

An election can only be made on or after 17 July 2013, but as indicated above it can take effect before that date. The lifetime and death elections are irrevocable. However, an election will cease to have effect if the electing person is later resident outside the UK for more than four full consecutive tax years (*s 267ZB(10)*). Legislation in the draft *Finance Bill 2016* clauses published in December 2015 indicated that this period is to increase to six consecutive tax years from 6 April 2017, although the government subsequently indicated in Budget 2016 that it intended legislating all non-UK domicile reforms in *Finance Bill 2017* instead.

HMRC guidance on elections for non-UK domiciled spouses and civil partners to be domiciled in the UK is included in the Inheritance Tax Manual (at IHTM13040 and following), including details of how to make an election (IHTM13043).

Note that it is only the domicile of the *transferee* spouse which is relevant in the above context of the exemption limit in *s 18(2)*. Thus the limit does not apply if both the transferor and spouse are not domiciled in the UK, or if the transferor is domiciled outside the UK but the spouse is domiciled in the UK.

Deemed domicile

1.7

> **Focus**
>
> For IHT purposes, a person can be *deemed* to be domiciled in the UK if either of the two rules below apply, even though he is domiciled elsewhere under general law (*s 267*).
>
> See also **1.3** above regarding the deemed domicile status of MPs and members of the House of Lords.
>
> The election for a person to be treated as domiciled in the UK is discussed at **1.6** above. In determining whether the person making the election is (or was) domiciled in the UK, the deemed domicile provisions in *s 267* are ignored (*s 267ZA(8)*). However, the election does not prevent the deemed domicile provisions applying in the normal way if a person who has elected to be treated as domiciled in the UK becomes deemed domiciled in the UK while the election is in force, by meeting the conditions in *s 267* (IHTM13040).
>
> The UK government announced in the summer Budget 2015 that it intended introducing new deemed domicile rules, with the aim of restricting non-UK domiciled individuals from being able to claim non-UK domicile status for an indefinite period of time. The new rules are expected to be introduced in *Finance Bill 2017*, and to apply for IHT purposes from 6 April 2017. The government intends that similar domicile reforms will cover income tax and capital gains tax.

There are presently two separate and alternative time-based tests for determining deemed domicile status for IHT purposes (*s 267(1)*):

- *The 'three-year' rule* – A person is treated as domiciled in the UK if he or she was domiciled in the UK at any time in the three years immediately preceding the time at which the question of his domicile is to be decided.

  HMRC's guidance at the time of writing states in the context of the above 'three year rule' (IHTM13024): 'For the rule to apply the taxpayer must have been domiciled in the UK both on or after 10 December 1974 and at any time within the three *calendar years* before the *relevant event* (the death or gift)' (emphasis added). However, the legislation refers to the three-year period immediately preceding the 'relevant time' (ie broadly when UK domicile is lost (*s 267(1)*).

  It is assumed that HMRC's guidance means the third anniversary of the relevant time (and not the alternative interpretation of three calendar years from 1 January to 31 December preceding that date), although the guidance could be clearer.

- *The long-term residence or '17 out of 20' rule* – A person will be deemed domiciled in the UK when he has been resident for 17 out of the 20 years of assessment ending with the present one (income tax rules broadly apply for the purposes of determining residence in the UK for any particular tax year). This rule is the most relevant to someone who has come from abroad to live in the UK.

Example 1.1—'Deemed' domicile: the 'three-year' rule

Christine is aged 40, and had been resident and domiciled in Scotland all her life. She leaves the UK on 31 March 2013 and settles in Spain permanently, acquiring a domicile of choice in Spain under general law.

Christine will cease to be domiciled in the UK for IHT purposes under the 'three-year' rule on 1 April 2016.

However, she will not lose her deemed domicile under the '17 out of 20' rule until she has been non-resident in the UK for three tax years and the fourth has begun. Her three years of non-residence would be 2013/14, 2014/15 and 2015/16. She will lose her deemed domicile under the latter rule on 6 April 2016 (ie at the start of the 2016/17 tax year).

Care may be needed in some cases, as it may be unclear when an individual has actually abandoned his or her domicile in one territory in favour of another, for the purposes of determining when the three-year period begins and ends.

Example 1.2—'Deemed' domicile: in two minds

Davor, who was born in Croatia, came to live in Scotland at a very early age and established a domicile of choice. Some years later, his lawyers found it difficult to establish whether he had acquired a new domicile of choice in France as soon as he left Scotland. The lawyers used a Latin tag for this situation: *sine animo revertendi* (loosely translated as: 'I really haven't yet made up my mind whether or not to return to Scotland').

The lawyers came to the conclusion that Davor had probably retained his domicile of choice in Scotland whilst he made up his mind. On that basis, any delay on his part could postpone the start of the relevant three-year period, because he would not lose his domicile in Scotland straight away.

Example 1.3—'Deemed' domicile: the '17 out of 20' rule

Joseph came to the UK to stay on 1 May 2000. The Inland Revenue (as it then was) considered him to be UK resident for the tax year 200/01 (ie Joseph was resident in the UK for more than 183 days in that tax year). He remained resident in the UK for 2001/02 and all later tax years up to and including 2015/16.

The tax year 2016/17 is the seventeenth tax year. If Joseph remains resident in the UK during 2016/17, he becomes deemed domiciled in the UK. A transfer of foreign situs assets by Joseph would then be caught for IHT purposes, unless exempt or potentially exempt.

Note: The government proposes to introduce legislation in *Finance Bill 2017* to reduce the number of years of UK residence, so that individuals who have been UK resident for at least 15 out of the last 20 tax years will be deemed UK domiciled. This change is to apply from 6 April 2017. However, for individuals leaving the UK before 6 April 2017, but who would be deemed UK domiciled under the '15-year rule' on that date, the government has indicated that the present rules will apply (see **1.10**).

1.8 However, there are exceptions to the application of the 'deemed domicile' rule. The rule does not apply in certain circumstances including the following:

- specified government securities in the beneficial ownership of persons not ordinarily resident (and in certain cases not domiciled) in the UK (*ss 6(2), 48(4)*);

- certain types of savings by persons domiciled in the Channel Islands or the Isle of Man (*s 6(3)*);
- certain pre-CTT double taxation agreements still in force by virtue of *s 158(6)*. Those agreements contain their own rules for domicile and for resolving the issue where both countries claim domicile (*s 267(2)*); and
- for the purposes of deciding whether property settled before 10 December 1974 is excluded property, and for certain other purposes (see *s 267(3)*).

In addition, as indicated at **1.7** above, the deemed domicile rules are ignored for the purposes of determining whether a spouse or civil partner making an election to be treated as domiciled in the UK (see **1.20**) is or was domiciled in the UK (*s 267ZA(8)*). Furthermore, the election provisions (in *ss 267ZA, 267ZB*) are ignored for the purposes of determining whether a person is or was domiciled in the UK under the deemed domicile rules (*s 267(5)*).

Following legislation introduced in *Finance Act 2013*, the concept of 'ordinary residence' is generally removed for tax purposes. However, the government stated (in its explanatory notes to the *Finance Bill 2013* legislation) that the above IHT provisions in *ss 6(2)* and *48(4)* will continue to apply to securities issued on the basis of exemption for persons not ordinarily resident provided that the beneficial owner acquired them before 6 April 2013. All UK government securities acquired on or after 6 April 2013 will be exempt provided the beneficial owner is resident outside the UK; domicile is relevant only to the issue of 3.5% War Loan (IHTM27241).

With regard to the third bullet point above, HMRC accept that domicile issues exclude deemed domicile when considering the double tax agreements with France, Italy, India and Pakistan. However, if there is a common law domicile in France, Italy, India or Pakistan, the deemed domicile rules can apply to chargeable *lifetime* transfers (IHTM13024).

Domicile reform

1.9

Focus

Following criticism that the tax regime for non-UK domicile persons favoured those who are long-term resident in the UK, the UK government announced at summer Budget 2015 that it would be bringing forward the point at which an individual is treated as deemed domiciled in the UK for IHT (and other tax purposes) to 15 out of 20 tax years.

> In addition, the government stated its intention to treat individuals with a domicile of origin in the UK (ie those born in the UK to a parent domiciled in the UK) as UK domiciled whilst they are in the UK. These changes are to be introduced from 6 April 2017.

HMRC guidance on the proposed changes ('Technical briefing on foreign domiciled persons changes announced at Summer Budget 2015') was published on 8 July 2015. The government broadly proposes the following two 'rules' with the aim of restricting persons from being able to claim non-UK domiciled status for an indefinite period of time:

- long-term residence (or '15-year rule') – a deemed domicile rule for long-term resident non-UK domiciled persons (see **1.10**); and
- a 'returning UK domiciles rule' (see **1.12**).

The proposed reform of the regime for non-UK domiciled persons extends beyond IHT to other taxes, and will affect those persons who are non-UK domiciled under general law.

Draft *Finance Bill 2016* clauses subsequently published in December 2015 included amendments to the IHT legislation, and the government announced that further legislation covering the income tax and capital gains aspects of the domicile reforms would follow. The changes were expected to be included in *Finance Bill 2016*, but the government subsequently indicated (in Budget 2016) that all non-UK domicile reforms would be legislated in *Finance Bill 2017*, and introduced from 6 April 2017.

The '15-year rule'

1.10 As indicated at **1.7** above, the deemed UK domicile rules broadly provide (among other things) that a person who is not domiciled in the UK under general law is treated as UK domiciled for IHT purposes if he is resident in the UK for 17 out of the last 20 tax years (*s 267(1)(b)*).

The government proposes to reduce the number of years of UK residence, so that individuals who have been UK resident for at least 15 out of the last 20 tax years will be deemed UK domiciled. The government has indicated that this will apply not only for IHT but for all UK tax purposes.

This rule is to apply from 6 April 2017, irrespective of when the individual arrived in the UK; HMRC guidance pointed out that there will be no special 'grandfathering' rules for those already in the UK.

For those leaving the UK before 6 April 2017, but who would be deemed UK domiciled under the '15-year rule' on that date, the present rules will apply.

1.11 The proposed changes mean that some individuals leaving the UK will continue to be subject to IHT on their worldwide estate for a significantly longer period than under the 'three-year' rule (see **1.7** above). The government has referred to this proposed extended period as the 'five-year rule', ie in broad terms once a deemed UK domiciled individual under the 15-year rule leaves the UK and spends more than five tax years outside the UK, he will at that point lose his deemed tax domicile. The same will apply to UK domiciliaries who leave the UK permanently after 5 April 2017, having been resident in the UK for over 15 tax years.

If, having spent more than five tax years abroad, the non-UK domiciliary returns to the UK temporarily but intends eventually to leave the UK (ie such that he remains foreign domiciled under general law), it was proposed that the individual will be able to spend another 15 years as a UK resident for tax purposes before becoming deemed UK domiciled again. However, this treatment will not apply to returning UK domiciliaries who are subject to the 'returning UK domiciles rule' (see **1.12** below).

The 'returning UK domiciles rule'

1.12

> **Focus**
>
> The UK government has declared the intention to make it more difficult for individuals with a domicile of origin in the UK to claim non-UK domicile status if they leave the UK and acquire a domicile of choice in another country, but subsequently return to the UK and maintain that they have retained a foreign domicile of choice.

Draft *Finance Bill 2016* clauses published in December 2015 include an amendment of the deemed domicile legislation (in *s 267*) such that a person is treated as domiciled in the UK for IHT purposes if he is a formerly domiciled resident for the tax year in which the relevant time falls. This legislation was not subsequently included in *Finance Bill 2016,* but is expected to be included in *Finance Bill 2017* instead.

A person is a 'formerly domiciled resident' for these purposes broadly if he was born in the UK, had a domicile of origin in the UK at birth, was resident in the UK for that tax year, and was also resident in the UK for at least one of the two immediately preceding tax years.

It is proposed that, in such circumstances, the individual will be taxed as a UK domiciliary on their return to the UK, irrespective of their domicile status under general law. In addition, returning UK domiciliaries will not benefit from any favourable tax treatment in respect of trusts set up while not domiciled in the UK.

The government intends that a returning UK domiciliary will be able to lose their UK tax domicile in the tax year after departure from the UK, but only if the following conditions are satisfied:

(a) they have not spent more than 15 tax years in the UK; and

(b) they have not acquired an actual UK domicile under general law during their return period to the UK.

HMRC's guidance indicated:

- If (a) above applies but not (b), the individual will be subject to the 'five-year rule' (see **1.11**), ie five years' non-UK residence will be required to lose their UK domicile.
- If (b) applies but not (a), the individual will be subject to the 'three-year rule' (see **1.7**), ie the individual will remain UK domiciled for IHT purposes for three years after acquiring a foreign domicile of choice under general law.
- If both (a) and (b) apply, the individual will be subject to both the 'five-year rule' and 'three-year rule', and can only lose UK tax domicile on the later of those events.

It is proposed that the 'returning UK domiciles rule' will affect all returning UK domiciliaries from 6 April 2017, including those who return before that date. The 'five-year rule' will affect UK domiciliaries leaving the UK after 5 April 2017.

The proposed changes are subject to legislation to be included in *Finance Bill 2017*.

WHAT IS CHARGEABLE TO IHT?

1.13 IHT is a direct tax on transfers of capital (eg lifetime gifts) made on or after 18 March 1986. It is broadly a cumulative tax charge on the following:

- the value transferred by a chargeable transfer made by an individual during his lifetime within the preceding seven-year period (ie broadly the loss to the donor), and on the value of his estate on death. A 'chargeable transfer' is any 'transfer of value' (see below) made by an individual, other than an exempt transfer (*s 2*); and

- certain events relating to settlements (eg gifts to a discretionary trust).

The IHT charge on death (and in respect of certain settled property) is brought into charge by deeming a transfer of value to have been made immediately before death, equal to the value of the person's estate (and the value of the settled property, if appropriate) (*ss 4(1), 52(1)*). The IHT legislation specifically precludes certain property from charge (see below).

CUMULATION AND THE IHT THRESHOLD

1.14 Chargeable transfers within the seven-year period ending with the date of the latest chargeable transfer are cumulated, for the purposes of determining the IHT rate (*s 7*). Where chargeable lifetime transfers and the individual's death estate do not exceed the IHT threshold (or 'nil rate band', as it is more commonly known) there is no IHT liability.

The nil rate band can normally be expected to increase annually by reference to an indexation factor. Previously this factor was the retail prices index (RPI) (but see below). The increase in the indexation factor in September in each year is applied to the rates of chargeable transfers made on or after 6 April in the following year (*s 8*). However, the UK Parliament may determine the nil rate band otherwise than by reference to the indexation factor, and in some previous Finance Acts have done so.

Legislation to move the default indexation factor for direct taxes, including IHT, from the RPI to the Consumer Price Index (CPI) was included in *Finance Act 2012*, which amended *s 8* with effect for chargeable transfers from 6 April 2015. However, automatic indexation of the nil rate band using the CPI is subject to override if the UK Parliament determines that a different amount should apply. The IHT nil rate band was initially frozen at £325,000 up to and including 2014/15.

In addition, the nil rate band was frozen at £325,000 for subsequent tax years up to and including 2017/18 (*Finance Act 2014, Sch 25, para 2*). Subsequently, the indexation of the nil rate band in *s 8* was disapplied again (in *Finance (No 2) Act 2015*), such that the nil rate band is to remain at £325,000 for the tax years 2018/19, 2019/20 and 2020/21.

The nil rate band for the current and recent tax years is as follows (*Sch 1*):

Table 1.1—The 'nil rate band'

Transfer of value	*Threshold*
	£
2009/10 to 2020/21	325,000
2008/09	312,000
2007/08	300,000

In addition to the IHT threshold or nil rate band above, the transferable nil rate band provisions (*ss 8A–8C*) broadly allow claims for the unused nil rate band of a deceased spouse or civil partner to be transferred to a surviving spouse or civil partner (who dies on or after 9 October 2007). The survivor's nil rate band can be increased by up to 100%, or one additional nil rate band.

An increased nil rate band is also available from 6 April 2017 where a residence is passed on death to a direct descendant. This 'residence nil rate band' will be £100,000 in 2017/18, rising to £125,000 in 2018/19, £150,000 in 2019/20, and £175,000 in 2020/21.

RATES OF IHT

Lifetime

1.15 Chargeable lifetime transfers are charged at half of the rate on death (*s 7(2)*). The 'death rate' of IHT for 2016/17 is 40%, and, therefore, chargeable lifetime transfers above the nil rate band are charged at 20%.

Death

1.16 Transfers made within seven years of death are charged at the rate on death, subject to taper relief for transfers made between three and seven years from death.

However, a lower IHT rate of 36% applies to a deceased person's estate in certain circumstances involving charitable legacies (*Sch 1A*). This reduced rate broadly applies where 10% or more of a deceased's net estate (after deducting liabilities, exemptions, reliefs and the nil rate band) is left to charity or a registered community amateur sports club. In such cases, the normal 40% rate is reduced to 36%.The relevant legislation was introduced in *Finance Act 2012*, and the lower rate of IHT has effect for deaths on or after 6 April 2012.

An 'Inheritance Tax reduced rate calculator' is included on the HMRC website (www.hmrc.gov.uk/tools/iht-reduced-rate/calculator.htm). In addition, HMRC's technical guidance on the reduced rate for charitable gifts (at IHTM45000 and following) includes an example of the wording of a clause that can be included in a Will which HMRC accepts will ensure that a specific legacy to charity will always meet the 10% test (see IHTM45008).

Grossing-up

1.17 IHT is based on the loss in value of the donor's estate as the result of a chargeable transfer. If the donor also pays the IHT on a gift, that payment results in a further loss to his estate. The tax must, therefore, be taken into account in the transfer of value. The gift (net of IHT) must be 'grossed-up' to determine the actual chargeable transfer.

Example 1.4—Lifetime transfers

Mr A transfers £129,000 to a discretionary trust on 1 May 2016, £219,000 on 31 December 2016 and a further £35,000 on 1 February 2017. He bears the tax and he has made no other chargeable transfers. His IHT position is as follows:

	£	£	£
Gift on 1 May 2016		129,000	
Deduct annual exemption			
– 2016/17	3,000		
– 2015/16	3,000	6,000	
		123,000	
Covered by nil rate band of £325,000			
Gift on 31 December 2016		219,000	
(Note: Annual exemption already used for 2016/17)			
Cumulative net transfers		£342,000	
Tax thereon:			
£0–£325,000		0	
£325,001–£342,000 (£17,000 × ¼)		4,250	
Tax on gift		£4,250	

Gift on 1 February 2017

	Gross	*Tax*	*Net*
	£	£	£
Cumulative totals			
	346,250	4,250	342,000
Add Latest net transfer of £35,000	43,750	8,750	35,000
	£390,000	£13,000	£377,000
Tax on £377,000			
£0–£325,000		Nil	
£325,001–£377,000 (£52,000 × ¼)		13,000	
		13,000	
Deduct tax on previous transfers		4,250	
Tax on latest gift		£8,750	

TRANSFERS OF VALUE

1.18 A transfer of value is a disposition by a person resulting in the value of his estate immediately after the disposition being less than it would be but for the disposition. The amount by which his estate is reduced is the measure of the transfer of value (*s 3(1)*). This is sometimes referred to as the 'loss to the donor' principle.

However, the transfer of 'excluded property' (see below) does not count for the above purposes (*s 3(2)*).

Focus

Some 'dispositions' (eg gifts or transfers) are not treated as transfers of value, where certain conditions are satisfied. These include:

- gifts without gratuitous intent (*s 10*);
- transfers for family maintenance (*s 11*);
- dispositions which are allowable for income tax or corporation tax purposes (*s 12*); and
- waivers of remuneration and dividends (*ss 14, 15*).

For further commentary on dispositions that are not transfers of value, see **9.12**.

POTENTIALLY EXEMPT TRANSFERS

1.19 Most types of gifts made during lifetime are potentially exempt transfers (PETs). A PET is broadly a lifetime transfer of value that satisfies the following conditions (*s 3A*):

- it is made by an individual on or after 18 March 1986;
- the transfer would otherwise be a chargeable transfer;
- for transfers of value before 22 March 2006, if it is either a gift to another individual or a gift into an accumulation and maintenance trust or a disabled person's trust;
- for transfers of value from 22 March 2006, if the transfer of value is made to another individual, a disabled person's trust or a 'bereaved minor's' trust on the ending of an 'immediate post-death interest' (see **Chapter 7**) (ie lifetime gifts into the vast majority of trusts do not qualify as PETs from that date).

A PET made more than seven years before death becomes an exempt transfer. Conversely, a PET becomes a chargeable transfer if made within seven years of death.

CHARGEABLE LIFETIME TRANSFERS

1.20 A lifetime transfer is broadly a disposition (eg a gift) made by a person resulting in a reduction in the value of the person's estate (*s 3(1)*). A chargeable transfer is a transfer of value by an individual, other than an exempt transfer (*s 2*).

As mentioned, most lifetime transfers are PETs, which are assumed will prove to be exempt when made, and which only become chargeable if the transferor dies within seven years of making them. A lifetime transfer that does not qualify as a PET will, therefore, generally be immediately chargeable to IHT. Examples include:

- transfers to a company;
- gifts to a discretionary trust; or
- lifetime gifts to an interest in possession settlement created on or after 22 March 2006.

Other transfers of value prevented from being PETs include transfers by a close company, and deemed dispositions on the alteration of share rights or capital of close companies (*ss 94, 98*).

With regard to lifetime transfers in general, see **Chapter 2**.

IHT ON DEATH

1.21 IHT is charged on the deceased's estate as if, immediately before his death, he had made a transfer of value. The value transferred is deemed to equal the value of his estate immediately before death (*s 4(1)*).

The estate for IHT purposes includes the value of all property to which the deceased was beneficially entitled, certain interests in possession in settled property (see **Chapter 7**) and any gifts with reservation of benefit (see **Chapter 5**), but not excluded property (see **1.22** below).

Changes in the value of the estate caused by the death may be taken into account (*s 171*). HMRC guidance (at IHTM04046) cites various examples, including a life assurance policy maturing on death, on the footing that it will often pay out a greater sum than the open market value of the policy immediately before the death.

Liabilities of the deceased may generally be deducted if imposed under a legal obligation, or if incurred for valuable consideration (*s 5(5)*), together with reasonable funeral expenses (*s 172*). However, certain restrictions on deductions for liabilities were introduced in *Finance Act 2013* and *Finance Act 2014*, including provisions in relation to the repayment of liabilities after a person's death (*s 175A*), where this occurs on or after 17 July 2013 (ie the date on which *Finance Act 2013* received Royal Assent). However, the provisions applicable to liabilities relating to certain 'relievable property' apply to liabilities incurred on or after 6 April 2013 (see **3.13**).

The amount of IHT chargeable on the death estate is subject to any IHT reliefs and/or exemptions to which the deceased's estate may be entitled (eg business or agricultural property relief, or the spouse or civil partner exemption), and depends on the total chargeable lifetime transfers and potentially exempt transfers made within the seven years before death.

With regard to IHT on death generally, see **Chapter 3**.

EXCLUDED PROPERTY

1.22 Some types of property are outside the scope of IHT. Such property is known as 'excluded property', and includes the following:

- Property situated abroad (and investments in an authorised unit trust or open ended investment company) if the beneficial owner is a non-UK domiciled individual (*s 6(1)* and *(1A)*).
- Settled property situated outside the UK, if the settlor was non-UK domiciled when the settlement was made (*s 48(3)*).

However, if a UK-domiciled person acquires an interest in possession in the settled property (from 5 December 2005) for valuable consideration, that interest is not excluded property (*s 48(3B)*). In addition, the excluded property and settled property provisions were amended (by anti-avoidance legislation in *Finance Act 2012*) with effect for arrangements entered into on or after 20 June 2012, to close certain schemes involving the acquisition by UK domiciled individuals of interests in excluded property trusts (*ss 48(3D), 74A–74C*).

In addition, legislation in the draft *Finance Bill 2016* clauses published in December 2015 broadly provided that from 6 April 2017 where the settlor was non-UK domiciled when the settlement was made, the property is not excluded property (under *s 48(3)* or *(3A)*) at any time in a tax year if the settlor was a 'formerly domiciled resident' for that tax year. However, the amending legislation was not subsequently included in *Finance Bill 2016*, as the government indicated (in Budget 2016) its intention to introduce its proposed tax reforms in respect of non-UK domiciliaries in *Finance Bill 2017*.

- Settled property (situated abroad or not) consisting of investments in an authorised unit trust or open ended investment company, if the settlor was non-UK domiciled when the settlement was made (*s 48(3A)*). However, if a UK-domiciled person acquires an interest in possession in settled property from 5 December 2005 for valuable consideration, that interest is not excluded property (*s 48(3B)*). See also the proposed exception regarding formerly domiciled resident settlors in the previous bullet point.
- A 'reversionary interest' (ie a future interest under a settlement) subject to certain anti-avoidance provisions (eg if the interest has previously been acquired for valuable consideration; see *s 48(1)*).
- Certain government securities owned by persons not ordinarily resident (and in certain cases, not domiciled) in the UK (*s 6(2)*) (although as to ordinary residence, see **1.8** above).
- National Savings certificates, war savings certificates, premium savings bonds or deposits with the National Savings Bank or a trustee savings bank of persons domiciled in the Channel Islands or the Isle of Man (*s 6(3)*).

However, as to the first two bullet points above, see **1.24** below on the government's intention to bring all UK residential property held directly or indirectly by non-UK domiciled persons into charge for IHT purposes, even where the property is owned through an offshore structure such as an offshore company or partnership.

There is also an exclusion from the death estate in respect of foreign (ie non-sterling) currency bank accounts of a person who was not domiciled, resident or ordinarily resident in the UK immediately prior to death (*s 157*). However, the condition as to ordinary residence is removed by *Finance Act 2013* for deaths on or after 6 April 2013.

In addition, certain other types of property are left out of account for IHT purposes:

- decorations for valour or gallant conduct, which have never been the subject of a disposition for consideration in money or money's worth (*s 6(1B)*) (Note – this provision replaced ESC F19 with effect in relation to transfers etc occurring from 6 April 2009 (*SI 2009/730, art 14*)); and
- certain compensation etc. for World War II claims.

Legislation introduced in *Finance Act 2016* (new *s 153ZA* and *Sch 5A*) replaces previous concessionary treatment (under ESC F20 'Late compensation for World War II claims'), in respect of qualifying payments of compensation and ex-gratia payments for World War II claims. The legislation also extends the scope of the concession to include one-off compensation payments of €2,500 made under the 'Child Survivor Fund', and allows the Treasury to add any further schemes by way of regulations. The legislation will operate as a relief rather than an exemption, as the IHT on the amount of the qualifying compensation or ex-gratia payment is allowed as a credit against the IHT arising on the chargeable value of the recipient's estate. ESC F20 had effect until 1 January 2015. The relevant legislation in *Finance Act 2016* is backdated to deaths occurring on or after 1 January 2015.

Settled property

1.23 The excluded property legislation refers to the settlor's domicile when the settlement was made.

HMRC take the view that, in the case of added property, a further settlement is made when that property is transferred. If the settlor was domiciled in the UK at that point, the property will not be excluded property. HMRC's Inheritance Tax Manual gives the following example (IHTM04272):

Example 1.5—Foreign settled property

S, when domiciled abroad, creates a settlement of Spanish realty. Later he acquires a UK domicile and then adds some Australian property to the settlement.

The Spanish property is excluded property because of S's overseas domicile when he settled that property. However, the Australian property is not excluded property as S had a UK domicile when he added that property to the settlement.

Care is also needed if settled property leaves an excluded property settlement, but that property (or property derived therefrom) is later reintroduced into the settlement. Such property may become subject to IHT (eg on the settlement's ten-year anniversary) if, when that property was reintroduced, the settlor had become UK domiciled (*Barclays Wealth Trustees (Jersey) Ltd and another v HM Revenue & Customs* [2015] EWHC 2878 (Ch)).

IHT is not charged on lifetime transfers of excluded property. Nor does excluded property form part of a person's estate on death; the same applies to a foreign-owned work of art situated in the UK for public display, cleaning and/or restoration (*ss 3(2), 5(1)(b)*).

However, excluded property is taken into account when measuring the loss in value of a person's estate if there is a transfer of non-excluded property.

Non-UK domicile and UK residential property excluded

1.24 As indicated at **1.2** above, non-UK domiciled individuals are liable to IHT, but only on chargeable UK property. Thus if the individual dies owning UK assets directly, their estate is liable to IHT at 40% on the value of those assets (subject to exemptions and the nil rate band, if available).

By contrast, property beneficially owned by a non-UK domiciled individual which is situated outside the UK is 'excluded property' for IHT purposes. Such property is generally taken outside the ambit of an IHT charge (*s 6(1)*).

Owning assets indirectly through an overseas company whose shares are situated abroad has been a popular strategy for non-UK domiciliaries, on the basis that the shares in the non-UK company are excluded property. If a UK asset such as a house (which is not excluded property) is held by the overseas company, its value would generally be taken outside the scope of IHT.

In addition, property comprised in a settlement and situated outside the UK will generally be excluded property for IHT purposes if the settlor was domiciled outside the UK when the settlement was made (*s 48(3)*). Thus a non-UK domiciled individual with assets abroad who is considering becoming domiciled in the UK (or is about to become 'deemed' domiciled in the UK under *s 267(1)(b)*) would often consider settling those assets before becoming UK domiciled, so that they can remain outside the scope of IHT.

Furthermore, if the non-UK domiciled settlor has UK assets such as residential property, consideration could be given to the trust owning the shares of an offshore company (which, as mentioned above, are generally excluded property if situated outside the UK), with the investment company owning the UK assets. The settled property would then be the foreign company shares, not the UK assets.

However, in the case of residential property, the prospect of increased stamp taxes, the annual tax on enveloped dwellings (ATED) and ATED-related capital gains tax (CGT) charges has made property ownership by such a 'non-natural person' potentially unattractive for other tax purposes (see **Chapter 15**).

1.25

> **Focus**
>
> The government announced in the summer Budget 2015 that it intended to legislate to ensure that, from April 2017, IHT is payable on all UK residential property owned directly or indirectly by non-UK domiciliaries (and regardless of their residence status for tax purposes). This change is aimed at blocking what HMRC describe as 'enveloping', ie holding property indirectly through offshore structures.

HMRC published guidance on the proposed changes ('Technical briefing on foreign domiciled persons/Inheritance Tax residential property changes') on 8 July 2015. Subject to consultation, the changes are expected to be included in *Finance Bill 2017*, to take effect from 6 April 2017.

1.26 It is intended that the excluded property provisions for IHT purposes will be amended, so that trusts or individuals owning UK residential property through an offshore company, partnership or other 'opaque vehicle' will be liable to IHT on the value of the UK property.

However, it is intended that the IHT position for non-UK domiciliaries and excluded property trusts will be unchanged in relation to UK assets other than residential property, as well as for non-UK assets.

The IHT charge on UK residential property

1.27 It was proposed that the IHT charge on UK property held indirectly would be based on the ATED provisions. However, unlike those provisions, there would be no minimum property value threshold for the purpose of the IHT charge.

Furthermore, the various reliefs available under the ATED regime would not be applicable for IHT purposes. Thus, it seems that (for example) indirectly owned UK residential property rental businesses would be within the scope of an IHT charge, notwithstanding that relief is available under the ATED rules (see *FA 2013, s 133*).

The scope of CGT was extended (by *FA 2015*) to include gains on the disposal of UK residential property interests by non-UK resident persons (or by individuals in the overseas part of a split year) from 6 April 2015. It was proposed that broadly the same properties covered by the CGT charge for non-residents disposing of UK residential property interests would be liable to IHT, subject to any necessary adaptations, where appropriate.

As with the above CGT charge, it was proposed that diversely held vehicles that hold UK residential property would not be within the scope of the IHT charge. However, any 'closely controlled' offshore company, partnership or similar structure would be brought within the IHT provisions.

It was proposed that IHT would be chargeable on the value of UK residential property owned by the offshore company, etc. This would include on the death of a non-UK domiciled individual who owns the company shares, or on a gift of the company's shares into trust. Relevant property trusts would be subject to IHT charges (eg ten-year anniversary and 'exit' charges) in relation to the value of the UK residential property. The gifts with reservation anti-avoidance provisions (see **Chapter 5**) may also need to be considered on the death of a donor or settlor who benefits from gifted UK residential property or offshore company shares within seven years prior to death.

1.28 Changes in the IHT legislation would effectively provide that shares of offshore companies or similar structures are not excluded property to the extent that they derive their value directly or indirectly from UK residential property, or to the extent that the value of the shares is otherwise attributable to UK residential property. The relevant property regime for trusts would also need to be amended accordingly.

Focus

In many cases, the offshore company, etc may own other assets in addition to UK residential property, such as foreign land, or UK commercial property. However, it was proposed that only the value of the UK residential property would be subject to IHT (less outstanding borrowings to purchase it).

Nevertheless, the proposed extension of IHT to UK residential property is likely to increase complexity and compliance burdens (eg in relation to reporting requirements to HMRC).

The HMRC guidance note (see **1.25** above) acknowledges that some non-UK domiciliaries and trustees may wish to 'de-envelope' UK residential property from offshore structures as a result of the proposed IHT changes, and into a simpler structure (outside the scope of the ATED and ATED-related CGT regimes). However, the guidance note also recognises that there may be significant costs in de-enveloping (eg if the property has significantly increased in value since 2013), and indicates that the government will consider such issues during the course of consultation.

EXEMPTIONS—SUMMARY

1.29 The following types of property are exempt and, therefore, outside the IHT charge:

- **Transfers between spouses or civil partners** (*s 18*)

  There is a complete exemption for all transfers (ie lifetime and on death) between UK-domiciled spouses.

  However, where the transferor spouse is UK domiciled but the transferee spouse is foreign domiciled, the exemption is restricted to a *cumulative* total of £325,000 (for 2016/17) (*s 18(2)*; see IHTM11033).

  If the non-domiciled transferee spouse subsequently becomes UK domiciled, unfortunately any preceding transfers to them are still considered to be subject to the above restriction. Following the *Civil Partnership Act 2004*, same-sex couples who enter into a civil relationship are given parity of tax treatment with married couples. A gift to a non-UK domiciled spouse that is within the gift with reservation rules may not be protected by spouse relief and may eventually prove to be chargeable.

  The above upper limit was increased to the prevailing nil rate band at the time of the transfer, with effect in relation to transfers of value made on or after 6 April 2013 (previously £55,000), following changes introduced in *Finance Act 2013*. However, there are provisions for an election to allow non-UK domiciled spouses to be treated as domiciled in the UK for IHT purposes, so that the inter-spouse exemption is unlimited but electing spouses are then generally subject to IHT on their worldwide estates.

  The broad effect is that, if no election is made to be treated as UK domiciled, the overseas assets of the non-UK domiciled spouse generally continue to be excluded property for IHT purposes, but transfers from their spouse or civil partner would be subject to the 'capped' exempt limit. By contrast, the effect of making an election in writing to HMRC will broadly be to avoid a possible IHT charge on the first death, but as mentioned the worldwide estate of the surviving spouse generally becomes liable to IHT on the second death.

The election must be made in writing, but there is no prescribed form for making the election. However, HMRC guidance states that the election should be made to HMRC Trusts & Estates Risk Team (Elections) in Nottingham, and must include the following information (IHTM13043):

- full name and address of the person making the election (or for whom the personal representatives are making an election);
- date of birth, and (if appropriate) date of death;
- full name of their spouse or civil partner who is domiciled in the UK; and
- date from which the election is to take effect.

The election is irrevocable, and continues to apply while the electing individual remains resident in the UK. However, an election ceases to have effect if the electing person is later resident outside the UK for more than four full consecutive tax years (*s 267ZB(10)*), although this period is likely to be extended to six years in *Finance Bill 2017*. Thus overseas assets may cease to be liable to IHT once more, subject to the person not being actually or deemed domiciled in the UK at that point.

- **Annual exemption** (*s 19*)

  Lifetime transfers of value up to £3,000 per tax year are completely exempt from IHT. Any unused part of the exemption may be carried forward for one tax year only, and deducted after the annual exemption has been fully used in that later year. If the value of the gift or transfer exceeds the annual exemption, the excess will either be a potentially exempt transfer or an immediately chargeable transfer.

- **Small gifts to same person** (*s 20*)

  Lifetime gifts in a tax year with a total value not exceeding £250 to any one person are exempt from IHT. If the total value of gifts to that person exceeds £250 in the tax year, the exemption is completely lost, eg it cannot be set against part of a larger gift. The gifts must be outright. For example, they cannot be gifts of premiums on a life policy that has been written in trust (although the exemption for normal expenditure out of income in *s 21* might well apply (see below)).

- **Normal expenditure out of income** (*s 21*)

  The exemption applies to lifetime gifts which:

  (a) form part of the normal expenditure of the person making it;

(b) were made out of income (taking one year with another); and

(c) left the donor with sufficient income to maintain their normal standard of living.

Unlike other lifetime exemptions (eg the annual exemption), the normal expenditure out of income exemption is not subject to an upper maximum, and is only restricted to the extent of the donor's gifts, which satisfy the above conditions. Evidence is crucial to support claims to this relief.

- **Gifts in consideration of marriage or civil partnership** (*ss 22, 57*)

  Marriage gifts are exempt within certain limits. The amount of the exemption depends on the donor's relationship to the bride, groom or civil partner. Gifts of up to £5,000 by a parent of a party to a marriage or civil partnership are exempt. In the case of gifts by a grandparent or remoter ancestor, or by one party to the marriage or civil partnership to the other, the exemption limit is £2,500. For marriage gifts made by any other person, the upper limit is £1,000. These exemptions apply per marriage.

  The gifts must be made on or shortly before the marriage or civil partnership, and must become fully effective on the event taking place. Gifts in excess of the above exempt limits are chargeable to IHT, but only to the extent of the excess.

- **Gifts to charities or registered clubs** (*s 23*)

  Gifts to charities or registered clubs are exempt from IHT, if certain conditions are satisfied. For periods prior to changes included in *Finance Act 2010*, it was necessary for a charity to be established in the UK.

  However, a statutory definition of 'charity' was introduced (in *Finance Act 2010, Sch 6*), which includes a four-stage test to determine if an organisation is eligible for UK charity tax reliefs. This includes a jurisdiction condition, which broadly allows the organisation to be located in the UK or an EU member state or specified country, of which Iceland and Norway are included (*SI 2010/1904*) and Liechtenstein was subsequently added from 31 July 2014 (*SI 2014/1807*). The *Finance Act 2010* changes apply for IHT purposes from 1 April 2012 (the *Finance Act 2010, Sch 6, Part 2 (Commencement) Order, SI 2012/736*) (Note – for HMRC guidance as to transfers before that date, see IHTM11112). The IHT charity exemption is relevant to outright gifts to charity or to certain charitable trusts, and applies to lifetime gifts or transfers on death with no upper limit.

  In *Routier and another v Revenue & Customs* [2014] EWHC 3010 (Ch), a charitable gift to a trust was held not to be eligible for the charity exemption, on the grounds that the trust was governed by Jersey law, as opposed to UK law. The High Court concluded that the expression 'held on trust for charitable purposes' in *s 23(6)* requires not only that the charitable purposes are UK law charitable purposes, but that the relevant trust must be subject to the jurisdiction of the UK courts as well.

It should be noted that the four-stage test mentioned above includes a 'management condition', which in turn includes a 'fit and proper person' test. This could deprive some organisations of their charitable status. There is no statutory definition of a 'fit and proper' person, although a helpsheet (and fit and proper person declaration) is available on the gov.uk website (www.gov.uk/government/publications/charity-tax-relief-model-declaration).

- **Gifts to political parties** (*s 24*)

  Transfers of value to qualifying political parties are exempt transfers for IHT purposes without limit. To meet the qualifying status the parties must, at the last UK General Election, have had two members of that party elected to the House of Commons or had one member elected to the House of Commons and obtained not less than 150,000 votes for their party candidates. At present, the rules do not allow for political parties to qualify under their achievements at a Scottish Parliamentary Election (see Overview **A8**).

- **Gifts to housing associations** (*s 24A*)

  Gifts of UK land to a registered housing association or registered social landlord are exempt without upper limit. For the purposes of the exemption, 'land' includes any buildings that are attached to that land (IHTM11211).

- **Gifts for national purposes** (*s 25, Sch 3*)

  An unlimited exemption applies to qualifying transfers of value to those bodies designated in *Sch 3* which includes the National Museums of Scotland, Scottish Natural Heritage, the National Trust for Scotland for Places of Historic Interest or Natural Beauty, and any university or college. Gifts to the nation (within *Finance Act 2012, Sch 14, para 1*) are also exempt (*s 25(3)*).

- **Gifts for public benefit** (*s 26*) (repealed)

  Gifts within certain specified categories to bodies not established for profit were exempt from IHT if the Board so directed. This exemption was repealed for gifts made from 17 March 1998.

- **Maintenance funds for historic buildings, etc** (*s 27, Sch 4*)

  Transfers of value (during lifetime or on death) into settlement for the maintenance, repair or preservation of historic buildings and assets of outstanding scenic, historic or scientific interest, etc are exempt subject to certain conditions, where HMRC so direct (under *Sch 4*). The exemption must be claimed within two years after the date of the transfer concerned, or within such longer period as HMRC may allow (*s 27(1A)*).

- **Employee trusts** (*s 28, 28A*)

  Transfers, by an individual, of shares or securities in a company to 'trusts for the benefit of employees' of the company (within *s 86*) are exempt from IHT, if certain conditions are satisfied (*s 28*).

  Furthermore, legislation dealing with companies owned by 'employee-ownership trusts' (introduced in *Finance Act 2014* from 6 April 2014), provides a transfer of shares in a company by an individual to a trust is exempt from IHT broadly if the company meets a 'trading requirement' as defined, the trust meets an 'all-employee benefit requirement', and the trust does not meet a 'controlling interest' requirement immediately before the start of the tax year of transfer but does so at the end of that tax year (*s 28A*).

- **Other exemptions**

  - Annuities payable on a person's death under a registered pension scheme, a qualifying non-UK pension scheme or to a 'section 615 scheme' (ie a superannuation fund within *ICTA 1988, s 615(3)*) or, prior to 6 April 2006, either a retirement annuity contract or a personal pension scheme to a spouse, civil partner or dependant, where a capital sum might at the deceased's option have become payable instead to his personal representatives (*s 152*).

  - 'Killed in war', etc exemption (ie broadly property of a member of the armed services (or certain associated services) passing on death caused by injury or disease received or aggravated whilst on active service (*s 154*)). This exemption was extended by *FA 2015*, broadly to include circumstances where armed service personnel die while responding to an emergency, or where their death is hastened by injury or illness resulting from that emergency.

    In addition, provisions introduced in *FA 2015* extended IHT exemption in relation to an 'emergency responder' (ie broadly emergency services personnel and humanitarian aid workers) who die from an injury sustained, accident occurring or illness contracted in the line of duty, or whose death is hastened by illness aggravated when responding to emergency circumstances (*s 153A*). A further IHT exemption applies in relation to police constables and armed service personnel who die from an injury sustained or illness contracted as a result of being attacked due to their status, or from an illness aggravated in such circumstances (*s 155A*). These extended exemptions, which include any additional IHT on death for chargeable lifetime transfers and potentially exempt transfers, have effect in relation to deaths occurring from 19 March 2014.

– Foreign currency bank accounts held on the death of an individual not resident, or domiciled in the UK *(s 157)* (see **1.18**). A further condition as to ordinary residence in the UK applies where the person died before 6 April 2013.

Aside from the above exemptions, it should be noted that certain dispositions do not represent transfers of value for IHT purposes, such as dispositions not intended to confer gratuitous benefit (*s 10*) and dispositions for the maintenance of family (*s 11*); see **9.12**.

TAPER RELIEF: OUTLINE

1.30 IHT on all lifetime transfers (chargeable lifetime transfers and PETs) made within seven years before death is subject to a potential reduction for taper relief, if the lifetime transfer was made more than three years before death. Note that the relief reduces the IHT that would otherwise be payable on a transfer, not the value of the transfer itself.

Tax on chargeable lifetime transfers is calculated at lifetime rates. If the transferor dies within seven years the tax is recomputed at full death rates, subject to taper relief where the death is more than three years after the gift. However, taper relief cannot reduce the tax payable below that originally charged.

In addition, IHT at full death rates is calculated at the time of death on any PETs made within seven years prior to death, subject to the availability of taper relief. The value of the transfer stays the same for taper relief purposes, but the full rate(s) of IHT charged are reduced to a percentage of those rates on the following scale (*s 7(4)*):

Table 1.2—Taper relief rates

Transfer:	3–4 years before death: rate reduced to:	80%
	4–5 years before death:	60%
	5–6 years before death:	40%
	6–7 years before death:	20%

1.31 However, if IHT on a chargeable lifetime transfer is recalculated on death with taper relief and produces a lower tax figure than the tax originally calculated at lifetime rates, the original figure stands (*s 7(5)*); in other words, no IHT repayments result from the application of taper relief. For further commentary on taper relief, see **10.2–10.3**.

QUICK SUCCESSION RELIEF: OUTLINE

1.32 Quick succession relief (QSR) is available on the death of an individual whose estate has increased in value as the result of a chargeable transfer (ie during lifetime or a transfer on death) made within five years before his death (*s 141*).

If the conditions for QSR are satisfied, the tax charge on the later transfer is calculated in the normal way. The relief is then given by reducing the IHT on death by a percentage of the tax attributable to the net increase (see below) in the deceased's estate from the original transfer. It is not necessary for the asset in question to be retained. The percentage varies according to the length of time between the dates of transfer and death, as follows:

Table 1.3—Quick succession relief

Period between transfer and death	*Relief percentage*
One year or less	100%
1–2 years	80%
2–3 years	60%
3–4 years	40%
4–5 years	20%

The earlier transfer can, for example, be a failed PET on which IHT becomes payable. The same rates of quick succession relief apply to successive IHT charges within five years on trust property with an interest in possession.

Note one practical point in calculating QSR, the reference above to 'the net increase'. Suppose that, on the earlier death, the tax on the transfer was actually paid by the residue of the estate. Gifts of UK assets will be 'free of tax', in the sense that tax is borne by residue, unless the will provides to the contrary. In such a case, what the beneficiary gets is the full value of the gift, so his estate is increased by the full amount, and on death soon after the full amount features in the calculation of QSR (IHTM22072).

By contrast, suppose that the will had put the burden of tax on the gift itself: in that case what the beneficiary inherits is effectively less, and QSR is reduced accordingly (see example at IHTM22073).

QSR is also available in respect of lifetime charges on the termination of a lifetime interest in settled property (*s 141(1)(b)*), where certain conditions are satisfied (in *s 141(2)*).

For further commentary on QSR, see **10.4–10.5**.

DOUBLE TAXATION RELIEF

1.33 Where IHT is chargeable in the UK and tax of a similar nature (or which is chargeable by reference to death or lifetime gifts) is charged in another territory on the same property, double taxation relief may be available.

Treaty relief

1.34 Relief is given if the UK has a double taxation agreement with the overseas territory containing provisions to eliminate the double taxation chargeable by reference to death or lifetime gifts (*s 158*).

A person can be deemed domiciled in the UK for IHT purposes even though he is domiciled elsewhere under private international law (ie under the '17 out of the 20' tax years rule, or if domiciled in the UK within the previous three years (see **1.7**)). That person may also be domiciled elsewhere under the domestic law of another state. The 'deemed domicile' IHT rule does not apply in all cases, such as where certain pre-CTT double taxation agreements are still in force (ie by virtue of *s 158(6);* see *s 267(2)*). Those agreements contain their own rules for domicile and for resolving the issue where both countries claim domicile.

As indicated at **1.8** above, HMRC accept that domicile issues exclude deemed domicile when considering the double tax agreements with France, Italy, India and Pakistan, although if domicile under common law is in France, Italy, India or Pakistan, the deemed domicile rules can apply to chargeable *lifetime* transfers (IHTM13024).

It should also be noted that an election to treat a non-UK spouse as domiciled in the UK (see **1.6**) does not apply for certain purposes, including when considering a person's domicile in connection with double taxation agreements with France, Italy, India or Pakistan (*s 267ZA(6)*; see IHTM13047).

The double taxation conventions between the UK and other countries in force for IHT purposes (under *s 158*) are listed in HMRC's Inheritance Tax Manual (at IHTM27161), and also on the gov.uk website (www.gov.uk/inheritance-tax-double-taxation-relief#11).

Unilateral relief

1.35 Where relief is not provided under a double tax agreement, credit is available against UK tax for tax suffered in an overseas territory, on the same property (*s 159*). Unilateral relief may also be claimed if it provides greater relief than by applying treaty relief (*s 159(7)*).

If the property is situated in the overseas territory and not in the UK, credit is available on the whole amount of overseas tax. However, if the overseas tax exceeds the UK tax, the excess is not repayable.

A measure of relief is also available if the property is situated as follows (*s 159(3)*):

- in a third territory; or
- both in the UK and the overseas territory (ie due to different laws on the situs of assets in the UK and that territory).

Relief similarly applies if tax is imposed in two or more overseas territories if the property is situated as follows (*s 159(4)*):

- neither in the UK nor those territories; or
- both in the UK and in each of those territories.

CLOSE COMPANIES

Transfers of value

1.36 Anti-avoidance provisions apply to transfers of value (eg sales at undervalue) by close companies. Only individuals can make a chargeable transfer for IHT purposes (*s 2(1)*). However, if a close company makes a transfer of value, the transfer is apportioned between the participators in that company (*s 94*). Each participator is deemed to have made an immediately chargeable transfer of value (ie not a PET) equal to the amount so apportioned. The company is primarily liable to pay any IHT liability arising (*s 202*).

However, if the participator's estate increases as a result of the transfer, that increase may be deducted from the amount so apportioned. The balance reflects the net decrease in value of the person's estate. Therefore, a transfer of value to a participator with a 100% interest in the close company should not normally result in an overall decrease in the value of his estate.

Focus

A transfer of value is not apportioned to participators in the following circumstances (*s 94(2)*):

- if the amount is liable to income tax or corporation tax (or would be taken into account but for exemption in respect of UK company distributions) in the recipient's hands, eg as employment income or dividend income of the individual; or
- the participator is not domiciled in the UK, and the relevant asset is situated abroad.

1.37 If the participator has less than 5% of the transfer apportioned to him, the transfer is not added to his cumulative total of transfers for IHT purposes (*s 94(4)*), and no IHT liability attaches to that person in respect of the transfer.

The tax is calculated by reference to the participator's IHT position at that time, although he cannot be held liable to pay the IHT if the company is in default (*s 202(2)*). The annual IHT exemption may be deducted (if not already used elsewhere) from the value of any amount apportioned (*s 94(5)*).

Alterations of capital

1.38 The IHT anti-avoidance rules for close companies also include provisions relating to alterations in unquoted share capital, loan capital or rights attaching to its unquoted shares or debentures.

Participators to whom those provisions apply are broadly treated as having made a disposition for IHT purposes, which is not a PET (s 98).

HMRC guidance on the provisions (at IHTM14855) includes two examples, the first involving two new classes of shares being created with one class each issued to two of the company's three existing shareholders, and the second illustrating the issue of shares which vary the proportions in which the company's share capital are held.

Chapter 2

Lifetime transfers

SIGNPOSTS

- **Exemptions, etc** – Certain lifetime transfers of value are exempt for IHT purposes, and some dispositions are not treated as transfers of value at all (see **2.1–2.4**).
- **PETs** – Potentially exempt transfers (PETs) are assumed to be exempt when made, subject to a seven-year survival period. Most lifetime gifts into trust ceased to qualify as PETs from 22 March 2006. PETs can be actual or 'deemed'. If a PET becomes chargeable, it also affects the individual's cumulative total of chargeable transfers (see **2.5–2.15**).
- **Chargeable lifetime transfers** – These are aggregated over a seven-year period. IHT is charged on a transfer as the highest part of the cumulative total. A lifetime gift is broadly valued based on the reduction in the transferor's estate. A 'gift with reservation' is treated as forming part of the donor's estate on death. There are also anti-avoidance provisions regarding 'associated operations' affecting transfers of value (see **2.16–2.24**).
- **'Pilot' trusts** – Anti-avoidance provisions are targeted at arrangements involving the use of multiple settlements and the addition of assets to those settlements on the same day, subject to certain limited exceptions (see **2.24**).
- **Calculating IHT** – In some cases, it may be necessary to look back at lifetime transfers up to a maximum of 14 years before the date of death. Chargeable lifetime transfers are subject to reporting requirements, unless certain exceptions apply (see **2.25–2.28**).

INTRODUCTION

2.1 IHT is a tax on 'chargeable transfers' made on or after 18 March 1986 during an individual's lifetime, and on the value of the death estate. A 'chargeable transfer' is any transfer of value made by an individual, other than an exempt transfer (*IHTA 1984, s 2(1)*; all statutory references in this chapter are to *IHTA 1984*, unless otherwise stated).

A 'potentially exempt transfer' (PET) becomes an exempt transfer seven years after the date of the gift. It is assumed that a PET will become an exempt transfer when the gift is made (*s 3A(5)*). An outright lifetime gift to another individual (or a trust for disabled persons, or a trust for bereaved minors in certain circumstances; see **1.15**) is a PET, which therefore only becomes chargeable to IHT if the donor dies within seven years of making the gift.

However, transfers to a company and gifts to a relevant property trust (ie discretionary trusts and, from 22 March 2006, most interest in possession trusts) are immediately chargeable lifetime transfers. IHT at the lifetime rate may become due (subject to any reliefs and exemptions) if the total value of those gifts exceeds the taxable IHT threshold or 'nil rate band' (£325,000 for 2016/17).

EXEMPT LIFETIME TRANSFERS

2.2 In addition to PETs made more than seven years before the donor's death, certain lifetime transfers are exempt from IHT.

For further information on IHT exemptions generally, see **1.20** and **Chapter 9**.

2.3 *Lifetime* exemptions are summarised below:

- Gifts between spouses or civil partners (note that the exemption is restricted if the transferor is domiciled in the UK but the transferee is domiciled outside the UK). The exempt transfer limit is the prevailing available nil rate band limit at the time of the transfer (from 6 April 2013; previously, the limit was £55,000). However, there is an election facility for the non-UK domiciled spouse or civil partner to be treated as UK domiciled for IHT purposes: see **1.6**) (*s 18*).
- Annual exemption for gifts not exceeding £3,000 in any tax year. If the total value of gifts in one tax year is less than £3,000, the excess can be carried forward to the next tax year, but no further (*s 19*).
- Small gifts in any tax year up to a total of £250 per donee, to as many recipients as the donor wishes (*s 20*).
- Normal expenditure out of income is exempt with no upper limit, if certain conditions are satisfied (broadly that the gifts are part of the donor's usual expenditure, were made out of income, and left the donor with sufficient income to maintain his normal standard of living (*s 21*)).

- Wedding or civil partnership gifts within certain limits (£5,000 if the donor is a parent of a party to the marriage or civil partnership, £2,500 if the donor is a remoter ancestor or is one of the parties to the marriage or civil partnership, or £1,000 for any other donor) (*s 22*).
- Gifts to charities or registered clubs (*s 23*).
- Gifts to qualifying parliamentary political parties (*s 24*) (see **1.21** and Overview **A8**).
- Gifts to registered housing associations (*s 24A*).
- Gifts for national purposes (eg the National Galleries of Scotland, National Museums of Scotland and the National Trust for Scotland) (*s 25, Sch 3*), and gifts to the nation (within *Finance Act 2012, Sch 14, para 1*).
- Transfers to maintenance funds for historic buildings, where HMRC so direct upon making a claim (*s 27, Sch 4*).
- Transfers of shares or securities by an individual to an employee trust (within *s 86*) subject to certain conditions (*s 28*). In addition, following legislation in *Finance Act 2014,* a transfer of shares in a company by an individual to an 'employee ownership trust' is exempt from IHT broadly if the company meets a 'trading requirement' as defined, the trust meets an 'all-employee benefit requirement' and the trust does not meet a 'controlling interest' requirement immediately before the start of the tax year of transfer but does so at the end of that tax year (*s 28A*).
- Transfers of national heritage property may be exempt from IHT where certain conditions are satisfied, ie 'conditionally exempt transfers' (*ss 30–35A*).

Dispositions that are not transfers of value

2.4 Certain actual and deemed 'dispositions' (eg gifts, payments or actions, such as the waiver of salary or dividends if certain conditions are satisfied) are not treated as transfers of value, and are therefore not taken into account for IHT purposes (*ss 10–17*) (see **Chapter 9**).

This includes dispositions which are not intended to confer a gratuitous benefit on anyone (*s 10*), and payments for the maintenance of certain family members, eg current or ex-spouse or civil partner, the donor's children (including adopted children and stepchildren) who are under 18 for their education and training, and relatives who are dependent due to old age or infirmity (*s 11*); as to the latter category of disposition, see *R McKelvey (personal representative of D V McKelvey) v HMRC* [2008] SSCD 944 (SpC 694), discussed at **15.22**.

'Maintenance' for the above purposes usually means making periodic payments rather than lump sum provision (see *Phizackerley v HMRC* [2007] WTLR 745).

In addition, following legislation (new *s 12A*) introduced in *Finance Act 2016*, where a person has failed to exercise their rights to draw designated pension funds from a 'drawdown fund' (including a flexi-access drawdown fund) during the person's lifetime (and as a result has unused funds when they die), this does not give rise to a deemed disposition (under *s 3(3)*) as an omission to exercise a right.

POTENTIALLY EXEMPT TRANSFERS

Definition and scope

2.5 A PET is a transfer of value made by an individual (as opposed to a 'person', which has a wider meaning, including a company), which would otherwise be a chargeable transfer. A PET made seven years or more before the transferor's death is exempt; any other PET is a chargeable transfer.

A PET is treated as exempt whilst the donor is alive, and in the seven-year period following the transfer it is assumed that the PET will become exempt (*s 3A(5)*).

In the case of a life insurance policy taken out or varied (since 26 March 1974) for the benefit of someone else, if an annuity was also taken out (before, at the same time or after the policy), then unless the taxpayer can show that the purchase of the annuity and the taking out of the policy were not associated operations (within *s 268*), a transfer of value of a specified amount is treated as having been made in taking the policy out for someone else, which can qualify as a PET (*s 263*; see IHTM20374).

This form of IHT planning (known as 'back-to-back arrangements') is otherwise intended to benefit from the 'normal expenditure out of income' exemption, although an anti-avoidance provision can deny the exemption (*s 21(2)*). HMRC practice is not to treat arrangements as associated operations (and not to disqualify the premiums from being normal expenditure for exemption purposes) if it can be shown that the life policy was issued on 'normal' terms. This means that full evidence of health must have been obtained, and that the terms on which the policy was issued would have been the same even if the annuity had not been bought (*SP E4*).

For back-to-back life policy arrangements involving husband and wife (or civil partners), full medical evidence should be obtained in respect of both parties (*Smith v Revenue and Customs Commissioners* [2008] STC 1649).

In addition, the capital element of a purchased life annuity (within *ITTOIA 2005, s 423*) purchased on or after 13 November 1974, which is exempt for income tax purposes (under *ITTOIA 2005, s 717*), is not regarded as part of the transferor's income for the purposes of the normal expenditure exemption (*s 21(3), (4)*).

Transfers before 22 March 2006

2.6 Before 22 March 2006, gifts qualified as PETs if made by an individual to:

- another individual (or to an interest in possession trust for another individual);
- an accumulation and maintenance trust; or
- the trustees of a trust for a disabled person.

Transfers from 22 March 2006

2.7 From 22 March 2006, gifts to an accumulation and maintenance trust (to the extent that such trusts remain in existence) ceased to be PETs, ie they are immediately chargeable transfers (*s 3A(1)–(1A)*). Gifts to interest in possession trusts are discussed below.

A 'transfer of value' is a disposition made by a person resulting in the value of his estate immediately afterwards being less than it otherwise would be; the difference is the value transferred. The measure of the transfer is, therefore, the reduction in the transferor's estate (*s 3(1)*).

A gift to another individual is a PET to the extent that the value transferred becomes comprised in that individual's estate, or to the extent that the transfer results in an increase in his estate (eg the forgiveness of a loan to another individual).

2.8

Focus

- A gift to a disabled person's trust is a PET to the extent that it becomes settled property within *s 89* ('Trusts for disabled persons') (*s 3A(3), (3A)*);
- A disabled person's interest within *s 89A* (Self-settlement by a person where it is reasonable to expect that the person's condition

would lead to that person falling within the definition of 'disabled person') is a qualifying interest in possession (ie within *s 49(1A)*), so the gift is effectively a non-event for IHT purposes, as it is treated as remaining part of the settlor's estate (*s 89B(1)(b)*);

- The same IHT treatment applies to an interest in possession which is self-settled on or after 22 March 2006 by a person with a condition expected to lead to disability, and to which the person is beneficially entitled, where certain conditions are satisfied as to the distribution of the settled property (*s 89B(1)(d)*);
- An interest in possession to which the disabled person became beneficially entitled on or after 22 March 2006 is also a qualifying interest in possession, where certain conditions are satisfied as to the distribution of the settled property (*s 89B(1)(c)*);
- A gift to a disabled person's trust by another individual constitutes a PET, within *s 3A(1), (1A)* (see IHTM42805).

In addition, a gift into a 'bereaved minor's' trust is a PET if made on the ending of an 'immediate post-death interest' (*s 3A(1A)(c)(iii)*) (see **Chapter 7**). Prior to 22 March 2006, a lifetime gift to an accumulation and maintenance trust was also a PET, if it became settled property within *s 71* ('Accumulation and maintenance trusts').

Certain transfers of value are specifically prevented from being PETs, including:

- transfers by a close company (*s 94(1)*; see IHTM14853);
- the deemed disposition on an alteration in the capital or share rights of close companies (*s 98(3)*);
- the release of a life interest between 18 March 1986 and 16 March 1987 (see IHTM04063);
- the gift of a purchased reversionary interest within *s 81A* (see **2.9**);
- the lifetime termination of an interest in possession (within *s 52*) to which *s 5(1B)* applies (ie where a UK domiciled person became beneficially entitled to the interest following a disposition which was prevented from being a transfer of value by virtue of *s 10* ('Dispositions not intended to confer a gratuitous benefit') (*s 3A(6A)*) (see **2.14**); and
- a transfer to the extent to which the property transferred consists of woodlands subject to a deferred estate duty charge (*Finance Act 1986, Sch 19, para 46*).

Purchased reversionary interests

2.9 If a reversionary interest (ie a future trust interest) in relevant property has been purchased for money or money's worth, or is held by the settlor or spouse or civil partner, a deemed disposal arises for IHT purposes when the reversionary interest ends and entitlement to an interest in possession begins. The resulting IHT charge is based on the value of the reversionary interest immediately before it ended. A gift of such a reversionary interest is prevented by legislation from being a PET (*s 81A*).

This rule applies to reversionary interests arising from 9 December 2009, but does not affect interests in possession outside the 'relevant property' regime, such as a disabled person's interest.

Deemed PETs

2.10 An exception to the general rule that occasions of IHT charge (ie where tax is charged as if a transfer of value had been made) are excluded from being PETs applies to charges under *s 52* ('Charge on termination of an interest in possession') (*s 3A(6)–(7)*). This exception relates to transfers of value from 17 March 1987. The release of a life interest is a PET in the circumstances outlined below.

Before 22 March 2006

2.11 The disposal or release of an individual's beneficial entitlement to an interest in possession in settled property by gift before 22 March 2006 is a PET in the following cases (*s 3A*):

- another individual becomes beneficially entitled to the property in question (or to an interest in possession in that property); or
- the property is settled on accumulation and maintenance trusts or trusts for the disabled; or
- the value of another individual's estate is increased.

From 22 March 2006

2.12 An interest in possession created before 22 March 2006 and disposed of or released by gift to someone else from that date is a PET as above, unless the rules for bereaved minors (*s 71A*) or 'Age 18-to-25 trusts' (*s 71D*) applied to the trust property in which the interest subsisted immediately before that disposal (*ss 51(1B), 53(1A)*).

If an individual has an interest in trust property, which remains comprised in his estate for IHT purposes (eg an 'immediate post-death interest'), if that interest is later terminated or gifted but he continues to enjoy the property thereafter, the rules regarding 'gifts with reservation' (in *Finance Act 1986, s 102*) apply. The individual is treated for the purposes of those anti-avoidance provisions as having made a gift of the interest terminated or given away (*Finance Act 1986*, s *102ZA(2)*).

In the case of an interest created on or after 22 March 2006, a subsequent disposal or release of the life interest by gift is a PET if it is an 'immediate post-death interest', a 'disabled person's interest' or a 'transitional serial interest' (*ss 3A(6A), 51(1A)*).

For further information on interests in possession generally, see **Chapter 7**.

2.13 Certain transfers are treated as if they were PETs, ie the lifetime cessation of a benefit in 'gift with reservation' property (*Finance Act 1986, s 102(4)*) (see **2.22**), and the discharge or reduction of a debt subject to abatement (see below).

The release of a life interest between 18 March 1986 and 16 March 1987 cannot be a PET and is, therefore, an immediately chargeable transfer. This is because a transfer of value was originally prevented (by *s 3A(2)*) from being a PET if it resulted in settled property becoming comprised in an individual's estate, or in an increase in the value of settled property already comprised in the estate.

A further deemed PET arises on the discharge, or reduction, of a debt subject to abatement under *Finance Act 1986, s 103* ('Treatment of certain debts and incumbrances') on or after 18 March 1986 (*Finance Act 1986, s 103(5)*).

Interests in possession under s 5(1B)

2.14 There is an exception from PET treatment in respect of an IHT charge under *s 52*, where a UK domiciled person purchased an interest in possession at arm's length. Such an IHT charge is prevented from being a PET (ie it is immediately chargeable), if the person's beneficial entitlement to the interest arose on or after 9 December 2009 (*s 3A(6A)*).

This is a targeted anti-avoidance rule, as the background note to the relevant clause in Finance Bill 2010 explains:

> 'HM Revenue & Customs (HMRC) became aware of arrangements that sought to avoid any IHT charges on assets that are put into a trust. The arrangement was designed to allow individuals who would normally be chargeable to IHT on transfers in to trust to purchase an interest in a trust

that had not been subject to UK IHT charges when property had originally been transferred in to it.'

A disposition which is not intended to confer gratuitous benefit (within *s 10*) is not a transfer of value. This could apply to the arm's-length purchase of an interest in possession. A lifetime interest in possession settlement made after 21 March 2006 (other than a disabled person's interest) does not generally form part of the estate of the person beneficially entitled to the interest (*s 5(1A)*). Without the above anti-avoidance rule, the arm's-length purchase of such an interest in possession could therefore have resulted in that interest falling outside a person's estate.

However, *s 5(1B)* provides that the interest forms part of the estate of a person who was domiciled in the UK upon becoming beneficially entitled to it, if that entitlement arose by virtue of a disposition within *s 10*. In addition, the lifetime termination of such an interest is an immediately chargeable transfer, since it is prevented from being a PET, as indicated above.

Further anti-avoidance provisions were introduced in *Finance Act 2012*, which target IHT avoidance schemes involving the acquisition of interests in excluded property trusts (see **3.5**).

Implications of PETs

2.15 As indicated at **2.1** above, it is assumed that a PET will become an exempt transfer when made. Prior to death, it is therefore only necessary to notify HMRC of the transfer if it is relevant to the application of the annual IHT exemption in respect of an immediately chargeable transfer (see below). However, the PET is not cumulated with the immediately chargeable transfer. A PET becomes an exempt transfer if the donor survives seven years after the date of the gift, but is otherwise chargeable to IHT if the donor dies within that seven-year period.

Notwithstanding the assumption that a PET will become an exempt transfer, in HMRC's view the annual exemption (if available) should be allocated against the PET when it is made. This appears to be on the basis that a transfer of value only qualifies as a PET to the extent that it would, apart from *s 3A*, be a chargeable transfer (eg if not covered by an exemption) (IHTM04024).

If an individual dies within seven years, the earlier PET becomes chargeable to IHT at the date of that gift. For the purposes of allocating the annual exemption, a chargeable PET is deemed to have been made later than any non-PET made in the same tax year (*s 19(3A)*). However, HMRC practice (see below) is to allocate the annual exemption to transfers of value in chronological order, at least initially.

For example, if an individual makes a PET (eg a gift to a sibling) earlier in the same tax year than a chargeable lifetime transfer (eg a gift to a discretionary trust), HMRC guidance (at IHTM14143) indicates that where tax is otherwise payable on the two transfers made on different days in the same tax year, the exemption should be applied to the earlier transfer, and that this would be the case irrespective of whether the transfers were PETs or chargeable when made.

If a PET becomes chargeable, IHT is calculated at the death rates applicable at the time of death, subject to any taper relief (see **10.2**). In addition, the transfer is cumulated with the death estate, and will also affect the individual's cumulative total of chargeable transfers (see **Example 2.1**).

Example 2.1—Death within seven years of a PET

Mr Smith died on 30 April 2016, having made the following lifetime gifts:

		£
1 June 2013	Cash gift to daughter	150,000
6 April 2015	Cash gift to discretionary trust	263,000

Lifetime IHT position of gifts

The IHT position on making the lifetime gifts is that the cash gift to Mr Smith's daughter on 1 June 2013 is a PET, which is not cumulated but uses his annual exemptions of £6,000 (ie £3,000 for 2013/14, plus £3,000 unused exemption brought forward from 2012/13).

The creation of the discretionary trust on 6 April 2015 was an immediately chargeable transfer, but the amount chargeable to IHT of £257,000 (ie £263,000 less £3,000 annual exemptions for 2015/16 and 2014/15) was less than the nil rate band, so no IHT was payable.

IHT position of lifetime gifts on death

(a) On the gift to Mr Smith's daughter:

	£
Gift to daughter	150,000
Less: annual exemption (× 2)	(6,000)
	144,000
Less: nil rate band (2016/17)	(144,000)
	Nil

(b) On creation of the discretionary trust:

	£
Cash gift to trust	263,000
Less: annual exemption (× 2)	(6,000)
	257,000
Less: nil rate band remaining	
(£325,000 – £144,000)	(181,000)
	76,000
IHT @ 40%	£30,400

Taper relief is not in point, as the gift was within three years of Mr Smith's death.

CHARGEABLE LIFETIME TRANSFERS

2.16 A chargeable lifetime transfer is a transfer of value made by an individual, which is not unconditionally or potentially exempt (*s 2(1)*). Hence this includes the following:

- transfers into relevant property trusts, such as discretionary trusts, or terminations of pre-22 March 2006 interests in possession in favour of such trusts (and, from 22 March 2006, lifetime gifts into most trusts); and
- transfers by close companies, which can be charged on the shareholders in some cases (*ss 94–97, 202*).

In addition, see **2.8** above for transfers of value that are chargeable on the basis that they cannot be treated as PETs.

A chargeable lifetime transfer is aggregated with other such transfers over a seven-year period, following which they fall out of the cumulative total. Business property relief and agricultural property relief may reduce the value of the gift, if the relief conditions are satisfied at the date of transfer (see **Chapter 11**). The rate of IHT is determined by reference to this total. Tax is charged (at half the rate at death) on the transfer as the highest part of the cumulative total, to the extent that it exceeds the nil rate band, after deducting any available reliefs and exemptions.

Where the transferor bears the IHT liability, the tax represents a further loss in the value of his estate, and the transfer must, therefore, be grossed-up to arrive at the overall amount of the chargeable transfer.

Example 2.2—Cumulation of chargeable lifetime transfers

Martin made the following lifetime gifts (after exemptions and reliefs):

			£
1 June 2007	–	Discretionary trust	50,000
6 April 2010	–	Discretionary trust	85,000
31 December 2014	–	Gift to daughter (PET)	100,000
6 April 2016	–	Discretionary trust	340,000

The transfer to the discretionary trust in 2007 was made more than seven years before the transfer in 2016, but the transfer in 2010 is taken into account. The PET in 2014 is ignored when calculating lifetime tax on the chargeable transfer in 2016.

If Martin agrees to pay the tax on his lifetime gifts, his IHT position is as follows:

1 June 2007 – Discretionary trust £50,000

The transfer is covered by the nil rate band.

6 April 2010 – Discretionary trust £85,000

The transfer (although cumulated with the earlier transfer on 1 June 2007) is covered by the nil rate band.

6 April 2016 – Discretionary trust £340,000

The transfer is cumulated with the earlier transfer on 6 April 2010. However, it is not cumulated with the transfer on 1 June 2007 (ie more than seven years ago). Nor is it cumulated with the gift to Martin's daughter on 31 December 2014 (ie a PET when made).

The IHT position is, therefore, as follows:

	£
IHT:	
£240,000 (ie £325,000 – £85,000) × nil	NIL
£100,000 × ¼ (ie grossed-up)	25,000
	£25,000

The gross value of the transfer is £340,000 + £25,000 = £365,000

2.17 Additional IHT becomes chargeable at the 'death rate' (40% for 2016/17) in respect of immediately chargeable lifetime transfers made within seven years from the death of the transferor. The gift is cumulated with immediately chargeable gifts and PETs in the preceding seven years. The resulting IHT (recalculated at the full death rate) is compared with the lifetime tax paid (if any), for the purposes of calculating any additional liability. However, if the recomputed figure is lower than the IHT paid at the time of transfer, no additional tax is payable, but the difference is not repaid.

Example 2.3—Chargeable lifetime transfers: position on death

Continuing the above example, suppose that Martin died on 5 October 2016. The additional IHT on death would be as follows (after reliefs and exemptions):

6 April 2010 – Discretionary trust £85,000

The transfer (cumulated with the earlier transfer on 1 June 2007) remains covered by the nil rate band.

31 December 2014 – Gift to daughter £100,000

The 'failed' PET is cumulated with the discretionary trust transfer on 6 April 2009 (but not the gift on 1 June 2007, which falls out of charge). The cumulative total (ie £100,000 + £85,000 = £185,000) is covered by the IHT nil rate band.

6 April 2016 – Discretionary trust £340,000

The transfer is cumulated with the transfers on 6 April 2010 and 31 December 2014. The additional IHT on the gross value of the transfer (ie £365,000) is calculated as follows (Note – the trustees pay the additional IHT liability):

	£
IHT:	
£140,000 (ie £325,000 – £185,000) × nil	NIL
£225,000 × 40% (note – no taper relief)	90,000
	90,000
Less: IHT paid at lifetime rates	(25,000)
Additional IHT due (paid by the trustees)	£65,000

2.18 The calculation of additional tax on death may be affected by considerations such as the following, which are discussed in subsequent chapters:

- the availability of relief for business and agricultural property (see **Chapter 11**);
- the application of other reliefs (if available). For example, a reduction in additional IHT on death may be claimed (ie by the person liable for the tax) if the value of an asset has fallen between the date of gift and the date of the transferor's death (or an earlier qualifying sale of the gifted property) (*ss 131–140* 'Transfers within seven years before death') (see **Chapter 10**); and
- whether the 'gifts with reservation' anti-avoidance rules apply (see **2.20** below).

VALUING LIFETIME TRANSFERS

General

2.19 The general rule is that assets are valued for IHT purposes at the price they might reasonably be expected to fetch if sold in the open market at the time of transfer (*s 160*).

The importance of obtaining accurate asset valuations cannot be overstated. HMRC have in recent years taken a much tougher approach to market valuations of property, especially where there might be development potential. HMRC has produced a toolkit to assist tax agents and others when completing the account Form IHT400 (www.hmrc.gov.uk/agents/toolkits/iht.pdf). The toolkit identifies particular areas of risk when completing an IHT400, and states: 'Valuations are the biggest single area of risk, accounting for a large part of our compliance checks'.

Inaccurate asset valuations carry the threat of possible interest and penalties, as well as further IHT liabilities. It is therefore advisable to obtain valuations for IHT purposes from at least one suitably qualified professional to help reduce such risks.

However, the value of a lifetime gift is measured by the reduction in value of the transferor's estate as a result of the transfer (but not normally taking into account the value of any excluded property ceasing to form part of the estate (*s 3(2)*)). The value of the gift will often equal the loss to the estate, but not always. For example, the loss to the estate of a 51% shareholder in a private company who makes a lifetime gift of 2% is greater than the value of the 2% gift; it is the value of the shareholder's loss of control in the company.

Liabilities are taken into account in valuing the estate at the date of transfer, if imposed by law or to the extent of being incurred for consideration in money or money's worth (*s 5(3), (5)*).

A liability attaching to a particular asset will generally reduce the value of that asset (*s 162(4)*).

However, *Finance Act 2013* introduced restrictions and conditions for deductions in respect of liabilities to be allowable, including rules determining how liabilities may be deducted in certain circumstances involving excluded property (see **1.18**), 'relievable property' (ie qualifying business or agricultural property (see **Chapter 11**) or property eligible for woodlands relief (see **10.24**)), and also rules concerning the repayment of liabilities after death.

Further legislation (introduced in *Finance Act 2014*) treats funds held in foreign currency accounts in UK banks which are left out of account in determining the value of a person's estate on death for IHT purposes (under *s 157*) in a similar way to excluded property for the purposes of the above provisions restricting how liabilities are deducted from the value of the estate for IHT purposes (*s 162AA*). The provisions regarding liabilities are outlined at **3.13**.

Valuing PETs

2.20 If property becomes comprised in another individual's estate, or becomes qualifying settled property, the value transferred by a PET is generally calculated by reference to the loss to the transferor's estate. There is no 'grossing-up' because the transferor is not liable for the tax on a PET.

The loss to the transferor's estate will often (but not always) be the same as the increase in value of the transferee's estate. For example, the forgiveness of a loan should result in a loss to the estate and corresponding increase. Conversely, HMRC cites the omission to exercise a right as a circumstance where the 'loss to transferor' principle may not apply (IHTM04066).

Valuing transfers by close companies

2.21 In the case of a close company transfer of value (see **1.27**), IHT is charged as if each individual participator had made a transfer of the amount apportioned to them by reference to their rights and interests in the company immediately before the transfer. The transfer is based on the net amount apportioned to each participator after taking account of any corresponding increase in that participator's estate following the transfer.

The annual exemption specifically applies to these transfers if not otherwise used elsewhere (*s 94(5)*), and the spouse or civil partner exemption is also available to the extent that the estate of the spouse or civil partner of a participator is increased (IHTM04068).

Alterations to a close company's unquoted share or loan capital (eg a subscription for valuable shares at par by an individual), or any rights attaching to its unquoted shares or debentures, are also treated as dispositions made by the participators (*s 98(1)*), which are apportioned among the participators in the same way as a transfer by a close company. The disposition is specifically prohibited from being treated as a PET (*s 98(3)*).

GIFTS WITH RESERVATION

2.22 The 'gifts with reservation' (GWR) anti-avoidance provisions (*Finance Act 1986, ss 102–102C, Sch 20*) apply to lifetime gifts in certain circumstances. The rules are designed to prevent 'cake and eat it' situations, whereby an individual gifts an asset but continues to have the use or enjoyment of it. As mentioned, most lifetime gifts to individuals are PETs if not otherwise exempt, which only become chargeable if the transferor dies within seven years of the transfer.

Without the GWR rules, if the transferor survived the transfer by seven years, the PET would become an exempt transfer, even though for all practical purposes the transferor may have continued to enjoy the gifted asset until their death.

The effect of the GWR rules is broadly to ensure that the property subject to a GWR is treated as forming part of the donor's death estate. If the benefit is ended during his lifetime, the donor is treated as having made a PET at that time when the benefit ends (*Finance Act 1986, s 102(4)*), which becomes a chargeable transfer on death within the following seven years.

However, because the PET is not actual but deemed (ie because there is no actual transfer of value when the GWR ceases) the annual exemption is not available to offset against it. The property transferred by the PET is valued on the basis of the loss to the transferor's estate (IHTM04073).

In the absence of provisions to the contrary, IHT could become chargeable on the initial lifetime transfer, and on the value of the relevant asset when the reservation ceased (eg upon death). However, the GWR rules are supplemented by regulations designed to prevent a double tax charge arising (*Inheritance Tax (Double Charges Relief) Regulations, SI 1987/1130*).

For further commentary on the GWR rules, see **Chapter 5**).

ASSOCIATED OPERATIONS

2.23 As mentioned, a transfer of value is any disposition made by a person as a result of which the value of his estate immediately after the disposition is less than it would be but for the disposition; and the amount by which it is less is the value transferred by the transfer (*s 3(1)*). A 'disposition' is defined (by *s 272*) to include a disposition effected by associated operations.

The 'associated operations' provision is a further anti-avoidance rule, which provides for transactions to be treated as being made (whether directly or indirectly) by way of two or more linked operations (*s 268*). Where this rule applies to transfers at different times, the combined effect on the value of the transferor's estate will be taken into account and treated as made at the time of the last transfer. The provision applies to transactions affecting the same property or a series of linked transactions, which need not be effected by the same person.

The following example is taken from HMRC's Inheritance Tax Manual (at IHTM14821):

Example 2.4—Associated operations

'T has a 100% shareholding in ABC Ltd. At 11 June 2011 it is valued at £100,000.

T transfers:

- a 33% holding to s on 11 June 2011
- a 33% holding to s on 12 June 2011 and
- a 34% holding to R on 13 June 2011

Following T's death in August 2011, the loss to the estate on each transfer is individually valued at:

- £43,000
- £26,000, and
- £17,000 respectively.

A total of £86,000.

The total of the individual transfers for inheritance tax is only £86,000 but T had effectively given away £100,000 worth of assets.

The legislation at *IHTA 1984, s 268* counters this in certain circumstances so that you can look at the overall effect of several events through the concept of "associated operations".'

2.24 However, case law has effectively restricted the scope of the associated operations rule in certain situations (see below).

The omission to exercise a right can be an 'operation' treated as an associated operation for these purposes (*s 268(1)*). However, the associated operations rule does not apply to associate the grant of a lease for full consideration in money or money's worth, with any operation effected more than three years after the grant (*s 268(2)*).

The value of a transfer made through associated operations is normally the overall loss to the transferor's estate, measured at the time of the last operation. However, if any of the earlier operations was also a transfer of value by the transferor, the value transferred by the earlier operation(s) (to the extent that the spouse or civil partner exemption is not available) is deducted from the overall amount (*s 268(3)*).

Property added to multiple trusts on the same day

With regard to the creation of settlements anti-avoidance provisions have been targeted at arrangements involving the use of multiple ('pilot') trusts and the addition of assets to those trusts on the same day.

Prior to the introduction of those provisions, in *Rysaffe Trustee Co (CI) Ltd v IRC* [2003] STC 536, the Court of Appeal held that as a matter of general law five separate discretionary settlements created on different dates (ie to maximise the availability of nil rate bands) on very similar terms constituted separate settlements for the purposes of the ten-year anniversary charge (under *s 64)*. The court rejected HMRC's contention of only a single settlement, existing by associated operations. The settlor had intended separate settlements. Hence each settlement was eligible for its own nil rate band, as each settlement had been created by a 'disposition'.

IHT planning arrangements involving the use of 'pilot' trusts are among those included in 'HMRC's general anti-abuse rule (GAAR) guidance' (see Part D – Examples at www.gov.uk/government/uploads/system/uploads/attachment_data/file/399271/3__HMRC_GAAR_Guidance_Part_D_with_effect_from_XX_November_2014_chm_171214v2.pdf). The guidance states (at D26.5.3): 'The practice was litigated in the case of *Rysaffe Trustee v IRC* [2003] STC 536. HMRC lost the case and having chosen not to change the legislation, must be taken to have accepted the practice'. It concludes: 'The arrangements accord with established practice accepted by HMRC and are accordingly not regarded as abusive'.

However, following a series of HMRC consultations on complexity and fairness issues relating to the IHT rules for trusts, draft Finance Bill 2015 anti-avoidance legislation published on 10 December 2014 included a provision broadly aimed at settlors creating pilot trusts and avoiding IHT through the availability of multiple nil rate bands. This provision is aimed at ensuring that where property is added to two or more settlements on the same day (and after the commencement of those settlements) the value of the added property, together with the value of property settled at the date of commencement (if the settlements are not related), is generally brought into account in calculating the IHT rate for the purposes of various chargeable events for trusts (ie ten-year charges (under *s 66*), exit charges before the first ten-year anniversary (under *s 68*), exit charges between anniversaries (under *s 69*) and the charge on 18/25 trusts (under *s 71F*)).

However, there is an exception from the same day additions rules in respect of same day transfers of value of £5,000 or less made during the settlor's lifetime, subject to an 'anti-fragmentation' rule (see *s 62A(2)–(4)*). The same day addition treatment is also subject to certain exceptions (see *s 62B*), including additions to 'protected settlements' (see below).

This anti-avoidance measure applies to the above relevant property trust charges arising on or after 18 November 2015 (ie the date on which *Finance (No 2) Act 2015* received Royal Assent).

However, the same day addition provisions do not apply to 'protected settlements' (*s 62C*). These are broadly relevant property trusts created before 10 December 2014 (ie the date when draft legislation was initially published), where the settlor has made no additions from that date. Note that whilst there is an exception from the same day additions rule for transfers of value of £5,000 or less (see above), transfers of value of *any* amount by the settlor from 10 December 2014 can result in protection from the same day additions rule for a protected settlement (under *s 62C(3)(a)*) being lost (eg a settlor addition to pay trust professional fees)).

A settlement is also protected if the settlor's same day addition was effected by a will executed before 10 December 2014, if the will provisions are in substance the same at the settlor's death as they were immediately before that date. However, this exclusion is limited to deaths before 6 April 2017, to allow affected individuals an opportunity to change their wills (*s 62C(3)(b)*).

CALCULATING IHT

2.25 The IHT rates for chargeable lifetime transfers for 2015/16 are shown in **Table 2.1** below (*s 7, Sch 1*), and remain unchanged from the previous tax year.

The IHT threshold (or 'nil rate band') was effectively fixed (in *Finance Act 2010, s 8*) at £325,000 for 2010/11 to 2014/15 inclusive.

From 2015/16, the consumer prices index (CPI) becomes the default basis for increasing the nil rate band, as opposed to the retail prices index (RPI) (*s 8*). Legislation to this effect was included in *Finance Act 2012*. However, the automatic indexation of the nil rate band using the CPI from 2015/16 is subject to override where Parliament considers it appropriate.

Subsequently, *FA 2014* included legislation to extend the effective freezing of the nil rate band at £325,000 up to and including 2017/18. Furthermore, the indexation of the nil rate band in *s 8* was once again disapplied in *Finance (No 2) Act 2015*. Consequently, the nil rate band is to remain at £325,000 for the tax years 2018/19, 2019/20 and 2020/21.

An additional nil rate band (or 'residence nil rate band') is potentially available when a home is passed on death to direct descendants of the deceased from 6 April 2017 (see **16.55–16.69**).

Table 2.1—Chargeable lifetime transfers on or after 6 April 2016: Tax on gross transfers

Gross taxable transfers £	*Gross Cumulative totals* £	*Rate*
First 325,000	0–325,000	NIL
Above 325,000	20% for each £ over 325,000	

Grossing-up of net lifetime transfers

Net transfers £	*Tax payable thereon* £	
First 325,000	NIL	NIL
Above 325,000	25% (or 1/4) for each £ over 325,000	

No IHT is payable if the chargeable transfers or failed PETs do not exceed the IHT threshold. If a transfer has become chargeable because of death, the IHT threshold and rate at the date of death is used to calculate the tax due.

If there has been a change in the IHT rate bands, the new rate bands are used to calculate the tax on a subsequent transfer. The cumulative totals of chargeable transfers may need to be restated where IHT is included, before this calculation can be made.

Chargeable transfers of value are cumulated; the IHT rate will depend on the total value of any such transfers made within the seven-year period ending with the latest transfer. After seven years, these transfers drop out of the cumulative total.

The '14-year backward shadow'

2.26 It may be necessary to look back at transfers made more than seven years before the date of death, up to a maximum of 14 years.

For example, if a PET was made (say) six years and 11 months before death, the period 13 years and 11 months prior to the death will need to be reviewed. However, the only transfers more than seven years before death which need to be considered are immediately chargeable ones.

Example 2.5—Cumulation of lifetime gifts

Mr Jones died on 1 December 2016, having made gifts (after reliefs and exemptions) of £100,000 to his daughter on 5 April 2005, £150,000 to a discretionary trust on 5 April 2008 and £263,000 to his son on 31 December 2014.

The additional IHT liabilities arising on Mr Jones' death are:

5 April 2005 – Gift to daughter £100,000

The gift to Mr Jones' daughter was a PET made more than seven years before death, which, therefore, became exempt. The gift is not cumulated with later gifts.

5 April 2008 – Transfer to discretionary trust £150,000

The gift to the discretionary trust was an immediately chargeable transfer, but no IHT was payable as the gross value was within Mr Jones' available nil rate band (£285,000 for 2007/08). The gift was also made more than seven years before death, and no tax is payable on that event.

31 December 2014 – Gift to son £263,000

The gift to Mr Jones' son was a PET made within seven years of death, which, therefore, becomes chargeable. The gift to the discretionary trust is cumulated, even though made more than seven years before death.

	£
5 April 2008 – Transfer to discretionary trust	150,000
Nil rate band remaining: £325,000 – £150,000 = £175,000	
31 December 2014 – IHT on gift to son:	
£175,000 × nil	NIL
£88,000 × 40%	35,200
	£35,200

No taper relief (death within three years of gift).

2.27 Taper relief is applied if appropriate (eg if a PET becomes chargeable, which was made more than three years before the date of death). See **Chapter 10**.

If more than one chargeable transfer is made on the same day and their order affects the transfer values, they are treated as made in the order which results in the lowest value chargeable.

For example, if two chargeable gifts are made on the same day, with tax being paid by the donor on one gift (ie such that 'grossing-up' applies) and by the donee on the other gift, the tax-bearing gift by the donor is treated as having been made first in order to ensure grossing-up at a potentially lower rate. This rule applies to lifetime gifts, but not to transfers on death (*s 266(3)*).

REPORTING CHARGEABLE LIFETIME TRANSFERS

2.28

Focus

Chargeable lifetime transfers are reportable on an Account for Inheritance Tax (Form IHT100 and supplementary forms), which must be submitted within 12 months from the end of the month of transfer (or three months after the person became liable, if later) (*s 216(6)(c)*; see **Chapter 6**).

However, there are exceptions from the requirement to submit an IHT100 account, normally in the circumstances below.

The reporting exceptions mentioned above are as follows:

- gifts or chargeable transfers made by an individual which are wholly exempt (eg gifts to a UK-domiciled spouse within *s 18*). HMRC's view is that this general rule is subject to a possible exception in respect of the normal expenditure out of income exemption (*s 21*), where an IHT liability would otherwise arise but for the availability of the exemption (IHTM10652);
- gifts or chargeable transfers of value (ie actual, not deemed) made by an individual as follows:
  - *for transfers of cash or quoted shares or securities* – if the value transferred, together with the value of any chargeable transfers made by the transferor in the preceding seven years, does not exceed the IHT threshold (note that if any other assets are included in the transfer, it cannot be excepted under this test); or
  - *for transfers of other assets* – if the value transferred, together with the value of any chargeable transfers made by the transferor in the preceding seven years, does not exceed 80% of the IHT threshold, and the value transferred by the transfer of value giving rise to the chargeable transfer (excluding business or agricultural property relief) does not exceed that IHT threshold less the value of chargeable transfers in the previous seven years (the *Inheritance Tax (Delivery of Accounts) (Excepted Transfers and Excepted Terminations) Regulations, SI 2008/605, reg 4*).
- 'excepted terminations' of interests in possession in the settled property of a specified trust. A 'specified trust' for these purposes is one in which the person's beneficial entitlement arose before 22 March 2006, or trusts for bereaved minors (within *s 71A*), or 'immediate post-death interests' (within *s 49A*), or trusts for disabled persons (within *ss 89* or *89A*), or a disabled person's interest (within *s 89B*) or 'transitional serial interests' (within *ss 49B–49E*). A termination is excepted in any of the following cases:
  - it is wholly covered by an exemption made available by the liferenter and notified to the trustees (eg if no chargeable transfers have been made personally); or
  - the interest related to cash or quoted shares or securities, and the value transferred by the termination, together with the value of any chargeable transfers made by the transferor in the preceding seven years, does not exceed the IHT threshold; or

– the value transferred by the termination, together with the value of any chargeable transfers made by the transferor in the preceding seven years, does not exceed 80% of the IHT threshold and the value transferred by the termination (excluding business or agricultural property relief) does not exceed that IHT threshold less the value of chargeable transfers in the previous seven years (*SI 2008/605, reg 5*).

Detailed HMRC guidance on excepted transfers and terminations is included in the Inheritance Tax Manual at IHTM06100 to IHTM06113.

For general guidance on the completion of form IHT100, see 'When to use form IHT100' in HMRC Booklet IHT110 ('How to fill in form IHT100'), which is available via the gov.uk website (www.gov.uk/government/uploads/system/uploads/attachment_data/file/375337/IHT110.pdf).

As indicated at **2.1** above, a PET is not immediately chargeable, and, therefore, does not need to be reported on form IHT100 when it is made.

Chapter 3

IHT on death

SIGNPOSTS

- **Notional transfer on death** – IHT is charged on the basis that a person makes a notional transfer of value of the whole estate on death. A person's estate potentially consists of the death estate, and certain types of settled property. Gifts with reservation are also taken into account. However, various IHT reliefs, exemptions and exclusions can apply on death, and certain liabilities may be deducted in determining the net estate (see **3.1–3.8**).
- **Deductions** – Liabilities may be taken into account in valuing a person's estate, subject to certain conditions and valuation rules. Funeral and limited other expenses may also be deducted (see **3.9–3.18**).
- **Valuations** – The general rule is that the value of assets comprised in a person's estate before death is their open market value immediately before death, but there are certain other provisions to consider, such as the 'related property' rules (see **3.19–3.20**).
- **IHT calculation** – Chargeable lifetime transfers and PETs within seven years of death are liable to IHT at death rates, subject to taper relief, if appropriate. The IHT threshold (or 'nil rate band') is taken into account, including any transferable nil rate band from a previously deceased spouse or civil partner. Quick succession relief and double tax relief may also be deducted in some cases (see **3.21–3.26**).
- **Chargeable and exempt estate** – If the death estate is partly exempt, special provisions apply to determine the extent and impact of IHT liabilities on the non-exempt part, and also how IHT should be borne by the beneficiaries, etc (see **3.27–3.41**).
- **IHT compliance** – HMRC's IHT Toolkit is designed to assist in the completion of account form IHT400 (see **3.42**).

INTRODUCTION

3.1 A person is treated as making a notional transfer of value of the whole estate immediately before his death, and IHT is charged accordingly (*IHTA 1984, s 4(1)*) (unless otherwise stated, all statutory references in this chapter are to *IHTA 1984*).

The tax charged on the estate broadly depends on the aggregate chargeable lifetime transfers and potentially exempt transfers (PETs) in the seven years preceding death. The estate generally consists of all the property to which the individual was beneficially entitled, less excluded property and liabilities.

The IHT liability will also depend upon the identity of the legatees of the net estate, ie whether the recipient is a chargeable person (eg a son or daughter), or an exempt person (eg a UK-domiciled spouse, or a qualifying charity).

If an individual dies without leaving a will, or if the will is invalid (eg if it is not signed by the testator or testatrix, or was not witnessed as required), the estate is subject to distribution in accordance with the laws of intestacy (see below).

(i) Scotland

Table 3.1a: Scotland: The distribution of intestate estate

The distribution of intestate estates in Scotland is governed by the Succession (Scotland) Act 1964 as amended by the Law Reform (Miscellaneous Provisions) (Scotland) Act 1968 and the Succession (Scotland) Act 1973 and by the Civil Partnerships Act 2004. New rules came into force on 1st February 2012 increasing the entitlement of a surviving spouse or civil partner. The legislation makes a clear distinction between heritable and moveable property. The current rules are as follows (see below for further proposed reform).

(a) Spouse/civil partner and issue survive

Spouse/civil partner receives:	*Issue receives (including remoter issue by representation):*
• **Prior Rights** (have priority) • Heritable dwellinghouse (in which the surviving spouse/civil partner was ordinarily resident) (i) where the value of the interest does not exceed £473,000, to that interest (or in certain cases to a sum equal to its value); or	

(ii) in any other case, to the sum of £473,000.	
• **Furniture and plenishings** of a dwellinghouse in which the surviving spouse/civil partner was ordinarily resident	
(i) where the value of the furniture and plenishings does not exceed £29,000, the whole furniture and plenishings; or	
(ii) in any other case, to such part of the furniture and plenishings, to a value not exceeding £29,000, as the surviving spouse/civil partner may choose	
• **Monetary Right** to the sum of £50,000	
• Legal Rights	• Legal Rights
One third of the net moveable estate	One third of the net moveable estate

(b) Spouse/civil partner survives without issue

Spouse/civil partner receives:	
• Prior Rights	
• Heritable dwellinghouse	
(in which the surviving spouse/civil partner was ordinarily resident)	
Spouse/civil partner receives	
(i) where the value of the interest does not exceed £473,000, to that interest (or in certain cases to a sum equal to its value); or	
(ii) in any other case, to the sum of £473,000.	
• **Furniture and plenishings** of a dwellinghouse in which the surviving spouse/civil partner was ordinarily resident	

(i) where the value of the furniture and plenishings does not exceed £29,000, the whole furniture and plenishings; or

(ii) in any other case, to such part of the furniture and plenishings, to a value not exceeding £29,000, as the surviving spouse/civil partner may choose

- **Monetary Right** to the sum of £89,000
- Legal Rights

One half of the net moveable estate

(c) Issue survive without spouse or civil partner

Issue receives:

- Legal Rights

One half of the net moveable estate

Rights of co-habitee in Scotland

If an individual dies intestate their co-habitee may make an application within six months of the date of death, under *s 29* of the *Family Law (Scotland) Act* 2006 for provision on death if the deceased was domiciled in Scotland immediately before their death. A cohabitee's award can never exceed the amount to which they would have been entitled had they been married to the deceased. The court carefully reviews the question of domicile as in *Chebotareva v Khandro 2008*. Land outside Scotland cannot be taken into account when evaluating a surviving partner's claim on the estate under s *29* of the *Family Law (Scotland) Act 2006* as *s 29* forms part of the Scots law of succession and thus deals only with estate governed by that law (see *Kerr* v *Mangan* (2014) ScotCS CSIH 69, 2014 SLT 866 and *Fulwood v O'Halloran* GWD 11-196, Sheriff H J L Miller at Glasgow).

Free Estate

After payment of debts and any Prior Rights, Legal Rights or Claims by a co-habitee the free estate is distributed in accordance with the order in *s 2(1) of the Succession (Scotland) Act 1964* which is as follows:-

(a) children

(b) parents and brothers and sisters (each class taking half)

(c) if no parents alive, brothers and sisters

(d) if no siblings alive, parents

(e) spouse/civil partner

(f) uncles and aunts

(g) grandparents

(h) grandparents' siblings

(i) remoter ancestors

If no relation can be identified the estate passes to the Crown as *ultimus haeres*.

Scottish Succession Reform

In April 2009 the Scottish Law Commission published its Report on the Law of Succession which contained many significant proposals for changing the Scottish Succession rules aimed to 'simplify the law radically by providing rules which are easily understood and which at the same time reflect the nature of family structures in contemporary Scotland' (Scottish Law Commission's Report on Succession News Release April 2009).

As a result of the Report, increased limits, shown above, for the surviving spouse's Prior Rights and Legal Rights entitlement were introduced on 1 February 2012.

Following consulation on the Report the *Succession (Scotland) Act 2016* was introduced which impacts the distribution of estates and IHT implications. The provisions included in the Act are:

- divorce now terminates the entitlement of a former spouse or civil partner under a Will or Special Destination. The former spouse is treated as having died before the testator subject to any contrary provision. Provisions regarding guardianship are not terminated (*ss 1* and *2*);
- rectification provisions where a Will prepared fails to accurately express the testator's instructions (*ss 3* and *4*), to enable the Will to be rectified to accurately reflect the initial instructions, such as the English case of *Marley v Rawlings* [2014] UKSC 2, where a husband and wife signed each other's will instead of their own;
- statutory replacement for the common law rule *conditio si institutus sine liberis decesserit*, providing that where a beneficiary, who is a direct descendant of the testator, is entitled to legacy in a Will, dies between

the Will being made and the testator's death, then the legatee's issue will inherit (subject to clear intention to the contrary) (*s 6*);

- detailed provisions regarding forfeiture rule stating that the offender shall be treated as having died before the deceased, persons acquiring property in good faith or for value directly or indirectly from a person who in relation to the property has incurred forfeiture shall be protected and providing power to the sheriff to order the sheriff clerk to execute documents if necessary (*ss 12–14*);
- where a liferent terminates other than on the death of a liferenter, if the fee has not vested in the fiar by the date the liferent was terminated then the fee vests in the fiar on that termination date (except for express provision otherwise in the deed or an obligation) (*s 7*); and
- changes to the survivorship rules (see **3.7**).

The Scottish government consultation in 2015 also considered the other aspects of the Scottish Law Commission Report including the suggested changes for testate estates which exclude children in the Will with two routes suggested: (i) that children would be entitled to 25% of what they would have inherited had the deceased died intestate, and (ii) that dependent children would be entitled to a capital sum calculated by reference to their maintenance needs.

The Report recommended that co-habitees be entitled to a percentage of what they would have received had they formerly been the deceased's spouse or civil partner, calculating the percentage on the length and quality of their relationship with the deceased.

The Scottish Government Land Reform Review Group published their Report in May 2014 entitled '*The Land of Scotland and the Common Good*' in which the Review Group recommended that the Scottish Government should, in the interests of social justice, develop proposals in consultation with the Scottish Law Commission for legislation to end the distinction between immoveable and moveable property in Scotland's laws of succession. This would have IHT implications and would also affect the distribution of estates. *The Land Reform (Scotland) Bill* proposes amendments to the succession rules for agricultural tenancies which would have a knock on impact for IHT.

The EU Succession Regulation (EU/650/2012) came into effect on 17 August 2015. The Regulation is intended to provide more certainty to individuals who have estate in more than one country and to allow them to determine the law to apply to succession to their assets. The UK has not adopted the Regulation; however, a UK national resident in Scotland could elect to have Scots law apply to their property within countries that have adopted the Regulation. Election into a particular country's system will also bring into effect any forced heirship rules such as the Legal Rights in Scotland detailed above.

(ii) England and Wales

Changes to the distribution of estates on intestacy under the *Administration of Estates Act 1925, s 46* were introduced in the *Inheritance and Trustees' Powers Act 2014* (see below), which received Royal Assent on 14 May 2014 and entered into force on 1 October 2014 (*Inheritance and Trustees' Powers Act 2014 (Commencement) Order, SI 2014/2039*). For the distribution of estates before and after these changes, see **Table 3.1b**.

Table 3.1b—England and Wales: The distribution of intestate estates

The distribution of intestate estates in England and Wales is governed by the *Administration of Estates Act 1925, s 46*. The following applies to England and Wales, and differ from those in Scotland (see (i) above) and Northern Ireland (see IHTM12162).

Deaths on or after 1 October 2014

Spouse or civil partner and issue survive:

Spouse or civil partner receives	*Issue receives*
• All personal chattels; • £250,000 absolutely (or the entire interest where this is less); • One half of residue (if any) in trust for the survivor absolutely.	• One half of residue (if any) on statutory trusts.

Spouse or civil partner survives without issue:

Spouse or civil partner receives

The residuary estate in trust for the survivor absolutely.

Deaths before 1 October 2014

Spouse or civil partner and issue survive:

Spouse or civil partner receives	*Issue receives*
• All personal chattels; • £250,000 absolutely (or the entire interest where this is less); • Life interest in one-half of residue (if any).	• One half of residue (if any) on statutory trusts plus the other half of residue on statutory trusts upon the death of the spouse.

Spouse or civil partner survives without issue:

Spouse or civil partner receives	*Residuary estate to*
All personal chattels;	The deceased's parents.
£450,000 absolutely (or entire estate where this is less);	If no parent survives: on trust for the deceased's brothers and sisters of the whole blood and the issue of any such deceased brother or sister.
One half of residue (if any) absolutely.	

Notes

1. For distributions prior to changes introduced in the *Inheritance and Trustees' Powers Act 2014,* the above fixed sums of £250,000 and £450,000 apply for deaths on or after 1 February 2009 (*Family Provision Act 1966, s 1*; *The Family Provision (Intestate Succession) Order, SI 2009/135*). Previously, the fixed sums were £125,000 and £200,000 respectively.

   If the intestate dies leaving a surviving spouse or civil partner but no issue, parents, brothers or sisters or their issue, the residuary estate is held in trust for the survivor absolutely.

2. For distributions following the introduction of the *Inheritance and Trustees' Powers Act 2014*, the *Family Provision Act 1966* is repealed, and the above fixed sum of £450,000 is no longer required. The fixed sum of £250,000 is determined by the *Administration of Estates Act 1925, Sch 1A*, and is subject to possible future amendment by statutory instrument.

3. The above provisions in favour of the deceased's spouse or civil partner are subject to a 28-day survival period (*Administration of Estates Act 1925, s 46(2A)*).

No spouse or civil partner survives:

Estate held for the following in order given with no class beneficiaries participating unless all those in a prior class have predeceased. Statutory trusts may apply except under (b) and (e):

(a) issue of deceased

(b) parents

(c) brothers and sisters (or issue)

(d) half-brothers and half-sisters (or issue)

(e) grandparents

(f) uncles and aunts (or issue)

(g) half-brothers and half-sisters of deceased's parents (or issue)

(h) the Crown, the Duchy of Lancaster or the Duke of Cornwall

Note: The *Administration of Estates Act 1925* was extended (by the *Civil Partnership Act 2004, Sch 4, paras 7–12*) to include the remaining surviving civil partner, who effectively acquires the same rights as a spouse in cases of intestacy.

HMRC's Inheritance Tax Manual includes guidance on intestacy as it applies in:

- England and Wales (IHTM12111–IHTM12129);
- Scotland (IHTM12141–IHTM12156); and
- Northern Ireland (IHTM12161–IHTM12179).

ESTATE ON DEATH

General

3.2 A person on death (after 17 March 1986) is treated as having made a transfer of value equal to the value of his estate immediately before death (*s 4(1)*). A person's estate consists of the following:

- *free estate* – the aggregate of all property to which the deceased was beneficially entitled, but without taking into account any excluded property; and
- *settled property* – certain settled property in which the deceased was beneficially entitled to an interest in possession (see below).

An interest in possession in settled property to which the deceased originally became beneficially entitled before 22 March 2006 forms part of the estate (*s 49(1)*). In addition, an interest in possession to which the deceased was beneficially entitled on or after 22 March 2006 is included in the death estate if it falls within one of the following categories (*s 49(1A)*):

- an 'immediate post-death interest' (ie within *s 49A*);
- a 'disabled person's interest' (see *s 89B*); or
- a 'transitional serial interest' (as defined in *s 49B*).

In addition, if an interest in possession is purchased by a UK-domiciled person at arm's length (on or after 9 December 2009), the interest forms part of that person's estate (*s 5(1B)*).

However, interests in property before 22 March 2006 to which the rules on trusts for 'bereaved minors' (*s 71A*) apply do not form part of the deceased's estate (*s 49(1B)*) – see **Chapter 7**.

Legal Rights (as detailed above, but not Prior Rights) are also available in testate estates. In testate cases an individual (spouse/civil partner/child or remoter issue by representation) may elect to claim their Legal Rights or accept their entitlement under the Will (if any).

3.3 Gifts with reservation (GWR) form part of the death estate by being treated as property to which the deceased was beneficially entitled (*FA 1986, s 102(3)*).

The IHT charge on death is a 'deeming' provision, ie it creates a transfer of value. In addition to exemptions which are only intended to apply to lifetime transfers (eg the annual and small gifts exemptions), HMRC do not consider that relief from IHT on death applies under provisions by which certain dispositions are not treated as transfers of value (*ss 10–17*), eg dispositions not intended to confer a gratuitous benefit, or for the maintenance of family members (IHTM04042) (see **9.12**). This is on the footing that the rules apply to actual dispositions, and therefore cannot apply to a charge which is based on a deemed transfer (eg death), unless the legislation specifically applies the provisions to the deemed transfer concerned (IHTM04151).

However, other types of IHT relief are available on the basis that a transfer of value includes a deemed transfer unless specifically excluded by statute (*s 3(4)*), such as business and agricultural property relief if the relevant conditions are satisfied (see **Chapter 11**). Various exemptions and exclusions from IHT also apply on death (see **3.4**), and certain liabilities may be deducted in determining the net estate (see **3.9**).

Exemptions and exclusions

3.4 Exemptions from IHT were summarised at **1.20** and are covered in **Chapter 9**. They are generally available on death, unless expressly excluded.

As mentioned at **3.3** above, certain exemptions relate to lifetime transfers only, and cannot therefore be claimed on death. These include the annual exemption (*s 19(5)*), the exemptions for small gifts (*s 20(3)*), normal expenditure out of income (*s 21(5)*) and gifts in consideration of marriage (*s 22(6)*).

An exemption may be subject to restriction (for deaths after 26 July 1989) if an exempt beneficiary (eg the surviving spouse or civil partner) settles any claim against the deceased's estate otherwise than out of the deceased's transfer on death, where the claim is not a deductible liability for IHT purposes (*s 29A*).

For example, if the surviving spouse directly settles a Legal Rights claim against the estate by the deceased's children, it is treated as a chargeable legacy (and not an allowable estate liability). The spouse exemption is restricted to the net benefit. This restriction removes the advantage of the spouse settling the claim out of her exempt share.

3.5 Some exemptions (eg the spouse or civil partner exemption in *s 18*, or the charity exemption in *s 23*) are available as a result of death. In addition, certain categories of estate property can be left out of the IHT account on death:

- Cash options under approved pension schemes – where under a registered pension scheme, a 'qualifying non-UK pension scheme' (within *s 271A*) or a '*s 615(3)* scheme' (ie a superannuation fund within *ICTA 1988, s 615(3)*) (or prior to 6 April 2006, either a retirement annuity contract or a personal pension scheme) an annuity becomes payable on a person's death to a spouse, surviving civil partner or dependant of that person, and a capital sum might at the deceased's option have become payable instead to his personal representatives, the deceased is not to be treated as having been beneficially entitled to that sum, with the result that it escapes liability to IHT (*s 152*).
- Overseas pensions – the value of certain pensions payable to the deceased by former colonial governments is not included in the death estate (*s 153*).
- Death on active service, etc – no IHT is payable on the death of a person from a wound, accident or disease sustained or aggravated whilst on active service (or other service of a warlike nature), if certified by the Defence Council or the Secretary of State (*s 154*). Following *FA 2015*, this exemption extends broadly to deaths caused or hastened by responding to an emergency.

  Further IHT exemptions (introduced in *FA 2015*) broadly apply in relation to emergency services personnel and humanitarian aid workers who die as a result of responding to an emergency, and police constables and armed service personnel who die as a result of being attacked due to their status (*ss 153A, 155A*; see **1.20**).
- Emoluments and tangible moveable property of visiting armed forces members, certain international military headquarters staff and (from 17 July 2012) certain EU civilian staff attached to such headquarters, are excluded property for IHT purposes (*s 155*).

- The balances of any qualifying foreign currency accounts are excluded if the deceased was not domiciled and not resident in the UK immediately before his death (*s 157*). This exclusion also applies if the deceased was beneficially entitled to an interest in possession in settled property which included the qualifying foreign currency account, unless the settlor was domiciled in the UK when he made the settlement, or if the trustees were domiciled or resident in the UK immediately before the beneficiary's death. In each case a further condition as to ordinary residence applies if the person died before 6 April 2013, (ie prior to changes introduced in *FA 2013*). A 'qualifying foreign currency account' means a non-sterling account with a 'bank' (as defined in *ITA 2007, s 991*). The balance on such an account is excluded, whether in credit or debit (IHTM04380).

In addition to the above, legislation introduced in *Finance Act 2016* broadly provides that IHT on certain qualifying compensation and ex-gratia payments for World War II claims (listed in Concession F20, which the legislation replaces and extends) and a one-off payment from the 'Child Survivor Fund' should be allowed as a credit against the IHT arising on the chargeable value of the recipient's estate.

Offshore (and certain UK) property is excluded property for IHT purposes if the beneficial owner is domiciled outside the UK (*s 6(1), (1A)*). A similar rule applies to settled property, if the settlor was non-UK domiciled when the settlement was made (*s 48(3), (3A)*). However, if the interest in possession was acquired by a UK-domiciled person (from 5 December 2005) for valuable consideration, that interest is not excluded property (*s 48(3B)*).

It should be noted that the UK government announced at summer Budget 2015 that it intended to legislate to ensure that, from April 2017, IHT is payable on all UK residential property owned directly or indirectly by non-UK domiciliaries (and regardless of their residence status for tax purposes). This change is aimed at blocking what HMRC describe as 'enveloping' (ie holding property indirectly through offshore structures).

Further anti-avoidance provisions introduced (in *Finance Act 2012*) with effect from 20 June 2012, are to be aimed at countering arrangements involving UK domiciled individuals who acquire an interest in settled excluded property, which would otherwise give rise to a reduction in the individual's estate (*ss 48(3D), 74A–C*). The arrangements covered include situations where a UK corporate settlor has settled assets as part of an avoidance scheme, and to arrangements where individuals retain the interests in settled property they have acquired. If the anti-avoidance provisions apply, the effect is broadly that the property ceases to be excluded property, and an IHT charge arises. For further information on excluded property and exempt transfers, see **1.18** and **Chapter 9**.

Secondary legislation (*The Taxation of Equitable Life (Payments) Order 2011, SI 2011/1502*) provides for the tax treatment of payments made under the *Equitable Life (Payments) Act 2010* to investors, and states that where a payment is made to the estate of someone who has died before the payment has been made, it is ignored for IHT purposes (*art 5(1)(a)*). Where personal representatives receive such a payment, there is no need for them to report it to HMRC (by contrast, where the payment is made to someone who is still alive, the money will form part of their estate and be subject to IHT in the normal way when disposed of either during their lifetime or on death; see IHTM10271). Further details of the Equitable Life payment scheme are available in Revenue & Customs Brief 26/11 (www.hmrc.gov.uk/briefs/cgt/brief2611.htm).

Woodlands relief

3.6 A specific relief is available for transfers of woodlands on death (*s 125*), to take account of the fact that trees may take several generations to grow. Where the relief is available, an election may be made to exclude the value of UK trees or underwood (but not the land itself) from the value transferred by the chargeable transfer on the deceased's death. IHT is instead payable when the trees are disposed of (ie by sale or gift), other than to the disposer's spouse or civil partner.

Following a disposal, tax is charged on a subsequent death in the usual way, unless another election is made. In effect, the relief is a deferral of the IHT otherwise due on death.

For further commentary on woodlands relief, see **Chapter 10**. However, if the woodlands form part of a business, business property relief may be available if the conditions for that relief are satisfied; see **Chapter 11**.

Survivorship

(i) Scotland

3.7 The *Presumption of Death (Scotland) Act 1977* and the *Succession (Scotland) Act 2016* provide clear rules on the deemed death of someone where they have disappeared, or on the balance of probabilities are dead, or where order of death is not clear.

Where two people die simultaneously or in circumstances in which it is uncertain who survived whom each person is treated as having failed to survive the other, regardless of whether they are spouses or civil partners or not (*ss 9–11 of* the *Succession (Scotland) Act 2016*) (before the Act where two people or more died in circumstances where the order of death was unclear, the younger was deemed to have survived the older except for spouses and civil partners where the rule was that neither was deemed to have survived the other).

The *Presumption of Death (Scotland) Act 1977* allows for court actions to be raised which may render a person being declared dead if it is thought he or she has died (eg an accident where body cannot be recovered) or he or she has not known to be alive for at least seven years. In the latter case the death is treated as having occurred seven years after the person was last known to be alive.

Title to heritable property may contain a special destination deeming the property to transfer to the survivor on the death of the first party. Title may be varied during lifetime or on death to remove the destination. If an individual dies after their marriage is terminated by divorce or annulment, or their civil partnership is terminated by dissolution or annulment, and titles to heritable property they own with their former spouse or civil partner contains a Special Destination, then *s 2* of the *Succession (Scotland) Act 2016* treats the former spouse as having predeceased.

(ii) England and Wales

The rule as to commorientes (in the *Law of Property Act 1925, s 184*) provides as follows (Note: this rule relates to England and Wales and does not extend to Scotland – see (i) above):

> 'In all cases where … two or more persons have died in circumstances rendering it uncertain which of them survived the other or others, such deaths, shall (subject to any order of the court) for all purposes affecting the title to property, be presumed to have occurred in order of seniority, and accordingly the younger shall be deemed to have survived the elder.'

This rule could give rise to double (or multiple) IHT charges on death (subject to 'quick succession relief' (*s 141*) if there was a chargeable transfer – see **Chapter 10**).

However, for IHT purposes, where it cannot be known which of two or more persons who have died survived the other or others, they shall be presumed to have died at the same instant. Therefore, the estate of the younger is not swollen (*ss 4(2), 54(4)*).

In some cases, the interaction of the IHT provisions and *LPA 1925, s 184* can result in the estate of an elder spouse or civil partner escaping IHT on simultaneous deaths. This point is illustrated in HMRC's guidance at IHTM12197 (which also points out that the treatment of simultaneous deaths in Scotland and Northern Ireland is different).

3.8 Double (or multiple) IHT charges (subject to Quick Succession Relief) may also arise on successive deaths (ie deaths which are not (or are not treated as) simultaneous but follow within a short period of each other, where it is ascertainable which person survived the other even if only for a relatively short time).

However, if under the terms of the will (or otherwise, such as under a settlement), property is held for any person ('Beneficiary A') on condition that he survives another for a specified period of not more than six months, and another beneficiary ('Beneficiary B') becomes entitled to property by reason of the survivorship condition (ie Beneficiary A has not complied with that condition), the IHT payable is the same as if Beneficiary B had taken the property direct, without the intervention of the survivorship condition. Beneficiary B is therefore deemed to have become entitled from the beginning of the survivorship period (*s 92*).

LIABILITIES

General

3.9 A liability may be taken into account in valuing a person's estate (unless otherwise provided by tax law) if it is legally enforceable and is:

- imposed by law (eg income tax and capital gains tax up to the date of death, and IHT liabilities in respect of chargeable lifetime transfers discharged by the deceased's personal representatives); or
- incurred for a consideration in money or money's worth (*s 5(5)*).

For example, if executors claim the deduction of a liability incurred shortly before death, HMRC may be interested to know the whereabouts of the money obtained by the deceased as a result of entering into the liability. If the money cannot be traced and there is no evidence that it has been given away, a deduction may be denied.

A deduction is given in the deceased's estate in certain circumstances where income tax liabilities arise as a result of death (ie involving offshore funds and deeply discounted securities (*s 174(1)*).

Mortgages or secured loans can generally be deducted from the property they are charged against (but see below). If the mortgage is for more than the value of the property, the excess can generally be deducted from the deceased's other assets (see 'How to value the debts and liabilities of someone who has died' at www.gov.uk/valuing-estate-of-someone-who-died#2 under 'Debts and liabilities'). However where a person with liabilities in excess of his assets is the liferenter of a fund his personal indebtedness cannot offset the value of the trust fund (*St Barbe Green v Inland Revenue Commissioners* [2005] EWHC 14 (Ch)).

Following changes introduced in *Finance Act 2013* and *Finance Act 2014*, there are certain conditions and potential restrictions in respect of the deduction of liabilities such as mortgages, to the extent that the liability was used to acquire, maintain or enhance certain types of property (*ss 162A–162C*). In addition, the deduction of liabilities discharged after death is subject to certain requirements (*s 175A*) (see **3.13**).

3.10 Following the introduction of the *Gambling Act 2005* from 1 September 2007, deductions for gambling debts are allowed if they can be legally enforced. Prior to 1 September 2007, gambling debts were not an allowable deduction, because the debt could not be legally enforced. This applies to gambling debts in Scotland, England and Wales, but not Northern Ireland (IHTM28130).

HMRC cite racecourse betting through the Tote as an example of a legally enforceable gambling debt that can be deducted (see www.gov.uk/valuing-estate-of-someone-who-died at section 4 ('Debts and liabilities') under 'Gambling debts').

Focus

An anti-avoidance rule in *FA 1986, s 103* ('Treatment of certain debts and encumbrances') restricts debts incurred or created by the deceased on or after 18 March 1986 when determining the value of an estate immediately before death, to the extent that:

- the money borrowed originally derived from the deceased; or
- the money was borrowed from a person who had previously received property derived from the deceased (eg an interest in a property is gifted from Miss X to Mr Y. Mr Y retains the property, takes out a loan secured on it and lends the proceeds back to Miss X, who dies more than seven years after the original gift of the property interest).

However, the above restriction does not apply if it can be demonstrated that:

- the original disposition by the deceased was not a transfer of value; and
- it was not part of associated operations (as set out in *FA 1986, s 103(4)*).

This anti-avoidance rule can affect estate planning (eg 'debt' or 'charge' arrangements), as illustrated in *Phizackerley v HMRC* [2007] STC SCD 328.

A disallowance of the debt may result in a double IHT charge.

Example 3.1—Effect of *FA 1986, s 103*

On 1 January 2014, Adam gifted cash of £50,000 to Bob. On 6 April 2014, Bob lends £50,000 to Adam. On 1 December 2016, Adam dies.

The cash gift from Adam to Bob is a PET which becomes chargeable as the result of Adam's death within seven years.

In addition, Adam's estate includes the £50,000 gifted back to him, but a deduction for the debt of £50,000 is denied under *FA 1986, s 103*, leading to a potential double IHT charge.

3.11 However, relief is given in such circumstances (*FA 1986, s 104(1)(c); Inheritance Tax (Double Charges Relief) Regulations 1987, SI 1987/1130, reg 6*).

The effect is broadly that whichever of the two transfers results in the higher overall IHT liability remains chargeable, and the value transferred by the other is reduced (ie either the debt is disallowed and the gift is correspondingly reduced (*reg 6(3)(a)*), or the gift is taxed and the debt allowed (*reg 6(3)(b)*)).

Examples illustrating the operation of these rules are included as a Schedule to *SI 1987/1130*, although they do not prevail over the regulations themselves (*reg 9*).

No liability (eg debts or premiums) in respect of life assurance policies are allowable unless the policy proceeds form part of the estate (*FA 1986, s 103(7)*).

Guarantee debts

3.12 A guarantee debt (ie a promise to pay the debts of a borrower if he is unable to repay those debts) to which the deceased agreed to act as guarantor may be deductible from the death estate if the loan remained outstanding at the time of death. However, before allowing a deduction, HMRC may seek to establish whether consideration was given for the debt (*s 5(5)*).

This will generally be the case with commercial loan arrangements, but possibly not in family situations (eg where a parent gratuitously agrees to guarantee a child's bank borrowings). In addition, HMRC may consider the financial resources of the borrower at the date of death, as a liability is only taken into account to the extent that reimbursement cannot reasonably be expected (*s 162(1)*).

HMRC may regard the giving of the guarantee as a lifetime transfer by the deceased. For example, if the borrower is a 'man of straw' with no financial resources, the outstanding liability will be deductible in full, but the guarantee may be a lifetime transfer up to the full amount of the liability.

Even if there is no outstanding liability at the date of the guarantor's death, HMRC consider that lifetime transfers may nevertheless arise if the guarantee was made within seven years of death and the guarantee was called in and paid within that time, depending on the borrower's financial position when the guarantee was given (IHTM28356–7).

RULES FOR AMOUNT OR VALUE OF LIABILITY

General

3.13 The IHT provisions allowing a deduction for liabilities were amended by *Finance Act 2013* (and by *Finance Act 2014*; see below). Those amendments mostly have effect for deaths and chargeable transfers on or after 17 July 2013 (ie the date on which *Finance Act 2013* received Royal Assent), and are therefore retroactive in the sense that they potentially affect liabilities which were already in place. However, the rules on liabilities in respect of 'relievable property' (see below) apply to liabilities incurred on or after 6 April 2013 (*Finance Act 2013, Sch 36, para 5(2)*).

The above changes introduce conditions and restrictions in the way that a deduction for liabilities is allowed in certain circumstances (see below).

The general rules for determining the amount or value of liabilities may be summarised as follows:

- A liability for which there is a right to reimbursement is taken into account only to the extent that reimbursement cannot reasonably be expected to be obtained (*s 162(1)*).
- If a liability will be discharged after the time at which it is to be taken into account, it must be valued when it is taken into account (ie at its discounted value (*s 162(2)*) – but see below regarding *s 162(3)*.
- In valuing the transferor's estate immediately after the transfer, his IHT liability is computed as follows (*s 162(3)*):
  - (i) without making any allowance for the fact that the tax will not be due immediately; and

(ii) as if any tax recovered otherwise than from the transferor were paid in discharge of a liability for which the transferor had a right to reimbursement.

- A liability which is an encumbrance on estate property must (as far as possible) be taken to reduce the value of that property (*s 162(4)*). However, following the changes introduced in *Finance Act 2013*, this rule applies to the extent that the liability has not been taken into account against 'relievable property' under new *s 162B* (ie broadly business or agricultural property, or woodlands), if applicable (see below).
- A liability due to a person not resident in the UK which neither falls to be discharged in the UK nor is an encumbrance on UK property must (as far as possible) be taken to reduce the value of property outside the UK (*s 162(5)*). However, this rule is subject to the same further condition mentioned in the previous bullet point, following *Finance Act 2013*.

The provisions introduced by *Finance Act 2013* potentially affect the deduction of liabilities broadly as follows:

- *Excluded property, etc* – A deduction is not generally taken into account for a liability that has been incurred directly or indirectly to acquire 'excluded property' (see **Chapter 9**) for IHT purposes. However, where the acquired property is no longer excluded property, or has been disposed of and the proceeds are chargeable assets in the deceased's estate, or where the liability is greater than the value of the excluded property, a deduction may be allowed in certain circumstances (see *s 162A*).
- *Non-residents' bank accounts* – A foreign currency bank account balance (within *s 157*) is left out of account on the death of a person who is not domiciled and not resident in the UK. Those funds are not excluded property as such. However, *FA 2014* included provisions (for transfers of value made, or treated as made, from 17 July 2014) to treat foreign currency accounts in UK banks in a similar way to excluded property for the purposes of restricting the deduction of liabilities. The effect is broadly that the liability is disallowed for IHT purposes if the borrowed money financed the relevant account balance. If the liability exceeds that balance, the excess may be allowed, provided that it has not arisen for the purpose of securing a tax advantage or an increase in the amount of the liability (*s 162AA*).
- *Relievable property* – If the liability was incurred directly or indirectly to acquire (or maintain or enhance) 'relievable property', being assets on which an IHT relief (ie business or agricultural property relief, or woodlands relief) is due, the liability reduces the value of those assets. The liability is matched against the assets acquired, and relief is restricted to their net value. Any excess liability is allowable as a deduction against the estate in general, subject to the rule (in *s 175A*) about liabilities on

death (see below). However, to the extent that a liability has already been taken into account in arriving at the net value of the business (under *s 110(b)*), the provision does not have effect for business property relief purposes (*s 162B*).

- *Liabilities on death* – In determining the value of a person's death estate, a deduction for a liability is only allowed to the extent that it is repaid to the creditor out of the deceased's estate or from excluded property owned by the deceased immediately before death (and there are no other IHT provisions that prevent it from being taken into account), unless it is shown that there is a real commercial reason for not repaying the liability, securing a tax advantage is not a main purpose of leaving the liability outstanding, and it is not otherwise prevented from being taken into account (*s 175A*).

3.14 There are provisions dealing with the partial repayments of liabilities used to acquire assets including excluded property (or assets which have become excluded property) and relievable assets before an IHT charge arises. Those provisions were also amended following the rules in *FA 2014* concerning liabilities to finance non-UK residents' bank accounts (see above).

In broad terms, in determining the value of an estate on death, any part of a liability which is not attributable to excluded property, relevant account balances or relievable property is treated as having been repaid first. If the partial repayment exceeds that part of the liability, the part of the liability which is attributable to relievable property is treated as having been repaid next, then to any part attributable to relevant account balances, with any remaining liability attributable to excluded property, or assets that have become excluded property, being treated as being repaid last (*s 162C(1A)*).

A similar priority rule applies to the partial repayment of a liability otherwise than on death (*s 162C*). However, *s 157* only applies on death, so any part of a liability that was attributed to financing a relevant account balance is treated as paid off before any part which would be restricted or disallowed.

There are also provisions dealing with the partial repayment of liabilities after death, where the liability was used to acquire assets including excluded property, relevant account balances (see above) or relievable property. Any part of the liability which is attributable to excluded property is treated as being repaid first. If the partial repayment exceeds that part of the liability, following the introduction of *FA 2014* the part of the liability which is attributable to relevant account balances is treated as being repaid next, followed by relievable property. If the partial repayment was greater than the part of the liability attributable to excluded property, relevant account balances and relievable property, the remainder of the liability can then be deducted against the chargeable estate (see *s 175A(7)*).

3.15 The above provisions in *s 175A* are as anti-avoidance measures to block schemes and arrangements aimed at exploiting the IHT rules on liabilities to reduce the value of an estate. Those arrangements broadly involved obtaining a deduction for a liability and either not repaying the liability after death, or acquiring an asset which is not chargeable to IHT.

For the purposes of business and agricultural property relief (see **Chapter 11**), in the case of a liability incurred for a non-relievable purpose, securing the debt on qualifying property generally has the effect of reducing the amount on which relief would otherwise be available. Such debts should therefore be secured on non-qualifying property, if possible.

HMRC guidance on liabilities is contained in the Inheritance Tax Manual (at IHTM28000 onwards) and in 'Valuing the estate of someone who's died' under 'Debts and liabilities' (www.gov.uk/valuing-estate-of-someone-who-died/valuing-debts-and-liabilities).

Funeral expenses

3.16 In determining the value of a person's estate immediately before his death, deductions can be made as below:

- reasonable funeral expenses (*s 172*), including the cost of a tombstone or gravestone (SP 7/87) and flowers (IHTM10372);
- a reasonable amount for mourning for the family. This deduction was originally given by concession (ESC F1). However, in its Technical Note 'Withdrawal of extra statutory concessions' dated 9 December 2009, HMRC stated that this concession would be withdrawn from 9 December 2010, but added: 'We believe that it may not in fact be a concession at all, rather a statement of what HMRC considers reasonable.' HMRC guidance also states (at IHTM10375):

  > 'ESC F1 which originally allowed the deduction of reasonable mourning expenses was withdrawn on 9 December 2010. This does not alter our practice and any reasonable mourning expense which was previously allowed under ESC F1 should be allowed under IHTA84/S172.'

What is 'reasonable' will broadly depend on the living standards of the deceased during his lifetime.

A deduction may also be allowed for the reasonable costs of refreshments for mourners (IHTM10377).

Other expenses

3.17 Further principles for determining the deductibility of expenses in certain circumstances are summarised below:

- Costs of administering the UK estate (eg Confirmation fees, estate agent or valuation fees) cannot be deducted for IHT purposes, as they arise after death.
- However, a deduction is allowed for the additional expenses incurred by the deceased's personal representatives in administering or realising property situated abroad. The allowance is deducted from the value of the property, up to a maximum of 5% of the property value (*s 173*). HMRC state that 'additional' in this context means the excess of the expenditure over and above which it would have cost to deal with the property in the UK (IHTM27050).
- A deduction is not normally allowable for professional fees in respect of work carried out after the date of death. However, there is an exception for post-death work undertaken in connection with tax repayments included as an asset of the estate. In that case, HMRC may allow a deduction by concession for fees not exceeding 10% of the repayment (IHTM28041).
- Provisions apply to charge IHT in the case of dispositions which are transfers of value made for partial consideration in money or money's worth and the transferor makes a payment more than one year after the disposition. The effect is that any chargeable part of each payment is treated as a separate transfer of value at the time it is made (*s 262*). If the transferor dies while there are still outstanding liabilities the personal representatives have to complete the remaining payments (*s 175*). However, a deduction is only given for the non-gratuitous part of the remaining payments (IHTM14874).

Focus

A liability that represents an encumbrance on property (eg a mortgage) should be deducted from the value of that property as far as possible, but only to the extent that (following changes introduced in *Finance Act 2013*) it does not reduce the value of certain 'relievable property' under *s 162B* (*s 162(4)*).

As intimated at 3.13 above, a debt incurred in respect of non-relievable property should be secured against such property (ie where possible and practical) in preference to property qualifying for, say, 100% business or agricultural property relief.

Debts owed by the deceased

3.18 The IHT account of the estate on death (form IHT400) includes a supplementary form (Schedule IHT419 'Debts owed by the deceased') if the deceased's personal representatives are claiming a reduction in the estate for the following types of debt:

- money spent on the deceased's behalf (eg by a close friend or relative), which is being claimed as a deduction from the estate (eg paying domestic bills);
- loans and liabilities (including loans from close friends and relatives);
- liabilities related to an insurance policy and/or an investment bond (ie where its value is not fully reflected elsewhere in the form IHT400);
- guarantee debts; and
- gifts to, and loans from, the same person (ie such that a deduction for the debt may be restricted (*FA 1986, s 103*)).

The purpose of the form is to provide HMRC with further information in support of the deductions claimed elsewhere on form IHT400, to establish whether a deduction is due. For example, if a loan was made to the deceased by a friend or family member, was it legally enforceable or made for consideration in money or money's worth? Was an outstanding loan secured on any property? The answers will help to determine the extent of any deduction for the liability. Form IHT419 can be downloaded from the gov.uk website (www.gov.uk/government/publications/inheritance-tax-debts-owed-by-the-deceased-iht419).

ASSET VALUATIONS: OUTLINE

3.19 The asset valuation rule is broadly that the death estate is valued based on a deemed transfer of value immediately before the deceased's death. The value of assets comprised in a person's estate is generally their open market value immediately before death (*s 160*).

Changes in estate value caused by death are taken into account when valuing the estate (*s 171(1)*). The changes to be taken into account can include the following (see IHTM04046 for specific examples):

- an addition to the property in the estate (eg the proceeds from a life policy);
- an increase in the value of any estate property; and
- a decrease in any estate property, other than a decrease resulting from an alteration in the capital or share rights of a close company (*s 98(1)*).

However, *s 171* does not apply to the termination on the death of any interest or the passing of any interest by survivorship (*s 171(2)*). An open market valuation of assets applies instead.

For the purposes of valuing a person's estate, HMRC's approach is that certain items of property may be taken together, even if held under separate titles (and irrespective of whether all the various parts of the estate are chargeable to tax) (IHTM04045). This principle mainly applies to valuations of unquoted shares, interests in land, undivided property interests and 'sets' of assets such as antique chairs.

For further commentary on the valuation of specific types of asset, see **Chapter 4**.

RELATED PROPERTY: INTRODUCTION

3.20 A particular rule deals with the valuation of property in an estate if other property exists which is related to it (*s 161*). It is intended to cover situations such as if a set of assets (eg antique chairs) is divided through an exempt transfer (eg a gift to the spouse), thereby reducing the value of the assets retained. The rule applies to both lifetime transfers and to deemed transfers on death.

'Related property' is broadly property included in the estate of a spouse or civil partner, or in certain cases property belonging to a charity or one of the political, national or public bodies to which exempt transfers may be made.

For more detailed commentary on the related property rules, see **Chapter 4**.

Relief is potentially available broadly if related property is sold by a legatee or the deceased's personal representatives to an unconnected person within three years of death for less than the related property valuation on death. If the relief conditions are satisfied, a claim may be made by the deceased's personal representatives to recalculate the tax at death based on the value of the asset concerned, without reference to the related property provisions (*s 176*). The relief only applies if the sale price (after adjusting for any change in circumstances) is less than the amount at which the property concerned was originally valued (*s 176(4)*).

For more detailed commentary on the relief for sales of related property, see **Chapter 10**.

CALCULATING IHT ON THE DEATH ESTATE

General

3.21 IHT on the death estate is calculated as follows:

Lifetime transfers

3.22 IHT on chargeable lifetime transfers is initially calculated at lifetime rates (see **Chapter 2**). If the transferor dies within seven years, the tax is recomputed at full death rates, subject to taper relief (see **Chapter 10**) where the death is more than three years after the gift. Taper relief cannot reduce the tax payable below that originally charged.

Tax at full death rates is calculated at the time of death on any PETs made within seven years prior to death, subject to the availability of taper relief. As PETs are assumed to be exempt transfers when made, no lifetime IHT would have been paid, and the PET did not enter into the transferor's cumulative total at that time. Upon the transferor's death within seven years of the PET, it becomes a chargeable transfer at the actual date of the gift.

When computing the tax on PETs which become chargeable, any chargeable transfers made within seven years of the PET must be cumulated, even if they were made more than seven years before death. If the PET was made before a chargeable lifetime transfer, the tax on that transfer may need recalculating, and the transferor's cumulative total will need to be revised.

The death estate

3.23 The deceased's estate is taken into account based on a notional transfer of value equal to its value immediately before death (*s 4(1)*).

IHT on death is charged according to the thresholds and 'death rate' as shown in Table 3.2 below (*s 7, Sch 1*). The IHT threshold may be extended by an additional nil rate band (or 'residence' nil rate band) if an interest in the home passes on death to lineal descendants of the deceased from 6 April 2017 (see **3.24**).

A lower rate of 36% may be charged on a deceased person's estate, broadly where 10% or more of the net estate has been left to a charity or a registered community amateur sports club (ie in relation to deaths on or after 6 April 2012 (*Sch 1A*).

Table 3.2—Transfers on death after 5 April 2016

Tax on transfers:

Gross taxable transfers	*Gross cumulative totals*	*Rate*
£	£	
First 325,000	0–325,000	NIL
Above 325,000		40% for each £ over 325,000

Grossing-up of specific transfers on death which do not bear their own tax

Net transfers	*Tax payable thereon*
£	£
First 325,000	NIL
Above 325,000	2/3 for each £ over 325,000

The personal representatives are assessed to IHT on the deceased's free estate (*s 200(1)(a)*).

If the deceased had an interest in possession in settled property which is deemed to form part of his estate on death (see **3.2**), the settlement trustees are liable to IHT in respect of the trust property (*s 200(1)(b)*).

Hence, the IHT calculated must be apportioned between the free estate and the settled property.

Example 3.2—Free estate and settled property

Mr Edwards died on 10 June 2016. His free estate consisted of net chargeable investment assets amounting to £273,000. In addition, he had a life interest in a trust originally created in 2001, which was worth £640,000. The IHT liability on death is calculated as follows:

	£
Free estate	273,000
Settled property	640,000
Chargeable to IHT	913,000
IHT:	
(£913,000 – £325,000) × 40% = £235,200	
The IHT is apportioned and payable as follows:	
Personal representatives:	
$\frac{£273,000}{£913,000} \times £235,200$	70,328
Trustees:	
$\frac{£640,000}{£913,000} \times £235,200$	164,872
	£235,200

Alternatively, an average 'estate rate' of IHT can be calculated and applied to the free estate and settled property, ie £235,200/£913,000 × 100 = 25.76%.

The application of these rules was seen in *Smith and others v HMRC* [2009] SpC 742, where it was found that a settlement existed of money in an account. Whilst the executors were not liable to tax in respect of the fund itself, there was an adjustment to the overall liability that affected the estate in their hands. The case is considered at **7.5**.

Transferable nil rate band and the residence nil rate band

3.24 The nil rate band of a spouse or civil partner may be wholly or partly unused on their death. Prior to the introduction of the facility to transfer unused nil rate bands, if all the deceased's assets were left to their UK-domiciled surviving spouse, the spouse IHT exemption may have resulted in the loss of the deceased spouse's nil rate band.

However, on the death of the surviving spouse (or civil partner) since 9 October 2007, a claim has been available for the unused proportion of the nil rate band from the earlier death to be added to the survivor's own nil rate band, so that a larger nil rate amount is available against their estate for IHT purposes.

The nil rate band to be transferred is expressed as a percentage (not exceeding 100%, as the limit is one additional nil rate band, even if there was more than one former spouse) of the amount unused from the earlier death. The nil rate band that applies on the death of the surviving spouse is increased by that percentage (*s 8A*).

Focus

A claim to transfer unused nil rate band must be made by the survivor's personal representatives, within two years from the end of the month in which the survivor dies or (if later) within three months of the personal representatives first acting as such, although HMRC may allow a longer period at their discretion.

In the absence of a claim by the personal representatives, a late claim may be made by any person liable to IHT on the survivor's death, subject to HMRC's agreement (*s 8B*).

There are potentially complicated rules for dealing with the transfer of the nil rate band and the calculation of IHT when certain IHT and capital transfer tax deferred charges (ie on heritage assets and woodlands) are triggered, where the deferred IHT is calculated by reference to the earlier deceased spouse (*s 8C*).

For periods prior to the date of changes introduced in *Finance Act 2011*, complex rules also apply to determine the amount of nil rate band available in calculating IHT where a dependant who inherits an alternatively secured pension fund dies or ceases to be a dependant (*ss 151A–151C*). However, with effect for deaths from 6 April 2011, IHT does not normally apply to drawdown pension funds remaining under a registered pension scheme, including when the individual dies after reaching the age of 75. The effective requirement to purchase an annuity by that age has been removed, and the complex rules mentioned above have been repealed.

Further information on transferable nil rate bands is available in HMRC's Inheritance Tax Manual (at IHTM43000 onwards), and also via the HMRC website (www.gov.uk/inheritance-tax/leaving-assets-spouse-civil-partner).).

The subject is also discussed in **Chapter 14**.

An increased nil rate band (or 'residence nil rate band') is available on death from 6 April 2017, where a residence is passed on death to a lineal descendant of the deceased (*ss 8D–8M*). The residence nil rate band, if available, is in addition to the IHT threshold (or standard nil rate band).

The residence nil rate band for 2017/18 is £100,000, increasing in stages to £175,000 in 2020/21. However, the residence nil rate band is subject to a taper threshold, which reduces the nil rate band available according to the value of the deceased's estate.This taper threshold is set at £2 million for 2017/18 and subsequent tax years.

If the deceased's estate does not include a qualifying residential interest, or if it does include such an interest but none of it is inherited by lineal descendants, the deceased's residence nil rate band is nil. However, the residence nil rate band that has not been used is available for transfer to a spouse (or civil partner) (*s 8F*). The transferable amount is expressed as a percentage, which is subject to an overriding maximum of 100%, or one additional residence nil rate band.

The transferable residence nil rate band must be claimed (*s 8L*). The claim should generally be made by the deceased's personal representatives within a permitted period. Alternatively, a claim may be made by any other person liable to IHT on the person's death within such later period as HMRC may allow.

Further legislation introduced in *Finance Act 2016* provides for the residence nil rate band to be available in certain circumstances involving downsizing where other assets are passed on death to direct descendants. The provisions apply to downsizing moves or disposals from 8 July 2015, in relation to deaths from 6 April 2017.

For further commentary on the residence nil rate band see **14.42–14.48**.

Quick succession relief

3.25 Relief for successive charges (or 'Quick succession relief': see **Chapter 10**) applies if the value of the deceased's chargeable estate for IHT purposes was increased by a previous chargeable transfer (either during lifetime or on death) made within five years before his death (*s 141*).

Quick succession relief reduces the total IHT chargeable on death by a percentage of the tax attributable to the net increase in the deceased's estate resulting from the previous transfer. The relief percentage depends on the length of time between the two occasions. The relief reduces the tax payable on the death estate. This includes any settled property in which the deceased had a life interest forming part of his estate. If IHT is payable on any part of the deceased's death estate, the relief is due regardless of which part of his estate the tax is chargeable.

If IHT is payable under more than one title (ie personally and as liferenter), the relief is apportioned accordingly (IHTM22045).

Note also the commentary on the relief at **1.23** and **10.4–10.5**.

Double tax relief

3.26 Property situated abroad may be liable to IHT and also to a similar tax imposed by another country or state. Double tax relief is available for all or part of the overseas tax. Relief may be given under the terms of a double tax agreement with another territory (*s 158*).

Otherwise, unilateral relief may be given for the tax paid in the overseas territory against the IHT due on the same foreign property, up to the amount of overseas tax paid on those assets (*s 159*).

See **Chapter 10**.

CHARGEABLE AND EXEMPT ESTATE

Introduction

3.27 The deceased's estate may be wholly exempt, partly exempt or wholly chargeable to IHT, depending on whether the beneficiaries under a will or intestacy are wholly or partly exempt. If a transfer on death is only partially exempt (eg because the deceased leaves part of his estate to his spouse or to charity), there are provisions (*ss 36–42*) to determine the extent and the impact of IHT liabilities on that part of the estate which is not exempt.

The rules can apply to lifetime transfers (eg gifting interests in an asset to exempt and non-exempt beneficiaries), but are more common and of greater relevance in relation to transfers on death.

Terminology

3.28 The value of the estate is divided for IHT purposes into 'specific' and 'residuary' gifts. A 'gift' in this context is the benefit of any disposition or rule of law by which any property becomes the property of any person or applicable for any purpose.

- A *specific gift* is any gift other than a gift of residue or a share of residue (*s 42(1)*), such as the deceased's residence, company shares or personal effects. Certain liabilities are also treated as specific gifts for these purposes (*s 38(6)*).
- A *residuary gift* is the balance of the estate after all specific gifts have been made.

- A specific gift may '*bear its own tax*', ie IHT comes out of the gift itself so that the beneficiary gets the property less the tax on it, or the IHT attributable to the gift falls upon the beneficiary (*ss 42(2), 211(3)*). A specific gift bears its own tax if the deceased's will so states (*s 211(2)*). Otherwise, a specific gift of UK property is 'tax free' (see below), but a specific gift of non-UK property bears its own tax (*s 211(1)*). Other property bearing its own tax includes joint property passing by survivorship, nominated property, 'gift with reservation' property and any other property which does not vest in the deceased's personal representatives (IHTM26126).
- Alternatively, the gift may be '*tax free*' (ie the beneficiary gets the full value of the gift, without reduction for the IHT on the gift, and the IHT is paid out of residue).

The value of a specific gift will normally be a specified sum (eg £50,000 cash) or the market value of a particular asset. However, partial exemption may produce a value of the gift when calculating the IHT due which is different from the specified sum or value of that asset.

If the total value of the specific gifts exceeds the total value of the estate, the specific gifts may need to be reduced so that their total value equals the value of the estate, by a process of 'abatement' (*s 37*).

For example, if an individual's estate is worth £400,000 and in his will he gifts £200,000 to charity, £200,000 to his daughter (bearing its own tax) and £400,000 to his wife, abatement will apply. The legacies total £800,000, but the estate is only worth £400,000, so each legacy is reduced by one-half.

Interaction with business and agricultural property relief

3.29 If an estate includes property attracting business property relief (BPR) or agricultural property relief (APR) (see **Chapter 11**), special rules apply for the purposes of valuing specific and residuary gifts if part of the estate is exempt. If the business or agricultural property is given by a specific gift, its value is reduced by BPR or APR (*s 39A(2)*).

However, if any residuary gifts (after 17 March 1986) include business or agricultural assets, any specific gifts of non-business or non-agricultural assets (eg cash gifts to chargeable parties) will be entitled to a due proportion of business or agricultural property relief (*s 39A*).

The value of such specific gifts is the 'appropriate proportion' of their value, which is calculated as follows (*s 39A(4)*):

Estate (after BPR/APR)	less	Specific gifts of business or agricultural property (net of BPR/APR)
Estate (before BPR/APR)	less	Specific gifts of business or agricultural property (before BPR/APR)

Settled property is excluded from the *s 39A* calculation (see HMRC examples at IHTM26110 and IHTM26158).

The above rule presents a potential pitfall, as BPR or APR is effectively wasted if given against exempt legacies, possibly resulting in a higher overall IHT liability.

Example 3.3—*Section 39A* pitfall

Richard died on 5 June 2016. His estate of £1,250,000 consists of shares in an unquoted trading company worth £700,000 together with cash and investment assets worth £550,000.

His will leaves cash and some of the other (non-business) assets of £400,000 to his spouse, with the residue to his son and daughter.

The value of Richard's estate (net of BPR) is £550,000. The 'appropriate proportion' (see above) of the spouse's exempt legacy is:

$$\text{£}400{,}000 \times \frac{\text{£}550{,}000}{\text{£}1{,}250{,}000} = \text{£}176{,}000$$

The non-exempt residue (ie the chargeable free estate) is £374,000 (ie £550,000 – £176,000). BPR is wasted to the extent that it reduces the legacy to Richard's spouse, which is exempt in any event (*s 18*).

The loss of BPR (or APR) such as in the above circumstances can be avoided by ensuring that specific gifts of business and agricultural assets which attract 100% relief are made to chargeable parties (possibly in addition to an amount up to the nil rate band if appropriate, although for surviving spouses or civil partners (who have died since 9 October 2007), it may alternatively be possible to transfer unused nil rate band from the first spouse to die).

If the deceased's will does not provide for such specific legacies, it may be possible to vary the dispositions in the will using a deed of variation within two years of the deceased's death, and to include a statement in the deed that it is to apply for IHT purposes (*s 142*).

Partly exempt gifts

3.30 The calculation of IHT where gifts are partly chargeable and partly exempt is potentially complex. HMRC's Inheritance Tax Manual (at IHTM26071 onwards) sets out a five-step process for applying the partly exempt transfer rules in the correct order.

Alternatively, a 'grossing up' calculator (at 40%) is available via the HMRC website (www.gov.uk/government/uploads/system/uploads/attachment_data/file/402972/G_up40_per_cent.pdf), which will calculate the chargeable estate in most circumstances, if the estate is partially exempt from IHT and there are tax-free legacies.

The five-step process mentioned is summarised in the table below.

Table 3.3—Partly exempt transfer rules: HMRC's five-step process

Step 1 – Value legacies

Set out the starting values of specific gifts.

Step 2 – Abatement (if applicable)

If the total value of specific gifts exceeds the value of the free estate, consider abatement (see **3.26**).

Step 3 – BPR/APR (if applicable)

The value of specific gifts may need to be reduced if business and/or agricultural property relief has been allowed (*s 39A*).

Step 4 – Grossing-up

The values of any chargeable specific gifts which do not bear their own tax are 'grossed-up' (see **3.31**).

Step 5 – Calculate residue

The total value of specific gifts (exempt and chargeable) is compared with the value of the free estate (after any business and/or agricultural property relief). If the free estate exceeds the specific gifts, the balance is the value of the residue. However, if specific gifts exceed the free estate, there is no residue, and abatement may apply.

Grossing-up

3.31 The process of calculating the chargeable part of the deceased's estate when specific tax-free gifts are made to a chargeable beneficiary and the estate is partly exempt is termed 'grossing-up'. It is therefore important to recognise which gifts bear their own tax and which do not (see **3.26**).

For the purposes of grossing-up, if the deceased's estate on death includes property under different title (eg free estate and settled property), the property chargeable under each title is considered separately and in isolation (*s 40*).

Simple grossing

3.32 'Simple' (or 'single') grossing applies only if specific chargeable gifts are all tax free and the residue is wholly exempt. The specific gift is a net transfer which must be grossed-up.

Example 3.4—Simple grossing (no lifetime gifts)

Daphne died on 6 May 2016. Her free estate is valued at £950,000. In her will, Daphne leaves £450,000 free of tax to her son, and the residue to her husband. She made no lifetime transfers in the seven years preceding her death.

The grossing calculation is as follows:

	£
Chargeable tax-free gift	450,000
IHT on gift:	
(£450,000 – £325,000) × 2/3	83,333
Value of estate (after IHT):	
£950,000 – £83,333	866,667
The net estate is divided:	
Son	450,000
Husband (£500,000 – £83,333)	416,667
	866,667

3.33 The above result can be checked by calculating IHT on the grossed-up tax-free gift, ie (£450,000 + £83,333) = £533,333 – £325,000 = £208,333 × 40% = £83,333.

If lifetime gifts have been made in the previous seven years but their total is less than the IHT nil rate band, the value of those gifts is deducted and the remaining nil rate band is used in the grossing calculation.

Example 3.5—Simple grossing (lifetime gifts below nil rate band)

The facts are as in **Example 3.4** above, except that Daphne made a PET of £150,000 on 24 December 2013. The grossing calculation becomes:

	£
IHT on gift:	
£450,000 – (£325,000 – £150,000) × 2/3	183,333
Value of estate (after IHT):	
£950,000 – £183,333	766,667
The net estate is divided:	
Son	450,000
Husband (£500,000 – £183,333)	316,667
	766,667

(Check: £450,000 + £183,333 IHT = £633,333 – £175,000 nil rate band remaining = £458,333 × 40% = £183,333).

3.34 If lifetime gifts made in the previous seven years exceed the nil rate band, the chargeable specific tax-free gifts are grossed-up by the fraction 5/3.

Example 3.6—Simple grossing (lifetime gifts above nil rate band)

The facts are as in **Example 3.4** above, except that Daphne made a PET of £400,000 on 24 December 2013. The grossing calculation becomes:

	£
£450,000 × 5/3	750,000

	£
IHT on gift:	
£750,000 × 40%	300,000
Value of estate (after IHT):	
£950,000 – £300,000	650,000
The net estate is divided:	
Son	450,000
Husband (£500,000 – £300,000)	200,000
	650,000

Double grossing

3.35 What if the residue is partly exempt and partly chargeable, or there are tax-bearing legacies? The tax-free legacies must be grossed-up using a procedure (in *s 38*) commonly referred to as 'double grossing-up'. This procedure is described in HMRC's Inheritance Tax Manual as 'The four stages' (see IHTM26152 onwards), upon which the following summary is based.

Table 3.4—'Double grossing' stages – Summary

Stage 1 – Grossing-up

Gross-up chargeable specific tax-free legacies, as if they were the only chargeable free estate.

Stage 2 – Calculate IHT rate

Using the gross value from Stage 1, calculate the chargeable free estate (ie including any specific chargeable gifts bearing their own tax). Add the value of any exempt specific gifts.

The initial value of the residue is the difference between the resulting total and the overall value of the estate for IHT purposes.

The value of the chargeable part of the residue is then determined (ie the total residue less the exempt residue).

The chargeable free estate for these purposes is the total of the chargeable specific gifts and chargeable residue. Calculate the tax on the chargeable free estate, to arrive at the estate rate.

Stage 3 – Re-gross at estate rate

Gross-up the chargeable specific tax-free gifts by the estate rate found in Stage 2.

Stage 4 – Calculate IHT on chargeable estate

Calculate the chargeable estate (ie the total of all chargeable specific tax-free gifts (Stage 3) and the total value of any chargeable specific gifts bearing their own tax).

Find the total value of all specific gifts (ie including any exempt specific gifts).

Find the value of the residue (ie the value of the estate for IHT purposes, less total specific gifts).

The chargeable residue is the total residue, less the exempt residue.

Calculate the IHT on the chargeable estate (ie the total of the chargeable specific gifts and the chargeable part of residue).

3.36 The following is a relatively straightforward example of the double grossing procedure for a free estate (ie no settled property, or joint property passing by survivorship) in which there is no business or agricultural property.

Example 3.7—Double grossing

Joe died on 30 April 2016, leaving a free estate of £1,500,000, comprising cash and investments. He made no lifetime gifts and had no other chargeable property such as trust interests.

In his will, Joe left £500,000 to his son tax-free, and the residue equally between his wife (exempt) and daughter (chargeable). The IHT payable on Joe's death and the distribution of his estate is set out below.

Stage 1 – Grossing-up

Gross-up the chargeable specific tax-free legacy (using the available nil rate band):

£325,000 × Nil

£175,000 × 2/3 = £116,666

The gross value is £500,000 + £116,666 = £616,666

Stage 2 – Calculate IHT rate

Calculate the chargeable free estate, the IHT thereon and the estate rate:

	£
Total free estate	1,500,000
Less: gross specific legacy	(616,666)
Value of residue	883,334
Less: exempt residue (1/2)	(441,667)
Chargeable residue	441,667
Chargeable free estate (£616,666 + £441,667)	1,058,333

IHT thereon:

£325,000 × Nil

£733,333 × 40% = £293,333

The estate rate is:

$$\frac{£293,333}{£1,058,333} \times 100\% = 27.7165\%$$

Stage 3 – Re-gross at estate rate

Gross-up the chargeable specific tax-free gift by the estate rate found in Stage 2:

$$100 \times \frac{£500,000}{100 - 27.7165} = £691,721$$

Stage 4 – Calculate IHT on chargeable estate

Calculate the chargeable estate:

	£
Total free estate	1,500,000
Less: gross specific legacy	(691,721)
Value of residue	808,279
Less: exempt residue (1/2)	(404,140)
Chargeable residue	404,139
Chargeable free estate (£691,721 + £404,139)	1,095,860

Calculate IHT on the chargeable estate:

£325,000 × Nil

£770,860 × 40% = £308,344

Summary

Estate rate:

$$\frac{£308,344}{£1,095,860} \times 100\% = \underline{28.1372\%}$$

Tax on gross legacy (£691,721 × 28.1372%) = £194,631

Tax on chargeable residue:

(£404,139 × 28.1372%) = £113,713

Residue:

	£
Total free estate	1,500,000
Less: gross legacy (£500,000 + £194,631)	(694,631)
Value of residue	805,369
Less: exempt residue (1/2)	(402,685)
Chargeable residue	402,684

Division of free estate:

	£
Legacy to son	500,000
Residue to wife	402,685
Residue to daughter (£402,684 – £113,713)	288,971
IHT (£194,631 + £113,713)	308,344
Total estate	£1,500,000

A more complicated example of the 'double grossing' procedures (ie including interaction with BPR (see **3.27**) and settled property) is featured in the Inheritance Tax Manual at IHTM26158.

Allocating the burden of tax

3.37 Having calculated the IHT in double grossing situations involving chargeable and exempt proportions, there are provisions to determine how the tax should be borne by the beneficiaries (*s 41*).

The rules expressly override the terms of the will or other disposition. They provide that no tax falls on any exempt specific gifts (or any exempt part of a specific gift), and that no tax attributable to the value of residue should fall on an exempt share of that residue.

3.38

> **Focus**
>
> The burden of tax can broadly be summarised as follows:
>
> - *Chargeable specific gifts bearing own tax* – the tax is deducted from the gift (*s 42(2)*).
> - *Exempt specific gifts* – the gift is made without deduction of tax (*s 41(a)*).
> - *Chargeable specific tax-free gifts* – the gift is made without deduction of tax (Note – HMRC's view is that the tax is paid out of residue, even if it is wholly or partly exempt; see IHTM26203).
> - *Residue is dealt with as follows*:
>   - the tax on tax-free specific gifts (see above) is deducted from the whole residue;
>   - the balance is divided according to the terms of the will or other disposition;
>   - the tax on any chargeable part of the residue is borne by that part (*s 41(b)*), despite any provisions to the contrary in the will.

Re Benham's Will Trust and *Re Ratcliffe*

3.39 The interpretation of wills in which the residuary estate is divided between gifts to exempt and chargeable beneficiaries was considered in *Re Benham's Will Trust* [1995] STC 210 and *Re Ratcliffe, Holmes v McMullan* [1999] STC 262.

The question of meaning concerns the proper construction of the following common type of clause in wills:

> 'I give devise and bequeath all my real and personal estate whatsoever and wheresoever not hereby otherwise disposed of unto my Trustees upon trust to sell and convert the same into money with power at their absolute discretion to postpone any such sale and conversion for so long as they shall think fit without being answerable for any loss and after payment thereout of my debts and funeral and testamentary expenses to stand possessed of the residue as to one half part thereof for my children in equal shares absolutely and as to the remainder of my estate upon trust for the following charities …'

Should such a clause be interpreted as meaning that the children should receive their residuary share of the estate subject to IHT, thereby receiving less than the charities?

Prior to *Re Benham* this was widely assumed to be the proper construction. The alternative construction (ie that the IHT should be paid and then the residue split) was disregarded, as it is prohibited (by *s 41(b)*) and therefore could not be effected. *Re Benham* held that there was a third construction which was not so prohibited (ie that the non-exempt beneficiary's share should be grossed-up so that after his share bore the IHT, he would receive an equal sum to the exempt beneficiary), albeit that this would result in more IHT being payable.

3.40 Subsequently, in *Re Ratcliffe* [1999] STC 262, it was held that on a proper construction of the common will clause, the non-exempt beneficiaries receive their share subject to IHT and without grossing-up.

Thus, in the case of wills drafted in accordance with *Re Ratcliffe*, the proper IHT treatment would be to calculate the residuary estate, deduct the exempt beneficiary's share, and calculate IHT on the balance.

Example 3.8—'Ratcliffe' will clause

Alice died on 30 June 2016, leaving an estate worth £800,000. She had made no lifetime transfers. In her will (which is drafted in accordance with *Re Ratcliffe*), Alice leaves her estate equally to her husband Albert and her daughter Beatrice.

IHT on Alice's estate is calculated as follows:

	£
Residuary free estate	800,000
Less: exempt residue (1/2)	(400,000)
Chargeable residue	400,000

	£
IHT on chargeable estate:	
£325,000 × Nil	
£75,000 × 40%	30,000
Division of estate:	
Albert	£400,000
Beatrice (£400,000 – £30,000)	£370,000

Construing wills

3.41 The Inheritance Tax Manual (at IHTM26131) states that grossing-up in accordance with *Re Benham* is 'very rare', but acknowledges (at IHTM26172) that 'It is perfectly possible, though unusual, for you to come across wills deliberately drafted to achieve a *Re Benham* result'.

Clearly, it would be better to avoid any doubt by reviewing and clarifying the will, to reduce the possibility that its meaning is given an alternative construction. The type of difficulty which can arise if a will is capable of being construed in different ways was illustrated in *RSCPA v Sharp* [2010] EWCA Civ 1474.

However, in some cases it may be possible to rectify the will following the testator's death by way of a variation (*s 142*). It should be noted that (following *FA 2012*) where a variation redirects property to a charity or registered club, the variation is not treated as made by the deceased unless the persons executing the variation show that the 'appropriate person' (ie charity, registered club or trustees) has been notified of it (*s 142(3A), (3B)*).

This condition applies where the person's death occurs on or after 6 April 2012. Copies of an exchange of letters between the parties to show that the charity or trustees are aware should be sufficient for these purposes (HMRC Trusts & Estates Newsletter, April 2012).

IHT COMPLIANCE

3.42 For information on IHT compliance in respect of the death estate (eg accounts and returns, payment of IHT), see **Chapter 6**.

HMRC have published an 'Inheritance Tax Toolkit', which is aimed at 'helping and supporting tax agents and advisers for whom Inheritance Tax Accounts do not make up a significant element of their work'. The guidance adds: 'Other agents may still find the toolkit helpful in validating their approach to this work and it may also be of use to anyone, including trustees and personal representatives, in completing form IHT400 Inheritance Tax Account'.

In the context of whether a penalty arises for an error in the IHT400 account, HMRC guidance on the gov.uk website ('Tax agent toolkits') states that whether 'reasonable care' has been taken in any particular case will be a question of fact and will not depend on whether a toolkit has or has not been used (www.gov.uk/government/collections/tax-agents-toolkits).

The Inheritance Tax Toolkit is available from the gov.uk website: www.gov.uk/government/uploads/system/uploads/attachment_data/file/382051/iht.pdf

HMRC have also published an 'online bereavement questionnaire', which is aimed at unrepresented individuals with a simple estate to administer and distribute. It covers income tax, child benefit and tax credits, as well as IHT and confirmation, and provides tailored, basic guidance (www.hmrc.gov.uk/tools/bereavement/index.htm). Improvements to HMRC's bereavement service were announced in its Trusts & Estates Newsletter for December 2014 (www.gov.uk/government/uploads/system/uploads/attachment_data/file/388356/141211_December_Newsletter-Final_draft_02.pdf).

Chapter 4

Valuation of assets

SIGNPOSTS

- **Valuation principles** – An 'open market value' generally applies for IHT purposes. However, a transfer of value is broadly measured by the reduction in a person's estate, which may differ (see **4.1–4.5**).
- **Related property** – The value of 'related property' must be taken into account if this results in a higher valuation. However, related property relief may be available if related property is sold to an unconnected person within three years of death for less than the related property valuation (see **4.6–4.10**).
- **Particular assets** – Certain assets are subject to particular valuation rules and principles. These include life policies, unquoted shares and securities and debts (see **4.11–4.35**).

GENERAL

4.1 IHT is charged on the value transferred by a chargeable transfer (*s 1;* unless otherwise stated all statutory references are to *IHTA 1984*).

As a general rule, the value of property for IHT purposes is the 'open market value', ie the price which the property might reasonably be expected to fetch if sold on the open market at that time. The price is not reduced on the basis that selling the property on the hypothetical open market at the same time would flood the market (*s 160*), and assumes a willing seller and a willing buyer, and sometimes a special buyer.

A 'special buyer' is a person prepared to pay more for an asset than anyone else (eg a 49% shareholder in a company wishing to acquire a further 2% of the company's shares to assume a controlling interest would probably be willing to pay more for those shares than another person acquiring the 2% holding in isolation).

A restriction or fetter on the freedom to dispose of property (eg a provision in a partnership agreement stating that a deceased's partnership interest passes on death to the retiring partners without cost) can reduce the value of a person's estate. However, the property is valued ignoring restrictions unless certain conditions are satisfied, including that consideration was given for the restriction or exclusion in money or money's worth (*s 163*).

For example, a stipulation in a testator's will that the grounds of his house are 'never to be sold for building land but always kept with the house' cannot restrict the value of that land if, at the date of death, it has 'hope value'. This is because the testator has received nothing as consideration for the restriction. It would be different if, for example, the testator had given the National Trust for Scotland covenants over the land for the benefit of some property belonging to the Trust.

Other valuation principles also need to be considered for IHT purposes, which are considered below.

HMRC's approach

4.2 HMRC considers valuation to be an area of 'high risk' in terms of the potential loss of IHT. This increases the risk of a challenge, where the valuation appears to HMRC to be too low (*Hatton v Revenue and Customs Commissioners* [2010] UKUT 195 (LC); although by contrast, see *Chadwick and another v Revenue and Customs Commissioners* [2010] UKUT 82 (LC)). In addition, a substantial undervaluation may result in the imposition of penalties. However, the tribunal decision in *Cairns v Revenue & Customs Commissioners* [2009] UKFTT 67 (TC) might offer some comfort in this context.

The generally preferred approach from HMRC's perspective is that taxpayers etc refer valuations to a qualified, independent valuer. However, this of itself may not be sufficient to satisfy HMRC that an asset has been valued satisfactorily. In its 'Inheritance Tax Toolkit' (www.gov.uk/government/uploads/system/uploads/attachment_data/file/382051/iht.pdf), HMRC advises (subject to certain exceptions – see below) as follows:

> 'For assets with a material value you are strongly advised to instruct a qualified independent valuer, to make sure the valuation is made for the purposes of the relevant legislation, and for houses, land and buildings, it meets Royal Institution of Chartered Surveyors (RICS) or equivalent standards.'

In terms of instructing an independent professional valuer, HMRC strongly advises that this is done 'properly', and recommends the following:

- 'Explain the context and draw attention to the definition in *s 160, Inheritance Tax Act 1984 (IHTA)* (market value).

- Provide all the relevant details concerning the asset, in particular ensuring the valuer is aware of the need to take into account any points in the bullet points under 'Risk' above.
- Ensure that copies of relevant agreements, or full details where only an oral agreement exists, are provided so misunderstandings do not arise.'

The importance of professional valuations was further emphasised in HMRC's Trusts and Estates Newsletter (August 2010), in the context of land and buildings (see **4.22** and subsequent paragraphs below). In a subsequent Trusts and Estates Newsletter (April 2011), HMRC also stated that it will take an 'appropriate penalty' if an application is made as an excepted estate, but the discovery of an undervaluation (or omission) leads to IHT being payable, where it is shown that personal representatives have failed to take reasonable care (or worse).

However, HMRC does not consider professional valuations to be necessary in all cases. The IHT toolkit also states:

> 'In limited circumstances you can provide self valuations for assets. For example, ordinary household goods where individual items have a value of no more than £500, and the use of publicly available data to obtain a valuation for second hand cars. Where you have provided a self valuation, explain how you have arrived at that value and why, if appropriate, a low or 'nil' valuation has been returned. Where there are antiques or collections and you are not obtaining a professional valuation provide us with a full description of the items and details of any sales proposed.'

4.3 Aside from this Chapter and HMRC's IHT Toolkit, further guidance on valuations for IHT purposes is available as follows:

- HMRC's notes to form IHT400 ('IHT400 Notes – Guide to completing your Inheritance Tax account') (www.hmrc.gov.uk/inheritancetax/iht400-notes.pdf);
- HMRC's Inheritance Tax Manual (eg at IHTM09701 onwards);
- HMRC's Shares and Assets Valuation Manual (eg at SVM111000 onwards, in the context of business property relief); and
- The Valuation Office Agency's (VOA) IHT manual, which can be accessed via the VOA website: (http://manuals.voa.gov.uk/corporate/publications/Manuals/InheritanceTaxManual/sections/toc.html).

The 'loss to estate' principle

4.4

> **Focus**
>
> The value transferred by a transfer of value is the amount by which a person's estate is reduced as a result (*s 3(1)*).
>
> This value will not necessarily be the actual value of an asset.

Example 4.1—Loss in value of estate

ABC Ltd has 100,000 issued ordinary £1 shares. The shares (shown as a percentage of the company's overall issued share capital) are valued as follows:

51%–75% = £25 per share

26%–50% = £14 per share

25% or less = £8 per share

Mr Scott owns 60,000 shares (ie 60% of the shares). He makes a gift of 20,000 shares to his daughter. The transfer of value for IHT purposes is as follows:

	£
Before (60,000 × £25)	1,500,000
After (40,000 × £14)	(560,000)
Value transferred	£940,000

Note that although the value of 20,000 shares in isolation is £160,000 (ie 20,000 × £8), for IHT purposes the reduction in Mr Scott's estate is higher as the result of losing his controlling interest in the company.

HMRC's IHT Toolkit lists the 'loss to the estate principle' as a 'risk' area for valuation purposes in respect of gifts, and sums up the principle as follows:

'When looking at the value of gifts you need to consider the "loss to the estate" principle. This means that you look at the value of the estate before and after the gift was made. The difference between those two figures is the loss to the estate and is the figure that needs to be included on the form IHT400'.

The 'estate concept'

4.5 A person's estate consists of all the property to which he is beneficially entitled (but not excluded property or a foreign-owned work of art situated in the UK only for the purpose of public display, cleaning and/or restoration) (*s 5(1)*).

The estate generally also includes property over which a person has a general power (*s 5(2)*), together with certain settled property in which the person is beneficially entitled to an interest in possession (see **3.2** and **Chapter 7**).

A beneficial interest in the net assets of an unadministered residuary estate also forms part of the estate (*s 91*), together with property subject to a 'gift with reservation' (*FA 1986, s 102(3)*).

Example 4.2—Estate assets

On Mr Johnson's death, his free estate included 2,000 ordinary £1 shares in XYZ Ltd, representing 20% of the company's issued share capital. He also had an immediate post-death interest under a will trust created on his wife's death in April 2005. The trustees held a further 6,000 ordinary shares in the company.

In valuing Mr Johnson's estate for IHT purposes, it is necessary to value 8,000 shares in XYZ Ltd, out of the company's issued share capital of 10,000 ordinary shares.

There is case law authority for the treatment of valuing property together (*Gray (surviving executor of Lady Fox) v IRC* [1994] STC 360), and for dividing estates into 'natural' or appropriate units (*Buccleuch v IRC* [1967] 1 AC 506) if doing so results in higher valuations.

When considering the value of land or buildings, the Valuation Office Agency will normally divide the estate so as to provide the highest value. HMRC may similarly decide how to divide certain other assets (eg wine collections) for estate valuation purposes (IHTM09715). In the context of wine cellars, HMRC state that the valuation must be open market value (under *s 160*) at the time of the relevant occasion of IHT charge, and not (as some had apparently thought) at the purchase price (HMRC Trust & Estates Newsletter, August 2010).

A person other than the sole legal owner of an asset such as land and buildings may claim to have a beneficial interest in that asset. Alternatively, property may be registered in joint names (eg unmarried co-habitants), but one of the parties may have a greater beneficial interest than the other, perhaps having contributed a larger proportion of the purchase price. In such cases, the parties may prefer the asset to be treated as owned by them in accordance with their respective beneficial shares. This principle is derived from two non-tax cases, *Oxley v Hiscock* [2004] EWCA Civ 546, [2005] Fam 211 and *Stack v Dowden* [2007] UKHL 17. In the latter case, Baroness Hale commented:

> 'The burden will therefore be on the person seeking to show that the parties did intend their beneficial interests to be different from their legal interests, and in what way. This is not a task to be lightly embarked upon.'

Following those cases, HMRC stated that the onus is upon the non-legal owner to demonstrate that they have any interest in the property, as if the claimant was presenting their case to a court of law (IHT & Trusts Newsletter–December 2007).

Subsequently, in *Pankhania v Chandegra* [2012] EWCA Civ 1438, the Court of Appeal had to consider whether an express declaration of trust was conclusive, or whether the rules of implied, resulting or constructive trusts in *Stack v Dowden* as reviewed in *Jones v Kernott* (see below) applied instead. In *Pankhania v Chandegra*, C and D purchased a property in 1987, which was the subject of an express declaration that C and D held the beneficial interest in the property as tenants in common in equal shares. The Court allowed an appeal from the High Court, and confirmed that an express declaration of trust is conclusive, unless it is set aside, varied or rectified.

In *Wade v Baylis* [2010] EWCA Civ 257, a couple commenced living together as man and wife in 1982, but separated in 2005. Following the split, Mr Wade claimed a 50% beneficial interest in the property, even though he had been removed from the deeds in 1986 at his own request. He had apparently made no contribution to the capital cost of the property, and contributed little to the mortgage repayments, although he had worked for free in a business run by Ms Baylis. The Court of Appeal dismissed Mr Wade's appeal against an earlier decision that Ms Baylis was the sole beneficial owner of the property in question.

Subsequently, in *Jones v Kernott* [2011] UKSC 53, the Supreme Court unanimously held that the beneficial interests of co-habitants in a property can change without their explicit intention. In that case, the co-habitants bought a house in 1985, and jointly owned it, without making any declaration as to how their beneficial interests should be apportioned. The relationship ended, and Mr Kernott moved out after the parties had lived in the property together for more than eight years. Ms Jones had originally contributed £6,000 of the £30,000 purchase price, and the balance had been funded by an interest-only mortgage. Following the separation, Ms Jones continued to live in the property, and assumed sole responsibility for the mortgage and outgoings, including repairs and maintenance. Mr Kernott later demanded a half-share of the house.

However, the County Court awarded Ms Jones 90% of the equity. Mr Kernott unsuccessfully appealed to the High Court. Subsequently, the Court of Appeal ([2010] EWCA Civ 578) held (by majority) that Mr Kernott and Ms Jones each had a 50% beneficial interest in the property. However, the Supreme Court overturned that decision, stating that an initial presumption of joint tenancy in law and equity can be displaced if the parties changed their intentions, and that a court can deduce their common intention from their conduct.

In *O'Kelly v Davies* [2014] EWCA Civ 1606, an individual who was the legal owner of a house was found on the facts to have held the beneficial ownership of the property on constructive trust for herself and her former cohabiting partner in equal shares.

A common intention to vary beneficial interests of the parties was subsequently inferred in *Barnes v Phillips* [2015] EWCA Civ 1056, such that the respondent was held to own an 85% interest and the appellant an interest of 15%.

There are specific IHT valuation rules, such as for quoted shares and life assurance policies, and also in the case of property that is related to property in the estate of a spouse or civil partner or the property of a charity.

RELATED PROPERTY

Rule of valuation

4.6

> **Focus**
>
> The value of 'related property' must be taken into account when valuing a person's estate if this results in a higher valuation (*s 161*).
>
> This rule applies to lifetime and death transfers, and prevents the division of an asset into less valuable parts by means of exempt transfers to reduce overall IHT liabilities.

Property is broadly 'related' for these purposes if it is:

- in the spouse's or civil partner's estate; or
- is (or was during the preceding five years) the property of a charity (or held on trust for charitable purposes only) (or a qualifying political party, housing association or national or public body, to which exempt transfers may be made) as the result of an exempt transfer (after 15 April 1976) by the individual, spouse or civil partner (*s 161(2)*).

The transferor's property and the related property are combined and valued as a single unit. The combined value of the estate property and related property is then apportioned to the estate property in the proportion that its value in isolation bears to the separate values when added together.

The related property rules are mostly used in practice to value transfers of unquoted shares and jointly owned property. They are one of the 'risk' areas for valuation purposes listed in HMRC's IHT Toolkit: 'Where there is "related property" ensure that this has been taken into account in the valuation following a lifetime event or on death'.

It should be noted that, for the purposes of determining whether shares or securities are deemed to give a person control of a company, shares or securities which are related property (within the meaning of *s 161*) are taken into account (*s 269(2)*).

How does the rule apply?

4.7 In the case of jointly owned property, the value of the combined unit is apportioned between the property in the individual's estate and the related property according to their separate values (*s 161(3)*). This general rule also applies for valuing other assets (but see below for a special rule in respect of shareholdings).

Example 4.3—Related property (land)

Derek owns land worth £15,000 and his wife Lisa owns adjoining land worth £25,000.

The combined value is £80,000.

The related property value of Derek's land is:

$$\frac{15{,}000}{15{,}000 + 25{,}000} \times £80{,}000 = £30{,}000$$

4.8 Should the value of jointly owned property be discounted to take into account the rights of the co-owner? The Inheritance Tax Manual (at IHTM04045) states HMRC's view as follows:

> 'It is often said that in order to sell either half share, the co-operation of the other joint owner is required and so a discount should be allowed to compensate for the uncertainty involved. Whilst in reality this may be

true, for IHT purposes the statute imposes the hypothesis that the deceased is beneficially entitled to the whole and it is the whole that is valued in accordance with Section 160 IHTA 1984. If tax is only chargeable on a fractional share (because, say, the other share is exempt) it is the arithmetic proportion that is taxed and not the value of the share involved.'

In the context of real, heritable or leasehold property, HMRC also comments (at IHTM09739):

> 'The related property rules apply because the interests of the spouses/civil partners are together worth more than the sum of their separate interests – the separate interests would normally be subject to a discount for joint ownership. The interests of the husband and wife, or civil partners, will normally be identical and will extend to the whole of the land and property so the value of the deceased/transferor's interest will be the appropriate proportion of the entirety value.'

The value to be included in the estate is the 'appropriate portion' of the value of the combined property (*s 161(1)*). There are two methods of calculating the appropriate portion: what HMRC refers to (in IHTM09734) as the 'general rule' (*s 161(3)*; see **6.7**); and the 'special rule' (*s 161(4)*; see below). HMRC's guidance points out that the general rule is used where the items of property being aggregated for valuation purposes are different (eg see **Example 6.3**). The special rule is mainly used for calculating the value of shareholdings where the value of the same shares can vary with the size of holding. However, HMRC may seek to use the special rule in other situations as well.

For example, in *Arkwright and another (Personal Representatives of Williams, deceased) v IRC* [2004] STC 1323, Mr and Mrs W owned a property as tenants in common. On Mr W's death, HMRC determined that IHT was due on 50% of the property's agreed open market value. The personal representatives appealed, contending that Mr W's interest should be valued at less than 50% of the vacant possession value, because his widow had the right to occupy the property and could not have it sold without her consent.

The Special Commissioner accepted this contention and allowed the appeal in principle, holding that the value of Mrs W's interest should be determined in accordance with *s 161(3)* (ie on the basis that both shares in the property were related, and that their values should therefore be aggregated, with the value of each property share being determined as if it did not form part of that aggregate). The Court of Appeal subsequently held that the Commissioner was entitled to conclude that the value of the deceased's interest in the property was not inevitably a mathematical one-half of the vacant possession value, rejecting HMRC's argument that *s 161(4)* applied to treat the land as 'units' and that the valuation ratio was one-half. However, the court considered that the value of Mr W's interest was a question for the Lands Tribunal to determine. The appeal was subsequently settled by agreement.

HMRC subsequently stated (in Revenue & Customs Brief 71/07) that, following legal advice, they would apply *s 161(4)* when valuing shares of land as related property in cases received after publication of that Brief (27 November 2007) and would consider litigation in 'appropriate cases', but that any existing cases would be dealt with on the basis of the Special Commissioners' decision in the *Arkwright* case as it relates to the interpretation of *s 161(4)*.

The 'general rule' was applied in *Price v Revenue and Customs Commissioners* [2010] UKFTT 474 (TC). In that case, the executor and trustee of his late wife's estate appealed against an IHT determination in respect of a property owned in equal half shares by husband and wife as tenants-in-common. The entire property was valued at £1.5 million, whereas the half shares of the property, valued independently, amounted to £637,500 each. The Executor argued (among other things) that 'the value of that and any related property' in *s 161(1)* meant the value of the two property interests valued independently of each other. HMRC argued that the above expression meant the totality of both interests treated as a single item of property. The tribunal held that the related property provisions hypothesise a notional sale and that the property interests were to be valued on the basis that they are offered for sale together and at the same time. If this resulted in a greater price than if the interests had been offered individually, then (if the sale would not have required undue effort or expense) the greater price must be attributed to the two items by applying the formula in *s 161(3)*. The appeal was therefore dismissed.

4.9 As indicated in **4.8** above the 'special' rule generally applies for the purposes of valuing shares and other securities of the same class (*s 161(4), (5)*). In that case, the apportionment of the combined value is based on the number of shares, not the value of the different holdings.

Example 4.4—Related property (shares)

On the husband's death on 31 October 2016, the share capital of a private company was held as follows:

Issued share capital – 10,000 shares

Husband	4,000	40%
Wife	4,000	40%
Others (employees)	2,000	20%
	10,000	100%

The value of an 80% holding is £80,000, while the value of a 40% holding is £24,000. In his will, the husband left his 4,000 shares to his daughter.

The related property rules apply to aggregate the shares of:

Husband	4,000
Wife	4,000
Related property	8,000 shares

Chargeable transfer on legacy to daughter:

IHT value of 8,000 shares (80%)	£80,000
IHT value attributed to legacy of husband's shares	$\frac{4{,}000}{8{,}000} \times £80{,}000 = £40{,}000$

This special rule applies not only to shares of the same class, but also to stock, debentures and other 'fungible' property, ie that which is capable of being divided into units of an identical nature, such as unit trusts or bottles of wine of the same vintage.

In the case of lifetime transfers, both the 'loss to estate' principle and the 'related property' rule apply in arriving at the value transferred (ie the related property rules are used to calculate the 'before' and 'after' estate values).

Related property relief

4.10 If related property is sold to an unconnected person within three years of death for less than the related property valuation, a claim may generally be made to recalculate the tax at death without reference to the related property (*s 176*). The relief is subject to certain conditions, and applies to a 'qualifying sale' as defined (*s 176(3)*; see IHTM09754).

The claim may be made by the deceased's personal representatives, or by persons in whom the property vested immediately after the death. Relief is also available if the property was valued with other property in the estate (eg if the deceased held property absolutely, together with property subject to an interest in possession (ie within *s 49(1)*)).

Note that related property relief does not substitute the value of the property at the date of sale. The valuation date is immediately before the death.

See **Chapter 10**.

PARTICULAR ASSETS

4.11 Certain assets have their own valuation rules. Some of the more common assets and situations are outlined below.

In some cases, the uncertain nature of an asset at a particular point in time can cause difficulties in its valuation. One such example is compensation payments received after the date of death. The right to pursue a compensation claim is an asset of the estate. The personal representatives should therefore disclose full information about the claim on form IHT400, together with a 'reasoned estimate' of the open market value of the right where they are able to do so (HMRC Trusts and Estates Newsletter, August 2013).

A list of specific types of property is contained in the Inheritance Tax Manual (at IHTM09702), together with references to detailed guidance elsewhere in the manual on how to value them.

Life policies

Lifetime transfers

4.12 The lifetime gift of a life policy or annuity (ie by assignment or declaration of trust) from one person to another constitutes a transfer of value. The value transferred is broadly the greater of the premiums paid (less any proceeds received under the policy or annuity contract prior to the transfer, eg on a partial surrender) and the open market value of the policy (ie normally its surrender value) (*s 167(1)*).

The above valuation rule does not apply to transfers of value on death (*s 167(2)(a)*) (see **4.13**). In addition, term assurance policies are excluded if the sum assured becomes payable only if the life assured dies before the expiry of a specified term (or before the expiry of a specified term *and* during the life of a specified person). However, if the specified term ends, or can be extended to end, more than three years after the policy is made and if neither the life assured nor the specified person dies within the specified term, the premiums must be payable during at least two-thirds of that term and at yearly or shorter intervals, and the premiums payable in any one period of 12 months must not be more than twice the premiums payable in any other 12-month period for this exclusion to apply (*s 167(3)*).

A separate rule applies for the purpose of valuing unit-linked policies. This broadly provides for a reduction in the value of the policy if the value of the units has fallen since the date of their allocation (*s 167(4)*; see example at IHTM20244).

A policy taken out for another person is also a transfer of value, normally based on the amount of the first premium, and on any subsequent premiums. If premiums are paid on a policy owned by somebody else, the amount of each premium is a separate transfer of value, subject to any exemptions due (eg the annual exemption (*s 19*) or the normal expenditure out of income exemption (*s 21*)).

Transfers on death

4.13 The proceeds of a policy taken out on the person's own life or for his own benefit, which are payable on death to the deceased's personal representatives are taken into account as part of the estate, based on the policy's open market value (*s 160*). The open market value will be the amount for which the policy could be sold, and might exceed its surrender value (IHTM20231).

If the proceeds from the life policy are payable to someone other than the life assured, and if that beneficial owner dies before the life assured, there will be a transfer on their death based on the value of the life policy.

'Back-to-back' arrangements

4.14 An anti-avoidance rule applies to cover circumstances in which an individual (who may be in poor health) purchases one or more annuities to enable him to take out one or more life policies written in trust for someone other than the life assured, and where the annuity payments feed the premiums for the life policy. If the life policy was taken out (or varied) since 26 March 1974 and the two events are associated operations, the IHT exemption for normal expenditure out of income does not apply (*ss 263, 21(2)*).

In addition, unless it can be shown that the purchase of the annuity and the taking out of the life insurance policy are not 'associated operations' (as defined in *s 268*), the purchaser of the annuity is treated as having made a transfer of value when the policy became vested in the other person. The amount of the transfer of value is the lower of the following:

- the cost of the annuity and any premiums (or other consideration) paid on or before the transfer; and
- the value of the greatest benefit capable of being conferred by the policy, calculated as if that time was the transfer date (*s 263(2)*).

However, HMRC should be prepared to accept that the two contracts are not 'associated operations' if the life policy is shown to have been underwritten on the basis of medical evidence without reference to the annuity (Statement of Practice E4; see IHTM20375). The easiest way to demonstrate that the two contracts were not 'associated' would be to take up the annuity and the policy with separate, unconnected life offices. If the same life office is used, the policy should be issued and the premiums fixed on the basis of full medical evidence.

In the case of joint life assurance policies (eg between husband and wife) full medical evidence is required in respect of both lives assured. In *Smith v Revenue and Customs Commissioners* [2008] STC 1649, it was held that Statement of Practice E4 did not apply to a joint life policy, where a medical report had not been obtained in respect of the wife's health. The Court upheld the earlier decision of the Special Commissioner that the purchase of the annuity and making of the life assurance policy were associated operations.

Discounted gift schemes

4.15 A discounted gift scheme broadly involves the gift of a bond, subject to retained rights such as withdrawals or successively maturing reversions. The retained rights are such that the 'gift with reservation' anti-avoidance rules (*FA 1986, s 102*) do not apply. The gift of the bond is a transfer of value, based on the difference between the amount invested in the bond and the open market value of the retained rights (*s 160*).

In May 2007, HMRC issued a Technical Note concerning the valuation and other issues relating to discounted gift schemes, which stated HMRC's view, *inter alia*, that if the settlor was uninsurable for any reason at the date of gift the open market value of the retained rights would be nominal, and the gift would be close to the whole amount invested. HMRC also stated that settlors older than 90 years of age would be considered uninsurable (www.hmrc.gov.uk/cto/dgs-tech-note.pdf).

However, in *Bower v Revenue and Customs Commissioners*, a 90 year old lady in relatively poor health took out a life annuity policy. She paid a premium of £73,000, and the policy was issued to a settlement she created, subject to the reserved right to a 5% life annuity. Mrs Bower died five months later. HMRC valued the reserved right at only £250, whereas the insurance company had valued the rights at £7,800. Her executors appealed. The Special Commissioner ([2008] SpC 665) considered that the open market value of the reserved rights to the annuity was £4,200. HMRC appealed.

In Business Brief 23/08, HMRC stated an intention to appeal to the High Court against the decision in the above case, and indicated that in the meantime new cases would continue to be dealt with in accordance with the May 2007 Technical Note mentioned above. Subsequently, the Court allowed HMRC's appeal in the *Bower* case ([2009] STC 510), on the grounds that the Commissioner was erroneous in law in concluding that he was required or entitled to assume hypothetical speculators or to indicate the price that the hypothetical buyer was assumed to have paid.

HMRC subsequently issued Revenue & Customs Brief 21/09 (dated 2 April 2009), confirming that cases would be dealt with in accordance with its technical note issued in 2007. The Brief also stated that '... there is nothing in the Inheritance Tax legislation which allows any withdrawals actually taken between the gift date and the date of death of the settlor to be offset against the sum invested'.

In *Watkins and another v Revenue & Customs* [2011] UKFTT 745 (TC), the deceased had created a discounted gift trust in December 2004, and settled a redemption bond obtained for a premium of £340,000. She died in March 2006, aged 91 years. The deceased's retained right in the settlement to an income stream was valued at approximately £49,033, but HMRC determined the value to be £4,250. The tribunal dismissed the appeal against HMRC's Notice of Determination, and held that although the appellants' formulations were 'ingenious' they were not identifiable with any type of open market which exists. The burden of displacing HMRC's valuation was on the appellants, and the tribunal held that this burden had not been discharged.

The ability of UK life insurers to charge different premiums (or determine different benefits) for males and females based on gender related factors was removed following a legal challenge to the European Court of Justice by the Belgian consumer's association Test Achats. HMRC subsequently stated (in its Trusts and Estates Newsletter for April 2011) that if the Test Achats decision resulted in changes from the market practice of life companies to take into account the gender of the life assured, HMRC would consult on how best to incorporate that change into its practice of valuing retained rights under discounted gift schemes.

HMRC later stated that, following the Test Achats case, the use of gender as a factor in setting insurance premiums is not permissible from 21 December 2012. HMRC therefore altered the mortality basis used in the calculation of the open market value of the retained rights, to reflect the change in open market premium rates. It also revised the current interest rate assumption within the calculation. The revised mortality (80% of AFC00 select mortality) and interest rate (4.5% per annum) basis applies to all transfers (or ten-year anniversaries, in respect of relevant property trusts) from 1 December 2013 (Revenue and Customs Brief 22/13).

Quoted shares and securities

4.16 HMRC's IHT400 Notes state (www.gov.uk/government/uploads/system/uploads/attachment_data/file/373508/IHT400_Notes.pdf):

'You do not have to get a professional valuation for quoted stocks and shares. You can value shares quoted on the London Stock Exchange by finding the price of the shares in the financial pages of a newspaper'.

Further HMRC guidance on the basis of valuation is included in the IHT manual (at IHTM18091 and following).

Quoted investments must be valued based on the general rule regarding open market value in *s 160*.

There is no special statutory basis (in *s 160* or otherwise) for valuing quoted shares and securities for IHT purposes. Historically, capital gains tax valuation rules were generally used in practice to ascertain the value of stocks and shares for IHT purposes (*TCGA 1992, s 272*).

Prior to 6 April 2015, the same valuation basis therefore applied for both capital gains tax and IHT purposes. However, the basis of valuation for listed shares, securities and strips for capital gains tax purposes was changed by statutory instrument from that date (see below); however, the statutory instrument does not apply for IHT purposes as well. At the time of writing, the valuation bases have not been aligned, so the pre-6 April 2015 basis of valuation for capital gains tax purposes continues to apply to IHT valuations (see IHTM18093).

From 6 April 2015, the market value of UK quoted stocks and shares for capital gains tax purposes is generally the lower of the two prices shown in the Stock Exchange Daily List as the closing price, plus one-half of the difference between those two figures, or (if the Stock Exchange was closed that day) that value on the last day on which it was open, unless the closing prices are not a proper measure of market value due to special circumstances (*Market Value of Shares, Securities and Strips Regulations 2015, SI 2015/616, reg 2*). Different valuation rules apply to securities or strips (but not shares) listed on a foreign exchange (*SI 2015/616, reg 3*).

For valuations prior to 6 April 2015, the lower of two figures is applied for capital gains tax purposes:

- The 'quarter-up' method, ie the lower closing Stock Exchange price plus one-quarter of the difference between the lower and higher closing prices (this can normally be obtained, for example, from the *Financial Times* or similar periodical for the day following the valuation date).

Example 4.5—Valuation of quoted investments: 'quarter-up' method

James owned 5,000 shares in Widgets plc at the date of his death. Their price range on that date was 110–122 pence. The valuation would be:

$$110 + \frac{1}{4}(122 - 110) = \underline{113 \text{ pence}}$$

The value of 5,000 shares would therefore be 5,000 × 113p = £5,650.

- Mid-price between the highest and lowest recorded bargains for the day of valuation. This is sometimes referred to as the 'mid-price bargain' or 'average bargain' rule.

If the transfer takes place on a day that the Stock Exchange is closed, the market value can be ascertained by reference to the previous day or the following day, and the lower valuation is taken.

If shares are transferred 'ex-dividend' (ie broadly dividends declared but not yet paid at the date of valuation), the right to the dividend represents an asset of the estate, which should therefore be taken into account unless the right to receive it is transferred.

These valuation rules can be applied both to lifetime transfers and for the purposes of valuing the death estate.

A special rule applies to holdings in Bradford & Bingley (B&B), in relation to former shareholders who died on or after 29 September 2008 and no longer held the shares but were entitled to compensation for the loss of them. Where the right to compensation was for a holding of 1,000 shares or less in B&B, HMRC indicated that the value offered may be accepted without enquiry, including a value of nil. For holdings of more than 1,000 shares, any valuation is likely to be referred to HMRC Shares and Assets Valuation (IHTM10073).

Unit trusts

4.17 The market value of unit trusts is the buying price, being the lower of two published values (ie the buying and selling price) for the date in question, or on the last previous business day if the transfer does not take place on a business day (*TCGA 1992, s 272(5)*) (see also IHTM18095).

Unquoted shares and securities

4.18

> **Focus**
>
> Unlike quoted shares and securities, there is normally no ascertainable or readily available value for unquoted shares and securities. The valuation of unquoted shares and securities is based on the price that they might reasonably be expected to fetch when sold in the open market (*s 160*).
>
> For the purpose of determining this price, it is assumed that a prospective purchaser possessed all the information that might reasonably be required if the purchase was from a willing vendor at arm's length (*s 168*).

Valuations may take into account relevant factors such as the size of the company and shareholding, its activities and profit levels, asset backing and dividend history. In practice, the IHT value is generally subject to negotiation with HMRC Shares and Assets Valuation.

HMRC guidance on valuation issues regarding unquoted shares is included in the Shares and Assets Valuation Manual (see SVM113000 and following in connection with the statutory open market, and SVM114000 and following concerning information standards).

If a valuation cannot be agreed, it will be subject to appeal before the Tax Tribunal.

4.19 In practice, HMRC Shares and Assets Valuation will not always consider and formally agree a valuation (eg if the share value is likely to be well within the transferor's available nil rate band, or if the shares qualify for 100% business or agricultural property relief (see **Chapter 11**)).

In the latter case, if HMRC agree that full relief may be deducted, this is not an indication that the share value has been accepted (Note: in those circumstances, the value has not been 'ascertained' for IHT purposes, and therefore cannot be relied upon in any subsequent CGT computations (*TCGA 1992, s 274*)). It should be noted that such share transfers are subject to the same reporting requirements as other types of assets, and that a reasonable valuation should still be advanced (see **4.2**).

Joint property

4.20 In Scotland jointly owned property is normally held with pro-indiviso shares and is known as common property (see **Overview A6** for Scottish

Property Issues). Common property may be held with a special destination which triggers a deceased's interest in the property to pass upon death by survivorship to the remaining owner(s). For titles without a survivorship destination the interest or share of any owner passes on death under their will or, if there is no will, under the rules of intestacy.

The *Succession (Scotland) Act 2016 , s 2* treats a former spouse as having died before the other spouse for survivorship destinations contained in heritable property titles that remain in place on death after divorce or on the dissolution of a civil partnership.

There are also the joint property rights of trustees and partners where they do not have identifiable shares (which accrue on death to the survivors) (see IHTM 15091).

Money accounts

4.21 Under Scots law, where bank or building society accounts are held in joint names, the special or survivorship destination does not by itself pass the ownership of the money in the account to the survivor. An account with a bank or building society is not a document of title (ie it is not a Deed of Trust in terms of the *Blank Bonds and Trusts Act 1696*). It is a contract between the bank and the customer. The question of the ownership of the funds in the account therefore falls to be determined according to the ordinary principles of ownership. The individual who deposited funds in the account remains the owner, unless a transfer of ownership has occurred (IHTM 15054). This applies to all bank or building society accounts governed by Scots Law, and therefore applies to taxpayers living in England, Wales and Northern Ireland with an account governed by Scots Law (IHTM15054).

In England and Wales, joint money account holders (eg with banks, building societies, etc) are normally regarded as beneficially entitled to the proportion of the account attributable to their contributions. In addition, HMRC accept that, as a general rule, if one individual places money in a joint account with another as joint tenants and retains the right to withdraw the whole of it, there will not be a lifetime transfer when the money is paid into that account (although there may be a transfer on a later withdrawal of funds for the other joint owner) (IHTM15042–3).

However, care should be taken when one or more beneficial interests in joint accounts are gifted to other individuals (particularly if those individuals are not exempt beneficiaries), to avoid the whole account being included in the transferor's estate (*O'Neill & O'Neill's Executors v CIR*, SpC [1998] SSCD 110; *Sillars v IRC* [2004] SSCD 180).

In *Taylor and another v Revenue and Customs Commissioners* [2008] SSCD 1159, the deceased was held to have a general power enabling her to dispose of the whole of two joint accounts. This was on the grounds (among other reasons) that there was no evidence that the other joint account holder was to benefit from the accounts on the particular facts of the case, and that the deceased was able to dispose of the whole balance in those accounts.

In *Matthews v Revenue and Customs Commissioners* [2012] UKFTT 658 (TC), Mrs Matthews died in January 2007. She initially held funds in an account in her sole name. In 1999, she opened a new account with her son at Abbey plc. Mrs Matthews withdrew all the monies in the account in her sole name, and deposited them in the new joint account. The account instructions included that either Mrs Matthews or her son could withdraw monies from the account without the other's signature being required, although no withdrawals were actually made prior to Mrs Matthews' death. The only deposits after the deceased's initial transfer into it consisted of interest credited, and small account bonuses. Each account holder declared half of the interest earned in their income tax returns each year. In addition, the IHT account on Mrs Matthews' death indicated that her share of funds in the account passed by survivorship to her son. The tribunal held that the whole of the funds in the account were liable to IHT as part of the deceased's estate under *s 5(2)*, or alternatively under the gift with reservation anti-avoidance provisions (*FA 1986, s 102*).

Land

4.22 As indicated at **4.2** above, HMRC considers land and property valuation to be an area of high risk in terms of the potential loss of IHT, particularly where the valuation is not undertaken by a qualified, independent valuer. However, even if a professional valuation is obtained, HMRC may expect it to be revisited in certain circumstances. HMRC's Trusts & Estates Newsletter (August 2010) states the following:

> 'If, having obtained a valuation and before you apply for a grant, you find out about other information that casts doubts on the initial valuation, you must reconsider it. For example, if you have a valuation that shows the property was worth £250,000, but when you try to sell the property you market it at £270,000 and receive some offers at that figure or more, it suggests that the open market value for the property may be more like £270,000.
>
> In these circumstances, HMRC recommends that you ask the valuer to reconsider and, if appropriate, amend the date of death value, taking into account such things as the length of time since the death and movements in the property market.'

For Scottish heritable property survivorship destinations may be revoked during lifetime by both parties or unilaterally in a will (subject to the financial contribution element to the initial purchase) and are terminated on divorce (*Succession (Scotland) Act 2016, ss 1* and *2*).

The case of *Phizackerley v Revenue & Customs [2007] UKSPC SPC00591* highlighted that HMRC will carefully consider the position of ownership, especially for heritable property. The case highlighted that where one party contributed wholly or mainly to the financing of the property any transfer into a trust and subsequent loan arrangement could be caught under *s 103 Finance Act 1986* and treated as not a deductible debt on the second deceasing spouse's estate if the property originally derived from their estate.

For Scottish common property, and in England and Wales if joint tenants (see above), purchase land with the help of a mortgage, unless there is an agreement to the contrary, their beneficial interests equate to their respective shares of the mortgage and the lender will normally expect the respective shares in the mortgage to mirror that of the property title.

On the transfer of an interest by a tenant in common (eg on death), that person's share could be eligible for a discount of between 10–15%, although the level of discount will be subject to the Valuation Office Agency (see **Overview A2.3** and the Valuation Office Agency's guidance 'Inheritance tax: undivided shares' at: www.voa.gov.uk/corporate/Publications/Manuals/InheritanceTaxManual/sections/r-section_18/b-iht-man-s18.html#TopOfPage)). HMRC's starting point for negotiating discounts is often to apply a flat £4,000, to reflect the potential costs of a Division and Sale Action. However, in the case of property held by spouses or civil partners (whether as joint tenants or tenants in common, albeit that joint property passing by survivorship may be subject to the spouse exemption in any event), HMRC may seek to challenge any discount claimed, based on the related property provisions (see **4.6** above).

4.23 On the death of a joint owner of property (eg the family home) where the title contains a survivorship destination the survivor takes title absolutely and by operation of law.

If the beneficial interests in land vary from the legal title, HMRC will require evidence of the parties' beneficial ownership (IHTM15044). See **4.5** above.

4.24 In *Wight v IRC* 264 *Estates Gazette* 935/82, the value of an interest in a dwelling house owned as tenants in common in equal shares was held by the Lands Tribunal to be its vacant possession value less a discount of 15% to reflect the restricted demand for this type of interest.

In *Price v Revenue and Customs Commissioners* (see **4.8** above), HMRC acknowledged that such a discount is appropriate when the interest being valued is an undivided share in property (but not if the valuation involves aggregating two undivided shares in property, when considering a valuation under the related property provisions in *s 161*).

In *Charkham v IRC* [2000] RVR vol 40, p 7, an individual held minority interests in a number of investment properties. The Revenue considered that the value should be discounted overall by between 10–15%. The taxpayer appealed. The Lands Tribunal held that there should be a single discount on each property, and that the appropriate discount should be 15% on some properties, and 20% or 22.5% on others. However, these larger discounts are exceptional: see **4.28** below.

4.25 As mentioned previously, in the context of farms, HMRC's IHT Toolkit highlights valuations as a potential risk area, and emphasises 'the need for separate valuations and details for the farmhouse, any other dwellings, any farm/outbuildings and their usage, the land and any amenity land and their rights such as fishing, shooting, mineral'. It also encourages the submission to HMRC of plans and photos of the farmhouse, buildings and land, in addition to copies of any professional valuation reports obtained.

Development value

4.26

> **Focus**
>
> HMRC made their view of development value very clear in their IHT Newsletter of 28 April 2006. The potential for development value must be accounted for where an estate contains land or buildings. The personal representatives should take all appropriate steps to disclose the value that the land may expect to achieve if sold on the open market and that value must reflect any feature that may make the land attractive to a builder or developer, for example a large garden or access to other land.

The personal representatives should consider all the evidence available when completing the IHT account. It is not enough just to obtain a professional valuation. If further information then comes to light, for example on advice about marketing the property, and if that later advice casts some doubt on the original valuation, the extra information should be disclosed.

In the IHT Toolkit, HMRC state that a 'risk' area in respect of land and buildings is 'the potential for the development of the land (in particular large gardens) and buildings (in particular dividing buildings into flats), the existence of tenancies, or occupation by people other than the deceased'.

4.27 It may happen that after the personal representatives have lodged form IHT400 based on the situation as they saw it as at the date of death, new information will come to light during the administration of the estate and before winding up the estate. If that affects the value as at the date of death, HMRC would expect to be notified as quickly as possible. Where it is clear that reasonable and adequate steps have not been taken to ascertain the open market value based on all the information that was available, the personal representatives may be liable to penalties.

That does not mean that the full development value is taxable. In *Prosser v IRC* DET/1/2000 [2001] RVR 170, it was realised that a house enjoyed a garden big enough to serve as an extra building plot. The district valuer suggested a figure as at the date of death of 80% of the value that the plot would have with planning consent, allowing for the fact that no application for planning permission had yet been made. That was considered to be wrong. The Lands Tribunal held that, at the date of death, there was a 50% chance of obtaining planning permission and that a speculator, in the absence of permission, would not offer 80% of the development value but would offer only 25%.

Discounts

4.28 As mentioned above, the Valuation Office Agency (VOA) generally applies discounts when valuing an undivided half-share interest. The Valuation Office Agency Inheritance Tax Manual does not specifically cover the application in Scotland, which can be significantly different given the opportunity for an action for division and sale (see **Overview A2.3**). Estate Practitioners and the Law Society of Scotland are keen to receive clearer valuation guidance from HMRC for Scottish properties.

The table below details the discounts relating to property in England and Wales (Valuation Office Agency Inheritance Tax Manual, Practice Note 2, para 9.7, which can be viewed online at: www.voa.gov.uk/corporate/Publications/Manuals/InheritanceTaxManual/pnotes/h-iht-man-pn2.html#P303_25440l):

Table 4.1—Discounts re undivided half-share interest in land

(a)	where the other co-owner(s) is (are) not in occupation and the purpose behind the trust no longer exists	10%
(b)	where the other co-owner(s) is (are) not in occupation but they have a right to occupy as their main residence and the purpose behind the trust still exists	15%
(c)	where the other co-owner(s) is (are) in occupation as their main residence	15%

The VOA Inheritance Tax Manual also indicates that a discount may be appropriate for a minority share, and even for a majority share. Practice Note 2, para 10.9 states:

> 'When valuing a minority share a larger discount than 10% may be appropriate in cases where
>
> **i** it is felt unlikely that a potential purchaser would seek an order for sale (under Section 14 TLATA 1996 or Section 30 LPA 1925) or, there is evidence that the majority of the share owners under a trust of land would oppose an application for an order for sale by a minority shareholder, and
>
> **ii** it is felt that there is potential for dispute concerning how the property is managed,
>
> However, the discount should not normally exceed 20%.'

The guidance goes onto state (at para 10.10):

> 'Clearly even a majority share has disadvantages compared with ownership of the entirety. There will be circumstances however, where a discount of less than 10% share should be considered – e.g. where it is known the co-owner(s) is/are keen to place the entirety interest on the market, or in cases involving large majority shares, such as a share of over 90% in a high value 'property'

The extent of any discount will therefore depend on the circumstances of each case.

As detailed above the law of special or survivorship destination in Scotland provides that if an asset is purchased jointly under which there is a contractual agreement that on death the property passes to the survivor and they have paid equally for the asset, the survivor will be entitled to the whole on the death of the first to die. If the price was not provided equally, the donor can revoke the survivorship destination by will. If one party provided the whole property, he retains ownership unless there is indication of intention to make an immediate gift to the joint owner (see IHTM15050).

Settled property

4.29 The value of settled property in which an individual has an interest in possession generally forms part of the estate on death, if he became beneficially entitled to it before 22 March 2006, or alternatively if he became beneficially entitled to an 'immediate post-death interest', a 'disabled person's interest' or a 'transitional serial interest' on or after that date (*s 49(1), (1A)*) (see **Chapter 7**).

If an interest in possession falls within one of the above categories, the individual is effectively treated as the absolute owner of that property, or the relevant proportion of it. The value of the life interest for IHT purposes is the value of the settlement property in which the individual's life interest subsisted.

An exception to this rule applies if the interest in possession is acquired for money or money's worth, ie the extent (if any) to which the giving of consideration is a transfer of value falls to be determined without regard to that valuation rule (*s 49(2)*).

4.30 The lifetime cessation of the above interests in possession is usually a PET, which becomes chargeable on the individual's death within seven years. If an immediate IHT charge arose at lifetime rates (eg if the settled property went into a discretionary trust) further IHT may become due at the rate on death, upon the individual's death within seven years.

Specific IHT legislation applies in respect of proper liferents of property (*ss 43(4), 46, 47*) (see IHTM16072).

If the individual's estate was increased by an earlier chargeable transfer of the settled property within the previous five years, 'quick succession relief' is available (**Chapter 10**). The IHT charged on death falls to be reduced by a percentage of the tax charged on the earlier transfer (*s 141*).

Gifts with reservation

4.31 Property may fall to be treated as forming part of a donor's estate for IHT purposes if the 'gifts with reservation' (GWR) rules apply (see **Chapter 5**).

For example, a parent may transfer his home into joint ownership with his adult daughter, but continue living there. Unless the parent pays a market rent for his continued occupation, or unless his daughter takes up co-occupation, there is a GWR.

A gift caught by the GWR rules at the individual's death is treated as part of the donor's estate, and is liable to IHT accordingly. In addition, where the gift was made within seven years prior to the transferor's death, or the reservation ended within that period, there is a further chargeable transfer in respect of the same gift. However, there are regulations to eliminate this double tax charge (*FA 1986, ss 102, 104*; *IHT (Double Charges Relief) Regulations, SI 1987/1130*), which effectively determine the value of the gift to be taken into account on the donor's death.

The lifetime termination of an interest in possession falling within the categories mentioned in **4.29** above is treated as a gift for GWR purposes. If the individual retains use or enjoyment of the settled property after their interest has ended, it remains part of their estate under the GWR rules as if they had owned the property outright and gifted it when the interest ended (*FA 1986, s 102ZA*).

Other assets

Debts

4.32 It is generally assumed that the right to receive a sum due under any obligation will be paid in full (ie the face value of the debt is included in the creditor's estate), unless that recovery is impossible or not reasonably practicable (eg if the debtor is insolvent).

It may be possible to include a reduced value on the death estate if either title to the debt or the amount due is in doubt. However, if a reduced figure is used, HMRC will probably require an explanation, including how that amount has been calculated and any evidence in support of the reduced amount shown.

No allowance is made if the recovery is in doubt because of any act or omission by the creditor (eg failing to enforce collection) (*s 166*).

The amount to be included in the death estate also includes interest due up to the date of death. If some or all of the debt has been written off, that amount is treated as a gift.

If the lender waives a loan (voluntarily and not for consideration), HMRC will generally expect the debt release to be effected by a deed before allowing a reduction in the lender's estate, clearly indicating that it is intended as a deed by the parties involved. The deed must be validly executed (usually by signature) by those persons. However, in Scotland the release of a debt does not need to be effected by deed (IHTM19110).

Household goods and personal effects

4.33 Household and personal goods are subject to the 'market value' rule (*s 160*), ie 'the price which might reasonably be expected to fetch if sold in the open market …'

In its *IHT Newsletter* (December 2004), Inland Revenue Capital Taxes (as it then was) stated:

> '… we will be paying particularly close attention to the values included for household and personal goods. In appropriate cases we will open an enquiry and ask you for further information to satisfy ourselves that all of the goods have been included and that they have been valued on the statutory basis.'

HMRC may seek to impose a penalty if the value of household or personal goods as returned for IHT purposes is estimated inaccurately, or if incorrect information is not corrected within a reasonable time. If preparing an IHT account (ie form IHT400 or IHT100) which includes the value of household and personal goods, it would therefore clearly be advisable to provide the fullest information possible in the circumstances. This should also reduce the possibility of enquiry by HMRC. In particular, references in the account to the valuation being made 'for Confirmation purposes' or for 'IHT purposes' should be avoided.

Whilst it is generally good practice to obtain professional valuations of assets, it is not considered necessary to do so in all cases, such as in respect of ordinary household goods where individual items have a value of no more than £500 (see **4.2** above).

Note that HMRC do not accept that the value of jointly owned household goods should be discounted as a matter of course, where the related property provisions (see **4.6** above) do not apply. HMRC's guidance states (at IHTM21043):

> 'Although we allow a discount as a matter of course for jointly owned land, we do not do this automatically for jointly owned chattels. This is because any discount is to reflect problems with disposing of less than a full share and, for chattels, the circumstances in which a sale could be obtained may vary.'

Values 'ascertained'

4.34 As explained in *Capital Gains Tax 2016/17* (Bloomsbury Professional), and as indicated at **4.19** above, if IHT was chargeable on the value of a person's estate immediately before death and the value of an asset forming part of that estate has been 'ascertained' for IHT purposes, that value is taken to be the market value for CGT purposes at the date of death (*TCGA 1992, s 274*).

However, where a value has been ascertained solely for the purpose of establishing the amount of transferable IHT nil rate band between spouses or civil partners, that value will not similarly apply for CGT purposes (see **Chapter 14**).

Valuation of liabilities; guarantees

4.35 It was noted at **3.9** that a liability may be taken into account to reduce the chargeable estate only to the extent that it was incurred for money's worth and is enforceable.

One area of regular difficulty is the valuation of a guarantee given by the deceased that has not been called upon at the date of death. HMRC strongly resist allowance of the full value guaranteed. For HMRC's approach on the calculation of allowable deductions for guarantee debts, see IHTM28355 and **3.12**.

The negotiation of that valuation generally involves considering:

- what security was given by the deceased to support the guarantee;
- the likelihood that the guarantee will be called upon; and
- the amount by which the original debtor will default, such that the guarantor must make it good.

This is unsatisfactory from the point of view of the guarantor, because an obligation has been assumed that no doubt restricts his freedom to deal with certain assets because they support the guarantee. It will often be better, from a tax point of view, simply to provide the money rather than a guarantee; but in family situations the donor/lender may be reluctant to do so.

Chapter 5

Gifts with reservation of benefit

SIGNPOSTS

- **Scope** – The 'gifts with reservation' (GWR) provisions are anti-avoidance rules, which apply to property given away from 18 March 1986. Gifts 'caught' by the GWR provisions are generally treated as remaining part of the donor's estate for IHT purposes (see **5.1–5.9**).
- **Interests in land** – The GWR provisions were extended in relation to gifts of interests in land from 9 March 1999 (see **5.10–5.15**).
- **Specific issues** – A GWR can be 'traced' in some cases by special rules ('substitutions and accretions'). The GWR rules can also apply to gifts into settlement, and specific rules apply in respect of insurance policies, and business and agricultural property (see **5.16–5.23**).
- **Exceptions and exclusions** – The general rule that gifts 'caught' by the GWR provisions are treated as remaining part of the donor's estate (**5.7**) is subject to various exceptions and exclusions (see **5.24–5.36**).
- **Double IHT relief** – The GWR provisions could result in a double IHT charge on the same property. However, relief from a double IHT charge applies in various circumstances (see **5.37–5.38**).
- **Separating income and capital** – Certain trust arrangements have been argued to escape the GWR rules (see **5.39**).

INTRODUCTION

5.1 An individual who gives away property on or after 18 March 1986 makes a 'gift with reservation' (GWR) broadly if:

- the recipient does not immediately enjoy possession of the property; or
- the donor continues to enjoy, or benefits from, the property gifted.

As indicated at **2.22**, the GWR rules (*FA 1986, ss 102–102C, Sch 20*) are anti-avoidance provisions designed to prevent 'cake and eat it' situations in which an individual makes a lifetime gift of an asset (which they hope to survive by at least seven years), but continues to have the use or enjoyment of it.

Property subject to the GWR rules on the individual's death is treated as part of the donor's estate, and charged to IHT accordingly. If the reservation ends during the individual's lifetime and before the end of the 'relevant period' (see **5.5**), the gift is generally treated as a PET at that time, which is subject to IHT upon death within seven years (*FA 1986, s 102(4)*).

The annual exemption cannot be used against the value of the 'deemed' PET (*s 19(5)*). In addition, the 'normal expenditure out of income' exemption does not prevent a gift being chargeable under the GWR rules (*s 21(5)*). HMRC regard the small gifts exemption (*s 20*) as only applying to outright gifts, in practice the mere fact that the donor has reserved a benefit in the gifted property should not, of itself, prevent the gift from being regarded as an outright one (IHTM14319).

Despite property subject to the GWR provisions being treated as part of the donor's estate on death for IHT purposes, the normal capital gains tax uplift in the value of the property (*TCGA 1992, s 62(1)*) does not apply on the donor's death. Furthermore, the same property will generally form part of the donee's IHT estate as well. The implications of the GWR provisions applying are therefore potentially wide ranging.

5.2

Focus

- If the transferor pays a full market rent for continued enjoyment or benefit of land or a chattel, the gift is not treated as a GWR (*FA 1986, Sch 20, para 6(1)(a)*). Note that this GWR exception applies specifically to land and chattels. Care should be taken with other assets (see **5.29**).
- A gift which is an exempt transfer (eg a straightforward transfer to a UK-domiciled spouse or civil partner, or a transfer subject to the small gift or marriage gift exemption) cannot normally be a GWR (*FA 1986, s 102(5)*).

Special rules apply if an individual disposes of an interest in land by gift (on or after 9 March 1999), where the donor or his spouse enjoys a 'significant right or interest', or is party to a 'significant arrangement' in relation to the land. In such cases, the gifted interest in the land is treated as a GWR, unless certain specific exceptions apply (see **5.10**ff).

Relief is available in certain circumstances where a double IHT charge would otherwise arise in respect of the same property (ie where the original gift was immediately chargeable), or as the result of a PET becoming chargeable within seven years of death, where that property is also included in the death estate for IHT purposes because it was a GWR (*Inheritance Tax (Double Charges Relief) Regulations SI 1987/1130*) (see **5.37** below).

Pre-owned assets

5.3 The 'pre-owned assets' income tax charge (or the 'charge to income tax on benefits received by former owner of property', to be precise) was introduced (by *FA 2004, s 84*, and *Sch 15*, and underpinned by subsequent Treasury Regulations) in response to certain IHT planning arrangements. The charge operates for 2005/06 and subsequent years, but applies with retroactive effect to 18 March 1986.

It should be noted that there is no 'pre-owned assets tax' charge if the GWR provisions apply (*FA 2004, Sch 15, para 11(5)*), or if an election is made (under *FA 2004, Sch 15, para 21*) to effectively 'opt out' of the income tax charge and into the GWR rules for IHT purposes.

A double IHT charge could arise if an election is made and the taxpayer dies within seven years of the original gift (ie both on the original transfer that must now be aggregated with the death estate, and on the property subject to the reservation). Double charge regulations (*Charge to Income Tax by Reference to Enjoyment of Property Previously Owned Regulations (SI 2005/724)*) therefore prevent a double liability (ie on the original gift and the GWR); the higher amount of tax is charged (*SI 2005/724, reg 6*).

HMRC have published a section on pre-owned assets in their Inheritance Tax Manual (IHTM44000–IHTM44116), albeit that the pre-owned assets regime relates to income tax, as opposed to IHT.

For further commentary on pre-owned assets, see **Chapter 16**.

SCOPE AND EFFECT OF THE GWR RULES

Scope of GWR rules

5.4 The GWR provisions are anti-avoidance rules designed to stop taxpayers decreasing the value of their IHT estates by making gifts whilst leaving their overall circumstances effectively unchanged.

The rules apply to gifts of property on or after 18 March 1986 by an individual ('the donor') if:

- possession and enjoyment of the property is not assumed ('bona fide' as the legislation puts it) by the recipient of the gift ('the donee') at or before the beginning of the 'relevant period' (see below); or
- at any time in the relevant period the property is not enjoyed to the entire exclusion, or virtually to the entire exclusion, of the donor and of any benefit to him by contract or otherwise (*FA 1986, s 102(1)(a), (b)*).

The requirement that the donee must assume 'bona fide' possession and enjoyment of the gifted property to prevent a GWR means that the beneficial interest in the gifted property must be duly transferred, and the donee must have had actual enjoyment of that property (eg through physical occupation, or the receipt of income generated therefrom), instead of just the legal right of enjoyment.

Chattel gifts are usually perfected by the delivery of the item to the donee. Several cases have examined what constitutes a valid gift, and from these we may perhaps see what amounts to the assumption of possession and enjoyment of the thing given. In *re Cole (a bankrupt)* [1964] Ch 175 as between husband and wife, the gift of such chattels as remained in the house was not a gift by delivery. The gift, in *re Lillingston* [1952] 2 All ER 184, of a key to a box was the gift of the contents of that box. Where the claimant had lived in a house where some furniture was situated, and there was a verbal gift of the furniture, that amounted to a valid gift because the donee lived there: *re Stoneham* [1919] 1 Ch 149. The question of whether gifts of assets (ie paintings) were effected by delivery was considered more recently for IHT purposes in *Scott v Revenue & Customs* [2015] UKFTT 266 (TC).

A gift of a chattel to a person living in the same house may be challenged, on the ground that the donor can still use it. Only special circumstances, such as the fact that the item is stored in the attic and the donor is too frail to have access to it, may displace the GWR argument.

5.5 The GWR rules can apply if the donor derives a benefit 'at any time' during the relevant period. The 'relevant period' is the period ending on the date of the individual's death and beginning seven years before that date, or (if later) on the date of the gift (*FA 1986, s 102(1)*).

For example, if the donor makes a gift eight years before his death (which satisfies condition *(a)* or *(b)* in *FA 1986, s 102(1)*), the relevant period is seven years before his death. However, if the gift was made four years prior to death, the relevant period is four years.

HMRC guidance (at IHTM14333) indicates that 'virtually' intends to take gifts outside the reservation of benefit rules if the donor's benefit is 'insignificant' in relation to the gifted property. The requirement that the gifted property must be enjoyed to the exclusion of any benefit to the donor 'by contract or otherwise' is considered by HMRC to be a separate requirement to the 'virtually' test, and applies to a benefit obtained by the donor through 'associated operations' (*FA 1986, Sch 20, para 6(1)(c)*). See **2.23**.

In *Buzzoni and others v Revenue & Customs* [2013] EWCA Civ 1684, the Court allowed an appeal by the deceased's executor and others against the conclusions of the First-tier Tribunal and Upper Tribunal that the grant in 1997 of a future underlease to a trust (Legis) out of a headlease was a gift with reservation (within *FA 1986, s 102(1)(b)*). The decisions of the Tribunals had been on the basis that the underlease was not enjoyed to the entire exclusion, or virtually the entire exclusion, of a benefit to the donor (Mrs Kamhi) by reason of positive covenants in the underlease which mirrored the covenants in the headlease.

The Court had to consider whether the benefit Mrs Kamhi obtained from the positive covenants affected Legis' enjoyment of the flat, but concluded that it made no difference whatsoever to their enjoyment of the underlease. The obligations in the positive covenants did not detract from the enjoyment of the underlease because the obligations imposed by those covenants did not add to the obligations already imposed. Even if it could be said that Mrs Kamhi obtained a benefit she had not previously enjoyed, it was not obtained at the expense of the donees' enjoyment of the underlease.

In allowing the appeal, Moses LJ commented as follows:

> 'To persist in the possibly over-baked metaphor, the size of the cake remained unaffected, because the portion Mrs Kamhi is said to have eaten had already been consumed by the Head Landlord. She gifted a property, the enjoyment of which was already subject to obligations which mirrored the obligations contained in the positive covenants which are said to constitute her benefit. The imposition of duplicate obligations on that property merely mirrored but did not add to the obligations which the Underlease already bore under the Licence to Underlet.'

By contrast, in *Hood v Revenue & Customs* [2016] UKFTT 59 (TC), at her death Lady Hood (LH) was entitled to the head lease of a property in London dated 21 September 1979, which expired in December 2076. A sub-lease was granted in June 1997, by which the property was sub-let for a term commencing on 25 March 2012 and expiring on 22 December 2076. The sub-lease was subject to the same terms, covenants, provisos and conditions as were contained in the head lease. LH (as sub-lessor) and her three sons (as sub-lessees) respectively covenanted to perform and observe those provisions as if they had been repeated in full in the sub-lease. LH died in March 2008. HMRC considered that the creation of the sub-lease was a GWR, and LH's executor appealed against HMRC's determination.

The dispute concerned *FA 1986, s 102(1)(b)*, and particularly the second limb of that provision, which the First-tier Tribunal expressed as: 'at any time in the relevant period the property is not enjoyed to the entire exclusion, or virtually to the entire exclusion, of any benefit to the donor by contract or otherwise'. The tribunal noted that, in contrast to the position in *Buzzoni*, the sub-lessees in the present case gave no direct covenants to the head lessor. The only positive covenants from the sub-lessees were those given in the sub-lease in favour of the sub-lessor (LH). Unlike the position in *Buzzoni*, the sub-lessees were under no obligation to the head lessor in respect of the covenants.

Furthermore, the tribunal did not accept that the circumstances of the present case were economically equivalent to those in *Buzzoni*. Nor did the tribunal accept that, as a matter of property law, the benefit of the sub-lessees' covenants formed part of LH's retained proprietary interest under the head lease, and not the donated property (ie such that LH was not enjoying any part of the donated property, and the case was thus outside *s 102(1)(b)*). The appellant's appeal was dismissed.

The scope of the GWR rules was extended in 1999 and again in 2003, to counteract IHT avoidance arrangements designed to exploit loopholes in the GWR provisions in connection with interests in land and the spouse exemption. Those provisions are considered later in this chapter.

'Property' and 'gift'

5.6 To determine whether a gift is subject to the GWR rules, it is first necessary to ascertain the property given away.

For example, if Mr X gave his home to Miss Y (his daughter) in 1998, and Miss Y decided to lease the house back to Mr X at a nominal rent, the 'property' would be the house, and the reserved benefit (subject to the GWR rules) would be the lease.

It was previously possible to make arrangements for gifts of an interest in land whilst continuing to enjoy a benefit from it. However, changes to the GWR rules were introduced (with effect from 9 March 1999) with the intention of blocking such arrangements (see **5.12**).

The GWR rules apply to 'gifts', which can include sales at undervalue. HMRC's view is that a sale for less than full value arising from a 'bad bargain' is not necessarily a gift with reservation. However, where the GWR provisions do apply to a sale at undervalue, they only apply in respect of the undervalue proportion (IHTM14316).

It is possible to reach the alternative conclusion that any element of undervalue is sufficient for the entire property to be 'caught' under the GWR rules. However, taxpayers and their advisers will no doubt wish to apply HMRC's more generous view, as illustrated below.

Example 5.1—GWR: sales at undervalue

Henry sold his home to his daughter Daphne on 1 September 2002 for £10,000, when the value of the property was £100,000. Henry continued living at the house rent free until his death on 15 June 2016, when the property had increased in value to £600,000.

Henry's sale of the property to Daphne at undervalue is a GWR. The value of the property disposed of by way of 'gift' was 90% of the value of the whole property. Therefore, 90% of its death value is treated for GWR purposes as property to which Henry was beneficially entitled, ie £600,000 × 90% = £540,000.

Effect of GWR rules

5.7 Without the GWR rules, if an individual could make a PET of property and survive at least seven years, the property would fall outside his estate and he could continue to enjoy or benefit from the gifted asset with impunity for IHT purposes.

The GWR rules therefore provide that if property subject to a reservation would not otherwise form part of the donor's estate immediately before his death, it will be treated as such (*FA 1986, s 102(3)*). The gift is deemed for IHT purposes to be property to which the individual was beneficially entitled immediately before his death, and is therefore ineffective to reduce the value of his IHT estate. However, this GWR treatment does not apply to excluded property (IHTM04072). See **5.33**.

Following the introduction of an additional nil rate band (or residence nil rate band) where a home is passed on death to lineal descendants of the deceased from 6 April 2017 (see **16.55–16.76**), if the property has been given to a person but is treated as forming part of the deceased's estate by reason of the GWR rules (under *FA 1986, s 102(3)*), the recipient is treated as having 'inherited' the property for the purposes of the residence nil rate band (*s 8J(6)*).

Example 5.2—'Caught' by GWR rules (1)

On 5 September 2008, Derek gave his house and its contents to his grandson Gerald, but continued to live in it with his wife Fiona, paying no rent. The house and contents were valued at £400,000 (after annual exemptions).

On 3 July 2016, Derek died leaving his estate of £400,000 by way of a specific legacy of £200,000 to Fiona, with residue to his granddaughter Hannah. The value of the house at that time was £600,000.

The IHT position is as follows:

5 September 2008 – Gift

Derek's original gift of the house to Gerald is a PET. However, the property is subject to the GWR rules.

3 July 2016 – Death

Derek's gift of the house to Gerald on 5 September 2008 is a PET which has become exempt, because it was made more than seven years before Derek's death.

However, the GWR rules apply to treat the house as forming part of Derek's death estate. IHT is charged on the value of the house on death. The chargeable estate is therefore £800,000 (ie the house worth £600,000, plus his other chargeable estate of £200,000 (the other £200,000 passing to his wife is exempt)).

	£
Chargeable transfer	800,000
IHT thereon:	
£325,000 × nil	NIL
£475,000 × 40%	190,000
	190,000

As indicated above, if Derek had died after 5 April 2017, the residence nil rate band would need to be taken into account in calculating the IHT liability on the value of the house, upon a successful claim being made.

5.8 In the above example, the original gift of the property was a PET made more than seven years before Derek's death. Had the gift been a chargeable

PET made within seven years before his death, a double IHT charge would arise (ie on the original gift, and on the property forming part of Derek's estate under the GWR rules).

Special rules therefore apply to prevent double taxation in such circumstances (*FA 1986, s 104*; *Inheritance Tax (Double Charges Relief) Regulations, SI 1987/1130*). The rules as they apply to a GWR are discussed at **5.37** below.

Example 5.3—'Caught' by GWR rules (2)

The facts are as in **Example 5.2**, except that the date of the GWR is 5 September 2013.

5 September 2013 – Gift

Derek's original gift of the house to Gerald (see previous example) is a PET. The property is subject to the GWR rules.

3 July 2016 – Death

Derek's gift of the house to Gerald on 5 September 2013 is a PET which becomes chargeable, because it was made within seven years of Derek's death. The house also forms part of Derek's death estate, so it is necessary to consider the double charges relief regulations.

Calculation (a) – Ignore PET and charge house in death estate

5 September 2013 – gift ignored: IHT = nil.

3 July 2016 – tax on chargeable death estate of £800,000 = £190,000 (see **Example 5.2**)

Calculation (b) – Charge PET and ignore house in death estate

5 September 2013 – IHT on £400,000:

	£
IHT thereon:	
£325,000 × nil	NIL
£75,000 × 40%	30,000
	30,000

3 July 2016 – tax on chargeable death estate of £200,000 (no nil rate band available):

£200,000 × 40% = £80,000

Total IHT (£30,000 + £80,000) = £110,000

Conclusion

A higher amount of IHT is payable on calculation (a) by charging the house as part of Derek's death estate. This amount (£190,000) is therefore charged, and the second IHT charge (£110,000) is reduced to nil (*SI 1987/1130, reg 5(3)*).

GWR and spouse exemption

5.9 As mentioned at **5.1** above, certain exempt transfers (eg to a spouse or civil partner) cannot generally be a GWR. However, legislation was introduced in *Finance Act 2003* (inserting *FA 1986, ss 102(5A)–(5C)* into the GWR rules) to block '*Eversden* schemes' resulting from the Court of Appeal's decision in *IRC v Eversden (exors of Greenstock, decd)* [2003] EWCA Civ 668.

In that case, a married woman (W) settled a 5% interest in the family home she owned for herself absolutely. The other 95% was settled on an interest in possession trust to benefit her husband (H) for life, following which the trust fund would be held on discretionary trusts for a class of beneficiaries including W. They continued to occupy the property until H's death four years later. The property was sold a year later, and a replacement property was bought together with an investment bond. The interests held by W and the settlement remained unchanged. W died five years later. The Court of Appeal held that the original gift of the property was an exempt transfer between spouses under *IHTA 1984, s 18*.

The effect of the GWR rules (following *FA 2003*) is that the donor is treated as making a gift when the life interest of their spouse or civil partner terminates. This means that if the donor subsequently occupies or enjoys a benefit from the settled property, the gift is one to which the reservation of benefit rules apply. For example, the rules affect a husband making a gift to a trust under which his wife takes an initial interest in possession, which is subsequently terminated in favour of a discretionary trust in which the husband is a potential beneficiary.

However, following changes to the IHT treatment of interest in possession trusts introduced in *Finance Act 2006*, these anti-avoidance rules are generally more likely to be relevant to interests in possession before 22 March 2006 (see **Chapter 7**).

Gifts of interests in land

5.10 As indicated at **5.6**, previously (ie prior to 9 March 1999) it was possible to make arrangements for gifts of an interest in land whilst continuing to enjoy a benefit from it.

Ingram schemes

5.11 A 'loophole' in the GWR rules at that time was highlighted in *Ingram (Executors of Lady Ingram's Estate) v IRC* [1997] STC 1234.

In that case, Lady Ingram gifted to her children a property, subject to a lease which she retained. The lease was created by the conveyance of the property to a nominee, followed by the grant of a lease to Lady Ingram for 20 years. The purpose was to enable Lady Ingram to continue occupying the property by reason of the lease, without making a gift of the freehold subject to the GWR provisions.

The House of Lords held that Lady Ingram had made an effective gift of the freehold reversion, in which no benefit had been reserved. She had simply gifted one property interest in which she reserved no benefit, and retained (or 'carved out') another interest which entitled her to remain in residence. Lord Hoffmann described the position in the following terms;

> '…although [section 102] does not allow a donor to have his cake and eat it, there is nothing to stop him from carefully dividing up the cake, eating part and having the rest. If the benefits which the donor continues to enjoy are by virtue of property which was never comprised in the gift, he has not reserved any benefit out of the property of which he disposed…'

Following the decision by the House of Lords in Lady Ingram's favour, changes to the GWR rules were quickly introduced by *FA 1999* with the intention of countering the effects of that decision (*FA 1986, ss 102A–102C*). The provisions apply to gifts of interests in land from 9 March 1999.

It should be noted that pre-9 March 1999 *Ingram* schemes considered effective for IHT purposes are generally subject to a pre-owned assets income tax charge (see **5.3**).

In addition, the general GWR provisions (*FA 1986, s 102(3), (4)*) discussed earlier are still capable of applying to 'straightforward' gifts of land (*s 102C(7)*).

The 'interests in land' rules

5.12 The GWR rules for gifts of interests in land (from 9 March 1999) provide that if the donor or spouse (or civil partner) enjoys a 'significant right or interest', or is 'party to a significant arrangement' in relation to the land during the 'relevant period' (as defined in **5.5**), the gifted land interest is a GWR.

A right, interest or arrangement is 'significant' only if it entitles or enables the donor to occupy all or part of the land, or to enjoy some right in relation to all or part of it, otherwise than for full consideration in money or money's worth (*FA 1986, s 102A(2), (3)*).

Thus, no GWR arises if, for example, a donor gifts the freehold interest in a house to another individual (a PET) but retains, or is immediately granted, a lease at a full rent.

There are exceptions from the GWR rule if the right, interest or arrangement (as appropriate) is not 'significant' if, ie:

- it does not and cannot prevent the enjoyment of the land to the entire exclusion, or virtually to the entire exclusion, of the donor (*FA 1986, s 102A(4)(a)*); or
- it does not entitle or enable the donor to occupy all or part of the land immediately after the disposal, but would do so but for the interest disposed of (*FA 1986, s 102A(4)(b)*);
- the right or interest was granted or acquired before the seven-year period ending with the date of gift (*FA 1986, s 102A(5)*).

An example of the second exception above is where the donor gifts a 20-year rent-free leasehold interest and retains the freehold reversion, as those rights do not entitle or enable the donor to occupy the land immediately after the disposal, but would do so but for the interest disposed of.

The third exception above means that a *Lady Ingram* type scheme is not caught by *FA 1986, s 102A* as a 'significant right or interest' if there is a gap of at least seven years between the creation of the lease and the gift of the freehold reversion. However, note that the exception does not preclude a 'significant arrangement' in relation to the land from being a GWR.

Reversionary lease schemes (England and Wales only)

5.13 IHT avoidance arrangements in England and Wales (Scots Law does not accommodate reversionary leases) involving reversionary leases in land originally came into being before 9 March 1999. The 'reversionary lease scheme' typically involves a donor granting a long lease for (say) 999 years to the proposed donee. The lease would not commence until a future date (ie normally beyond the donor's life expectancy, but less than 21 years to avoid problems under the *Law of Property Act 1925, s 149(3)*).

To fall within the GWR exception in *FA 1986, s 102A(5)* mentioned above, a gap of at least seven years would need to be left between the date of purchase of the land and the date of the grant of the lease.

HMRC state (in the Inheritance Tax Manual at IHTM14360) that such schemes '… had previously escaped the GWR provisions' before 9 March 1999, although reversionary lease schemes were one of the targets of the 'pre-owned assets' income tax provisions covered in **Chapter 16**.

HMRC's guidance on pre-owned assets in the Inheritance Tax Manual states (at IHTM44102):

> 'Where a reversionary lease scheme is established before 9 March 1999 … the arrangement succeeds in avoiding the reservation of benefit provisions so long as the lease does not contain any terms that are currently beneficial to the donor, such as covenants by the lessee to, say, maintain the property. Consequently, the donor will be subject to the POA charge under FA04/Sch15/Para3(2).'

With regard to reversionary lease schemes established on or after 9 March 1999, HMRC's guidance distinguishes between situations where the donor grants a reversionary lease more than seven years after acquiring the freehold interest, and where the reversionary lease is granted within that seven-year period:

> 'Where a reversionary lease scheme is established on or after 9 March 1999 it was originally considered that FA86/S102A … would apply because the donor's occupation would be a "significant right in relation to the land". If that were correct, the reservation of benefit rules would apply and there would be no POA charge.
>
> However, where the freehold interest was acquired more than 7 years before the gift … the continued occupation by the donor is not a significant right in view of FA86/S102A(5), so the reservation of benefit rules cannot apply and a POA charge arises instead.
>
> It follows that if the donor grants a reversionary lease within 7 years of acquiring the freehold interest, FA86/S102A may apply to the gift depending on how the remaining provisions of that section apply in relation to the circumstances of the case – for example, if the donor pays full consideration for the right to occupy or enjoy the land, that would not be a significant right in view of FA86/S102A(3), so the reservation of benefit rules cannot apply and a POA charge arises instead.'

Where the pre-owned assets provisions apply, it may nevertheless be possible to elect out of an income tax charge, and into the GWR provisions instead.

The GWR provisions will apply in any event if the lease contains terms which are currently beneficial to the donor. However, the decision in *Buzzoni and others v Revenue & Customs* [2013] EWCA Civ 1684 should be noted. There was no reservation of benefit in that case, on the basis that the covenants given by the donee that benefited the donor did not adversely affect the donees' enjoyment of the gifted property. By contrast, in *Hood v Revenue & Customs* [2016] UKFTT 59 (TC), the grant by an individual to her sons of a sub-lease of premises was held to be a GWR on the particular facts of that case (see **5.5**).

'Share of interest in land'

5.14 The GWR rules were extended in *FA 1999* to cover gifts of an undivided share of an interest in land (from 9 March 1999), such as where a sole owner gifts a half interest to another individual (*FA 1986, s 102B*). The share disposed of is a GWR (*FA 1986, s 102(3)* and *(4)*).

There are exceptions from this GWR rule if:

- the donor does not occupy the land (*FA 1986, s 102B(3)(a)*); or
- the donor occupies the land to the exclusion of the donee for full consideration in money or money's worth (eg a full market rent) (*FA 1986, s 102B(3)(b)*); or
- both donor and donee occupy the land, and the donor receives no (or negligible) benefit from the donee in connection with the gift (*FA 1986, s 102B(4)*).

Focus

- The first exception above means that, provided the donor does not occupy the land, there is no reservation of benefit even if the donor otherwise benefits from the gifted interest (eg the gift is of a share in an investment property).
- The third exception above means that if, for example, an individual gifts an interest in the property to his daughter who lives with him and shares the property outgoings, there is no GWR (Note: the daughter should not contribute in any way to the father's share of the household upkeep and expenses. There is nothing to prevent the father continuing to pay all the running expenses of the property).
- There is also an exemption from the 'pre-owned assets' income tax charge in circumstances such as those described in the previous bullet point (*FA 2004, Sch 15, para 11(5)(c)*), see **Chapter 16**.
- If *FA 1986, s 102B* applies, the other GWR rules (*FA 1986, ss 102* and *102A*) do not (*FA 1986, s 102C(6)*).

Other points

5.15 Supplemental rules (*FA 1986, s 102C*) linking the 'interests in land' rules with the general GWR rules provide that exempt gifts (listed at **5.25**) fall outside both sets of rules (*FA 1986, s 102C(2)*).

In addition, the donor's occupation of land is expressly disregarded if certain conditions (see **5.31**) are all satisfied (*FA 1986, s 102C(3)*, and *Sch 20, para 6(1)(b)*).

As indicated above, the exception for exempt transfers to spouses or civil partners in *FA 1986, s 102(5)* is applied to the GWR land rules (*FA 1986, s 102C(2)*). However, the spouse exemption is limited in its application for GWR purposes (*FA 1986, s 102(5A)–(5C)*) (see **5.9**).

It should be noted that the provisions in *FA 1986, ss 102A–102C* apply to interests in land (including a share in land); they do not apply to chattels. However, the general GWR provisions (*s 102, Sch 20*) are still relevant to chattels.

'Tracing' GWRs

5.16 There are complicated GWR rules dealing with situations whereby the donee does not retain the gifted property until the donor's death or until the benefit ends, eg the property is sold, exchanged or otherwise disposed of (*FA 1986, Sch 20, paras 2–4*).

For GWR purposes, it is necessary to determine whether the original subject matter of the gift can be traced and substituted. These rules (entitled 'substitutions and accretions') prevent what might otherwise be simple IHT avoidance.

For example, a mother may give Property A to her daughter, who may exchange it for Property B, and allow her mother to live there rent free. The tracing rules mean that the mother has reserved a benefit by occupying Property B.

5.17 The tracing rules do not apply to absolute gifts of cash (*FA 1986, Sch 20, para 2(2)(b)*).

However, HMRC consider that if individual A gives £250,000 cash to B which B uses to purchase A's residence (worth £250,000), with A remaining in occupation rent free until his death, this may constitute a GWR of the residence, under the 'associated operations' rules in *IHTA 1984, s 268* (see **2.23**) (see HMRC's example 'Anna' at IHTM14372).

The scope of the associated operations rules was effectively diminished (albeit in a different context) by the Court of Appeal in *Rysaffe Trustee Co (CI) Ltd v IRC* [2003] STC 536. Nevertheless, this remains a point that HMRC appear to take.

The GWR provisions only apply to the property originally given. Thus if, for example, individual C gives land to individual D, and individual D builds a house on that land, if the GWR rules are in point they apply only to the extent of the gifted land, though interesting valuation issues may arise where the development has increased the value of the subject matter of the gift.

If the donee gifts the relevant property to someone else or voluntarily disposes of it for less than full consideration (other than back to the donor), the donee is treated as continuing to have possession and enjoyment of the property (*FA 1986, Sch 20, para 2(4), (5)*).

If the gifted property was shares or debentures, any bonus and rights issues are generally treated as comprised in the gift (*FA 1986, Sch 20, para 2(6), (7)*), subject to a deduction for consideration paid by the donee for the shares in valuing the property comprised in the gift (*FA 1986, Sch 20, para 3*).

If the donee predeceases the donor, or dies before the benefit ends, then unless the property is settled by will or intestacy, the GWR rules apply as if he had not died, and the actions of his personal representatives are treated as his own. Any property taken under the donee's will or intestacy is treated as a gift made by him on death (*FA 1986, Sch 20, para 4*).

Settled gifts and GWR

5.18 The GWR rules also potentially apply to settled property. However, a pre-18 March 1986 settlement is not subject to the rules (even if it would have been caught if made after 17 March 1986), unless further gifts into settlement are made after that date, in which case the GWR provisions will only apply to the property settled by those further gifts (IHTM14311).

If a donor makes a gift by way of settlement, the type of property is immaterial. The property comprised in the settlement needs to be considered instead. The normal 'tracing' rules described above do not apply to a gift of settled property, although the GWR rules potentially apply instead to the settled property at the date of the donor's death (or when the GWR ceased), unless it is unrelated to the original gifted property (*FA 1986, Sch 20, para 5(1)*) (see **5.20**).

The donor should be excluded from being a beneficiary, in terms of avoiding a GWR (for example, see *Lyon's Personal Representatives v HMRC* ([2007] SSCD 675). Furthermore, if there is a settlement power to add beneficiaries, any argument by HMRC that the GWR rules apply can be avoided if the trustees are expressly prevented from adding the donor as a beneficiary.

In addition, it may be good practice to ensure that the trust deed is drafted so as to ensure that there is no possibility of the settled property reverting to the settlor by default, in terms of preventing any contention that the settlor can benefit under a resulting trust. Whilst HMRC (or the Inland Revenue, as was) previously indicated (in a letter dated 18 May 1987) that no reservation of benefit is considered to arise in such circumstances, there may be other issues to consider, such as whether any income tax implications arise.

Focus

- If the donor creates a discretionary settlement in which the donor's spouse or civil partner (but not the donor) is a potential beneficiary, this is not, of itself, a GWR.
- However, a trust distribution to the spouse or civil partner may be a GWR, if the donor can share in the benefit of that distribution.
- The GWR rules can apply not only if the donor is a beneficiary of the settlement, but also if a gift is made into trust for others, to the extent that the donor's beneficial interest is not completely lost, or if the property can revert back to the donor.

Interests in possession and GWR

5.19 GWR rules dealing with the lifetime termination of interests in possession were introduced by *FA 2006* (*FA 1986, s 102ZA*). The rules apply to:

- pre-22 March 2006 interests in possession; or
- a post-21 March 2006 interest in possession which is an immediate post-death interest, disabled person's interest or a transitional serial interest (for further discussion, see **Chapter 7**).

The GWR rules apply to gifts, whereas the lifetime termination of an interest in possession is a transfer of value. The effect of these rules is that the lifetime termination of the interest is treated as a gift of the settled property (*FA 1986, s 102ZA(2)*). See **13.17**. If the individual retains use of the settled property after their interest in possession has ended, the property remains part of their estate under the GWR rules as if they owned it outright.

The lifetime creation of an interest in possession trust on or after 22 March 2006 is not normally a potentially exempt transfer (*s 3A(1A)*), with the trust entering the 'relevant property' regime as for discretionary trusts. If the trust is settlor-interested, there is arguably no GWR on the value of the settled property upon the settlor's death under *s 102(3)*. This is on the basis that the settlor has given away the remainder interest in which no benefit is reserved, but there is no gift of the right to receive the income because the donor has always had it, ie there is no GWR but rather a 'carve-out' (*Trust Taxation,* 4th Edition by Emma Chamberlain and Chris Whitehouse (Sweet & Maxwell) at 39.32).

'Tracing' the settled GWR

5.20 There are also 'tracing' provisions under which the GWR rules may apply if the property subject to the deemed gift continues to be settled property immediately thereafter and is replaced by other assets; or if all or part of the settled property ceases to be settled while the reservation still exists; or if gifted property is not settled directly by the donor but subsequently becomes settled by the donee.

In the latter case, the period between the original gift and settlement by the donee is subject to the normal tracing rules, but from the date of settlement by the donee, the tracing rules for settled property apply instead (*FA 1986, Sch 20, para 5;* see IHTM14403).

On the lifetime termination of an interest in possession to which *FA 1986, s 102ZA* applies (see **5.19**), if the property continues to be settled, the individual's deemed gift for GWR purposes is the settled property at the 'material date' (as defined in *FA 1986, Sch 20, para 1(1)*), or property representing or derived from it. However, accumulated trust income arising after that time is not treated as derived from that settled property (*FA 1986, Sch 20, para 4A(5)*).

Settlor as trustee and GWR

5.21 A trustee's duties are of a fiduciary nature (ie to safeguard the interests of the beneficiaries). Thus, as a matter of trust law, and for GWR purposes, there is normally no objection to the donor (or spouse or civil partner) being one of the trustees, as long as he acts in the interests of the beneficiaries and not himself.

In addition, HMRC accept that a donor can receive reasonable remuneration for his duties as a trustee without constituting a GWR (IHTM14394). This is despite the decision in *Oakes v Comr of Stamp Duties of New South Wales* [1954] AC 57, an Australian case in which it was held that remuneration paid to the settlor as trustee was a benefit.

If company shares are settled and the settlor is a trustee and also a paid director of that company, the gift does not, of itself, constitute a GWR. There is a possible GWR argument if the settlor settles shares onto a trust and *then* obtains a paid position as director or employee of the company. In that situation, the settlor should obtain no more than reasonable remuneration for the work done.

HMRC accept that the continuation of reasonable commercial remuneration arrangements entered into before the gift does not of itself constitute a reservation, provided that the benefits were in no way linked to or affected by the gift. However, a new remuneration package may be challenged as a GWR 'by contract or otherwise' if the gift was taken into account as part of the arrangements (IHTM14395).

Insurance policies

5.22 There are also GWR rules specifically in respect of insurance policies, which can apply if there is a gift relating to a policy of insurance on the life of the donor, the spouse or civil partner or joint lives, where the resulting benefits to the donee vary according to benefits to the donor, spouse or civil partner. If those GWR provisions apply, the property comprised in a gift relating to the insurance policy is treated as a reserved benefit for the donor (*FA 1986, Sch 20, para 7*).

Note that this rule can apply to policies from which the donor's spouse (or civil partner) can benefit. This is an exception to the general rule that property from which the donor's spouse (but not the donor) can benefit or enjoy is not, of itself, a GWR (see **5.18**).

However, if a donor effects a whole life policy on his own life in trust, and the trustees' power of appointment over the trust fund can be exercised in favour of the donor's spouse (but not the donor), HMRC's position is that *FA 1986, Sch 20, para 7* does not apply (see Example 2 at IHTM14453). This is on the basis that the provision is only relevant if benefits can accrue to the donor or spouse under the policy itself, not where the spouse can only benefit under the trust (even though the trust assets include the insurance policy).

If an insurance policy is taken out for another person, the date of gift is the date on which the insurance contract is taken out. Gifts made before 18 March 1986 are not subject to the GWR rules. However, HMRC consider that if the policy is varied on or after that date, all premiums paid after 17 March 1986 (not just those paid after the variation) are subject to the GWR rules (IHTM14433).

Business and agricultural property

5.23 The availability of business property relief (BPR) or agricultural property relief (APR) (see **Chapter 11**) on gifts charged as a GWR depends on whether the property is qualifying business or agricultural property (eg land or buildings) or qualifying shares or securities in a company (Note: if the shares or securities subject to the GWR charge do not qualify for APR, they may qualify for BPR instead).

For the purposes of establishing entitlement to BPR or APR in terms of the minimum period of ownership requirement (*ss 106, 117*), ownership by the transferor before the GWR is treated as ownership by the donee (*FA 1986, Sch 20, para 8(2)(a)*), and occupation by the transferor (ie before and after the GWR) is treated as occupation by the donee (*para 8(2)(b)*).

The question whether BPR or APR is available (and, in the case of APR, at what rate) is determined on the basis that a notional transfer of value had been made by the donee (*FA 1986, Sch 20, para 8(1A)(b)*). As to the availability of APR for shares or securities in farming companies, see below.

HMRC will consider whether the BPR or APR conditions were satisfied at the date of gift (and by reference to the donor's ownership history), and also when the GWR charge arises, ie on the death of the donor, or when the benefit ceases (IHTM25381, IHTM24200).

For shares or securities in farming companies, if the GWR rules apply, the availability of APR is subject to separate requirements (*FA 1986, Sch 20, para 8(3)*). These are, broadly, that the shares or securities qualified for relief when the GWR was made, the donee has retained ownership of the shares between the dates of the gift and GWR charge, and the shares or securities qualify for relief on the basis of a notional transfer of value by the donee.

As indicated above, the conditions for APR (or BPR) in respect of shares or securities must be satisfied at the time of gift, and also when the GWR charge arises (*FA 1986, Sch 20, para 8(1A)(b)*). In addition, for shares within *IHTA 1984, s 122(1)* ('Agricultural property of companies') the donee must retain ownership of the shares between the date of gift and the date of the GWR charge (*FA 1986, Sch 20, para 8(3)(b)*).

The availability of BPR on shares or securities is generally determined on the basis that they remained in the donor's ownership, ie as if the gift had never been made (*para 8(1A)(a)*). The normal requirement that the donee must retain the gifted property until the time of the GWR charge is subject to tracing provisions, as discussed above. However, if the gifted property is shares or securities constituting a control holding in a company with agricultural assets within *s 122(1)*, HMRC consider that any substitute property will not qualify for APR (or BPR) due to the ownership requirement in *FA 1986, Sch 20, para 8(3)*. HMRC states (at IHTM24206): 'advice should be taken on any case where it is claimed that agricultural or business relief should apply in respect of substituted property'.

If the donee dies prior to the GWR charge, the donee's personal representatives or beneficiaries of the GWR property are treated as the donee for the above purposes (*FA 1986, Sch 20, para 8(5)*).

EXCEPTIONS AND EXCLUSIONS FROM CHARGE

Gifts made before 18 March 1986

5.24 The GWR rules do not apply to gifts before 18 March 1986, even if there is a reservation of benefit thereafter.

For example, a pre-18 March 1986 discretionary trust which would have been caught by the GWR provisions had it been made after 17 March 1986 will escape the GWR charge, unless further gifts into trust are made after that date (in which case the GWR rules will apply to those later gifts).

Gifts which are exempt transfers

5.25 The GWR rules do not apply to certain exempt transfers (*FA 1986, s 102(5)*). The exemptions are listed below (all references are to *IHTA 1984*):

- transfers between spouses or civil partners (but see **5.26**) (*s 18*);
- small gifts (*s 20*);
- gifts in consideration of marriage or civil partnership (*s 22*);
- gifts to charities or registered clubs (*s 23*);
- gifts to political parties (*s 24*);
- gifts to registered housing associations or registered social landlords (from 14 March 1989) (*s 24A*);
- gifts for national purposes etc (*s 25*);
- gifts for public benefit (although this relief has now been repealed) (*s 26*);
- maintenance funds for historic buildings, etc (*s 27*); and
- employee trusts (*s 28*).

5.26 Before changes to the GWR rules were introduced (*FA 1986, ss 102(5A)–(5C)*), arrangements were possible to take advantage of the exception from the GWR provisions for exempt gifts between spouses. *Eversden* schemes (such as outlined at **5.9**) used the spouse exemption (*IHTA 1984, s 18*) to avoid a GWR on the gift of an asset to a trust. Such schemes were blocked by the above GWR changes (with effect for disposals from 20 June 2003), and pre-existing schemes are potentially subject to an income tax charge under the pre-owned assets regime (see **Chapter 16**).

Whilst the GWR rules do not necessarily apply to a gift (eg to a discretionary trust) in which a benefit is reserved by the donor's spouse or civil partner (ie as a potential beneficiary), if enjoyment of the gift is effectively shared by the donor (eg if distributions from the discretionary trust are paid into a joint bank account of the donor and spouse/civil partner), the GWR provisions will need to be considered.

In the context of joint money accounts (eg between mother and son), care is needed if the funds were provided by one of the parties. Otherwise, the whole of the funds may be treated as part of the donor's estate on death, either under *IHTA 1984, s 5(2)* or the GWR provisions (*Matthews v Revenue and Customs Commissioners* [2012] UKFTT 658 (TC); see **4.21**).

5.27 It should be noted that the following categories of exempt gift can fall within the GWR rules:

- PETs made more than seven years before the donor's death (*IHTA 1984, s 3A(4)*);
- the £3,000 annual exemption (*IHTA 1984, s 19(5)*); and
- the normal gifts out of income exemption (*IHTA 1984, s 21(5)*).

For example, if there is a GWR and the reservation ceases with the gift becoming a PET, there can be no £3,000 exemption when the reservation ends, as *s 19(5)* effectively precludes the annual exemption from applying to the resulting deemed transfer (IHTM14343). This exclusion is perhaps logical in the sense that the gifted property actually passed to the donee at the time it was made, not when the reservation ceased.

De minimis exceptions

5.28

> **Focus**
>
> As indicated at **5.4**, one of the conditions to avoid a GWR is that the gifted property must be enjoyed by the donee to the entire exclusion, or virtually to the entire exclusion, of the donor (*FA 1986, s 102(1)(b)*).
>
> There is no definition of 'virtually' in the legislation. However, in HMRC's view, the expression 'virtually to the entire exclusion' covers cases in which the benefit to the donor is 'insignificant' in relation to the gifted property.

Examples of situations in which HMRC consider that the donor can benefit to some extent without the GWR rules applying are illustrated in *Revenue Interpretation 55*, and are reproduced below:

Table 5.1—GWR: *de minimis* exceptions (Revenue Interpretation 55)

- a house which becomes the donee's residence but where the donor subsequently:
  - stays, in the absence of the donee, for not more than two weeks each year; or
  - stays with the donee for less than one month each year;
- social visits, excluding overnight stays made by a donor as a guest of the donee, to a house which he had given away. The extent of the social visits should be no greater than the visits which the donor might be expected to make to the donee's house in the absence of any gift by the donor;
- a temporary stay for some short-term purpose in a house the donor had previously given away, for example:
  - while the donor convalesces after medical treatment;
  - while the donor looks after a donee convalescing after medical treatment;
  - while the donor's own home is being redecorated;
- visits to a house for domestic reasons, for example babysitting by the donor for the donee's children;
- a house together with a library of books which the donor visits less than five times in any year to consult or borrow a book;
- a motor car which the donee uses to give occasional (ie less than three times a month) lifts to the donor;
- land which the donor uses to walk his dogs or for horse riding provided this does not restrict the donee's use of the land.

The above guidance warns taxpayers that if a benefit escalates into something more significant, the GWR provisions may apply (eg a house in which the donor then stays most weekends, or for a month or more each year).

Full consideration

5.29 If the donor gives full consideration in money or money's worth there should generally be no reservation in the case of land and chattels. The retention of a benefit by the donor is disregarded if the donor is in actual occupation or actual enjoyment and pays full consideration in money or money's worth (*FA 1986, Sch 20, para 6(1)(a)*), eg a 'commercial lease' pursuant to which the donor pays a full arm's-length rent for the lease or tenancy retained.

Full consideration is required throughout the period, and regular rent reviews should take place to ensure that this condition is satisfied. HMRC accept that 'full' consideration falling within 'normal' valuation tolerances will be acceptable (*Revenue Interpretation 55*), although there is no statement of what is regarded as 'normal' in this context.

Note that the above GWR exception applies specifically to land and chattels. Care should be taken with other assets. HMRC's Inheritance Tax Manual (at IHTM14336) cites an example in which A, who is a partner, withdraws capital from his partnership capital account and gives it to B. B then lends the partnership an equivalent cash sum. HMRC consider that this is a GWR, and state that even though A may pay B a commercial rate of interest for the loan, this payment will not prevent the loan being a reservation (see also *Chick v Commissioner of Stamp Duties of New South Wales* [1958] AC 435).

5.30

> **Focus**
>
> To reduce the possibility of a GWR challenge by HMRC, the 'full consideration' in relation to land or chattels should be negotiated at arm's length between parties with separate professional advisers in accordance with normal commercial criteria at the time.

HMRC guidance on 'full consideration' can also be found in *Revenue Interpretation 55* (see **5.28**), and specific examples are included in the Inheritance Tax Manual (at IHTM14341).

There is a similar full consideration let-out from the pre-owned assets income tax charge (see **Chapter 16**) in relation to land and chattels (ie where the consideration is paid under a legal obligation), but not intangible property (*FA 2004, Sch 15, paras 4(1), 7(1)*).

The donor's occupation of gifted land is not a GWR if it represents reasonable provision for an infirm relative, if certain conditions are all satisfied (*FA 1986, Sch 20, para 6(1)(b)*) (see **5.15** and **5.31**). There is also an exemption from a pre-owned assets income tax charge in those circumstances (*FA 2004, Sch 15, para 11(5)(d)*).

Provision for old age and infirmity

5.31 As indicated at **5.15**, the donor's occupation of *land* is expressly disregarded if the following conditions are all satisfied (*FA 1986, s 102C(3)*, and *Sch 20, para 6(1)(b)*):

- it results from unforeseen changes in circumstances of the donor since the gift (eg a sudden serious illness, but not merely getting old); *and*
- the donor is unable to maintain himself through old age, infirmity, etc; *and*
- it represents a reasonable provision by the donee for the donor's care and maintenance; *and*
- the donee is a relative of the donor or his spouse (or civil partner).

It should be noted that the above conditions are cumulative, and therefore potentially onerous.

In addition, it may be difficult in practice to determine what constitutes a 'reasonable' provision by the donee for the donor's care and maintenance; this will depend on the particular facts of the case.

Instruments of variation

5.32 The GWR rules cannot apply to a disposition which is subject to a variation by the beneficiary (ie within *IHTA 1984, s 142*).

The variation is treated for IHT purposes as having been made by the deceased person whose estate is the subject of the variation, not the persons entitled under his will.

Example 5.4—GWR exception: deed of variation

Mr Baker died on 2 January 2015, leaving property under his will to Mrs Baker.

On 1 June 2016 (ie within two years), Mrs Baker varied her late husband's will (ie by an instrument of variation within *s 142*), so that the property became settled on a discretionary trust for Mrs Baker and her adult children.

The discretionary trust is treated for IHT purposes as having been made by the deceased, Mr Baker. Therefore, the GWR rules cannot bite.

The government announced at summer Budget 2015 that it intended reviewing the use of deeds of variation for tax purposes, due to concerns that the tax rules are being abused. Following that review, the government stated that it would not be introducing new restrictions on how deeds of variation can be used for tax purposes. However, the government also pointed out that it would continue to monitor the use of deeds of variation for such purposes.

Non-UK assets of non-UK domiciliary

5.33 The 'excluded property' of a non-UK-domiciled person (see **1.18**) is not subject to the GWR rules (but see **5.37** below for a possible future exception in respect of UK residential property held indirectly, such as by an offshore company).

Example 5.5—GWR exception: excluded property

James was born and domiciled in New Zealand. In 2007, he gave away an investment property portfolio in Wellington to his daughter Mary. The lettings income was shared equally between them. James died in 2016, still domiciled in New Zealand.

The gifted property was subject to a reservation at James' death. However, it was situated outside the UK, and James remained domiciled outside the UK throughout. The property is therefore excluded property (*IHTA 1984, s 6(1)*), and the GWR charging provisions do not apply.

However, HMRC's view (see IHTM14318, at Example 3) appears to be that if the donor makes a gift subject to a reservation and subsequently becomes UK domiciled, there may be a GWR claim on death; or alternatively if the reservation ceased in the donor's lifetime, a deemed PET may be treated as being made. This is on the basis that the donor is domiciled in the UK when the GWR charge arises, and that the excluded property rule in *s 6(1)* does not then apply.

As to domicile generally, including the government's proposed 'returning UK domiciles' rule from 6 April 2017, see **Chapter 1**.

5.34 A popular IHT planning point has been that if a non-UK domiciliary held assets abroad, those assets could be gifted into trust if there was any possibility of the individual becoming actually or deemed domiciled in the UK (eg settling the non-UK situs assets on discretionary trust with the settlor as a possible beneficiary), in order to continue benefiting from excluded property status. It was commonly thought that the GWR rules could not apply, because the excluded property rules prevailed. HMRC's guidance in the Inheritance Tax Manual created uncertainty on this issue for some time.

However, HMRC's guidance (at IHTM14396) was subsequently amended, and now states the following:

> 'Where the settlor was domiciled outside the UK at the time a settlement was made, any foreign property within that settlement is excluded property and is not brought into charge for inheritance tax purposes.
>
> This rule applies where property is subject to a reservation of benefit even though the settlor may have acquired a domicile of choice in the UK, or be deemed to be domiciled in the UK, at the time the GWR charge arises.'

5.35 The rationale for HMRC's approach in the above circumstances is that the property is comprised in a settlement when the GWR charge arises. If property comprised in a settlement is situated outside the UK, it will generally be excluded property if the settlor was not domiciled in the UK when the settlement was made (*s 48(3)(a)*).

The guidance goes on to provide the following example:

> '*Example*
>
> Henry, who is domiciled in New Zealand, puts foreign property into a discretionary trust under which he is a potential beneficiary. He dies five years later having acquired a domicile of choice in the UK and without having released the reservation. The property is subject to a reservation on death but it remains excluded property and is outside the IHT charge.'

However, if the trustees in the above example had sold the foreign property and invested the proceeds in UK situs assets, the property comprised in the trust on Henry's death would no longer be situated outside the UK, and the excluded property treatment in *s 48(3)* would not then apply.

If the individual becomes domiciled in the UK and adds property to the settlement, HMRC will regard the donor as creating a separate settlement. Thus the foreign assets settled when the donor was non-UK domiciled continue to be excluded property, but all assets (UK and foreign) settled when the donor was domiciled in the UK will be subject to IHT under the GWR provisions.

5.36 If gifted assets are subject to a reservation which is subsequently lifted during lifetime, the donor is treated as making a PET at that time (*FA 1986, s 102(4)*).

HMRC's view (at IHTM14396) is that no account is taken of excluded property which ceases to form part of the person's estate as the result of a disposition (*s 3(2)*), and therefore provided the assets were still excluded property when the deemed PET was made, they are excluded from an IHT charge. This is subject to exceptions, such as if the foreign assets had been replaced by UK situs property.

As already indicated, assets which are added to an excluded property trust after the settlor has become UK domiciled will not themselves be regarded by HMRC as excluded property. Further guidance on HMRC's approach to excluded property trusts is contained in *Revenue Interpretation 166* ('Excluded property settlements by people domiciled overseas').

An anti-avoidance rule was introduced in *Finance Act 2006* to counteract 'deathbed' IHT planning. This planning broadly involved an individual purchasing an interest in a pre-existing settlement created by a non-UK domiciled individual. Prior to 5 December 2005, a purchased interest in settled property was not precluded from being excluded property. However, the effect of the anti-avoidance rule is broadly that the exemption in *IHTA 1984, s 48(3)* is removed if a UK domiciled individual's beneficial interest in excluded trust property has been purchased on or after 5 December 2005 (*s 48(3B)–(3C)*).

Further anti-avoidance provisions (subsequently added by *Finance Act 2012*), affect certain arrangements in respect of settled excluded property from 20 June 2012. The provisions are broadly aimed at avoidance schemes involving a UK domiciled individual acquiring an interest in relevant settled property that would otherwise be excluded property, where there is a 'relevant reduction' in the value of the individual's estate. The scope of the legislation includes arrangements where a UK corporate settlor has settled assets as part of an avoidance scheme, and where individuals retain the interests in settled property they have acquired. The effect of the provisions is broadly that the relevant settled property is no longer treated as excluded property, ie it is treated like a UK trust (*IHTA 1984, s 48(3D)*). Furthermore, the reduction in value of the individual's estate falls to be charged to IHT as if a transfer of value had been made directly to a relevant property trust (*ss 74A–74C*).

As indicated at **7.32**, the government announced at summer Budget 2015 that it intended to legislate to ensure that, from April 2017, IHT is payable on all UK residential property owned directly or indirectly by non-UK domiciliaries. This change is aimed at blocking the holding of such property indirectly through offshore structures (or what HMRC describes as 'enveloping').

Consequently, shares in a 'closely controlled' offshore company will not be excluded property of the non-UK domiciliary to the extent that the shares derive their value directly or indirectly from UK residential property, or to the extent that the value of those shares is otherwise attributable to such property.

The GWR provisions will also need to be considered. For example, if a non-UK domiciled individual has retained a benefit in UK residential property gifted to an offshore company, based on the government's proposals it appears that the property would fall to be treated as remaining in the individual's estate for IHT purposes under the GWR rules.

The government's technical briefing on the proposed changes published on 8 July 2015 indicates that if shares in the offshore company owning the UK residential property were gifted into trust, the GWR provisions may be in point on the settlor's death unless he was excluded from benefit.

The government is to legislate its reforms to the taxation of non-domiciled individuals in *Finance Bill 2017*.

GWR AND DOUBLE IHT RELIEF

5.37 As indicated at **5.2** above, the GWR rules give rise to the possibility of a double IHT charge in respect of the same property. However, there are provisions (*FA 1986, s 104*; the *Inheritance Tax (Double Charges Relief) Regulations, SI 1987/1130*) which provide for relief in those circumstances.

The regulations provide for the avoidance of a double charge in the following circumstances involving a GWR (*SI 1987/1130, reg 5*):

- an individual makes a gift caught by the GWR rules (which may be a PET or a chargeable lifetime transfer) and the property is (by reason of the GWR rules) also subject to a deemed transfer which is chargeable as a result of the transferor's death; or
- facts as above, except that the donor's benefit ends before death (ie a deemed PET under the GWR rules), which becomes chargeable on the donor's death within seven years.

In both cases, two calculations are performed as a consequence of the death:

- charging the GWR in the death estate, and ignoring the lifetime transfer (*reg 5(3)(a)*); or
- charging the lifetime transfer and ignoring the GWR (*reg 5(3)(b)*).

5.38 Whichever transfer produces the higher amount of tax remains chargeable. However, provision is made for credit to be given for any lifetime tax already paid (*reg 5(4)*). See the example (**Example 5.3**) at **5.8**. In addition, the regulations include a schedule with worked examples of the double IHT relief rules as they apply to GWRs, although the examples do not prevail over the rules as stated in the regulations (*SI 1987/1130, reg 9*).

As indicated at **5.3**, the 'pre-owned assets' income tax legislation (see **Chapter 16**) also provides a measure of relief from IHT in certain very specific circumstances, where the taxpayer elects for those provisions not to apply and if two IHT charges otherwise arise on the same underlying asset value (*Charge to Income Tax by Reference to Enjoyment of Property Previously Owned Regulations, SI 2005/724, reg 6*). The double charges relief provisions effectively retain the charge on the transfer that produces the higher overall amount of IHT, and reduce the other transfer to nil.

Further provisions (*Inheritance Tax (Double Charges) Regulations, SI 2005/3441*) were designed to deal with the double IHT charges that may arise for taxpayers who decide to dismantle a 'double trust' arrangement and return to the position they were in previously. Once again, IHT is charged on the transfer producing the greater amount of tax, with the other transfer being reduced to nil.

GWR AND 'SHEARING' ARRANGEMENTS

5.39 There is always a fine line to be drawn between 'shearing' (or 'carving out') and GWR. At its simplest, shearing has been described thus: if Mr A owns three assets and gives two of them away, he does not reserve a benefit out of the third; he simply does not give it away.

Focus

In the context of more subtle arrangements, it has been suggested that it may be possible to separate capital from income, such as by a settlement in which the settlor retains a right to income but excludes himself from the possibility of benefiting from the capital.

Some commentators have suggested that such a trust might hold an interest in commercially let property, with the settlor retaining an interest by receiving the income stream.

HMRC may consider this to be fairly aggressive tax planning: the draftsman should issue the client with a suitable 'health warning'. Note that the section in HMRC's guidance concerning 'carve-out arrangements' (at IHTM14314) in relation to commercial property has been withheld from public access under the *Freedom of Information Act 2000*.

Chapter 6

Compliance

SIGNPOSTS

- **IHT: Interest** – Amendments have been made to the IHT late payment interest provisions, to complement future changes in secondary legislation to support the digitisation of IHT and the introduction of an online IHT service (see **6.2**).
- **Accounts and returns** – IHT100 and its supplementary forms need to be filed on lifetime gifts in some circumstances (see **6.4–6.9**).
- **Accounts and returns** – IHT400 and its supplementary forms report transfers on death (see **6.10–6.15**).
- **Excepted estates** – In certain circumstances the completion of Forms IHT100 and IHT400 can be dispensed with (see **6.16– 6.20**).
- **Payment of IHT** – Due dates and instalment options (see **6.25–6.36**).
- **Penalties** – An explanation of HMRC's new tougher approach to penalties and the potential pitfalls for advisers (see **6.38–6.54**).
- **Determinations and appeals** – An outline of 'what to do' if a dispute with HMRC arises (see **6.56–6.67**).

LIABILITY AND INCIDENCE OF TAX

6.1 Liability is the duty to pay the tax due, from the assets that lie to hand and it concerns the relationship between HMRC and the accounting party. Incidence is the allocation of the burden of the tax between beneficiaries; thus an executor or trustee will be concerned with the rules as to incidence when administering an estate where, for example, the residue passes partly to non-exempt persons and partly to charity. In that situation the executor is liable for the tax but must apply the rules of incidence to ensure that, subject to the terms of the will and to the rules in *Re Benham's Will Trust* [1995] STC 210 and *Re Ratcliffe* [1999] STC 262, the tax is actually suffered by the non-exempt persons. For analysis of these decisions, see **3.39–3.40**. *Finance Act 2006* has thrown up some anomalies in this area and reference should be made to 'A sting in the tail' at **7.42**.

ACCOUNTS AND RETURNS

The forms

6.2 The main control documents are:

- C1, Confirmation form to be completed if the deceased lived in Scotland;
- IHT100, the account for lifetime transfers of value; and
- IHT400 (which replaced IHT200), the HMRC Account for IHT at death.

These are supplemented by administrative forms that apply in situations, especially on death, where an estate is of substantial size but where no tax is in fact chargeable (and the estate does not fall with any of the exempt estate categories). The forms are updated regularly and there have been several changes in the last few years alone, so it is important always to use the most recent version which can be downloaded from the HMRC website at www.hmrc.gov.uk.

For death estates Form IHT 400 need not be submitted to HMRC if the criteria for Form C5 or C5(SE) are met, in which cases the C5 or C5(SE) is lodged with the Sheriff Court directly.

Form C5 may be used for individuals domiciled in the United Kingdom at the date of death where the gross value of the estate for inheritance tax purposes is less than (i) the excepted estate limit or (ii) is two times the excepted estate limit and form IHT217 (*Claim to transfer unused nil rate band for excepted estates)* is being submitted or (iii) is less than £1,000,000 and after deduction of liabilities and spouse or civil partner and/or charity exemption only (taking account of no other relief) the estate is below the IHT threshold.

Form C5(SE) may be used for individuals domiciled in the United Kingdom at the date of death where his or her estate qualifies as a Small Estate under the Small Estates Acts (see 6.18).

Focus

To use the website forms to best advantage, practitioners may wish to purchase editing software. Alternatively there is now a range of bespoke software developed by commercial providers.

The IHT400 series takes account of common practices such as the gift of personal effects to charity, which is dealt with in form IHT408, which is actually a 'one-off' variation of the dispositions of the estate and as such should be read in conjunction with any other variation contemplated by the personal representatives. Extra information, which was hitherto set out in a supplemental sheet, can be shown on pages 15 and 16 of form IHT400.

The schedules to include the main control document IHT400 are regularly amended and in February/March 2016 minor adjustments were made specifically to forms IHT 403, 408 and 421. Current versions of the full suite of forms are available from the HMRC website.

It should be noted that HMRC have identified an increasing number of errors made in completing form IHT403 where reliance is placed on securing the gifts out of income exemption. HMRC have stated that where the exemption is being claimed:

- full details of the gift must be included;
- full details of the deceased's income and expenditure during the period the gifts were made must be included on the form or be supplied by separate attached schedule; and
- relevant documents should be sent in support of the information stated on the form.

HMRC have made it clear that they will and in fact do pursue tax geared penalties for careless errors (or more serious misdemeanours) in the event of any loss of tax.

The current Form IHT407, formerly IHT409 'Household and personal goods', is more user friendly than its predecessor but its proper completion will be much more demanding than most families will expect or enjoy.

Form IHT409, 'Private and occupational pensions on death', now asks more pertinent questions, particularly concerning binding nominations that oblige pension scheme trustees to make a payment to a nominee where trustee discretion may be effectively overridden.

There is an ongoing government commitment to a 'digital strategy' to improve the process of interaction between HMRC and their 'customers' and HMRC's administration of taxes generally, including IHT. The government has carried out its intention first announced in the 2013 autumn statement that HMRC would move towards providing an online IHT return submission service in 2015/16. HMRC are continuing to work on the development of this service through limited public testing first implemented in late autumn 2015.

The service is now available for use by personal representatives, trustees, agents and other persons who are liable to IHT and/or who need probate to administer an estate. In late May 2016, HMRC indicated their intention to verify the source identity of the online IHT filer by sending an access code to their mobile phone and has added the following safeguards, requiring the filer to also:

- enter a User ID and password as noted on the Government Gateway service; and
- on first registration only, answer a series of identity verification questions.

Having registered for electronic filing, any request to withdraw consent for HMRC to communicate via electronic means must be made in writing.

Prior to 2 November 2015, any person delivering the online account had to declare that the information was correct and complete to the best of their knowledge and belief. As a result of adverse comments from the professional bodies, HMRC issued revised directions effective from 2 November 2016 which make it clear that where an agent is submitting electronic IHT information on behalf of the client, the agent is confirming that the client, not the agent, has approved the information of a Return.

To support the introduction of the IHT online service, various legislative changes are necessary in the primary and secondary IHT legislation, to facilitate online processes and align the treatment of interest and penalties for IHT purposes with other taxes. As part of the above changes, amendments to the legislation concerning late payment interest were included in the *Finance (No 2) Act 2015*, to come into force from a date to be specified in regulations. In particular, the changes extend the power to make regulations (under *Finance Act 1986, s 107(4)* and *(5)*) to the late payment interest provisions where IHT is payable by instalments in *Finance Act 2009, Sch 53* (*para 7(7)* and *(8)*) and update the provisions relating to financial institutions and companies. The changes will enable regulations to be made so that the late payment interest provisions in *Finance Act 2009, Sch 53* relating to IHT instalment payments can be updated.

In addition, the period from which late payment interest is charged (in *Finance Act 2009, Sch 53, para 9*) on amounts payable under *IHTA 1984, s 147* (Scotland: legitim, etc) in sub-para *(4)* is corrected by the changes, so that it refers to the end of the month in which the testator died (as opposed to the date of the testator's death). This amendment aligns the date with the late payment interest provisions in *IHTA 1984, s 233(1)(b)*. Other legislative changes are expected to be made by later regulations and appointed day orders to support the digitisation of IHT, with a view to ensuring that the relevant late payment interest provisions are updated and apply correctly to the online service.

The duty of notification on creation of offshore trusts stipulated by *s 218* should not be overlooked. Those concerned with the creation of such trusts, with the exception of barristers, must inform HMRC within three months. There is no prescribed format and such notifications can be made by way of simple letter.

Compliance

6.3 Legislation was introduced in *Finance Act 2008, Pt 7* ('Administration') and *Schs 36, 37, 39* and *40* (dealing with inspection powers, record keeping, time limits for assessments, claims etc and amendments to the rules on penalties for errors etc). *Finance Act 2009, s 96* and *Sch 48 (Appointed Day, Savings and Consequential Amendments) Order 2009 SI 2009/3054,* applicable from 1 April 2010 extended the rules as to information and inspection powers to IHT: see CH20150; and for a useful summary of commencement dates, see the links there set out.

The general scope of the legislation is to amend the rules on record keeping and the information and inspection powers. The general thrust of the more readily seen compliance checks is to reassure the majority who do comply that the system is fair and to ensure that taxpayers know what their obligations are in relation to registration for tax.

Taxpayers should understand what records are needed in order to calculate the tax due and, in the context of the administration of estates, the preparation of proper executorship accounts must come high on the list. The checks are also intended to understand where people are unsure of the law and put that right; and to eradicate weaknesses in the systems and processes which are used by taxpayers, correcting mistakes and discouraging people from non-compliance.

The checks are also very much intended to expose deliberate understatement of tax and that whole approach is driven by what HMRC perceive to be the risk involved. On the one hand, as for example with valuation of chattels, the risk may only involve a small amount of tax each time, but errors may be widespread. Alternatively, there may be segmental risk where, for example, taxpayers in a particular category or holding a particular type of asset may exhibit behaviour leading to risk which can be addressed through work with representative bodies or trade organisations.

The new basis includes the following features:

- flexibility according to the way taxpayers behave;
- going easy on the compliant majority;
- cracking down on the minority who deliberately understate their tax;
- greater clarity and consistency across the various taxes;

- clear definitions of HMRC powers and safeguards against inappropriate use.

To some extent, none of this is all that new.

For example, HMRC were able to use existing legislation very effectively against the taxpayer in *Smith v HMRC* [2008] SpC 680, where the Inspector examined private bank accounts to trace credit card expenditure of £47,500 and other unexplained transfers of £410,000 from companies controlled by the taxpayer. He extrapolated backwards into (more than six) earlier years to estimate the full level of under-disclosure of tax.

In *Sokoya v HMRC* [2008] ChD STC 3332, the taxpayer complained unsuccessfully from the decision of the Special Commissioner against a request from HMRC for documents to check 'nil' entries in his return. The burden of proof to be satisfied by HMRC is not that of the criminal courts: see *HMRC v Khawaja* [2008] ChD STC 2880. The Inspector need not be clairvoyant, so the inclusion of a round sum as a loss is not sufficient notice that the taxpayer has been using a tax scheme to create an artificial loss, such that time runs against HMRC in discovering it: *Corbally-Stourton v Revenue and Customs Commissioners* [2008] STC (SCD) 907 (SpC 692).

Note, however, that the First-tier Tribunal can take a robust and practical line, as it did in *Cairns v Revenue & Customs* [2009] TC00008, an investigation into the estate of a former Chief Examiner with the Estate Duty Office. The deceased's house was in extremely poor condition and had been valued shortly before death at about £400,000. The personal representative adopted that figure in the IHT account (form IHT200, as it then was), not considering it necessary to revalue, since on sale the price achieved would very likely be substituted anyway. Following sale for £600,000, which was then agreed to be the value at date of death, HMRC pressed for penalties for delivery of an incorrect account. Fraud was not alleged; instead HMRC alleged negligence on the basis that the personal representative should have obtained another valuation.

Not so, held the Tribunal which found that the account was not negligently delivered. The value specified should have been shown as provisional but that was a mere technical error which had no consequence whatsoever. There was no loss to the public purse because in fact IHT had been overpaid and was later repaid. Any finding of negligence would have been the merest technicality. A proportionate approach would have been a nominal penalty.

A detailed consideration of the legislation, which appears at *Finance Act 2008, ss 113, 115–117* and *Schs 36–37* is beyond the scope of this book, but is included in Chapter 1 of *Capital Gains Tax 2016/17* (Bloomsbury Professional). In practical terms, help has been rolled out to practitioners by HMRC in the form of 'checklists' for various taxes.

HMRC have published an 'Inheritance Tax Toolkit', which, it is stated, is aimed at 'helping and supporting tax agents and advisers in completing Inheritance Tax account form IHT400, although it may be of use to anyone, including trustees and personal representatives, in completing this form'.

The Toolkit is an aide memoire and thus does not need to be used in order to demonstrate that 'reasonable care' has been taken, if the matter of penalties arises due to an error in the IHT400 account. However, HMRC's website states that use of the Toolkit 'can also be used to help demonstrate that 'reasonable care' has been taken' www.hmrc.gov.uk/agents/toolkits-background.htm).

HMRC announced changes to their compliance checks in their December 2013 Trust and Estates Newsletter. If a case has been selected for a compliance check, an initial letter will be sent to the practitioner explaining that a case has been so selected. HMRC stated that they will aim to complete the check within eight to ten weeks of receipt of the IHT account. The investigator will make contact with the practitioner by phone with the aim to agree a case plan to resolve the matter more quickly.

Finance Act 2014 contains legislation which imposes up-front penalties on taxpayers who have used marketed tax avoidance schemes that are under open investigation or litigation. Taxpayers who have used an avoidance scheme similar to one that a court has already overruled will have to pay the amount HMRC say they owe. Taxpayers who continue the dispute will incur penalties, unless they ultimately win their case. The accelerated payment scheme applies to tax in dispute under arrangements which fall within the Disclosure of Tax Avoidance Scheme (DOTAS) rules and cases challenged by the new General Anti-Abuse Rule (GAAR).

Lifetime transfers

6.4 The requirement as to when to deliver an account of a lifetime transfer is not sufficiently well known, though HMRC have issued reminders from time to time (see **2.28**). No account is needed for a PET irrespective of its monetary value but there may be a requirement to report a lifetime chargeable transfer even though seven years may elapse before the death of the transferor.

Where the transfer is immediately chargeable and not exempt from reporting under the rules described below, the account is to be delivered by the transferor. If he does not pay the IHT by the due date, other persons become liable such to include the donees, trustees and beneficiaries under settlements, though they do not have to deliver the account themselves. In those rare cases where a close company makes a transfer of value, IHT is calculated as if the participators in the company had made the transfer; nonetheless the company is liable for IHT thereon but it has no requirement to deliver an account: see *IHTA 1984, ss 94* and *202* and the commentary at **1.27** (all subsequent statutory references are to *IHTA 1984*, unless otherwise stated).

Finance Act 2006 greatly increased the number of transactions that now fall to be chargeable transfers, even though in a great many cases, no immediate tax results. As a consequence the level of disclosure was revised and reduced by the *Inheritance Tax (Delivery of Accounts) (Excepted Transfers and Excepted Terminations) Regulations 2008 SI 2008/605* and the *Inheritance Tax (Delivery of Accounts) (Excepted Settlements) Regulations 2008* SI 2008/606. These regulations, which came into force on 6 April 2008 apply in the case of the former with regard to chargeable events occurring on or after 6 April 2008 and in the latter with regard to chargeable events occurring on or after 6 April 2007. These are discussed in more detail below.

The changes caught many taxpayers out but not (see *Marquess of Linlithgow and Earl of Hopetoun v HMRC* [2010] CSIH 19) those who acted promptly (or with prescience). That case turned on the effective date of a transfer of land under Scots law. Two documents detailing dispositions to an accumulation and maintenance trust, dispositions, were executed on 15 March 2006, so just days before the changes; but were not recorded in the Register of Sasines until October and November of that year. An attempt by HMRC to treat the transfers of value as chargeable failed: Following the estate duty case of *Thomas v Lord Advocate* [1953] SC 151, the date of transfer was that of the disposition, not registration.

Excepted transfers and terminations

6.5 The regulations as to excepted transfers and excepted terminations removed the obligation to deliver an account for those transactions covered by the regulations unless HMRC served a notice requiring one but there is a duty:

- in a trust scenario, on trustees to file an account in respect of failed PETs; and
- in a trust scenario, on trustees and others to file an account on the termination of a settlement which would have been a PET, but fails under the seven-year rule; and
- on other lifetime gifting, to file a return where the parties thought that the transfer was excepted within the new rules and it turned out not to be.

Excepted transfers

6.6 An excepted transfer under the new rules must be one made by an individual and must be an actual transfer, not a deemed transfer as defined for IHT purposes. There are two categories.

(a) Fixed-value transfers

Where the transfer is either cash or quoted shares or securities the transfer will be excepted if the value transferred, together with values of chargeable transfers made by that transferor in the preceding seven years, do not exceed the current nil rate band.

(b) Transfers of uncertain value

Where the transfer includes assets other than cash or quoted shares or securities (ie heritable property) the transfer is exempt where:

- its value, together with other transfers by that transferor in the preceding seven years do not exceed 80% of the nil rate band (upper level of £260,000 based on the 2016/17 nil rate band of £325,000); and
- the value transferred by this particular transfer does not exceed the nil rate band after deducting the value of all the previous chargeable transfers.

For this purpose neither BPR nor APR is to be taken into account, so to be excepted the entire value must be within the limits prescribed.

Example 6.1—Gift of a share in a flat

Louis wishes to give his grandchildren a one-third interest in a flat in Edinburgh which is let. The flat as a whole is worth £660,000. On 30 June 2016, he settles that one-third interest, which might seem to be a gift of £220,000 (ie £660,000 × 1/3) but the value for the lifetime transfer must be calculated on the loss to estate rule. Before the transfer his estate includes the full (100%) value of the property but post transfer his estate holds a 67% (two-thirds share) which should be discounted by say 15% to reflect multiple ownership and is therefore worth £374,000 ((660,000 × 2/3) × 85%). The loss to his estate is £286,000 (660,000 – 374,000).

Given the current 2016/17 nil rate band of £325,000 the limit above which the transfer must be reported is £260,000 namely 80% of £325,000. Louis' transfer must be reported; it is not £220,000, which would have been within the limit, but £286,000. Even the availability of two annual exemptions (current and prior year) would not help here.

Example 6.2—Excepted transfers: generous grandfather

Harry, having used his annual exemptions, set up a series of small discretionary trusts totalling £39,500 in the years 2010 to 2013. Some were of cash, some of assets but all of that was below the old filing threshold. In November 2016, he proposes to settle another £150,000 in cash and quoted securities (he has already utilised his annual exemption such that this is no longer available). This will bring his cumulative total to £189,500 (150,000 + 39,500) which is less than the 80% limit.

Harry also has a remaining nil rate band pre transfer of £285,500 (325,000 – 39,500). Harry need not file an IHT100.

Excepted terminations

6.7 The rules as to excepted terminations apply only to 'specified' trusts, ie:

- interest in possession trusts (qualifying interest) that existed before 22 March 2006;
- trusts for bereaved minors under *s 71A*;
- IPDI trusts within *s 49A(1)(d)*;
- disabled persons trusts; or
- TSI trusts within *ss 49B–49E*.

The termination of a qualifying interest in possession in a trust can be a chargeable transfer, but it need not be reported in one of three circumstances described below.

(a) Small or exempt transfers

The transfer may be small, for example within the annual exemption, and the liferenter may have served notice under *s 57(3)* that an exemption is available. If the amount of the transfer is within the specified exemption, there is no need to submit an account.

(b) Nil rate band: fixed-value fund

Where the trust property is cash or quoted securities and the total of the value of the fund in respect of which the termination takes place, and the value of other chargeable transfers made by the liferenter in the seven years preceding the event are within the nil rate band, there is no need to submit an account.

(c) Variable value funds

Where the trust fund does not consist wholly of cash or quoted securities there is still no need to submit an account if the value of the 'termination fund' and of previous chargeable transfers by the liferenter in the previous seven years do not exceed 80% of the nil rate band.

As with the rules for excepted settlements, these termination rules take no account of APR or of BPR. The 2008 Regulations replaced those made in 2002 in relation to lifetime transfers made on or after 6 April 2007.

Excepted settlements

6.8 The rules as to excepted settlements reduce the filing requirements in respect of pilot trusts and small settlements in which no qualifying interest in possession subsists (ie the settlement is a relevant property trust). As such there is no need to submit an account in respect of such trusts where the transfer is of cash of £1,000 or less to a UK-resident settlement and there are no related settlements.

Apart from such pilot trusts the regulations have also removed the obligation to file a return in respect of:

- UK trusts (which continue to remain UK resident); by
- settlors domiciled in the UK at the time the settlement is made; who
- remain domiciled here until either the chargeable event or the death of the settlor whichever first happens; where
- there are no related settlements; and
- one of the following conditions are met.

Extra condition 1 – The ten-year charge: The trust is excepted where the value in the trust is not more than 80% of the nil rate band (disregarding liabilities or reliefs such as APR or BPR).

Extra condition 2 – The exit charge in the first ten years of the trust: The language of the Inheritance Tax (Delivery of Accounts) (Excepted Transfers and Excepted Terminations) Regulations 2008 SI 2008/605, reg 4(5) is somewhat obscure but it concerns the value that is transferred by the notional chargeable transfer which is one element of calculating the exit charge in the first ten years of the relevant property trust. For a transfer to be excepted, the calculation of value disregards liabilities or reliefs such as APR and BPR. On an exit charge in the first ten years of a relevant property trust, there is no need to submit an account if the value released from the trust does not exceed 80% of the trust available nil rate band in force at the event date.

Extra condition 3 – The exit charge after the first ten-year anniversary: There is no need to submit an account if the value of the transfer does not exceed 80% of the trust available nil rate band in force at the event date.

Extra condition 4 – The exit charge from an 18-to-25 trust: There is no need to submit an account where the chargeable transfer is within 80% of the trust available nil rate band in force at the event date.

A trap for unwary trustees

6.9 There is one circumstance that could easily catch trustees out. It is described in IHTM06130 and arises on the death of a transferor. Trustees may have received sums which are well within the settlor's nil rate band and may have appointed funds out, again well within the levels that are now exempt from reporting. If this is the only chargeable transfer made by the settlor, there is no problem, but if the settlor had made PETs which now fail by reason of his death within seven years there will be a 'knock-on' effect for the trust. This is because, when seen in the context of the failed PETs, the transfers that were previously exempt from reporting must now be shown in an account. Depending on the value there might not be any extra tax to pay, but an account must be filed.

Example 6.3—Death affecting prior transactions

Jessica gave her daughter Celia a plot of land in 2011. This was a PET, so there was no requirement to submit an account. There was some prospect that Celia could get planning permission on the land, but she and her mother assumed that the value of the gift was £60,000. On 1 July 2014 Jessica settled £235,000 on trust being partly cash and partly quoted securities. Seen in isolation that was an 'excepted transfer' and there was no need to submit an account.

On 15 May 2014, the trustees advanced £80,000 to John, a beneficiary, to help him buy a house. The settlement had been within the nil rate band on creation so there would be no exit charge under normal principles.. Applying the rules, 80% of the nil rate band at that time was £260,000 so an appointment that could conceivably give rise to an exit charge need not be reported under the new rules because in this example the original fund, at £235,000, is well within the reporting limits.

Jessica died on 6 August 2015, so the 2011 PET to Celia fails. That triggers a review of the tax charges on the settlement. The effect will depend on the value finally agreed for the transfer of the land. If the value is, as claimed, £60,000, the notional aggregate of chargeable transfers goes up to £295,000. That is still within the nil rate band, so there will be no exit charge on the appointment made by the trustees, but the figures now exceed the limits in the new regulations so the trustees will have to deliver an account.

Greater difficulties will arise if it transpires that the likelihood of planning permission was so great at the time of the gift that the true value of the land was much more than £60,000. A significant increase in the valuation of the gift of the land could easily bring the tax rates applicable to the trust up to the level where an exit charge would be due on the £80,000 that was advanced to John.

There is detailed and useful guidance, with further illustrations, inserted into the IHT Manual at IHTM06100 to IHTM06130. See for example the detailed guidance on discounted gift schemes and their valuation at IHTM06105: where the discount is later found to be set at too high a level, a duty to file may arise on discovery within six months.

Settlors sometimes try to circumvent the chargeable transfer rules using the *s 21* 'normal expenditure out of income' exemption. Under the 2008 Regulations, there is no duty to submit an account if the transfers are covered by exemptions but the position is not so straightforward in the case of the normal expenditure out of income exemption (IHTM14231) where the exemption is only available '… to the extent that it is shown …' that the exemption applies. For this purpose HMRC interpret 'shown' as meaning 'shown to the satisfaction of HMRC'. Where denial of the exemption would still not breach the limits for a cash transfer it is not necessary to submit an account. HMRC will consider whether the *s 21* exemption is due if the matter is material when a later transfer is made or on death. However, in other cases where denial of the exemption in respect of the transfer would mean that there is a liability to IHT, an account should be delivered so that the availability of the exemption could be agreed: see IHTM06106.

Discovery and catch-up: a taxpayer may have thought that a transfer was outside the filing rules and realise the error later. If so, he has six months to put things right.

Transfers on death and failed PETs

6.10 **Chapter 1** explained how a lifetime transfer not otherwise immediately chargeable (a PET) might become chargeable if death occurred within seven years (a failed PET). The primary duty to complete returns rests with the personal representatives, who owe a duty of care to complete the return to the best of their knowledge and belief, subject to a test of reasonableness. HMRC's 'Inheritance Tax: Customer Guide' contains guidance to encourage consistency between HMRC's approach to the penalty legislation for IHT (www.hmrc.gov.uk/cto/customerguide/page22.htm).

Example 6.4—Accounting for a gift (and illustration of some rules)

Joe died on 17 May 2016, leaving his estate to his daughter Emma. He had made simple, outright, cash lifetime gifts as follows:

1: January 2009	£20,000 to Emma
2: June 2009	£16,000 to his son Philip
3: December 2009	£3,000 between his grandchildren
4: December 2010	£3,000 as before
5: December 2011	3,000 as before
6: May 2012	£10,000 to the National Trust
7: December 2012	3,000 as before
8: December 2013	£3,000 as before
9: May 2014	£20,000 to Philip
10: December 2015	£3,000 as before

Under a registered Continuing Power of Attorney which contained the power to make gifts, Philip continued the pattern of gifts at Christmas and also made, on behalf of his father, gifts as follows:

11: January 2015	£15,000 (personal effects to Emma)
12: May 20156	£25,000 between grandchildren

The executors can claim relief under *s 21* (ie normal expenditure out of income) for all the Christmas gifts up to 2015. *Gift 1* is more than seven years before death and out of the reckoning. The gift, even though made outside the seven-year period, will none the less absorb the annual exemption for that year, leaving less to set against gifts that do fall within the seven-year period.

Gift 2 enjoys £3,000 of annual exemption, so is a failed PET of £13,000 net. It is set against the nil rate band. *Gift 6* is to a charity and exempt. *Gift 9* benefits from two annual exemptions, leaving £14,000 to go against the nil rate band.

Of the gifts under the power of attorney, those at Christmas are probably exempt both under *s 21* and because they were habitual and therefore reasonable for the attorney to continue. *Gift 11* may also have been reasonable within the terms of the power, if Joe was moving into a nursing home and the alternative was to sell the chattels.

Gift 12 fails in every sense. It goes beyond what is reasonable under a power, unless there was specific authority.

In England and Wales, the power of an attorney under an LPA is more closely defined than used to be the case under an EPA: see *MCA 2005*, *s 12*, which provides that there is no general power to make gifts but that, subject to any express limitation in the power, the attorney may make gifts on customary occasions to persons related to or connected with the donor, including the grantee of the power; and may make certain charitable gifts. 'Customary occasion' means births, birthdays, marriage, formation of civil partnership or any other customary occasion, which allows cultural flexibility. This will bring the deeds in line with the Scottish position for Continuing and Welfare Powers of Attorney granted under the *Adults with Incapacity (Scotland) Act* 2000 and registered with The Office of the Public Guardian in Falkirk.

Reporting lifetime transfers after death: the duty of care

6.11 Personal representatives should enquire into the history of lifetime transfers by the deceased but how far they should pry depends on the circumstances. Having established the extent of the property remaining in the estate at death, executors should call for back statements on bank and similar accounts to check the pattern of withdrawals. They should make enquiries of relatives, professional advisers and close business colleagues. If, in the course of those enquiries, their suspicions are raised that gifts may have been made that were not disclosed by other papers of the deceased, their enquiries should continue until they are reasonably sure that they have identified all the gifts made by the deceased.

A particular problem concerns the date and nature of the gifts. In relation to 'old' gifts, their date will be material, perhaps to show that a gift was made more than seven years before death. Equally, a gift may have been made out of property that was at that time held jointly with some other person who has since died. The gift may therefore have been of only one half or some other fraction of the property given away.

Lifetime gifts may qualify for exemption under *ss 18, 19, 20, 21, 22* or *23* and following. Form IHT403 suggests a checklist of information that should be supplied and when it is correctly completed it can save an enquiry into the return. The difficulty, which has been noted before, lies in page 6 of IHT403, which attempts to help the personal representative to claim relief under *s 21* by setting out columns for each tax year prior to the death to show the available income so that gifts may be allocated to tax years and set against the relevant income. If the deceased died on 5 April, the form works fine; but if on any other day in the year an extra column may be needed, if the deceased made gifts on a regular basis – as is implied by reliance in *s 21* anyway. As an alternative for the practitioner's own use, the following (partly completed) table may be prepared as a spreadsheet to help to calculate the amount of nil rate band available after the lifetime gifts have been brought into account on death.

Focus

Rules introduced by *Inheritance Tax (Delivery of Accounts)(Excepted Estates)(Amendment) Regulations 2011 (SI 2011/214)* provide that where someone dies after 1 March 2011, an account may have to be delivered, even though the value of the estate is below £150,000, if reliance is sought on *IHTA 1984, s 21* (See **6.18**).

Example 6.5—Checking lifetime gifts

Susan died on 17 December 2016 having made the following lifetime gifts:

- June or July in each year: £2,000 to her niece;
- September 2009: 12,000 to her godson;
- February 2010: £10,000 to a niece;
- May 2011: £5,000 to her nephew;
- September 2012: £4,000 to a friend.

Her income was steady, at about £30,000 per annum after tax. She lived frugally, taking a holiday (cost £3,000) only in alternate years. Her living expenses were £15,000 per annum in the 'non-holiday years'. The table, which should be created as a spreadsheet, can be used to sort the gifts and to claim the reliefs before completing IHT400. Note that gifts that are clearly exempt need not be set out in IHT400 itself but this form ensures that none are forgotten.

Period	*Income* See note below*	*Gifts*	*Annual Exemption*	*s 21 Claim*	*Other Claims*	*Chargeable*
Part year 18.12.2009 – 5.4.2010	4,375	10,000				10,000
Year to 5.4.2011	12,000	2,000	3,000	2,000		
Year to 5.4.2012	15,000	7,000	5,000	2,000		
Year to 5.4.2013	12,000	6,000	3,000	2,000		1,000
Year to 5.4.2014	15,000					
Year to 5.4.2015	12,000					
Year to 5.4.2016	15,000					
Part year 6.4.2016 –17.12.2016	8,500	None**				
Total chargeable						11,000
NRB unused						314,000

* For this purpose 'income' means disposable income not necessarily taxable income thus will income for example ISA income, and a preliminary filter or table is needed to establish the sum each year or part year that was truly available to fund gifts.

The table is an example of the situation where there are actually eight periods for consideration, as noted above. The nil rate band at date of death was £325,000. The regular gifts form part of a pattern and are exempt under *s 21*. The isolated gift of £12,000 in September 2009 falls entirely out of account, but the annual exemption for that year and for the previous year will have been used up. Therefore, the gift in February 2010 of £10,000 has to be set against the nil rate band.

**Gifts by attorneys should be examined with care. Cheques uncashed at death are not effective gifts and their value is still part of the estate at death.

In real life there may be formidable obstructions to the proper performance by the personal representatives of their duties and this should not be underestimated. Families may be secretive, especially where one sibling knows that she has received more by way of lifetime gifts than the others or chattels may be taken from the residence to avoid burglary during the funeral and somehow are not returned to be included in the Confirmation inventory or IHT valuation (if indeed there is one). All of this will place an extra burden on the executor who must be seen to take 'reasonable care' so as to avoid penalties.

Normal expenditure out of income

6.12 Claims under *s 21* (normal expenditure out of income) meet resistance from HMRC where the evidence is, frankly, thin and without foundation. The taxpayer must show that:

- the gift was made of part of normal expenditure;
- it was made out of income; and
- the transferor was left with enough to live on and maintain his normal lifestyle.

Note that form IHT403 ('Gifts and other transfers of value') includes nursing home fees as an expense to be met out of income. This is consistent with the decision in *Nadin v IRC* [1997] STC (SCD) 107, but takes no account of the views expressed in *Stevenson (Inspector of Taxes) v Wishart* [1987] STC 266, where nursing home fees were substantial. The issue causes regular difficulty and is discussed at **1.20**, **2.3** and **9.8–9.9**.

It is not necessary to set gifts against the annual exemption in priority to making an *s 21* claim: thus, in the example above, where Susan made a gift in May 2008 that used up the annual exemption for that year, she could make gifts in the following year of £3,000 and still have available £15,000 (more or less) to set against gifts in respect of which an *s 21* claim was made.

6.13 To satisfy the test as to normal expenditure there must be:

- regularity;
- a pattern of gifts; or
- a commitment to make regular gifts; and preferably all three.

The scope for 'overs and shorts' under *s 21(1)(b)* is interpreted narrowly by HMRC. They will to a limited extent permit 'storing up' of income to support later gifts but HMRC will resist claims to relief unless there is evidence of intention to make particular gifts. They strongly resist a claim based on averages which relies on bringing back into a year the income of a later period but the legal authority for this resistance is unclear and should be challenged: the legislation only requires the taxpayer to show 'that (taking one year with another) [the gift] was made out of [the taxpayer's] income'. The leading case on the allowability of exemption under *s 21* is *Bennett v IRC* [1995] STC 54 and it requires careful reading as it is more generous to the taxpayer than generally realised. That having been said each case will turn on its own facts and on the quality of records which in many cases are seldom complete or even available.

HMRC have recently substantially re-written their guidance on gifts out of income (IHTM14231 to IHTM14255), which reflects their approach to closer scrutiny of this exemption. See **9.10**.

> **Focus**
>
> - Where reliance is placed the exemption under *s 21*, it is recommended that an annual record of income and expenditure is kept.
> - This can be recorded either by using a spreadsheet or form IHT403.

Personal effects

6.14 Another area of difficulty is personal effects, where HMRC consider that there may previously have been insufficient or somewhat superficial disclosure. The true value to be shown is governed by the market value rule in *s 160* and there is no such thing as 'Confirmation or Probate value': the value to be disclosed is 'the price which the property might reasonably be expected to fetch if sold in the open market' at the date of death. That is the gross selling price, not the net. Here, in particular, Form IHT407, asks searching questions even down to the registration number of the deceased's car; whether chattels that have been sold were purchased by relatives; and how the value of other chattels was arrived at.

Estimates

6.15 There is statutory authority in *s 216(3A)* for the use of estimates. The personal representatives must make very full enquiries but, if unable to arrive at the exact value, they must:

- say that they have made full enquiries;
- supply a provisional estimate of the value; and
- undertake to deliver a further account as soon as the value is ascertained.

For an example of litigation on these issues and on the costs of the litigation itself, see *Robertson v CIR* [2002] STC (SCD) 182 and *Robertson v CIR (No 2)* [2002] SSCD 242. For a case that highlighted the duty, see *Cairns v Revenue & Customs* [2009] UKFTT 67 (TC) TC00008, noted at **6.3** above.

Focus

HMRC are taking a much more aggressive stance against estimates.

- It is advisable, if not a necessity, to obtain robust valuations from qualified professionals, ideally so called 'Red Book Valuations'. This is more so now given the introduction of the new penalty regime (see **6.38–6.45**).
- In relation to land, 'development value', 'hope value' and the state of repair of a property all need to be addressed and recorded. In such situations photographic evidence is particularly useful.
- As of April 2011 it became mandatory for chartered surveyors who provide 'Red Book Valuations' to sign up to a registration scheme. Alternatively a member of the Institute of Rating, Revenue and Valuation will comply with the requirement of The Red Book.

EXCEPTED ESTATES

Bare trusts

6.16 Following *FA 2006*, there was a resurgence in the popularity of bare trusts, since these were outside the scope of the relevant property regime and as is always the case, some advisers pushed the boundaries of what might be considered to be a bare trust. Perhaps in response to this, HMRC revealed that they were considering one analysis of such trusts where there was, either expressly or by implication, a duty on the trustees to accumulate the income where such arrangements might be thinly disguised substantive trusts caught by *Finance Act 2006*.

This suggestion provoked uproar among professional advisers, who considered it to be wrong in law. The core of the HMRC argument turned on the effect *s 43(2)(b)* and its reference to accumulations. There is perceived to be inconsistency between the established treatment of bare trusts for income tax (see, for example, TSEM1031) and as proposed for IHT, thus cautious advisers in England and Wales may decide to exclude *TA 1925, s 31* to weaken the suggestion that there is a substantive trust.

The issue now seems to have been resolved and it is accepted that a simple bare trust of capital for a minor beneficiary is not settled property and thus cannot be relevant property. HMRC have formally commented:

> 'We confirm that our view is that where assets are held on an absolute trust (ie a bare trust) for a minor the assets so held will not be settled property

within the meaning of section 43 IHTA 1984 and that this will be the case whether or not the provisions of section 31 Trustee Act 1925 have been excluded.'

Transfers on death

6.17 There are now three categories of excepted estate, see *Inheritance Tax (Delivery of Accounts) (Excepted Estates) Regulations 2004 (SI 2004/2543)*. Many practitioners fail to take advantage of the regulations, preparing form IHT400 where it is not needed thereby incurring additional administration, cost and time which could all have been avoided. This apparent ignorance of the regulations is not encouraged by HMRC, because it just makes for unnecessary work that yields no tax. The reporting levels were increased by *Inheritance Tax (Delivery of Accounts) (Excepted Estates) (Amendment) Regulations 2006 SI 2006/2141* with effect from 1 September 2006 and *Inheritance Tax (Delivery of Accounts) (Excepted Estates) (Amendment) Regulations 2011 SI 2011/214* with effect from 1 March 2011.

Category One: small estates: the traditional form

6.18 For the shorter and simpler Form C5 (SE) to be used instead of Form IHT400 the conditions are:

(1) The deceased was UK domiciled and died on or after 1 September 2006.

(2) The estate relates to property in the following categories:

- it passes under the will of the deceased or on his intestacy;
- it passes under nomination taking effect on death;
- it is contained in one settlement only in which the deceased had an interest in possession; or
- it was joint property and passes by survivorship.

(3) Of the property passing on death:

- no more than £100,000 was situated overseas; and
- no more than £150,000 was trust property.

(4) In the seven years before death the deceased made transfers which, before deduction of business or agricultural property relief, did not exceed £150,000.

Note: For deaths on or after 1 March 2011 gifts under *s 21* (normal expenditure out of income) in excess of £3,000 in any one tax year will be treated as chargeable gifts for reporting purposes.

(5) The whole estate, including certain categories of transfer, did not exceed the IHT threshold which for this purpose means:

   (a) where death occurred on or after 6 April and before 6 August or where an application for Confirmation is made after 5 April and before 6 August in that year, the nil rate band applicable in the prior tax year; or

   (b) in any other case the nil rate band in force for the year in which death occurred.

(6) The deceased had not made a gift with reservation of benefit, nor had an IHT charge arisen on an alternatively secured pension.

There are two categories of transfers referred to in this last condition. 'Specified transfers' are defined in *SI 2004/2543, reg 4(6)* to mean chargeable transfers in the seven years up to death consisting only of:

- cash;
- personal chattels or moveable property;
- quoted shares or securities; or
- interest in land (with qualifications).

The same regulations define 'specified exempt transfers' as those made in the seven years up to death which are exempt under one of the following headings:

- transfers between spouses;
- charities;
- political parties;
- gifts to housing association;
- gifts to maintenance funds for historic buildings;
- employee trusts.

Category Two: estates: spouse/charity exemption

6.19 *SI 2004/2543* created a new category of excepted estate of a gross value of up to £1 million where, post offset of the spouse or charity exemption, the estate was still within the IHT threshold. To comply with this category the following conditions must be satisfied.

(1) The deceased was UK domiciled and died on or after 6 April 2004.

(2) The value of that person's estate is attributable wholly to property passing:

- by will or on intestacy;
- under a nomination taking effect on death;
- under a single settlement of which the deceased was tenant for life; or
- by survivorship in a special destination.

(3) The estate included:

- not more than £100,000 foreign property;
- not more than £150,000 of settled property but ignoring settled property that on death passes to a spouse or to charity; and
- that in the seven years leading up to death the deceased did not make chargeable transfers other than specified transfers not exceeding £150,000 before deduction of business or agricultural relief.

(4) The estate did not exceed £1,000,000, including within that figure:

- the gross value of the estate;
- the value transferred by specified transfers;
- the value transferred by specified exempt transfers.

(5) Applying the formula A – (B + C), the total does not exceed the IHT threshold. For this purpose:

- A is the aggregate of the estate, specified transfers and the specified exempt transfers.
- B is the total value transferred on death that qualifies for exemption as passing to a spouse or charity, but subject to qualification of that rule in relation to Scotland.
- C is the total liabilities of the estate.

IHT threshold: transferable nil rate band

6.20 *SI 2011/214* allows personal representatives to claim the benefit of the transferable nil rate band (TNRB) and apply for a grant as an excepted estate provided that a number of conditions are met. The TNRB in an excepted estate must be claimed using form IHT217. The conditions that must be met are:

- the deceased survived the earlier death of their spouse or civil partner and was married to, or in a civil partnership with, them at the earlier death;

- importantly, none of the nil rate band must have been used by the earlier death, so that 100% is available for transfer;
- a valid claim is made and is in respect of one earlier death only;
- the first deceased person died on or after 13 November 1974, where the deceased was the spouse of the first deceased, or on or after 5 December 2005, where the deceased was the civil partner of the first deceased person.

The estate of the first deceased person must also meet the following conditions:

- the first deceased person died domiciled in the UK;
- their estate consisted only of property passing under their will or intestacy and jointly owned assets;
- if their estate included foreign assets, their gross value did not exceed £100,000;
- agricultural and business relief did not apply.

Where an estate meets the above conditions and a valid claim is made:

- in a 'standard' excepted estate, the gross value of the estate must not exceed double the applicable nil rate band; or
- if the estate is an exempt excepted estate, the gross value of the estate must not exceed £1 million and the net chargeable value of the estate (after deduction of liabilities and spouse or civil partner exemption and/or charity exemption) must not exceed double the applicable nil rate band.

Category Three: small foreign estates

6.21 This category of estate is one where the deceased was never domiciled or deemed domiciled in the UK for IHT purposes and the UK estate comprises only cash or quoted shares or other securities with a total value not exceeding £150,000. It is necessary to state the value of worldwide estate and if the level is below the IHT threshold, domicile is less likely to be examined in detail as there is no tax at stake.

The personal representatives of an excepted estate, where the person died on or after 1 September 2006 with their permanent home abroad and limited assets in Scotland, are not entirely excused from supplying information. In all such cases they must complete the short form C5 (OUK). This may in any event serve a separate function by offering some protection to beneficiaries, especially charities, because without C5 (OUK) there might actually be no formal inventory of the estate.

PARTICULAR COMPLIANCE POINTS

Development value of land

6.22 Cases such as *Prosser v IRC* (DET/1/2000) have shown that the value of land for IHT must reflect some, but not necessarily full, account of 'hope' value where appropriate. In that particular case a garden plot in respect of which planning permission was eventually obtained, was held to be worth 25% of its ultimate value for probate purposes. The IHT Newsletter of 28 April 2006 stressed that development value must be accounted for, and that the value of a house should reflect any feature that makes it attractive to a builder or developer. If new information comes to light that enhances the value, the personal representatives should declare it, on pain of penalties for failure to do so.

Note that HMRC do now take the point that, if an asset is sold relatively soon after the death for substantially more than the value reported for IHT, the personal representatives may have failed in their duty of disclosure and penalties may result. Certainly with such a disparity in values it will invite HMRC interest.

Focus

- In 2012/13 HMRC saw a 23% rise in the amount of money raised by challenging the valuation of estates.
- HMRC are now asking executors how much care they took when getting an independent valuation – see earlier reference to 'Red Book' valuations on property.
- HMRC now consider that executors have a duty to draw the valuer's attention to specific features of the property that may affect its price.

Annuities

6.23 There will seldom be any residual value of an annuity, but where payments do continue after death, as where the annuitant dies before the end of the guaranteed period, that right to the income stream must be valued. Whilst personal representatives may value as they think fit, many will want to make use of the HMRC calculator on their website, giving a reasonable estimate of the value under *s 160*; see www.hmrc.gov.uk/cto/forms/g_annuity.pdf

Joint property

6.24 Property owned jointly with a special destination passes to the surviving owner without the need for Confirmation or a disposition. That does not mean, however, that no IHT is due. If the surviving joint owner is neither the spouse nor the civil partner, the value may be taxable. Form IHT400 will be appropriate, with form IHT404 annexed.

The deceased may have opened an account jointly with their grown up child, perhaps for convenience through frailty or failing capacity. Payment of money into such an account is not necessarily a gift of half to that child: but the withdrawal of funds by the child for her own purposes will usually be a transfer for IHT and should be brought into account. HMRC explained, in IHT Newsletter for December 2006, that they, not surprisingly, look critically at accounts opened shortly before death. See also *Taylor v HMRC* [2008] SpC 704, noted at **4.21**. Furthermore for Scottish accounts where funds have been contributed jointly, unlike in England and Wales, the surviving account holder will not inherit the deceased's share by survivorship. The deceased's share will pass in accordance with the Will or intestacy.

PAYMENT OF IHT

6.25 In the past, the main IHT event was triggered by death with tax payable on the death estate whilst bringing into account failed PETs made within the previous seven years. *Finance Act 2006* has now caused that position to quietly shift as a direct consequence of the new rules which brings most lifetime trusts and caused many existing settlements to migrate into the relevant property regime of exit charges and periodic charges.

Lifetime transfers

6.26 Hitherto most transfers, by number and possibly by value, have been PETs, so that tax on them would arise only if they failed by reason of the donor's death within seven years. The 'top-up' death charge that arises on the failure of a PET is charged, see *s 199(1)*, on:

- the transferor;
- the transferee whose estate is increased by the transfer;
- the recipient of the property in whom it is vested, whether for his own benefit or not, at any time after the transfer;
- anyone enjoying an interest in possession in the transfer;
- anyone for whose benefit the property or its income is applied where the property has become settled.

6.27 On the death of the donor, the first in line is the donee but, if he does not pay the tax within 12 months of the end of the month in which the donor died, *s 204* transfers that liability to the personal representatives. That can cause a real problem for executors, who may not know the full facts. HMRC indicated, in a letter dated 13 March 1991 to the Law Society, that they will not normally pursue personal representatives who have made the fullest enquiries, as reasonably practicable, to discover lifetime transfers; have done all they can to make full disclosure and have obtained the certificate of discharge and have distributed the estate all before a chargeable transfer comes to light.

There is a special rule for woodlands: see *s 208*.

Due date: lifetime transfers

6.28 This filing deadline for lifetime chargeable transfers that were made prior to 6 April 2014 were:

- for chargeable events occurring after 5 April but before 1 October the due date was 30 April in the following year; and
- for chargeable events occurring after 30 September but before 6 April the due date was six months after the end of the month in which the chargeable event occurred.

Finance Act 2014 addressed the issue that the time limits for reporting IHT periodic and exit charges for relevant property trusts differed from the time limits for paying any IHT due. Therefore for chargeable events occurring within a trust scenario on or after 6 April 2014, the time limit for both submitting an account and paying any IHT due is fixed at six months from the end of the month in which the transfer was made.

Payment by instalments

6.29 The tax may be paid by ten equal yearly instalments on 'qualifying property' where certain conditions apply. 'Qualifying property' for this purpose means:

- land;
- shares or securities within *s 228*; or
- business or an interest in a business.

The conditions are:

- the transfer is made on death; or,
- the tax is being paid by the person who benefits from the transfer; or

- the transfer comes within the relevant property regime (which will be more common in the post-*FA 2006* era), and either the tax is borne by the beneficiary or the property remains in the settlement.

At first sight this would seem to exclude IHT due arising on failed PETs but actually the instalment option is available, see *s 227(1C)*, where:

- the property was owned by the transferee from the date of the transfer to the death of the transferor (or if earlier of a transferee); or
- the charge arises under clawback of APR or BPR following the death of the transferor.

'Section 228' shares

6.30 Four categories of shares or securities of a company qualify for the instalment option:

- shares giving control;
- unquoted shares which attract (together with tax due on other instalment assets for which the same person is liable) not less than 20% of the tax chargeable by that person in the same capacity;
- unquoted shares where the tax cannot be paid without undue hardship; and
- other shares neither giving control nor unquoted but where the value of the transfer is over £20,000 and the shares are at least 10% of the nominal value of all the shares in the company at that time, or they are ordinary shares and their nominal value is at least 10% of the nominal value of all the ordinary shares of the company at that time.

Interest

6.31 Interest is added to each instalment, running from the date at which the instalment is payable unless it is land (excluding a business asset qualifying for BPR or agricultural property qualifying for APR) or shares/securities in companies whose business is wholly or mainly dealing in securities, stocks or shares, or making or holding of investments: see *s 234(2)*.

Loss of the instalment option

6.32 Curiously, advance payment of more than the instalment currently due can cause the loss of the instalment option in total. If it suits the taxpayer to pay extra at any time, the extra should be sent under cover of a separate letter as money to be put on deposit pending the due date for payment. It should also be remembered that the right to pay by instalment belongs to the beneficiary, who can claim against an executor or trustee in circumstances where the latter have caused the instalment basis to forfeit by early settlement of instalment payments.

However, if the executor releases property to the beneficiary in advance of the instalment payment he remains liable: see *Howarth's Executors v IRC* [1997] STC (SCD) 162, where a lawyer was personally liable for the outstanding and unpaid instalments of tax due on property that he had earlier released to the beneficiaries.

The 'Inland Revenue' charge

6.33 In England Wales only where tax charged on the value of a chargeable transfer is unpaid *s 237(1)* imposes a charge in favour of HMRC on the relevant property. It is known by statute as the 'Inland Revenue charge', see *s 237(1)*, rather than the 'HMRC charge'. The rules were updated by *s 237(3C)* in relation to certain specialised forms of charge. The Inland Review Charge is not applicable in Scotland.

Payment of IHT on death

6.34 The personal representatives are liable and the tax is treated as part of the administration expenses of the estate. The *Administration of Estates Act 1925* sets out the order in which the tax is charged against the assets in the estate but that rule is limited by *IHTA 1984, s 211* to the value of property in the UK that vests in the personal representatives of the deceased and was not comprised in a settlement immediately before the death. There are separate rules for recovery of tax where property is vested in another person.

IHT direct payment scheme

6.35 Since 31 March 2003 and by arrangement between HMRC and certain financial institutions, it has been possible for personal representatives to access funds in the name of the deceased before Confirmation is granted. This is a great help because tax must be paid 'up front' on all property except property that qualifies for the instalment option. Where, for example, a dispute about the will prevents the issue of a grant of Confirmation, this facility still allows the tax to be timely paid whilst avoiding the need to raise loans from third parties (ie banks).

The scheme is voluntary, so whilst most of the mainstream organisations do participate not all financial institutions (including some banks) are willing to assist. It applies only to accounts held in the sole name of the deceased and, if the deceased has several accounts, the institution will not release more than the net value (ie after setting off overdrafts or credit card liabilities). The number of the account must be nominated on the form. IHT423 using a separate form for each financial institution from which the funds will be applied.

Acceptance of property in lieu of tax

6.36 This is a specialist topic, but in outline it is possible to offer heritage property in satisfaction of tax liabilities. It must be of outstanding quality but the procedure is protracted, although it does secure for the nation valuable objects that might otherwise have been sold to overseas buyers to pay tax. As an incentive, the taxpayer receives a credit that slightly exceeds the net of tax commercial value of the item. This is known somewhat archaically as the 'douceur' (under a tax law rewrite it would perhaps be better described as a 'cashback').

DISCLOSURE OF TAX AVOIDANCE SCHEMES (DOTAS)

6.37 In January 2011 the *Inheritance Tax Avoidance Schemes (Prescribed Description of Arrangements) Regulations SI 2011/170* were published. The effect is that from 6 April 2011 transfers into trusts are within the DOTAS regime for IHT.

A useful flowchart to determine whether a particular scheme is subject to DOTAS has been published by HMRC in their guidance notes (see www.hmrc.gov.uk/aiu/dotas.pdf). To determine whether DOTAS applies HMRC have published a four-stage test in their guidance:

- **Test 1**: Are there arrangements or proposals for arrangements which result in property becoming 'relevant property'?
- **Test 2**: Are those arrangements or proposals for arrangements such that they enable a 'relevant property charge advantage?
- **Test 3**: Is the tax advantage a main benefit of the arrangements?
- **Test 4**: Is the arrangement not on the list of grandfathered schemes and schemes that are not within the regulations. If so it may have to be disclosed. The list of grandfathered schemes can be found in the guidance.

The main aim of the extension of the disclosure rules is to restrict disclosure to those schemes which are new or innovative. This is achieved by exempting from disclosure those schemes which are the same or substantially the same as arrangements made available before 6 April 2011.

Legislation was included in *Finance Act 2014* to impose advance penalties on taxpayers who entered into a tax avoidance scheme. In such cases where the tax avoidance scheme involved is notifiable to HMRC under DOTAS, or is counteracted under the GAAR, HMRC have from 17 July 2014 the power to issue a Notice to Pay. This requires the taxpayer to pay the tax that HMRC consider to be due; even though the taxpayer has appealed against the assessment and does not believe that he will owe any tax. Controversially this also applies to those who entered into tax schemes many years ago where the dispute has not yet been settled.

It was further announced that users of defeated avoidance schemes will be required to disclose their use to HMRC and pay any tax in dispute upfront. Penalties will apply for non-compliance.

Finance Act 2014 included measures against so-called high risk promoters of tax avoidance schemes awarding HMRC two new powers. The first enables HMRC to issue a promoter a 'conduct notice' demanding full details about a particular tax-planning product and its intermediaries and users. The second allows HMRC to issue 'monitoring notices' to selected promoters to provide details of all their products, intermediaries and users within five days of being asked to do so. 'Monitoring notices' will require the approval of the First-tier Tribunal.

On 31 July 2014 HMRC issued a consultation document 'Strengthening the Tax Avoidance Disclosure Regimes' and a summary of responses was later published in December 2014. The 2014 Autumn Statement contained a proposal for the introduction of a new threshold condition to ensure that promoters do not use the DOTAS regime as a way of obtaining advance clearance by repeatedly tweaking schemes and re-submitting them for consideration. The new threshold condition would consider how often a promoter contacts HMRC to gain approval of a scheme.

Specifically aimed at IHT which hitherto had been largely unscathed by the DOTAS rules, it is intended that the disclosure requirements will be more keenly focused on those IHT avoidance schemes which operate outside the normal planning routines involving available reliefs and exemptions.

On 2 September 2015 HMRC issued new Guidance Disclosure of Tax Avoidance Schemes which brings readers up to date with the changes introduced in *Finance Act 2014* and *Finance Act 2015*. The latter changes include:

- increasing the penalty for persons using schemes which do not comply with reporting requirements;

- protecting persons who voluntarily provide information about potential failures to comply with DOTAS;
- requiring promotors to notify HMRC if their details or those of one of their schemes change;
- enabling HMRC to publish information about schemes and promoters that it receives under the DOTAS rules;
- giving HMRC powers to obtain details of users of undisclosed schemes from introducers; and
- creating a new power requiring additional information to be sent to clients.

Following responses made to the consultation on its proposed draft changes to the hallmark regulations, which closed in September 2015, HMRC has made a number of amendments which changes became effective from 23 February 2016. In April 2016 HMRC issued a further consultation document which provided welcome examples of ordinary IHT planning which could secure a tax advantage but which HMRC considered to be nonetheless outside the DOTAS hallmark because such tax planning was neither contrived nor abnormal – these included:

- straightforward outright gifts;
- lifetime transfers into flexible or discretionary trusts;
- investment into assets that qualify for IHT reliefs;
- arrangements that are within a statutory exemption, ie paying full consideration for the continued use of a gifted asset;
- certain routine insurance-based arrangements, ie loan trusts.

The consultation closed on 13 July 2016 and the outcome is not expected for release until late autumn.

PENALTIES

A new (and tougher) approach

6.38 Another part of the modernisation of powers, deterrents and safeguards was the reform of penalties. Whereas other aspects of the modernisation did not specifically concern IHT, as was noted at **6.3** above, IHT was included in *Finance Act 2008*. The intention of the new legislation was described during the HMRC consultation as being to influence behaviour, to be effective and to be fair. There are five areas of concern:

- incorrect returns;

- failure to notify a new taxable activity;
- late filing and late payment;
- record keeping and information powers failures; and
- other regulatory failures.

The legislation in *Finance Act 2008* is not the end of this particular story. It concerns failure to notify and understatement and does not fully address the issue of the failure to submit returns at all. The structure of the legislation is to amend *Finance Act 2007, Sch 24*. *Finance Act 2008,* extended the existing schedule of taxes affected so as to include for IHT purposes accounts under *IHTA 1984, ss 216* and *217*, information or documents required by *IHTA 1984, s 256* and statements or declarations in connection with deductions, exemptions or reliefs. Beyond that, legislation was included in *Finance Act 2009, s 106* to impose penalties for late filing and, as a separate matter in *Finance Act 2009, s 107*, to penalise late payment of tax (see *HMRC v Evans* [2014] UKFTT 628 (TC)).

In IHT situations, there is often shared responsibility for information gathering. The most obvious example concerns lifetime gifts.

The penalty rules for inaccuracies generally apply for IHT purposes in respect of the following (see the Finance Act 2008, Schedule 40 (Appointed Day, Transitional Provisions and Consequential Amendments) Order 2009 SI 2009/571):

- documents relating to periods commencing from 1 April 2009, for which the filing date is on or after 1 April 2010; and
- relevant documents produced under regulations under *s 256* ('Regulations about accounts etc'), where the date of death is on or after 1 April 2009.

Example 6.6—Penalties: a difficult estate to administer

Philip had led a long and colourful life and a relationship whilst at medical school gifted him a daughter, Alice. He paid for her upkeep for a few years before leaving the UK to practise medicine in Africa, where his first marriage brought him a son, Brian, and daughter, Celia. That marriage ended in divorce and he returned to the UK. The length and bitterness of his divorce was exacerbated by a relationship with Dorothy, with whom Philip lived until his death.

Philip's will was prepared whilst he was still in Africa and named two of his then colleagues as executors. The terms of the will made no provision for Dorothy.

In his last years, Philip sought some reconciliation with each of his children, in particular Alice who (she said) cared for him in his latter years. His mental capacity was failing; he signed a continuing power of attorney in favour of Alice. By the time of his death serious difficulties had arisen between Alice, Brian, Celia and Dorothy. The estate was complicated, involving assets in Africa and in the UK and serious issues arose as to whether certain gifts had or had not been made and whether, at the time of gifts, Philip had had capacity to make them.

The executors in Africa face very significant difficulties in discharging their obligation under *IHTA 1984, s 216* to deliver an account that specifies all the appropriate property and its value.

This situation is addressed by *para 1A* inserted into *Finance Act 2007, Sch 24*. Most of the schedule centres on the obligations of a person identified in *para 1(1)* of the schedule as P. The penalties in *para 1A* concern a different person, T, and address the situation where the inaccuracy in the return made by P is attributable to false information that is deliberately supplied, either directly or indirectly to T or where T deliberately withholds information from P.

The inaccuracy is one which results in:

- an understatement by P of the liability to tax; or
- a false or inflated statement of a loss (which would not normally apply to IHT though debts at death have a similar effect); or
- a false or inflated claim to repayment of tax.

Thus, in the example of Philip the obligations would be shared by the executors and the family and if, for example, it transpired that Philip had made a substantial gift to Alice which Alice kept quiet about, the burden would lie on Alice.

Degrees of culpability

6.39 *Finance Act 2007, Sch 24* had already set out the new classifications, but the wording is tidied up by the amendments in *Finance Act 2008, Sch 40.*

Penalties may arise if 'reasonable care' has not been taken in preparing an IHT account or excepted estate return, or if any inaccuracy is discovered but reasonable steps are not taken to inform HMRC about it. HMRC consider that personal representatives will have taken reasonable care in the following circumstances (see HMRC Inheritance Tax and Trusts Newsletter, April 2009):

- The executors follow the guidance provided about filling in forms such as the IHT400 and C5, C5(SE) and C5(OUK).
- They make suitable enquiries of asset holders and other people (as suggested in the guidance) to establish the extent of the deceased's estate.
- They ensure correct instructions are given to valuers when valuing assets.
- They seek advice about anything of which they are unsure.
- They follow up inconsistencies in information they receive from asset holders, valuers and other people.
- They identify any estimated values included on the form.

If the executors leave the account or return to an agent, they are nevertheless required to check the entries carefully. Merely signing a form completed by an agent is not reasonable care.

The penalty regime identifies three categories of behaviour that can give rise to penalties for an inaccuracy in an account or return:

- The lowest level of culpability, described as 'careless', is where the taxpayer fails to take reasonable care in completing the return.
- The 'middle' level of culpability is 'deliberate but not concealed' where the return is wrong and it results from the deliberate action of the taxpayer, but the taxpayer makes no arrangements to conceal the inaccuracy.
- Finally, the most serious level of wrongdoing is that which is 'deliberate and concealed' where the taxpayer has deliberately sent in a wrong return and deliberately tries to conceal the parts of the return that are wrong, for example by submitting false evidence in support of false figures.

When it turns out that a return was inaccurate, the taxpayer will be treated as careless, even though he may not have been at the time of the return if he discovers the inaccuracy some time later and does not take reasonable steps to inform HMRC.

In this summary of the law, the word 'return' has been used but the rules apply in the much wider context of documents that, whether or not returns, fix the liability to tax.

The level of penalties

6.40 These maximum levels were established by *Finance Act 2007, Sch 24*, but their scope was extended by *Finance Act 2008*:

- The 30% rate: a penalty of 30% of the potential lost revenue applies where the taxpayer was careless.
- The 70% rate: a penalty of 70% applies where the action of the taxpayer was deliberate but not concealed.
- The 100% rate: a penalty of 100% applies where the action of the taxpayer was deliberate and concealed. This can apply in two circumstances. Under *Finance Act 2007, Sch 24, para 4(C)* the full penalty could apply to 'deliberate and concealed action'. That penalty still stands but is extended to cover 'third party' acts such as might apply to the family of Philip in **Example 6.6** above. The collection of tax lost through third-party inaccuracy was extended by *Finance Act 2008,* so that it includes any inaccuracy that results from the supply of false information or the withholding of information.

The penalty regime in *Finance Act 2007, Sch 24* did not previously apply to IHT, so specialists in that area of practice may not have become familiar with the scheme of that schedule. In a situation where there are various errors, such as could easily apply in the administration of an estate, careless inaccuracies are corrected before deliberate inaccuracies; and deliberate but not concealed inaccuracies are corrected before deliberate and concealed inaccuracies. In calculating the lost tax, account is taken of any overstatement in any document given by the taxpayer that relates to the same tax period.

The case of *Timothy Clayton Hutchings v HMRC* [2015] UKFTT 9 (TC) is a stark lesson in the manner in which the penalties operate and it highlights HMRC's significantly tougher approach. In that case, the taxpayer deliberately withheld information relating to a substantial gift of an offshore bank account and as the disclosure was prompted, a hefty penalty of 35% was imposed on the taxpayer.

Example 6.7—Penalties: too casual an approach to compliance

Henry, a widower whose late wife had used her nil rate band died on 1 January 2016, leaving a house, a share in an investment partnership and personal effects. There were no liabilities, Henry having taken out funeral costs insurance. His son John as sole executor knew that Henry had always used his annual exemption and was aware of lump-sum gifts of £70,000. John completed IHT400 thus:

	£
House	313,000
Partnership share	100,000
Personal effects	12,000
Gifts	70,000
	495,000
Less nil rate band	325,000
Taxable	170,000
Tax liability	68,000

John had been in a hurry to get a grant of Confirmation, anxious to catch the property market before his father's house fell in value. He did not get a professional valuation but he did not use the 'estimates' box in the return as he thought he knew property prices in the area. Actually, it turned out that an area of land to the side of the house had realistic prospect of development and that, if sold separately, with the benefit of planning permission, it might realise £100,000 without taking any value off the house. Applying the valuation rule in *Prosser v IRC*, this added £25,000 to the estate and £10,000 to the tax liability.

It also transpired that the investment partnership had made certain losses in respect of which it was entitled to a refund of tax, so £20,000 would be added to the value of the estate when the returns were settled. John told HMRC as soon as he had the right figures. No business relief was available in respect of the investment partnership, so this added £8,000 to the eventual liability.

John knew that his father had given his sister, Sarah, the family yacht, some eight or nine years before his death. It had then been worth £30,000. John had not the slightest interest in sailing and had never been concerned with the arrangement between his father and his sister, and assumed that the gift need not be disclosed because it was outside the seven-year period. He did know that his father continued to sail with his daughter, but it never occurred to him that that might constitute a reservation of benefit out of the gift within *Revenue Interpretation 55*. Sarah complained occasionally that she had to bear all the costs of running the boat whilst her work as a matrimonial lawyer prevented her from taking time off to sail, whereas her father in retirement made extensive use of the vessel. When the reservation of benefit point was raised in correspondence on another aspect of the estate, John immediately realised that there was a problem and disclosed the gift.

John was less forthcoming about the cheques that he had signed in his capacity as attorney for his father. For the last four years of his father's life, acting under a continuing power of attorney, John had regularly drawn off £1,000 per month into a separate account and had used the money towards the cost of his children's education. He thought that the gifts would be covered by *IHTA 1984, s 21* relief for normal and reasonable expenditure of the deceased. It was only when HMRC called for copy bank statements that the £48,000 of gifts were discovered and it was established that Henry had insufficient income for *s 21* to apply. Adding the gifts back to the estate increased the tax liability by £19,200.

The valuation error was careless. It was held in *Robertson v CIR* [2002] STC (SCD) 182 that a material understatement of value did not trigger penalties, but in that case the executor had indicated in the return that the value was an estimate and was therefore, in *Robertson v CIR (Number 2)* [2002] SSCD 242, able to recover handsomely from HMRC. In the present case, a penalty of up to £3,000 arises because the error is not simply the difference between one person's view of a value and that of another; there is a fundamental error in the basis of valuation which would have been avoided if John had been in less of a hurry and had obtained a proper valuation in the first place.

The restatement of value of the partnership interest probably does not attract a penalty at all. John showed the value of the partnership as he understood it at the date of death, and it is only after some negotiation with another branch of HMRC that the tax refund materialises. John has disclosed the change as soon as aware of it, so it is simply a case of paying the tax and interest, but not a penalty.

John did not disclose the reservation of benefit in connection with the boat, which was careless because he should have thought about the issue and the form of the return contains ample prompts on the issue. Sarah has made no secret of the fact that her father has had some benefit from the boat that he has given away, so she is not to blame. Tax is chargeable subject to negotiation as to value, remembering the option of HMRC to treat the gift as a chargeable transfer or to treat it as part of the estate at death. Where an asset falls in value, HMRC will probably prefer to treat the gift as a failed PET and tax the value at the time of the gift. On that basis, there is extra tax of £12,000 to find and the penalty could be another £4,000, subject as below.

In relation to the school fees, John's action is deliberate and concealed, so the penalty (subject to the observations below) is 100% of the tax: an extra £19,200.

Finance Act 2007, Sch 24, para 6 requires an initial calculation of the careless inaccuracies, here the £10,000 on the valuation issue and possibly the £8,000 in respect of the business. Next in gravity comes the £12,000 on the boat and finally the £19,200 on the school fees. As to mitigation, see below.

Strengthening civil deterrents for offshore tax avoidance

6.41 The offshore penalty regime strengthens existing penalties for:

- failure to notify;
- inaccuracy on a return; and
- failure to file a return in time.

There are three penalty levels, which depend on the territory in which the income or gain arises:

- Where the income or gain arises in a territory in 'Category 1' (which includes most of Europe and the United States), the penalty regime will be the same as under the existing legislation and the maximum penalty is 100% of the tax.
- Where the income or gain arises in a territory in 'Category 2', the penalty rate will be 1.5 times that in the existing legislation, up to 150% of tax.
- Where the income or gain arises in a territory in 'Category 3', the penalty rate will be double that in the existing legislation, up to 200% of tax.

There are no penalties for those who have taken reasonable care or have a reasonable excuse for the failure to notify taxable income and gains.

HMRC have announced that consultation will take place on further proposals for a 'strict liability' rule for offshore under-declarations which would provide:

- an automatic assumption of tax evasion without the need to establish fraud;
- enhanced penalties linked to the value of the overseas asset rather than the tax involved;
- new and wider penalties to include criminal sanctions aimed at 'enablers' of tax evasion and organisations who facilitate or fail to prevent such evasion.

The *Finance Act 2015* effective from 26 March 2015, included the proposals as announced in the Autumn 2014 Budget to extend the offshore penalty regime to:

- include IHT;
- apply to domestic offences where the proceeds of UK non-compliance are hidden offshore;
- update the territorial classification system; and
- introduce a new aggravated penalty, up to a further 50% of tax lost, for moving hidden funds to circumvent international tax transparency agreements.

However, *Finance Act 2015* also increased the level of penalties for offshore tax avoidance from 30% to 37.5%, 70% to 87.5% and 100% to 125% respectively (see 6.40 above) and introduced a new country category known as 'category 0'. This will include countries previously in category 1 that have since adopted the common reporting standard (CRS), a process by which countries automatically provide to HMRC annual information on offshore bank accounts, investments and structures. Irregularities relating to category 0 countries will be liable to the normal penalty regime associated with domestic misdemeanours. For IHT purposes, the territory where the assets are situated immediately after the transfer of value that gives rise to the IHT is the determinant for the relevant categories 0 to 3. If more than one territory is involved in an offshore transfer the penalty is determined by reference to the territory in the highest category, thus maximising the penalty.

As well as strengthening existing penalties, *Finance Act 2015*, now includes fresh legislation, applicable from 27 March 2015, which extends to include IHT (as well as the other taxes) and focuses on assets that are moved from a 'specified territory' to a 'non-specified territory'. A list of relevant jurisdictions has not yet been published but this will be addressed in a later statutory instrument. There are three conditions for the new penalty regime to apply:

1 A penalty for deliberate behaviour is due, known as the 'original penalty'.

2 There is a 'relevant offshore asset move' after the 'relevant time'.

3 The main purpose of the offshore asset move, or at least one of them, is to prevent or delay HMRC discovering the asset.

Where:

- A relevant offshore asset move is triggered where the person, in reality, remains the beneficial owner of the asset and:
  - the asset is moved from a specified to a non-specified territory;

- the owner ceases to be resident in a specified territory and becomes resident in a non-specified territory;
- ownership appears to change.

The relevant time for IHT purposes is when the liability for the tax first arises.

The penalty itself is a flat rate of 50% of the original penalty, but it is nonetheless regarded as an entirely separate penalty to which the normal rules apply regarding HMRC's ability to assess, time limits and appeals etc.

Reduction in penalties for disclosure

6.42 The purpose behind *Finance Act 2007, Sch 24, para 9* is to set bands of penalties and to allow some reduction within the band but, which is an important departure from previous practice, not total reduction in the more serious cases. *Paras 9* to *12* of *Sch 24* were updated by *Finance Act 2008*. There are reductions in penalties where a person, including a third party, discloses inaccuracy in a tax document. This may be by simply telling HMRC about the situation; or giving HMRC reasonable help to quantify the inaccuracy; or giving HMRC access to records to enable the inaccuracy to be corrected.

Where the disclosure is made by the taxpayer at a time when he has no reason to believe that HMRC have discovered or are about to discover the inaccuracy, that disclosure is classified as 'un-prompted'. The effect of this is that an unprompted disclosure of a careless error can reduce the penalty to nil. Applying the example of John's estate, the revaluation of the business following the obtaining of the tax refund, if disclosed promptly, may avoid a penalty entirely.

Mitigation of 30% penalties

6.43 Where the disclosure is prompted, a careless error, attracting a penalty of 30%, may be reduced, but not below 15%. The error by John in valuing his father's house was careless – see **Example 6.7** above. If he had notified HMRC as soon as he discovered that the property was significantly more valuable than he thought, that might be treated as an unprompted disclosure. However, the mechanism of valuation in deceased estates relies on disclosure which in turn includes answering the question whether the property is to be offered for sale. The value of the property is routinely referred to the Valuation Office. If it is known that a property is to be sold within a reasonably short time of the death, then it is quite common for the gross sale proceeds to be taken as the value at the date of death. There is scope for arguing that John, in **Example 6.7** above, merely put forward an opinion of the value of the property that turned out to be wrong and that he was, in effect, disclosing as part of the estate whatever price would eventually be received on sale, on the basis that the sale price would be substituted for the valuation. However, that is a weak argument and by his carelessness John has certainly risked a penalty of at least £1,500.

Mitigation of 70% penalties

6.44 Where the action of the taxpayer was deliberate but not concealed the starting point for penalties is 70% but it may be reduced to a minimum of 20% (*Finance Act 2007, Sch 24, para 10(3)*). The mitigation will depend on the 'quality' of the disclosure, which is defined by *Finance Act 2007, Sch 24, para 9(3)* as including timing, nature and extent.

In the case of Henry's estate in the **Example 6.7** above the failure to disclose the gift with reservation was careless; however it was not actually concealed but neither was it unprompted. It arose only from the detailed correspondence on the administration of the estate. Had John volunteered details of the gift, the penalty could have been reduced to 20% but under *Finance Act 2007, Sch 24, para 10(4)* a penalty that is otherwise chargeable at 70% cannot be reduced below 35%. On the face of it, therefore, John is at risk of a penalty of £4,200 in respect of the boat.

Mitigation of 100% penalties

6.45 Similar, but sharper rules apply to errors that fall into the 100% regime. Where disclosure is unprompted the minimum penalty is 30%, but where the disclosure arises only after HMRC have raised questions the penalty cannot be less than 50%. In relation to the undisclosed, unauthorised transfers to pay school fees from Henry's estate John has done nothing much to help HMRC. He did finally supply copies of his father's bank statements, but only after he had been asked a couple of times. He attempted to 'explain away' the payments. He will be lucky to escape with a penalty of much less than £18,000.

There is facility for 'special reduction' of a penalty in *Finance Act 2007, Sch 24, para 11* if HMRC think it right to reduce a penalty because of 'special circumstances', but that does not include inability to pay, nor the fact that the increased liability of one taxpayer may reduce the liability of another.

There is a 100% cap on penalties, introduced by *Finance Act 2008,* which inserts the limitation into *Finance Act 2007, Sch 24, para 12*. This is necessary where, for example, a penalty could be charged against both the taxpayer and a third party. Thus, in the example of Henry's estate, in **Example 6.7** above, if Sarah had kept quiet about her father's use of the boat and John had been careless about the issue of reservation of benefit, a penalty could apply to both of them but either way it would not exceed 100% of the tax in issue.

Failure to file

6.46 A penalty of £100 applies for failure to deliver an account on time, and is now regularly claimed (*s 245(2)*). A further penalty of not more than £60 per day may be claimed, though this is much less common. This is per day of default running from the day on which the failure to deliver the account has been declared as a default, either by a court or by the Special Commissioners. The daily charge runs up to the day on which the account is delivered. Usually, HMRC will give notice of an action to seek penalties so the taxpayer has one last chance to comply. If an account is delivered more than six months after the due date but before HMRC have taken proceedings before the tribunal the penalty is increased to £200. If the account is delivered more than 12 months after the due date a penalty of up to £3,000 may be charged.

The penalty is not imposed where the taxpayer can show reasonable excuse. The procedure involves the simple completion of a form setting out the circumstances, but the penalty will be charged unless the taxpayer delivers the account without unreasonable delay after the excuse has ceased: see *s 245(7)*. The mere fact that the estate is complicated is not itself a factor: there must be some other element.

Example 6.8—Late filing of return

Josiah's estate comprised his many business interests, investments and properties, all in the UK. His will appointed as executors his daughter, who had worked in the businesses with her father; and his friend, who was qualified as a registered trust and estate practitioner. Josiah died on 1 September 2015 and the normal filing date under *IHTA 1984, s 216(6)(a)* for form IHT400 was therefore 12 months from the end of the 'death month' ie 30 September 2016.

The account was late. It seemed for a time that, by a codicil, Josiah's estranged wife might be appointed executrix, but the difficulty was resolved by 7 May 2016 without her having to act. Had she become an executrix, she could have argued, under the 'three-month' rule in *s 216(6)(a)*, that time did not run against her until appointed, but: (a) she did not act anyway; and (b) the executors as a body are jointly liable for penalties, so the daughter and friend had no excuse. The size and complication of the estate are not excuses *per se*: the daughter knew all about the assets and the practitioner had the specialist knowledge to deal with the account.

Where the failure relates to non-resident trustees the risk is perceived to be higher and the penalties greater. The rules as to disclosure are in *s 218* and failure to make a return may trigger a penalty of up to £300 plus £60 per day of default (*s 245A*).

Penalties will not be claimed from a deceased person who had not been compliant, but that in no way exonerates delinquent personal representatives as confirmed in HMRC Enquiry Manual, EM1395 which states: 'Where an error or failure offence has occurred after the date of death in respect of the deceased's estate and this offence is attributable to the personal representatives you should seek to impose a penalty on the personal representatives.' The Compliance Handbook, at CH402000 also adds:

> 'If a penalty assessment, raised prior to a person's death, remains under appeal then negotiations to conclude any appeal must continue with personal representatives.'

Incorrect returns

6.47 The penalties for failure to make returns are modest by comparison with those where incorrect information is supplied. Under *s 247(4)*, any person assisting in the production of an account that he knows to be incorrect is liable to a penalty of up to £3,000. The person who actually makes the return wrongly may be liable for a penalty of up to 100% of the tax in issue, where the inaccuracy is both deliberate and concealed. If that person makes the return, but is not himself liable for the tax he may still be liable to a penalty of up to £3,000.

Errors are prevalent in completing form IHT404 (joint property) with approximately 10% of IHT return forms IHT400 meriting detailed examination. Form IHT407 (chattels) and IHT405 (property) are also often a fruitful source of enquiry for HMRC.

6.48 It is in the nature of executry work that the full story does not emerge immediately but it is drawn together over time. That is recognised (see **6.15** above) in the provisions for the use of estimates but it is also recognised by HMRC in connection with the delivery of an account which is later found to be incorrect. In such cases errors must be corrected without 'unreasonable delay' (see *ss 217* and *248(1)*) otherwise the person liable to deliver the account will suffer the same penalty as someone who delivers an account negligently. Correction may be made on form C4(S) but, if there are a number of small changes and the overall value is not significant, the changes can be dealt with more swiftly by correspondence.

The pre-*Finance Act 2007* rules as to calculation and mitigation of penalties allow practitioners to negotiate mitigation of the penalty by up to 30% for disclosure, up to 40% for co-operation and up to 40% in respect of seriousness (ie size and gravity), but all that changes for inaccuracies in returns for periods covered by the new rules described in this chapter.

Interest

6.49 Traditionally, executry lawyers never worried much about interest on late paid IHT. It was virtually regarded as a normal expense of administration and the work would be done as the works schedule permitted. Until the changes in *Finance Act 2009 (s 101, Sch 53)* the level at which interest was charged on IHT was less than the charge in respect of other taxes. That helped advisers, but personal representatives and beneficiaries are now much less tolerant of this easy-going attitude on the part of lawyers. Clients are aware of the due dates and expect lawyers to administer estates more promptly to mitigate the burden of interest and in many cases it can be avoided by the use of the direct payment scheme mentioned at **6.35** above. Under *Finance Act 2009, s 101(1)* the rate applies to any tax, so the rate of interest for IHT is aligned with that for other taxes and will track Bank of England Base Rate. The new rules also set the late payment start dates for certain IHT instalments (ie under *IHTA 1984, ss 227, 229*). In consultation the professional bodies argued that the same rate should apply to repayments as to late payments, but the government have rejected that idea.

Interest is inevitable where payment of the tax itself is made by instalments on certain designated assets (see **6.31**). Where tax and interest arise on death, *s 233(1)(b)* charges interest from the day after the end of six months running from the end of the month in which the death occurred but there are special rules in relation to specialised forms of property. Interest charged by HMRC is not allowable as a deduction in calculating any income profits or losses for any tax purposes.

That, however, is different from the situation where the executors have taken out a loan specifically in order to pay IHT (ie where they have not used the direct payment scheme). Where a specific loan account is taken out (not merely an overdraft) the interest paid for the first year may be deductible in calculating the income tax liability of the executors on untaxed estate income arising during the administration period (*ITA 2007, s 403*). This facility relates only to the initial loan to fund the tax payable before a grant of Confirmation can be issued and does not relate to any further loans taken out by the personal representatives at any other time.

Suspension of penalties

6.50 The new penalty regime includes an 'enabling' facility to encourage better compliance, where the error in a return is careless, but results from a faulty procedure or misunderstanding on the part of the taxpayer that can be put right. Penalties can be suspended where, by notice under *Finance Act 2007, Sch 24, para 14*, HMRC specify the action to be taken and the period for which it must be taken. This is unlikely to apply to family members who act as executor.

Shifting the blame onto the adviser

6.51 It has long been the complaint of taxpayers that 'I left it to the accountant/solicitor/adviser to get the forms right.' The prevalent reluctance of taxpayers either to pay tax or to give sufficient time to form filling suggests that sometimes such a complaint is unjustified, but *Finance Act 2007, Sch 24, para 18(3)* only exonerates the taxpayer who can show that he took reasonable care to avoid inaccuracy or unreasonable failure.

Penalties for late payment

6.52 *Finance Act 2009, s 106, Sch 56* introduced a more sophisticated penalty regime to tackle the issue of late payment. No doubt it will mainly affect 'ordinary' taxpayers more than trusts and estates, but the regime will be tougher. Where, as for IHT, the obligation to file is occasional rather than annual, the regime will provide:

- 5% of the tax penalty one month after the filing date;
- 5% more at six months;
- 5% more at 12 months; but
- suspension where the taxpayer agrees an arrangement for time to pay (though that does not apply to IHT, being inappropriate).

For a tax on capital, where there may be little liquidity, these are potentially serious amounts of extra money to find. The penalty provisions have already been introduced in respect of certain other taxes, but not for IHT purposes at the time of writing.

Penalties for late filing

6.53 *Finance Act 2009, s 105, Sch 55* applies penalties simply for late filing. The new regime already applies to certain taxes, but is now extended to IHT thus:

- £100 straight after the due date;
- £10 for each day that the failure to submit a return continues, for up to 90 days (but only if HMRC 'decide' that the penalty should be payable and issue a notice to that effect;

- 5% of the tax due (or £300, if greater) for prolonged failure (ie at six months);
- 5% more (or £300, if greater) at 12 months;
- 70% of the tax due where a person fails to submit a return for over 12 months and has deliberately withheld information that HMRC need to assess the tax due; and
- 100% where there has been concealment.

The latter two tax-based penalties are subject to potential reduction for disclosure. It is not uncommon for family to be so affected by bereavement that there is a delay before the formalities of Confirmation are even approached, let alone tackled. Where the estate is complex, these new penalties in effect force the family to begin the task of gathering information with what may feel like unseemly haste.

TIME LIMITS FOR HMRC ASSESSMENTS

6.54 *Finance Act 2009, s 99* and *sch S51* introduced extended powers for HMRC to issue assessment notices in relation to IHT matters.

They are as follows:

	IHT (account and payment submitted)	*IHT (no account and payment submitted)*
Careless loss of tax	6 years	20 years
Deliberate loss of tax	20 years	No limit
Other reason	4 years	20 years

If there is deliberate loss of tax and no account and payment has been submitted the legislation is silent on time limits for an assessment notice. It therefore is implied that there is no time limit.

RECORD KEEPING

6.55 The absence of records can be a major headache for personal representatives. Specific instances have already been described at **6.8** where the executors have a duty to notify HMRC of events of which they have had no personal knowledge before taking office. It is of course good practice for any person who has an estate that may on his death become taxable to maintain personal records of gifts etc in a form that will be intelligible to the personal representatives. That has become more important as many more transfers have been treated as chargeable since 22 March 2006.

Capital taxation long enjoyed a separate and more relaxed compliance regime than now applies, for example under self-assessment. However, prior to the changes introduced in *FA 2008* (*s 113* and *Sch 36*), the information-gathering powers of HMRC were just as strict as the corresponding provisions under self-assessment. There were previously powers to require information under *s 219*, to call for documents under *s 219A* and to inspect property under *s 220*. However, the information and inspection powers in *FA 2008, Sch 36* were extended to apply for IHT purposes by *FA 2009* (*s 96* and *Sch 48*), with effect from 1 April 2010.

Practitioners will usually keep executry and trust files for a very long time. In relation to trusts the papers will be kept because of the ongoing nature of the matter and because of the record-keeping requirements under self-assessment. In relation to estates, it is not uncommon that queries will arise some time later, for example where assets have been appropriated to beneficiaries *in specie* and where the IHT value has not been notified to the beneficiary or, if it has, the beneficiary has lost the record. The value for tax purposes at which the beneficiary acquired the asset will normally be its IHT value under the rule in *TCGA 1992, s 274* (where the value was 'ascertained' for IHT).

Finance Act 2008, Sch 37 contains new obligations as to record keeping, but they do not affect IHT. There were proposals for this in the initial consultation, but the professions doubted the validity of a proposal for documents to be kept for two years from the date of preparation of returns because (a) the time limit did not sit easily with others; and (b) most papers were retained anyway, so there was no need to legislate. Budget Note 89 to the Budget 2009 confirmed that in the light of these comments the government would not pursue the idea of special record-keeping requirements for IHT, so with the more general IHT rules set out in *ss 254–261* continue to apply.

DETERMINATIONS AND APPEALS

Procedure

6.56 In practice, the issue of a Notice of Determination will rarely come as a surprise to the taxpayer. After the usual examination of a return and correspondence about matters such as value, a disagreement as to treatment will arise where the positions of HMRC and the taxpayer are so far apart that they cannot be reconciled. There is a review procedure, under which the taxpayer may ask for the HMRC file to be passed to a separate officer to consider the issues in dispute: see **6.62** below. This can result in agreement without formal proceedings, so it should be considered in the first instance.

Example 6.9—Progress of a dispute with HMRC (I)

John Davis was an engineer working in the Middle and Far East. At the age of 45 he returned to Scotland and purchased a small farm. Adjoining the house were a range of farm buildings and 50 acres of land which he put to profitable use. He kept sheep and poultry but in later life he discontinued the poultry operation because it was no longer profitable. Age and infirmity eventually forced him to take on help with the flock, which he sold to a neighbour who continued to graze them on his land on an arrangement which, if it had been committed to writing, would have been more like a partnership or contracting agreement than a tenancy or licence. Those farm buildings that had not fallen into disrepair were used partly by his grandson for the repairing of vehicles but otherwise for the management of what remained of the farming business. There was some development value on part of the land.

Following his death his executors claimed that the house, buildings and land were a farm and that agricultural property relief should be available on the entirety. Mindful of the decision in *McCall v Revenue and Customs Commissioners* [2008] STC (SCD) 752, it was agreed that no business property relief would be available, but the claim to agricultural property relief was pursued.

HMRC quoted *Re Antrobus (No 2)* [2005] Lands Tribunal DET/47/2004: buildings used for car repairs are not occupied for the purposes of agriculture. They were willing to allow agricultural property relief on the land, and on one of the farm buildings, but not on the house, nor on the remainder of the property because, in effect, the deceased had given up farming some years before he died. His residence was merely a house with land rather than a farm. Correspondence ensued: see continuation of this example at **6.64** below.

The form of the notice

6.57 There is some latitude: it can include:

- the date of the transfer;
- the value transferred;
- the value of any property to which the value transferred relates;
- the transferor;

- the tax chargeable;
- the person liable to tax or part of it;
- the amount that anyone has overpaid tax and the date from which that overpaid tax carries interest;
- 'any other matter that appears to the Board to be relevant for the purposes of [*IHTA 1984*]'.

The notice specifies a time limit for appeal and the way in which the appeal can be made. Essentially, this makes the taxpayer decide exactly what to appeal against and why. That appeal is covered by *s 222* and must be made within 30 days by notice in writing given to the Board. Since 1 April 2009, appeals have normally proceeded to the First-tier Tax Tribunal.

6.58 Under the new appeals process introduced by the *Tribunals, Courts and Enforcement Act 2007* (only part of which extends to Scotland) there is a primary filter in *rule 23* under which all cases must be allocated to a category, viz:

- default paper;
- basic;
- standard; or
- complex.

The treatment of a 'default paper' appeal

6.59 Within this category will come late returns and fixed percentage surcharges for late payment, so this may affect few IHT situations. There will be a statement of the case, which can include a request for an oral hearing; a reply, which likewise could request a hearing; possibly listing for hearing but otherwise consideration of the papers and a decision.

The treatment of a 'basic' appeal

6.60 'Basic' will include appeals: from penalties; from information notices; for leave to appeal late; to postpone payment of tax pending appeal; or to close an enquiry; so again not really affecting many IHT situations. These will just be listed for hearing without statement of case or reply.

The treatment of a 'standard' appeal

6.61 This is the more likely territory for IHT practitioners, where say such a question as 'is it a farmhouse?' is considered. There will be a statement of case, and at that point the case may be designated as 'complex'. A list of documents must be produced. There may be a case-management hearing but in its absence the case will be listed for hearing. It is likely that many cases that would in the past have gone to the Special Commissioner will follow this route to a hearing.

The treatment of a 'complex' appeal

6.62 These will be rare. They will be treated like standard cases, but may enjoy specific directions before any case management hearing or the hearing itself.

Internal reviews

6.63 A system of 'internal reviews' by HMRC was introduced to coincide with the Tax Tribunals regime from 1 April 2009. Internal reviews broadly provide an alternative means for taxpayers and HMRC to resolve disputes by agreement, rather than through the auspices of a tribunal hearing. If an appeal has been submitted to HMRC and the issue cannot be settled, the taxpayer can notify the appeal to the Tribunal. Alternatively, the taxpayer may ask HMRC to review the point at issue, or HMRC may offer the taxpayer a review (*TMA 1970, s 49A*).

If the taxpayer requests a review, HMRC must respond by stating their original view within 30 days, or possibly a longer period if this is reasonable. If HMRC offer a review, the taxpayer has 30 days in which to accept. Otherwise, HMRC's original view generally stands (*s 49C*).

If a review takes place, HMRC may uphold, vary or cancel their original view of the case, and notify the taxpayer of their conclusion within the following 45 days, or other agreed period (*s 49E*). If HMRC's review is unfavourable, the taxpayer may notify an appeal to the Tribunal within 30 days, or outside this period with the Tribunal's permission.

Appeal

6.64 Appeals may be brought out of time with the consent of HMRC if there is reasonable excuse see *s 223*. Equally, the taxpayer may have second thoughts about the grounds for appeal. The Special Commissioners could, under the old rules, allow him to put forward ideas that were not specified in the notice of appeal provided that the omission was neither wilful nor unreasonable and could then decide the matter.

Under the new system, which is designed to be seen to be totally independent of HMRC, it is likely that that facility will continue, but it is necessary to wait and see how the new tribunals exercise their powers.

Example 6.10—Progress of a dispute with HMRC (II)

[Continuing from **Example 6.9** above]

Following a review of the facts, the executors give up the claim to relief on the farm buildings that were virtually empty but pursue the main claim, relief on the house which has not yet been sold. A meeting is fixed between HMRC, the Valuation Office, the valuer acting for the executors and the executors themselves. At that meeting the valuers agree the open market value of the farm house, the value of the buildings in respect of which no relief is claimed, and without prejudice to the dispute also agree the value of the house for the purposes of agricultural property relief. They also agree that, if the arrangement for sheep farming really was a partnership rather than a tenancy, there was enough agricultural land to support the claim that the house was a farmhouse; and that, on that basis, the house was of 'character appropriate'. That just leaves one issue to be decided: quite what was the arrangement between the deceased and his neighbour? On that now hangs the entire claim to APR on the house.

One week later, whilst still under the 'old' regime, HMRC issue the Notice of Determination. One week after that the executors appeal, arguing that the deceased was a farmer to the date of his death. The case is designated a 'standard' appeal because it turns entirely on questions of fact; but see below as to the progress of the matter. See continuation of this example at **6.65**.

Costs

6.65 The main concern of taxpayers, apart from the decision itself, is costs. This is currently the subject of informal consultation, to see if the present arrangements work fairly. Following the introduction of the First-tier and Upper Tax Tribunal regime from 1 April 2009, there are provisions for the award of costs in certain specific circumstances. The rules for the First-tier Tribunal (*The Tribunal Procedure (First-tier Tribunal) (Tax Chamber) Rules, SI 2009/273*) provide for costs if (among other circumstances) a party to the appeal (or their representative) has acted unreasonably in bringing, defending or conducting the proceedings. In addition, if a case falls into the 'complex' category, the taxpayer may effectively 'opt out' of costs or expenses by written request to the Tribunal within 28 days (*rule 10*). The Upper Tribunal Rules also make provision for the award of costs following unreasonable behaviour, but do not include an 'opt out' facility.

Under the previous appeals regime *SI 1994/1811, reg 21* provided, in relation to the old tribunals, that a tribunal might award costs against any party to the proceedings including one who has withdrawn his appeal if that party had acted 'wholly unreasonably'. For an example of this rule applied in favour of the taxpayer, see *Robertson v CIR (No 2)* SpC [2002] SSCD 242 (SpC 3130). The Revenue won, however, against an unreasonable taxpayer in *Phillips v Burrows* SpC [2000] SSCD 112 (SpC 229, 229A).

Costs were an issue in the case of *Wells (Personal Representative of Glowacki (deceased)) v Revenue and customs Commissioners* [2008] STC (SCD) 188, which decided in favour of HMRC that a slightly curiously drafted deed of variation did not have the effect of removing a house from the estate of the deceased by means of a non-chargeable deemed lifetime transfer. In the event, Malcolm Gammie QC as Special Commissioner quashed the determination that was the subject of the appeal but acknowledged, see para 48 of the decision, that the next step would be a further determination, based on his decision in the instant case. He ruled that neither party had acted unreasonably and that he could therefore make no order as to costs.

No order for costs is made without giving that party a chance to make representations. The tribunal can order one party to pay all the costs of the other. If not agreed they are taxed in the county courts like county court costs. There are special rules in Scotland.

The Special Commissioner appeal procedure has in the past been helpful both to HMRC and to the profession. It was very appropriate in deciding how the law should be applied in particular circumstances where the law was unclear. Strictly speaking, the decision of a Special Commissioner bound neither him in a subsequent case nor any other commissioner nor any court. However, the costs of an appeal are such that taxpayers, and no doubt HMRC and the new tribunals, will be guided by previous decisions of the Special Commissioners where the facts of the current case are broadly similar to one that has already been decided.

Do the changes represent a better way?

6.66 Classification of cases as 'default paper' or as 'basic' should allow for cheaper decisions. There is virtually no risk that precedents will be set, whether good or doubtful.

HMRC hope that their introduction of the internal review process mentioned above will reduce the number of disputes that go to appeal. The review will be done 'at a distance from caseworkers', something no doubt harder to achieve within the fairly narrow compass of IHT officers. Taxpayers can appeal from what they see as an unsatisfactory review.

Example 6.11—Progress of a dispute with HMRC (III)

Continuing from **Example 6.10** above,

The executors correspond with HMRC to identify the issues that are relevant to the hearing and, where possible, to agree the facts of the case. The executors obtain a proof of evidence from the neighbour and research the financial transactions between the deceased and the neighbour. It turns out that a diligent junior employee of the accountants had attended a meeting between the deceased and the neighbour some time previously, at which the basis of the farming arrangements was discussed. Prompted by the employee, a contemporaneous note was made of the arrangement, initialled by both parties and the accountant!

This shows that in fact the deceased remained the main decision maker, that he was responsible for various aspects of management of the flock and that the neighbour provided occasional help when required.

The tax in issue is not substantial. There is an internal review by the dedicated HMRC review team, whose decision can bind their case workers. After discussion between the executors and HMRC the matter is compromised on terms that require the taxpayer to pay some money, but not as much as tax on the entire farmhouse.

Chapter 7

Trusts: interest in possession

SIGNPOSTS

- **Substance v form** – The formal title of an interest in possession can be challenged in light of the action or indeed lack of action, by the trustees. This is particularly relevant where the main trust asset is the whole or a share of the former home (see **7.1–7.6**).
- **The old-style trust interest** – The full impact of the *Finance Act 2006* trust reforms must be considered in the context of any IHT planning routine involving variation or termination of an established (qualifying) pre-22 March 2006 interest in possession or Accumulation & Maintenance trust (see **7.10–7.13** and **7.27**).
- **The post-*Finance Act 2006* trust interest** – The trust reforms principally affect the IHT code with a beneficial knock-on effect for CGT – the income tax treatment remains unaffected. The current categories and restrictive use of the IPDI, BMT and 18-to-25 must be distinguished from their predecessors (see **7.7–7.10**; **7.19–7.21**; **7.31**).
- **Reversionary interests** – The penal anti-avoidance rules can produce costly and unintended results for the reversionary and purchased interests (see **7.22–7.26**).
- **Excluded property** – The application of the rules can still work in the taxpayer's favour but great care must be taken to avoid the not so obvious pitfalls (see **7.32–7.35**).

IHT TREATMENT

The old law: how an interest in possession was taxed

7.1 The 'old law' refers to the position that applied before the changes introduced in *Finance Act 2006*.

IHTA 1984, s 49 treated a person who was entitled to an interest in possession in settled property as if that person was beneficially entitled to the property in which that interest subsisted. This had IHT consequences (particularly on division of a fund between the liferenter and the beneficiaries for whom the fund was to be held in fee,) that were difficult to explain to the lay client. One illustration of the difficulty is *Executors of Patch deceased* [2007] SpC 600, which is reviewed at **13.50.** The issue of the existence of an interest in possession (such term to include an Immediate Post Death Interest (IPDI)) is frequently litigated.

Note: All statutory references in this chapter are to *IHTA 1984* unless otherwise stated.

Example 7.1—Half share of a house in a trust

Chris and Les, who were married to each other, owned their matrimonial home as tenants in common in equal shares. Each made a will leaving their half share in the house to their adult children without any restriction on use or alienation in the hope that there would be no interest in possession in that half share by the surviving spouse given that the latter would be living there by virtue of their own half share. It was intended that the value of the gift might use all or part of the nil rate band of the first spouse to die (Note: the benefit of this tax planning routine has been largely eroded by the introduction of the transferable nil rate band effective from 9 October 2007– see **Chapter 13** for existing schemes and **Chapter 14** for the position going forward).

Whilst there is no case directly in point, the robust view is that there is no interest in possession by the surviving spouse in the half house owned by the children as the former's continued occupation is by virtue of their own half share. The downside is that the CGT principal private residence relief is not available on the children's share if the house is later sold at a profit.

Of course, in Scotland, any owner of a pro indivisio share of a heritable property has a right to occupy the whole and apply to the courts for an action of division and sale if agreement cannot be reached.

7.2

Focus

Exercise of trustees' discretion to permit beneficiary occupation of a trust property does not necessarily create an interest in possession.

In *IRC v Lloyds Private Banking Ltd* [1998] STC 559, considered further at **15.46**, a mother gave her share in the house to her daughter but contrary to the example above, out of natural caution the will contained provisions restricting the daughter from disposing of that half share in the house during the father's lifetime. The daughter successfully argued before the Special Commissioner that her father did not gain significant advantage from the will because he was now responsible for all the outgoings instead of only half as before. However, on appeal, the High Court held that the father had, during widowhood, enjoyed the exclusive use of the mother's half share in the house and therefore had an interest in possession in it, thereby nullifying the intended tax advantage.

Interpretation of the law in *Judge v HMRC*

7.3 In *Judge (personal representatives of Walden deceased) v Revenue and Customs Comrs* [2005] SSCD 863 (SpC 506), the Special Commissioner had to consider a badly drawn will. The case, which is analysed in more detail at **15.38**, is of particular interest because it reviews several important and practical issues. The material part of the will gave an interest in a property:

> '...free of tax ... upon trust with the consent in writing of my wife during her lifetime to sell the same with full power to postpone the sale for so long as they shall in their absolute discretion think fit ... and I declare my trustees during the lifetime of my wife to permit her to have the use and enjoyment of the said property for such period or periods as they shall in their absolute discretion think fit pending postponement of sale she paying the rates taxes and other outgoings and keeping the same in good repair and insured against fire to the full value thereof...'.

7.4 The question posed was did this give the widow an interest in possession? Clearly she had a substantial economic interest because she could effectively restrict sale. On her death her executors considered that the widow did not have an interest in possession as her interest could have been terminated at any time by the trustees and thus they concluded that the property was held on discretionary trust.

The Commissioner agreed.

Had the trustees required the widow to vacate, they still could not have sold the house but they could have perhaps let it. The Commissioner disregarded the external evidence of the way that the advisers had treated the trust and looked only at the (unsatisfactory) terms of the will, inserting one or two words to complete its sense but giving effect to the intention of the testator as expressed in the terms of the whole will. There was nothing to go on as far as extrinsic evidence of the intentions of the testator was concerned.

7.5 An 'interest in possession' was defined adopting the tests in *Gartside v IRC* [1968] AC 553 and in *Pearson v IRC* [1980] STC 318. In *Pearson* it was described as '...a present right to the present enjoyment...' of something. Later cases such as *Woodhall (Woodhall's Representative) v IRC* [2000] SSCD 558 (SpC 261) and *Faulkner (Adams Trustee) v IRC* [2001] SSCD 112 (SpC 278) have shown that a right of occupation could constitute an interest in possession. In the *Judge* case the widow's right to occupation could be terminated, so she did not have an interest in possession but it should be carefully noted that the *Judge* case is limited to its specific facts and for that reason it should not be regarded as a blueprint for all cases. In particular it does not indicate whether Statement of Practice 10/79, reviewed below, is good law, nor comment on the effectiveness of the 'debt or charge' scheme – the latter is examined in detail at **15.52**.

One more recent 'finding' of an interest in possession was in *Smith and others v HMRC* [2009] SpC 742, where an account formerly held in the name of the late husband of the deceased had been transferred into the joint name of the son and the deceased. The intended purpose (but never committed to writing) was that the deceased would receive the interest during her life but on her death the capital would belong to the son – the reasoning was that the son helped his parents with both time and money. The account funds were not included in the estate of the deceased but its existence was later notified to HMRC, who issued a Notice of Determination that the executors were liable for IHT on its value. The son was assessed in his separate capacity as both executor and the recipient of the funds. The other executor appealed, partly because he had not received nor benefited from the funds.

The Commissioner found that the account had become settled property before the mother's death, being held for her and for the son in succession within *IHTA 1984, s 43(1)(a)*. As a result, the executors were not liable to IHT on the fund itself, so to that extent their appeal succeeded; but the son was liable as trustee. The executors were liable, however, for additional tax as adjusted for the amount due on the fund itself (ie the increase that resulted from aggregation of the settled fund with the free estate).

This outcome should be contrasted with the decision in *Davies and Rippon v HMRC* [2009] UKFTT 138 (TC) TC00106, where the existence of an interest in possession was asserted but not proved to the satisfaction of Judith Powell, sitting as judge in the First-tier Tribunal. The nature of the case is such that perhaps it is of greater interest to lawyers and will writers than to tax specialists, but it nonetheless establishes a useful reference point. The key facts are set out below.

Mrs Rhona Goodman, the mother of the appellants, was the widow of Geoffrey Goodman, who had died in 1969. Following the death of Mrs Goodman, it was argued that estate duty surviving spouse relief should apply to certain assets, though HMRC considered that they were part of Mrs Goodman's estate for IHT. The taxpayers argued that, by his conduct, Mr Goodman had, in effect, settled certain property on his wife for life, with the fee to his daughters; an alternate argument ran that Mr and Mrs Goodman had executed mutual wills, with the result that property later inherited by Mrs Goodman on her husband's death was held under trust and could not be alienated by her except in accordance with that mutual agreement.

The evidence supported that the wills of husband and wife were similar but not identical. During her widowhood Mrs Goodman formed a friendship with a Mr Dodd but was concerned to protect her daughters' inheritance; she did not spend the capital that she also inherited from Mr Dodd when she survived him.

The judge held that, for the claim to succeed, the appellants must show that the property had been settled and that the surviving spouse must not have been competent to dispose of it. The burden of proof of a secret trust is on those who assert it; see *re Snowden Deceased* [1979] Ch 528. Past evidence is admissible: see *Blackwell v Blackwell* [1929] HL 318. There must be 'clear and satisfactory evidence' to support mutual wills: see *re Cleaver* [1981] 2 All ER 1018. The judge considered the arguments as to a secret trust; and as to mutual wills but found no evidence to support either contention. There was no written trust and accordingly, all the property was taxable as part of Mrs Goodman's free estate.

Statement of Practice 10/79

7.6 Statement of Practice 10/79 has never been tested in court. Put simply, it states that where, pursuant to their powers, trustees of a discretionary trust permit the trust beneficiary to rent trust property or to have non-exclusive occupation of it, that does not create an interest in possession if full rent is paid or even if the tenancy is for less than full consideration. If, in the exercise of a power drawn widely enough, the trustees use that power so as to provide a beneficiary with a permanent home, HMRC will treat that as creating an interest in possession.

In *Judge*, Statement of Practice 10/79 was not in point because the trustees had not exercised any power. In *IRC v Eversden (exors of Greenstock, decd)* [2002] EWHC 1360 (Ch), [2002] STC 1109 there was an opportunity to rely on SP 10/79 which was not taken by the court. *Eversden*, which is discussed at **5.9**, went in favour of the taxpayer but was nullified by *Finance Act 2003, s 185*, which inserted *sub-s (5A)* into *Finance Act 1986, s 102* (the 'gifts with reservation' legislation).

Changes under *Finance Act 2006*

7.7 *Section 156* of the *Finance Act 2006* introduced amendments to *Finance Act 1986, Sch 20,* which changed the IHT treatment of many forms of interests in possession. It had become common, in settlements and even more so in wills, for any life interest to a spouse or civil partner to be subject to overriding powers of appointment. Occasionally, these powers were included for family reasons, such as where, following second marriage, the testator had strong reasons to protect the capital of the fund from the second spouse for the benefit of children of the first marriage. Whilst that might have been unobjectionable, one very common result of the structure was that, during widowhood, the trustees could exercise their powers to terminate the interest in possession and yet allow the widow(er) to continue to live in trust property but not by any right as a beneficiary.

Equally, where a wealthy, divorced man/woman had late in life married a much younger spouse, he/she could effectively use the younger spouse as a 'bridge' for substantial gifts to his/her children. Whilst he/she might not meet the required seven years survival period, giving the new spouse a short-term interest in possession could provide that the indirect gifts to his/her children in fee would likely escape tax assuming that their step-parent would live seven years from the date on which her/his interest in possession ceased. This is specifically countered by *Finance Act 1986, s 102ZA*, though some doubts have been expressed as to whether that section in fact closes all possible loopholes in this area.

7.8 With effect from 22 March 2006 most lifetime interest in possession trusts attract the IHT (and hence CGT) treatment always afforded to discretionary trusts – for IHT purposes the correct term is a 'relevant property' trust. Transitional rules were introduced in respect of pre-March 2006 trusts, most of which applied up to 5 April 2008. This chapter does not attempt to do justice to all the issues that have been raised, particularly since some are unresolved, though *Finance Act 2008, s 140* did contain some amending legislation (see at **7.27** below).

IPDI

7.9 An interest in possession trust created on death will generally continue to be taxed under the old rules by virtue of *s 49A*. This preserves most of the hallmarks of the pre 22 March 2006 treatment in that the spouse or civil partner exemption will continue to be available to shelter life interests under wills.

The conditions of *s 49A* ('Immediate post-death interest' (IPDI)) are as follows:

(1) The settlement must be effected by will or on intestacy.

(2) The liferenter must become beneficially entitled to an immediate interest in possession on the death of the testator or intestate.

(3) The trusts must not currently be for bereaved minors and the interest must not be that of a disabled person.

(4) Condition (3) must have been satisfied at all times since the liferenter became entitled to that interest in possession.

The concept of the IPDI is retained as part of the overall anti-avoidance scheme of *Finance Act 2006*. Thus, if the trustees use overriding powers to terminate the life interest of the spouse or civil partner to create ongoing trusts for adult beneficiaries, that will trigger an IHT charge and the funds will then migrate to the relevant property IHT regime described in **Chapter 8**. The specific target of abuse of 'bridging' was countered by *Finance Act 1986, s 102ZA*. This treats the termination of an interest in possession as a 'gift' by the liferenter, thus bringing the 'gift with reservation rules' into play.

Example 7.2—House in a nil rate trust

Under her will Sarah left her house to a discretionary trust of which her friend John is a member of the class of beneficiaries. Within two years of the death the trustees allow John to occupy the property. That does not automatically give John an interest in possession: it will depend on the facts, as it did in *Judge v HMRC*, reviewed at **7.3–7.5**.

If more than three months but less than 24 months from the date of Sarah's death, the trustees appointed the house to John absolutely, then for IHT purposes alone *s 144* would treat that appointment as effective from Sarah's death and hence as if read back into the will. Equally if they gave John an IPDI within 30 days of Sarah's death that would be effective in the same way but note there is no three-month waiting period for the latter IPDI creation, thus the impact of *Frankland v IRC* [1997] STC 1450 is neatly avoided.

If, however, John was residing in the house before Sarah's death and had just never moved out, but the trustees did nothing and simply allowed the situation to continue, the trustees could not be said to have exercised their powers to create an IPDI.

But consider what if John was a part owner of the house – how could the trustees throw him out? In such a case, HMRC would look carefully and decide the case on its specific facts.

Although the more common case will be that of beneficial ownership of a house which passes into trust under the terms of a will, some property is held within trusts that give a general power of appointment and usually to the tenant for life. The exercise of that power to create an immediate interest in possession can be an IPDI.

Example 7.3—IPDI by default

Ursula's will leaves shares in the family property company to her nephew, Tom and the residue of her estate to her niece Yolande for life, with remainder in fee to her great-nieces. Tom promptly disclaims his gift such that the shares fall back into residue. Yolande's resulting interest in the increased residue is an IPDI.

Example 7.4—Pilot trust

During his lifetime, Hank set up a pilot trust of £100 for his son for life with remainder in fee to the grandchildren. By his will Hank left his estate to that pilot trust. The net estate passing under the will and now held on the trust is an IPDI: it was in effect settled on death, not when the pilot trust was formed (though if it should ever be relevant, the trust began when the £100 went in).

'Old' interests in possession

7.10 Questions arise as to whether an interest in possession that existed before 22 March 2006 (an 'old style' IIP or more correctly qualifying IIP) remains within *s 49(1)*, ie is it treated today in the same way it always was? The issue is whether, by virtue of *s 49(1A)* that old treatment is displaced where the interest in question is one to which the beneficiary first becomes entitled after that date. Is it a new interest? The problem may gradually cease to be relevant but is best understood by illustrative examples.

Example 7.5—'Old' interests in possession: coming of age

A trust was created in 2002 giving Bill, who was born on New Year's Day 1988, the capital if he should attain 25 and income from 18. Bill reaches age 18 on 1 January 2006 and the trustees, in making their return to 5 April

2006, show that for part of the year (the period from New Year's Day 2006) the income has been due to Bill. This situation continues even when Bill reaches age 25 in 2013 – he has no different interest from that held on 22 March 2006: there is only one interest.

It follows that, if he had wished, Bill could have created a 'transitional serial interest' (TSI; see below) in favour of A N Other before 6 October 2008 and could even after then give away his interest which would be treated as a potentially exempt transfer (PET).

Example 7.6—'Old' interests in possession: protected heiress

A trust fund created in the same year (2002) is also held for Bill's twin Celia on terms where, if she attains age 25, the capital is applied for her benefit, but only for life, with remainder in fee for any children she may have.

Celia, like her brother Bill, also has an 'old' IIP achieved at age 18 on New Year's day 2006. In 2018 she will still have an old IIP, even though the particular trust provision under which income is paid to her is actually one that becomes operative only then. This would still be the case if the further trusts were in a separate clause in the trust document: Celia has an old IIP.

Example 7.7—'Old' interests in possession: long delayed enjoyment of the fund

David was 25 early in 2006 and had an established qualifying IIP by 22 March in that year. However, the trust ties up the capital so that, even though David becomes entitled to it at age 40, the trustees can at any time take it away from him by exercising a power of appointment in favour of his younger sister, Emma.

What is David's interest at age 40 in 2021? His qualifying IIP is, in one sense, replaced by a new but precarious capital interest that can be withdrawn at any time. The trust fund is still settled because the trustees could take the capital away. It is a defeasible interest in the capital. *Section 49(1)* still applies: he still has a qualifying IIP.

Example 7.8—Using the TSI facility but still controlling the capital

Frances had a qualifying IIP and once the terms of *Finance Act 2006* became clear she agreed to the creation of a Transitional Serial Interest (TSI) on terms that the fund was to be held to pay the income to her daughter Harriet, now 21, until age 35. At 35, Harriet is not to get the capital outright: there are overriding powers that could take the capital away.

Harriet has a TSI now and will still have a TSI once she is 35.

The common thread running through these examples, which are taken from an exchange of questions and answers between STEP/CIOT and HMRC (available via the STEP website: www.step.org/default.aspx?page=955), is that the interests stem from the original trust document and not from action taken by the trustees at some later point. The parties are not artificially prolonging the trust beyond what was originally provided.

DISPOSAL OF INTEREST IN POSSESSION

The basic rule

7.11 *Section 51(1)* provides that the disposal of an interest in possession by the person who is entitled to it is not the transfer of money/assets but instead is to be treated as the termination of the interest in possession, triggering the provisions of *s 52*. The single exception, see *s 51(2)*, is a disposition for the maintenance of a family member under *s 11* but in practice, claims that dispositions are covered by *s 11* are rare.

The *s 52* charging regime imposes a tax charge on the capital of the fund in which the interest in possession subsisted. If, for example, the person disposing of the interest was entitled to half the income, it is half the trust capital that is taxed. If the liferenter sells his interest for money, the money is then part of his estate and the tax on the fund is reduced by the amount of that money. However, that does not affect the valuation of an interest in fee in the property.

Example 7.9—Partition of a life interest fund

Sally, aged 60, enjoys a life interest under the will of her late husband and on her death the property will pass to her daughter Jane. Given Sally's life expectancy, actuaries determine that the commercial value of her interest is equal to 55% of the fund. Sally and Jane agree to divide the fund equally between them with Jane paying Sally cash equal to 5% by way of equalisation.

The IHT treatment is not what they might expect. Sally and Jane, having read about *s 10*, thought that this was a transaction at open market value and was not a gift at all. *Section 52*, however, treats the entire fund as belonging to Sally and not just the actuarial 55% element. There is therefore a transfer by her to Jane of 45% after taking account of what Jane has paid her (100% less 50% retained by Sally = 50% less 5% purchased by Jane = 45%). This was the very point in issue in *Executors of Patch deceased* [2007] SpC 600: see **13.50**.

Exceptions from charge on disposal

Focus

Finance Act 2006 radically altered the IHT position on the termination of an interest in possession and its impact must be fully understood when considering any trust tax planning routine.

7.12 There are exceptions from the *s 52* charge and these are examined in more detail when considering the 'true' termination, rather than the 'deemed termination', of an interest in possession, but are:

- excluded property (see **7.32** and following below);
- exchange of one interest in possession for another;
- reverter to settlor;
- spouse/civil partner relief.

Under the current rules virtually all post 21 March 2006 lifetime life interests will fail to be treated under the relevant property regime for IHT purposes. Accordingly, *Finance Act 2006, Sch 20, para 15* restricted the application of *s 52* so that the charge is confined to the coming to an end of an interest which is within the *Finance Act 2006* restricted class of favoured life interests (those which fall outside the relevant property regime), namely:

- an IPDI;
- a disabled person's interest (see **Chapter 8**); or
- a transitional serial interest (see **7.27** and **7.29** below).

Similarly, *Finance Act 2006, Sch 20, para 14* amended *s 53* so that tax is no longer chargeable under *s 52* where:

- the tenant for life was entitled to the interest before 22 March 2006;
- that life interest was terminated after that day; and
- immediately before the termination of that life interest, the *s 71A* (bereaved minors) or *s 71D* (18-to-25 trusts) provisions applied to the property in which the interest subsisted.

This is part of the regime that limits favoured life interests to 'simple' life interest for spouses followed by absolute interests for children on attaining the age of 18 (bereaved minors trust) or by short-term follow on trusts that end by age 25 (18-to-25 trust). *Schedule 20, para 14* made consequential amendments where a person becomes entitled to an interest in settled property on or after 22 March 2006 and the interest is not that of a disabled person and therefore not favoured under the current regime.

Finance Act 2010 introduced legislation that contains anti-avoidance measures to combat the exploitation of the rules as to excluded property trusts. This is discussed in greater detail at **7.24** below.

TERMINATION OF INTEREST IN POSSESSION

The old law

7.13 *Section 52* provided for a deemed transfer by the liferenter of the property in which they had an interest in possession. The exceptions from charge on a disposal of a qualifying interest in possession have been noted at **7.12**. There are also exceptions from charge when an interest in possession comes to an end in circumstances where:

- the liferenter becomes absolutely entitled to the property;
- the liferenter obtains some other interest in possession in the property;
- the capital of the fund reverts to the settlor;
- the capital of the fund passes absolutely to the spouse of the settlor; the capital of the fund passes absolutely to the widow or widower of the spouse of the settlor where that settlor has died within two years earlier and the widow or widower is domiciled in the UK.

There are qualifications to these rules in certain specified circumstances: see *s 53(5)–(8)*.

7.14 In addition to the general exceptions from the charge on deemed termination there were, under the old law, other exceptions in *s 54* which broadly mirrored the *s 53* exceptions thus:

- reversion of the fund to the settlor during the lifetime of the settlor – the value of the fund is not to be included as part of the estate of the liferenter;
- the passing of the fund on the death of the liferenter to the UK-domiciled spouse of the settlor absolutely – again, the capital of the fund is to be left out of account through the availability of the spousal exemption;
- the passing of the fund to the UK-domiciled widow or widower of the settlor where the settlor had died less than two years earlier – the capital of the fund is left out of account.

These exceptions are subject to qualification in the (somewhat rare) circumstances provided by *s 53(5)* and *(6)*. The even rarer situation of *commorientes* will also apply here.

Reverter to settlor

> **Focus**
>
> *Finance Act 2006* has negated the benefits previously enjoyed under the reverter to settlor rules.

7.15 This type of settlement has long been popular in appropriate circumstances. At its simplest consider A settled funds on B for life, with remainder to A. There was no IHT charge on B's death if A was still alive, which was logical because the property was returning to its original owner, A. However, this device was often used in relation to the family home or a share in it thus consider A, married to B, left his share of the house to their child, C, absolutely. Following A's death C would settle the share of the house on B for life, with remainder back to C and again there was no IHT charge on B's death if C was still alive, which was logical because the property was returning to its original owner, C. Thus, a share in the house might pass down the generations whilst still being occupied by the surviving parent without being taxed on the second death.

This did not always work for CGT. If the house was sold during B's lifetime, any gain might be sheltered by the principal private residence exemption under *TCGA 1992, s 225*; but if it was unsold at the time it reverted to C there was no tax-free uplift on B's death because of *TCGA 1992, s 73*. To avoid that situation arising, the settlement was drafted so that it did not end on B's death, but the fund passed to C for life with gifts over and powers of appointment of capital. That sidestepped *s 73* and, instead, *TCGA 1992, s 72* gave the desired uplift on B's death.

Finance Act 2006 spoilt this structure. On B's death a relevant property trust will now arise unless, to avoid that, it is arranged that the property is to vest absolutely in C; but if it does the CGT problem revives. The trustees, with the concurrence of the parties, must do their sums. Which is the greater evil, CGT or IHT? Action must be taken whilst B is still alive or it will be too late. These things cannot always be engineered, but a good solution might be to crystallise the gain whilst it is still protected by *TCGA 1992, s 225*. That would be possible if B was willing to move house, perhaps to sheltered accommodation or even to a place offering substantial care but of course practicality must take precedence over tax savings.

There can be no tax-free uplift on B's death although if the trustees leave the ongoing trusts in place, a sale soon after B's death might be substantially sheltered from CGT by *TCGA 1992, s 225*. However, as mentioned above the old IHT exemption secured under the reverter to settlor trust rule cannot apply because a relevant property trust has arisen, but if the funds are promptly appointed out to C, the IHT charge may be moderate, even nil.

There is still one occasion where the CGT uplift may be achieved. This arises under *s 53(4)*, which provides that there is no *s 52* charge on termination of an interest in possession if, on that termination, either the:

- UK-domiciled spouse or civil partner of the settlor; or
- UK-domiciled widow/former civil partner, if the settlor has died

becomes beneficially entitled to the settled property. In these circumstances the property is still in trust, so it is *s 72* that is in point rather than *s 73*; and *s 72(1)(b)* excludes a chargeable gain.

Finance Act 2006, s 80 changed *para 11(9)* and inserted *sub-paras (11)–(13)* into *Finance Act 2004, Sch 15*. *Paragraph 11(12)* prevents relevant property from being treated as comprised in the taxpayer's estate for the purposes of the *para 11(1)* or *para 11(2)* exemptions 'at that subsequent time'. The situation may not often arise and it is accepted that the new rules are difficult to follow.

No qualifying interest in possession trusts can be created post 21 March 2006 (except for disabled persons or in quite specialised circumstances or on death) so maybe the point is merely academic at this moment in time. One specific, but rarefied, problem arises where a settlor interested trust owns a company that in turn owns a residence where a POAT election will cause the assets to be treated as part of the taxpayer's estate. It could bring assets within the IHT net which previously may have been sheltered from IHT exposure under the situs rules.

Some of the heat has now been taken out of the problem as HMRC comment that the words 'at any subsequent time' in *para 11(11)* do not literally mean 'at any later occasion'. Instead this should be interpreted more 'at any later time after value leaves the donor's estate, thereby reducing his estate, but returns to it because property is purchased with that value and the taxpayer has an interest in possession in the property'.

As a result there should be no difficulty where:

- X settled cash on himself before 22 March 2006; or
- Y, being a disabled person, did the same on/after that date,

and in either case, the trustees:

- bought a house for X (or Y, as the case might be) to live in; or
- sold that house and bought another; or
- used some of the proceeds of the house to buy shares, etc.

That leaves only the problem of the discretionary trust that was later appointed onto interest in possession trust. In this latter instance, an election is the only way to avoid POAT.

Anti-avoidance rule

7.16 As will be seen in **Chapter 8**, the creation of a discretionary trust is nearly always a chargeable lifetime transfer and thus elaborate provisions are included to prevent taxpayers deliberately manoeuvring to avoid this charge.

Consider the actions of a taxpayer who had already made substantial chargeable lifetime transfers and now wished to set up a further discretionary trust, but realised that this would trigger an immediate and unacceptable IHT charge. Under the pre-*Finance Act 2006* law without legislative intervention the device employed could see the settlor create a short-term interest in possession trust in favour of a person (the 'poor relation') who still had the full use of their available nil rate band; and thereafter for the fund to be held on full discretionary trusts (the intended aim from the outset). The purpose of this routine would enable the new trust to be chargeable to IHT by reference to the poor relation, under the rules described in **Chapter 8**, and at much lower rates than are otherwise the case.

The language of *ss 54A* and *54B* is obscure and not easily understood at first sight but it is very much designed to frustrate this tactic. *Finance Act 2006, Sch 20, para 16* introduces changes that give effect to the post 21 March 2006 regime.

Use of annual exemption

7.17 Pre-*Finance Act 2006* the release by the liferenter to another of their interest in part of the trust fund was a potentially exempt transfer (PET). Accordingly, if not used elsewhere, the liferenter's annual exemption may be set against this transfer, provided that they notify the trustees that they wish to do so. *Section 57(4)* seems to suggest that such notice should be in some special form but that is misleading and although there was originally a form for this purpose its use has long since been discontinued. All that is currently required is a letter from the life tenant to the trustees indicating that the former has available an annual exemption (or two, as the case of the prior years unused allowance) and that they wish to set it/them against the intended transfer.

Maintenance funds

7.18 There are special provisions where, on the termination of an interest in possession, property passes to a designated maintenance fund. Such a fund is connected with the maintenance of heritage property and use of the relief is, as a consequence, very rare. Notwithstanding, the anti-avoidance measures in *Finance Act 2010*, described at **7.25** below, contain a 'let out' for transfers to maintenance funds.

The law since 22 March 2006

7.19 *Finance Act 2006, Sch 20* redefined the classification of potentially exempt transfers (PETs) made on or after 22 March 2006 so that lifetime transfers which can be PETs are henceforth limited to outright gifts to individuals or gifts into disabled trusts – disabled trusts are those falling within the definition in *s 89.*

This is a fundamental change which must be fully embraced as part of IHT planning through the use of trusts. Effectively all lifetime gifts into trust are now immediately chargeable (disabled trusts excluded) unless covered by exemptions or other pertinent reliefs (ie business property relief). As a result, those trust interests that confer a life interest thus come under the category of an IIP trust and are now within the relevant property regime for IHT purposes. The death of the life tenant no longer triggers a charge to IHT through aggregation with their estate – there is no need as the trust is now within the scheme of periodic and exit charges described in **Chapter 8**. The exceptions are:

- an IPDI;
- a disabled person's interest;
- a transitional serial interest (see **7.27** and **7.29** below).

Termination of IPDI

7.20 The termination of a qualifying IPDI is governed by the normal rules which applied to the old style qualifying interest in possession. Tax is charged under *s 52* on the whole or any part of the fund affected. The same rule applies to a disabled person's interest or, see **7.27** below, to a transitional serial interest.

Under the new rules there is, however, an exception from the *s 52* charge where:

- the interest of a person who was entitled as life tenant before 22 March 2006 now comes to an end; and
- immediately before it does so, the fund is within the new provisions of *s 71A* (trusts for bereaved minors); or
- the fund is within *s 71D* (18-to-25 trusts); see again *Sch 20, para 13*.

Prior to 22 March 2006, accumulation and maintenance trusts for children were (perhaps simplistically) treated by practitioners as if they were within the IHT regime applied to the old interest in possession trusts. That is certainly no longer the case and A&M trusts are therefore examined in detail in **Chapter 8**.

Exceptions from charge under the rules from 22 March 2006

7.21 The exceptions from charge that were noted at **7.12** are now restricted. They apply only where the interest concerned is a disabled person's interest or a transitional serial interest (TSI). A modified version of the exception from charge is now specified by *s 54(2B)* whereby the value of the fund is left out of account in fixing the value of the estate of the life tenant where:

- the life tenant was entitled to the interest in possession on or after 22 March 2006 and dies thereafter; and
- the interest in possession held by the life tenant was an IPDI; and
- the settlor of the IPDI died before the life tenant but less than two years before; and
- on the death of the life tenant the fund passes to their or the settlor's UK-domiciled widow or widower or surviving civil partner.

The anti-avoidance rule noted at **7.15** is adapted so that it applies only to a disabled person's interest or a transitional serial interest.

The rules relating to maintenance funds for heritage property are adapted so as to apply only to an IPDI, a disabled person's interest or a transitional serial interest.

REVERSIONARY AND PURCHASED INTERESTS

The general rule

7.22 The basic rule is that a fee interest is not part of the estate of the person who holds it because for a qualifying interest in possession or later IPDI trusts, it is already treated as part of the estate of the liferenter. However, the market value rule in *s 10*, which would normally exclude a transaction from being a transfer of value, does not apply to an acquired or purchased fee interest. The law has been made a good deal more complicated by anti-avoidance rules introduced by *Finance Act 2010, s 53* and described at **7.24** below.

The rule in *Melville v IRC* and its aftermath

7.23 *Section 55A* was introduced (in *Finance Act 2002*) to counter a perceived abuse in relation to purchased settlement powers. It applies where a person becomes entitled to a 'settlement power' or has the right to exercise a power over a settlement or the ability to restrict such a power. The disposition, by which the taxpayer acquires that power, for money or money's worth, does not qualify for the market value rule in *s 10*, nor can it be treated as exempt by virtue of spouse relief or the reliefs relating to charities and other gifts for public benefit.

The use and retention of settlement powers is less common in UK-based trusts than in trusts for certain non-UK domiciliaries, especially US citizens but even so this is a powerful anti-avoidance provision. The legislation arises out of the decision in favour of the taxpayer in *Melville v IRC* [2001] EWCA Civ 1247, [2001] STC 1271. The case turned upon a scheme involving a gift of a substantial portfolio of securities. A simple outright gift without a trust structure would have triggered an unacceptably large CGT charge but no immediate IHT consequence (by reason of its PET status). In contrast, the transfer to a discretionary trust would have paved the way for CGT holdover but would have triggered an exceptionally large IHT charge (immediate chargeable lifetime transfer). The scheme pivoted on the use of a discretionary trust, enabling the capital gains to be held over but with the trust terms crucially including a power over the settlement for the benefit of the settlor. This power had the effect of devaluing/depressing the chargeable transfer, thus mitigating the IHT charge. The scheme was nullified by *s 47A*, which defined 'settlement power', and by *s 55A*, which addressed the scheme itself.

Purchase of interests in trusts

7.24 *Finance Act 2010, s 52* inserted *s 81A* into *IHTA 1984* with the sole intention of preventing perceived abuse of trusts. Where a person:

- transfers property into a trust in which they or a spouse or civil partner has a future interest in reversion; or
- buys a reversionary interest,

the new legislation imposes an IHT charge when that future interest comes to an end and the property vests.

The guidance notes to the legislation employ the term 'future interest' interchangeably with 'reversionary interest' for fee interests. When the interest comes to an end and the person becomes actually entitled to the trust interest there is a charge if that person:

- actually bought the reversionary interest; or
- is the settlor of the trust or the spouse or civil partner of the settlor and becomes entitled to the reversionary interest.

By *s 81A(2)*, the gift of a reversionary interest in this situation as defined in *s 81A(1)* is a chargeable lifetime transfer, not a PET. These rules are effective as from 9 December 2009, being the date of the Pre-Budget Report which first announced the rules. The rationale for the new legislation is that neither a purchased reversionary interest nor a settlor's reversionary interest in trust property is excluded property. Each forms part of a person's estate whereas since *Finance Act 2006* an interest in possession does not normally form part of his estate by virtue of *s 5(1A)*. A possible IHT saving could arise on the vesting of an interest in possession because the reversionary interest was no longer held. As a result of the changes it will no longer be possible to avoid an IHT charge by making a gift of a purchased reversionary interest before the interest actually vests. These rules do not apply to those interests in possession which are protected by *Finance Act 2006* and do not form part of the relevant property regime. Thus disabled trusts, for example, are outside the scope of these changes.

Changes to the tax treatment of interests in possession

7.25 *Finance Act 2010, s 53* reviews *IHTA 1984, s 3A* which sets out which transfers are potentially exempt (PET) and which are not a chargeable lifetime transfer. A purchased interest in possession is, by *Finance Act 2010, s 53*, treated as part of the estate of the person who buys it. Whereas normally under *s 3A* dealings with an interest in possession fall within the PET category, *Finance Act 2010, s 53(2)(a)* alters the thrust of *s 3A* by removing the reference to *s 52* and by inserting *s 3A(6A)*. As will be seen from the account that follows as a general rule purchased trust interests are best avoided.

The result of the *Finance Act 2010* legislative amendments is that a transfer of value under *s 52* will be a PET except where it arises in respect of an interest that, under the new rules, is treated as part of a person's estate (ie by virtue of *s 5(1B)*. Therefore, where such a trust comes to an end and the capital is paid out, the transfer of value is treated as a chargeable transfer for IHT and no longer a PET.

Section 5(1)(a)(ii) is also amended so that where an interest in possession falls within the current definition in *s 5(1B)*, it will be treated as part of a person's estate. *Section 5(1B) sets out* a fresh category of interests in possession. These are interests that are included as part of a person's estate, being:

- those to which a person is entitled;
- who is domiciled in the UK;
- where that person acquired the interest in a transaction at arm's length.

For this purpose 'arm's length' is as defined in *s 10*. Thus the holder of a purchased interest in possession within *s 5(1B)* is now treated as entitled to the property, as under, *s 49(1A)*, so on death the value of the fund will be aggregated with the free estate.

There is, as a result, a change to *s 51(1A)*. That section normally provides that where a person disposes of an interest in possession that disposal is not regarded as a transfer of value, though an IHT charge could arise under *s 52*. However that does not apply to all interests but by virtue of *Finance Act 2010*, now apply to purchased life interests within *s 5(1B)*.

The regime for IHT charges when an interest in possession comes to an end during the lifetime of a beneficiary is mainly regulated by *s 52(2A)* and *(3A)*. Those charges now apply only to certain qualifying interests in possession, but the category of interest to which the charge can apply is now extended to include purchased interests within *s 5(1B)*. The gift of a purchased life interest or its termination will trigger a chargeable event for IHT.

But the changes go further. There can be relief under *s 57A(1A)* in relation to the IHT charge on an interest in possession where, somewhat unusually, the trust property is transferred to a heritage maintenance fund within two years of the death of the liferenter. There are actually very few heritage maintenance funds in existence, so the point is somewhat esoteric, but the relief is now extended by *s 5(1B)* to purchased life interests. There is a similar extension by way of an amendment to *s 100(1A)* in relation to reconstruction of the share capital of a close company and to slightly similar changes to company capital contemplated by *s 101(1A)*.

Section 102ZA(1)(b)(ii) of *Finance Act 1986* builds on the gift with reservation rules as they apply to the holder of an interest in possession. This provision is changed by *Finance Act 2010, s 53(8)* so as to include purchased life interests within *s 5(1B)*.

This extremely complicated anti-avoidance legislation is designed to frustrate the exploitation of the excluded property rules as they apply to trust interests that are not subject to IHT charges in the UK. Simply put, if a non-UK domiciled person sets up a trust of foreign property which includes an interest in possession, that interest is excluded property; but if a stranger buys that interest that stranger will come within the new regime and will not reap any of the benefits of the excluded property regime.

Purchase of interests in offshore trusts

7.26 The excluded property rules (which are considered below) do not apply where:

- a person is entitled to an interest in possession; and
- that person is domiciled in the UK; and
- the trust interest was purchased on or after 5 December 2005 (*s 48(3B)*).

It matters not whether the interest was paid for by the liferenter or another. The purchase may be direct or indirect (perhaps by way of inheritance from the purchaser). These rules are expanded by *Finance Act 2010, s 53*, amending *s 5* to introduce *s 5(1B)* and making amendments where necessary so as to include reference to *s 5(1B)*. *Finance Act 2012* includes draconian legislation intended to target perceived abuse through acquisition of interest of settled property in offshore trusts.

TRANSITIONAL PROVISIONS, 2006–2008

Transitional serial interests: property other than life policies

> **Focus**
>
> The IHT treatment of a pre-22 March 2006 (qualifying) interest in possession can be preserved under the TSI rules but the conditions are tightly drawn with narrow application.

7.27 *Section 49C* sets out four conditions under which an interest in possession could benefit from the tax treatment that applied an old-style interest that was in existence before 22 March 2006. However, the rules relate to transactions before 6 October 2008 and for a fuller account, readers are referred to earlier editions of this work.

The *s 49C* conditions are:

(1) The trust began before 22 March 2006 and immediately before that date the property was subject to an interest in possession ('the prior interest').

(2) The prior interest came to an end at some time between 22 March 2006 and 5 October 2008.

(3) The beneficiary became entitled to an interest in possession ('the current interest') at the time that the prior interest ended.

(4) This was not the settlement for a disabled person nor for a 'bereaved minor' (see below).

Care had to be taken in creating successive interests, perhaps for children, to ensure that the original liferenter was excluded from further benefit otherwise the termination of an interest in possession after 21 March 2006 could be a gift with reservation even if the interest in possession arose after that date.

Illustrative examples are as follows.

Example 7.10—TSI: making the beneficiary wait for the capital

Reginald had an established qualifying (pre-22 March 2006) life interest and the trust terms provided for entitlement to capital at age 30. The trustees doubted his business acumen and exercised their power to advance the fund onto a new trust which would give Reginald direct access to capital only when he attained 50, ie long after April 2008. This is a valid TSI.

Example 7.11—No TSI: spinning out the fund

Susan enjoyed the income of the trust, the terms of which provide that on her death the capital would pass to her brother Tom absolutely. Tom is wealthy and has assigned his interest to another established trust in which his own sons have life interests. Susan's interest was terminated before 6 April 2008, whereupon the fund came to be held on interest in possession trusts for her nephews. They do not have a TSI as their interest is in another trust.

Example 7.12—Continuing interest: sharing out the fund

The Goldsworthy fund, invested in stocks and shares, was held for Mike and Jim in equal shares, each having a life interest. The trustees created sub-funds by dividing the portfolio down the middle. That operation did not bring to an end the interest of either Mike or Jim.

One issue that could cause difficulty was deciding when an existing interest had been replaced by a new interest for the same beneficiary. There were many issues of detail to clarify and CIOT and STEP collectively led the process of elucidation of the most difficult areas, of which the examples above are good illustrations.

One particular anomaly, which arose where an a qualifying IIP was replaced by a new IIP for the same beneficiary, was addressed in *Finance Act 2008, s 140* and resulted in the rewriting of *s 53(2A)* retrospective to 22 March 2006. It provided that the exception from an IHT charge under *s 52* on termination of an interest in possession, which could apply if the person became entitled to another interest in the same trust, was available where a person became entitled to a new trust interest but only if that new interest was a disabled person's interest or a TSI. That would apply regardless of whether the original interest, which terminated, was a qualifying IIP, or an interest that came into being on or after 22 March 2006.

Example 7.13—Simple creation of a TSI

Under the will of Leonard, who died on 1 December 2005, his widow Marian became entitled to the income of the residue of his estate for life, with the fee to their grandchildren for life. The will gave the trustees power to advance capital in favour of any beneficiary who had a life interest and the fee would pass to the great grandchildren insofar as capital had not been advanced to grandchildren during their lifetimes.

Marian was well provided for in other ways and hoped to live at least another seven years and thus on 17 May 2006, she surrendered her life interest in favour of her grandchildren. Her interest was the 'prior interest'. The new life interests that then arose in favour of the grandchildren are 'current interests'. Those current interests fall to be treated as interests in possession under the old rules by virtue of the TSI provisions.

The youngest grandchild, Zac, is now five years old. The treatment of interests in possession as it was before 22 March 2006 could therefore continue for many years. If in due course Zac were to marry, the trustees could, no doubt with his consent, appoint capital to him which he could then give to his wife, enabling them to enjoy a fund equal to twice the nil rate band then in force without risk of an IHT charge on it. Other possibilities may be imagined.

Section 49D contained special rules to apply where a person becomes entitled to an interest on the death of a spouse or civil partner. The conditions are:

- the trust was in being before 22 March 2006;
- before 22 March 2006, there was a prior life interest;
- the prior interest ends on the death of its holder on or after 6 October 2008;
- the prior holder was the spouse or civil partner of the present liferenter;
- the present liferenter becomes entitled to the life interest as soon as the prior interest ceases;
- it is not a bereaved minor trust (BMT) (see below) nor a disabled person's interest.

Example 7.14—Availability of spouse relief

George was already the liferenter of a fund on 22 March 2006. On his marriage to Celia in September 2007 he gave up an interest in half of the trust fund in her favour, so that Celia became entitled to an interest in possession. That transfer was covered by spouse exemption and was a TSI.

In May 2016 George inherited funds from another family trust and decided to give up the remainder of his original life interest in favour of Celia. He surrendered it to her so that she became entitled to the income of the whole of the fund. Although in trust law Celia is entitled only to income, the second transfer is outside the transitional rules as it took place after October 2008. It is not an IPDI, being a lifetime settlement and under the rules from 22 March 2006 it is treated as a relevant property trust, thus a chargeable transfer; and since the fund does not increase Celia's estate it is not covered by spouse relief.

Addition of funds to existing trusts: special rules for policy trusts

7.28 The transitional provisions did not generally allow qualifying interest in possession funds to be augmented and remain within the old regime. The addition of new assets to an existing trust is, for one exception, instead treated as the creation of a new settlement under the new regime. This might simply be the transfer of extra funds by the settlor or an indirect benefit, such as the release by the settlor of a debt owed to him by the trustees.

On 29 October 2013, HMRC published updates to its IHT Manual (IHTM) which amongst other items included new guidance on additions of property or value to qualifying interest in possession trusts (see IHTM16074–16078). The new guidance contains useful examples of the HMRC approach to the additions thus on the case of mixed funds HMRC will consider an apportionment of values determined on a just and reasonable basis; an outline of circumstances in which HMRC may investigate loans made to the trustees after 21 March 2006; clarification on the treatment of third party settlement of trust expenses where the trust lacks liquid funds.

The one exception relates to insurance policies. The payment of premiums simply to keep an existing policy on foot is not regarded as the creation of a new settlement. Even so, depending on the circumstances, the payment of policy premiums may be exempt falling within *s 21* under the normal expenditure out of income rule.

7.29 *Section 49E* provides a special form of TSI for existing, but not new, trusts of insurance policies. For example, it can apply where 'C' has an interest in possession in a policy 'the present interest', before 22 March 2006 and certain conditions apply:

(1) It is a trust created prior to 22 March 2006; before 22 March 2006 the property in the trust was a policy; and C (or perhaps more likely some other person) had a life interest ('the earlier interest').

(2) The earlier interest ended on or after 6 October 2008 ('the earlier interest end-time') on the death of whoever was entitled to it and C became entitled to the interest on one of the following occasions:

- at the earlier interest end-time;
- at the end of an interest in possession occurring on the death of the previous liferenter; or
- when one of a series of interests in possession ends, where the first belonged to someone who became entitled to it at the earlier interest end-time and where each life interest came to an end when the holder of that interest died; or alternatively
- C became entitled to the interest that C now has on one of the following occasions:
  - when a transitional serial interest ends by death; or

- when the last of several consecutive interests ends and the first of them was a transitional serial interest, each ending by death.

There are two further conditions:

(3) The policy rights were in the trust from 22 March 2006 until C became entitled.

(4) This is neither a bereaved minor's trust nor one for a disabled person.

Associated operations

7.30 The use of insurance policies was examined in the case of *Smith v Revenue and Customs Commissioners* [2008] STC 1649, where husband and wife took out 'back-to-back' annuity and life policies with the same insurer in circumstances where the annuity income funded the life policies, which in turn were gifted to their children. There was no express reference in any policy to any other, but the total package of documents provided by the insurer made the connection plain. It was held that the policies taken together were a transfer of value.

Bereaved minors and age 18-to-25 trusts

7.31 The provision of funds for young people in the context of the new treatment of A&M trusts is dealt with more fully in **Chapter 8**. *Section 71C* defines 'bereaved minor' as a person not yet 18 and in respect of whom at least one parent (or guardian in loco parentis) has died. This definition is central to the *Finance Act 2006* IHT regime. As a result of strong professional representations that the age of 18 was perceived as far too young to manage substantial capital, the original structure of IHT, which would have made the tax treatment of capital much more favourable where the young person became absolutely entitled at 18, is toned down albeit marginally.

The introduction of *s 71D* for 'Age 18-to-25 trusts' has given parent settlors and indeed trustees a choice. These trusts are considered in detail at **8.7**. It seems likely that many families will accept the burden of the IHT regime for relevant property trusts as the price to be paid for securing the capital in the short to medium term.

Wills can be drafted with flexibility to take advantage of the new rules.

Example 7.15—Trusts for bereaved minors: 'wait and see how they turn out'

Betty died on January 2012 leaving funds to her husband Alfred for life (an IPDI) with the fee on discretionary trust for her children. The trustees appoint the fee fund onto a trust that complies with *s 71A*. That will be good enough: the *s 71A* trusts need not actually be set out in the will. Furthermore, it does not matter that capital might be appointed out to Alfred: whilst he has an IPDI the trusts of the fee are not tested.

EXCLUDED PROPERTY TRUSTS

Focus

The valuable IHT benefits secured through the use of an excluded property trust must form a central part of IHT planning routine for the non-domiciliary. However, the complexity of the rules, the increasing raft of anti-avoidance legislation and the impact of the *Finance Act 2008* changes which paved the introduction of the remittance charge mean that the position must be constantly monitored. The impact of *s 80* should not be underrated (see **7.35** below).

Fee/Reversionary interests

7.32 These have already been considered at **7.22**. A fee or reversionary interest is excluded property unless (see *s 48(1)*) it is:

- purchased; or
- one to which either the settlor or his spouse is beneficially entitled; or
- an interest expectant on the determination of a lease where that lease is treated as a settlement by virtue of the special rules in *s 43(3)*.

In the case of purchased reversionary interests, careful note should be taken of the anti-avoidance provisions of *Finance Act 2010, s 53* described at **7.24** and **7.25** above.

Foreign assets

7.33 The other more common category of excluded trust property is described in *s 48(3)* and concerns property situated outside the UK. There are two conditions:

- The property itself, but not a reversionary interest in it, is excluded provided that the settlor was not domiciled in the UK when the settlement was made.
- The rules in *s 6(1)* apply to a reversionary interest in the property, but do not otherwise apply to it (see below).

Section 6(1) states: '…Property situated outside the United Kingdom is excluded property if the person beneficially entitled to it is an individual domiciled outside the United Kingdom…'. The conditions required for property to be excluded within *s 48(3)* would therefore be satisfied if the present liferenter was domiciled in the UK, but the person entitled to the fee was not so domiciled.

However, it was announced in the summer Budget 2015 that it is intended to legislate to ensure that, from April 2017, IHT is payable on all UK residential property owned directly or indirectly by non-UK domiciliaries. This change is aimed at blocking the holding of property indirectly through offshore structures. Consequently, shares in a 'closely controlled' offshore company will not be excluded property of the non-UK domiciliary to the extent that the shares derive their value directly or indirectly from UK residential property, or to the extent that the value of those shares is otherwise attributable to such property. As at date of publication no further detail or draft legislation has been released. Accordingly, the exact detail of the proposal and its scope has yet to be examined.

In the case of *Bowring v HMRC* [2015] UKUT 550, the Upper Tribunal decided that capital payments made to UK beneficiaries of a UK trust that had in turn received funds from an offshore trust were free of the capital gains that had originated in that offshore trust. This overturned the decision of the First-tier Tribunal that interpreted *TCGA 1992, s 97(5)* so widely as to apply to beneficiaries who received distributions from the UK trust and were subject to tax under *ss 87* and *91* because they had received the capital payments indirectly from the offshore trust.

7.34 The excluded property rules may seem to be something of an anomaly.

Example 7.16—Excluded property trusts: benefiting from the rule years later

Anton fled to the UK during the Hungarian uprising in 1956. He had been a successful engineer and on arrival in the UK settled his commercial interests in both Hungary and in Switzerland in trust for the benefit of his wife Josefina for life with the fee to their son Maxim for life with gifts over in remainder. All this happened at a time when Anton still hoped eventually to return to the country of his birth and when he had been in the UK for only three years – thus Anton had non-UK domicile status at that time of trust creation.

Although Anton remained in the UK for many years after making the trust, such that he became deemed domiciled here (under the then '17/20 year' rule under *s 267)*, he did not add any further funds to the trust. In due course the composition of the trust fund changed and included indirect holdings in UK companies but the rules of situs were observed in such a way that at all times the trust property was situated outside of the UK. Anton died before 22 March 2006.

Josefina became deemed domiciled in the UK some years ago but on her death in 2016 it was acknowledged that the fund was excluded property.

Maxim was born in the UK and on reaching late teens made it clear that he adopted the UK as his country of domicile. For IHT purposes, that does not matter – the trust is still outside the IHT regime because of the circumstances of its creation and it has avoided later tainting because there has been no addition to the fund at a time when the settlor was domiciled in the UK.

In **Example 7.16**, the tax treatment would be different if Anton had purchased the interest after 5 December 2005 (see *s 48(3B)*).

Professional advisers have long debated the precise relationship between the rules as to excluded property and those for gifts with reservation, and with good reason. A 'non-UK domiciliary' may set up a trust of offshore assets from which they continue to benefit, by drawing the income. If the excluded property rule takes priority over the gift with reservation rule, the settlor continues to draw an income from property that is not taxed as their estate on death, even though they may meanwhile become deemed domiciled here under the 17/20 year (or post-5 April 2017 the 15/20 year) residence rule. The slightest indication of HMRC thinking was the original wording of paragraph IHTM14396 of the IHT Manual, which was unclear and cast some doubt over the interaction of the excluded property and gift with reservation codes. However, the current version of IHTM14396 makes it clear that the excluded property provisions do take priority over the gifts with reservation code (see **5.34**) even so the tightening of and introduction of new anti-avoidance legislation for the non-domiciliary must make this an area to monitor.

It was always perceived that difficulty could come from a non-fiscal source. By a press release dated 14 October 2009, the European Commission published proposals that if enacted, had the potential to impact directly on the procedures for inheritance within the EU through international recognition of rights to succession. This proposal posed fundamental problems for Scottish lawyers, with their concepts of domicile, executors, trusts and testamentary freedom who would want to be certain that lifetime gifts could not be clawed back to satisfy 'forced heirship' rules. The French would not lightly give up rules that protect children from disinheritance whilst English law does not accept 'habitual residence' as determinative of the legal system that should govern inheritance. These deep-founded traditions were already on a collision course with the EU when the UK made known that it was unwilling to be bound by the new rules if enacted. However, this area remains fluid and all the more so given the recent referendum decision to exit from the EU. Accordingly, developments in this area should be closely monitored.

What should settlors and their trustees do now? *Finance Act 2008, ss 24* and *25* and *Sch 7*, introduced a much sharper regime for the taxation of the non-UK domiciled taxpayer by raising the financial stakes on the favourable remittance basis, although that mainly affects income tax and CGT rather than IHT. The law is in a state of flux: thus there are cases on residence that declare the law as it applied to past situations but it does not reflect the current position. HMRC6 ('Residence, Domicile and the Remittance Basis') which replaced Booklet IR20, set out fresh guidance for income tax and CGT bolstered by HMRC victory in the now infamous Supreme Court decision against Gaines-Cooper, Davies & James (*R (on the application of Davies) v Revenue and Customs Commissioners* [2011] UKSC 47). In the case of *Peter Daniel v HMRC* [2014] UKFTT 173 HMRC's inconsistent application of the then IR20 residence rules was challenged but failed mainly due to the lack of credibility of the taxpayer, a senior banker with Morgan Stanley – the Tribunal stated it was '…surprised and troubled that every piece of objective evidence in this case, such as fax and email correspondence, presentations, letters and the very existence of at least three computers…' was unavailable.

This case underpins the view that the strength of the technical argument must be supported by facts rather than statements. However, looking to the future, progress has been made and the long awaited statutory residence test came into effect on 6 April 2013. Nevertheless, the rules remain complicated involving the application of a raft of automatic tests with particular unexpected twists dependent on personal factors, and despite the issue of initial HMRC guidance (see HMRC website 'What's new?' 8 May 2013) and supplemented by a revised HMRC guidance note released in September 2013, it will still be some time before the new framework becomes or feels comfortable.

The residence of trustees for CGT was reviewed in *Smallwood and another v HMRC* [2010] EWCA Civ 778. The case turned on exactly where the trust was resident when gains were made; on the facts, that was Mauritius, which had sole taxing rights under the double taxation agreement then in force. The appeal by Mr Smallwood and the trustees was allowed in the High Court

([2009] EWHC 777 (Ch)), but that decision was subsequently overturned in the Court of Appeal.

The statutory residence rules affect IHT through the test for 'deemed domicile' in *s 267(1)(b)*, which turns on residence: *Finance Act 2008, Sch 7* adjusted the 'day counting' rules.

Loss of excluded property status: the *s 80* problem

7.35 *Section 80* ('Initial interest of settlor or spouse or civil partner') imposes a primary fiction on all trusts set up since 27 March 1974, where a settlor or his spouse is entitled to a prior qualifying interest in possession in property before reverting to fresh relevant property trust terms on the death of that surviving spouse. That property is not initially treated as joining the trust fund for the purposes of IHT regime for relevant property trusts but its joining is postponed. However, once the qualifying interest of the settlor or spouse comes to an end when the property moves from a spousal IIP to a fresh trust interest (ie 18 to 25), it is at that point treated as joining a separate trust, made by the person who last had the qualifying interest in possession. 'Spouse' means spouse, widow, widower or civil partner of a settlor (*s 80(2)*).

The wording of *s 80* was amended and tightened by *Finance Act 2014* such that the wider term 'an interest in possession' is replaced with the narrower and more precise term 'a qualifying interest in possession'.

Example 7.17—Disclaimed interest: trigger of relevant property trust regime

On 30 June 1979, Geoff, domiciled in Scotland, settled £150,000 on trust for his wife Maud for life, with the fee on discretionary trust for his children and grandchildren. Maud enjoyed the income until 31 May 2005, when she disclaimed her interest, at which time the trust fund was worth £700,000, with the intention that her family should benefit. There is an immediately chargeable lifetime transfer by Maud of £700,000. That would also be the result if the disclaimer took place after 21 March 2006.

Example 7.18—Pre-22 March 2006: side-stepping the relevant property trust regime

The facts are as in **Example 7.17** above, only instead of a simple disclaimer the change is effected, not by Maud but by the trustees (on 31 May 2005) under a power in the deed. They appoint funds onto a new life interest trust for the children and onto old style A&M trust for the grandchildren. This time no discretionary trust arises, and as this occurred prior to 22 March 2006 there is no immediate chargeable transfer. It is a PET by Maud. However, see below as to the effect where the event occurs post 21 March 2006.

Under the post-*Finance Act 2006* regime, *s 80(4)* has the effect that, where the trigger event under *s 80(1)* happens on or after 22 March 2006, it will apply, not to the coming to an end of an interest in possession, as hitherto, but on the occasion of the ending of any 'postponing interest', by which is meant any type of qualifying interest in possession, even (see *s 80(4)(b)*), an IPDI or a disabled person's interest. This will severely cut down the freedom of trustees of offshore trusts for erstwhile non-UK domiciliaries to keep the fund outside the IHT net.

As mentioned above, *Finance (No 2) Act 2014* tightened the wording of *s 80* to correct an unintended effect which permitted a successive spousal non-qualifying IIP to potentially escape IHT charge because the trust assets were neither part of the successor's estate nor comprised within a relevant property trust. The term 'interest in possession' is now replaced with the term 'qualifying interest in possession' – the latter referring to an interest that is a pre-22 March 2006 established interest, an IPDI, transitional serial interest (TSI) or a disabled person's interest as set out in *s 59*. Accordingly, where one party to a couple succeeds to a life interest to which their spouse or civil partner was previously entitled during their lifetime, *s 80* will continue to apply at that time.

Example 7.19—The effect on an excluded property trust

The facts are as in **Example 7.17** except that: Geoff was domiciled in New Zealand in 1979 (and had been for more than 3 years); the disclaimer of Maud's interest occurred on 31 May 2016; and by this time both Geoff and Maud are both deemed to be domiciled in Scotland. The fund loses its excluded property status, because it is retested as a transfer made on 31 May 2016 by Maud.

Thus, by stealth, the advantages of excluded property trusts will, for many families, disappear. Certainly all trustees of excluded property trusts must regularly consider their position and continue to monitor developments in this changing arena.

INSURANCE POLICY TRUSTS

Existing policy trusts

7.36 The scheme for trusts as finally enacted in *Finance Act 2006* imposes on professional tax advisers (to include financial advisers) a duty to understand the taxation of trusts and the ability to explain it. *Section 46A* now deals with existing life interest policy trusts. The conditions are:

- the settlement and the life policy both existed before 22 March 2006;
- premiums are payable, or there is a variation of the policy which is permitted by the new rules, some time on or after 22 March 2006;
- there were pre-existing settlement rights, now defined as a 'transitionally protected interest';
- by virtue of continued payment of premiums or of a variation of the policy, rights under the policy become settled as part of the transitionally protected interest; and
- the only variations to the policy are those allowed by the legislation in 2006.

For the purposes of the legislation a variation is 'allowed' only where it takes place by operation of the exercise of rights that existed before 22 March 2006. A 'transitionally-protected interest' means only a pre-existing life interest or a transitional serial interest. Where all of these conditions are satisfied, the payment of any more premiums on the policy is a transfer of value made by the individual who pays it and the transfer of value at that time is a PET.

Transitional provisions

7.37 The same treatment will apply in an existing situation where the policy is not held on life interest trusts but on old-style A&M trusts. The relevant legislation is *s 46B* and it adopts the pattern of *s 46A*, so the conditions are as follows:

- the settlement and the policy must have existed before 22 March 2006;
- a premium is paid on the policy after that date;
- rights under the policy were settled on A&M trusts established before 22 March 2006; and
- further rights (ie those attaching to the next premium) become settled after 21 March 2006 and there is a variation on or after that date of the policy so as to increase the benefits or extend the term of the insurance, but that variation is an 'allowed one'.

Where the conditions are satisfied, A&M provisions may continue notwithstanding the general changes to A&M trusts introduced by *Finance Act 2006* thus the payment of a further premium is treated as a PET. For the purposes of policies subject to A&M trusts a variation is 'allowed' only where it represents the exercise of pre-existing rights under the policy.

7.38 There is a further level of protection of pre-existing policy trusts. This protects the eventual release of funds. The conditions are:

- pre-existing settlements and life policies;
- premiums paid or allowed variation on or after 22 March 2006 where the trusts fall within the 'new' *s 71A* (bereaved minors) or *s 71D* (18-to-25) trusts which were previously A&M trusts and which became *s 71A* or *s 71D* trusts; and
- a further premium was paid, the policy was varied in an allowed manner so as to increase or extend the benefits but only by exercise of pre-existing rights.

These rules apply to property in an 18-to-25 trust only where that property was previously in an A&M settlement which migrated to *s 71D* whilst still in the same settlement. If the settlements are bereaved minor trusts then the transitional provisions apply only where they migrate from A&M trusts under the terms of *Finance Act 2006* or where they would have been in 18-to-25 trusts, but cease to be held on those trusts because the trustees decided to modify the rights so as to comply with the restrictions for bereaved minors: in other words, they let the grandchildren have the money early, ie at age 18 rather than at the preferred age of 25.

New trusts

7.39 Post-*Finance Act 2006* insurance policy trusts, even if expressed to be interest in possession trusts, are treated as relevant property trusts for IHT purposes and will become subject to the regime of entry charges, periodic charges and exit charges. This regime is described in more detail in **Chapter 8**.

Pensions

7.40 The IHT treatment of pensions before 22 March 2006 was that benefits might be settled under a discretionary trust. The death benefits were not relevant property, during the lifetime of the policyholder by virtue of *s 58(1)(d)*, whether the pension was a regulated one or one within *ICTA 1988, s 615* (a '*section 615* scheme').

Equally, under *Finance Act 2004, Sch 29*, the death benefit was 'a defined lump sum benefit' if paid out within two years of death, see *para 13(c)*; or 'a non-crystallised lump sum death benefit' if paid out within the same period: see *para 15(1)(c)*. The language of the pensions simplification legislation is itself anything but simple but the effect was that the tax treatment for discretionary trusts did not apply, if the lump sum, of either kind, was payable at the discretion of the trustees and the funds were distributed within two years of the death. Where the funds were paid by the pension scheme trustees to a second trust, IHT became chargeable when the second trust released the benefits but subject to the two-year rule. Where the life tenant was the former spouse or civil partner, the IHT treatment reflected that and usually the funds were released so as to take advantage of that exemption.

The tax treatment following *Finance Act 2006* is that where the funds are transferred at the discretion of the pension scheme trustees to a second trust, that trust will be treated as a relevant property trust and the fund may therefore be subject to an exit charge on distribution, with the normal rules described in **Chapter 8** to apply the proportionate fraction. One particular difficulty may be in establishing whether the funds are released by the pension trustees to the second trust at their discretion, or whether effectively they have no choice.

There was a slight relaxation in *Finance Act 2007*. Lump sums, whether arising under regulated schemes or *s 615* schemes, will not come within the IHT rules for relevant property trusts if distributed within two years of the earlier of:

- the day on which the death was known to the trustees or those in charge of the scheme; or
- the day on which they could first be expected to have known of the death.

The taxation of pension savings was revisited in *Finance Act 2008, s 91* and *Sch 28*. These changes are considered in the context of 'lifetime planning' in **Chapter 12**.

For a long time there had been a difficulty for the owners of pension rights in deciding, on approaching retirement, whether or not to accept the annuity rates currently on offer; or to go into drawdown; or to carry on working. The last option might be in the hope of restoring the value of the fund to what it had been before the recession or other reason for depressed values. *Section 3(3)* imposed a charge to IHT where, by failure to exercise the right to draw the pension, the taxpayer brought about a situation where, on his death soon afterwards, the fund would otherwise pass free of IHT to close relatives.

This dilemma was keenly illustrated in *Fryer and others (PRs of Arnold Deceased v HMRC* [2010] UKFTT 87 (TC) 00398. Mrs Arnold could draw her pension on 8 September 2002, her sixtieth birthday. She was at that time diagnosed with a condition likely to prove terminal. Although she received details of the pension choices open to her, she did nothing. She died in September 2009. The First-tier Tribunal held that Mrs Arnold deliberately omitted, at her sixtieth birthday and thereafter until her death, to exercise her pension rights. Her estate in her lifetime lost the value of those rights, so there was a transfer of value within *s 3(3)*. The value transferred was the loss to the estate, ie the value of the right to opt to take the benefits. A hypothetical purchaser of those rights would opt to take the lump sum plus a guaranteed annuity for ten years; taking into account Mrs Arnold's health: all of that to be discounted 25%.

Practitioners had long worried about this issue: when was the failure tested to exercise the right to take the pension? The most difficult outcome of the *Arnold* case is to answer this question 'anytime until death', with the result that, since such a time must fall within two years of death, all future failures to draw pensions would be caught. It seems it was necessary to begin to draw the pension before death; or risk its exposure to IHT later. That interpretation, if correct, was harsh.

However, as part of the wider pensions reform from 6 April 2011 a charge under *s 3(3)* is disapplied (by *s 12(2ZA)*) where a member of a registered pension scheme (or qualifying non-UK pension scheme or *s 615(3)* scheme) omits to exercise pension rights under the scheme.

Life policies

7.41 There is no change to the treatment of discretionary trusts of life policies. Where the trusts are A&M trusts, care should be taken to note the identity of the beneficiaries as at 6 April 2008 because after that date a variation can bring the fund within the relevant property regime. As was noted at **7.28** above, there should be little difficulty with existing trusts. The main problems will concern new policies, especially those where the premiums are substantial. **Chapter 6** outlined the relaxation of the reporting requirements for new discretionary trusts. Once the policy trusts are in being, the usual regime described in the next chapter will apply.

It is of course part of the nature of a life policy, especially one of term assurance, that its value reflects the state of health of the life assured. As will be seen in **Chapter 8** the charging regime of relevant property trusts requires valuation of the fund on the eve of the tenth anniversary of creation. If at that date the life assured is seriously ill the value of the trust may exceed the nil rate band. The same could apply if death occurred just before a tenth anniversary. In relation to particular schemes, such as discounted gift schemes and loan trusts it will be necessary to go back to first principles and establish the exact nature of the rights under the policy and under the trusts before applying the charging provisions.

A sting in the tail

7.42 Finally, there is an anomaly of which both trustees and beneficiaries should take note. The issue of burden and incidence of tax was discussed at the beginning of **Chapter 6**. On death, liability for IHT is, see *s 200(1)*, on:

- the executors, for the free estate;
- the trustees, for trust property;
- any person in whom the property is vested, whether beneficially or not, or who has an interest in possession; or
- anyone for whose benefit a trust fund is held.

Section 201 deals further with trust property and *s 201(1)(b)* makes a person liable for tax if they are entitled to an interest in possession whether or not that interest is a qualifying interest.

These rules do not sit easily with the principle that many post-21 March 2006 liferenters will not have a qualifying interest and this will not be treated as entitled to the underlying trust capital. Although they may have an interest in possession for the purposes of trust law and even for CGT, for IHT it will be taxed as the interest of a beneficiary of a relevant property trust. Why treat them differently from 'true' discretionary trust beneficiaries? HMRC do not really defend the situation: they have commented:

> 'Although an IIP holder whose interest arose before 22 March 2006 has been regarded as owning the underlying property for inheritance tax purposes, in reality he has only ever owned a limited interest. The Finance Act 2006 changes do not alter the IIP owner's real position.'

This seems to recognise the anomaly but does not redress the balance.

Chapter 8

Relevant property trusts

SIGNPOSTS

- **Post-March 2006 categories** – Despite its rigid construction, the BMT and its more flexible 18-to-25 sister present a more palatable IHT option to the full-blown discretionary trust when considering will provision for children. However, great care must be taken to avoid the less obvious pitfalls (see **8.6–8.8**).
- **Migration – the new era** – It is crucial to understand the impact of the new law on the old style trust, to appreciate the impact of transitional relief provisions, to be aware of tax treatment going forward and in particular to consider the impact of later funding (see **8.22–8.25**; **8.17**).
- **The relevant property regime –** Given the extent of the *FA 2006* trust reforms most lifetime trusts will now fall to be taxed under the IHT code of periodic and exit charges; thus familiarity with the charging provisions must now be a prerequisite rather than option for the trust practitioner (see **8.26–8.60**).
- **Relevant property trusts** – Earlier proposed reforms designed to simplify the periodic charge calculation and block the effective use of multiple trusts will take effect for charges arising on or after Royal Assent (see **8.26**).
- **The 'Frankland' trap** – Appointments made out of trusts within three months of death in favour of the deceased's surviving spouse/civil partner will qualify for the spousal exemption (see **8.26**).
- **Interaction of APR and BPR** –The demarcation lines of myth and fact must be clearly drawn when considering the use of these valuable headline reliefs in the context of the charging regime applicable to relevant property trusts (see **8.61–8.66**).

TYPES OF DISCRETIONARY OR RELEVANT PROPERTY TRUSTS

Full relevant property trusts: history of the legislation

8.1 This book is mainly about IHT, but where trusts are concerned IHT and CGT closely interact and it is therefore necessary to comment on that interaction. Although at one time it was relatively easy to holdover gains on transfers into and out of trusts, this facility has been eroded in two ways:

- through the *Finance Act 2003* changes restricting hold over in connection with settlor-interested trusts and trusts of real estate residence; and
- through *Finance Act 2004* introducing *TCGA 1992, s 169B* in relation to trusts for minors which are treated as settlor-interested following *Finance Act 2006*, so that in effect there can be no holdover on gifts to children by way of trust. This restricts the advantage that was previously available on transfers of business property under *TCGA 1992, s 165* and of property in general under *TCGA 1992, s 260*.

The oft-forgotten upside of the *Finance Act 2006* changes to IHT that bring more trusts within the relevant property regime is to make holdover relief more readily available: see **8.6**. By *Finance Act 2008*, some of the restrictions on settlor-interested UK-resident trusts were also removed because until 22 June 2010 a single CGT rate of 18% applied across the board. In the post-22 June 2010 era with a second, higher CGT rate applied to trusts, estates and higher rate taxpayers this may pave the way for the reintroduction of the settlor-interested rules formerly contained in *TCGA 1992, s 77*.

The individual as the taxable entity

8.2 The preferred subject matter for IHT is the individual and the size of their estate. Thus an outright transfer from one individual to another is taxed on a simpler, if not necessarily more favourable, basis than a transfer which reduces the estate of one person without at the same time increasing the estate of any other. The distinction between potentially exempt transfers (PETs) and chargeable lifetime transfers (CLTs) was examined in **Chapter 1**. The effect of *IHTA 1984, ss 3* and *3A* is that the transfer of funds to a relevant property trust (namely a trust subject to the IHT regime of periodic and exit charges) is a chargeable transfer. The amount of the transfer (net of available exemptions) will initially be set against the transferor's unused nil rate band. Any excess will be chargeable initially at the lifetime rate and, in the event of the death of the transferor within three years, at the unabated death rate but where the transferor's death occurs more than three and within seven years, at the tapered death rate.

(Note: all statutory references in this chapter are to *IHTA 1984*, unless otherwise stated).

How relevant property trusts work

> **Focus**
>
> The rules for relevant property trusts need to be considered for the interests of the beneficiaries and the tax consequences.

8.3 The normal, straightforward type of relevant property trust will provide for a termination date, and an accumulation period, usually 21 years (21 being the maximum specified number of years for accumulation in Scotland although minorities of children may result in longer periods). The settlor transfers assets to the trustees, who then have complete freedom to decide which of the beneficiaries is to receive anything from the trust, whether it be capital, income or the use of an asset.

Commonly the settlor will give the trustees (of whom he may be one) a letter of wishes (see **Example 8.48**). The letter of wishes is not binding on the trustees. It is a subsidiary document. Significant debate surrounds the issue of whether such a letter is actually a trust document: clearly, it is of interest to all beneficiaries and to tax-gatherers in any jurisdiction.

Although many jurisdictions specifically protect such documents from prying eyes, there is some authority for the view that, if the disclosed principal trust document is so blandly or opaquely drawn that it is meaningless without the letter of wishes, that letter must be a trust document and as such belongs to the beneficiaries as a body, so they can, in fact, demand to see it. The view is advanced in some quarters that disclosure might be forced under the *Data Protection Act 1998*, but most practitioners disagree. The Data Commissioner has not made a ruling on the point. Certainly, most trustees will be guided by it and may find it useful in resisting repeated claims from one beneficiary in particular to preferential treatment. Good trustees can 'stand up to' the beneficiaries and preserve their independence. That having been said, the successful beneficiary's right to information on the trust composition was pivotal in the recent case of *Blades v Isaac & Alexander* [2016] EWHC 601 (Ch) which considered whether costs incurred by both the trust and pursuer by reason of that action should be borne by the trust fund.

A discretionary trust comes to an end on the termination date unless the trustees take earlier action. Normally the trust deed will provide that, in default of exercise of their discretion, the fund will at the end of the trust period be held for a particular person absolutely. However, the trustees can bring the trust to an end earlier simply by distributing all the funds in their hands.

The Scottish Law Commission's current wide-ranging review on Trusts is likely to bring about changes to trust operation and administration. The current law is based to a large extent on the *Trusts (Scotland) Act 1921* and late 19th century cases and the Commission recognises that the social and business background is very different now.

CGT and relevant property trusts

Focus

The *Finance Act 2006* extension of the relevant property regime has provided a welcome CGT planning opportunity to secure access to general holdover relief on chargeable assets transferred into most post 21 March 2006 lifetime trusts.

8.4 Apart from the IHT impact, relevant property trusts do attract CGT benefits. *TCGA 1992, s 260* provides that general gains (as opposed to gains on business assets) may be held over, both on transfers into relevant property trusts (but beware the restriction for transfers into settlor interested trusts) and transfers out.

Example 8.1—Tax charges on setting up a trust

Alice owns a small parade of shops with flats above which she inherited from her husband many years earlier and which have risen substantially in value since then. She wishes to benefit her grandchildren Bella, Catherine and David. The present value of the combined parade of shops and flats is £700,000 whilst the flats are together worth £300,000 and the shops £350,000 (Note: valued separately, the flats and shops are worth less than their combined value of £700,000). Alice transfers the flats to a relevant property trust. Although the flats are worth £300,000 the reduction in Alice's estate is £400,000 – that is the value of the transfer on the 'loss to the estate' principle. Alice utilises her nil rate band for 2016/17 of £325,000 and the annual exemption for this year and last thus leaving a chargeable transfer of £69,000. As the trust has no liquid assets from which to meet the IHT charge Alice agrees to settle the liability, thus requiring the net value of the asset to be grossed up for IHT purposes. The grossed-up value of £86,250 (£69,000 × 100/(100 – 20)) charged at 20% triggers an IHT charge of £17,250 (an effective rate equal to 25% of the net transfer).

Although the transfer to the trustees is a disposal for CGT purposes, Alice may avoid paying that tax herself by electing to hold over the gain – the trustees will acquire the flats at the adjusted base cost (the later of March 1982 value or Alice's original cost basis) rather than market value for the purpose of later disposal (that might be by sale or by transfer out to the beneficiaries). If the transfer out of trust ownership is itself a chargeable transfer (which in all normal circumstances it would be) the trustees could, subject to joint agreement with the beneficiary hold over the gain, so that the beneficiaries as the trustees before, acquire the asset at its adjusted base cost. If there are several beneficiaries, the fragmentation of the gain, the perhaps reduced rate of tax charged on individuals and the potential availability of the individual annual exemption may make for good planning.

Old accumulation and maintenance trusts

8.5 These trusts in their original form no longer exist as a separate category, having become interest in possession trusts or relevant property trusts, according to the circumstances prevailing when *Finance Act 2006* came into force. Virtually all A&M trusts, whether established in lifetime or by will, have migrated to the post March 2006 regime albeit perhaps with modified IHT impact and all new such trusts, with very few exceptions, are relevant property trusts. The exceptions to that rule are:

- disabled trusts;
- trusts for bereaved minors;
- age 18-to-25 trusts; and
- IPDI trusts.

The regime of A&M trusts under *s 71* was terminated with effect from 6 April 2008, except as still provided for bereaved minors under *s 71A* and 18-to-25 trusts under *s 71D*.

Bereaved minors' trusts (BMTs)

Focus

The post 21 March 2006 BMT and its extended 18-to-25 sibling cannot be created in lifetime and thus can never be viewed as a modern version of the old-style A&M trust.

8.6 It is important to appreciate that the BMT does not replicate the old style A&M trust. The essential features of a BMT are:

- It can arise only on death.
- It may arise on intestacy or under deed of variation or by way of appointment under *s 144*.
- The only possible beneficiary is a minor child of the testator or where the testator is acting in loco parentis. A grandchild is not a child for this purpose. Parent is defined in *para 71H of Sch 20* as an individual who immediately before death had parental responsibilities for the child in relation to the *Children (Scotland) Act 1995*. There is some provision for substitution of beneficiaries, but only under the rules of intestacy and not under the terms of a will.
- There is no need for an interest in possession in the income and thus income may be accumulated. However, the capital and all accumulations of income must vest at 18. It is not possible to exercise discretion between one beneficiary and another. Effectively, it is sub-funded for each beneficiary from the outset (though not in the full sense of that term).
- CGT holdover relief is available on vesting or asset appointment, as with any other relevant property trust (*TCGA 1992, s 260(2)(da)*).
- There must be no general power of advancement and in particular no power to make a 'settled advance'.

Example 8.2—The test of a BMT

Fred died intestate and was survived by his two children under the age of 16. If both reach the age of 16 they become absolutely entitled under the intestacy rules and the BMT requirements are satisfied.

In the unlikely event that one of them died in childbirth before obtaining majority, the intestacy rules would provide that the grandchild would step into the shoes of their parent and again be entitled to capital at age 16. The BMT rules would be satisfied.

By contrast, if Fred had made a will that provided for his children at age 18 but with substitution clauses in favour of a grandchild that would not comply with the requirements of BMT and the funds would be treated as held on relevant property trusts.

Example 8.3—Further tests of a BMT

On her death, Celia left her house to her minor daughter Jessica absolutely on reaching age 18 but, if Jessica should die before that age then to Celia's brother David, currently aged 23. The usual clause extending powers of advancement was not included in the will. As a result, the gift is a BMT. The substituted beneficiary is an adult and the other requirements are satisfied.

However, if Celia had instead specified that the house was to go to her daughter at age 21, that would have breached the BMT requirements and the result would be the creation of a relevant property trust (albeit perhaps one that met the conditions of an 18-to-25 trust).

Returning to the original scenario, shortly before the daughter is 18 the trustees decide that she is too young to have control of the house. They move half of the value of the house onto interest in possession trust terms. That goes beyond what HMRC approve, not being considered an appointment '…to the like effect…'. There is no precise or case driven dicta as to interpretation of this latter phrase other than from Statement of Practice E7: The appointment therefore triggers the special charge on an A&M trust (or indeed a BMT) under *s 70*: see **8.67** below.

If the will had included the clause extending advancement to the whole of the fund, that would have likely satisfied '…to the like effect…' and there would have been no BMT from the outset.

Example 8.4—Wording to create a BMT or 18-to-25 trust

Beverley's will left property 'to such of my children as reach 18 and if more than one in equal shares'. One of her children, Alice, survived her but tragically died at 17. Alice's share passed to her siblings at 18.

HMRC consider that this does not prejudice the shares, which can be treated sibling by sibling. The same treatment would result for 18-to-25 trust purposes.

18-to-25 trusts (including conforming A&M trusts): overview

8.7 Broadly, the flexibility of a vesting age between age 18 and age 25 comes at a tax cost. If the beneficiary receives the capital at 18 then the fund is IHT neutral during its lifetime up to vesting. If the capital vesting age is between age 18 but no greater than age 25 there will be a partial IHT exposure – no IHT charge will trigger before age 18 and that of course is an advantage over a fully relevant property trust, but thereafter the fund will attract an exit charge when capital vests (or on capital advancement) on or before age 25. In such circumstances, the benefit of the 'appropriate fraction', as described at **8.12** below, has the effect that the exit charge cannot exceed 4.2% and in practice may well be very much less. If the capital does not vest until, say, age 28, the trust is fully within the IHT rules for relevant property trusts from the outset and thus will attract both the periodic charge and exit charge throughout its life.

These rules apply to existing trusts as well as to new will trusts. Importantly, no new lifetime trust can come within this narrow class which can only be created on death: it will be a relevant property trust from the outset. However, an immediate life interest trust under a will may qualify as an IPDI and, if it does, it will be treated for IHT purposes as within the 'old' pre March 2006 regime (see **Chapter 7**).

The conditions for 18-to-25 trusts

8.8 The conditions for an 18-to-25 trust are:

- property is held on trust for someone under age 25;
- a parent (or where loco parentis applies) of that person has died;
- the trust is in a will of the parent who has died, or is under the Criminal Injuries Compensation Scheme and meets the '*subsection 6*' conditions (see below);

  The '*subsection 6*' conditions are:

  (i) the beneficiary will, by age 25 or earlier, be absolutely entitled to the capital and all income arising and all accumulated income;

  (ii) their share of the trust fund has been sub-funded so that their fund has never been available to anyone else.

The 18-to-25 rules do not apply to other categories of trust property, such as that for bereaved minor's trusts, existing interest in possession trusts, IPDIs or disabled trusts.

Particular points of difficulty affecting BMTs and 18-to-25 trusts

8.9 HMRC guidance has emerged on three troublesome issues:

- who is a 'the bereaved minor' (or 'B' in the legislation);
- how the legislation deals with the class closing rules; and
- the treatment of settled powers of advancement.

In *s 71A* 'the bereaved minor' can mean all the beneficiaries in the class who are alive and under the age of 18 when the trust takes effect. This will assist in the common form of bequest to all children who reach age 18 in shares appointed by the trustees, where the power of appointment is limited to prevent augmentation or depletion of a share of a child over 18. As a result the fund could be paid out in unequal shares; but age 18 is an effective cut-off point for the further exercise of the power of appointment to that child. Any further 'favouritism' is limited to the children under 18.

Example 8.5—Reallocation of capital share

Henry died young leaving his estate to such of his sons, Charles and Trevor and his daughter Alice as should survive him and attain age 18, but with power of appointment among them. Initially, the trustees treated all three children the same; but Henry's brother Iain then died, leaving his estate to his nephews but nothing to Alice (at this point all three are still under age 18). To balance matters, the trustees now want to allocate a nominal 1% of the fund each to Charles and Trevor with the remainder to Alice.

This will not prejudice the BMT status of the interests. Charles and Trevor could still, up to age 18, benefit if the power in favour of Alice were to be revoked, because they are still 'B' for the purpose of the legislation.

The mere existence of a power of advancement does not prevent a BMT or 18-to-25 trust classification: it is the exercise of that power in such a way as to defer the vesting of capital that will cause a relevant property trust to arise.

IHT charge on 18-to-25 trusts (including conforming A&M trusts)

8.10 The IHT charge on an 18-to-25 trust is set out in *s 71E*. It will not apply if the beneficiary takes absolutely at age 18, or dies under that age, or if the trust property becomes subject to the rules for a BMT before the beneficiary becomes age 18 (perhaps where the trustees vary it so that it will vest at age 18) or the fund is used for the beneficiary before he is aged 18 or as soon as he is aged 18. This allows the trustees to bring an otherwise non-compliant trust within the rules to escape IHT. In all other cases the charge will apply when the fund leaves the trust or the trustees enter into a depreciatory transaction. There is no tax charge on a depreciatory transaction if at arm's length or if it is the grant of an agricultural tenancy within *s 16*.

The tax itself is calculated under *s 71E* when property comes out of the trust, either passing to the beneficiary absolutely or applied for his benefit after the beneficiary is 18; or he dies. The legislation uses a formula multiplying the 'chargeable amount' by 'the relevant fraction' and by the 'settlement rate'. To find the settlement rate the trustees must establish a notional transfer similar to that described later in this chapter in relation to periodic and exit charges.

Chargeable amount

8.11 This is the reduction in the value of the trust fund as a result of the transfer. Importantly, where the IHT is to be paid out of the remaining fund rather than out of the asset so released, the value of the transfer is the grossed-up amount.

Example 8.6—18-to-25 trust: simple release

On 31 May 2004 Cyril set up an A&M trust which provided for capital entitlement at age 25 such that in the post-21 March 2006 era it conforms to the 18-to-25 rules. It holds £400,000 for Cyril's eight grandchildren, hence £50,000 for each. Rachel, age 22, needs money to reduce her student loan, so the trustees pay her £20,000 on the basis that she will meet any IHT due. The chargeable amount attracting the IHT exit charge is £20,000.

Example 8.7—18-to-25 trust: net release

Continuing the above example, Rachel's brother would like a car costing £20,000 to celebrate his 21st birthday. He has asked the trustees for the funds to buy it and for the trust to pay any IHT exit charge that may be due on that sum. There is no income available to distribute thus the payment must come from capital which must be grossed up to bear its own tax. Assuming that the settlement rate is 18% and that the appropriate fraction (see below) is 12/40 the position would be as follows:

Tax rate –	18% × 30% × 12/40 = 1.62%.
Tax thereon –	£20,000 @ 1.62% = £324
Tax grossed up –	£324 @100/(100 – 1.62) = £329
Gross transfer –	£329 + £20,000 = £20,329

Thus a transfer of £20,329 would attract a tax charge of £329:

£20,329 × (18% × 30%) × 12/40 = £329, leaving a net £20,000.00.

Example 8.8—18-to-25 trust: fall in value of the fund

Dimitri's fund holds only shares in the family investment property company. His son Alexei aged 22 is now joining the board of directors, so the trustees want him to have some shares in his own right.

Owing to the different values of holdings, the fall in value of the fund is in fact greater than the value of the shares themselves. Notwithstanding, it is that greater value that is the transfer value for IHT purposes (but not for CGT purposes).

Relevant fraction

8.12 The relevant fraction for the purpose of the exit charge calculation for an 18-to-25 trust (to include a pre-March 2006 conforming A&M trust) is dependent upon the time elapsed from the date on which the beneficiary reached age 18 (or 6 April 2008 if later) to the date of the chargeable event, reckoned in complete quarters. The fraction is 30% of X/40 where X is the number of complete quarters counted from age 18 (or 6 April 2008 if later).

Example 8.9—18-to-25 trust: fractions, timing and risk

(i) Conforming A&M trust – Rachel's brother

This was illustrated in the example of Rachel's brother (see **Example 8.7**), who suffered tax based on the fraction 12/40. Rachel herself is aged 22: if she is in fact only two months short of her 23rd birthday, the fraction applicable to her is 19/40 (period 18 to 22 = 4 years = 16 period 10 months = 3 quarters thus 16 + 3 = 19 complete quarters).

(ii) Non-conforming A&M trust

The position is different for a non-conforming pre-March 2006 A&M trust. Consider that an A&M trust was established on 1 March 1998 (no other trusts were created on the same day and there was no settlor cumulative transfer history) which provided for income only at age 25 with capital at trustees' discretion – this would not conform to an 18-to-25 trust under *Finance Act 2006* and thus it formally 'migrated' to the relevant property regime on 6 April 2008 thereafter exposed to ten-year and exit charges. The next ten-year charge post-21 March 2006 would have fallen on 1 March 2008, but the relevant property regime did not actively apply to the trust until 6 April 2008. The trustees, having made no prior capital distributions, want to terminate the trust as soon as they safely may, but there are large gains and a simple chargeable asset appointment would trigger a CGT charge. How soon can they appoint assets and hold over the gains, relying on *TCGA 1992, s 260*?

The bold answer is 'as soon as they like', on the basis that any appointment that is a chargeable transfer qualifies as a chargeable transfer for the purposes of *TCGA 1992, s 260(2)(a)*. A transfer from a trust which, as in this case, was within the available trust nil rate band is still a chargeable transfer albeit at 0% and holdover relief is therefore in point. However that is different to the position of an appointment where no IHT is due because that transfer is not an IHT event, namely that it is made within the first quarter (period of three months) during which the relevant property regime applies.

The 'exit' charge is calculated under *s 65(1)*, but importantly such charge is disapplied (*s 65(4)*), if the appointment is made in a quarter beginning with the date of commencement or beginning with the date of the ten-year anniversary of the trust. . Accordingly, even though the result for IHT in economic terms is the same as a charge at 0% ie no IHT due, holdover under *TCGA 1992, s 260* is no longer in point – there is no occasion of charge for IHT purposes. The transfer should be delayed but by how long? Certainly until 1 June 2008 or later ie more than three complete months counting from the trust ten-year anniversary of 1 March 2008. Note that a 'quarter' is defined by *s 63* as any period of three months, so it can begin on any day and not just a 'quarter day' as such.

In this case the trust entered the relevant property regime on 6 April 2008 pursuant to *Finance Act 2006, Sch 20, para 3. Section 69(2)(b)* provides for the situation where property was in a trust at the last ten-year anniversary (in this case as at 1 March 2008); but was not then relevant property (the trust was not within the relevant property regime on that anniversary date) and has since become relevant property (the trust entered the relevant property regime on 6 April 2008). The tax in such a situation is charged at the 'appropriate fraction' of the rate, ie X/40 where X is the number of complete quarters from the last ten-year anniversary up to the date of the appointment; (see *s 69(4)*). What about the period from 6 April 2008 to 1 June 2008? That is not three months; but *s 68(3)(b)* treats a part-quarter as a full one (note the difference for a conforming 18 to 25 trust where only completed quarters count and from 6 April 2008 or later 18th birthday). On that basis the trustees can safely distribute after 1 June and hold over the gain.

Most trustees and many advisers will play safe and let a further, clear, full quarter elapse, so as to avoid the complexities of this legislation. In any event the IHT charge may be very small compared with the CGT in issue.

Settlement rate

8.13 This is the effective rate, namely the tax expressed as a fraction of the notional chargeable transfer and it can be found only after other calculations have been performed. Although the multi-step calculation is difficult to grasp, it can be performed by using the form IHT100 with the working sheet IHT100(WS) and the guide IHT113. These can be downloaded at the HMRC website: www.gov.uk/government/organisations/hm-revenue-customs.

The notional transfer

8.14 As with relevant property trusts generally, there are a number of components namely:

- the original value of the trust to include the value of non-relevant property contained therein (but with the latter excluded for chargeable events occurring post 17 November 2015);
- the value of any related trust (with non-relevant related trusts excluded for chargeable events occurring post-17 November 2015); and
- the value of any property added to the trust post creation and before the event now being taxed.

Example 8.10—Grandchildren's trust: the notional transfer

Sean, who had not utilised his annual exemption, divided £400,000 between two trusts that he set up the same day on 6 April 2015: one for his daughter Megan in liferent and the other a discretionary trust for the benefit of Megan's children. On 16 June 2016, having made no other gifts but fearful of a rise in CGT, he put quoted shares worth £26,500 into the grandchildren discretionary trust.

	£	
Transfer to the grandchildren trust	200,000	
Less: half of annual exemption	(1,500)	
	198,500	
Transfer to related trust as above	198,500	
Original notional transfer	397,000	(A)
Addition		
	26,500	
Less: annual exemption	(3,000)	
	23,500	(B)
Revised notional transfer (A + B)	420,500	

Life interest trusts

Focus

Most lifetime interest in possession trusts created post-21 March 2006 will now fall within the relevant property regime.

8.15 Sometimes a change in tax law proves particularly difficult for practitioners and their clients to grasp and there is a tendency to hearken back to the old law. A classic example is the treatment of gifts under estate duty where taper relief applied to reduce the value of the gift itself in order to arrive at the value on which estate duty was charged. This rule was changed to the point of complete reverse under IHT such that chargeable lifetime gifts are now set initially against the nil rate band with taper relief, where in point, applied to the tax rate and not to the value of the gift. Notwithstanding the nearly 40 year passage of time elapsed, there is still adherence to the memory of that old estate duty treatment. In this same way, there will be many practitioners and their clients who will have a fundamental difficulty in accepting that a newly created life interest trust, treated as such for many purposes such as:

- matrimonial proceedings; or
- the taxation of income; or
- the taxation of gains where main residence may be in point;

is not treated as an old, 'estate' interest in possession trust for IHT purposes but is instead treated as a relevant property trust. The difficulty may be compounded by anti-avoidance legislation, which often employs the concept of a double negative: see for example the complex changes introduced by *Finance Act 2010, ss 52* and *53*, noted at **7.24** relating to reversionary interests and purchased life interests.

Except where it is a disabled trust, a BMT, 18-to-25 or IPDI, an interest in possession trust will now fall within the relevant property trust regime unless saved by the existing or transitional rules. In this chapter unless preceded by 'qualifying' or 'old style', the term 'interest in possession trust' in which a beneficiary has a right to income is, a trust for IHT purposes which is treated as a relevant property trust under the post-21 March 2006 regime. The conditions for an IPDI are set out in **Chapter 7**.

Post-21 March 2006 virtually any life interest trust established during the lifetime of the settlor and even if settlor interested will be treated as a relevant property trust for IHT purposes and thus its creation will be an immediate chargeable transfer. The trust will be subject to the periodic (ten-year anniversary) charge described at **8.38** and may incur the proportionate (exit) charge described at **8.26** and following below. Contrary to the traditional treatment of interest in possession trusts, there will (except in relation to purchased interests and reversions of settlor-interested trusts) be no aggregation of the capital of a life interest trust with the estate of the liferenter. There will, for CGT, be some holdover relief such that there will be scope for tax planning opportunities.

Example 8.11—Life interest trust: lifetime transfer failing to comply with new rules

Henry, who has made no previous chargeable transfers and has not used his current or prior annual exemptions (current and previous year), settled £331,000 on trust for his wife for life with the fee to their children at 25. The trust was made on 6 May 2016 during Henry's lifetime.

This cannot be an IPDI because it is a lifetime settlement. The result is that it must be treated as a relevant property trust. That in turn means that Henry's wife is not deemed to be the owner of the trust fund for IHT purposes as would have been the case under the old rules. As a result, the spousal relief is not available. Fortunately, after taking account of the two annual exemptions available, the amount of the settlement is within Henry's unused nil rate band ((£331,000 – (£3,000 + 3,000) = £325,000), so its creation does not trigger an IHT charge. However, Henry must keep good records for the future in case he decides to make any other settlements later.

THE RELEVANT PROPERTY IHT REGIME

The range of charges

8.16 There are three main occasions of charge on a relevant property trust:

- Entry charges:
  - On creation: use event form IHT100a.
  - On any addition to the fund, other than an exempt addition such as one within *s 21* (normal expenditure out of income): use event form IHT100a.
- Exit charges:
  - Before the first ten-year anniversary: use event form IHT100c.
  - Between ten-year anniversaries: use event form IHT100c.
- Ten-year charges:
  - Use event form IHT100d.

Other charges to IHT can apply, when for example:

- a qualifying interest in possession comes to an end and a relevant property trust arises; or
- a special charge arises, for example on a heritage fund; or
- woodland that was previously exempt is felled; or
- a chargeable event arises on a pension that has been 'alternatively secured' (prior to the abolition of those pension rules in *Finance Act 2011*); or
- a purchased reversionary interest vests;

but these are all outside the scope of this chapter.

TRANSFERS INTO TRUST: THE ENTRY CHARGE

Simple cases

Commencement

8.17 It is important for many of the IHT calculations involving relevant property trusts to know the trust commencement date but that will not always be easy to establish. The legislation is brief: '..references to the commencement of a settlement are references to the time when property first becomes comprised in it..'. This rule is not subject to *de minimis*, so the creation of a pilot trust with an initial £100 will be the commencement of that trust even though the bulk of funds are not added until, say, a death many years later. The importance of the commencement date is highly relevant to those old A&M trusts which fall foul of the post-21 March 2006 trust regime which from 6 April 2008 became subject to the ten-year anniversary charge (see **Example 8.9 (ii)**).

A slightly different but important rule applies where a trust is initially 'favoured' in some way but becomes a relevant property trust at a later date. Under *s 80(1)* the property is treated as joining a new settlement at the time when the first, favoured, interest ends – unusually, it is treated as a transfer made by the person holding the qualifying interest in possession at the time of change and not the original settlor. This does not affect the commencement date of the original trust which is relevant for counting of subsequent ten-year anniversaries. However, difficult questions arise where there has been more than one settlor and property has been added at various times. The general approach for the practitioner must be to recommend a new trust for each major transfer of property: the initial cost will be recouped in savings later.

Example 8.12—Transfer into trust: small family trust

On 7 December 2005, Hubert set up an old style A & M trust for the benefit of his grandchildren with £100, and on the same day he made a will leaving to it a further £300,000 – Hubert died on 3 February 2006. A review of the trust in the light of the *Finance Act 2006* showed that, in the particular circumstances given the ages of the relevant beneficiaries, unless appointments were made promptly half of the funds would be held on a relevant property trust from 6 April 2008 onwards.

The trustees thought the risk of dissipation of the fund by young beneficiaries was much greater than possible IHT charges. They anticipated that the nil rate band would increase, so they did nothing before 6 April 2008 and nothing was paid out. The first ten-year charge fell due on 7 December 2015 (but tax is calculated by reference to only part of the ten-year period namely from 6 April 2008 when it first entered the new regime).

Example 8.13—Migration of a trust to relevant property regime

As at 21 March 2006, Iain was the established liferenter of a trust established by him on 31 December 1986. On 30 June 2016 the trustees at his request terminated his interest and relevant property trusts arose for his grandchildren. The capital of the fund is treated as passing to a new trust on 30 June 2016 and the event is a chargeable transfer by Iain, but the next ten-year anniversary will be on 31 December 2016 (anniversary of original trust creation) not 30 June 2026 (anniversary of creation of new trust).

Example 8.1 concerned the setting up of a relevant property trust by Alice and of the calculation of IHT on that occasion. The initial charge on establishing a settlement is relevant in later computations but at this stage is quite straightforward with PETs ignored because they may fall out of account if the seven-year survival test is met. The annual exemption (and that for the previous year if available) is set against the first transfer made in any given tax year: see *s 19(3)(b)* and where there are no earlier chargeable transfers the nil rate band is applied to the balance of the gift with the excess taxed at 20%. The only complicating issue is to observe whether the gift is gross, here meaning that the donee will pay any IHT on it, or net, in which case the donor will pay the extra tax on the grossed up gift.

Example 8.14—Simple gross gift

On 13 April 2016 Sandra settles investment properties worth £370,000 on relevant property trusts. The previous tax year, she used her annual exemption but she has made no other gifts. She tells the trustees that they must pay any IHT due.

	£
Value transferred	370,000
Exemption 2016/17	(3,000)
	367,000
Nil rate band 2016/17	(325,000)
Excess	42,000
IHT @ 20%	8,400

Grossing-up

8.18 If the donor agrees to pay the tax that tax is established by grossing-up the value of the intended net transfer by the IHT due thereon. On lifetime transfers the grossing-up fraction for the tax is one-quarter; on death transfers the grossing-up fraction is two-thirds. In calculating the tax any previous chargeable transfers must be taken into account.

Example 8.15—Net gift following previous chargeable transfer

On 4 April 2016 Tanya gives trustees £280,000 cash to hold on relevant property trust similar to the trust to which she had made a chargeable transfer in the previous year of £100,000. She has used her annual exemption in each year. The gift is to be 'tax free'.

		£
Value transferred		280,000
Annual exemption fully utilised		
Nil rate band 2015/16	325,000	
Less: previous chargeable transfer	(100,000)	
Remaining nil rate band		(225,000)
Net transfer		55,000
Gross transfer £55,000 × 100/80		68,750
IHT £68,750 @ 20%		13,750

8.19 Although the tax charged on the initial lifetime transfer is calculated at the lifetime rate that rate is subject to review to take account of the higher death rate of 40% if the death of the donor subsequently occurs within seven years. However, despite the disparity in the rates, the review may not result in an increased charge and this is typically the case where the available nil rate band has increased in the interim: to the extent that the review results in a lower charge then there is no refund of the earlier tax.

Example 8.16—Death within three years of a small chargeable transfer

Una died on 31 March 2012. She had made a relevant property trust on 4 April 2009 of £330,000 gross. She had already used her annual exemption (current and prior year) but had made no prior chargeable transfers. When the trust was set up, the entry charge was:

	£
Value transferred	330,000
Nil rate band 2008/09	(312,000)
Excess	18,000
Tax @ 20%	3,600

Death occurs within three years, so it is necessary to recalculate using the 'death' rate as required by *s 7(4)*:

	£
Value transferred	330,000
Nil rate band 2011/12 (year of death)	(325,000)
	5,000
Tax @ 40%	2,000
Deduct tax already paid	(3,600)
Additional tax charge	NIL

8.20 Where the figures are larger, it is much more likely that death within three years, where no taper applies, will trigger a charge to additional tax.

Example 8.17—Death within three years of a large chargeable transfer

Victor died on 31 March 2012 and having made a relevant property trust on 5 April 2009 of £750,000 gross. He had already used his annual exemptions. On setting up the trust, the tax charge was:

	£
Value transferred	750,000
Nil rate band 2008/09	(312,000)
Excess	438,000
Tax at 20%	87,600

Death occurs within three years. Apply the death rate, at the rates then in force thus:

	£
Value transferred	750,000
Nil rate band 2011/12	(325,000)
	425,000
Tax @ 40%	170,000
Less tax paid earlier	(87,600)
Balance now payable	82,400

8.21 The final factor that can affect the entry charge is the existence of prior transfers which, though a PETs when made, become chargeable (as a failed PET) because the donor's death occurs within seven years thereof and thus have first call on the nil rate band.

Example 8.18—Review of earlier tax charge and re-computation at death rates

Willie, who died on 31 December 2016, always used his annual exemption and had made a number of lifetime gifts, thus:

	£
31 March 2008: cash to his daughter (outright)	150,000
31 January 2010: cash to his son	172,000
28 February 2014: investment property to a relevant property trust	330,000

No IHT was paid on the cash gifts, being PETs.

Tax was paid on setting up the relevant property trust as follows:

	£
Value transferred	330,000
Nil rate 2013/14	(325,000)
Excess	5,000
Tax at 20%	1,000

On death the gift in 2008 falls out of account as it was made more than seven years earlier but the PET in 2010 has now failed and is chargeable. The nil rate band otherwise available is first used towards and wholly covers this gift, so there is no tax to pay, but the position for the 2014 transfer into the relevant property trust must now be revisited following the repositioning of the nil rate band against the earlier gifts.

	£	£
Value transferred		330,000
Nil rate band 2013/14 (event date)	325,000	
Less: used for gift to son	(172,000)	
		(153,000)
Balance		177,000

	£	£
Lifetime tax at 20% (but see below)	35,400	
Less paid earlier	(1,000)	
Payable now in respect of original event (subject as below)		34,400

Death has occurred within three years so it is necessary to adjust the calculation for the increased death rate.

	£	£
Value transferred		330,000
Nil rate band 2016/17	325,000	
Less: used for gift to son	(172,000)	
		(153,000)
Excess		177,000
Tax at 40%	70,800	
Less: paid originally	(1,000)	
Less: payable at lifetime rates	(34,400)	
Excess payable at death rates		35,400

In the above example it was not strictly necessary to recalculate the tax at the lifetime rates to establish the further burden of tax but circumstances may be imagined where, because of periodic changes in the rates, each step in the calculation is necessary.

Migrations from the pre-2006 regime: the general position

8.22 The intention of *Finance Act 2006* was to extend the IHT relevant property regime to now include those various trusts that previously were outside that regime such as interest in possession trusts subject to overriding powers and A&M trusts where capital did not vest until post age 25. The position of qualifying interest in possession trusts is protected until that pre March 2006 interest expires (or even longer in a transitional serial interest). On the termination of those interests there will be an IHT charge if the property remains settled and irrespective of whether it then falls, as is most likely, to be held on relevant property trusts or not.

By *s 51(1A)*, the disposal of a post-21 March 2006 interest in possession is a transfer of value unless that interest is an IPDI, a disabled person's interest or a TSI. By *s 51(1B)*, the disposal of a pre 22 March 2006 interest in possession is a transfer of value unless immediately before that disposal the trust as a whole complies with the requirements of *s 71A* trusts for bereaved minors or *s 71D*: in other words, that on the disposal the trust will become either the property of minors at the age of 18 or the property of others no later than age 25.

Migration of interest in possession trusts to the relevant property trust tax regime

8.23 *Section 52* provides the general rule that there is a charge to tax on the coming to an end of a qualifying interest in possession, but with the condition that where that interest is sold the proceeds of sale are set against the value that would otherwise be taxed. *Section 52(2A)* provides that in relation to 'new' interests in possession, *s 52(1)* and *(2)* apply only where the interest being terminated is an IPDI, or a disabled person's interest, or a TSI. The same applies to depreciatory transactions.

Section 53(1A) provides for an exception from the general charge to tax on the fund under *s 52* in relation to an established qualifying interest in possession which continues after 21 March 2006 where, on the latter cessation of that interest, the requirements of a BMT or an 18-to-25 trust are met. The structure that results is that the termination of a qualifying interest in possession that existed before 22 March 2006 is still to be treated under the old pre-22 March 2006 rules thus:

- on that termination the fund becomes part of the estate of another person and it is a PET; and
- on that termination the trust continues and relevant property trusts arise (as is most likely the case) it is a chargeable transfer deemed made by the person giving up their qualifying interest, namely the liferenter.

On the other hand, the termination of an interest in possession which has only come into being after 21 March 2006 (thus a non-qualifying interest unless an IPDI) will be a chargeable transfer unless it is brought within the exceptional regime for a TSI or a BMT.

Migration of A&M trusts to the relevant property trust tax regime

> **Focus**
>
> Those old style A&M trusts the terms of which were timely amended to provide for capital (as opposed to income) entitlement at age 25 will only attract a modified exit charge – they will not be subject to a ten-year charge irrespective of the passage of time post-5 April 2008 before entitlement occurs.

8.24 The beneficial IHT treatment previously enjoyed by the old style A&M trust was terminated with effect from 22 March 2006. Any beneficiary who had already obtained an interest in possession at that date could happily continue to benefit from the old treatment.

However, a beneficiary who by accident of date of birth had not achieved an interest in possession by 22 March 2006 would henceforth be treated as a beneficiary of a relevant property trust, making their interest potentially subject to periodic and exit charges. This could cause significant disadvantage as between one beneficiary and another thus the provisions were softened a little to provide the trustees with a limited range of options.

Example 8.19—A&M trust: no election by the trustees

Hannah had four grandchildren for whom, in 1999, she set up an A&M trust. It was in simple form such that the children became entitled to income at the age of 18 and to capital at age 25. The trustees were either unaware of the right to elect into the 'at 18 (BMT)' regime or considered it unwise for family reasons.

By 22 March 2006 the eldest grandchild, Isaac, was 25 and had already received his one quarter capital share. Thus he was not affected at all by the post-21March 2006 regime and there was no *TCGA 1992 s 260* holdover relief for CGT purposes.

Jessica was aged 24 on 22 March 2006 and thus had an established income entitlement. She did not suffer an IHT charge on her one third share of the remaining fund when she became entitled to the capital in March 2007 as this occurred before the watershed of 6 April 2008. Conversely, there was no *TCGA 1992 s 260* holdover relief for CGT purposes.

Karen was 18 in January 2008 and as she had not established an interest in possession as at 21 March 2006, her one half of the remaining fund entered the relevant property regime on 22 March 2006. The delayed impact of the *Finance Act 2006* measures until 6 April 2008 ensured that there was no IHT charge when she became entitled to that interest in January 2008. However, the original freedom from IHT exit charges enjoyed by her elder sisters was lost post-5 April 2008 such that her fund suffered tax on the 18-to-25 basis when she became entitled to the trust capital in January 2015. As a consequence there was *TCGA 1992 s 260* holdover relief for CGT purposes.

Jenny was age 18 in December 2009 and as she had not established an interest in possession as at 21 March 2006, the remainder of the trust fund comprising her share entered the relevant property regime on 22 March 2006. There was no IHT impact when she became entitled to interest in December 2009 as the trust continued in existence but her fund suffers tax on the 18-to-25 basis when she becomes entitled to the trust capital in December 2016. As a consequence there will be *TCGA 1992 s 260* holdover relief for CGT purposes.

8.25 The transitional provisions were set out in *s 71(1A)* and *FA 2006, Sch 20, para 3*. If the terms of the trust were changed so that the age for vesting capital was reduced to 18, its A&M status could be preserved. The time for this has now passed but the following illustration may be relevant to understanding the tax treatment.

Example 8.20—Transitional provisions: action by the trustees

Referring back to the **Example 8.19** above, although the trust entered the relevant property regime on 22 March 2006 there was actually no exit charge when Jessica became entitled to the capital in March 2007 because of the transitional provisions of *Finance Act 2006, Sch 20, para 3(3)* which deferred active entry into the relevant property regime until 6 April 2008. The reason is one of timing of charges. Under the transitional provisions the capital was not treated as being within a relevant property trust until 6 April 2008. Capital that vested before that date therefore escaped the charge. Interests in possession that arose after that date did so within the context of a relevant property trust; they were not an occasion of charge.

THE PROPORTIONATE OR 'EXIT' CHARGE DURING THE FIRST TEN YEARS

> **Focus**
>
> Whilst the exit charge is only applied to the capital distribution itself, the rate of that charge is dependent on a combination of established values and time elapsed between date of trust creation and date of distribution. A nil rate band trust can therefore still produce a positive exit charge.

General considerations and the procedure

8.26 The taxation of relevant property trusts could have been made very much simpler by applying a single tax rate to all such trusts, regardless of size. Instead, the deliberate intention to tax settlements that are larger or that are derived from a larger estate, more heavily than smaller ones, has led to the introduction of complex rules. A fund that is within the nil rate band and remains so is infinitely easier to manage than a larger fund. The rate of tax is stipulated in *s 68(1)*, referring to:

- 'the appropriate fraction' of
- 'the effective rate' applied to
- the type of transfer identified in *s 68(4)*, but as varied by
- *s 68(6)* in relation to old trusts.

Perseverance is demanded in order to grasp the principles. This is one of the few areas where HMRC will help with the calculation and as a consequence some practitioners will be less inclined to become involved in the actual computation. However, this approach will severely curtail the ability to check the accuracy of any HMRC assessment and that must remain a concern. This is recognised within the professional organisations, such that both the Chartered Institute of Taxation (CIOT) and the Society of Trust and Estate Practitioners (STEP) now require new members to demonstrate much more than a basic level of competence in dealing with this subject.

There is no doubt that the complexities of the charges triggered under the relevant property regime have been heightened by the *Finance Act 2006* trust legislation. Responding to the concerns of professional advisers, it was announced in the March 2012 Budget there would be a consultative process launched to explore possible options for simplifying the calculation of the IHT periodic and exit charges on trusts that hold or dispose of relevant property. HMRC subsequently published a consultation document on 13 July 2012 to which the various professional bodies' response was invited and the outcome of that consultation was published in March 2013. It identified a number of areas of concern, simplification and potential reform to include standard treatment of accumulations, problems with poor historic records and the need for a uniform approach to multiple trusts. However, whilst HMRC rejected out of hand some suggestions ie a reversion to the pre-March 2006 rules for old style A&M trusts and exclusion of the non-qualifying IIP trusts and 18-to-25 trusts from the relevant property regime, HMRC did accept that there was a real need to make the system more workable and user friendly and acknowledged that more work was needed. A further consultation will be published in the coming months concentrating on:

- a simplified method of calculating the ten yearly and exit charges;
- clearer rules concerning the treatment and recognition of accumulated income; and
- the alignment of IHT trust charges, filing and payment dates.

On 31 May 2013 HMRC released a follow up consultative document (see '*Inheritance tax: simplifying charges on trusts – the next stage*', 31 May 2013) which provided more detail to the proposed method of reforms for the above three headings namely:

(i) Ten-year charge:

- dropping the seven-year settlor cumulative history;
- ignoring non-relevant property;
- dividing the nil rate band by the total number of settlements created by the settlor whenever created; and
- introduction of a standard 6% rate.

(ii) Accumulations:

Giving statutory recognition to capital status of accumulated income not distributed by the end of the second year in which the income arises.

(iii) Compliance alignment:

Alignment with the self-assessment framework for filing and payment dates.

On 10 December 2013 HMRC formally advised that following representations made by the key interest groups who participated in the consultation process, changes had been made to the original proposals namely:

(1) to introduce a new rule proposing to treat income that has remained undistributed for more than five years at the date of the ten-year anniversary as if it was part of the trust capital for the purposes of the ten-year anniversary charge;

(2) to align filing and payment dates to a uniform six months after the end of the month in which the event occurred;

(3) consult further on alternative proposals to split the nil rate band that will meet trustees' concerns whilst maintaining tax revenues and as a result:

- put the simplification of the calculations on a slightly slower track so that any new legislation would be introduced in the Finance Bill 2015; and
- defer the proposal to require trustees to 'self-assess' IHT due until Finance Bill 2015.

Finance Act 2014 gave statutory authority (i) for accumulations and (ii) for compliance alignment introduced with effect from 6 April 2014 but it was intended that (i) would be subject to further consultation. However, on 6 June 2014 in a fresh and unexpected development, HMRC published a third consultation document on IHT trust simplification. It contained new proposals aimed at thwarting the popular use of pilot trust by preventing taxpayers from reducing their IHT liability through setting up multiple trusts each using a separate nil rate band. HMRC proposed applying a single nil rate band (to be known as a 'settlement nil rate band') to all relevant property trusts created by the same settlor since 6 June 2014 but with the ability of the settlor to elect how that settlement nil rate band should be allocated. HMRC also restated their intention to introduce a standard fixed 6% charge to ease the complications of the current system.

More surprises were to follow when the December 2014 Autumn Budget stated that yet again the proposals previously announced (settlement nil rate band) were to be scrapped. In their place new measures would apply, intended to remove the need to recognise the value of non-relevant property when calculating the ten-year charge/exit charge and introducing rules dealing with the same-day addition of later added property to multiple trusts. The measures also included changes to the relevant property trust legislation intended to provide more certainty and to ease the effect/complexity of the legislation – in particular *s 144* would be amended so that the provisions of *s 65(4)* which prevent an IHT exit charge arising in the first three months after the will trust commenced (the *Frankland* trap) would not apply to appointments so made thereby allowing the appointment to be read back into the will and claim the benefit of the spousal exemption where appropriate.

Further, the value of non-relevant property would no longer be included in the ten-year charge calculation. The proposed measures, were contained in the Finance Bill 2015, and were intended to apply to all charges arising on or after 6 April 2015 in respect of relevant property trusts created on or after the publication of draft legislation on 10 December 2014. To prevent any pre-emptive steps, it would also apply to such trusts created before 10 December

2014 where additions were made to more than one trust on the same day. It was intended that this latter provision would not apply to transfers into pilot trusts on death occurring before 6 April 2016 provided they were made under the terms of a will which was put in place immediately before 10 December 2014). This latter measure initially raised concerns that post-December 2014 codicils could result in a loss of protection but this was later clarified in subsequent HMRC exchange.

However, due to the general election in May 2015 affording little time to debate the Finance Bill provisions on its passage through Parliament, none of the above intended trust measures made their way into *Finance Act 2015*. However, this has been partially addressed by the summer *Finance (No 2) Act 2015* which now provides for the following:

(i) Exclusion of non-relevant property

The calculation of the periodic and exit charges will be simplified by removing the need to include the (historic) value of non-relevant property (namely that property not subject to the IHT system of ten-year and exit charges) within the notional transfer total. This applies to all chargeable events arising on or after 18 November 2015 (date of Royal Assent).

(ii) Same-day additions

Aimed at negating the benefit of multiple trusts (pilot trusts) use, the rule will operate to ensure that where property is added to more than one relevant property trust on the same day (on or after commencement of those trusts) that added value together with the original value of that trust when first settled (to the extent not already recognised as a related settlement) will be brought into account in calculating the rate of tax for the purpose of the ten-year and exit charges. There is a *de miminis* exemption where the same-day addition is £5,000 or less (*s 62(2)–(4)*). The new provision will not apply to a will executed before 10 December 2014 where the death occurs before 6 April 2017 and will apply to all chargeable events taking place on or after 18 November 2015 (date of Royal Assent).

The above anti-avoidance legislation does not apply if either (or both) trust A and trust B is a 'protected settlement' (*s 62C*) namely a trust is which commenced before 10 December 2014 and either of two conditions (A or B) is satisfied:

- Condition A is broadly that the settlor has not added value to the settlement since 10 December 2014.
- Alternatively, Condition B is that the settlor makes a transfer on or after 10 December 2014 resulting in the value of the property being increased, where the transfer arises (under *s 4*) on the settlor's death before 6 April 2017 by reason of a 'protected testamentary disposition' (ie under the

settlor's will, where its provisions are substantially the same as they were immediately before 10 December 2014).

It should be noted that it still remains possible for the settlor to create a new relevant property trust every seven years, each with its own nil rate band (assuming that no other chargeable transfers or potentially exempt transfers have been made in the intervening periods). Furthermore, consideration could be given to adding business property to an existing trust, although as indicated such additions should generally be made on different days.

(iii) The 'Frankland' trap

The three-month waiting period for an absolute appointment out of a will trust (in which no qualifying interest in possession exists) to the surviving spouse or civil partner will be withdrawn paving the way for full spousal relief. This action reflects the treatment already afforded to the carve-out of an interest in possession in favour of the surviving spouse or civil partner. The new rules will apply to the testator's death on or after 10 December 2014. The Petition of *Nickson, Houldsworth and Lewis Petitioners* [2016] CSOH 119 seeking rectification of a 2012 deed of appointment caught under the old rules and the 'Frankland' Trap was disallowed rectification.

(iv) *Section 80* rejigged

The wording of *s 80* has now been amended to correct an unintended effect which permitted a successive spousal non-qualifying interest in possession to potentially escape IHT charge because the trust assets were neither part of the successor's estate nor comprised within a relevant property trust. The term 'interest in possession' will now be replaced with the term 'qualifying interest in possession' – the latter referring to an interest that is either a pre-22 March 2006 established interest, an IPDI, transitional serial interest (TSI) or disabled person's interest as set out in *s 59*. Accordingly, where one party to a couple succeeds to a life interest to which their spouse or civil partner was previously entitled during their lifetime, *s 80* will continue to apply at that time.

8.27 Where the fund value is greater than the nil rate band but the circumstances are simple, the computation is still manageable. The legislation, which is contained in *ss 64–69*, delivers little practical guidance since it expresses the charge without the use of formulae or examples. A more helpful tool is the actual form IHT100 itself – this can be simply downloaded together with the related forms IHT100d and IHT100 (WS) accompanied by completion instructions. In contrast, the similar calculation required for an 18-to-25 trust, is clearly set out in *s 71F*, it does use a formula and it is slightly easier to follow – perhaps this style has benefited from a more modern draftsperson.

In a simple case the settlor will not have added any funds to the trust since its creation. However it is distressingly common for this 'rule' to be breached and this does make the calculations more complicated – see **Example 8.29** below.

Further complications arise where the relevant property trust is also used as the vehicle for holding family assets which are the subject of pre March 2006/ TSI or interest in possession trusts: see **Example 8.24** below. Following the changes in *Finance Act 2006*, this is perhaps likely to be less of a problem in time because it will no longer be possible to create new lifetime interest in possession trusts outside of the relevant property regime.

Establishing the 'hypothetical transfer'

8.28 The complete calculation is dependent on a series of steps which taken together achieve a graduated tax burden. The first step in the calculation is to determine a hypothetical transfer as required by *s 68(4)*. The process may become clearer by working through several illustrative examples. Elements of the hypothetical transfer include (see *s 68(4)(b)):*

- the initial transfer into trust itself;
- the initial value of other settlements made on the same day (excluding non-relevant property settlements for chargeable events on or after 18 November 2015); and
- funds added later.

The following notes relate only to settlements established after 26 March 1974, thus avoiding the complexities of *s 68(6)*.

Example 8.21—The hypothetical transfer: simplest version

Alfred had used his annual exemptions and the other reliefs to the full but had made no chargeable transfers until 31 October 2015, when he put a small investment property, worth £260,000, into a relevant property trust for his grandchildren.

The hypothetical transfer comprises:

	£
• value of property in trust at commencement	260,000
• value of property in any related settlement	NIL
• value of any added property	NIL
Total	260,000

This is within the nil rate band then in force (£325,000 for 2015/16) so, as will be seen later, no IHT will be payable on transfer out of the fund during the first ten years of its life (provided there are no later additions).

8.29 The transfer is made up of the full value of the property, even though reliefs or exemptions may apply to the settlor – it should be remembered that no tax is actually being paid at this stage thus the taxpayer is not disadvantaged. *Section 62* defines a 'related settlement' as one made on the same day by the same settlor, except where one is for charity or covered by the spousal exemption.

Example 8.22—The hypothetical transfer: related settlement and business property

Bernard transferred a block of properties to a relevant property trust (No 1) created on 31 October 2015. It comprised a factory occupied by Bernard's family company (in which Bernard has a controlling shareholding) and some terraced cottages adjoining. The factory was worth £200,000, the cottages £150,000. The same day Bernard settled £50,000 cash on a separate relevant property trust (No 2).

The hypothetical transfer comprises:

	£
• value of the property in trust at commencement (No 1)	350,000
• value of property in related settlement (No 2)	50,000
• value of any added property	NIL
Total	400,000

Following through the point mentioned above, although BPR at 50% is in point with regard to the factory, that relief is ignored when (and only when) calculating the hypothetical transfer.

8.30 A common concern is whether the tax borne by the trustees on the transfer in of trust property should be deducted from the value of the trust fund for the purposes of the hypothetical transfer.

Example 8.23—The hypothetical transfer: allowance for tax debt

Celia owned a block of flats worth £415,000 and settled it on a relevant property trust on 31 October 2015 on terms that the trustees would pay any IHT due thereon. Celia had made one chargeable transfer of £50,000 (net of the annual exemptions for that and the previous year) earlier that year which was not connected with the trust.

The IHT on the transfer into trust is by reference to:

	£
• the transfer itself	415,000
• the earlier 'unconnected' transfer	50,000
	465,000
less: nil rate band 2015/16	(325,000)
chargeable excess	140,000
20% of excess (the 'entry' charge):	28,000

The hypothetical transfer comprises:

	£
• value of property in trust at commencement	415,000
• less the entry charge	(28,000)
	387,000
• value of property in related settlement	NIL
• value of any added property	NIL
Total	387,000

There is no statutory authority for the deduction of tax but it is a logical approach – the value of the trust fund must be the actual value received. Note that at this point it is not necessary to consider the prior chargeable transfer (in this example £50,000) – that may be relevant later but is not a component of this stage of the calculation and is not included within the elements set out in *s 68(5)*.

8.31 Where (in the case of trusts established before 22 March 2006) part of the trust fund was not held on relevant property trusts, logic suggests that that value should be excluded but this was not the case until 18 November 2015 (see **8.26** above). Of course since 22 March 2006 the entire fund will likely be a relevant property trust, so this particular issue will disappear in time but it remained on the radar until 18 November 2015.

Example 8.24—The hypothetical transfer: mixed (but not exempt) settlement

On 31 March 2006, Dennis created a trust, valued at £540,000 of which one half of the fund is for his niece in liferent whilst the remainder is held on discretionary trust terms. The hypothetical transfer for events taking place before 18 November 2015 comprises:

	£
• 100% value of property in trust at commencement	540,000
• value of property in related settlement	NIL
• value of any added property	NIL
Total	540,000

The fact that one half of the fund was a PET on creation (under the old pre 22 March 2006 rules) did not impact on the hypothetical transfer in this example. However, by virtue of the new rules contained in *Finance (No 2) Act 2015*, which excludes recognition of related non-relevant property, this will impact on events taking place after 17 November 2015.

Example 8.25—Trust migrating to the relevant property regime under the new rules

Doreen had made chargeable transfers totalling £75,000 in 1995 and created two settlements on 31 July 1996. The first, of £100,000, provided for a liferent interest for her son Eric. The second, of £350,000, was on old style A&M trusts for her grandchildren. By virtue of *Finance Act 2006* the A&M trust migrated to the relevant property regime on 6 April 2008 and its first ten-year charge fell due on 31 July 2016.

The hypothetical transfer comprises:

	£
• Value of property in A&M at commencement	350,000
• Value of property in related settlement	100,000
• Value of any added property	NIL
Total	450,000

8.32 Related settlements (but restricted to relevant property-related settlements only post-17 November 2015) can greatly affect the rate and this will be relevant in relation to A&M trusts that migrated to the IHT regime under *Finance Act 2006*, where it will now be necessary to look at the element that is caught by the new rules in the context of the trust as a whole. The way in which this rule can work is discussed below. However, by virtue of the new rules contained in *Finance (No 2) Act 2015,* which excludes recognition of related non-relevant property, this will impact on events taking place on or after 18 November 2015 (date of Royal Assent).

Example 8.26—The hypothetical transfer: death same day as settlement

Eric made a relevant property trust (No 1) of £400,000 on 30 November 2015 and died later that day, leaving an estate of £500,000 on a separate relevant property trust (No 2). No reliefs were available on death.

The hypothetical transfer comprises:

	£
• value of the fund at commencement (No 1)	400,000
• value of property in related transfer (No 2)	500,000
• value of any added property	NIL
Total	900,000

8.33 An exemption is treated differently from a relief. Whereas reliefs do not affect the hypothetical transfer, exemptions may, as seen in the next example.

Example 8.27—The hypothetical transfer: death same-day as settlement

On 30 November Frances made an interest in possession trust (No 1) of £100,000. She died later that day having by her will left £100,000 on trust (No 2) for her local church, £200,000 to her husband absolutely and the residue of £350,000 on discretionary trust (No 3).

The hypothetical transfer comprises:

		£
•	value of the fund at commencement (No 1)	100,000
•	value of property in related settlement (No 3)	350,000
•	value of any added property	NIL
Total		450,000

8.34 Where funds are left on trust for a charity 'without limit of time' there is, as noted earlier, no aggregation: see *s 62(2)*.

Example 8.28—The hypothetical transfer: exempt share of the trust

On her death on 30 November 2015 Gina left £600,000 in trust as to one half on IPDI terms for her husband Gregory for life and the other half on discretionary trust. She had made no previous chargeable transfers during her lifetime. The hypothetical transfer comprises:

		£
•	50% value of relevant property fund at commencement	300,000
•	value of property in related transfer	NIL
•	value of any added property	NIL
Total		300,000

This position, where the spousal exemption comes into play, should be contrasted with the example of Dennis above.

8.35 Curiously, even where an asset is added to the trust but is later distributed, it still affects the calculation. For valuation purposes it would seem that each asset is valued in isolation.

Example 8.29—The hypothetical transfer: extra funds for a while

On 30 November 2013 Henry settled a property worth £300,000 on discretionary trust. On 30 April 2014 he added £100,000 cash, of which £75,000 was released at Christmas 2015. The trustees paid the appropriate exit charge at that time. This calculation, like the others in this section, concerns only the hypothetical transfer by reference to a further release of funds, deemed to be made on, say, 31 October 2016.

The hypothetical transfer comprises:

	£
• value of relevant property fund at commencement	300,000
• value of property in related transfer	NIL
• value of added property	100,000
Total	400,000

Example 8.30—Failed PET coming to light

Celia (**Example 8.23**) died on 20 May 2016. It was established that she had made a PET of £100,000 (net of exemptions) on 31 August 2010 which now 'fails' and becomes chargeable by reason of death within seven years. The calculation of the entry charge on her transfer into trust on 31 October 2015 is revised.

The IHT entry charge on the transfer, to calculate the hypothetical rate for the later exit charge, is now:

	£
• the transfer in to trust	415,000
• the now failed PET	100,000
• the earlier recognised transfer	50,000
	565,000
• less: nil rate band on trust creation (2015/16)	(325,000)
• Chargeable excess	240,000
• Tax at 20% of excess	48,000

All of this tax relates to the establishment of the trust, because the earlier transfers have first bite of the nil rate band.

The hypothetical transfer comprises:

	£
• value of property in trust at commencement	415,000
• less IHT liability of trustees	(48,000)
	367,000
• value of property in related settlement	NIL
• value of any added property	NIL
Total	367,000

Calculating the 'effective rate'

8.36 Even though the preceding examples involve a tax computation, they are but the first step in the overall process of establishing the final calculation. The second step is to now calculate the tax on the hypothetical transfer but again this is not real tax but merely part of the process.

The purpose of this particular set of sums is to fix the charge on assets leaving a relevant property trust. The rate of tax used is the rate in force at the time of the transfer, not at the time that the trust was set up. All that this computation achieves is to identify the 'effective rate' and even that is not the rate at which tax will be charged: only a proportion will be charged.

It is important to note that the lifetime rate of 20% is always used even where the transfer was on death – the death rate of 40% is never a component of the ten year exit charge.

Example 8.31— The 'effective rate' for distribution made 31 October 2016

	£
Alfred (Example 8.21):	NIL
Bernard (Example 8.22):	
Value of hypothetical transfer	400,000
Nil rate band at the time of the exit charge (2016/17)	(325,000)
Notional chargeable transfer	75,000
Tax @ 20%	15,000
Effective rate 15,000/400,000	3.75%

	£
Celia (original calculation at **Example 8.23**):	
Value of hypothetical transfer	387,000
Nil rate band (2016/17)	(325,000)
Notional chargeable transfer	62,000
Tax @ 20%	12,400
Effective rate 12,400/387,000	3.20%
Celia (revised calculation at **Example 8.30**):	
Value of hypothetical transfer	367,000
Nil rate band (2016/17)	(325,000)
Notional chargeable transfer	42,000
Tax @ 20%	8,400
Effective rate 8,400/367,000	2.28%
Dennis (Example 8.24):	
Value of hypothetical transfer	540,000
Nil rate band (2016/17)	(325,000)
Notional chargeable transfer	215,000
Tax @ 20%	43,000
Effective rate 43,000/540,000	7.96%
Eric (Example 8.26):	
Value of hypothetical transfer	900,000
Nil rate band (2016/17)	(325,000)
Notional chargeable transfer	575,000
Tax @ 20%	115,000
Effective rate 115,000/900,000	12.77%
Frances (Example 8.27):	
Value of hypothetical transfer	450,000
Nil rate band (2016/17)	(325,000)
Notional chargeable transfer	125,000
Tax @ 20%	25,000
Effective rate 25,000/450,000	5.55%

	£
Gina (Example 8.28):	
Value of hypothetical transfer	300,000
Nil rate band (2016/17)	(325,000)
Notional chargeable transfer	Nil
Tax at 20%	NIL
Effective rate	0%
Henry (Example 8.29):	
Value of hypothetical transfer	400,000
Nil rate band (2016/17)	(325,000)
Notional chargeable transfer	75,000
Tax @ 20%	15,000
Effective rate 15,000/400,000	3.75%

Calculating the 'appropriate fraction' and the actual tax charge

8.37 The 'effective rate' is not the final tax rate.

Property may not have been subject to relevant property trust regime for a full ten years: indeed it cannot have been for the proportionate charge to apply. Each period of ten years is divided into periods of three months – a quarter. A fraction is calculated based on the number of complete quarters during which the property has been subject to relevant property trust regime throughout that ten-year period (comprising 40 quarters). That fraction is applied to the effective rate: see *s 68(2)*.

The following principles should be applied:

- *Section 68(2)*: calculate the number of complete successive quarters from the commencement of the trust to the exit date = A.
- *Section 68(3)*: look for anomalies, such as a period (complete quarters) during which the property was not subject to relevant property trusts; or when the property was in a different trust = B.
- Calculate the period of that anomaly and exclude it from the earlier calculation = A – B.

- With regard to periods of anomaly, where A – B = 0, but A is at least 1, tax at 30% of the effective rate multiplied by 1/40.
- Assess accumulations of income, disregarding income that has not been formally accumulated (see Statement of Practice 8/86) but (with effect from events occurring 6 April 2014) add back accumulations which arose more than five years prior to the ten-year anniversary date.
- Apportion the capital distribution that triggers the exit charge across the property that represents it.
- If the part now distributed was always subject to discretion then reduce it by the fraction A/40. *But*
- If, and to the extent that the above is not the case and an anomaly applies to part, apply the fraction (A – B)/40 to that part.
- Charge tax on the property at 30% of the effective rate, reduced by the A/40 or (A – B)/40 fraction, as appropriate.
- With regard to periods of anomaly, where A – B= 0, but A is at least 1, tax at 30% of the effective rate multiplied by 1/40.

Example 8.32—(Continued from the previous scenarios)—in each case there is a distribution of £50,000 cash on 31 October 2016

(1) For two examples (Bernard and Celia) the period from 31 October 2015 to 31 October 2016 is 12 full months thus four complete quarters, as required by *s 68(2)*; from mid November 2014 to March 2015 is similarly only one full quarter. Thus the position is as follows:

£50,000 × 440 × 30% = £1,500 multiplied by the effective rate in each case.

(2) For three examples (Eric, Frances and Gina) the period from 30 November 2015 to 31 October 2016 is 11 full months thus only three complete quarters, as required by *s 68(2)*. Thus the position is as follows:

£50,000 × 3/40 × 30% = £1,125 multiplied by the effective rate in each case.

(3) For one example (Henry) the period from 30 November 2013 to 31 October 2016 is 35 full months thus 11 complete quarters, as required by *s 68(2)*. Thus the position is as follows:

£50,000 × 11/40 × 30% = £4,125 multiplied by the effective rate in each case.

(4) Doreen's example is omitted because it illustrates a slightly different point.

(5) In Dennis's example the period from 31 March 2016 to 31 October 2016 is seven full months thus two complete quarters, as required by *s 68(2)*. Thus the position is as follows:

£50,000 × 2/40 × 30% = £750 multiplied by the effective rate in each case.

Alfred's trust (**Example 10.21**): £1,500 @ 0%	= 0
Bernard's trust (**Example 10.22**): £1,500 @ 3.75%	= £56.25
Celia's trust, on the revised figures (**Example 10.30**): £1,500 @ 2.28%	= £34.20
Dennis' trust (**Example 10.24**): £750 @ 7.96%	= £59.70
Eric's trust (**Example 10.26**): £1,125 @ 12.77%	= £143.66
Frances' trust (**Example 10.27**): £1,125 @ 5.55%	= 62.43
Gina's trust (**Example 10.28**): £1,125 @ 0%	= 0
Henry's trust (**Example 10.29**): £4,125 @ 3.75%	= £154.69

THE PERIODIC OR 'TEN-YEAR' CHARGE

Simple cases: first ten-year anniversary

8.38

Example 8.33—Reporting the charge

Sarah is domiciled in the UK. She creates a relevant property trust for her adult children and her grandchildren and settles an amount equal to 75% of the then nil rate band – there are no related settlements. The UK trustees invest the fund on a fairly conservative basis such that its value ten years later equates to some 85% of the nil rate band at that time. During that first ten-year period there have been distributions of income but not of capital. Although there is a duty on the trustees to complete form IHT100 in respect of the ten-year charge (as the fund exceeds 80% of the nil rate band the exceptions rule does not apply – see the *Inheritance Tax (Delivery of Accounts) (Excepted Settlements) Regulations), SI 2008/606, reg 4*)), there will be no tax to pay.

In complying with *s 64* and to the tax fund under *ss 66* and *67,* the completed form IHT100 will show the value of the fund on the eve of the tenth anniversary after taking account of any exemptions or reliefs applicable to the trust ownership (note that settlor additions to the trust exempted from entry charge under the regular gifts out of income rule does not apply as it belongs to the settlor and not to the trust). As would be the case with an estate on death, the fund is divided between assets on which tax must be paid immediately and those where the instalment option applies.

8.39 Form IHT100d identifies the date (see commentary at **8.16** above) on which property became subject to the relevant property trust regime and its value at the ten-year anniversary, again providing where appropriate for the instalment option. The form then puts the settlement into its gift context. In a simple case the transferor will have made no previous chargeable transfers in the seven years ending before the settlement was established and will have made no other settlements on the same day as the one which is the subject of the ten-year charge calculation.

In a process similar to that considered above for the exit charge, the ten-year charge involves a step-by-step calculation. It is again necessary to establish the 'hypothetical chargeable transfer' but in this case the component parts are different. The rate of charge established at the ten-year anniversary determines the rate of exit charge applied to interim capital distributions made in the following ten years up to the next ten-year anniversary. The tax rate is established by calculating tax on the hypothetical transfer (but adjusted for exclusion of non-relevant property where the ten-year anniversary takes place on or after 18 November 2015 (date of Royal Assent to *Finance (No 2) Act 2015*)) and applying it to the amount on which tax is charged, producing the 'effective rate'. However, one particular difficulty is the need to put the settlement in the context of other gifts.

Establishing the 'hypothetical transfer'

8.40 Special rules apply, see *s 68(6)*, where the settlement commenced before 27 March 1974. The rules are merely mentioned here for completeness but are not included in any of the illustrations. Those dealing with these old relevant property trusts are referred to the complex legislation in *s 68(6).*

For all other settlements it is necessary to establish the cumulative total of the following (see *s 66(4)*):

- the transfer value (market value) for the periodic charge;
- the value (historic value) of funds not subject to the relevant property regime (note the comments at **8.26**);
- the value (historic) of property in related settlements.

The transfer value

8.41 This relates to the value that will form the basis of the actual tax computation once the hypothetical transfer and the effective rate have been calculated. It is the value of that part of the property in the settlement immediately before the ten-year anniversary which is regarded as relevant property – *market value basis*. For ease of identification this is called 'the relevant property trust fund' in the calculations that follow.

When calculating the relevant property trust fund, no account should be taken of excluded property (see *s 58(1)(f)*) or property passing to charitable and similar trusts. Furthermore, favoured property qualifying for BPR or APR must be included at their value post relief. The case of *Gilchrist v RCC* [2014] UKUT 0169 (TCC) addressed the issue of whether the proceeds of a scrip dividend should be treated as capital and therefore liable for the ten year charge. It was held that the scrip dividends were not liable to tax for the ten year charge.

Other funds within the trust

8.42 This now only applies to chargeable events taking place before 17 November 2015. This relates to the value of property that is neither now within the relevant property regime, and has never been subject to the relevant property trust regime, but which is within the main settlement. The value is taken immediately after that property joined the trust – *historic basis*. For ease of identification this is called the 'sub-fund' in the computations that follow.

Related settlements

8.43 This relates to a separate trust which commenced on the same day as the main settlement and has the same settlor (but where it is a non-relevant property trust, this is excluded for chargeable events taking place on or after 18 November 2015). It will also take account of later added property – see **8.26** above. A charitable trust is not a related settlement for this purpose. The value is taken immediately after that property joined the trust but ignoring the availability of APR or BPR (see for example IHTM42165 for HMRC's view) – *historic basis*. For ease of identification, this is called 'the related fund' in the computations that follow. However, it should be noted that the impact of this factor has been severely affected by the *F(No 2)A 2015* legislation concerning the recognition of same-day funds added to existing settlements (see **8.26**). Developments in this area should be carefully monitored.

8.44 Importantly, there is one category of property that is specifically excluded from the hypothetical transfer cumulation. This is property in the settlement that was originally subject to the relevant property regime but which later became excluded or exempt without attracting any exit charge. A common example is relevant property that became held on permanent charitable trusts.

The following example is a model computation skeleton for the position post-17 November 2015 though in practice it is most likely that only some of the elements referred to will be needed.

Example 8.34—Form of computation of the hypothetical transfer required to calculate the ten-year charge on or after 18 November 2015

Elements:

1 Market value of the relevant property trust fund, eg:

- quoted securities
- cash (excluding accumulated undistributed income)
- unquoted securities
- residential property
- business interests
- business assets
- farming interests

Less:

- liabilities set against the fund; and
- value of excluded property
- assets held on charitable trusts
- BPR or APR on qualifying fund assets

2 Historic value of the related relevant property fund.

3 Hypothetical transfer = (1 + 2).

8.45 The following examples take each element of the computation in turn. The first is a simple situation, typical of that found in practice.

Example 8.35—Computation of the hypothetical transfer (ten-year charge)

On 28 February 2006, Elsie settled cash of £200,000 (which has never been invested by the trustees) and a holding of shares in an unquoted trading company, into a discretionary trust – she made no other settlements that day.

At the ten-year anniversary on 28 February 2016 the shares are worth £75,000. The entire fund is held and has been held throughout on relevant property trusts for Elsie's grandchildren.

		£
1	Value of 'the discretionary trust fund':	
	Cash	200,000
	unquoted securities	75,000
		275,000
	Less:	
	BPR (unquoted securities)	(75,000)
		200,000
2	Value of the related fund –	NIL
Hypothetical transfer:		200,000

8.46 Matters become considerably more complicated where APR or BPR is involved and where prior to 18 November 2015 the fund included non-relevant property.

Example 8.36—Computation of the hypothetical transfer (ten-year charge)

On 28 February 2005, Yolande set up a trust of which 50% was held on interest in possession terms for her sister and 50% held on discretionary terms for the benefit of her grandchildren. She made no other chargeable transfers during her lifetime. Into the trust she transferred quoted securities valued at £160,000 and worth £220,000 as at February 2015, a pair of cottages valued at £150,000 and worth £180,000 as at February 2015 and a share of some agricultural pasture valued then and still at £20,000. The hypothetical transfer as at 28 February 2015 is as follows:

1	Value of 50% of the trust fund:		
	value of the relevant property fund :		£
		quoted securities	110,000
		residential properties	90,000
		farming interests	10,000
			210,000
Less:			
		APR (pasture)	(10,000)
	Total		200,000
2	Value of the related fund (historic value)	165,000	
	Net value of the related fund		165,000
	Hypothetical transfer		365,000

The availability of APR is ignored in establishing the historic value.

Had the trust instead been created one year later on 28 February 2006 with a ten-year charge triggered on 28 February 2016, the impact of the *Finance Act 2015* exclusion of the non-relevant property element would have reduced the hypothetical transfer to £200,000.

8.47 Related trusts are not all that common but *Rysaffe Trustee Co (CI) Ltd v IRC* [2002] EWHC 1114 (Ch); [2002] STC 872 and on appeal [2003] EWCA Civ 356, [2003] STC 536 neatly illustrates the perils of related trusts and the tax planning routinely employed to avoid them. Where related trusts do exist (but restricted to related relevant property trust for chargeable events taking place on or after 18 November 2015), the hypothetical transfer is greater by reason of aggregation.

Example 8.37—Computation of the hypothetical transfer (ten-year charge):

Grete's trust was created on 28 February 2006 and on the first ten-year anniversary on 28 February 2016 comprised unquoted shares in a trading company worth £1,000,000, the premises from which the company trades worth £860,000 and cash of £100,000. BPR is available at 100% on the shares but at only 50% on the building. Grete settled £100,000 on a separate relevant property trust created on the same day in February 2006.

		£
1	Value of the discretionary trust fund:	
	Cash	100,000
	unquoted securities	1,000,000
	business assets	860,000
		1,960,000
Less:		
BPR (at 100%/50% on shares/premises)		(1,430,000)
		530,000
2	Value of the non-relevant property sub-fund	NIL
3	Value of the related relevant property fund	100,000
	Hypothetical transfer	630,000

8.48 Excluded property is a complication but it does not increase the hypothetical transfer.

Example 8.38—Computation of the hypothetical transfer (ten-year charge)

On 28 February 2006, Walter, who was not domiciled in the UK, settled on discretionary trust, a German vineyard worth £400,000 (February 2016), cash amounting to £600,000 (February 2016) and a house in Scotland worth £150,000 (February 2016) – he made no other settlements on that day.

		£
1	Value of the discretionary trust fund:	
	Cash	600,000
	Residential property	150,000
	Other property interests (the vineyard)	400,000
		1,150,000
Less:		
Value of excluded property (non UK situs)		(400,000)
		750,000
2	Value of the sub-fund	NIL
3	Value of the related fund	NIL
Hypothetical transfer		750,000

Note: BPR (unlike APR, which until *Finance Act 2009* was restricted to the UK, Channel Islands and Isle of Man, and woodland relief, which until the same legislation was restricted to the UK) is available on worldwide qualifying assets and thus in this example might have been available in respect of the vineyard.

Example 8.39—Computation of the hypothetical transfer (ten-year charge)

On 28 February 2006, Vera made two settlements – the first was held on qualifying interest in possession terms however, the liferenter died in 2007 after which the fund continued on discretionary trust; the second was held on discretionary terms. The current value (February 2016) of the original discretionary fund is a share portfolio worth £360,000. The other former IIP fund was valued at £50,000 on creation.

1	Value of the discretionary trust fund:	£
	Quoted securities	360,000
2	Value of the sub-fund	Nil
3	Value of the related relevant property fund	50,000
	Hypothetical transfer	410,000

Example 8.40—Comparison of position of non-relevant property exclusion post-Finance (No 2) Act 2015

On 30 November 2005, Thomas, having made no previous chargeable lifetime transfers in the previous seven years, settled cash of £1 million on an A&M trust for his three grandchildren Albert, Betty and Carol, which provided for income at age 25 and capital at trustee discretion. Under the pre-March 2006 rules that then prevailed this was a PET and hence no IHT fell due for payment and as Thomas survived the PET by seven years the transfer achieved full exempt status.

On 1 March 2006, Albert became entitled to an interest in possession (IIP) in one-third of the fund. As the IIP was established before 22 March 2006 it is a qualifying IIP.

On 6 April 2008, Betty and Carol's remaining two-thirds of the fund entered the relevant property regime.

On 30 November 2015, the trust reached its ten-year anniversary and Betty/Carol's two-third share was valued at £1.5 million.

(i) 6 April 2015 – ten-year charge pre-*Finance (No2) Act 2015* enactment

MV value of relevant property fund	1,500,000
Non-relevant property fund	330,000
(£1 million × 33%)	
Total	1,830,000
Nil rate band (2015/2016)	(325,000)
	1,505,000
1,505,000 @ 20%	301,000
301,000/1,830,000 x100	16.44%
(16.44 × 30)%	4.93%
Ten-year charge:	
1,500,000 @ 4.93% × 30*/40	55,462

* Complete quarters in the period 6 April 2008 to 30 November 2015

(ii) Ten-year charge post-enactment of *Finance (No 2) Act 2015*

MV value of relevant property fund	1,500,000
Non-relevant property fund	Exempt
Total	1,500,000
Nil rate band (2015/2016)	(325,000)
	1,175,000
1,175,000 @ 20%	235,000
235,000/1,500,000 x100	15.66%
(15.66 × 30)%	4.69%
Ten-year charge:	
1,500,000 @ 4.69% × 30*/40	52,762

* Complete quarters in the period 6 April 2008 to 30 November 2015

Previous transfers

> **Focus**
>
> The total of chargeable transfers made by the settlor in the seven years prior to the original date of trust creation will, unless a greater figure can be substituted (see **8.52** and **8.53**), always be a constant of the calculation for both the first and subsequent ten-year anniversaries.

8.49 As to be expected at this stage, this computation is not straightforward and involves five considerations:

- increases in the settlement;
- transfers before the settlement was created;
- bringing additions to the fund into account;
- assembling the total figure for the transfers; and
- bringing failed PETs into account.

Additions to the fund

8.50 The statutory authority for this part of the computation is *s 67(1)*. The legislation requires recognition of chargeable transfers made both after the settlement began and before the ten-year anniversary, as a result of which the value of any property in the settlement is increased, whether or not that property is subject to relevant property trusts.

A transfer that was not primarily intended to increase the value of the settlement and did not in fact increase the value of the trust property by more than 5% of its value immediately before transfer, is disregarded (*s 67(2)*). Furthermore, an exempt transfer is ignored, whether it is exempt by virtue of the small expenditure or annual exemptions or is made out of income within *s 21*. This is important where, for example, the settlor pays annual premiums on an insurance policy that is held by the trust.

Transfers by the settlor in the seven years before the trust

8.51 The total is required of any chargeable transfers made by the settlor in the period of seven years prior to the date of the trust's creation – this mirrors the seven year backward shadow applied to lifetime gifts in the event of the donor's death. The statutory authority here is *s 66(5)(a)*. This total will be a permanent inclusion in future ten-year charges but may in turn be replaced by a greater total – see **8.52** below.

Before 18 March 1986, the relevant period was ten years and in current financial times there must exist the possibility that this longer period may be reinstated.

Transfers preceding additions to the fund

8.52 If there have been any additions to the fund post trust creation then the history of transfers by the settlor in the seven years before each addition must be re-examined and if this gives a greater total than the original seven-year cumulative figure (see **8.51**) then this former will be used going forward. If there have been any chargeable transfers by the settlor in any such period of seven years, ending on the day before the addition to the fund, the amount are excluded except in so far as they have already been brought into account in the computation of the hypothetical transfers.

Assembling the totals

8.53 There is no aggregate total to carry forward (except in respect of additions to the fund) where a settlement commenced before 27 March 1974. However, if in the case of such settlement there have been some additions to the fund, the total of these additions is added to the total of the transfers in the seven years that immediately precede them.

For all other later created settlements, the computation depends entirely on whether there have been any additions to the fund. In the simple case where there have been no such additions, the relevant sum is the total of the chargeable transfers by the settlor in the seven years before the date on which the trust began. Where there have been additions to the fund, two calculations are needed – (i) the sum of transfers made by the settlor in the seven years before the trust and (ii) the total of the transfers made by the settlor in the seven years that precede the additions to the fund. The relevant figure is the greater of the two (*s 67(3)*).

Bringing failed PETs into account

8.54 Where the settlor of a relevant property trust made PETs and died within seven years thereof, such failed PETs (which now become chargeable transfers) must also be taken into account for this purpose, and this can complicate the tax calculation. Thus in summary:

- If the death of the settlor occurs after the ten-year anniversary and it appears that he has made additions to the fund before that anniversary, and has died within seven years of those additions, the history of his gift before those additions must be re-examined.
- If in the seven years before the additions to the relevant property trust there was a PET which has failed, that failed PET must be brought into account in the calculations described above.

This can have the effect of increasing the aggregate of the transfer by the settlor which will feed through to a higher ultimate tax liability. In the example below, the 'aggregate transfer' is the extra value to be brought into the tax computation.

Example 8.41—Calculating the aggregate transfer: previous transfers

On 28 February 2011, Ulrich set up a relevant property trust of £300,000 (gross). He had made two earlier gifts of £56,000 to his daughter on 31 August 2009 and of £12,000 to his son on 31 May 2010. He died on 31 January 2016 without having added any funds to the settlement.

The cash gifts, originally PETs, become chargeable:

	£
31 August 2009 (net of annual exemptions for 2008/09 and 2007/08)	50,000
31 May 2010 (net of exemption 2010/11)	9,000
	59,000

The aggregated transfer is calculated:

Additions to the fund	NIL
Transfers seven years before the trust	59,000
Aggregate transfer	59,000

Example 8.42—Calculating the aggregate transfer: addition to a trust

On 1 February 2006, Tom, who made no previous gifts, settled £100,000 on relevant property trusts. On 31 August 2006 he gave his son £30,000 and on 31 May 2007 he added £200,000 to the trust. He died within seven years of the gift to his son, so the PET became chargeable:

	£
Gift 31 August 2006	30,000
Less exemption (2006/07)	(3,000)
	27,000
The aggregate transfer is calculated:	
Additions to the fund 31 May 2007	200,000
(Exemptions utilised)	
Transfers preceding addition to the fund	27,000
	227,000
Transfers in seven years before the trust:	NIL
Aggregate transfer	227,000

Note: this type of transfer may in certain circumstances be adjusted in accordance with *s 67(4)(b)* and *s 67(5)*. Those sections apply only to trusts created before 27 March 1974 and, as was noted at **8.28** above, this chapter concentrates on trusts created after that date. The section brings into account transfers in the seven years before the chargeable transfer but disregards any value already subject to an exit charge.

Distributions from the trust: special cases

8.55 There are additional rules to calculate the total distributions. The first step requires a total of the amounts which attracted an exit charge during the first ten years of the life of the trust. However, this will exclude distributions which were otherwise exempt.

The second step requires a review of each occasion when property that was in the settlement at the ten-year anniversary had ceased to be subject to a discretion. This situation could arise where funds were taken from the relevant property trust and set aside for a beneficiary to provide them with an income and that beneficiary died before the ten-year anniversary. Equally, it could apply under the old rules where funds were appointed onto A&M trusts in favour of a beneficiary who then died. In such a case the total of distributions which is the subject of this part of the calculation must be reduced. The amount of the reduction is the lower of:

- the amount on which the exit tax was charged; or
- the value of the relevant fund on which the ten-year charge would otherwise be levied.

The purpose of this rule is to prevent double-counting of the same property.

8.56 The third step is rarely seen in practice but is included here for completeness. If the trustees have purchased heritage property and have obtained conditional exemption for it, the price paid for the heritage property must be included in the aggregate now being calculated as if it were subject to an exit charge.

Calculating the 'effective rate'

8.57 The foregoing has been preparation of a hypothetical transfer so as to establish one component of the tax charge, the 'effective rate'. The notional transfer is:

- one made by a transferor immediately before the ten-year anniversary;
- who had in the previous seven years made other chargeable transfers that were equal in value to the aggregate brought forward from the earlier calculations in **8.49**; and taking account of
- the distributions calculated by reference to **8.55**.

The result of the calculation is best illustrated as follows.

Example 8.43—The effective rate

On 31 January 2006, Sam made a relevant property trust of £250,000, having always used his annual exemptions and having made a chargeable transfer to another trust of £50,000 a year before. He did not add any funds to either trust, nor make any other PETs before his death on 28 February 2013. It is now necessary to consider the periodic charge on the fund at 31 January 2016.

The fund in the 2006 trust includes investments now worth £700,000 of which £100,000 are in unquoted trading companies, acquired more than two years before January 2016. No part of the fund has been appointed onto interest in possession trusts, nor is any of it excluded property. £70,000 of capital was distributed in December 2013.

Computation of the hypothetical transfer

		£	
Value of the discretionary trust fund		700,000	
Less: BPR (unquoted shares)		(100,000)	
		600,000	(A)
Value of relevant property sub-fund		NIL	
Value of related relevant property fund		NIL	
Hypothetical transfer:		600,000	(B)
Review of other transfers			
Previous chargeable transfer	50,000		
Additions	Nil		
Transfers before addition	Nil		
Distributions	70,000		
Total		120,000	
Notional transfer:		720,000	(C)
Nil rate band at 31 January 2016		(325,000)	
Excess		395,000	
Notional tax @ 20%		79,000	
Effective rate: 79,000/600,000(B) × 100		13.17%	

Calculating the actual tax

8.58 In the above example it can be seen that the inclusion of the settlor's cumulative seven-year transfers together with account of the distributions in effect erodes the availability of the nil rate band and thus increases the charge levied on the hypothetical transfer.

Yet again, there is a need to review the history of the trust. It might be thought that it was enough merely for the trustees to maintain proper accounts of capital and income (though many trustees will not even do as much as that, until forced to review the situation by the need to complete tax returns). In addition to knowing which part of the fund is capital and which is income, for IHT purposes the trustees must also know which part of the trust fund at any one time was subject to their discretion and which was not.

Equally, the trustees must take a view on the subject of income. The HMRC view is that any income which is accumulated is to be treated as comprised in the settlement from the date that the accumulation occurred: see Statement of Practice 8/86 which also notes that undistributed and unaccumulated income should not be treated as a taxable trust asset but will retain its income character. There is a fine distinction between income of a previous year that has simply not been distributed and income that has, by some action of the trustees or by virtue of the terms of the trust instrument, become accumulated at some interval after it was received by the trustees. This thorny issue and the complications that it raises was referred to in the trust consultation process (see **8.26**) and *Finance Act 2014* contains measures which treat income which has remained undistributed for more than five years at the date of the ten year anniversary as trust capital for the purpose of computing the ten-year charge. Harshly, tax will be charged at the full rate without the proportionate reduction to reflect the period in which the income has been retained thus where this is likely to apply the trustees should perhaps consider formally accumulating that income to ensure that the charge is scaled back to only apply from that date of formal accumulation.

Problems of identification can occur where there is unaccumulated income but later income distributions have been made. HMRC have stated that in such circumstance a first in, first out (FIFO) approach should be adopted but such direction does not have statute authority.

8.59 Fortunately, this is a somewhat rarefied area of the law but in practice HMRC appear to accept a reasonable computation put forward by the trustees that can be justified by the record of their actions. For the purposes of this discussion of the taxation of relevant property trusts, it is assumed that any cash held by the trustees at the ten-year anniversary represents undistributed but capitalised income rather than retained accumulations of income.

Putting the income question to one side, there still remains the issue of whether capital has been subject to the discretion of the trustees throughout the whole ten years or whether, for example, it was added to the settlement at some interim point during that ten-year period. For each 'chunk' of capital so affected, it is necessary to calculate the appropriate fraction following a similar manner to that described at **8.37**. The result is to apply the tax charge only for the period during which the property was subject to the relevant property regime.

The effective rate is then reduced by 30% and applied to the full value of the fund if it has been subject to the relevant property regime for the whole ten years or as reduced by the appropriate fraction otherwise. As can be appreciated this is not a straightforward calculation.

Example 8.44—The tax charge

Continuation of **Example 8.42** of Sam's 2006 trust.

All the property in the trust at 31 January 2016 has been within the relevant property regime since the trust began.

	£
Value of the fund on 31 January 2016 (net of BPR)	600,000
Effective rate 13.17% (ie 79,000/600,000 × 100)	
Tax: £600,000 × (30 × 13.17)%	23,706.00

Example 8.45—The tax charge where funds have been added to the trust

Referring back to the example of Tom (see **Example 8.41** above) it is noted that part of the fund has not been in the trust for ten years. At the date of the ten year anniversary the fund is worth £600,000 of which only £200,000 can be identified with the original capital (and hence held within the trust for the full ten years) with the balance of £400,000 identified with the funds added later (and hence not held within the trust for the full ten years). All income has been distributed, but there have been no capital distributions.

Calculate the hypothetical transfer

	£	
Value of the discretionary trust fund	600,000	
Value of related fund	NIL	
Hypothetical transfer	600,000	(A)
Review of other transfers		
Previous chargeable transfers	NIL	
Aggregate transfer as previously calculated (see earlier example)	227,000	
Deduct the value attributable to property now in the fund (*s 67(3)(b)* read with *s 66(4)*)	(200,000)	
	27,000	(B)

	£
Notional transfer: (A + B)	627,000
Nil rate band, 31 January 2016	(325,000)
Excess	302,000
Notional tax: 20%	60,400
Effective rate: 60,400/600,000(A) × 100	10.06%
Charge on the initial fund (held for ten years):	
£200,000 × (30 × 10.06)%	6,036.00
Charge on the later added funds:	
Held subject to discretion from 31 May 2007 to 31 January 2016: 35 complete/part quarters.	
Fraction is therefore 35/40	
£400,000 × 35/40 × (30 × 10.06)%	10,563.00
Total tax charge	16,599.00

Example 8.46—Ten-year charge where there has been a distribution

On 30 November 2005, Brian, who had made no earlier chargeable transfers, created a discretionary trust with cash of £255,000 gross with the trustees paying any IHT entry charge. No further funds have been added. There have been interim income distributions to the grandchildren with the tax credit wholly met from the tax pool and subject to later repayment in their hands because the payments were covered by their personal allowances.

On 10 June 2011, the trustees advanced capital of £60,000 to Sally to help her buy a flat.

At 30 November 2015 the trustees held:

	£
Quoted stocks and shares	200,000
Dividends (ex-dividend)	1,000
Government stock	50,000
Unquoted shares	50,000
Dividends held by brokers	5,000

	£
Property, let	175,000
Cash	30,000
Gross fund	511,000

The trustees had wisely arranged before the anniversary for valuations to be made. Their cost, at £275, was due at the valuation date. There was also income tax due on rental income of £400. The dividends held by the brokers are not relevant property unless appropriated to capital, which they have not been, because the trustees have pursued a policy of making regular distributions. Similarly, of the cash amount sum, £13,000 is actually undistributed income which arose during the last five years. The unquoted shares are in a company that used to trade, but which now concentrates on property investment, so a claim for BPR is unlikely to pass muster.

A significant problem in dealing with the IHT liability on relevant property trusts is relating the text of the statute to the calculation and then to the return itself. In this example, reference is made to the various box numbers, with the intention that that will help in following the calculation. The fund is shown on the supplemental forms thus:

D32, stocks and shares:

SS1 total values £200,000 and 1,000 dividends (to boxes E1 and E5 in form IHT100);

SS2 total value £50,000 (to box E2);

Unquoted shares £50,000 (to box F10).

D36, land etc:

Value shown £175,000 (to box F1).

IHT100, the account:

Event form IHT100d will be appropriate, see below. After details of Brian's tax reference and that of the trust, the only supplementary pages used are as shown above plus perhaps D40. Cash is shown net of the undistributed income at £17,000 (box E8). The assets not qualifying for instalment relief are, gross, £268,000 (box E15) and after offset of the liabilities of £675 are £267,325. There are no exemptions, so the total appears at box E19. There are no liabilities to set against the instalment option property so the total at box F17 is £225,000.

Thus:

		£
(a)	Non-instalment option property:	
	Stocks and shares:	200,000
	Dividends	1,000
	Gilts	50,000
	Cash	17,000
Less liabilities:		
	Valuation fee	(275)
	Tax due	(400)
Sub-total (E19)		267,325
(b)	Instalment option property	
	Unquoted shares	50,000
	Land	175,000
Subtotal (F17)		225,000

Event form IHT100d:

A proportionate charge has arisen in the preceding ten years in respect of the £60,000 distribution to Sally, all of which was taxable albeit the exit charge rate was set at 0% thus resulting in a nil tax charge (Q1.5). Brian had made no prior chargeable transfers and had added no funds to the trust. Nothing went into the trust that was not subject to the discretion of the trustees, so form IHT100d is fairly straightforward to complete.

Inheritance tax worksheet IHT100(WS):

There is no requirement to fill this in: as already noted, HMRC will do the calculation, but that leaves the adviser vulnerable. In this example, the totals brought across from the main account (£267,325 + £225,000) yield a value for tax of £492,325 (box WSB7). In this (simple!) case the only extra item at this point is Sally's £60,000 (box WSB15) bringing the taxable total to £552,325 (box R12) against which may be set the nil rate band as at 19 November 2013 of £325,000 to leave tax (for the purpose only of calculating the effective rate) on £227,325 at 20% of £45,465 (box R16) which is not adjusted for Sally's £60,000 and therefore enters the fraction (45,465/492,325) × 30% to produce an effective rate (rounded to three decimal places) of 2.770% (box R24).

That rate, applied to the non-instalment assets of £267,325, yields tax of £7,404.90 (box TX41) and on the other assets, £225,000 of £6,232.50 (box TX48) to which must be added any interest now due; the detail can be calculated using the structure set out in boxes IT1 to IT9 of IHT100 (WS), but by now the reader must be tiring of this example, so the detail of that calculation, and its division between the different categories of property, is ignored for the present purpose.

The tax amounts to (£7,404.90 + £6,232.50): £13,637.40, which is a light burden for a fund of over £500,000 to bear.

To summarise:

Fund of non-instalment property:	£267,325
Real property – instalment property:	£225,000
Taxable fund:	£492,325
Distributions:	£60,000
Tax rate charged:	2.770%
Tax on non-instalment property:	£7,404.90
Tax on the land – instalment property:	£6,232.50

Later ten-year anniversaries

8.60 The legislation at *s 64* provides for an IHT charge in relation to any ten-year anniversary without distinction between the first and later anniversaries. It is, (see *s 66*) charged at 30% of the effective rate on the chargeable transfer as described in *s 66(3)*. Importantly, the individual components of historic value of related settlements, historic value of property not subject to discretion and settlor's seven-year cumulative total of chargeable transfers (but see **8.52**) will always remain as a fixed part of the calculation irrespective of the passage of time but post enactment of *Finance (No 2) Act 2015*, the previous historic value of non-relevant property will be disregarded.

Additions of property are covered by *s 67* except where within the *de minimis* 5% rule of *s 67(2)(b)* or where there was no intention to increase the value of the fund, within *s 67(2)(a)*. This can arise on, for example, the waiver by the settlor of a dividend which indirectly benefits the trust.

THE IMPACT OF APR AND BPR

Focus

Whilst BPR/APR can reduce the rate of charge (and hence exit charge) on the first and subsequent ten-year anniversaries, it is ignored in establishing the exit charge rate applied to capital distributions made in the first ten years alone. This can produce a distortive and unexpected tax charge.

Effect at commencement

8.61 As previously discussed, relevant property trusts benefit from APR and BPR so that, when applying tax to a transfer of value, the otherwise chargeable amount of that transfer is reduced by that relief. However, as was seen in the example of Bernard (**Example 8.22**), when calculating the exit charge in the first ten years alone, the availability of APR or BPR is wholly ignored in establishing the hypothetical transfer. Once the trust is established and the transfer to be considered is at the first tenth anniversary or later, APR or BPR can reduce the size of the hypothetical transfer which has the beneficial effect of reducing the exit charge for later capital distributions.

APR or BPR is claimed by reference to the ownership of the trustees since unlike the life tenant of an interest in possession (whether established pre or post-March 2006), a discretionary beneficiary of a relevant property trust can never be deemed to be the owner of the trust assets.

Control

8.62 Control of a company can be relevant to BPR (see **Chapter 11**). Given that an unquoted shareholding of any size can potentially qualify for 100% relief, control is mainly important in determining access to relief under *s 105(1)(d)* in relation to land/other business assets personally owned by the shareholder and used in the business carried out by the relevant company, or under *s 122* in relation to farming companies, where control is essential for the relief to be available at all: see *s 122(1)(b)*. 'Control' of a company for IHT purposes is generally determined according to the specific provisions in *s 269*.

There is some difficulty in deciding whether trustees of a settlement have control of a company only by reference to the shares in that particular settlement or whether other settlements may be taken into account. This was one of the issues considered in *Rysaffe Trustee Co (CI) Ltd v IRC* [2003] EWCA Civ 356, [2003] STC 536.

Reduction in the tax charge

8.63 If a relevant property trust holds qualifying business or agricultural property, the exit charge post the first ten-year anniversary may be reduced (see **8.61**). If the occasion of the charge is the release of property which itself qualifies for APR and/or BPR, this will reduce the value on which the tax is charged but will not as such reduce the rate of tax established at the ten-year anniversary.

Example 8.47—Release of farmland

Sean's relevant property trust holds farmland eligible for APR at 100%. The entire farm is worth £1,500,000 and the records of the settlement show that the effective tax rate established at the previous ten-year anniversary was 4%.

The trustees transfer one-third by value of the farm to a beneficiary *in specie*. The remaining two-thirds of the farm is not devalued by this release, so the amount of the transfer, applying 'estate before less estate after' principles, is £500,000. The availability of APR reduces the chargeable value to nil and even though the exit charge is set at 4%, when applied to the nil chargeable value, it still results in a nil IHT charge.

One capricious element of APR and BPR in the context of an exit charge post a ten-year charge is its effective cut-off date. If the conditions for that relief are satisfied at the time of the chargeable transfer in general terms it does not matter that thereafter the transferee is not entitled to relief going forward. In the example just shown, the beneficiary could immediately sell the farm and there would be no tax clawback charge on the trustees. However, if the beneficiary died some three years later his estate would not include any property qualifying for relief – it should also be remembered that even if the property did continue to qualify by reference to the beneficiary's continued farming activities, a minimum two-year ownership period would be required to secure access to APR and/or BPR in his estate.

If the parties realise from the outset that it is likely that the relevant asset will be sold, it is better for it to be distributed *in specie* than for the trustees to make the sale.

Example 8.48—Distribution of cash

On its tenth anniversary on 31 March 2016 Daniel's relevant property trust comprised cash of £1,512,000 and unquoted shares (valued at £200,000) in the family trading company qualifying for 100% BPR. There are no other complicating factors (ie settlor's seven-year chargeable transfers or earlier capital distributions etc). The ten-year charge rate is calculated as follows:

	£	£
Cash		1,512,000
Shares	200,000	
BPR	(200,000)	
Net		Nil
Fund value		1,512,000
Nil rate band (2015/2016)		(325,000)
Taxable		1,187,000
Ten-year charge: 1,187,000 × (30 × 20)%	= 71,220	
Exit rate: 71,220/1,512,000 × 100	= 4.710%	

On 31 October 2016 the trustees distribute cash of £500,000. The tax payable (assumed met from the appointed cash) is calculated as follows: £500,000 @ 4.710% × 2/40 = 1,177.50

Reduction in the rate of tax

8.64 The availability of APR or BPR can reduce the overall tax burden, not only by reference to specific release of property but to the overall context of the settlement. The rate of a periodic charge on a relevant property trust can be reduced as a result of the fact that the amount on which the charge is imposed is itself reduced by BPR or APR. The result will be that on any exit charge in the next ten years there will be a reduction whether or not the distribution that triggers the exit charge is of property that qualifies for APR or BPR. Contrast this with the exit charge triggered prior to the first ten-year anniversary.

Clearly, where the subject matter of the distribution itself qualifies for 100% relief, there will be no need for any calculations.

Clawback

> **Focus**
>
> The tax impact of clawback can be costly and great care should be taken to preserve the qualities of APR/BPR during the seven year run-off period.

8.65 The clawback rules, which are one of the more difficult features of the APR and BPR regime, can affect trusts originally created by PETs under the old regime but which for IHT purposes have now become relevant property trusts by *FA 2006* (ie old-style A&M trusts). The later PET failure at a time when neither APR or BPR apply will cause the donor's cumulative history to be revised to reflect the PET value pre APR/BPR. It should be noted that the clawback rules do also affect trusts that were always relevant property trusts where the impact is restricted to the additional tax due as a consequence of the loss of APR/BPR on the original chargeable transfer but the donor's cumulative history is not affected. This is because *ss 113A* and *124A* each refer to value transferred by a PET.

Consider that a settlor had transferred property into trust that would have originally qualified as a PET (after 17 March 1986 but before 22 March 2006) in circumstances where APR or BPR would have been in point, but then died within seven years of that transfer. Clawback may apply if the trustees, who are the transferees for the purposes of the clawback rules, no longer own that property such that the potential to re-test that asset for BPR/APR is lost. This will have a double effect:

- the trustees will suffer IHT on the original transfer to them, except in so far as it was within the nil rate band; and
- there will be an increase in the calculations of exit charge and other transfers that have already been set out in this chapter.

Acquisition of relievable property

8.66 It is just as useful for trustees of a relevant property trust to acquire property that qualifies for APR or for BPR as it is for individuals in their later years. If trustees have invested the entire fund in assets that qualify for APR or BPR and have satisfied the period of ownership (two years (BPR) or seven years (APR)) appropriate for the type of property, the fund will escape the impact of the ten-year charge by reason of nil taxable value and as a consequence later distributions will also escape the impact of the exit charge by reason of this nil rate.

THE SPECIAL CHARGE UNDER *SECTION 70*

Background to the special charge

8.67 In certain cases, it was considered expedient for the legislation to include a special rate of charge which arises outside the usual regime of ten-year and periodic charges. Initially, the main trigger was the situation where property was settled for charitable purposes only until the end of some specific period but this scenario can now be extended to other situations – see **8.71** below. Since that period could be quite long, the rate of charge is expressed as a percentage which increases with the passage of time and which can relate to a period of 50 years or more.

The rate of charge

8.68 The charge is fixed by reference to the 'relevant period' which is usually a period that begins with the later of: the day on which the property came within *s 70*; or 13 March 1975; and ends with the day before the event that triggers the charge. The rate of tax is:

- For each of the first 40 complete successive quarters 0.25%
- For the next 40 quarters 0.20%
- For the next 40 quarters 0.15%
- For the next 40 quarters 0.10%
- For the next 40 quarters 0.05%

If the property was excluded property at any time during the period under consideration, then the period of one quarter during which it was excluded property is excluded from the calculation of the relevant period (*s 70(7)*).

8.69 The calculation is built up by applying the percentages set out above to the relevant period. For the first ten years, assuming that none of the property is excluded property, the rate, when expressed as a percentage, is the same as the period expressed as whole years and quarters. For other periods the following rate will apply:

- 15 years 14%
- 20 years 18%
- 25 years 21%
- 30 years 24%
- 35 years 26%

- 40 years 28%
- 45 years 29%
- 50 years or more 30%

Actually, these rates are in many instances higher than the normal rates of charge, but the fact that they can be calculated without the multi-step computations set out earlier in this chapter may be some compensation. There is however no election available to the taxpayer: the regime under *s 70* applies whenever the legislation states that it applies and not otherwise.

Variations on the rate of charge

8.70 Where a trust includes property qualifying for BPR or APR that relief can apply to mitigate the charge under *s 70*. There are also special provisions where property was previously in a maintenance fund for heritage property. Those special provisions are of limited application and the reader is referred to specialist works on the subject.

When the special charge will apply following *Finance Act 2006*

8.71 At **Example 8.3**, the example of Celia showed that trustees could use the statutory power of advancement. That triggered the special charge under *s 70*. It was always the case for A&M settlements that *s 70* would apply where property in an A&M settlement left it otherwise than in accordance with the main provisions of that section or where the trustees entered into a depreciatory transaction. Such occasions were rare and the application of *s 70*, as a result, is probably little known to general practitioners.

The position changed following *Finance Act 2006*. *Section 71B* now applies where settled property ceases to qualify as being held for a bereaved minor under *s 71A*. Tax will not be charged where the property leaves the trust because:

- the bereaved minor becomes 18;
- or dies; or the property is applied for his benefit.

Similarly, although there is a general regime which has been described in this chapter for the charge under *s 71E* on 18-to-25 trusts, there is a residual basis of charge under *s 71G* which applies the rates in *s 70* where, see *s 71G(1)(b)*, tax does not fall to be calculated under the system set out in *s 71F*.

Letter of wishes

8.72 Often the settlor will also wish to be a trustee of their trust but in many cases perhaps due to age or disinclination, they may prefer to leave the task to others. In either case the settlor may wish to guide the trustees as to how to exercise their discretion. Detailed below are examples of the type of letter that might be appropriate in connection with lifetime settlements, discretionary will trusts of both the nil rate band and latterly of residue, as was common before the introduction of the transferable nil rate band that is described fully in **Chapter 14**.

All too often in the latter case, the family used the fund, by default, for the benefit of the surviving spouse, even mandating income to them. Such conduct would enable HMRC to argue that the widow(er) enjoyed an interest in possession thereby perhaps negating any tax planning routine. There is also a trap here for those who now release funds to the surviving spouse in the mistaken belief that this will retrospectively put them in the position of being able to claim two nil rate bands on the second death: this will not be the case unless that release is sheltered by *s 144*.

Sometimes a will contains precatory words and occasionally even, in effect, the text of a letter of wishes. This is bad practice: it denies the testator any flexibility later, and the words used may come back to haunt the draftsman; see for example *s 143*.

Example 8.49—Letters of wishes

Note: Form A is a (somewhat antiquated in its view) example for a standard lifetime settlement. Form B (albeit in modified form) is still often seen, dating back to the 'pre-*Finance Act 2008*' situation (ie prior to the introduction of the transferable nil rate band facility), such as an existing will; and Form C is more appropriate for a recently drawn will.

Form A

This letter is confidential to my Trustees and is not the property of the beneficiaries.

In my Will that I have made today I have created a discretionary trust for my immediate family. I am one of the trustees but this letter is intended to guide my trustees after I am no longer a trustee for any reason. The trustees can at their discretion at any time share out the trust fund, either capital or income, between my daughter Susan and my sons Peter and John, with provision for grandchildren. My thinking in setting up the trust was as follows.

Susan is not working at present and her husband will only with difficulty afford to cover their household bills, so I would like the trustees to provide for Susan and her family occasional 'extras', even luxuries such as holidays. They cannot afford private education but I would be happy to see money set aside for when their children go to university.

Peter is no better at managing money at the age of 40 than he was as a child. The trustees should only in exceptional circumstances release capital to him. Far better to make an allowance to his dear and long-suffering wife Sally, who I know will use it for the family's benefit.

John is too level-headed and successful to need much help from the trust but should not be penalised on that account. His children deserve a good start in life so the trustees should be willing to help, even with golf or flying lessons if that is what they want.

Of course, this is only a guide. The trustees must exercise their discretion as they see fit according to the circumstances prevailing at the time.

Dated this day   of September 2016

Signed……………………

Form B

In my Will dated ……… September 2007 I have created a discretionary trust of 'the nil rate sum' for my immediate family. Apart from that, my Will gives my son Peter my interest in the family company and gives the rest of my estate to my wife Maureen for life. After Maureen's death, the trustees can at their discretion share out the rest of my estate between my daughter Sarah and Philip, with a provision for grandchildren. None of us can know exactly what assets we shall have at the date of our death, but my thinking in preparing the Will this way was as follows.

I want Maureen to be well provided for but I appreciate that if I leave the whole of my estate to her I have effectively 'thrown away' the nil rate band. I therefore hope that the Trustees of the nil rate sum, whilst always having an eye to what Maureen needs, will try to avoid the situation where Maureen is regarded as effectively the only beneficiary of the discretionary trust. It will be wise to encourage Maureen to use up some of her own resources first, to reduce her estate, before the trustees come to her aid.

As to my personal effects, for example, which are part of the nil rate sum, if I still own the yacht at the date of my death, I would like the trustees to consider Sarah having it, if she would like it, whilst Peter and his growing family might like the Volvo estate. Otherwise I hope that Sarah and Peter will agree between themselves if they would like any of my personal possessions.

Apart from that, my gift to Peter recognises that he has given his life to working for the family business. Giving him my interest in the business will, I hope, give him some security. It is also my hope that he will effectively receive that benefit tax free, so that it would not form part of the nil rate sum.

It would therefore be my wish that the Trustees, in deciding whom to benefit when exercising their discretion over the nil rate sum, should first compensate Sarah and her family to even up the benefit between my two children.

I do not think that there will be a substantial balance of residue over and above the nil rate band after taking account of the gift of the business. However, if there is, again I would like the Trustees to compensate Sarah if, in terms of value, she has received less than Peter.

The Trustees have a complete discretion over the nil rate sum and over the residue of my estate. I leave it to them to exercise that discretion as they think best in the circumstances that arise. This letter is only intended as a guide to my thinking in making my Will.

Dated this day of 2007

Signed……………………

[Testator]

Form C

In my Will dated [Date] I have created a discretionary trust of 'the nil rate sum' for my immediate family. Apart from that, my Will gives my son Peter my interest in the family company and gives the rest of my estate to my wife Maureen for life. After Maureen's death, the trustees can at their discretion share out the rest of my estate between my daughter Sarah and Philip, with a provision for grandchildren. None of us can know exactly what assets we shall have at the date of our death, but my thinking in preparing the Will this way was as follows.

I want Maureen to be well provided for and I appreciate that as far as I leave my estate to her I am preserving the nil rate band for use on her eventual death. I therefore hope that the Trustees of the nil rate sum, will always have an eye to what Maureen needs and in particular will consider, before the expiry of two years from my death, whether to release capital to Maureen.

As to my personal effects, which are part of the nil rate sum, Maureen should have anything she wants and needs but if I still own the yacht at the date of my death, I would the Trustees to consider Sarah having it, if she would like it, whilst Peter and his growing family might like the Volvo estate.

Apart from that, my gift to Peter recognises that he has given his life to working for the family business. Giving him my interest in the business will, I hope, allow him some security. It is also my hope that after business relief he will effectively receive that benefit tax free, so that it will not form part of the nil rate sum.

It would therefore be my wish that the Trustees, in deciding whom to benefit when exercising their discretion over the nil rate sum, should first compensate Sarah and her family to even up the benefit between my two children.

I do not think that there will be a substantial balance of residue over and above the nil rate band after taking account of the gift of the business. However, if there is, again I would like the Trustees to compensate Sarah if, in terms of value, she has received less than Peter.

The Trustees have a complete discretion over the nil rate sum and over the residue of my estate. I leave it to them to exercise that discretion as they think best in the circumstances that arise. This letter is only intended as a guide to my thinking in making my Will.

Dated this [day] of [month] 201

Signed……………………

[Testator]

Chapter 9

Exemptions and excluded property

SIGNPOSTS

- **Lifetime exemptions** –The annual exemption of £3,000 (see **9.7**) and the normal expenditure out of income exemption (see **9.9–9.10**) can help to reduce a future IHT liability.
- **Dispositions that are not transfers of value** – Dispositions for the maintenance of family are often overlooked (see **9.12–9.15**).
- **General exemptions** – Spouse exemption and gifts to charities exemption offer a useful shelter for IHT (see **9.16–9.19**).
- **Death exemptions** – No IHT is payable on the death of a person whilst on active service, even if the death occurs many years later but somehow can be linked to injuries inflicted or a disease contracted during active service (see **9.26–9.28**).
- **Excluded property** – Assets situated outside the UK and owned by non-UK domiciled individuals and in some cases even assets situated in the UK and reversionary interest may escape a charge to IHT (see **9.29–9.40**).

INTRODUCTION

9.1 IHT exemptions can be divided into three categories, those that only apply on death, those that apply on lifetime transfers only and those that can apply during lifetime or on death, here called 'general' exemptions. A PET is not an exempt transfer, but may become one seven years after the gift is made (see **Chapter 2**). Some exemptions apply to lifetime transfers and death.

Lifetime exemptions

9.2 *Lifetime* exemptions only apply to lifetime transfers and they are examined in more detail below. These are (all references are to *IHTA 1984*, unless otherwise stated):

- potentially exempt transfers (*s 3A*; see **Chapter 2**);
- annual exemption for gifts not exceeding £3,000 in any tax year (*s 19*);
- small gifts in any tax year up to a total of £250 per donee (*s 20*);
- normal expenditure out of income with no upper limit, if certain conditions are satisfied (*s 21*; see **Chapter 1**);
- wedding or civil partnership gifts within certain limits (*s 22*).

Dispositions that are not transfers of value

9.3 Certain dispositions do not constitute transfers of value if certain conditions are satisfied, including the following (see **9.12**):

- dispositions for maintenance of family (*s 11*);
- dispositions allowable for income tax or conferring retirement benefit (*s 12*);
- dispositions by close companies for the benefit of employees (*s 13*).

General exemptions

9.4 *General* exemptions, ie those which apply to both lifetime and death transfers are as follows:

- gifts between spouses or civil partners (*s 18*);
- gifts to UK based charities;
- gifts to qualifying Parliamentary political parties (*s 24*);
- gifts to registered housing associations (*s 24A*);
- gifts for national purposes (eg The National Galleries of Scotland, National Museums of Scotland and the National Trust for Scotland) (*s 25*);
- transfers to maintenance funds for historic buildings, where HMRC so direct upon making a claim (*s 27*);
- transfers of shares or securities by an individual to an employee trust, subject to certain conditions (*s 28*);
- transfers of national heritage property may be exempt from IHT where certain conditions are satisfied, ie 'conditionally exempt transfers' (*ss 30–35*).

Death exemptions

9.5 *Death* exemptions: There are three exemptions which are only available on transfers on death:

- death on active service exemptions and emergency personnel and humanitarian workers responding to emergencies (*ss 153A, 154, 154A* and *155A*);
- decorations for valour, if never transferred for consideration in money or money's worth (*s 6(1B)*);
- wartime compensation payments (*s 153ZA* formerly ESC F20).

Excluded property

9.6 *Excluded property* is property which has been specifically excluded from IHT (see *s 6*). Following *s 3(2)* transfers of value do not take into account the value of any excluded property. Excluded property is also not included in a person's estate following *s 5(1)*. In determining whether property is 'excluded property', one not only has to look at the situs of the property and the domicile of the transferor, but also at the type of property transferred. Excluded property comprises two main types of property:

(a) non-UK situs property beneficially owned by a non-UK domiciled individual; and

(b) non-UK situs property settled in a trust made at the time when the settlor is a non-UK domiciled individual.

It is important not to confuse exempt property with excluded property. While 'excluded property' will not form part of a person's estate for inheritance tax purposes, the application of exemptions depends very much on the recipient of any transfer of value. Note however the amendment in *s 5(1B)* introduced by *FA 2010, s 53* in respect of purchased trust interests.

From 6 April 2017 the Government intends to introduce legislation which provides that all UK residential property held through an offshore structure or trust will be chargeable to IHT – this will be in addition to ATED introduced in 2013: see **1.27**.

LIFETIME EXEMPTIONS

Annual exemption

9.7 Transfers of value during the lifetime of a person up to a total of £3,000 per tax year are exempt from IHT (*s 19(1)*).

- Where the annual exemption is not used in any one tax year it can be rolled forward for one year only.
- Where a gift exceeds the £3,000 limit, the excess must:
  - if the gifts were made on different days, be attributed, so far as possible, to a later rather than an earlier transfer; and
  - if the gifts were made on the same day, be attributed to them in proportion to the values transferred by them.

Where a transfer is a PET, in the first instance the annual exemption is left out of account. However if the donor dies within seven years of making the gift, the gift becomes a chargeable transfer. If two transfers are made on different days in the same tax year, the annual exemption is first applied to the earlier transfer. It does not matter whether the transfers are PETs or chargeable transfers when made (IHTM14143).

Example 9.1—Annual exemptions and PETs

Mrs Smith died on 30 April 2016, having made the following gifts to her daughter:

	£
1 June 2014	2,500
6 April 2015	1,500
15 April 2016	4,000
IHT position of lifetime gifts on death	
1 June 2014 gift:	2,500
Deduct 2014/15 exemption	3,000
Chargeable transfer on death	NIL
£500 can be carried forward	
6 April 2015 gift	1,500
Deduct 2015/16 exemption	3,000
Chargeable transfer on death	NIL

Only £1,500 can be carried forward. The annual exemption for the current tax year must be used before any unused annual exemption brought forward from the previous year (IHTM14144). The £500 unused exemption from the previous year can only be used during the 2015/16 year. It cannot be carried forward.

	£
15 April 2016 gift	4,000
Deduct 2016/17 exemption	3,000
Deduct unused 2015/16 exemption	1,500
Chargeable transfer on death	NIL

Small gifts exemption

9.8 The small gifts exemption under *s 20* covers transfers of value to any one person up to a total of £250 per tax year. The gift can consist of settled property and it may include free use of property. This exemption applies to any number of gifts up to £250 to separate persons, but it cannot be used to cover part of a larger gift.

This exemption can be used in addition to the annual exemption of £3,000, as long as the gift of £250 is made to a separate person. The current rule means that where the only transfer of value made is an outright gift of £3,250, the small gifts exemption cannot be used on the excess over £3,000 (assuming no carry-forward of the annual exemption from a previous year). Therefore, £250 will be chargeable to IHT.

Normal expenditure out of income exemption

9.9 Under *s 21* a lifetime transfer is exempt from IHT if it can be shown that:

- it was made as part of the normal expenditure of the transferor; and
- it was made out of his income; and
- after allowing for all transfers of value forming part of his normal expenditure, the transferor was left with sufficient income to maintain his usual standard of living.

Generally, HMRC will judge each case on its facts, therefore evidence to support a claim for this exemption is essential. The case *Bennett v IRC* [1995] STC 54 considered *s 21* in detail and the court identified several points to consider:

- 'Normal expenditure' means expenditure that was part of the settled pattern of expenditure adopted by the donor.

- A 'settled pattern' can be shown from the expenditure of the donor over a period of time *or* by showing that the donor has assumed a commitment, *or* adopted a firm resolution, in relation to future expenditure *and* has then made gifts in accordance with that commitment. One payment will be viewed as sufficient if clear evidence can be shown to support the claim that regular payments were intended.
- There is no fixed minimum period to establish the relief.
- Where there is no formal commitment or resolution, it may be necessary to show a series of payments.
- There can be some variation in the pattern, but to claim the relief it must be shown that the donor intended a pattern to exist and remain for a period of time.
- The amount of the transfer does not have to be fixed; the amount may be fixed by a formula such as a percentage of earnings or a figure such as 'what is left after paying all my outgoings'.
- Tax planning does not disqualify the expenditure; in contrast, if the taxpayer entered into a series of payments after taking advice, it may support his claim.

Gifts may also be made by a Continuing attorney who has sufficient powers in the Power of Attorney deed, and the same rules will apply (as highlighted by the case of *McDowall v IRC (2004)*). HMRC will usually request a copy of the deed to check the powers. On applying for a guardianship order a proposed guardian could include such powers in their application to the Sheriff Court.

9.10 Details of income and expenditure have to be listed to support a claim for this exemption on supporting schedule IHT403 to Form IHT400 (formerly D3a as added to Form IHT200). It is seen as good practice, if someone wishes to rely on this relief, to prepare a short document which explains that the donor has surplus income and that he therefore intends to make regular gifts out of income. See **Chapter 6** as to duty of care.

A premium on a life insurance on the donor's life paid directly or indirectly by the donor will not qualify under the 'normal expenditure out of income' exemption if at any time an annuity was purchased on the donor's life, unless it can be shown that the purchase of the annuity and the making or varying of the insurance were not associated operations (see *s 21(2)*).

As long as the above conditions are satisfied, the donor can pass funds to a donee limited only to the extent of the donor's available surplus income (IHTM14231–14251).

In the case of *McDowell and others (McDowell Executors) v CIR* [2004] STC SCD 22 it was held that a power of attorney does not give the attorney an authority to make gifts out of income.

The introduction of the *Inheritance Tax (Delivery of Accounts) (Excepted Estates) (Amendment) Regulations 2011, SI 2011/214* at first sight looked as if the facility of making gifts out of income under *s 21* has been curtailed. This regulation is not a change in the law as such but a change in the reporting requirements of such gifts. The main regulations about whether an estate needs an inheritance tax return are the ones in 2004 which provide that the parameters for an excepted estate were satisfied (among other things) where a person died who had not made chargeable transfers in the period of seven years before death exceeding £150,000. The new regulation says that certain gifts will be treated as chargeable transfers for reporting purposes. These are gifts that:

- in any year exceed £3,000;
- fall in the seven years prior to death; and
- are exempt only by virtue of *s 21*.

This means that under the new rules, it might be necessary to complete an IHT return where previously that might not have been necessary.

There is another point which has not been clarified. It is likely that in future it will become necessary to report gifts to be sheltered under *s 21* on income tax returns from year to year.

HMRC have recently substantially re-written their guidance on gifts out of income – see IHTM14231 to IHTM14255. HMRC now advise staff to deny taxpayers' claims that the exemption applies on gifts made out of several years of accumulated income.

Partial withdrawals from investment bonds (even if they are within the 5% annual allowance), while they may assume the character of income, are now deemed to be capital payments and do not qualify for the exemption under *s 21*.

Focus

- Competent professional advisers advise their clients to keep records of such gifts – Form IHT403 is useful as an indication of the type of information HMRC require.
- It also is good practice to prepare a short document explaining that the donor has surplus income and that he intends to make regular gifts out of income.
- An annual ledger of income and expenditure which shows surplus income will assist.
- Regular withdrawals from investment bonds count as capital for the purposes of the normal expenditure out of income exemption.

- HMRC's IHT Manual has now been updated – IHTM14250 deals with the issue whether income may have lost its income nature.

Gifts in consideration of marriage/civil partnership exemption

9.11 Gifts in consideration of marriage are exempt from IHT on the value transferred up to the following limits (*s 22*):

- £5,000 by a parent of either party to the marriage/civil partnership. Each parent can give £5,000 to the couple.
- £2,500 by one party to the marriage/civil partnership to the other or by a grandparent or remoter ancestor.
- £1,000 in any other case.

The gift must be made before, or contemporaneously with, the marriage/civil partnership. If it is made after the marriage/civil partnership it must be made in satisfaction of a prior legal obligation. If the marriage does not occur, the donor must have the right to recover the gift, otherwise a charge to IHT may occur.

The exemption applies to gifts to an illegitimate child, an adopted child and a stepchild.

This exemption can be used to settle property on trust, but only if the beneficiaries of the trust are limited to the couple, any issue and the spouses of such issue (*s 22(4)*).

DISPOSITIONS WHICH ARE NOT TRANSFERS OF VALUE

Disposition for maintenance of family

9.12 A disposition for the maintenance of family is not a transfer of value and it is therefore exempt from IHT (*s 11*). HMRC's view is that this exemption is limited to lifetime transfers only, so it is uncertain whether payments to the recipient would be covered under this exemption if the payer dies. The following payments are excluded from IHT:

- By one party to the marriage for the maintenance of the other party.
- By one party to a marriage for the maintenance, education or training of a child of either party. This includes stepchildren and adopted children. The maintenance can continue beyond 18 years, if the child is in full-time education.

- The provisions extend to the maintenance of an illegitimate child and to the maintenance of other people's children until they reach the age of 18 years.
- The exemption also covers reasonable provision made for the care or maintenance of a dependent relative who is incapacitated by old age or infirmity from maintaining himself. Mothers and mothers-in-law who are widowed or separated are always dependent relatives for this exemption. This has been confirmed in the case of *R McKelvey (personal representative of D V McKelvey) v HMRC* [2008] SSCD 944 (SpC 694), where a terminally ill daughter transferred properties to provide for her elderly mother.

Unfortunately, 'maintenance' has not been defined and, until the *McKelvey* case, it was uncertain whether the transfer of capital assets (ie the former matrimonial home), would be covered by this exemption. As the above case illustrates, it can also be difficult in practice to quantify what constitutes 'reasonable provision' for care or maintenance, as this will often be a question of judgement.

Section 13 exempts dispositions of property to trustees in favour of employees of close companies.

Following concession ESC F12 a disposition has been treated as exempt under *s 11(3)* if the disposition is made for an unmarried mother, who is genuinely financially dependent on the child making the disposition. This concession has now been superseded by a change of definition of 'dependent relative' in *s 11(6)(b)*, to include *'his mother or father or his spouse's or civil partner's mother or father'*.

Example 9.2—Disposition for family

Susan, a young mother of two children, is terminally ill. Her main asset is the family home, which she inherited from her parents and a small share portfolio. Both assets push her above the available nil rate band. The previous year she separated from Simon, who now lives in rented accommodation.

Her main concern is to provide for her two children who would be forced to leave the family home if IHT were to become payable. By relying on *s 11*, she could transfer her assets to the children during her lifetime. As this will not be a transfer of value, the transfer may not become chargeable to IHT on her death.

> **Focus**
>
> This exemption has been used successfully where a terminally ill child has looked after an elderly relative.

Allocation of exemptions and interaction with reliefs

9.13 Where a transfer qualifies for any of the exemptions considered above, the question often arises how to apply these exemptions and how they interact with other reliefs.

First, there is the question of how business and agricultural reliefs (see **Chapter 11**) fit in with the exempt transfer rules such as those relating to the annual exemptions. This can best be illustrated by an example.

Example 9.3—Annual exemption and business property relief

Mr Miller died on 30 April 2016, having transferred a tenanted agricultural property, which qualifies for 50% relief, to his son in January 2014.

	£
1 January 2014 gift:	100,000
Deduct	
50% APR	50,000
Unused 2013/14 exemption	3,000
Chargeable transfer	47,000

APR and BPR are applied first and the annual exemption is then used to reduce the remaining chargeable transfer.

9.14 As indicated at **9.7**, there is an HMRC practice as to the allocation of exemptions where more than one of the exemptions considered above are involved (see IHTM14143). Where tax is payable, if two transfers are made on different days in the same tax years, the exemption ought to apply first to the earlier transfer. If two transfers are made on the same day, apportion the exemption between them.

Example 9.4—HMRC's Inheritance Tax Manual, at IHTM14143

Ajani makes transfers of £4,000 and £8,000 on the same day. The total value transferred is £12,000. Only the current tax year's annual allowance is available.

£4,000/£12,000 × £3,000 = £1,000 exemption on the £4,000 transfer

£8,000/£12,000 × £3,000 = £2,000 exemption on the £8,000 transfer

9.15 Where a number of different exemptions apply, the order of applying the transfers is as follows:

- normal expenditure out of income;
- marriage gifts;
- £3,000 annual exemption.

This provides the transferor with the opportunity for some forward planning to use the exemptions in the most efficient manner. Should the transferor wish to allocate the exemptions in a different order, HMRC will consider the matter accordingly.

GENERAL EXEMPTIONS

Spouse or civil partnership exemption

9.16 Transfers of value between UK-domiciled spouses/civil partners are exempt from inheritance tax (*s 18*):

- where property becomes comprised in the transferee's estate, by the amount by which the transferor's estate is diminished; or
- in any other case (eg payment by the transferor of his spouse's/civil partner's debt) by the amount by which the transferee's estate is increased.

The spouse/civil partner exemption for IHT applies when property is held on trust for the transferee spouse/civil partner under an 'immediate post-death interest' (see **Chapter 7**). However, following changes introduced in *FA 2006*, the exemption does not apply to the lifetime creation of an interest in possession in favour of spouses or civil partners from 22 March 2006, as such transfers do not become comprised in that individual's estate.

The spouse/civil partner exemption is qualified where the transfer passes under a testamentary or other disposition, usually a will, and:

- the disposition takes effect on the termination, after the transfer, of any interest or period; or
- the disposition is conditional on the happening of some event that is not satisfied, or does not take place, within 12 months after the transfer (*s 18(3)*).

9.17 Following *Finance Act 2005* the spouse exemption applies to same-sex couples who have entered into a civil partnership by virtue of the *Civil Partnership Act 2004.*

Following the introduction of the *Marriage and Civil Partnership (Scotland) Act 2014* any reference to marriage, married couple, spouse etc in existing legislation in Scotland is to be read as including marriage of a same sex couple.

By contrast, in *Holland (Exor of Holland Deceased) v IRC* [2003] STC (SCD) 43, the Special Commissioner decided that a couple who had lived as husband and wife for 31 years did not qualify for the spouse exemption.

In the case of *Burden v United Kingdom* [2008] STC 1305, it was decided that the spouse/civil partner exemption does not extend to co-habiting siblings.

Finance Act 2008 introduced provisions which enable the survivor of a married couple or civil partnership to inherit the unused proportion of the nil rate band of the first to die (*s 8A*). See **Chapter 14**.

Finance Act 2013 introduced new provisions which increase the spouse exemption for non-UK domiciled spouses or civil partners to the nil rate band in force at the time (£325,000 for 2015/16).

For transfers until 5 April 2013:

- if immediately before the transfer, the transferor but not the transferor's spouse or civil partner, was domiciled in the UK the spouse or civil partner exemption was limited to a cumulative total of £55,000, without grossing-up for tax (*s 18(2)*);
- if a lifetime transfer to a non-domiciled spouse or civil partner exceeded £55,000, the excess was treated as a PET and may become chargeable if the transferor dies within seven years;
- this restriction does not apply if both spouses or civil partners are non-UK domiciled individuals.

Finance Act 2013, s 177 inserted s*s 267A* and *268A* which amend these provisions for transfers from 6 April 2013 as follows:

- the non-UK domiciled spouse or civil partner can elect to be treated as UK domiciled, if one of two conditions is met:
  - condition A ('the lifetime exemption'): the person's spouse or civil partner must be UK domiciled at the time of the election and the person must not be UK domiciled; or
  - condition B ('the death exemption'): the person's spouse or civil partner died UK domiciled on or after 6 April 2013 and the person was not UK domiciled at that time and the election is made within two years of the UK domiciled spouse's date of death,
- if these conditions are met the restricted spouse or civil partner exemption is increased to the same amount as the nil rate band (£325,000 for 2014/15);
- the election can be backdated for a period up to seven years but not a date before 6 April 2013.

The election is irrevocable and brings the person's worldwide assets into the UK IHT net. Although the election cannot be revoked, if the person making the election is not UK resident for the purposes of income tax for the whole of any 'period specified', the election ceases to take effect. The 'period specified' is any period of four successive tax years beginning:

- in the case of a lifetime election, at any time after it takes effect; or
- in the case of the death exemption, at any time after the election is treated as having effect.

HM Treasury issued a further consultation paper on the draft legislation included in the Summer Budget 2015 in relation to deemed domicile. One of the proposals includes amendments to *s 267* in that from 6 April 2017 the qualifying period for a person resident in the UK to become deemed will be reduced from 17 out of 20 years to 15 out of 20 years. This will extend the 'period specified' mentioned above from four years to five years. The practical effect of this is that a person who elected to be treated as domiciled in the UK remains domiciled for a five-year period on ceasing to be UK resident. It was also announced that individuals who were born in the UK and who have a UK domicile of origin will revert back to their UK-domiciled status for tax purposes while resident in the UK.

Care needs to be taken on lifetime gifts, as the election must state the date from which it is supposed to take effect to ensure that any gift benefits from the full spouse exemption.

Example 9.5—Spouse exemption and domicile

Scenario 1: death prior to 6 April 2013

Mr Jones, who is UK domiciled, dies on 30 April 2012. In 2003, he married Maria Hofer, who is Austrian and moved to the UK following the marriage. Maria finds the British climate challenging and both she and her husband spend considerable time in Austria. She therefore remains domiciled in Austria, although she is resident in the UK. Mr Jones' estate was valued at £1 million and his will left his whole estate to his spouse:

IHT position on Mr Jones' death

	£
Estate	1,000,000
Less: nil rate band	325,000
Less: limited spouse exemption	55,000
Net estate	620,000
IHT @ 40%	248,000

Scenario 2: death on or after 6 April 2013

Mr Jones dies on 30 April 2016. Maria can elect to be treated as UK domiciled and the estate can benefit from an unrestricted spouse exemption, which would save £248,000 of IHT.

However, as this will bring Maria's worldwide estate into the UK IHT net, it has to be considered carefully, especially as there is no IHT equivalent in Austria.

If Maria decides to make the election and moves back to Austria in November 2016, she will retain her UK domicile status by election, despite being non-resident, until 6 April 2022.

Gifts to charities

9.18 Gifts to charity are exempt from IHT (*s 23*). This exemption was limited to gifts to UK-based charities, but see below. Following *Finance Act 2002*, the definition of 'charity' has been extended and now includes community amateur sports clubs, if they are registered and open to the whole community, are organised on an amateur basis and have as their main purpose the provision of facilities for, and the promotion of participation in, one or more eligible sports.

By *s 23(6)*, the property that is the subject matter of the transfer must actually become the property of the charity, or must be held for charitable purposes. Where the value transferred (ie the loss to the transferor's estate as a result of the disposition), exceeds the value of the gift in the hands of the charity, the exemption extends to the whole value transferred (see Statement of Practice E13).

9.19 *Section 23(2)* includes various restrictions to this exemption to prevent the abuse of charitable relief. The relief is not given, if the testamentary or other disposition by which it is given:

- takes place after any other transfer of value has had effect for any interest or period; or
- is conditional on something that does happen for 12 months after the transfer; or
- is defeasible, ie can be taken away from the charity after the gift for any reason.

Another restriction has been imposed in *s 23(4)* where the donor of the property wishes to continue living in the property after he has given it to the charity. The general rule is that the exemption does not apply if the donor, his or her spouse or a person connected to the donor has the right to possession of the property or to occupy the whole or part of the land rent free or at a rent that is below the market value.

A transfer that has not been defeated 12 months after it is to have taken effect and that, after that time, is indefeasible, is treated as charitable and secures the exemption.

Finance Act 2010 extended UK charity relief to certain EU organisations and community amateur sports clubs in the EU and the European Economic Area countries of Norway and Iceland, following a judgment in the European Court of Justice in January 2009. The extended definition of 'charity' applies for IHT purposes. HMRC (in their guidance to completing the IHT400 account) helpfully summarise the position as follows: 'All lifetime gifts and bequests on death to qualifying charities are exempt provided the gift was made to the charity outright'. They add: 'A qualifying charity is one that meets the following conditions:

- it is a charity established in the European Union or other specified country;
- it meets the definition of a charity under the law of England and Wales;
- it is regulated in the country of establishment, if that is a requirement in that country (see *Routier and another v RCC* [2014] EWHC 3010 (Ch));

- its managers are fit and proper persons to be managers of the charity.'

As there are different charitable governing bodies for England, Wales, and Scotland, the charitable status test and tax exemption position has become more complicated. The Office of the Scottish Charity Regulator has authority to grant charitable status to Scottish Charities but has no control over the tax status – this rests with HMRC (see **Overview A7**).

An entire estate left to a qualifying charity will be completely exempt from IHT, subject to any Legal Rights claims by children (or issue of a predeceasing child).

Gifts to political parties

9.20 All gifts made to qualifying political parties are exempt from IHT (*s 24*). A political party qualifies for the exemption if, at the last general election preceding the transfer of value:

- two members of that party were elected to the House of Commons; or
- one member of that party was elected to the House of Commons and not less than 150,000 votes were given to candidates who were members of that party.

Restrictions are the same as applied to charitable gifts.

In considering the exemption particular care must be given to the qualifying criteria especially for Scottish political parties (see **Overview A8**).

Gifts to housing associations

9.21 Under *s 24A*, transfers of value to registered social landlords, as defined by the *Housing Associations Act 1985* or *Housing Act 1996* or *Housing (Northern Ireland) Order 1981, SI 1981/156 (NI 3)* are exempt to the extent that the value transferred is attributable to land in the UK.

Again, the restrictions are the same as applied to charitable gifts.

Gifts for national purposes

9.22 Gifts to certain national bodies are exempt from IHT (*s 25*). The list of national bodies can be found in *Sch 3* and includes, among others, the National Galleries of Scotland, the National Museums of Scotland and any UK university.

Again, the restrictions are the same as applied to charitable gifts.

Transfers to maintenance funds for historic buildings

9.23 Transfers into settlements for the maintenance, repair or preservation of historic buildings and assets of outstanding scenic, historic or scientific interest are, subject to certain conditions, exempt (*ss 30–35A, Sch 3*). There is a two-year time limit from transfer to bring the claim, which can be extended by HMRC concession.

Transfers of shares or securities by an individual to an employee trust

9.24 Following *s 28*, subject to certain conditions, transfers to trusts for the benefit of employees of a company without interests in possession are exempt from IHT and will escape ten-yearly IHT charges (*s 58(1)*). Such transfers can be made by individuals, close companies and settlements.

The trusts of the settlement must fit the requirements of *s 86(1)*. The conditions are that the settled property is held on trusts, which, either indefinitely, or until the end of a period, do not permit that property to be applied otherwise than for the benefit of:

- people of a class that is defined by reference to employment in a particular trade or profession; or
- people of a class defined by employment by, or holding an office with a particular body carrying on a trade, profession or undertaking; or
- people of a class by reference to marriage to, or a relationship to, or dependence on people of a class defined above; or
- other charitable purposes.

In addition, *s 28(1)(b)* determines that the exemption only applies if all or most of the people working for that body can benefit, or if the trusts fit a profit-sharing scheme that has already been approved by HMRC under *ICTA 1988, Sch 9*, or for trusts which are approved share incentive plans within *ITEPA 2003, Sch 2* (*s 86(3)*).

9.25 *Section 28(2)* imposes a number of additional restrictions, which are as follows:

- the trustees must hold at least half the shares in the company; and
- the trustees must have a majority of votes in the company; and

- there must be no provisions that effect the company or its management or its shares or securities under which this power of ownership or of voting can be brought to an end without the consent of the trustees.

Finally, no participator (ie someone who owns at least 5% of any class of the shares comprised in its issued share capital and on winding-up of the company is entitled to 5% or more of its assets) may benefit from the trust.

HMRC in their Revenue & Customs Brief 18/11 summarised their approach in relation to close companies. IHT charges therefore may arise if the disposition is intended to confer a gratuitous benefit under *s 10*. There is both a subjective and an objective test both of which must be met. The subjective test is not met if there is the slightest possibility of a gratuitous intent when the contribution is made. The objective test must satisfy the conditions that the transaction must have been made at arm's length between persons not connected with each other, or was such as might be expected to be made in a transaction at arm's length between persons not connected with each other. This means that for close companies these conditions are rarely met in HMRC's view.

Section 28(A) was introduced by *Finance Act 2014* and creates a new exemption for employee-ownership trusts (EOTs). It provides that a transfer of shares by an individual is an exempt transfer to the extent that the value transferred is attributable to shares in or securities of a trading company if the settlement meets all-employee benefit requirements and the shares transferred give the EOT control of the company at the end of the tax year in which the transfer is made.

DEATH EXEMPTION

Death in service

9.26 Following *s 154*, no IHT is payable on the death of a person whilst on active service against an enemy or other service of a warlike nature. The Defence Council or the Secretary of State must certify that the person concerned:

- died from a wound that was inflicted when that person was on active service; or
- died from an accident that occurred during such service; or
- died from a disease contracted when the person was on that service.

Where a disease was contracted at some previous time, but it was aggravated during active military service and therefore death was brought on more quickly, the exemption also applies.

This exemption was invoked in the case of *Executors of 4th Duke of Westminster (otherwise Barty-King) v Ministry of Defence* QB [1978] STC 218 where the 4th Duke of Westminster died of cancer many years after his war wound. Although there was no direct causal connection between the war wound and the cause of his death, the exemption was successfully invoked.

All that is required is to find a 'reasonable link' which may have caused the death. For example a limp following a war injury may have caused a fall which resulted in death.

The following amendments were included in *Finance Act 2014* to take effect for deaths on or after 19 March 2014:

- A new *s 153A* was introduced which covers the death of emergency and humanitarian aid workers responding to emergency circumstances.
- A new *s 155A* extends the IHT exemption to constables and armed service personnel targeted because of their status.
- *Section 154A* extends the relief for armed forces personnel to injuries sustained when responding to emergencies.
- *Finance Act 2015, s 75* extended the death in service exemption to IHT payable on lifetime gifts that arises as a result of the death.

Decorations for valour or gallant conduct

9.27 Formerly ESC F19, now enacted in *s 6(1B)*, a decoration or other award if awarded for valour or gallant conduct and it has never been subject of a disposition for a consideration in money or money's worth is 'excluded property' for IHT.

Finance Act 2015, s 7 treats all medals and decorations awarded by the Crown or a country or territory outside the UK to armed forces personnel, emergency service personnel and individuals for achievements and services in public life as excluded property. The changes affect all transfers of values made on or after 3 December 2014.

Wartime compensation payments

9.28 This relief was originally only available to recipients of the £10,000 payment for Japanese prisoners of war, but has now been extended to a range of payments to victims of wrongs suffered during World War II. A list of qualifying payments can be found in *s 153ZA* (formerly Extra Statutory Concession F20).The amount of compensation received is assumed to be included in the deceased's assets. In effect, for any recipient of relevant compensation payments, the nil rate band for IHT is increased by the amount of compensation received.

New *s 153ZA* includes detailed provisions to enact this concession, which are backdated to 1 January 2015.

EXCLUDED PROPERTY

9.29 No transfer of 'excluded property' is chargeable to IHT following *ss 3(2)* and *5(1)*. The main categories of 'excluded property' are listed in *s 6* and are mentioned below.

Property situated outside the UK

9.30 Following *s 6* property situated outside the UK is excluded property if the person entitled to it is an individual who is domiciled outside the UK for the purposes of IHT. For the definition of domicile, see **Chapter 1**.

Settled property that is situated outside the UK is 'excluded property' if the settlor was domiciled outside the UK when the settlement was made (*s 48(3)*). The recent case of *Barclays Wealth Trustees (Jersey) Ltd and another v HMRC* [2015] EWHC 2872 confirms that the domicile status of the settlor needs to be re-examined if further funds are introduced into an excluded property settlement.

Following *s 82*, if the settlor retains an interest in possession either for himself or his spouse, and a discretionary trust arises on the termination of that interest, an additional test is imposed on the determination of the interest in possession. It will be necessary to ascertain where the settlor and his spouse are domiciled when their interests end and the discretionary trust arises.

Example 9.6—Settlement of excluded property

Hans, a German national, settles shares in a German company on a life interest trust for his wife Gemma in 1993. Both Hans and Gemma are domiciled in Germany. At the date of settlement, the shares are excluded property, being property situated outside the UK and settled by a non-UK domiciliary. However, the trust document determines that on the ending of Gemma's life interest, the trust assets should be resettled on discretionary trusts for Hans' grandchildren. It will therefore be necessary to revisit the settlement, when Gemma's interest ends (it ends in 2013).

Hans and Gemma decided that they prefer the Scottish climate and moved to Scotland in 1995. When Gemma's life interest ends in 2013, both Hans and Gemma are deemed UK domiciled for IHT. The German shares therefore will not qualify as 'excluded property' when Gemma's interest ends and a charge to IHT will occur, if the shares are valued above the nil rate band at that time.

If the trustees had used their power of appointment to resettle those same shares on discretionary trust prior to Hans and Gemma becoming deemed domiciled, the shares would have remained 'excluded property' and the settlement would have escaped the relevant property regime.

Property that is excluded or exempt despite being situated in the UK

Government securities

9.31 Following *s 6(2)* exempt government securities are excluded property if they are in the beneficial ownership of a person who satisfies the conditions for exemption attached to the stock. The exemption depends on the qualifying person having beneficial ownership and not the mere legal title.

Settled exempt government securities are excluded property if a person who satisfies the conditions for exemption is entitled to a qualifying interest in possession in the settlement (*s 48(4)*). 'Qualifying interest in possession' means an interest in possession to which an individual is beneficially entitled, or an interest in possession to which a company is beneficially entitled as a result of the commercial purchase of the interest in certain circumstances. If an annuitant (or other person entitled to part only of the income of the settled property) domiciled and resident abroad dies, or if his interest terminates at a time when the settled property is exempt government securities, the relevant 'slice' of the property is excluded property.

Settled exempt government securities not subject to a qualifying interest in possession will only be excluded property if the trustees can demonstrate that all known persons for whose benefit the settled property, or income from it, has been or might be applied, or who are or might become beneficially entitled to an interest in possession in it, are persons who satisfied or satisfy the exemption conditions for the beneficial owner of the securities.

These conditions previously included the requirement that the beneficial owner must be domiciled and ordinarily resident outside the UK. However, for deaths and other chargeable events on or after 6 April 1998, all government securities (with the exception of 3½% War Loan stock) are excluded property for IHT purposes by reference only to the ordinary residence of the beneficial owner, ie domicile is no longer relevant (see IHTM04291 and IHTM27241).

Holdings in an authorised unit trust and shares in an open-ended investment company

9.32 A holding in an authorised unit trust and a share in an open-ended investment company are excluded property if, in either case the person beneficially entitled to it is an individual who, for the purposes of IHT, is domiciled outside the UK, in relation to transfers of value or other events occurring after 15 October 2002 (see *s 6(1A)*).

An authorised unit trust is a scheme authorised as such under the *Financial Services and Markets Act 2000, s 243*.

An open-ended investment company is such a company within the meaning of the *Financial Services and Markets Act 2000, s 236* and which is incorporated in the UK.

Certain property owned by persons domiciled in the Channel Islands or Isle of Man

9.33 Some types of national savings contracts are excluded property if the beneficial owner is domiciled in the Channel Islands or Isle of Man. 'Domicile', for this purpose, has its ordinary meaning, and not the extended meaning given to it for certain IHT purposes. The consequence will be that no IHT is payable on the death of the owner, or on any lifetime transfer of the savings. The savings contracts in question are (see *s 6(3)*):

- war savings certificates;
- national savings certificates (including Ulster savings certificates but not national savings income bonds);
- premium savings bonds;
- deposits with the National Savings Bank or with a trustee savings bank;
- certified contractual savings schemes within the meaning of *ITTOIA 2005, s 703(1)* (ie, SAYE schemes).

Visiting forces

9.34 *Section 6(4)* allows limited reliefs from IHT for visiting forces and the staff of allied headquarters. The reliefs fall into two categories. First, certain items of property belonging to visiting forces and staff are excluded property. Secondly, certain periods of residence in the UK are disregarded for IHT purposes. Details can be found in *s 155(1)* and are beyond the scope of this book.

Overseas pensions

9.35 Following *s 153*, some categories of foreign pensions relating to service in certain foreign colonial territories or relating to service for the government of an overseas territory are excluded property. The rule applies on death only and has the effect that the pension is left out of account in determining the value of a person's estate immediately before his death. The effect is that no IHT will be payable on the death of the pensioner, wherever he is domiciled and whatever the nature of his entitlement (eg a repayment of contributions due to the deceased's estate).

Non-sterling bank accounts

9.36 *Finance Act 1982, s 96* introduced a statutory exemption from capital transfer tax in relation to qualifying foreign currency bank accounts held by individuals who are non-UK residents and non-UK domiciled. The exemption is now provided by *IHTA 1984, s 157* and is only available on death.

A 'foreign currency account' is any account other than one denominated in sterling.

A 'qualifying' foreign currency account is a foreign currency account with the Post Office, the Bank of England, an institution authorised under the *Banking Act 1987*, a relevant European institution, or an international organisation of which the UK is a member which is designated as a bank by Treasury order.

These foreign currency accounts were used to sidestep restrictions for the deductibility of liabilities introduced by *FA 2013,* which disallow a deduction of liabilities used for acquiring 'excluded property'. For deaths occurring on or after 17 July 2014 (the date of Royal Assent to *FA 2014*) no deduction will be allowed for liabilities incurred to fund foreign currency bank accounts.

Foreign works of art

9.37 ESC F7, as modified by Ministerial Statement dated 25 February 2003, previously provided that there would be no liability to IHT on a work of art normally kept overseas and beneficially owned by a foreign domiciliary, if it is situated in the UK at the date of death and was brought to the UK solely for the purposes of public exhibition, cleaning or restoration, or if it would otherwise have left the UK to be kept overseas but is retained in the UK solely for these purposes. The concession also applied to waive the periodic charge to tax if the work of art is comprised in settled property in which there is no interest in possession.

This concession was withdrawn (by *The Enactment of Extra-Statutory Concessions Order 2009, SI 2009/730, art 13*) with effect from 6 April 2009, but legislative effect is given to it in *ss 5(1)(b)* and *64(2)* respectively.

Property owned by diplomatic agents

9.38 The *Diplomatic Privileges Act 1964, s 2(1)* gives the force of law to Articles of the *Vienna Convention on Diplomatic Relations. Article 34* of the *Convention* provides that a diplomatic agent is exempt from all taxes with certain exceptions. These exceptions include dues and taxes on private immovable property situated in the territory of the receiving state, dues and taxes on private income having its source in the receiving state and capital taxes on investments made in commercial undertakings in the receiving state.

It would seem therefore that tax will not be chargeable on any transfer *inter vivos* by a diplomatic agent of property situated in the UK, but that it will in strictness be leviable on his death on his immovable property situated here, and on any movable property unless its presence in this country can be attributed solely to the deceased's presence as a member of a mission. Thus, his personal chattels would be exempt, and (presumably) his personal current bank account, but (probably) not any investment capital assets.

Reversionary interests

9.39 Following *s 48(1)* a reversionary interest is excluded property unless:

- it has at any time been acquired, either by the person entitled to it or by a person previously entitled to it, for a consideration in money or money's worth; or
- it is one to which the settlor or his spouse is or has been beneficially entitled; or
- it is an interest expectant on the determination of a lease of property which is for life or lives, or for a period ascertainable only by reference to a death and not granted for a full consideration in money or money's worth.

Provided that the above conditions are satisfied, the situs of the trust property, and the domicile of the settlor and reversioner, are irrelevant.

In addition, even if those conditions are not satisfied, a reversionary interest is excluded property if the interest, as distinct from the fund in which it subsists, is situated outside the UK and the person who owns the reversion, whether or not it has been acquired by purchase, is domiciled outside the UK.

9.40 *Section 48* was amended by *Finance Act 2006*, which inserted *s 48(3B)*. This provides that where property situated outside the UK is excluded property, such property will not continue to be excluded if a UK-domiciled individual purchases an interest in possession in the excluded property for consideration in money or money's worth after 5 December 2005. This in effect is an anti-avoidance measure against 'deathbed' arrangements to prevent UK-domiciled individuals with a limited life expectancy (eg elderly or infirmed individuals) purchasing excluded property shortly before death.

Example 9.7—Reversionary interest (I)

A fund consisting entirely of non-UK situs property is held on trust for Arthur for life, with the fee to Bertie. Bertie dies.

There is no charge to IHT on Bertie's death. The domicile of the settlor and Bertie's domicile are irrelevant.

Example 9.8—Reversionary interest (II)

A fund consisting entirely of non-UK situs assets is held on trust for Arthur for life, with the fee to Bertie. Bertie has sold his interest to Charlie. Charlie dies.

IHT is payable on the value of the reversion as part of Charlie's estate, as the condition in *s 48(1)(a)* has been breached.

The fund will escape a charge to IHT if, following *s 48(3)* the settlor was a non-UK domiciliary, Charlie was domiciled abroad at the date of his death and the reversion can be regarded as excluded property under *s 6(1)* (ie the trust is non-UK resident).

Example 9.9—Reversionary interest (III)

A fund is held on trust for Arthur for life, with the fee to Bertie. The fund contains (*inter alia*) reversions purchased by the trustees as investments. Arthur dies.

There is a charge to IHT on Arthur's death except in so far as it consists of excluded property. If the settlor was domiciled outside the UK when the settlement was made, the reversion should be excluded property if (but only if) it is situated abroad.

Anti-avoidance provisions have been introduced in s 81A. Where a reversionary interest in relevant property, which was acquired for consideration by an individual, or his spouse or civil partner, comes to an end, and the individual, his spouse or civil partner become entitled to an interest in possession in the relevant property, this will be treated as a disposition of the reversionary interest at that time.

Chapter 10

Reliefs – General

SIGNPOSTS

- **Taper relief** – Available on lifetime transfers which exceed the nil rate band for inheritance tax and are made more than three years before death (see **10.2–10.3**).
- **Quick succession relief** – Provides relief against two charges to IHT where there was more than one chargeable transfer within a five-year period (**10.4–10.5**).
- **Related property relief** – If property was valued on death as 'related property' and is sold within three years at less than that valuation a claim can be made (see **10.6–10.7**).
- **Fall in value relief** – If the value of a PETs or lifetime chargeable transfer has fallen since date of gift and date of death within seven years, relief can be claimed (see **10.8–10.12**).
- **Post-death reliefs on the sale of shares** – If there is a fall in value since date of death and date of sale within 12 months, Executors can claim relief (see **10.14–10.16**).
- **Post-death relief on the sale of land** – Relief can be claimed (subject to certain conditions) to substitute the sale value with the probate value (see **10.17–10.18**).
- **Woodlands relief and heritage property relief** – Subject to a number of conditions these reliefs may be useful albeit rare (see **10.24–10.30**).

INTRODUCTION

10.1 In addition to the reliefs listed in **Chapter 9** and business property relief and agricultural property relief detailed in **Chapter 11** there are a number of other reliefs which can reduce a charge to IHT (see also **1.21**) (all statutory references in this chapter are to *IHTA 1984*, unless otherwise stated):

- Taper relief is available on both chargeable lifetime transfers and potentially exempt transfers made more than three years before death (*s 7*) (see **1.21**).
- Quick succession relief provides relief against two charges to IHT where there was more than one chargeable transfer within a five-year period (*s 141*) (see outline in **3.25**).
- Property valued on death as 'related property' (see **3.20**) may qualify for relief if it is sold within three years of death at less than that valuation (*s 161*).
- Relief is available when the market value of property transferred within seven years before death is lower at the date of death than at the time of the chargeable transfer (*ss 131–140*).
- Relief is available if quoted securities are sold within 12 months of death for less than their date of death IHT value (*ss 178*ff), and if land is sold within four years of death for less than its date of death IHT value (*ss 190*ff).
- Where the transferor is liable to IHT charges on the same assets in two jurisdictions, double tax relief may be available in certain circumstances.
- *The Inheritance Tax (Double Charges Relief) Regulations 1987, SI 1987/1130* and the *Inheritance Tax (Double Charges Relief) Regulations 2005, SI 2005/3441* prevent a person being charged to IHT twice on the same property in certain circumstances.
- An election can be made which enables the IHT chargeable on death in respect of growing timber and underwood to be deferred until sale (*ss 125–130*).
- Heritage property relief is a 'conditional exemption' which may be available on transfers of national heritage property if certain conditions are met (*s 30*).

These reliefs are covered in detail below.

TAPER RELIEF

10.2 IHT on all lifetime transfers (PETs and chargeable lifetime transfers) made within seven years before death may be subject to taper relief if the lifetime transfer was made more than three years before death, thereby reducing a potential charge to IHT. The taper relief rates are as follows (*s 7(4)*):

Table 10.1—Taper relief rates

Transfer:	3–4 years before death:	80%
	4–5 years before death:	60%
	5–6 years before death:	40%
	6–7 years before death:	20%

IHT at full death rates is calculated at the time of death on any PETs made within seven years prior to death, subject to the availability of taper relief. The value of the transfer stays the same for taper relief purposes, but the full rate(s) of IHT charged are reduced by taper relief.

10.3 Tax on chargeable lifetime transfers is calculated at lifetime rates. If the transferor dies within seven years, the tax is recomputed at full death rates, subject to taper relief where the death is more than three years after the gift, but using the rates in force at the date of death.

However, if IHT on a chargeable lifetime transfer is recalculated on death with taper relief and produces a lower tax figure than the tax originally calculated at lifetime rates, no IHT repayments will result from the application of taper relief (*s 7(5)*).

Example 10.1—Taper relief on PETs made within seven years of death

In September 2010 Alice made a gift of £110,000 to her son Alistair. In October 2010 she made a gift of £110,000 to her daughter Jennifer. Alice then decided to give her second son James £115,000 in November 2010 and in December 2012 she gave her youngest daughter Eleanor £110,000.

Alice died in June 2016, so all four PETs become chargeable transfers. No annual exemptions are available.

Alistair's and Jennifer's gifts escape a charge to IHT, as they are within the nil rate band of £325,000. The IHT payable by James and Eleanor will be calculated as follows:

	£
James's gift	115,000
Available nil rate band 2016/17 (£325,000 – £220,000)	105,000
Taxable gift	10,000
Tax charge @ 40%	4,000
Taper to 40%	1,600
James' IHT liability therefore will be £1,600	
Eleanor's gift	110,000
The nil rate band has been used up, therefore available NRB	0
Taxable gift	110,000
Tax charge @ 40%	44,000
Taper to 80%	35,200
Eleanor's IHT liability therefore will be £35,200	

Example 10.2—Taper relief on chargeable lifetime transfers made within seven years of death

In July 2011 Alice's husband Felix made a potentially exempt transfer of £200,000 to his daughter Jennifer. He made a transfer to a discretionary trust of £500,000 in September 2012 and IHT at the lifetime rate of 20% was paid on this chargeable transfer. Felix died in August 2016 having made no other lifetime transfers. No annual exemptions are available.

The IHT on the transfer to the discretionary trust payable during Felix's life is calculated as follows:

	£
Gift to discretionary trust	500,000
Deduct:	
Nil rate band 2012/13	325,000
	175,000
IHT payable at the lifetime rate of 20%	35,000

Following Felix's death the PET to Jennifer in July 2011 will become chargeable. This will use up part of the nil rate band. The additional IHT on the chargeable lifetime transfer to the discretionary trust is calculated as follows. The IHT on the trust at death rates is:

(£500,000 – (£325,000 – £200,000)) × 40% = £150,000.

This is now subject to taper relief at the rate of 80%.

£150,000 × 80% = £120,000

From this must be deducted the lifetime IHT payment of £35,000 to arrive at additional IHT of £85,000 payable as a result of Felix's death.

QUICK SUCCESSION RELIEF

10.4 Quick succession relief (QSR) provides relief against two charges to IHT where there was more than one chargeable transfer within a five-year period (*s 141*).

QSR is given on death, where the value of a person's estate was increased by a chargeable transfer made within the previous five years. The previous chargeable transfer may have been made *inter vivos*, or on death. The property subject to the first chargeable transfer does not have to be part of the deceased's estate for the relief to apply, ie it may have been given away by the deceased, but still form part of the deceased's estate for IHT as a chargeable PET.

10.5 In relation to settled property, the relief is only available where the later transfer is of settled property and the transferor had an interest in possession in the property under the pre-*Finance Act 2006* rules. In relation to settlements the relief can be granted on death and *inter vivos* transfers.

QSR reduces the tax payable on the later transfer and the formula to calculate the relief can be found in *s 141(3)*. In essence it is calculated as follows:

$$\text{Percentage} \times \frac{(\text{Gross chargeable FT} - \text{Tax on FT})}{\text{Gross chargeable FT}} \times \text{Tax on FT}$$

FT = First transfer

The percentages for the periods between transfers are as follows:

- 100% if the period beginning with the date of the first transfer and ending with the date of the later transfer does not exceed one year.

- 80% if it exceeds one year, but does not exceed two years.
- 60% if it exceeds two years, but does not exceed three years.
- 40% if it exceeds three years, but does not exceed four years.
- 20% if it exceeds four years.

Example 10.3—QSR in action

On 1 July 2013 Anna's father Fred gifted Anna £40,000 (his favourite son Freddie having received a gift of £400,000 earlier in the year). Anna's father died shortly afterwards and Anna paid IHT of £16,000 on the failed potentially exempt transfer received from her father.

Anna's mother died on 15 June 2014 and Anna was entitled to an interest in possession (an immediate post death interest (IPDI)) in her mother's estate. Her mother had a net estate of £450,000 on which IHT of £50,000 ((£450,000 – £325,000) × 40%) was paid.

On 1 June 2016 Anna dies leaving assets valued at £500,000. Her life interest in her mother's estate passes to her brother James and is valued at £275,000.

IHT on Anna's estate (before QSR):	£
Free estate	500,000
Settled property	275,000
Anna's estate	775,000
Deduct	
Nil rate band (2016/17)	325,000
Taxable estate	450,000
IHT payable @ 40%	180,000

Quick succession relief

The PET from Fred was made more than two years but less than three years before Anna's death and therefore quick succession relief of 60% applies.

$$60\% \times \frac{(£40{,}000 - £16{,}000)}{£40{,}000} \times £16{,}000 = £5{,}760$$

Anna's mother died more than one year but less than two years before Anna's death and therefore quick succession relief of 80% applies.

$$80\% \times \frac{(£450{,}000 - £50{,}000)}{£450{,}000} \times £50{,}000 = £35{,}556$$

Tax payable on Anna's death

		£
IHT on Anna's estate		180,000
Deduct		
	Quick succession relief on PET from Fred	5,760
	Quick succession relief on life interest	35,556
Total IHT payable		138,684

RELATED PROPERTY RELIEF

10.6 If property was valued on death as 'related property' under *s 161* (see **3.20** as to the valuation of 'related property') and is sold within three years at less than that valuation, a claim can be made to substitute that valuation with the value it would have been had it not been determined together with the related property or the other property in the estate (*s 176*). The following conditions must be complied with for the relief to apply (*s 176(3)*):

- the vendors are the persons in whom the property vested immediately after the death, or are the personal representatives of the deceased;
- the sale is at arm's length, for a price freely negotiated, and is separate from any sale of related property;
- no vendor (or any person having an interest in the sale proceeds) is, or is connected with, any purchaser (or any person having an interest in the purchase); and
- neither the vendors nor anyone having an interest in the sale proceeds obtain, in connection with the sale, a right to acquire the property sold or any interest in or created out of it.

10.7 Where the relevant property consists of shares in or securities of a close company, the relief is not available if, at any time between the death and the qualifying sale, the value of the shares or securities is reduced by more than 5% as a result of an alteration in the company's share or loan capital or in any rights attaching to shares in or securities of the company (*s 176(5)*). This provision was introduced as an anti-avoidance measure.

The relief is given only if claimed, and the claim must be made within four years after the date on which the IHT was paid, with effect from 1 April 2011 (*s 241*). Prior to that date, the time limit was six years.

The two examples below illustrate related property relief.

Example 10.4—Related property relief (I)

Husband owns land worth £15,000 and his wife owns adjoining land worth £25,000.

The combined value is £80,000.

The related property value of the husband's land is calculated as follows:

$$\frac{15{,}000}{15{,}000 + 25{,}000} \times £80{,}000 = £30{,}000$$

The above calculation was made to ascertain the value of the husband's land following his death. The husband's property is sold for £20,000 within three years of his death, so a claim can be made to substitute the date of death value of £30,000 with £15,000.

Example 10.5—Related property relief (II)

On the husband's death on 31 October 2016, the share capital of a private property investment company was held as follows:

Issued share capital – 10,000 shares		
Husband	4,000	40%
Wife	4,000	40%
Others (employees)	2,000	20%
	10,000	100%

The value of an 80% holding is £80,000, while the value of a 40% holding is £24,000. In his will, the husband left his 4,000 shares to his daughter.

The related property rules apply to aggregate the shares of:

Husband	4,000
Wife	4,000
Related property	8,000

Chargeable transfer on legacy to daughter

IHT value of 8,000 shares (80%)	£80,000
IHT value attributed to legacy of husband's shares	$\frac{4,000}{8,000} \times £80,000 = £40,000$

Focus

- In **Example 10.5** above if the 4,000 shares are sold within three years of the husband's death for less than £40,000, a claim can be made to substitute the value of £40,000 with £24,000 to reclaim some of the IHT paid.
- A detailed calculation will assist when deciding which action to take.
- Advice from a share valuation specialist or suitably qualified accountant may be required.

TRANSFERS WITHIN SEVEN YEARS BEFORE DEATH

The relief

10.8 Where market conditions have changed following a PET or a chargeable transfer and the value of the property transferred is less at the time of the transferor's death (or on a prior sale by the transferee or his spouse) than at the time of his gift, relief is available in certain circumstances when computing the IHT or additional IHT, so that the tax or additional tax is charged on the reduced value (*s 131*).

The relief is available in the following circumstances:

- tax or additional tax is chargeable on the value transferred by a chargeable transfer or a potentially exempt transfer because of the transferor's death within seven years of the transfer; and
- all or part of the value transferred is attributable to the value of property which, at the date of the death, remains the property of the transferee or of his spouse, or has before the date of the death been sold by the transferee or his spouse by a qualifying sale.

10.9 For the purposes of the relief, it is important that:

- any transaction was an arm's length transaction for a price freely negotiable at the time of the sale; and
- the vendor (or any person having an interest in the proceeds of the sale) is not the same as or connected with the purchaser (or any person having an interest in the purchase); and
- no provision is made, in or in connection with the agreement for the sale, that the vendor (or any person having an interest in the proceeds of sale) is to have any right to acquire some or all of the property sold or some interest in or created out of it.

In order to avoid giving too much relief, there is a special rule for calculating the relief where the property also qualifies for business or agricultural relief. In this case the market values of the transferred property on the two dates that are compared to establish the reduction in value must be taken as reduced by the percentage appropriate to any available business or agricultural relief.

10.10 When valuing property transferred in order to ascertain whether relief should become available, no account should be taken of the related property under *IHTA, s 161* or property passing under another title with which it was originally valued (IHTM14626).

In the case of a transfer that was immediately chargeable at lifetime rates, the relief does not give rise to a repayment or remission of the tax that has already become payable during the transferor's life.

The relief also does not apply where the property has before the death been given away by the transferee or his spouse.

Wasting assets

10.11 The relief is not available if the transferred property is tangible movable property which is a wasting asset, such as a motor car (*s 132*). An asset is a wasting asset if immediately before the chargeable transfer it had a predictable useful life not exceeding 50 years having regard to the purpose for which it was used by the transferor.

Plant and machinery is always regarded as a wasting asset unless it is incorporated in the structure of the building, in which case it is immovable property.

'Fall in value' relief

10.12 Relief will only be given in respect of a fall in the value of shares or securities because of adverse market conditions. Therefore, if the value of the shares fell subsequent to capital payments, calls and corporate reorganisations, the relief will not be available. This prevents the relief being available if the value of the shares has been reduced deliberately by making capital payments by the company to its shareholders.

Example 10.6—Fall in value of property and shares

Mr Jones died on 8 June 2016. He made two PETs which are now chargeable to IHT. On 1 July 2012 he gifted a property, valued at £500,000, to his daughter Alice. On 1 July 2013 he passed his shares in ABC plc to his son Thomas. The shares were valued at £250,000.

Both investments have fallen in value since the PETs were made. When the assets were revalued on Mr Jones's death, it transpires that the property is only worth £450,000 and the shares are worth £125,000.

IHT payable on the PETs that are now chargeable is calculated as follows:

	£
PET of property to Alice	500,000
Deduct	
2 annual exemptions	6,000
Fall in value	50,000
	444,000
Deduct: Nil rate band (2016/17)	325,000
Chargeable to IHT	119,000
PET of shares to Thomas	250,000

Deduct		£
1 annual exemption		3,000
Fall in value		125,000
Chargeable to IHT		122,000
Total value of PETs		241,000
IHT payable	(£241,000 @ 40%)	96,400

Apportionment of tax:

PET of property to Alice $96{,}400 \times \frac{119{,}000}{241{,}000} = £47{,}600$

PET of shares to Thomas $96{,}400 \times \frac{122{,}000}{241{,}000} = £48{,}800$

The overall IHT saving in this example is £70,000. The relief can be extremely valuable in times when house prices and/or share prices fall.

Setting aside PETs/and chargeable transfers

10.13 In exceptional circumstances PETs may be set aside, as was the case in *Griffiths (Deceased): Ogden and another v Trustees of the RHS Griffiths 2003 Settlement and others* [2008] STC 2008. Mr Griffiths made gifts in April 2003 and February 2004. However later in 2004 he was diagnosed with terminal cancer and died in April 2005 as a result of which both PETs failed. The High Court decided that the later gift was to be set aside on the grounds of mistake. Lewison J said that 'The operative mistake must, in my judgment, be a mistake which existed at the time when the transaction was entered into.'

Strangely, HMRC did not contest this case, especially as the tax at stake was in excess of £1 million. In cases where the deceased died unexpectedly after having made substantial PETs it may be worthwhile considering whether they can be set aside, but it is uncertain whether the lenient approach in *Griffiths* will be repeated.

In *Pitt and another v Holt and another* [2010] EWHC 45 (Ch) the second defendant was HMRC, taking an interest in opposing the reliance of the receiver under the *Mental Health Act 1983* on the *Hastings-Bass* principle. Mrs Pitt made a settlement on behalf of her husband but in so doing failed to take IHT into account and later regretted her action. The second claimant was the husband's executor. At first instance the judge held that the *Hastings-Bass* principle need not apply only to trustees: a receiver was in a similar position to a trustee, and exercised a fiduciary power. The critical point here was that it was for Mrs Pitt to decide whether or not it was in the interest of her late husband for her to pass his property to the trustees. The case fell squarely within the tests imposed in *Mettoy Pension Trustee v Evans* [1990] 1 WLR 1587 and in *Sieff v Fox* [2005] 1 WLR 3811. The transfer was set aside, but HMRC appealed.

On 9 March 2011 the Court of Appeal allowed the appeal in the combined appeal of *Pitt v Holt and Futter v Futter* [2011] EWCA Civ 197 in which the Court re-examined the scope and application of the rule in *Hastings-Bass*. It was held that in *Pitt v Holt* the resulting tax liability was not a mistake to the legal effect of the disposition but as to the consequences and therefore it was not a mistake that could invoke the equitable jurisdiction to set aside a voluntary disposition for mistake.

The taxpayers in *Pitt* appealed to the Supreme Court which allowed the appeal on the grounds of mistake and set aside the trust stating that she was intending to create 'precisely the sort of trust to which parliament intended to grant relief by *s 89 IHTA 1984*', (see *Pitt v HMRC* and *Futter v HMRC* [2013] UKSC 26). For a more detailed discussion see **12.10**.

In contrast the Supreme Court unanimously dismissed the appeal in *Futter* stating that a Court should only intervene when trustees acted in such a way as to amount to a breach of their fiduciary duty. In this case the trustees' exercise of the power of advancement had been valid, but they relied on apparently competent professional advice which turned out to be wrong.

The ratio in *Pitt v Holt* was successfully relied upon in the recent case of *Freedman v Freedman others* [2015] EWHC 1457 (Ch). The settlement was set aside on the ground of equitable mistake as the solicitor had advised to transfer properties into an interest in possession trust in the mistaken belief that such transfer was a potentially exempt transfer and therefore escaped an immediate lifetime charge to IHT.

Rectification of a deed of variation which did not include the election that *IHTA 1984, s 142(1)* shall apply was ordered in the case of *Vaughan-Jones and another v Vaughan-Jones and others* [2015] EWHC 1086 (Ch).

Focus

Advisers need to be aware that the Court of Appeal's decision may put strict limits on the rule in *Hastings-Bass* and its future application.

However, a number of recent cases successfully relied on the grounds of equitable mistake rectifying deeds or setting aside transactions which resulted in avoidable tax charges.

POST-DEATH RELIEFS

Post-death relief: shares (*ss 178–189*)

10.14 When 'qualifying investments' (quoted shares and securities, holdings in an authorised unit trust and shares in a common investment fund (ie funds managed by the Public Trustee)) are sold within 12 months after death for less than their probate valuation on death, the personal representative, or anyone else who is liable to pay the IHT on the shares, may claim a repayment for IHT. The shares or securities must be listed on the Stock Exchange, so the relief does not apply to private company shares. Incidental costs of sale cannot be deducted.

All the investments sold within 12 months after death have to be taken into account, when the relief is claimed. Therefore, where investments have fallen in value since date of death, and where the relief would affect the amount of IHT payable, a personal representative should review the estate portfolio in good time before the 12-month period expires and:

- consider selling within 12 months of the death all holdings of quoted shares and holdings in authorised unit trusts and shares in any common investment fund ('qualifying investments') which have dropped in value since the death;
- keep qualifying investments which have risen in value since the death.

10.15 The relief is also available for shares, which are cancelled without replacement within 12 months of death, when the deemed sale value will be a nominal consideration of £1 at the date of cancellation. If shares are suspended within 12 months of death and remain suspended on the first anniversary of death, relief can be claimed on a deemed sale of the suspended investment at the value immediately before the first anniversary.

If during the 12-month period, the personal representative purchases qualifying investments, the original loss on sale relief is reduced proportionately. The reduction on the original relief is calculated as follows (*s 180(1)*):

$$\frac{\text{Value of reinvestment}}{\text{Sales proceeds}} \times \text{Original reduction in value}$$

10.16 The inheritance tax value of each of the investments sold will have to be adjusted both for inheritance tax and capital gains tax to the gross sale proceeds, plus the relevant proportion in the fall in value.

Example 10.7—Sale of shares by executors

Anna died on 31 January 2015 leaving a substantial share portfolio to her nephews and nieces. A number of shares have fallen in value and her executors decided to sell those shares and to claim the relief.

The inheritance tax value of the shares sold was £100,000, while the sale proceeds were only £25,000.

The executors purchased a new holding in A plc for £15,000 on 31 March 2015.

The estate included shares in B plc, which had an inheritance tax value of £1,000, but they were cancelled on 1 April 2015.

The shares in C plc, which had an inheritance tax value of £2,500, were suspended on 1 December 2015. On 31 January 2016 these shares were still suspended with an estimated value of £99.

		£
Value of investments at probate value:		
	Shares which have fallen in value	100,000
	B plc	1,000
	C plc	2,500
	IHT value	103,500
Sales proceeds		
	Shares which have fallen in value	25,000
	B plc (deemed value of £1)	1
	C plc (estimated value of £99)	99
	Sales proceeds	25,100
Reduction in estate value		78,400

Therefore, the executors would initially be able to claim a reduction of £78,400.

However, following the purchase of the shares in A plc, the 'reduction in the estate's value' will be restricted as follows:

$$\frac{15{,}000}{25{,}100} \times £78{,}400 = £46{,}853$$

The total relief claimed is therefore £31,547 (£78,400 – £46,853).

Post-death relief: land (*ss 190–198*)

10.17 Similar to the relief on quoted securities, where an 'interest in land' is sold within three years of death, a claim can be made by the personal representatives to substitute the sale value with the inheritance tax value using Form IHT38. *Section 197A* introduced a restriction for sale in that the election is not available for sales in the fourth year, if the sale value would exceed the inheritance tax value.

Following *Jones (Ball's Administrators) v IRC* [1997] STC 358, exchange of contracts for English and Welsh properties does not qualify as a sale for this relief.

No claim can be made if:

- the sale value differs from the value on death by less than the lower of £1,000 and 5% of the value on death (*s 191(2)*);
- the sale is by a personal representative or trustee to the following:
  - a person, who, at any time between death and sale, has been beneficially entitled to, or has an interest in possession in, property comprising the interest sold, or
  - the spouse, child or remoter descendant of such a person, or
  - a trustee of a settlement under which such a person has an interest in possession in property comprising the interest sold;
- the vendor obtains a right in connection with the sale to acquire the interest sold or any other interest in the same land (*s 191(3)*).

10.18 If an estate comprises a number of interests in land, the loss relief claim cannot be made until four months have elapsed from the date of sale of the last interest in land, as there is the possibility of further purchases of land. If an estate only has one interest in land, the relief is available and HMRC Inheritance Tax will make a provisional payment of tax, but HMRC will not issue a certificate of discharge until the expiry of the statutory four-month time limit.

Expenses of sale, ie estate agent fees or legal fees cannot be deducted.

Example 10.8—Sale of land interests by executors

Peter's estate (he died on 31 January 2013) includes four parcels of land.

The inheritance tax value of the land is as follows:

	£
Blackacre	100,000
Whiteacre	150,000
Greenacre	300,000
Peter's home	500,000
	1,050,000

In the four years since Peter's death, his executors sell all his interests in the above land. On 5 May 2015, a compulsory purchase order was made to purchase Peter's home to build a by-pass. The acquisition of Peter's home is finalised on 15 February 2017 and the executors receive £400,000 (expenses of sale cannot be deducted):

	£
Blackacre sold 1 July 2013	99,100
Whiteacre sold 15 December 2015	125,000
Greenacre sold 1 February 2016	300,100
Peter's home	400,000
	924,200

The claim

The sale of Blackacre is disregarded in the claim, as the loss on sale (£900) is less than 5% of £100,000 (£5,000) and is lower than £1,000.

Greenacre will be disregarded because it is sold in the fourth year since Peter's death and the sale proceeds are larger than the inheritance tax value.

The loss on Peter's home following the compulsory purchase order however can be included in the claim, as the compulsory purchase order was made within three years of Peter's death, although it was finalised more than four years after his death.

The overall allowable reduction therefore is £125,000 (£25,000 for Whiteacre and £100,000 for Peter's home).

If the executors purchase further interests in land within a period beginning with the death and ending four months after the date of the last sale, the available relief has to be reduced. Unlike for the relief on quoted securities, one has to revisit each interest to recalculate the relief, which is complex and beyond the scope of this book.

If the land sold was held in joint ownership and a discount of between 10 and 15% was allowed on this joint interest, care needs to be taken when making a loss relief claim, as the discount does not apply post-sale.

Example 10.9—Loss of relief claim and discount on joint-ownership

Suzy and Fiona are sisters, both widowed. They decide to purchase a property which they both occupy and own jointly. On Suzy's death the property is valued £500,000, before any discounts, and it passes to Fiona. Suzy's half share is valued at £250,000 and after the 10% discount, the value for IHT purposes is £225,000. Fiona, who cannot look after herself any longer, sells the property for £470,000. Suzy's estate's half share of the sale proceeds is £235,000. If a loss relief claim is submitted, the discount is disapplied and there will be IHT due of the additional £10,000 above the discounted value of £225,000.

DOUBLE TAXATION RELIEF

Introduction

10.19 Double taxation of gifts and inheritances can arise in a number of ways, and knowledge of the relevant provisions will become more relevant given the increase in the ownership of foreign property and the number of UK-domiciled persons moving abroad.

Below are a few examples where double charges to IHT may arise:

- A UK-domiciled person who makes a gift of a foreign asset may be liable to a foreign gift tax on the disposal and may also be liable to IHT in the UK either immediately if it is a chargeable transfer or, if the gift is a potentially exempt transfer, on his death within seven years.

- A person not domiciled in the UK may be liable to IHT in the UK, as well as gift tax or inheritance tax in his own country, if he dies while owning assets situated in the UK.
- A UK-domiciled person moving abroad with the intention of living there permanently remains UK domiciled for at least three years (*s 267(1)*), and therefore remains subject to IHT on his estate wherever it is situated. Should he die during that period he may be liable both to IHT in the UK and to foreign estate tax in his country of residence.
- Similarly, a non-UK domiciled individual who has been resident in the UK for at least 17 of the last 20 tax years (the UK Government proposes to reduce these rules to 15 of the last 20 years from April 2017) and who goes to live abroad permanently may be deemed to be domiciled in the UK for up to three years (increasing to five years from April 2017) following his departure. Should he die during this period, his estate may be liable both to IHT in the UK and IHT in his country of residence.

10.20 Where IHT is chargeable in the UK and a similar tax is charged by another country on the same property, relief may be available in two ways:

- under the specific terms of a double tax agreement between UK and that country, following *s 158*; or
- under the unilateral double tax relief provisions in the UK legislation under *s 159*.

Double taxation agreements

10.21 The following countries have entered into double taxation agreements with the UK:

- France (*SI 1963/1319*);
- India (*SI 1956/998*);
- Italy (*SI 1968/304*);
- Ireland (*SI 1978/1107*);
- the Netherlands (*SI 1980/706* and *SI 1996/730*);
- Pakistan (*SI 1957/1522*);
- South Africa (*SI 1979/576*);
- Sweden (*SI 1981/840* and *SI 1989/986*);

- Switzerland (*SI 1957/426* and *SI 1994/3214*); and
- USA (*SI 1979/1454*).

Under these treaties, the country in which the transferor was domiciled is generally entitled to tax his whole estate. The other country is usually restricted to tax the property situated in that country, for example, land and buildings. Relief is then available on the double taxation of the same property.

Care ought to be taken, as some double tax agreements override the deemed domicile rules in *s 267* (see **1.3**).

Unilateral relief by UK

10.22 In the absence of double tax agreements, relief may be obtained by means of a credit for the foreign tax charged against the UK inheritance tax. This relief may also be important in cases where it is greater than the relief obtained under a double taxation agreement (*s 159*).

Unfortunately, in cases where the overseas tax suffered exceeded the UK liability before relief, no IHT will be payable in the UK, but the excess would not be repayable.

DOUBLE CHARGES RELIEF

10.23 The *Inheritance Tax (Double Charges Relief) Regulations, SI 1987/1130* prevent a person being charged IHT twice on the same property in various circumstances, where the event or transfer occurred after 17 March 1986.

Double charges relief applies in the following circumstances:

- where someone has made a lifetime transfer which following his death is a chargeable transfer and he has subsequently been given back the property comprised in the transfer (eg under the will of the donee) and he still owns the property on his death; or
- where someone has made a gift with reservation where the original gift was or turns out to be a chargeable transfer and the property comprised in the gift is also charged to IHT as property subject to a reservation; or
- where someone has died owing a debt which is wholly or partly non-deductible under *FA 1986, s 103* and has made a lifetime transfer to the person to whom the debt was owed which was or turns out to be chargeable.

The *Inheritance Tax (Double Charges Relief) Regulations* are complicated, partly because of the extensive use of cross-references. The *Schedule* to the Regulations therefore includes helpful examples of how they are supposed to operate.

WOODLANDS RELIEF

The relief

10.24 An election can be made which enables the IHT chargeable on death in respect of growing timber and underwood to be deferred until sale. The relief is only available on death and does not extend to the IHT in respect of the land upon which the trees are growing.

Following *s 125(1)* certain conditions need to apply for woodlands relief to be available:

- the woodland must be based in the UK or, following *FA 2009*, elsewhere in the EEA; and
- the woodland does not qualify for agricultural property relief under *s 115(2)*. The District Valuer will be able to advise on this point; and
- the deceased must have owned the land throughout the five years up to his death or have acquired the land otherwise than for consideration in money or money's worth, ie through inheritance or gift; and
- an election for relief must be made in writing to HMRC within two years of the death or such longer time as they may allow.

The relief is given by leaving the value of the timber out of account in determining the value transferred on death. The value of the timber is then not taxed until the timber, or any interest in it, is disposed of.

Calculation of IHT on disposals of trees or underwood

10.25 Where woodlands relief has been given on death, if the whole or any part of the trees or underwood is disposed of, IHT is charged on the following amounts:

- if the disposal is a sale for full consideration in money or money's worth, on the net proceeds of the sale; and
- in any other case, on the net value, at the time of the disposal, of the trees or underwood.

The IHT is chargeable at the rate or rates at which it would have been chargeable on the death if that amount, and any amount on which IHT was previously chargeable in relation to the death, had been included in the value transferred on the death, and the amount on which the IHT is chargeable had formed the highest part of that value.

References to the net proceeds of sale or the net value of any trees or underwood are references to the proceeds of sale or value after deduction of any expenses allowable in *s 130(2)*.

Example 10.10—Sale of timber following woodlands relief claim

Alice died in June 2015 leaving a net estate of £1,000,000, which included woodlands worth £500,000, of which £200,000 related to the land on which they stood (the value of the timber is £300,000). Her nil rate band was not available. Alice left her estate to her son Benedict, who elected for woodlands relief. In August 2017, Benedict sold timber from the woodlands for £500,000, incurring costs for felling of £100,000, sales commission of £10,000, and replanting expenses of £75,000.

The IHT chargeable on the death of Alice was £280,000 (Alice's taxable estate was £700,000 (ie £1,000,000 less value of the timber £300,000)). On the sale of the timber by Benedict, further IHT becomes payable as follows:

Gross proceeds of sale	£500,000
Deduct: Expenses incurred in disposal:	
Felling	£100,000
Sales commission	£10,000
Expenses incurred in replanting	£75,000
	£185,000
Net proceeds of sale (£500,000 – £185,000)	£315,000
The IHT chargeable on the disposal is calculated:	
IHT on £315,000 @ 40%	£126,000

Planning

10.26 Woodlands relief is generally less attractive than BPR, as it only postpones an IHT liability. Therefore, if the woodlands are managed on a commercial basis and if the other conditions for BPR are satisfied (see **Chapter 11**), BPR should be applied for rather than woodlands relief.

If BPR is not available it may, in certain circumstances, still be a difficult choice whether to make an election for woodlands relief or not:

- Where the woodland passes under the will to a spouse or to a charity, an election will not be appropriate, as the woodland will be exempt for IHT purposes in any event.
- If someone dies leaving a life interest in woodland to an elderly relative, whose estate (excluding the woodland) is just below the nil rate band, and there is little chance of a disposal during the elderly relative's lifetime, it may be better to defer the payment of IHT to avoid a charge to IHT.
- On the other hand, if someone dies leaving newly planted woodlands with a low value to a minor beneficiary, and the IHT rate is low (or nil) it would be better to pay a small amount of tax (or no tax), rather than elect and chance a much larger charge especially if the woodland is expected to increase in value.

In most cases, therefore, it is necessary to weigh the cash-flow advantages of an election and the possibility of avoiding the payment of tax altogether, against the possibility of having to pay a much larger amount of tax at the deceased's top tax rate on a greatly enhanced value at some future date.

CONDITIONAL EXEMPTION: HERITAGE PROPERTY

10.27 On certain conditions transfers of national heritage property (eg works of art, print or scientific objects) can be exempted from IHT (*s 30*). This conditional exemption applies to transfers of value made in lifetime and on death as well as to settled property. The conditional exemption cannot be claimed in relation to a potentially exempt transfer, unless and until the transferor dies within seven years of the transfer and it becomes a chargeable transfer.

The relief works as follows:

- An application for conditional exemption is made to HMRC within two years of the transfer, or within two years of death of the transferor.
- HMRC designate the property as 'heritage property' under *s 31*.
- An undertaking has to be given to HMRC.
- Death, disposal or a breach of the undertaking can be a chargeable event giving rise to a claim for IHT (*s 32*) (IHTM04115).

10.28 The following objects can be 'designated' as 'heritage property' within the conditional exemption:

(a) any relevant object which appears to HMRC to be pre-eminent for its national, scientific, historic or artistic interest;

(b) any collection or group of relevant objects which, taken as a whole, appears to HMRC to be pre-eminent for its national, scientific, historic or artistic interest;

(c) any land which in the opinion of HMRC is of outstanding scenic or historic or scientific interest;

(d) any building for the preservation of which special steps should in the opinion of HMRC be taken by reason of its outstanding historic or architectural interest;

(e) any area of land which in the opinion of HMRC is essential for the protection of the character and amenities of such a building;

(f) any object which in the opinion of HMRC is historically associated with such a building as is mentioned in (d) above.

10.29 In addition to the designation by HMRC, it is necessary for an undertaking to be given by the transferee – that is, the intended beneficial owner. Where the property will be subject to a trust, the trustee is also required to give the undertaking. With regard to pictures, prints, books, manuscripts, works of art, scientific collections and other things not producing income, the requisite undertaking is that, until the person beneficially entitled to the property dies or the property is disposed of, whether by sale or gift or otherwise:

- the property will be kept permanently in the UK and will not leave it temporarily except for a purpose and a period approved by HMRC; and
- steps will be taken for the preservation of the property and for securing reasonable access to the public, as agreed between HMRC and the person giving the undertaking.

10.30 The requirement of access to the public can give rise to considerable expense and difficulty where the objects are kept in a private house or flat. Where an undertaking is given after 30 July 1998, the steps agreed for securing reasonable access to the public must ensure that the access that is secured is not confined to an appointment-only basis. Although this only applies to post-*Finance Act 1998* undertakings, it should be noted that *FA 1998* also introduces provision for pre-*Finance Act 1998* undertakings to be varied so that there is public access without prior appointment.

The provisions *of IHTA 1984 Schedule 6, paragraph 4(2)* have been amended so that where the conditional exemption under *IHTA 1984, s 30* is granted on death, this will no longer make absolute an earlier exemption under the old estate duty regime. From 16 March 2016, HMRC will have the choice of raising either estate duty or IHT where the chargeable event happened on death. A change to the allocation of tax under *Finance Act 1930, s 40(2)* brings in a charge on objects which have been exempted from Estate Duty but which have been lost. This is subject to HMRC's discretion not to levy a charge, where the loss is not due to the negligence of the owner. In essence the same approach will apply as is currently in place in the case for conditional exemption from IHT.

This is a specialised topic and the general practitioner is referred to specialist books on the subject and in particular to the decision of the Special Commissioner in the case of *Re an application to vary the undertakings of A; Re an application to vary the undertakings of B* [2004] SpC 439; [2005] STC (SCD) 103. There is also some useful information on tax-exempt heritage assets on HMRC's website.

Chapter 11

Business property relief and agricultural property relief

SIGNPOSTS

- **Scope** – An understanding of the broad scope of these headline reliefs and in particular when they apply, when they overlap, and when they fall into breach, is critical to any tax planning routine (see **11.1; 11.24**).
- **BPR and the business** – The differing treatment applied to a business structure must be appreciated to determine the applicable rate and preserve continuing access to BPR (see **11.3–11.4; 11.6; 11.21**).
- **Qualification** – The basic rules of ownership, usage, classification, sale and replacement must be continually monitored to ensure compliance (see **11.9–11.16; 11.36–11.39; 11.49**).
- **APR and the farmhouse** – The rules in this area are complex, confusing and constantly changing – an awareness of case law is crucial (see **11.27–11.28; 11.31–11.34**).

SCOPE OF BUSINESS PROPERTY RELIEF

Unincorporated businesses

11.1 In the past it had always been considered that *IHTA 1984, s 105(1)(a)* confined relief to a 'business or an interest in a business' and in October 2012 HMRC published draft legislation to extend business property relief to businesses carrying on the business of a market maker, as defined within the Markets in Financial Instruments Directive (2004/39/EC). Notwithstanding, further reading of *s 105* suggested that this should be interpreted as referring to an unincorporated business with the focus centred on the business itself rather than the underlying assets. The position has now been unequivocally clarified by the case of *HMRC v Trustees of the Nelson Dance Family Settlement*: [2009] EWHC 71 (Ch) see **11.7** below.

Section 105(3) excludes investment-type businesses. In this respect property management itself may be a business, but only where the business is the supply of the service of management rather than the more passive management of assets belonging to that business – the distinction is fine but critical: see *Clark and Southern (Clark's executors) v HMRC* [2005] SpC 502; [2005] SSCD 823, *Trustees of the Zetland Settlement v HMRC* [2013] UKFTT 284 (TC) and more recently *Best v HMRC* [2014] UKFTT 77 (TC). Equally farming is a business, but where such activity is confined to passively managing land so as to produce a crop of grass, then that too is an investment-type business: see *McCall and Keenan v Revenue and Customs Commissioners* [2009] NICA 12 examined in greater detail at **11.14**.

The businesses of authors, painters, sculptors, musicians, and similar merit special attention because it is arguable that the income from copyright is not the business itself, but income from an investment asset. IHTM25153 requires Inspectors to refer such cases to the Technical Group for guidance. Where the ongoing business is the exploitation of existing work it may be possible to show that it outlives the originator, for example where executors go to great lengths to ensure that a musician's catalogue is regularly performed in order to encourage the flow of fresh royalties to the estate.

Difficulties commonly arise because an enterprise may well be a business for the purposes of income tax, or CGT, but yet not qualify for BPR under the IHT code – an obvious example is lettings of holiday cottages where the activities supporting the income source are subject to critical review (see also **11.15** for discussion on the *Pawson* case and the more recent case of *ACC Green v HMRC* [2015] UKFTT 0236 (TC). Owning one holiday cottage, which is used by the family for the most popular weeks of the year and is otherwise occupied by friends on a 'break-even' basis, is not regarded as a business for the purposes of BPR. However, owning and managing a seasonal holiday park, providing for short lets and offering catering, entertainment and other ancillary services will usually meet the criteria for relief.

Section 103(3) demands that the business must be carried on for gain (although the profit motive is not a requisite for APR as demonstrated in the *Golding* case discussed at **11.35**) – this is a pre-eminent qualification. Accordingly, the passive management of a collection of classic cars which are only occasionally exhibited or used for films etc and produce an income stream which barely covers the costs of storage and insurance, is unlikely to qualify for BPR through lack of profit motive.

Note: All statutory references in this chapter are to *IHTA 1984* unless otherwise stated.

> **Focus**
>
> The transfer of 'mere' assets can qualify for BPR to the extent such assets are used in the business and that business continues post transfer.

11.2 Until the decision in the *Nelson Dance* case it was widely thought and indeed generally accepted within professional circles that an interest in a business did not include a 'mere asset': see **11.7** below. A business may still exist even where a trade, even the principal trade, has been sold: see *Brown's Executors v IRC* [1996] STC (SCD) 277. The interest of a partner is an interest in the business unless and until the partner retires (see *Beckman v IRC* [2000] SSCD 59), whereupon the value of that partnership interest becomes a mere loan to the business that attracts no relief.

The position in relation to Lloyd's underwriters is complicated but may be summarised by the general principle that the assets that are actually at risk will qualify for BPR, whereas assets that secure a guarantee but far exceed in value the amount needed to support that guarantee will not so qualify. See, for example, *IRC v Mallender (Drury-Lowe's Executors)* [2001] STC 514 and in relation to the treatment of losses see *Hardcastle (Vernede's Executors) v IRC* [2000] STC (SCD) 532.

11.3 *Section 267A* governs the treatment of limited liability partnerships (LLPs) introduced by the *Limited Liability Partnerships Act 2000* with affect from 6 April 2001. Thus:

- Property belonging to the partnership is treated as the property of its members.
- Property occupied or used by the limited liability partnership is treated as occupied or used by the members.
- Business carried on by the limited liability partnership is treated as carried on in partnership by the members.
- An incorporation of the limited liability partnership is treated in the same way as formation of partnership, and changes are treated as they would be for a partnership.
- A transfer of value made by a limited liability partnership is treated as a transfer by its members.
- A transfer of value to a limited liability partnership is treated as a transfer to the members of the partnership.

HMRC guidance on LLPs states the following in relation to BPR (IHTM25094):

'…an interest in a LLP is deemed to be an interest in each and every asset of the partnership, while an interest in a traditional partnership is a "chose in action", valued by reference to the net underlying assets of the business. This may require you to consider issues of situs of property. In cases of doubt refer to HMRC's Technical Group for advice.

However, in considering if an LLP is an investment business the nature of the business underpinned by those assets should be looked at, rather than the nature of the assets themselves, to see whether IHTA84/S105(3) is in point.

Thus, in the case of an LLP investing in unquoted shares in trading companies, it would be inappropriate to allow relief on the basis that the underlying assets constitute business property: the true position is that the nature of the business conducted by the LLP falls within IHTA84/S105 (3) so that relief is not available.'

A Jersey LLP may be a partnership or a company: (see *R v IRC ex p Bishop* [1999] STC 531). However, HMRC seem inclined to treat them as 'opaque' (see *Tax Bulletin* Issue 83 (June 2006)), which is more in the nature of a body corporate than a partnership but this view has yet to be tested.

In the past, if a family wanted HMRC clarification on the availability of BPR before entering into planning transactions, this was simply not available – HMRC were not resourced for that purpose. For example, if an estate was spouse-exempt such that no IHT was payable regardless of the nature of the assets HMRC would not consider the relief as IHT was simply not in point: see IHT Newsletter 25 August 2006. This put taxpayers and their advisers on the spot.

Example 11.1—Frustrated appropriation or variation

On her death in May 2016 Samantha's estate was left in her will with cash equal to the unused available nil rate band to her children and with the residue of her estate to her husband, Peregrine. Samantha had made no lifetime gifts. The estate included (unquoted) shares in a business which had originally specialised in the provision of sunbeds and reflexology. Over the years, the profits were reinvested in premises and latterly there has been some repositioning of the business with the result that part became franchised with many of the outlets occupied on short leases. The bulk of the profits now come in the form of rents and franchise fees with very little derived from hands-on work and it is with this backdrop that the satisfaction of the 'wholly or mainly' test is worrying the family: see **11.10** below.

If BPR is available, Peregrine would be happy to see the company shares, now worth approximately £700,000, allocated to the children instead of the lower cash sum; but if not he will take the shares and make lifetime gifts of those shares over time in the hope of meeting the seven-year survival test. Well within the two-year period required by *s 142*, half the shares (value of approximately £350,000) are redirected to the children pursuant to a valid deed of variation, which is lodged on the basis that if BPR is denied, IHT will be due: in effect asking for a ruling in circumstances where if there is no BPR the IHT in point will at worst be only £10,000 ((£350,000 – £325,000) @ 40%).

HMRC will probably not be drawn into considering the relief not least since the tax in issue, after the exercise of valuation, is marginal. Rather HMRC may seek to read the variation back into the will: take the view that what is given is initially the nil rate band with the excess representing a gift from Peregrine; and that they will examine the issue of relief on his death. It is not an ideal situation but the family must nail their colours to the mast and decide whether or not to transfer the rest of the company's shares to the children.

A limited but valuable form of help by way of clearance is now available in situations of genuine difficulty. The procedure is described by HMRC on their website (www.gov.uk/guidance/non-statutory-clearance-service-guidance) and requires an application, preferably by e-mail, with supporting information. The following information must be supplied:

- particulars of the applicant;
- IHT reference, if any;
- details of the business, including UTR or company registration number;
- details of interest in the business held;
- contact details;
- what the application is about;
- why the transaction arises;
- description of the proposed transaction;
- what HMRC are being asked to clear;
- likely date of the transaction;
- contingencies involved;
- how important tax is to the transaction;
- the reason for doing the deal this way;

- other related clearances;
- the commercial importance of the issue to the business;
- two years' business accounts;
- the legislation in point;
- the doubt as to the application of the legislation, with reference to published guidance and case law;
- legal advice obtained that the taxpayer is willing to disclose;
- details of previous HMRC advice.

The broad description of the service suggests that the process has limited application and is aimed predominantly at those cases of genuine difficulty – that it is no substitute for a thorough study of the law and of guidance as to its application. Applications properly made and fully supported with appropriate documentation tend to be dealt with promptly and can give much valued certainty. Some practitioners may simply find the completion of the application for clearance a useful tool for considering the matter in more detail and that, having thought the issues through, it may not then be necessary to proceed with clearance.

A checklist and further guidance on HMRC's BPR clearance service is available via HMRC's website (www.gov.uk/government/uploads/system/uploads/attachment_data/file/377648/annex-c.pdf).

Interests in companies

> **Focus**
>
> 'All that glitters is not gold'. The definition of 'unquoted' for BPR purposes is not as wide as may be first thought – whilst it includes shares quoted *solely* on the alternative investment market (AIM) it excludes those quoted on 'any recognised stock exchange'. It is therefore perfectly possible for such shares to 'drift in and out' of qualification with potentially costly IHT consequences.

11.4 The chief and most accessible category of property qualifying for BPR, see *s 105(1)(bb)*, is 'any unquoted shares in a company' (but see **11.10** for a more detailed discussion on excluded activities). Other categories are mentioned below. For this purpose, 'shares' means any kind of share – this can include a preference share, but tax practitioners should take great care to draft the company documents in such a way as to ensure that the share has all the attributes of a share and is not really a loan to the company disguised as a share. There is no case directly in point but the drafting must be robust.

'Unquoted' for this purpose has a defined meaning, see *s 105(1ZA)* and whilst in relation to UK companies this will usually mean not quoted on the full list of the London Stock Exchange it will also require non listing on *any* recognised exchange. This has given rise to considerable investor interest in small companies in light of the trust reforms contained in *FA 2006* which now bring more trusts within the relevant property regime.

Income Tax Act 2007, s 1005 was amended with effect from 19 July 2007 so as to allow HMRC to regard as a 'recognised stock exchange' any investment exchange that the Financial Services Authority designates as a 'recognised investment exchange'. This power was exercised, for example, in relation to part, but not all, of the market formerly known as OFEX, now ISDX. The result is confusing: some shares on ISDX qualify for BPR, while others do not and as a consequence great care should be taken in this area.

Since 2013, HMRC designated the following as recognised stock exchanges for IHT purposes:

- The Channel Islands Securities Exchange Authority (20 December 2013);
- GXG Main Quote (23 September 2013);
- Global Board of Trade (30 July 2013);
- GXG Official List (16 May 2013);
- ICAP Securities & Derivatives Exchange Ltd (25 April 2013);
- European Wholesale Securities Market (18 January 2013);
- National Stock Exchange of Australia (19 June 2014);
- Singapore Exchange Securities Trading Limited (7 October 2014);
- Singapore Exchange Derivatives Trading Limited (7 October 2014); and
- Euronext London (4 February 2015).

Example 11.2—Diversified investments

Richard dabbled in stock market investments. On his death on 20 May 2016 his estate included holdings in the following fictional companies:

Microworks

IBC

Notel

Café Direct

Churchill Ware

Abraham

Of these, the first three holdings are of shares listed on a 'recognised stock exchange'. Unless in each case the holding is sufficiently large to give control, the shares will not qualify for BPR.

The other three holdings may all qualify for the relief. Café Direct is traded only on ETHEX, a matched bargain exchange. Churchill Ware is only on the Alternative Investment Market (AIM). Abraham is only on the part of ISDX that is not a recognised exchange.

Provided these last three companies are not simply investment companies, then subject to the point mentioned below, their shares may qualify for BPR because they are not deemed 'listed', even though prices for them are quoted regularly in the financial press. Note that where a company, say a mining enterprise, seems to qualify because its shares are traded on AIM, but it is also listed on another foreign stock exchange, BPR will nonetheless be denied if that other exchange is a 'recognised' one.

11.5 Shares or securities in a quoted company will qualify for BPR where they together comprise a controlling holding: see *s 105(1)(cc)*. Unquoted securities of a company which either by themselves or with other securities give the transferor control of that company, will qualify for BPR under *s 105(1)(b)*.

In every case, *s 106* requires that the securities must have been held by the transferor for a minimum period of two years or must qualify for a holding period by virtue of the replacement provisions of *s 107* or the succession provisions of *s 108* or the provisions as to successive transfers in *s 109*.

Trading assets

11.6 BPR is also available under *s 105(1)(d)* and *s 105 (1)(e)* on business assets that are not in themselves an interest in the business but are so used in the business. The asset categories which include land or buildings, machinery or plant, will qualify for relief according to the basis of ownership. BPR is available on:

- assets used for the business of a company controlled by the transferor;
- assets used by a partnership of which the transferor is a member;
- assets used for a business carried on by the transferor but owned by a trust in which he has an interest in possession.

The last of these categories, as exemplified by *Fetherstonaugh v IRC* [1984] STC 261, may be of less importance in the future as the popularity of interest in possession trusts continues to decline as a consequence of the *FA 2006* trust reforms.

The distinction between BPR on an *interest* in a company or partnership and BPR on the *assets* used in that company or partnership but now owned by that company or partnership is important in two ways. First, BPR on the externally owned trading assets used in the company or partnership is given at a lower 50% rate. Second, BPR on trading assets is available only where the asset is still held at the time of transfer and is not at that date subject to any binding contract for sale (the date of registration/recording for property is key – see **Overview A6.2**). Where, however, the claim is made in respect of the business rather than its assets, it does not matter that a particular asset may be in the course of sale at the time of transfer because that does not necessarily bring the business itself to an end: the principle is illustrated in the case of *Brown's Executors v IRC* [1996] STC (SCD) 277 mentioned above.

11.7 As mentioned at **11.1,** the long held view that BPR under *s 106(1)(a)* was confined to an interest in a business, rather than an asset of that business was dramatically overturned in *Trustees of Nelson Dance Family Settlement v Revenue and Customs Commissioners* [2009] EWHC 71 (Ch). Mr Dance, a farmer, transferred land to a settlement. Agricultural relief (APR) was not in issue here rather the taxpayer wanted BPR because the land had development value. HMRC denied relief on the basis that the subject matter of the transfer was not an interest in his farming business but a 'mere asset'.

The taxpayer successfully argued that it was necessary to look not at the actual asset transferred, but at its transfer of value based on the 'loss to the estate' principle. The estate of Mr Dance was reduced by the transfer: what was reduced was the value of his farming business; he had been in farming for many years; so the transfer of value fell to be reduced by BPR.

At first instance the Special Commissioner could see a distinction between those cases, such as spousal relief where the recipient is important, and the present situation where the basis of relief is determined by the transfer, not the underlying asset, commenting (at para 16):

> '…All these form part of an overall scheme. Everything turns on the loss in value to the donor's estate, rather than what is given or how the loss to the estate arises, except where the identity of the recipient is crucial to a particular exemption….'

As expected HMRC appealed to the High Court contending that the reference in the legislation to the value of business property implied that the transfer must be of business property, not merely business assets. Sales J dismissed the appeal.

It was sufficient that a possible and proper characterisation of the value transferred was that such value was attributable to the value of a business. The source of that value did not require an exclusive type of characterisation and thus it did not matter that the attribution could be to the value of the land transferred, as long as it could be said that the attribution could also be to the value of a business. That interpretation was simple and certain and sat well with *s 110* and with the 'loss to donor 'principle in *s 103*.

Does this mean that any transfer of a mere asset now attracts BPR? No: for example, such an asset owned jointly by sisters, one of whom does not trade, may not attract BPR. To rely on the rule now established, taxpayers must study the case report and bring themselves precisely within its facts.

It has to be said that a sole trader is in an advantageous position; in effect, he 'is' the business and he need make no distinction between those assets he trades with and others: he may not actually show all assets in his balance sheet and yet be using them for his business. To determine whether a particular asset is a business or a 'mere asset' it may still be necessary to refer to those old cases that were so relevant to the former CGT retirement relief but which may now enjoy a revival of interest in applying CGT entrepreneurs' relief, for example *McGregor (Inspector of Taxes) v Adcock* [1977] STC 206; *Mannion (Inspector of Taxes) v Johnston* [1988] STC 758; *Atkinson v Dancer* [1988] STC 758 and *Pepper (Inspector of Taxes) v Daffurn* [1993] STC 466. In addition, for a more recent case directly concerning entrepreneurs' relief, see *Gilbert (t/a United Foods) v Revenue & Customs Commissioners* [2011] UKFTT 705 (TC).

Timing is important if not critical in relation to gifts of shares and assets in family businesses.

Example 11.3—Order of gifts: getting it wrong

Jason owned 60% of Fleece Ltd, the family business, his sons Artemis and Theseus each owning 20%. Fleece Ltd traded from an industrial estate which Jason also owned. Jason wished to keep the parts of the trading estate that were let to third parties but was tiring of the risks of business itself and wanted to hand over the company with its factory premises to his two sons.

He had intended all this as a celebration of his retirement on reaching the age of 80, but in the event the lawyers were slow to deal with the transfer of the land and this took place some weeks after the actual handover celebrations concerning the company itself.

The transfer of the shares qualified for BPR, but the later transfer of the factory premises did not, because at that later time Jason was no longer a (majority) shareholder in the company. Artemis and Theseus were therefore at risk of a liability to IHT until Jason had survived the gift by seven years. Understandably, they required the lawyers to pay them compensation equal to the cost of insuring Jason's life for that period for a sum sufficient to pay the IHT at risk.

Rate of relief

11.8 BPR at the rate of 100% applies to the following categories of property:

- business;
- interest in a business;
- unquoted securities of a company giving control;
- unquoted shares.

BPR at the reduced rate of 50% applies to the following categories of property:

- controlling holding of quoted company;
- land, building, machinery or plant used in the business of a company controlled by the transferor or a partnership of which the transferor is a member;
- similar trading assets used for a business carried on by the transferor but owned by a trust in which he has a life interest.

CONDITIONS

Period of ownership

Focus

Qualifying replacement property can 'piggyback' on the time qualification of the original asset in order to meet the two year holding requirement and this can provide a platform for a useful planning strategy .

11.9 As previously stated, property will not qualify for BPR unless owned throughout the two years immediately preceding the transfer; see *s 106*. It may however be treated as satisfying that condition (see *s 107*) where it replaces other property that would have otherwise qualified for BPR.

There is scope for a gap in ownership. *Section 107(1)(a)* requires the property held at the time of transfer and the property which it replaces to have been owned by the transferor for at least two years out of the five years immediately prior to the transfer. The replacement property concerned must qualify for BPR in all respects other than the period of ownership. It is important to note that there is generally no scope for 'trading up' within this rule. Capital reconstruction can be disregarded so as to 'look through' a period of ownership.

Example 11.4—Replacement property: business angel

Returning to the example of Richard (see **Example 11.2**), it appears that Richard had held the shares in Café Direct for only 18 months. However, the money that he used to buy the shares came from the sale, only two months before, of shares in Coffee Ltd which, at the relevant time, was quoted on the Alternative Investment Market (AIM), and from Beans Ltd, an ISDX company. The records of those companies show that they were unquoted trading companies throughout the relevant time. As a result, BPR is available on the shares in Café Direct (the replacement property), even though those shares had not yet been owned for two years.

This does illustrate that investors who hope to secure the benefit of BPR by investing in unquoted shares must be vigilant and alert to change: companies migrate from smaller exchanges to larger as they develop, and it is only rarely (see for example Young and Company Brewery plc which moved from the main exchange to an AIM listing) that they move the other way. Small companies by their very nature will always be vulnerable to takeovers thereby forcing the investor to seek new BPR opportunities.

Example 11.5—Period of ownership: capital changes

Jason, in **Example 11.3** above, had formed Fleece Ltd from a family partnership comprising himself and his sons. The partnership had been trading for a number of years before the incorporation but at the time of the share transfer, Jason had only held the shares for one year. However, his period of ownership of an interest in the partnership also counts when considering the time ownership test in *s 106*.

The period of ownership was the main issue in *The Executors of Mrs Mary Dugan-Chapman and another v Revenue and Customs Commissioners* [2008] SpC 666. The taxpayer had hoped that the use of a rights issue to capitalise a loan might effectively sidestep the two-year ownership rule by deeming the shares acquired under that rights issue to be treated as part of an existing shareholding which had been owned for the requisite period by relying on the reorganisation provisions of *Taxation of Chargeable Gains Act 1992, s 126* when read with *s 107(4)*. The case turned on its own very special facts, the description of which occupies 31 paragraphs of the report but it is nonetheless worth reading. Actions taken under extreme time pressures did not, it was held, achieve the effect that had been hoped for.

The general principles that practitioners may draw from the case are self-evident namely:

- the paperwork must be correct;
- keep only one (correct) record of the transaction, not two conflicting notes; and
- *do not delay.*

In this case the parties had considered tax planning in light of the health concerns of the elderly shareholder but the latter then seemed to recover her health and at the instigation of her family there was delay. As a consequence precious weeks were lost, leaving everything to be done in a rush just before Christmas as her health deteriorated. At the end, the transactions were construed, not as a rights issue, but as a cash subscription for shares, with the result that on the shareholder's death days later she had not satisfied the requirements of *s 106*.

The aftermath of that decision returned to the High Court as *Vinton and others v Fladgate Fielder* [2010] EWHC 904 (Ch) where the daughters of Mrs Dugan-Chapman sued the solicitors for damages to recover both the IHT now payable and the costs of the unsuccessful tax appeal. The solicitors applied to have the claim struck out as 'fanciful'. The court considered the pleadings and evidence but refused to strike out the claim.

It is important to be aware that even if a rights issue is properly undertaken, there should still be a commercial need for cash, since otherwise the money subscribed for the new shares will be treated as an excepted asset within *s 112* (see **11.22** below). The directors should record the need for funds for the purposes of the business of the company.

Not investment business

Background

> **Focus**
>
> There can be a real threat to preservation of BPR where a business has multiple interests which combine active trading and passive investment. The extent of the latter could cause the business to fail the 'wholly or mainly' test such that BPR is lost in totality rather than simply restricted (see 11.22).

11.10 It cannot be stressed too strongly that this is an area of great practical difficulty for advisers. A young business may comprise trading assets, intangible assets and may be burdened with substantial debt. A mature business may hold the undistributed profits earned over many years which have been reinvested in 'safe' assets such as property, perhaps because the tax burden on distribution was unacceptably high. The problem thus comes in two forms: at its most extreme, BPR is denied on the entire company because it is no longer mainly trading but has moved into a predominantly investment vehicle. In a more moderate form, BPR is restricted under the rules as to excepted assets considered below.

BPR is denied by *s 105(3)* where the business of the trading entity, whether incorporated or not, '…consists wholly or mainly of one or more of the following, that is to say, dealing in securities, stocks or shares, land or buildings, or making or holding investments…'. Relatively few cases arise on simple land dealing whereas the directors of pure investment companies recognise that a claim to BPR would be hopeless. The main disputes arise where the accounts of the company show some trading activity and the receipt of some rental income.

Cases concerning lettings

11.11 For background reading, see the following cases and specialist works on the subject:

- *Martin (Moore's Executors) v IRC* [1995] STC (SCD) 5; *Burkinyoung (Burkinyoung's Executors) v IRC* [1995] STC (SCD) 29 and *Trustees of David Zetland Settlement v HMRC* [2013] UKFTT 284 (TC) all concerned businesses that were primarily making an income from lettings.
- See also the caravan park cases *of Hall (Hall's Executors) v IRC* [1997] STC (SCD) 126; *Powell v IRC* [1997] STC (SCD) 181;

Furness v IRC [1999] STC (SCD) 232; *Weston (Weston's Executors) v IRC* [2000] STC 1064 and *IRC v George* [2003] EWCA Civ 1763, [2004] STC 147.

Two cases are worthy of mention. In the *Trustees of David Zetland Settlement v HMRC* [2013] UKFTT 284 (TC) the taxpayer claimed that the level of services carried out to the tenants of Zetland House meant that it ought to be classified as a business for the purposes of BPR. Access to the relief was very relevant since the Settlement was approaching its ten-year anniversary charge. Zetland House was originally a multi-storey factory occupied by a number of printing firms but the property had outlived its original purpose. There were a number of long-term leases and by 1997 one quarter of the building was unoccupied – gross rents were £510,000 per annum.

The taxpayer acquired the premises and transformed them by offering flexible space for computer, media and high technology businesses all of which required major changes to both the physical appearance and the usage/occupation of the tenant. He made office space more available, offered attractive short-term leases and made the individual offices smaller. The gross rents and service charges in the year ended 5 April 2007 were approximately £2.4 million. The taxpayer hired more staff to provide a wider range of services and facilities to the tenants. The building had a restaurant, gym, cycle arch, Wi-Fi, portage, 24-hour access, meeting rooms, media events, outdoor television screens and an art gallery – it was run on the basis of a community with regular barbeques and social gatherings.

HMRC argued that the purpose of the additional services was to increase occupancy and hence increase the rental receipts – the services were no more than incidental to the core business of collecting rent and service charges. The tribunal looked closely at the income and profit of the various activities which clearly indicated that the bulk of income, well in excess of 50%, derived from the rent and service charge. It was held that the activities were predominantly investment activities or relate to investment. The services provided were mainly of a standard nature aimed at maximising income through short-term tenancies. The non-investment side was incidental to the core business and the services were insufficient to make the business one that was mainly non-investment. The purpose of the activities was largely to improve the building and its fabric, to secure the tenancy and to keep the occupancy rates high.

In *Best v HMRC* [2014] UKFTT 77 (TC) Bullick Developments Ltd owned a business centre in County Antrim which was financed in part by the Local Enterprise Development Unit – the latter it was argued did not finance mere investments. The centre included offices, showrooms, industrial and warehouse space, from very small to quite large units. It was agreed that one self-contained area, bringing in 15% of the income, was an investment, 10% was offices, the rest light industrial or warehousing. In total 400 people worked there.

The standard form licence agreements did not give exclusive possession of the land. Services were listed in two schedules but it was agreed that most of those in the first schedule were of a type commonly provided by a landlord. Further services were listed in the second schedule and much emphasis was placed on the availability of a forklift driver.

It was an identifiable weakness of the case that no copy invoices were provided. The company employed:

- a full-time site maintenance person, receptionist and a forklift driver;
- two part-time people; and
- three full-time security guards.

Most of the units had no separate landline, so calls were put through by the receptionist and many units were accessible only to small vehicles, making the forklift useful, though the extent of that use was not proved.

Income of £611,472 was broken down into:

Licence fees	£447,068
Service charges	£53,335
Sundry	£4,517
Equipment hire	£4,452
Heat and light	£31,284
Telephone	£45,568
Postage	£20,056
Parking	£5,192

Applying the tests in *George, McCall* and *Pawson*, the tribunal considered that the provision of office-like facilities and of the forklift was not significant enough to save the business from its investment nature. Those services did not predominate when considering the business as a whole and it was considered that the business was 'well towards the investment end of the spectrum'. BPR was denied.

Landed estates

11.12 The leading case is *Farmer (Farmer's Executors) v IRC* [1999] STC (SCD) 321, which considered an estate run as one business where the majority of income came from lettings or licence fees but the main capital value was held in the farmland, farmhouse and farm buildings. After detailed consideration BPR was granted on the basis there was a business of running a landed estate. That case concerned a substantial acreage but such decided cases do not provide a steer on how small an estate may qualify for BPR on this principle. There are doubtless many landholdings in the range of five to 50 acres where a Tax Tribunal decision would be welcome clarification of the law.

The decision in the *Farmer* case has been reinforced by the Scottish case of *Brander (Representative of Earl of Balfour deceased) v HMRC* [2010] UKUT 300 TCC. In *Brander* two issues arose: whether the requirements of *s 107* as to replacement property were satisfied (they were); and whether the business failed the 'wholly or mainly' test of *s 105(3)*. It was held that the lowland landed estate in question fully satisfied the tests for BPR: in particular the late Earl, in managing the tenancies of estate cottages, had selected tenants who could be of service to the estate rather than always going for the highest available rent, so the running of residential property was integrated into the overall business purpose of managing the estate. The case is very interesting given the diversity of the business components and it is strongly recommended that the full case be reviewed for its content and commentary.

Inter-company loans

11.13 A case of specialist interest is *Phillips & others (Phillips' executors) v HMRC* [2006] SpC 555; [2006] SSCD 639 where an unquoted company lent money to related family businesses. HMRC denied BPR under *s 105(3)* but an appeal to the Special Commissioner succeeded, on the basis that the company was the 'banking arm' for in-house transactions. Few would treat money-lending as a mere investment activity. The company was making loans, not investing in them, so BPR was allowed.

This is another interesting case for advisers. Commonly an elderly entrepreneur may be happy to give up the active cut and thrust of daily commerce to his children but might still be happy to support their activities by providing finance, even though that may involve him in significant commercial risk. Access to BPR will, of course, depend on the facts of each case.

The business of providing a crop of grass

11.14 The released report of key cases which come before the courts or tribunals regularly demonstrate that the particular tax issue has been considered with great care leading to a decision that is particularly helpful in establishing general principles, even if that decision is not always the result the taxpayers might hope for. It is probably no coincidence that several such cases have been argued by William Massey QC (the successful advocate in the *Nelson Dance* case mentioned above). He represented the taxpayers in *McCall and Keenan v Revenue and Customs Commissioners* [2009] NICA 12, where a parcel of land had an agricultural value, at the date of death, of £165,000 but a market value of £5,800,000. It was therefore important for the executors to show that at the date of death there was a business qualifying for BPR to soak up the development value rather than a mere agricultural interest with its lower APR coverage.

The evidence showed (just) that the son-in-law of the deceased had spent time looking after the land, which lay on the edge of a town. The work involved walking the land, repairing the fencing, cleaning drinking troughs, clearing the drainage systems of mud and leaves, cutting and spraying weeds. For these purposes, the son-in-law had a tractor and reaper and a knapsack sprayer. He probably worked no more than 100 hours per year but some work was contracted out. The grazier fertilised the fields.

At first instance the Commissioner reviewed the authorities, including several mentioned above and in particular the *indicia* noted by Gibson J in *Customs and Excise Commissioners v Lord Fisher* [1981] STC 238. He concluded that the son-in-law's activity of tending the land: '…was, just, enough to constitute a business.… but was it a trade? The letting of the land was earnestly pursued, the work of tending the land was modest but serious, the letting and tending were pursued with some continuity, the income was not insubstantial, the letting was conducted in a regular manner although the use of [the son-in-law's] time was something which is not a feature of an ordinary business, and the letting of land for profit is a common business. To my mind the *Lord Fisher indicia* point towards a business…'

However, the taxpayers' case fell, both at first instance and on appeal, because it was held that the business consisted wholly or mainly of holding investments, within *s 105(3)*. After a detailed consideration of the nature of farming arrangements under the law of Northern Ireland which may not be of general application the Commissioner held that:

> '…The test to be applied is that of an intelligent businessman, not a land lawyer. Such a person would be concerned with the use to which the asset was put. The deceased was making the land available, not to make a living on it but from it; the management activities related to letting the land; it was unlike "hotel accommodation for cattle" as suggested by Mr Massey; nor was it like a "pick your own" fruit farm after months of weeding, fertilising spraying and pruning, customers are licensed to enter to take the produce and pay by the pound for what they take away; in the business of letting the fields there was less preparatory work, the fields were let for the accommodation of the cattle as well as for the grazing, and the rent was paid by the acre rather than by the ton of grass eaten….'

The Court of Appeal in Northern Ireland agreed. The Commissioner had properly understood the law. The test was that of the intelligent businessman (interestingly this phrase also surfaced in the recent *Pawson* case discussed at **11.15** below), who would look at the use to which the land was put – a landowner who derives income from land or a building will be treated as having a business of holding an investment even though he may carry out incidental work to obtain the income. Here, the activities of the son-in-law were in the nature of maintenance work to achieve a successful letting. The use of the land by graziers was exclusive, so the owner could not use the land for any purpose that interfered with the grazing. The appeal was dismissed.

Holiday lettings

11.15 Great care is needed when dealing with holiday lettings but there is no doubt that the ability of BPR to be secured against that activity has been severely reduced following several high-profile cases all found in HMRC's favour. Original HMRC guidance indicated that BPR would generally be allowed if the lettings were short term (ie weekly or fortnightly) *and* there was substantial involvement with the holidaymakers both on and off the premises. This applied even if the lettings were for only part of the year.

However, current HMRC guidance (IHTM25278) was amended in late 2008, and at the time of writing states: '...Recent advice from Solicitor's Office has caused us to reconsider our approach and it may well be that some cases that might have previously qualified should not have done so. In particular we will be looking more closely at the *level and type of services, rather than who provided them'* (emphasis added). The guidance goes on to indicate that cases involving claims for business property relief on holiday lettings should be referred to HMRC's Technical Team (litigation) – it is clear that there is a great deal of unease within HMRC.

Although following a period of consultation, the *FA 2010* has restored in part the favourable income tax treatment of furnished holiday lettings this did not impact on the IHT position which has always been dealt with quite separately under the IHT code. Nonetheless, any claim to BPR in respect of furnished holiday lets is always carefully scrutinised by HMRC and it must be said, with more than a jaundiced approach. It is clear that HMRC do take a strong stance and thus the practitioner must be prepared to mount a robust defence.

The narrowness of the HMRC position was challenged in *Pawson (deceased) v Revenue and Customs Commissioners* [2012] UKFTT 51(TC). In this case the deceased had 25% interest (with the remaining ownership held by other family members) in a picturesque large seaside holiday letting cottage in respect of which the executors claimed BPR. The income from the property in recent years had steadily increased producing a small taxable profit in all but one year due to expenditure on necessary repairs etc. The property was fully furnished with heating and hot water turned on before the arrival of visitors, the well-equipped kitchen was kept in good working order, the cleaner attended the property between each letting and the gardener was hired to ensure that the grounds were kept in good order at all times during the letting season – the family owners dealt with the letting arrangements personally and attended the property on a regular basis. In a surprising decision at the First-tier Tribunal it was held that the activities amounted to a business and the claim to BPR was allowed. However, as expected, HMRC appealed to the Upper Tribunal and were successful in their bid to overturn the earlier decision.

This effectively restores the position to that determined under *Stedman's Executors v IRC*; *CIR v George and another* namely that the rental exploitation of land with a view to profit is still fundamentally a business of holding the property as an investment. It is generally accepted that the *Pawson* case was rather weak such that the appeal decision was probably the correct one on the facts as they stood. However, the concern is that the Upper Tribunal commentary is sufficiently damming as to be likely to prevent a BPR claim in any furnished letting case. Leave to appeal was refused by the Court of Appeal in October 2013 on the fairly damming grounds that there would be no realistic prospect of any such appeal succeeding.

A further death knell has been delivered in the recent case of *ACC Green v HMRC* [2015] UKFTT 0236 (TC) which considered the availability of BPR on transfer of 85% of the appellant's interest in an established self-contained holiday business. The appellant's team argued that a wide spectrum of businesses involved the use of property which at one end involved the granting of a tenancy and at the other end the running of a hotel or a shop but the tribunal were not swayed that the business in question fell on the hotel side. The Tribunal placed heavy reliance on the authorities set out in the cases of *Pawson v HMRC* [2012] UKFTT (TC), *McCall v HMRC* [2009] NICA 12 STC 990 and *Best v HMRC* [2014] UKFTT 077 (TC) and concluded that 'the extra services provided are insufficient to demonstrate that the business is other than mainly one of holding the property as an investment'.

Other types of lettings involving land may also fall foul of *s 105(3)* in HMRC's view. Its guidance states (at IHTM25280): 'Consider whether investment holding is in point where exploitation of land ownership in other ways is involved, eg moorings or beach huts, and seek the views of Technical Group (TG).'

Small company group

11.16 A strict examination of *s 105(4)(b)*, with its emphasis on holding 'companies' rather than 'assets' suggests that where a holding company has no trade of its own but holds only:

- shares in a trading subsidiary; and
- the premises from which that company trades,

the shares in the holding company would appear to fail the test for BPR. What is the holding company 'wholly or mainly' doing? The problem would not arise if there were a trade within the holding company, but here there is none. Suppose that the trade is of little value relative to the value of the premises: does that make a difference? Would it be wise to set up a second subsidiary, just to hold the premises?

It might be. However, it is necessary to look at the situation in the round: if the group as a whole is regarded as trading, and the land is held only to facilitate the trade, there should be no problem. HMRC appear to agree with that view, though of course each case will turn on its own facts.

VALUATION, EXCEPTED ASSETS

11.17 If the property is of the type identified at **11.22** as qualifying for 100% BPR, it might seem that valuation is not an important issue. Sometimes, that will be the case but where there are excepted assets it is still necessary to undertake the full valuation exercise to establish the quantum of that relief.

Shares

11.18 The vast majority of claims to BPR on shares will be on unquoted shares and related securities. The general principles of valuation of assets that are subject to restrictions will apply, as seen for example in *IRC v Crossman* [1936] 1 All ER 762. In practice there may be a conflict between arguments that were raised in valuing company shares for CGT purposes, especially as at March 1982 where the taxpayer may want to value high, and the value that may apply for inheritance tax, particularly where there is some restriction on relief and the taxpayer is valuing low.

Difficulties arise, as in *I C McArthur's Executors v HMRC* [2008] SpC 700, where 'clever' structures are used. There the main shareholder lent money to companies on terms that linked the loans to options to purchase other shares. On his death, HMRC required the valuation of the loans to reflect the value of the options. Although the executors argued that the options had little or no value, the Special Commissioner disagreed. There was evidence, in the form of 'writs' of the debtor, that there were loans and conversion rights. The unit of valuation was the loan plus the relevant conversion rights.

11.19 The level of information that would be available to a purchase of shares and many of the other general principles of valuation were considered in *Caton's Administrators v Couch* [1995] STC (SCD) 34. There the Special Commissioner had to decide: how much unpublished information would be available to a purchaser; the value of the shares on the date of Mr Caton's death; and whether professional costs including the appeal itself might be allowable in computing the chargeable gain. The Commissioner concluded that the purchaser of a small block of shares would not normally expect to receive as much information as a larger investor. He would get no more than the published data and be restricted to what he could find out without questioning the directors.

11.20 Family companies can involve competing factions and that competition can affect the value of the shares. These principles were examined in detail in *Hawkings-Byass v Sassen (Inspector of Taxes)* [1996] STC (SCD) 319 and in *Denekamp v Pearce (Inspector of Taxes)* [1998] STC 1120. A dispute in *CVC/Opportunity Equity Partners Ltd v Almeida* [2002] UKPC 16, forced the Privy Council to consider the valuation basis where a company in the nature of a limited partnership had expelled one of the partners. The court decided that in such a case the majority may exclude the minority only if they buy them out at a fair price. The continuing shareholders had to pay the expelled partner a value on a going concern basis without discount. For a contrary view, see *Phoenix Office Supplies v Larvin* [2002] EWCA Civ 1740, [2003] 1 BCLC 76, where a discount did apply.

The determining factor seems to be that there must actually be someone in the market who has a special reason for buying the shares. The valuer should consider whether there is, in the circumstances of the company, another shareholder who is prepared to offer full market value without discount. Arguably some discount will always be appropriate: see the decision in *Re Courthorpe* KB 1928 7 ATC 538. Although there has from time to time been comment to establish a rule of thumb, there is no hard and fast rule and the value must be negotiated each time.

Net value

11.21 One clear rule is established by *s 110*, though it seems to apply only to unincorporated businesses (see the reference to 'a business or an interest in a business'). The value of the business is the net value and as a result, all liabilities incurred 'for the purpose of business' are set against the value of the company assets, whether or not secured on them. This same rule also applies to unincorporated businesses. There is a distinction between debts incurred 'for the purposes of the business' and liabilities that are incurred in acquiring the business itself.

Example 11.6—Net value of business

(i) Charles sets up in business as a solicitor. Having no real capital resources, the premises and equipment are rented. At the end of his second year of trade, Charles correctly recognises the value of some of his work in progress that has not been billed out because it related to work done partly by him and partly by assistants. However, there is no money to pay the tax, so the firm goes into overdraft. On a valuation of the business at that date the overdraft would be netted off against the value of the work in progress.

(ii) David gives up his job as a solicitor and buys a will-writing business. Having no capital, he negotiates a loan from his bank, secured on his house, to buy a franchise interest, comprising a fireproof safe, a collection of 500 wills and a software package of precedents. On a later valuation of the business for BPR, the loan secured against the house is not deducted from the value of the business, because it was a loan incurred to buy the business rather than for running the business.

(iii) Charles wants to retire and agrees to sell his business to David, who takes out a further loan. On a valuation of David's business some time later, the second loan probably would be deducted from the value because the purchase of Charles's business could be seen as a mere extension of the existing business so that the cost of finance was for the purposes of the business that David already owned.

Subject to the rule illustrated above, and prior to the *FA 2013*, there was a general principle that a debt lies against the asset on which it is secured. Accordingly, repositioning a debt could affect relief, especially APR where the rule in *s 110* has no parallel and since this was a 'snapshot' test and not time based, repositioning the debt to gain unrestricted APR/BPR on the underlying asset only days before death could save significant tax. This device has now been curtailed by a surprise measure in *FA 2013* which operates to automatically offset the liability used to acquire the BPR/APR relievable asset before application of the BPR/APR relief). Originally intended to be operative with immediate effect, following representation amendments incorporated in the Act ensure that the new measures only apply to transfers of value on and after 17 July 2013 but with effect from 6 April 2013 to new liabilities incurred. It is important to note that the new rules apply not only to new borrowings after 5 April 2013 but to any refinancing after that date: see IHTM 28011.

Excepted assets

> **Focus**
>
> BPR cannot be secured by simply placing non-business assets in a business wrapper – the nature of the asset must be reviewed and tested on its merits.

11.22 *Section 112* requires a double valuation exercise. First, the value of the business is calculated under general principles. It is then recalculated excluding the value of 'excepted assets', ie those assets that are neither used wholly or mainly for the purposes of the business nor required at the time of transfer for future use.

Slightly different rules apply to incorporated and unincorporated businesses. For companies it has been robustly and successfully argued that *s 112* will seldom apply because the business of a company is indivisible and therefore, if the asset contributes to the overall business success of the company, its value ought not to be excluded when calculating BPR unless the asset falls to be treated as a 'luxury' asset falling within the specific exception at *s 112(6)*. If the business is not incorporated, this argument does not apply and it becomes easier for HMRC to exclude an asset from relief.

11.23 In any event, there are specific exceptions to the 'robust' argument. The first is cash. In *Barclays Bank Trust Co v IRC* [1998] STC (SCD) 125 it was held that surplus retained cash did not qualify for BPR. In that case a substantial cash balance remained unused many years after the valuation date. The court held that, in the circumstances, cash was not 'required' for future use for business purposes within *s 112(2)(b)*. Despite Government encouragement, the continued reluctance of high street banks to lend will have persuaded some owners of small businesses to retain and stockpile cash to see them through the recession. However, such greater levels of prudence are not embraced by HMRC and as a consequence this may have a detrimental impact when considering the tests for *s 112*.

The second exception applies where an asset is not used for business purposes at all, such as a holiday flat used exclusively by the family of the majority shareholder – this falls squarely within *s 112*. A more borderline issue is whether certain 'passive' assets are excluded, for example, surplus funds for the company invested in quoted securities will probably not be excluded assets if they are moderate in value compared with the capital of the company as a whole. It is more difficult where perhaps over a number of years surplus profits have been invested in building up a portfolio of freehold investment properties. After a time, the existence of such substantial or non-trading assets can threaten the whole claim to BPR under the rule already noted relating to 'wholly or mainly holding investments' in *s 105(3)* – this is indeed a potential danger.

From initial review of the facts in *Executors of Marquess of Hertford v IRC* [2004] SpC 00444, it might have seemed that the rules as to excepted assets might be in point. In this case, HMRC sought to disallow BPR on the value of that part of Ragley Hall which was not open to the public, thus reducing a claim to BPR on the value of the business of opening the house to the public which itself had been the subject of a lifetime gift. However, it was successfully argued that the whole of the house was an asset of the business – visitors saw the whole of the outside and most of the interior and the entire building was thus an integral part of the business. *Section 112(4)* was not in point because that concerned a building that would, but for relief, qualify for no BPR at all.

The placing of assets within a company group can be significant when claiming BPR. The interaction of *ss 105(4)* and *111* has the effect that it may be best, in appropriate circumstances, for the 'working' properties of a group to sit with the top company and for any properties that are more in the nature of investments to be spread around the group.

In summary, great care must be taken in this area to ensure that the balance is correct –assumption and complacency have no place. Whilst tax cases provide a valuable insight into the broader parameters, the outcome will inevitably turn upon the facts present in each individual case.

SCOPE OF AGRICULTURAL PROPERTY RELIEF

Agricultural property

11.24 One basic but important distinction between BPR and APR is that the exclusion (subject to the *Nelson Dance* case) from BPR of a 'mere asset' in the context of a business has no parallel in APR. Essentially, APR is only granted on 'mere assets' but of particular categories detailed as follows:

- agricultural land;
- pasture;
- woodland occupied with agricultural land or pasture where occupation is ancillary;
- buildings used for intensive stock or fish rearing where occupied with agricultural land or pasture and occupation is ancillary;
- farm cottages and their land of a character appropriate;
- farm buildings and their land of a character appropriate;

- farm houses and their land of a character appropriate;
- stud farms;
- land in habitat schemes;
- a 'look through' provision to the assets of farming companies.

11.25 In practice, problems often arise through lack of scale of the farming enterprise. Land may have been sold off and the operation scaled down as the farmer grows older and becomes less agile. Interestingly, and despite HMRC contention, from an APR viewpoint there is nothing in the legislation which requires the farming operation to be profitable (and this view was supported in the *Golding* case – see **11.35**). Many will argue that the mere growing of crops is now not enough to support a farming enterprise and that viability can be achieved only with a combination of growing of crops, and/or of stock, the use of various rural initiatives and the exploitation of grant schemes. The principal difficulties arise where the main, if not the only, source of income is the entitlement to Single Farm Payment and where, in reliance on that scheme, the farmer has sold all his farm machinery and other equipment. In such a situation, farm buildings may well have become redundant and as such will lose APR, being no longer 'occupied for the purposes of agriculture' within *s 117*.

11.26 Furthermore, property may be of the appropriate type, but may nevertheless fail to qualify for APR because of the specific requirements of *s 115* which when read with the ownership conditions of *s 117* require that the land be occupied for the purposes of agriculture. For example, woodland may qualify if it adjoins meadow land and if it provides shade for 'meat' animals grazing nearby, but an isolated coppice which is effectively used only for shooting will not qualify because its occupation is not ancillary to that of agricultural land. Equally, as demonstrated in *Williams (Williams Personal Representative) v HMRC* [2005] SSCD 782; [2005] SpC 500, a building used for the intensive rearing of poultry does not qualify for APR where it stands on and dominates a small landholding because its use is not 'ancillary' to the land on which it stands.

The occupation test frequently gives rise to other problems, particularly in connection with cottages and houses.

Example 11.7—Loss of APR on farmhouse

Geoffrey farmed for many years and his house was the hub of the business. It adjoined a traditional range of farm buildings, some of which over the years had been adapted to allow the storage of modern farming equipment. It had been a small mixed farm, but over the years Geoffrey sold his stock and let some of the buildings as stabling and two of the fields as paddock. Eventually, he scrapped the redundant farm machinery and sold the rest. He entered into an informal letting agreement with his farmer neighbour for the rest of the land.

On Geoffrey's death APR can be secured on the land let to the neighbour for farming (subject to the ownership requirement) but not on the paddocks because they are not occupied for the purposes of agriculture. The horses are not 'meat' animals, but family pets and thus APR is denied on the stable buildings. Finally, APR is denied on the farmhouse because it is no longer the hub of a farming business – it had become no more than the house where a retired farmer lived until the date of his death.

Farmhouses

11.27 Tax cases dicta coupled with HMRC approach have made this a difficult but fluid area of law. With the exception of a heritage house open to the public, there is virtually no other form of residence that can escape a charge to IHT (albeit limited relief is now afforded in 2017/18 et seq in the form of the residence nil rate band – see **Chapter 3**) and this in itself makes it very popular for taxpayers to claim that their personal residence should be treated as a farmhouse – it is and remains a contentious area. Farmhouses are often well situated, having slightly more seclusion than normal residential properties, so they can command a 'charm' premium. That seems certainly to have been true in the *McKenna* case, considered at **11.34** below. There are fewer working farms than in the past, so the likelihood that the occupier of a farmhouse makes his living from the adjoining land is much less now than it was even 50 years ago. Much greater use is now made of farming contractors than formerly and a farmer may live some distance from the field where his business is carried on.

11.28 The combination of all these factors can result in a situation where arguably the basis for the original relief has perhaps long since been lost. If income from farming activities consists partly or even mainly of the Single Farm Payment there is now really no particular link between the house where the farmer lives and the land in respect of which the payment is earned. Some of these tensions are well reflected in the observations, admittedly *obiter*, of the Lands Tribunal in *Antrobus (No 2)* [2006] RVR 138, as was recognised in the *McKenna* case. Certainly practitioners are continuing to encounter regular challenge by HMRC to APR claims on farmhouses on grounds that there is really no viable business to be run from the house in question; and for this purpose HMRC also rely heavily on the *McCall* case to disregard a 'farming' business that consists only of owning land that is subject to grazing licences.

Section 115(2) allows APR on 'such cottages, farm buildings and farmhouses, together with the land occupied with them, as are of a character appropriate to the property'. This tends to show that the relief can apply not only to the house, but also to its garden and that for the relief to be available there must be 'the property' and crucially there must be some link between the farmhouse and 'the property'.

Consider the important decision in *Hanson v Revenue & Customs Commissioners* [2012] UKFTT 95 (TC), which was soundly upheld before the Upper Tribunal on 15 April 2013. After a detailed examination of the facts and careful analysis of the legislation the Upper Tribunal held that when determining whether a farmhouse qualifies for APR, both it and the land (to which the farmhouse is of 'character appropriate') must be in the same occupation but not necessarily, as HMRC argued, in the same ownership.

The facts of the case were straightforward. Immediately before his death in December 2002 Joseph Charles Hanson was the liferenter of a trust created by his father in 1957. The trust held a property which HMRC agreed was a 'farmhouse' for APR purposes with an agreed market value in December 2002 of £450,000. Mr Hanson's son lived in the farmhouse which he had occupied since 1978 under a rent-free licence. From there the son farmed 215 acres of land of which 128 acres was owned by the son and a mere 25 acres was part owned by Mr Hanson. The remainder of the 215 acres comprised 20 acres rented by the son from a third party and a further 42 acres whose ownership was unspecified. The only land in common ownership and common occupation with the farmhouse was the 25 acres part owned by Mr Hanson and farmed by the son.

Following Mr Hanson's death his executors claimed APR on the value of his interest in the farmhouse. HMRC denied the relief on the basis that there was insufficient agricultural land (25 acres) in both common ownership and common occupation with the farmhouse for the farmhouse to pass the 'character appropriate' test. The son appealed the decision in his capacity as sole trustee of the trust arguing that common occupation (the son in his capacity as farmer of the land) was the only connecting factor required between the farmhouse and the agricultural land to which it was of a character appropriate (namely the combined 25 acres owned by the deceased and the 215 acres owned by the son/A N Other). The Tribunal agreed with the son.

This was a landmark defeat for HMRC but it is a welcome decision which restores faith in good judgment based on a practical understanding of the farming operation. It will be of significance in situations where a downsizing farmer has moved out of the farmhouse and gives away much of the agricultural land.

Farming business? What farming business?

11.29 As previously commented and in contrast to BPR there is nothing within the legislation which actually stipulates that there must be a viable (profitable) farming business. An unpublished decision of the Special Commissioners in 1994 stated that '…whether or not one can make a living from a given acreage of land cannot be determinative of the question whether a building is a farmhouse…'. However, no relief is given on any agricultural property in the absence of its occupation for the purposes of agriculture as required by *s 116*.

A claim to APR on a home, irrespective of its title and location, can never be in point unless there is at least some recognisable farming activity. See, for example, *Dixon v IRC* SpC 297 [2002] SSCD 53 concerning a cottage, its garden and orchard of which the total area was 0.6 acres and the gross cash turnover (ignoring bartering arrangements) was £70 per year. It was held that the activities were consistent with the use of the property as a residence and garden, not for agriculture. The property was primarily a cottage with garden and orchard. APR was refused.

For a long time, it was HMRC practice to enquire closely into claims for APR on houses worth £250,000 or more where the land holding was 100 acres or less, but this value limit has now been eroded. The current approach now routinely met in practice is to deny relief on any farmhouse where the farm land does not seem extensive enough to support a viable business; and of course where values are moderate such cases may not reach the courts.

11.30 There may in the past have been a farming business, but it may no longer relate to the dwelling. Thus, in *Rosser v IRC* SpC 368, [2003] SSCD 311, the relevant dwelling had for many years been a farmhouse for 41 acres comprising agricultural land, the house itself and a barn. Fatally, as it turned out, the deceased and her husband gave 39 acres of land to their daughter, who was married to a farmer and who then farmed that land with other land. That effectively 'demoted' the retained residence from its status of a farmhouse to that of a retirement home.

There is a restricted argument resulting from the decision of the Court of Appeal in *Starke (Brown's Executors) v IRC* [1996] 1 All ER 622. There the farmhouse had become separated in ownership from the adjoining farmland which was owned through the medium of a company. In that case the argument turned on a technicality, so the decision in *Starke* will not always decide the matter. In summary, a claim to APR on a dwelling will always be dependent upon first proving that there is a farming business and, as will be seen below, and second, that the house is the place from which that business is run – past usage and current title have no impact if these two key requirements are not in place.

Unoccupied farmhouses cause problems: see the review at **11.38** below of *Harrold v IRC* [1996] STC (SCD) 195 and of *Atkinson v HMRC* [2010] UKFTT 108 (TC) TC00420. The latter case is of particular interest not least for its initial unexpected decision in favour of the taxpayer, a member of a farming partnership until his death but prevented from continued occupation of the farmhouse through ill health necessitating offsite residential care. Not surprisingly HMRC appealed the case to the Upper Tribunal but the executors of Mr Atkinson, concerned over costs, chose not to attend. HMRC's appeal was allowed thus soundly overturning the decision of the First-tier Tribunal (*HMRC v Atkinson and another* [2011] UKUT B26 (TCC)).

'Character appropriate'

11.31 There are many houses that look like farmhouses, but fail the test as to 'character appropriate' because they are disproportionate in size or quality to the farming business that purports to support them. The legislation originally included a category of dwelling that qualified for relief – mansion houses – but the removal of that category has strengthened the HMRC argument that grand houses should not qualify for APR. The test is whether the property is in substance a fine house surrounded by land, in which case APR will be hard to justify, or is a land holding that happens to contain a house, where the chances of APR will be better.

11.32 In *Higginson's Executors v IRC* [2002] STC (SCD) 483 found in HMRC's favour, a property was set in a landed estate of 134 acres, of which only 63 were agricultural land. The gardens extended to three acres and there were 68 acres of woodland and wetland. This was a special property and, although it had for many years been occupied as a farmhouse for some time before the death of the owner, the farmland had been let and the woodland and wetland were made areas of nature conservation. The estate was not economically viable and was sold for £1,150,000, a price described from a farming perspective as being 'an appalling investment in terms of yield', being well beyond farmers' means.

Antrobus

11.33 In *Lloyds TSB (Personal representative of Antrobus) v IRC* [2002] STC (SCD) 468 (*Antrobus (No 1)*) Cookhill Priory, which was within 126 acres of freehold land plus 6.5 acres of tenanted land, had been occupied by the Antrobus family since 1907. The original nunnery had been founded in 1260. The six-bedroom house dated to the mid-sixteenth century with an extension in 1765 and was altered in 1785, in the Georgian period and in 1910. Father farmed the land until 1942, his widow died in 1959, Miss Antrobus, occupied 124 acres and acquired the property from relatives in 1959, then farming it until her death. It was held that she was definitely a farmer. It was agreed that the land and buildings were agricultural property but the claim in respect of two let houses and Cookhill Priory was fiercely disputed by HMRC. Doctor Brice summarised the relevant questions to be answered in relation to any claim for APR on a farmhouse and that checklist was updated in the *McKenna* case, considered below.

McKenna

11.34 *Arnander (Executors of McKenna Deceased) v HMRC* [2006] SpC 00565 is a valuable and very thorough examination of the issues outlined above, to which this summary cannot do justice and for that reason the author recommends that the full case transcript is read.

Rosteague House, Cornwall, overlooked the sea. It was in poor condition but nevertheless listed Grade II and '...at the very top end of the size of a farmhouse...', even in the context of the many fine examples in the district. It stood in 187 acres which included 52 acres of coastal slope and over a mile of sea frontage. It dated back in part to 1597, according to contemporary maps. It was a very substantial building with impressive gardens and there were farm buildings.

The farming history could be traced back to 1365, though recently it had been conducted by agents and through contract-farming arrangements. The woodland area was extended with the help of a planting grant. The farm buildings were little used as such, but did house garden implements.

The owner spent perhaps an hour a day on farm work until illness prevented him and eventually the estate was sold, but not as a farm, for £3,050,000. Later evidence showed that urgent repairs would cost the purchaser nearly £200,000.

Against that background, Dr Brice found as follows:

- It was not a farmhouse. She quoted with approval the decision in *Rosser v IRC*. She approached the views of the Lands Tribunal in *Antrobus No 2* 'with some caution' as *obiter*, but held that the principle that '...the farmer of the land is the person who farms it on a day-to-day basis rather than the person who is in overall control of the agricultural business conducted on the land is a helpful principle...'. After a review of all the cases she set down the following principles:
  - A farmhouse is a dwelling for the farmer from which the farm is managed.
  - The farmer is the person who farms on a day-to-day basis, not the manager.

  - The purpose, not the status, of occupation is what matters.
  - If the premises are extravagantly large, then even though occupied for the purpose of agriculture they may have become something more grand.
  - Each case turns on its own facts, judged by ordinary ideas of what is appropriate in size, content and layout, taken in context with the buildings and the land.

  Based on this, Dr Brice found that the actual farming was not done from the house, which was too grand for the much-reduced farming operations carried on.

- It was not of a 'character appropriate' anyway. After referring to the *Antrobus* principles and to *Higginson* Dr Brice reviewed the elements as follows:
  - There were many fine farmhouses in Cornwall, some quite large and with very pleasant gardens.
  - Rosteague House was large and despite its condition had 'an interior of grace and charm'.
  - The farm buildings were not really used as such.
  - There was not enough land.
  - A layman would think of it as a large country house; it was in effect marketed as such.
  - On sale, 65% of the price realised was for the house, part for tenanted properties and only 12% for the agricultural land. It would not attract commercial farmers needing to make a living from the land.
- It was not occupied for the purposes of agriculture. Neither Mr McKenna, nor Lady McKenna had been able to farm actively during the relevant two-year period.
- Most of the farm buildings were not occupied for the purposes of agriculture. One was a dung stead, latterly used in connection with livery, but livery of horses is not an agricultural purpose. On the facts, however, some were used for agriculture.

It would be more than sensible to consider the full impact of this decision before advising on fine houses in future, but undeniably it makes a claim for a 'lifestyle' farmer in respect of a charming country house that much harder to pursue.

11.35 In *Executors of D Golding Deceased v Revenue & Customs Commissioners* [2011] UKFTT 352 (TC) the reverse scenario was considered.

In this case, the deceased had for many years until his death at age 81, farmed a smallholding of just 16.29 acres – the diverse farming trade comprised some 600 chickens, seven to ten cattle, harvesting of fruit from trees and growing vegetables. The farm produced milk and crops of wheat and barley were produced for sale. It was accepted that old age and infirmity led to scaling back of activities confined to selling of eggs, fruit and vegetables which produced a net profit of approximately £1,500 pa on average over the last five years – equal to less than 25% of the deceased's sustainable income. Even so in the early years the farm had been sufficient to sustain a family albeit not to any great state of luxury. The farmhouse was small in size, without electricity in parts and in a very poor state of repair. HMRC had implied acceptance that the house in which the deceased lived and from which he carried out his farming activities, was a farmhouse for agricultural purposes but disputed that the property was of 'character appropriate' – the argument rested to a great extent on the profitability of the farm. In a refreshingly simple and clear analysis of the facts as presented, the tribunal in finding for the taxpayer stated '...we do not accept that the lack of substantial profit is detrimental to the decision that the farmhouse was of character appropriate...'.

Rather belatedly and in response to the outcome of the *Golding* case HMRC have added new guidance to their IHT manual (see IHTM24036 et seq and HMRC Guidance reported at STEP UK News Digest 13 May 2013) which discusses the entitlement of a farmhouse to APR under the character appropriate test.

Farm buildings

11.36 It was noted earlier that farm buildings do not automatically qualify for APR by virtue of their use but rather such buildings must be ancillary to the main land holding. This was confirmed in *Williams (Williams Personal Representative) v HMRC* [2005] SSCD 782; [2005] SpC 500.

CONDITIONS FOR APR

Period of ownership or occupation

11.37 Unlike its stronger BPR sibling where a single test is required, APR is denied unless the property complies with one of two conditions as to ownership and occupation (*s117*). The first condition is occupation by the transferor for the purposes of agriculture throughout the period of two years ending with the date of transfer. This can lead to slightly surprising results.

Example 11.8—Period of occupation: deathbed purchase

James and Phillip were brought up on their father's farm and eventually inherited it from him. James lived on in the family house whilst his brother moved into the bungalow which had been his father's home in retirement. For a time they tried to run the farm between them, but there were differences of temperament and in reality the land holding was not really big enough to support them both thus they agreed to partition the land between them. James thereafter owned the main farmhouse plus half the land which he farmed in hand and rented the remainder of the farmland from his brother.

Some years later James was forced to sell part of his land to the Highways Authority, generating a substantial cash compensation receipt. Though no longer in good health he continued to farm the remaining land, including the land rented from his brother and used the compensation to buy out his brother's land. James died only days after the transaction was completed.

APR will be allowed in respect of the whole acreage, including land that had only been in James's estate for a matter of days before his death as the two-year occupation test has been met by reason of James farming of the land throughout.

11.38

Focus

Unlike its stronger BPR sibling where direct involvement is required, the landowner can secure APR by 'piggy-backing' on the qualification of the underlying tenant.

The second and alternative qualification for APR under *s 117* is that the property was owned by the transferor throughout the seven years ending with the date of transfer and throughout that period was occupied for the purposes of agriculture. For this second test, it does not matter whether the land was occupied by the owner or by some other person. APR qualification under this route is most likely to be in relation to bare land rather than a farmhouse because of the arguments already noted in relation to farmhouses but certainly if the farmhouse is occupied by the tenant farmer then relief will be secured and also by virtue of the decision in *Hanson* (see **11.26** above), such relief is now secured even if the farmhouse and the land farmed by the occupier of the farmhouse are in different ownership.

Example 11.9—Period of occupation: small let farm

Alwen's family have always been farmers. The holdings were small hillside properties and the main occupation was sheep farming. Alwen's uncle eventually moved out of his 90-acre property, letting it (house, land and farm buildings) on a commercial basis to a neighbour. By his will the uncle left the property to Alwen who thereafter drew the rents continuing to own the property until her own death more than seven years later.

APR will be allowed on the land and on the house (at its tenanted value) since the entire holding has been occupied for the purposes of agriculture throughout the qualifying period.

Contrast the above outcome with **Example 11.7** which illustrated the circumstances in which APR was denied on the farmhouse since it was not occupied by the tenant farmer to whom the land was tenanted.

The need for actual occupation has been tested in two 'farmhouse' cases. The first, *Harrold v IRC* [1996] STC (SCD) 195, was a 'clawback' case triggered by death within seven years of a gift. A building that in all respects satisfied the farmhouse tests nevertheless failed because it had not, at the relevant time, been renovated to habitable standard. It was not occupied for agriculture because it was not occupied at all.

In *HMRC v Atkinson and another* [2011] UKUT B26 (TCC), referred to at **11.30**, the bungalow had been occupied, as part of a larger unit, by a farming partnership but at the date of death the farmer, Mr Atkinson a partner in the business, was in a nursing home. Evidence showed that he still took an interest in farm business. However, it was held that the occupation was not merely by the farmer but by the partnership, and the partnership had ceased to occupy the bungalow when Mr Atkinson moved into the care home. It was necessary to identify a strong connection between the use of the bungalow and the agricultural activities being carried out on the farm – the mere housing of personal possessions and occasional attendance by the partners to oversee the property could not be said to amount to occupation in the true sense.

Successions

11.39 When farming property passes on death, the person inheriting it is treated as owning it from the date of death and, if they later occupy the property, as having occupied it from the date of death whether they actually did or not; *s 120(1)(a)*. Importantly, where the inheritance in point is between spouses/

civil partners the person inheriting the farming property is also credited with the period of occupation of the previous owner (but note that this does not apply to lifetime gifts between spouses/civil partners).

Example 11.10—Successions: keeping it in the family

Sarah ran a small stud farm and equestrian centre with arable land and pasture. Her lifelong companion Margaret helped with the horses. As soon as they were able to do so they formalised their relationship by registration as a civil partnership. Sarah left the property to Margaret on her death and Margaret herself died some 18 months later leaving the property to her niece.

APR, if allowable on the farming enterprise at all, is allowable just as much on the death of Margaret as it had been on that of Sarah since the combined period of two years' occupation has been met.

Replacements

11.40 There is not much turnover in farm property since as a general observation, when people sell farmland they tend to move away from farming altogether. Nevertheless, *s 118* operates to preserve entitlement to APR in circumstances where a person who previously owned agricultural property exchanges it (directly or indirectly) for other agricultural property and occupies one property (or the other) for the purposes of agriculture for periods which together comprise at least two years within the five years ending with the date of transfer. This is in substitution for the two-year occupation condition in *s 117(A)*.

11.41 There is a corresponding provision by which replacement property may qualify for the purposes of *s 117(B)*. Where agricultural property is replaced, the test is satisfied if the new property and the old were held for periods together comprising at least seven years in the last ten prior to transfer and were occupied by someone for the purposes of agriculture.

Importantly, it should be noted that *s 118* does not generally allow for 'trading up'. The relief is restricted to the extent that the new property replaced the old.

Example 11.11—Replacements: trading up

Quentin's farm was small and inconvenient but he put up with it for many years until he came into some money from an inheritance. He then sold the farm for £400,000, purchasing a slightly larger and much more convenient property for £600,000. There was then a general downturn in the value of all farms.

On Quentin's death soon afterwards, the new farm was worth only £550,000 and APR was allowed only on £366,630, being the proportion of the value of the new farm that was referable to the earlier holding (£400,000/600,000 × 100 = 66.66%); see *s 118(3)*.

The valuation of the transfer

11.42 All agricultural property must be valued twice for IHT (see **11.46**). Under the general rule in *s 160* the taxpayer must show the price the property might reasonably be expected to fetch on the open market at the time of transfer. That means the gross open market value and importantly not an off the cuff discounted 'IHT' value. It also means that where several parcels of land are concerned as is often the case, the appropriate value is that which would be achieved by offering the land in lots and thereby likely to yield the best value overall.

This issue is examined in detail in *Ellesmere (Earl) v IRC* [1918] 2 KB 735 and *Buccleuch (Duke) v IRC* [1967] 1 AC 506 and more recently, when considering two interests in the same parcel of land, the case of *Gray (surviving executor of Lady Fox) v IRC* [1994] STC 360. In this latter case, discussed in greater detail at **11.43** below, the Lands Tribunal considered that the 'natural unit' for sale would be to offer both the land itself and a partnership interest in it as the same item – this was on the basis that the hypothetical vendor must be regarded as having done whatever was reasonably necessary to get the best price including taking separate properties, or separate interests in property, and selling them together.

11.43 The open market value will however take account of the existence of any tenancy and that tenancy, even though not marketable or capable of assignment, will likely have a value. In *Baird's Executors v IRC* [1991] 1 EGLR 201 George Baird had given up the tenancy of an agricultural holding in favour of his daughter-in-law and his grandson. The tenancy had first been granted in 1921 and the transfer, to which the landlord consented, was in December 1977. Mr Baird died in 1985. The gift of the tenancy was a chargeable transfer under the rules in *Finance Act 1975* and the Lands Tribunal had to decide whether the 'rump' of the lease had any value.

It was held that the lease could have a value and in fact did carry a value. The District Valuer's figure was 25% of vacant possession value, having regard to what the landlord might pay to get the land back, what a tenant might pay in a sale and leaseback, the sort of figure paid to a tenant on compulsory purchase of land and on prevailing rents of other similar land. The case, being brought in Scotland, was particularly concerned with *s 177*, which provides that in certain circumstances value of a lease may be left out of account.

11.44 In the *Lady Fox* case discussed above, the Court of Appeal reviewed the decision of the Lands Tribunal. Lady Fox owned an agricultural estate farmed by a partnership which had an agricultural tenancy. She was entitled to 92.5% of the partnership profits and on her death HMRC assessed capital transfer tax (CTT) on the basis that her interests in the land and her partnership share could be valued together. The vacant possession of the land could be discounted in a number of ways and the result of that argument was to produce a much higher valuation figure than would apply to the land if the partnership share had been disregarded.

The Lands Tribunal had originally decided that the assets should be valued separately but had also considered what the value would be if the assets were taken together, in accordance with the method that was approved by the Court of Appeal. Taking open market vacant possession value, the District Valuer deducted the amount that the partners other than Lady Fox would accept to sell their share of the tenancy. He took a percentage of the difference between a vacant possession of value and tenancy value and discounted it to compensate for risk and delay in obtaining vacant possession.

The Tribunal, applying the rules as required by the Court of Appeal, felt that there was no guarantee that the minority partners would accept the particular sum suggested by the District Valuer and would have been willing to accept a slightly larger discount for the uncertainty, but there was no evidence from the taxpayer on that point.

11.45 Every valuation of agricultural land will turn on its own facts. Where there is in existence an 'old' tenancy, (one established before 1 September 1995) APR will be given at the lower 50% rate unless Extra-statutory Concession F17 is in point. The latter will permit access to the higher 100% APR rate where possession of the land can be obtained within 24 months or where, notwithstanding the terms of any tenancy, the land is valued at an amount broadly equivalent to its vacant possession value. This situation can arise where the tenant is a company and where the transferor controls the company.

Example 11.12—Rate of APR: ESC F17 in action

David owned 52% of the shares in Hanley Farms Ltd, having given a 24% shareholding to each of his sons Eric and Fred. The company held the tenancy of Old Hanley Farm, which was owned by David. Late in life David remarried – his new wife, Geraldine, was very much younger than he and showed little interest in farming. Her tenacious personality resulted in the transfer of half of Old Hanley Farm into her name, but subject to the existing lease.

By his will David left his shares in Hanley Farms Ltd to Geraldine for life with remainder to Eric and Fred. Geraldine, who was the sole executor and trustee of the will, was advised of ESC F17 – she claimed that the farm should therefore be valued at open market value with APR relief available at the 100% rate. ESC F17 conveniently ignores the fact that a surrender of the lease by the company, which lies in Geraldine's power by virtue of her controlling shareholding, would be action oppressive of the minority because it would take away value from the holdings of Eric and Fred.

As stated above, APR at 100% will be in point where vacant possession can be obtained within 12 months or within 24 months under ESC F17 notwithstanding that the tenancy was granted before the 1 September 1995 watershed. However, in the case of farming partnerships, it is becoming increasingly common practice for HMRC to challenge the 100% relief where the partnership occupies land and that occupation is not otherwise supported by formal documentation which defines the precise terms of occupation and/or there is no formal partnership agreement.

The value for relief

Focus

APR is not applied to market value but restricted to the, usually, lower agricultural value, as determined. If BPR is in point, it can be used to soak up the shortfall.

11.46 The second valuation of agricultural land is required by *s 115(3)* and is '…the value which would be the value of the property if the property were subject to a perpetual covenant prohibiting its use otherwise than as agricultural property…'. In short, for the farmhouse this could mean an adjusted lower value of perhaps 70% of open market value unless particular circumstances dictate otherwise, as will be seen from the discussion below of the leading case, referred to many times in this chapter, of *Lloyds TSB Private Banking plc (personal representative of Rosemary Antrobus deceased) v Twiddy* (IRCT) [2005] DET/47/2004 ('*Antrobus Number 2*').

Example 11.13—Agricultural value: farmhouse in Argyll

Lower Kilmartin Farm comprises a four-bedroomed detached house with single garage standing in a quarter of an acre adjoining a range of modern farm buildings – the farm itself is 175 acres of arable land. The journey time from the farm to Glasgow Queen Street station is slightly over three hours, allowing for the distressed state of certain country roads. It is five miles to the nearest petrol station and seven miles to the nearest regular public transport network. Although the land is very productive the scenery is featureless and the existence or absence of an agricultural restriction would make little difference to the value of the property. It has no particular aesthetic charm and is so far from any centre of employment or of education that it would be of little interest to any purchaser who still had to earn a living or had teenage children. In the circumstances, the agricultural value of the property must be almost the same as the open market value.

Example 11.14—Agricultural value: farmhouse in Forfar

Torrin Farm is set in picturesque landscape, although not listed, the property retains many original features and is set in small but well-managed gardens as part of a holding of 50 acres all of which are managed by a farm contractor. The journey time to Dundee is under one hour and the station itself is only 12 minutes away. There are good shopping and restaurant facilities, schools within 15 miles.

The land is not enough to support a farming family, but that is irrelevant – the house and its setting is magnificent. The property, commands a premium by virtue of its situation, the ease with which it can be managed and what was described in *Higginson's Executors v IRC* [2002] STC (SCD) 483 as 'a case where the property has a value greater than ordinary, not because of development potential but rather because of its "amenity value"'. In such a case the agricultural value of the farmhouse could be perhaps as low as 55% of its full market value.

11.47 For a time HMRC attempted to establish a rule of thumb that the agricultural value of a farmhouse was set at 70% of its open market value and many tax liabilities were settled on that basis until the welcome decision of the Lands Tribunal in *Re Antrobus (No 1)*. The outcome of this case, noted at **11.33** above, was that the house in question, Cookhill Priory, was indeed a farmhouse, however, the decision of the Lands Tribunal must be read carefully and taken in context. It is only a decision on value, though the Tribunal did consider certain wider issues in order to arrive at their decision. The open market value of the farmhouse and gardens was £608,475. HMRC, adopting the 70% approach argued that APR should be available on only £425,932 and the tribunal fixed the agricultural value at that figure.

11.48 The case was very fully and forcefully argued. The taxpayer sought APR on the entire value by arguing that some purchasers actually welcomed a restriction on the use of property because it kept other people away. However, these were perhaps not 'true' farmers but 'lifestyle' farmers who have perhaps made money in some other occupation and could therefore afford to pay a premium for the seclusion of an agricultural property. There was evidence that offers had been made for Cookhill Priory of £935,000 and eventually £1,035,000. The Valuation Office argued for a discount of 30% because the terms of *s 115(3)* are even more restrictive than a 'planning tie' – the latter can eventually be lifted, whereas the effect of *s 115(3)* is permanent. No true agricultural purchaser would deliberately 'overpay' for a house because as a farmer he would have to buy land to go with it. The over bid for the farmhouse, with a small area of land adjoining it, from non-farming residential purchasers should be excluded since that over bid or excess would depend on matters such as location, setting, views etc which did not impact on the viability of a farming operation.

11.49 To arrive at their decision, the Lands Tribunal considered what a farmhouse actually was and its link to the farm. They decided that '…a farmhouse is the chief dwelling house attached to a farm, the house in which the farmer of the land lived…'. but went further to define the farmer as '..the person who lives in the farmhouse in order to farm the land comprised in the farm and who farms the land on a day-to-day basis..'. Based on that, the Tribunal was able to ignore the premium price that would be paid by a 'lifestyle' farmer. It had already been established that lifestyle farmers were a substantial part of the market for this type of property, so if they were excluded the value of the property fell to only 70% of the open market value.

Here, as in many other aspects of APR, practitioners should consider HMRC's current guidance on APR (www.hmrc.gov.uk/manuals/ihtmanual/IHTM24000.htm). However, it is important to note that as with all such HMRC guidance, it represents HMRC's view, and by that token it is not actually law. Nevertheless, to take a line that is inconsistent with HMRC's approach must put the adviser on a collision course which may end before the First-tier Tribunal and perhaps not even there. Clients should be informed that in Scotland binding missives for sale are a binding contract which instantly terminates the BPR or APR qualification.

LOSS OF BPR AND APR

> **Focus**
>
> A binding contract of sale will deny access to APR/BPR irrespective of the qualities of the business.

11.50 It is critical to the planning process to appreciate that neither BPR nor APR is available where the subject matter of the transfer is itself already subject to a binding contract for sale at the very time of the chargeable/potentially chargeable event: see *s 113* (for BPR) and *s 124* (for APR). In that sense there is a loss of relief, in that the owner of the property can no longer claim APR/BPR on a transfer made after the contract has been entered into. This point was keenly illustrated in the negligence case of *Swain Mason v Mills & Reeve* [2012] EWCA Civ 498 and operates as a salutary warning.

The provisions cause difficulty, especially in partnership situations where it may be suggested that there is, by virtue of the terms of a partnership deed, a binding contract under which surviving partners can and must buy in the share of the deceased partner. If all else fails, it will be necessary to look carefully to see if there has been a partnership change effected, not by deed, but by conduct. If there has, an argument that it is now a partnership at will only, should suffice to drive a coach and horses through the old partnership deed. Alternatively, consider the Statement of Practice 12/80 and/or IHTM25292 for the HMRC view.

Another important occasion of unintended loss of relief is where there is some change in the nature of the asset during its period of ownership prior to transfer, perhaps where an unquoted trading company goes public and lists on a recognised stock exchange. Again there is loss of BPR in the sense that on a subsequent transfer it will no longer be available, where a controlling shareholder who owns property used by an unquoted trading company reduces his shareholding with the result that the conditions for BPR on the other assets are lost. As has been noted, there can be loss of APR on a farmhouse where it ceases to be the hub of a true farming business or where its occupation is separate from the end user of the land.

However, all these are instances of not so much of loss of relief previously granted but more where relief which might have been available is no longer in point. This section is concerned with clawback of relief under *ss 113A* and *124A* and although there is a separate code for BPR and APR, their wording is so similar that they are taken together with commentary.

BPR or APR may be lost where, following a transfer which would otherwise qualify for relief, certain conditions are not satisfied at point of later test – the relief that would have otherwise sheltered the transfer from tax is in effect clawed back. Clawback applies in two circumstances, namely:

- where a PET is made within seven years of the death of the transferor and that PET fails; or
- where there is a chargeable lifetime transfer (usually by transfer into a relevant property trust) and death occurs within seven years thereof.

It operates by applying the concept of a 'notional transfer' made by the transferee of the property immediately before the death of the transferor or, if earlier, of the transferee. On the occasion that triggers clawback, the notional transfer tests the continued availability of the relief that was originally in point – if the conditions for relief are not satisfied at that point of test it will be clawed back.

The conditions are:

- that the original property was owned by the transferee throughout the period beginning with the date of the chargeable transfer and ending with the death of the transferor; and
- that, subject to one exception, specific to shares in relation to a notional transfer of value made by the transferee immediately before the death, the property would qualify for relief but for satisfaction of the requirement as to ownership or occupation.

Example 11.15—Clawback of BPR

(i) Olive gives Renee a 30% holding of unquoted shares which would have qualified for BPR at time of gift. Olive dies within seven years, so the PET fails and must be taken into account. If Renee still holds the shares and they still meet the BPR qualification at the date of Olive's death all is well and BPR will be in point to shelter the gift. However, if Renee has in the meantime sold the shares no BPR (assuming the replacement provisions are not in point) will be available – there is no asset to test.

(ii) Albert gives Denise a 15% holding in an unquoted trading company which later becomes listed on the London Stock Exchange. The shares qualified for BPR at the date of the gift but, even though Denise may still own them at the time of Albert's death within seven years, BPR is not available because on the notional transfer at that date of Albert's death the conditions for BPR are no longer satisfied (*s 113A(3A)(b)*).

There are rules for substitution/replacement of property in the BPR and APR codes: these are considered by HMRC in RI95, to which reference should be made and also discussed at **11.9** and **11.40**.

Computation of the tax

11.51 Where a gift of business property is a failed PET its testing of BPR qualification is always by reference to the position of the donor except in the case of shares or securities. Where clawback applies, this will affect the history of chargeable transfers by the donor – the cumulative clock.

Where the transfer was a chargeable lifetime transfer that originally benefited from APR or BPR but no longer qualifies at point of later test, clawback operates to charge extra tax on the original gift on the basis that no APR (or BPR) is available. In this circumstance there is no change to the history of chargeable transfers by the donor, because the value of the property before relief has not changed – the cumulative clock remains unchanged.

Special rules apply to a gift of shares or securities which qualified for BPR at the time of gift and are now retested at the time of the donor's death under the clawback rules. It does not matter that the shares may qualify for relief by reference to a different subsection of *s 105* provided that the qualification is determined by reference to the donee.

Example 11.16—BPR: gift of minority shareholding

Sidney controls a quoted company and on 30 November 2014 he gifted a small minority holding of shares in it to his son Alfred. In Sidney's hands those shares qualified for BPR at 50% under *s 105(1)(cc)*.

Alfred keeps the shares and still owns them when Sidney dies only two years later on 30 November 2016. In Alfred's hands no BPR would normally be available in respect of a minority holding in a quoted company. However, the gift was of quoted shares within *s 113A(3A)(a)*, rather than within *s 113A(3A)(b)*, so that brings into play *s 113A(3)(b)* thus in relation to the notional transfer that Alfred is deemed to make, it is not necessary to satisfy the earlier test.

Alfred, in effect, manages to keep the original claim to BPR at 50% on shares in a quoted company and suffers no clawback. The distinction between different classes of interest in a company used to be more important where the rate of relief was not always 100%.

11.52 One major area of difficulty used to concern gifts into trust. For the purposes of the clawback rules, it is important to note that the donee of the property is the trustee, not the underlying beneficiary. Under the rules in force prior to *FA 2006*, a transfer to a lifetime trust other than a relevant property trust would be a PET and would therefore come within *s 113A(1)* or *s 124A(1)*, so clawback could apply.

If the trustee appointed the property to a beneficiary within seven years of its entry into trust and if the donor died within seven years of that transfer into trust there was a risk of clawback that the trustee could have avoided simply by not making the appointment. That option was not available where, for example, the trust was an A&M settlement prior to 22 March 2006, as seen in the example below.

Example 11.17—A&M trust: partial BPR clawback

Dawn set up an A&M settlement for her grandchildren on 3 March 2005 and transferred to the trustees shares in her trading company, Roller Doors Ltd. At the time of the gift the eldest beneficiary was aged 17. One year (and before the 22 March 2006 watershed) later the eldest beneficiary on attaining age 18, becomes entitled to an interest in possession in part of the fund. All the other beneficiaries are much younger.

On Dawn's death in March 2011 six years from the original settlement creation, the notional transfer by the trustees is examined. At that point the trustees still hold all the shares but, in relation to the eldest beneficiary, the shares are now treated by virtue of *s 49* (prior to the amendments in *FA 2006*) as being part of the estate of the eldest beneficiary. To that extent the trustees no longer holds them and relief in respect of that part of the fund is clawed back. There is no clawback of the relief of the remainder of the fund because the trustees still holds it.

11.53 Over the years there have been difficulties with clawback because of changes in the definition of 'quoted' affecting shares on the old Unlisted Securities Market. Such shares so listed are now treated as unquoted for the purposes of clawback throughout the period from the date of transfer to the date of the notional transfer. The effect of a change in 1996 is to avoid clawback where it might otherwise have applied. However, as previously mentioned, if a company listed on AIM acquired a second listing, perhaps on a major foreign and 'recognised' stock exchange, it would lose its favoured BPR status and clawback could apply.

Comparison of PETs and chargeable transfers and the treatment for clawback

11.54 The following checklist may help to assess the effect on the transfer of business or agricultural property (CLT = chargeable lifetime transfer).

	PET Treatment	*CLT Treatment*
On lifetime gift: immediate charge to IHT?	No	Only on value as reduced by BPR/APR as appropriate
Death within seven years of transfer: assets retained by donee and continue to qualify for reliefs	No IHT: full relief secured	No IHT: full relief secured
Death within seven years of transfer where clawback applies: effect on the transfer itself	IHT charge, subject to availability of nil rate band. Charge is on the full amount of the original transfer.	IHT charge, subject to availability of nil rate band. Charge is on the full amount of the original transfer.
Death within seven years of transfer where clawback applies: effect on aggregation with later transfers	Full value is aggregated – cumulation principle	The value is nil and there is no cumulation with later gifts
Transferor lives seven years from gift and no benefit has been reserved	No IHT: transfer has become exempt	No IHT: transfer falls out of cumulation

Chapter 12

Lifetime planning

SIGNPOSTS

- **Reliefs** – Careful planning and a structured approach using all available lifetime reliefs will minimise a future IHT liability (see **12.1**).
- **Child Trust Funds, Junior ISAs and New ISAs ('NISAs')** – A generous gesture by the government which is often overlooked, but can build up a sizeable fund which can grow outside the parents' or grandparents' estate (see **12.2**).
- **Potentially exempt transfers** – One of the most tax efficient ways of reducing a large estate for as long as the donor survives seven years. PETs are sometimes used in more aggressive schemes, which ought to be approached with care (see **12.3–12.11**).
- **Disabled persons' trusts** – An IHT efficient way of planning for persons with disabilities (see **12.12–12.19**).
- **Protected gifts without trusts** – As *FA 2006* severely restricted the use of trusts without triggering IHT charges, pensions and family limited partnerships may be worth investigating (see **12.20–12.26**).
- **Traditional protected gifts** – In addition to making lifetime gifts into trust, insurance policy trusts, discounted gift schemes and flexible insurance trusts are an alternative for estate planning purposes (see **12.27–12.34**).

USE ALL THE RELIEFS

Lifetime reliefs

12.1 The taxation of lifetime transfers was discussed in **Chapter 2**. The main exemptions and exclusions were described in **Chapter 9** and the reliefs of general application in **Chapter 10**. There is, naturally, some overlap between this chapter and **Chapter 14**, relating to the nil rate band. The cardinal rule for IHT planning, if not of all tax planning, is first to use all of the reliefs that the legislation provides.

Finance Act 2006 restricted the scope for lifetime giving, making it more urgent for taxpayers with substantial estates to consider their options and to exercise them. However, several factors tend to restrict the use of lifetime gifts, all of which contribute to difficulties for taxpayers later in life. They can be seen from the following extended example (all statutory references are to *IHTA 1984*, unless otherwise stated).

Example 12.1—Case study (I): background

Ian worked for many years in local government and is now in his early sixties. He took early retirement, which has provided him with a useful pension pot that he will soon draw. He now works from home, providing consultancy services to his former employer and to other local authorities. He was first married to Sarah. They had a daughter, Sam, now a chartered accountant, and a son, Jon, who is employed by the NHS. Ian and Sarah were divorced many years ago. Ian eventually achieved a clean break settlement. He now lives with Prudence, but they are not married. Their only son, Ben, is a student.

Prudence came out of her own divorce with some savings, now worth £100,000. Ian has no worthwhile savings apart from his pension, but he does own the house in which they live, worth £1,000,000.

Ian gets on fairly well with Sam and Jon. Sam and her husband would really like to start a family but their present mortgage is such that they both need to work to fund it. Jon is in rented accommodation and finding it difficult to get onto the property ladder. Prudence does not really object to the idea that Ian might make some provision for the children of his first marriage provided, of course, that Ben's interests are protected.

Example 12.2—Case study (II): existing wills etc

Prudence's will leaves her estate to Ben. Ian's will leaves the house to Prudence for life with the fee to Sam, Jon and Ben in equal shares. Ian has nominated Prudence as the main beneficiary of his pension if he dies before drawing it. His will leaves the residue of his estate, which would include the value, if any, of his consultancy, to Prudence.

If Prudence died first, there would be no IHT on her estate, which would pass to Ben free of tax. It is, however, assumed that Ian dies first. His pension provision was nominated to Prudence many years ago and falls outside his estate. The consultancy is worth £20,000, comprising the benefit of work in progress and some other realisable assets: these are all genuine trading assets and 100% BPR is available in respect of them. By then, the house is assumed to be worth £1,100,000. No gifts have been made, the nil rate band of £325,000 is set against the value of the house, leaving in charge £775,000 and giving rise to a tax charge at 40% of £310,000.

Although Prudence would have the benefit of a reduced pension, and could use her own savings to pay part of the IHT, she might decide that the house must be sold and ask the trustees to buy something more modest. If she were to die shortly thereafter, the estate to be considered would be her own capital of £100,000, the money realised from the consultancy plus the net value of the remaining trust fund, say £790,000 ignoring expenses. The IHT bill, if she died within a year of Ian's death, would reflect the benefit of quick succession relief.

As Ian left a Will Prudence has no right to make a claim through the courts for any further/additional part of his estate under the *Family Law (Scotland) Act 2006* as these provisions only relate to intestate estates.

Example 12.3—Case study (III): marriage and downsizing

If Ian and Prudence had taken tax advice, things might have been rather different. Although they were living together they were not married. If he and Prudence married, spouse relief could be available on the first death of either of them.

Second, following Ian's retirement there is no real need for them to continue to live in where they are. Ian's consultancy is not worth a significant amount. It therefore makes sense for Ian to sell the house and to buy something that is quite big enough for him and Prudence (and for Ben when he comes home from university). They find a suburban property, which they purchase in their joint names as tenants in common for £500,000.

Example 12.4—Case study (IV): gifts and wills

That leaves Ian with cash of £600,000 and increases Prudence's estate to £350,000. Ian gives £100,000 each to Sam and Jon. Ben has found a property in the university town where he is studying that could be bought for £250,000. Ian therefore gives Ben £100,000 as a deposit on the house.

Ben establishes that, even in the present market, with a substantial deposit a 'student/buy to let' mortgage is on offer at quite favourable terms.

Having obtained confirmation of the rates available in the open market, he then borrows £150,000 from Ian on terms that are quite good for Ian but actually give Ben a significantly better interest rate than he could have secured elsewhere, so there is no reservation of benefit in the transaction.

Ben has student friends who will rent two-thirds of the property. The rent will be almost enough to pay the interest to Ian.

That leaves Ian with £150,000. He invests £100,000 on the advice of a stockbroker friend in blue-chip securities. The last £50,000 is invested in a small AIM company providing services to local authorities in a commercial field that Ian happens to know about and which he thinks is reasonably safe.

Prudence changes her will. She now leaves £100,000 to Ben outright, then leaves the balance on an immediate post-death interest trust for Ian, and on Ian's death absolutely to Jon, Sam and Ben in equal shares. Ian makes a will leaving the AIM shares to his children. He gives his executors power not to call in the mortgage on Ben's property. He leaves the residue of his estate to Prudence for life with power to advance capital for her with the fee to his children. This ensures that not only the transferable nil rate band is available, but also the residence nil rate band (from April 2017).

Example 12.5—Case study (V): the tax effect of lifetime planning

Broadly, the effect of these arrangements is to make full use of the transferable and residence nil rate band, as was the case under the previous part of the illustration, but this time there is no crippling IHT charge on Ian's death. If Prudence were to die first the gift to Ben would be tax-free. The saving is substantial.

On the assumption that Ian dies first during 2016/17, his estate is as follows:

	£	£
Half share in house		250,000
Quoted shares		100,000
Unquoted shares		50,000
Consultancy		20,000
Loan		150,000
Sub total		570,000

	£	£
Recent gifts (£150,000 less £6,000 exempt)		294,000
Estate before reliefs		864,000
Deduct		
BPR on shares	50,000	
BPR on consultancy	20,000	70,000
Estate after reliefs		794,000

The estate suffers no IHT, being exempt or relieved. Distribution is as follows:

Gross estate for distribution as above	864,000
Deduct balance of nil rate band (see below)	31,000
Residuary fund (below)	833,000
Spouse relief	833,000

The nil rate band is £325,000. From it are deducted the three gifts to the children totalling £300,000, less two annual exemptions of £6,000.

The specific gift of the AIM shares avoids the difficulties of *s 39A*: for more detail see **3.39**, **Example 3.3** and **13.25**.

Example 12.6—Case study (VI): incidental benefits for the family

The result of this arrangement is that Sam can reduce her mortgage and think about starting a family. Jon can put a deposit down on a property. Ben has secure accommodation whilst he is a student and, if he sells at a profit after he graduates, main residence relief will be available on the whole of the gain. In the meantime he can claim rent-a-room relief.

The family as a whole will benefit from BPR on the eventual disposal of the consultancy and on the investment in the AIM company. If the AIM company does no more than hold its value the saving after two years will be tax of £20,000 (though that saving only lasts if shares are still owned by Ian at the date of his death and if at that date the company is still an unquoted company).

Prudence's position is more secure. She now owns half of the house she lives in and has a life interest in the other half. If she wanted to move, main residence relief should be available both to her and to the trustees. She has the income from the quoted securities and from Ben's mortgage. If Ben sells his house well when he graduates, he will have a substantial deposit and should find it easy to borrow in the open market, releasing £150,000 to the trustees.

If Prudence finds that she does not need all of the income from the trust fund, she has one or two choices available to her. She may simply authorise the trustees to pay away to the family any income in so far as it exceeds a certain sum that she needs to live on. That would be entirely within the rule in *Bennett v IRC* [1995] STC 54 and the payments would quickly gain relief under *s 21*. Alternatively, she may release part of her life interest, allowing the children to become absolutely entitled. That would be a PET against which, if she gave notice to the trustees, she could set her annual exemption under *s 57*.

The estate will benefit from the transferable nil rate band (although small if Ian dies within seven years of the gift to his children) and potentially the residence nil rate band.

The Child Trust Fund, Junior ISAs and NISAs

12.2 The Child Trust Fund (CTF) was a casualty of the Coalition Government following its election in 2010, when government contributions were reduced and then stopped altogether in January 2011. Existing CTFs will carry on building up, largely tax-free, to age 18, and friends and family will continue to be able to pay in up to £1,200 a year. It offers substantial scope for saving income tax, capital gains tax and IHT. Although the amounts may seem modest the effects of full use of the allowance and of accumulation of income may be greater than is generally realised. On 26 October 2010 the government announced that it would introduce a new tax-advantaged account for saving for children, to be known as a Junior ISA. Junior ISAs were launched on 1 November 2011. They were available for any UK-resident child. From 1 July 2014 ISAs were reformed into a simpler product, the NISA, and all existing ISAs will become NISAs.

The CTF, Junior ISAs or NISAs are essentially UK-based gross roll-up funds. Normally, a parent achieves no advantage from a settlement on his unmarried minor child, as any income of such a settlement is assessable on him if it exceeds £100 per parent (*ITTOIA 2005, s 629*). The CTF, Junior ISA or NISA avoids this difficulty. For CTFs the parent, or indeed any family member, was able to add £100 per month to the fund without the tax penalties that would otherwise apply. The limit of £1,200 per year was calculated by reference to the child's birthday, not the tax year. The limit for Junior ISAs was £3,840 per annum until 30 June 2014 increasing to £4,000 per annum from 1 July 2014 for NISAs. The allowance for 2016/17 is £4,080.

The government allows savings kept in a CTF to be transferred to a Junior ISA from April 2015. The CTF scheme was closed to new deposits in 2010.

Example 12.7—Child trust funds, junior ISAs and NISAs: generous but forgetful grandfather

Robert's children had blessed him with several grandchildren, some born after 31 August 2002. On 1 May 2008, to celebrate his eightieth birthday he gave each of his grandchildren £500. For each of the younger children this was promptly added to the CTF that the parent had taken out. In late March 2009, having read about the CTF, Robert quickly sent £1,000 to the parent of each younger grandchild, to catch the end of the tax year. As Robert has a generous pension, he also adds £500 annually to Junior ISAs, or now NISAs.

In each case, if the pattern continues and depending on Robert's level of income and expenditure, it may be possible to argue that the gifts form part of Robert's normal expenditure and are within *IHTA 1984, s 21,* rather than PETs.

12.3 The drawback of the scheme is that there is no way of deferring the enjoyment of the CTF, Junior ISA or NISA beyond the age of 18.

In the past, private secondary school education has often been funded by grandparents through A&M trusts. The facility of doing that is cut down significantly by *FA 2006*. If, therefore, the burden, for those who choose it, of funding secondary education falls more heavily on parents than on grandparents, the grandparents could use the CTF, Junior ISA or NISA to help with the cost of further education.

Focus

- Most banks and building societies are actively marketing ISAs.
- A wealth of information explaining the details and rates can be found on the internet.

INDIVIDUAL SAVINGS ACCOUNTS (ISAs), INHERITED ISAs, LIFETIME ISAs, FLEXIBLE ISAs AND INNOVATIVE FINANCE ISAs

12.4 Individual Savings Accounts (ISAs) have become more flexible and ISAs are seen by many as a simple tax-efficient way to save for retirement. The annual investment limit was £15,000 in 2013/14 and increased to £15,240 in 2015/16. *FA 2016* contains provisions which keep the subscription limit for ISAs at £15,240 for 2016/17.

The Individual Savings Account (Amendment No 2) Regulations, SI 2015/869 took effect on 6 April 2015, which provides that the spouse or civil partner of a saver who died on or after 3 December 2014 can benefit from an additional ISA allowance equal to the value of the ISA at the holder's date of death, also called an 'additional permitted subscription' (APS). This is in addition to the surviving spouse's or civil partner's own ISA allowance and the APS can be used within three years from the date of death. This allows for the deceased's ISA to be transferred to the surviving spouse/civil partner.

The government further announced a new ISA, the Help-to-Buy ISA. First-time buyers will be able to save up to £200 per month towards the purchase of their first home. For every £200 saved the government will contribute £50. The bonus will be available on home purchases of up to £450,000 in London and £250,000 elsewhere.

Since 6 April 2016 savers have been able to withdraw from an ISA and then replace the amount withdrawn in the same year. Not all banks are offering this Flexible ISA so it is important to check.

Legislation is included in *FA 2016* to amend *ITTOIA 2005, s 694A* in that it extends the income tax and CGT free exemption to estates during the administration period.

FA 2016 also introduces a new pension savings account, called the Lifetime ISA (LISA). The LISA will be available from April 2017 for individuals under the age of 40, who will be able to contribute £4,000 per year with a 25% bonus received from the government.

Individuals will be able to make LISA contributions and receive the 25% bonus from the Government from the age of 18 up to the age of 50. This means that over their lifetime individuals can save up to £128,000 with a £32,000 bonus. Funds can be withdrawn to:

- purchase a first home worth up to £450,000 at any time after 12 months from opening the account; and/or
- draw on the fund from the age of 60.

On the face of it this sounds quite attractive but early withdrawals which are not used to purchase a first home will suffer a 5% charge and the bonus will need to be repaid.

The *Individual Savings Account (Amendment No 2) Regulations 2016* includes a list of qualifying investments for the new Innovative Finance ISA (IF ISA). This will be extended to debt securities issued by companies and offered via crowdfunding and possibly equity crowd funding. The IF ISA is high risk, as unlike other ISAs it is not protected, but it does offer returns up to 6%, which might make it attractive to some.

BPR and APR

12.5 The rate of BPR and APR has not always been as much as maximum 100%. Future Governments may consider reducing the rate if increased tax revenues are required.

12.6 The difficulty for families will be that the assets that qualify for BPR are those that involve some element of risk. Sometimes such assets are held more for the possibility of capital growth than for income. As a result, an elderly estate owner may wish to keep the assets that are safe and that yield a good income, whilst disposing of other assets. If IHT mitigation is the only consideration, the estate owner should probably do the opposite. If at his death his estate comprises entirely assets that qualify for APR or BPR there will be no IHT to pay except in so far as lifetime gifts, originally PETs, become chargeable. The exceptions are those gifts that by their very nature prejudice subsequent claims to relief. See the example 'Getting it wrong' at **Example 11.3** and of loss of relief on farmhouse at **Example 11.7**.

Another factor that will often influence the subject matter of gifts is the availability, or lack of it, of hold-over relief for CGT purposes. *TCGA 1992, s 165* offers fairly wide scope for holdover relief of business assets and is extended.

Shares traded on the Alternative Investment Market (AIM) qualify for BPR once the investor has owned the shares for two years. A number of providers offer AIM portfolio IHT plans which spread the risk. However AIM shares are a higher risk, long-term investment, as AIM has less stringent rules and AIM company shares may be less liquid than those listed on the London Stock Exchange.

Another option is to invest in companies which benefit from the Enterprise Investment Scheme (EIS). EIS shares also qualify for BPR after the investor has held the shares for two years, but again the risk associated with such investment has to be weighed up carefully.

Example 12.8—BPR: recycling business property into investments

Alan invested in unquoted trading company shares, gradually building up a portfolio worth £800,000 in which all the holdings had been held for at least two years. He then transferred them all to his son, such that the transfer was a PET that might be subject to clawback of BPR if he died within seven years. None of the companies had a secondary listing on any recognised stock exchange, so the transfer attracted 100% relief, but subject for the next seven years to the clawback rule in *s 113A*.

The son was wary of such investments, fearing lack of liquidity and risk generally. He realised that a clawback charge could apply in the event of Alan's death, if they no longer held assets that qualified for 100% BPR, so he took out term insurance. Having done that, he sold all the shares and bought gilts and investment properties to stabilise the portfolio.

SHARES LISTED ON THE ALTERNATIVE INVESTMENT MARKET (AIM) AND ENTERPRISE INVESTMENT SCHEME (EIS) SHARES

12.7 The Enterprise Investment Scheme (EIS) is designed to help smaller higher risk trading companies to raise finance by offering a range of tax reliefs, including IHT, to investors.

Guidance can be found on www.gov.uk/government/publications/the-enterprise-investment-scheme-introduction. If certain conditions are complied with, such shares will benefit from BPR, once held for two years.

Shares listed on the Alternative Investment Market (AIM) and shareholdings in OFEX companies also qualify for BPR after the transferor held them for two years.

For more information, please see *Tax Planning 2016/17* (Bloomsbury Professional).

Focus

Both EIS shares and AIM listed shares potentially may be more volatile; and they may be more difficult to liquidate.

OUTRIGHT GIFTS

True outright gifts

12.8 Many people of moderate wealth will accept the present regime and will suffer the tax on discretionary trusts as the price to be paid for preserving family property from dissipation as a result of vesting at age 18, which can be compared against the advantages of outright gifts which are:

- simplicity;
- cheapness, in terms of legal fees saved;
- the transfer is a PET;
- holdover relief from CGT may be available under *TCGA 1992, s 165,* avoiding the complexities of *TCGA 1992, s 169B* that arise on gifts to settlor interested settlements.

The trouble with simplicity is its transparency. No formal deed is necessary to make a gift of cash: let the donor just write out a cheque and, mindful of the rule in *Curnock (Curnock's Personal Representative) v IRC* [2003] STC (SCD) 283, do it soon enough that it can be encashed before death. A gift of shares in a plc held in certificated form requires no more than a stock transfer, again delivered timeously to avoid the rule in *Rose, Re, Rose v IRC* [1952] 1 All ER 1217. For a gift of land to an adult, a transfer is enough; in Scotland, the date of the disposition is the effective date, not the later date of registration (*Marquess of Linlithgow and Earl of Hopetoun v HMRC* [2010] CSIH 19). A car or a valuable chattel may be given by simple delivery, but it might be safer to execute a deed of gift (and to be mindful of the reservation of benefit rules).

Many of these transactions generate little in professional fees but are effective none the less. If reliance is to be placed on the *s 21* exemption, what is needed is not so much a formal deed as a record of the intention to make regular gifts and its execution over a period of years. Good record keeping showing that these gifts are made out of excess income is essential (see **9.9**).

Unwise gifts

12.9 A gift is perceived as being unwise where family assets as a result can be at risk of claim in matrimonial proceedings or at the suit of creditors. Apart from that, gifts may be unwise where they prejudice APR or BPR. This was illustrated in the **Example 11.3** of Jason where the transferor no longer had control of the company at the time of a gift of an asset used by that company.

This is illustrated in the case of *Rosser v IRC* SpC 368, [2003] SSCD 311, discussed at **11.30**. It is also illustrated by the considerations that have just been described above in relation to the choice of asset to give away.

12.10 There are other circumstances where a gift may prove to have been unwise. The example of Willie in **Example 8.18** shows how gifts may be taxable in the context of a discretionary trust. Certainly, if an outright gift has been made nearly seven years ago and the transferor is considering establishing a trust now, which will be treated as a discretionary one under the rules in *FA 2006*, it makes sense to allow the seven years from the earlier gift to run off so that it does not affect the calculation of the hypothetical transfer, see the example of Celia at **Example 8.3** where a failed PET came to light.

Care needs to be taken when money is gifted into a joint bank account for the donor and donee. Even if there is an intention to make the gift, but if the account is operated so that the donor potentially can withdraw the full amount, there might be a reservation of benefit and the whole account may remain within the donor's estate for IHT purposes (see *Sillars v IRC* (2004) STC (STD) 180 and *Matthews v Revenue and Customs Commissioners* [2012] UKFTT 658 (TC)).

Example 12.9—Failed PET: a gift that should not have been made

Henry, whose late wife had used her nil rate band in full, settled £400,000 on discretionary trusts on 18 June 2008. On 22 July 2013, he gave his daughter Jennifer a cheque for £160,000. When he died on 30 June 2016 his estate was £500,000 and had the benefit neither of APR nor BPR. The chargeable transfer to the discretionary trust was more than seven years before the death and therefore itself fell out of aggregation with the estate at death. However as there was a chargeable transfer followed by a PET, there is a potential trap for the unwary advisor.

The PET in 2013 was less than three years before the death and outside the scope of taper relief. IHT on the PET is calculated by reference to the situation on the day that it was made. On that date the cumulative total of transfers was £400,000, so IHT on the failed PET is based on £560,000. The nil rate band is that on death, £325,000, leaving all of the £160,000 in charge at 40%, tax therefore £64,000.

The estate for IHT purposes is £500,000. The failed PET of £160,000 must be taken into account. After allowing for the nil rate band in force at the date of death of £325,000, the tax is £134,000 (ie £500,000 – (£325,000 – £160,000) × 40%). This liability is in addition to the IHT on the failed PET.

The situation could have been better if the gift had not been made and instead there had been equivalent provision by will. Assuming that the

£160,000 had not been spent and that none of the income from it was saved, the estate at death might then have been £660,000. The tax on that would be £134,000. There would have been no failed PET and therefore no tax charge on it.

The moral of the story is that someone who has made a substantial chargeable transfer must weigh up quite carefully the advantages of early giving and the risk that a charge on his estate may apply by virtue of *s 7(1)*. Lifetime gifting has the advantages of using annual exemptions.

For a time, it seemed that if a taxpayer made a mistaken gift, there was some scope for 'putting the toothpaste back in the tube' by relying on the principle in *Hastings-Bass Deceased, Hastings v CIR* [1974] 2 All ER 193. If, say, trustees had mistakenly appointed out funds on the wrong day, they could apply to have the deed set aside on the ground that they had not appreciated the full effect of the document when entering into it. Thus, Abacus Trust Co were twice before the courts, once with NSPCC and again with Barr, to seek help.

In *Sieff v Fox* [2005] WLR 3811 Lloyd LJ reformulated the *Hastings-Bass* principle as it relates to exercise by trustees of their discretion. The court will interfere '… if it is clear that [the trustees] would not have acted as they did had they not failed to take into account considerations which they ought to have … or taken into account considerations which they ought not …' He also observed that it might help the court if HMRC did not always decline the invitation to take part when such matters were litigated.

In *Tax Bulletin* 83 (June 2006), HMRC indicated that they would in future consider joining in litigation if much tax is in issue. They feel that where, as in *Abacus Trust Co (Isle of Man) Ltd v NSPCC* [2001] STC 1344, the trustee takes tax advice but fails correctly to implement it, there should be no relief. That would (though of course the *Bulletin* does not use such language) effectively blow many such cases out of the water. A mistake as to the intended tax effect of a document is unlikely to be the subject of rectification by the court (see *Allnutt and another v Wilding and others* [2007] EWCA Civ 412).

Litigation was joined in *Pitt v Holt* [2010] EWHC 45 (Ch) and *Futter and Futter* [2011] EWCA Civ 197, see the recent Supreme Court decision in *Pitt v HMRC; Futter v HMRC* [2013] UKSC 26.

In *Futter* the trustees of the two discretionary trusts exercised their power of advancement with the intention of transferring assets out of the settlement in such a way as to avoid a charge to CGT. The trustees' decision was made following professional advice which overlooked the provision in *s 2(4)* which provides that allowable losses within a settlement cannot be set off against gains attributed to beneficiaries, thereby resulting in unexpected CGT charges.

The Supreme Court unanimously dismissed the trustees' appeal and held that the trustees' exercise of the power of advancement had been valid and that it would be contrary to principle and authority to set aside the decision by trustees who acted on wrong professional advice.

In *Pitt* the issue was whether a transfer of assets into a settlement can be set aside. Mrs Pitt, whose husband suffered serious head injuries in an accident in 1990, on advice of solicitors, transferred the damages received, into a settlement. However the form of settlement suffered substantial IHT liabilities. Mrs Pitt applied to the Court to set aside the settlement and a related settlement.

The Supreme Court unanimously upheld the appeal, holding that a voluntary disposition can be set aside on the grounds of equity. Based on the facts of the case the settlement could have been drafted so as to fall under the definitions of 'disabled trusts' under *s 89*. This approach was confirmed in the recent case of *Kennedy v Kennedy* [2014] EWHC 4129 Ch.

More subtle schemes

12.11 The steady rise in house prices has forced planners to explore ways of sheltering the home from IHT. At its least aggressive, this may involve the gift of a share in the home to a child who continues to live there and is likely to remain permanently.

If the sale is to an unconnected third party, pre-owned asset tax (POAT) will not be a problem, though it will otherwise be, unless the transaction took place before 7 March 2005, or (which is rather contrived) the consideration is not for money or readily convertible into money (*SI 2005/724, reg 5*).

More adventurous is the creation of a lease, followed by the sale of the property and a gift of the proceeds of that sale. This level of planning must carry a health warning and must be carefully executed.

A variant of this idea is the sale of a share in the house followed by gift of the proceeds, but again it will have to be to a stranger, or not for cash, to avoid POAT.

Boldest of all is:

- the sale of the house (or perhaps an investment property) to a spouse;
- the price is satisfied by a debt; and
- the debt is given away (eg to adult children).

It has been argued that there was no gift with reservation, because:

- a sale is not a gift;
- the deduction should be allowable, unless *FA 1986, s 103* happens to be an issue; there will potentially be LBTT to pay, but no POAT, because it is an excluded transaction.

However *FA 2013* includes new IHT provisions which amend *s 162(4)* and *(5)* and disallow a deduction from the value of an estate for liabilities owed by the deceased on death in the following circumstances:

- excluded property – no deduction will be allowed for a liability to the extent that it has been incurred directly or indirectly to acquire property which is excluded from the charge to IHT. However, where the acquired property has been disposed of or where the liability is greater than the value of the excluded property, the deduction may be allowed providing certain conditions are met – see new *s 162A*; or
- where the liability has been incurred to acquire assets on which a relief such as BPR, APR or woodlands relief is due, the liability will be taken to reduce the value of those assets that can qualify for relief. The deduction for the loan will be matched against the assets acquired and relief will be restricted to the net value of the assets. Any excess liability will be allowable as a deduction against the estate in general subject to the new rule about unpaid debts – see new *s 162B*; or
- a deduction for a liability will be allowed only to the extent that it is repaid to the creditor, unless it is shown that there is a commercial reason for not repaying the liability and it is not left unpaid as part of arrangements to get a tax advantage – see new *s 175 A*.

The measure has effect for transfers of value, including transfers arising on death, made on or before 17 July 2013 the date on which *FA 2013* received Royal Assent. The provisions in *s 162B* dealing with liabilities in relation to relievable property only apply to liabilities incurred on or after 6 April 2013.

DISABLED PERSONS' TRUSTS

12.12 Disabled persons' interests ('DPI') escaped some of the changes in *FA 2006*. The tax code for DPIs is complex and confusing following a series of changes in *FA 2006, FA 2013* and *FA 2014*.

There has long been a code for disabled trusts, which has been little used because it was inflexible and many of the advantages could be achieved through normal discretionary trusts.

Original *s 89* Disabled Persons Interest

12.13 The original DPI is defined in *s 89 IHTA 1984*:

'(1) This section applies to settled property transferred into settlement after 9 March 1981 and held on trusts –

(a) under which, during the life of a disabled person, no interest in possession in the settled property subsists, and

(b) which secure that not less than half of the settled property which is applied during his lifetime is applied for his benefit.

(2) For the purposes of this Act the person mentioned in subsection (1) above shall be treated as beneficially entitled to an interest in possession in the settled property.

(3) The trusts on which settled property is held shall not be treated as falling outside subsection (1) above by reason only of the powers conferred on the trustees by *section 32* of the *Trustee Act 1925* or *section 33* of the *Trustee Act (Northern Ireland) 1958* (powers of advancement).

(4) The reference in subsection (1) above to a disabled person is, in relation to any settled property, a reference to a person who, when the property was transferred into settlement, was—

(a) incapable, by reason of mental disorder within the meaning of the Mental Health Act 1983, of administering his property or managing his affairs, or

(b) in receipt of an attendance allowance, or

(c) in receipt of a disability living allowance'

Therefore until 22 March 2006 only discretionary trusts qualified as DPIs under *s 89 IHTA*.

Finance Act 2006 changes

12.14 *Finance Act 2006* introduced three further types of DPIs:

- *IHTA 1984, s 89A* – self-settlement on discretionary trust on or after 22 March 2006 by person with a condition expected to lead to a disability;
- *IHTA 1984, s 89B(1)(c)* – DPI on interest in possession created by anyone during the lifetime of a settlor on or after 22 March 2006 for the benefit of a disabled person; and
- *IHTA 1984, s 89(B)(1)(d)* – self-settlement on interest in possession trust on or after 22 March 2006 by person with a condition expected to lead to a disability.

Therefore after *FA 2006* there were four different DPIs. A transfer into these types of trust therefore is treated as a potentially exempt transfer for IHT rather than a chargeable transfer. In addition these types of trust do not suffer ten yearly charges or exit charges for IHT.

IHTA 1984, s 49(1) provides that the disabled person will be deemed to be the beneficial owner of the trust fund with the result that the trust fund will be aggregated with the disabled person's other assets on death.

Following changes introduced by *FA 2014 s 60 a* capital gains tax free uplift on death under *TCGA 1992, s 72* applies to DPIs with underlying interests in possessions for deaths on or after 5 December 2013.

Focus

- A major disincentive for creating *s 89* trusts was that half the income had to be paid to the disabled person, thereby making it less flexible than discretionary trusts. Following *FA 2013* this is now even more restrictive, as for DPIs created on or after 8 April 2014, all the capital needs to be applied for the disabled beneficiary subject to an "annual limit" of the lesser of £3,000 or 3% of the settled property.
- The potential double charge to IHT and CGT on the death of the disabled person with an interest in possession in the settled fund was another disadvantage. The CGT disadvantage has been addressed in *FA 2014 s 60.*

Section 89A – self-settlement under *FA 2006*

12.15 This type of trust was introduced to permit persons to provide for themselves in the anticipation of a future disability. This type of trust is useful when someone suffers from a degenerative illness.

The legislation defines this type of DPI as follows:

'(1) This section applies to property transferred by a person ("A") into settlement on or after 22nd March 2006 if—

(a) A was beneficially entitled to the property immediately before transferring it into settlement,

(b) A satisfies the Commissioners for Her Majesty's Revenue and Customs that, when the property was transferred into settlement, A had a condition that it was at that time reasonable to expect would have such effects on A as to lead to A becoming—

(i) a person falling within *section 89(4)(a)* above,

(ii) in receipt of an attendance allowance mentioned in *s 89(4)(b)* above, or

(iii) in receipt of a disability living allowance mentioned in *s 89(4)(c)* above by virtue of entitlement to the care component at the highest or middle rate, and

(c) the property is held on trusts—

(i) under which, during the life of A, no interest in possession in the settled property subsists, and

(ii) which secure that Conditions 1 and 2 are met.

(2) Condition 1 is that if any of the settled property is applied during A's life for the benefit of a beneficiary, it is applied for the benefit of A.

(3) Condition 2 is that any power to bring the trusts mentioned in *subsection (1)(c)* above to an end during A's life is such that, in the event of the power being exercised during A's life, either—

(a) A or another person will, on the trusts being brought to an end, be absolutely entitled to the settled property, or

(b) on the trusts being brought to an end, a disabled person's interest within *section 89B(1)(a)* or *(c)* below will subsist in the settled property.

(4) If this section applies to settled property transferred into settlement by a person, the person shall be treated as beneficially entitled to an interest in possession in the settled property.'

This type of DPI has to be a discretionary trust settled during someone's lifetime in expectation of a disability for his own benefit provided:

- If any capital is distributed during the settlor's lifetime, it will be distributed for the settlor's benefit, or
- If the trust is brought to an end during the settlor's lifetime, the settlor is entitled to the trust fund, or someone else is entitled to the trust fund, so that it will form their estate for IHT purposes.

Alternatively the settlement can be brought to an end in favour of another DPI's interest.

Section 89B as introduced by *Finance Act 2006*

12.16 *Section 89B of IHTA 1984* extends *IHTA 1984, ss 89 and 89A* to include interest in possessions to qualify as DPIs.

'(1) In this Act "disabled person's interest" means—

(a) an interest in possession to which a person is under section 89(2) above treated as beneficially entitled,

(b) an interest in possession to which a person is under section 89A(4) above treated as beneficially entitled,

(c) an interest in possession in settled property (other than an interest within paragraph (a) or (b) above) to which a disabled person becomes beneficially entitled on or after 22nd March 2006, or

(d) an interest in possession in settled property (other than an interest within paragraph (a) or (b) above) to which a person ("A") is beneficially entitled if—

(i) A is the settlor,

(ii) A was beneficially entitled to the property immediately before transferring it into settlement,

(iii) A satisfies Her Majesty's Commissioners for Revenue and Customs as mentioned in *section 89A(1)(b)* above,

(iv) the settled property was transferred into settlement on or after 22nd March 2006, and

(v) the trusts on which the settled property is held secure that, if any of the settled property is applied during A's life for the benefit of a beneficiary, it is applied for the benefit of A.'

Section 89B(1)(c) applies to interest in possession trusts created by anyone during the settlor's lifetime for the benefit of a disabled person. This type of trust cannot be created on death, as the provisions in *IHTA 1984, s 49A* which create immediate post death interests take priority.

Section 89(1)(d) is similar to *s 89A IHTA 1984* in that it allows for self-settlement in expectation of a disability, but on interest in possession trusts rather than discretionary trusts. Again this type of trust will be outside the relevant property regime for IHT.

New DPIs created or additions to existing DPIs on or after 8 April 2013

12.17 *Section 216 and Sch 44 of FA 2013* made the following main amendments to the existing regime:

- alignment of income and capital requirements imposed by the income tax, capital gains tax and IHT treatment for vulnerable beneficiaries (see **12.19**)
- inclusion in the definition of a DPI of persons who are in receipt of the new Personal Independence Payment.

A statutory meaning of 'disabled person' was amended by *FA 2013* with effect from 6 April 2013 (*FA 2005, Sch 1A*). A disabled person therefore is someone who falls into one or more of the following categories:

(a) incapable of administering his property or managing his affairs by reason of mental disorder within the meaning of the *Mental Health Act 1983*; or

(b) receiving attendance allowance; or

(c) receiving a disability living allowance by virtue of entitlement to the care component at the highest or middle rate; or

(d) receiving personal independence payment by virtue of entitlement to the daily living component; or

(e) receiving an increased disablement pension; or

(f) receiving constant attendance allowance; or

(g) receiving armed forces independence payment.

The requirements as to the allowances and payments etc in (b) to (g) above are set out in the legislation (*Sch 1A, paras 2–7*).

The legislation is confusing, as the 'new definition' of disabled person applies from 6 April 2013 and not 8 April 2013 when the *Welfare Reform Act 2013* was enacted. The new rules relating to income and capital requirements only came into force on 17 July 2013. This means that DPIs created between 6 April 2013 and 17 July 2013 will have the new definition of disabled person but the old rules as to income and capital conditions.

Income and Capital Requirements for DPIs

12.18 For lifetime DPIs created prior to 8 April 2013 only 50% of capital had to be given to the disabled person. This meant that prior to *FA 2013* DPIs could be set up for a disabled person but with a wide class of beneficiaries, for example to include siblings, spouses, widows/widowers and children with the benefit that the trust did not qualify as a relevant property trust. As distributions now are limited to the 'annual limit' (see below), families will have to think carefully whether to opt for DPIs.

For DPIs created between 22 March 2006 and 7 April 2013 distributions to beneficiaries other than the disabled beneficiary which exceed the 50% rule and were made during the lifetime of the disabled person will be deemed to be potentially exempt transfers by the disabled beneficiary.

Finance Act 2013 amended the income and 50% capital rules in that for trusts created from 8 April 2013 all the capital needs to be applied for the disabled person subject to the exception of the 'annual limit' which is the lesser of £3,000 or 3% of the settled property applied for the benefit of another person during each tax year.

Distributions to beneficiaries other than the disabled beneficiary in excess of the 'annual limit' on or after 8 April 2013 will be subject to IHT exit charges on the excess above the annual limit.

Special income tax and capital gains tax treatment

12.19 The special income and capital gains tax regime for vulnerable beneficiaries introduced in *FA 2005, ss 23–45* applies to all four types of DPIs (see **8.2** and **8.3** above). Care needs to be taken that the capital and income requirements post 8 April 2013 are not breached, as otherwise the special treatment does not apply.

DPIs qualify for special treatment for income tax and capital gains tax purposes, if a vulnerable person election has been made and is effective for the tax year in question (*FA 2005, s 34(2)*). The election has to be made on Form VPE1 and signed jointly by the trustees and the beneficiary. The election is irrevocable and will continue until one of the following events occur:

- the vulnerable beneficiary ceases to be a vulnerable person;
- the trusts in relation to which the election is made cease to qualify; or
- the trusts are terminated.

On the occurrence of any of the above events the trustees are required to give notice to HMRC within 90 days of the event.

Where a claim for special treatment has been made, the regime provides that no more tax is paid in respect of the relevant income and gains of the trust for the tax year in question than would be paid had the income and gains accrued directly to the beneficiary.

The income tax liability of the trust is reduced to the actual income tax liability the beneficiary would pay if the income had been received directly in his own right. However the liability remains the liability of the relevant trust; it is merely the calculation of the liability that is affected.

For the special capital gains tax treatment to apply, the following conditions must be satisfied:

- Chargeable gains arise in the tax year to the trustees on the disposal of trust property held on qualifying trusts for the benefit of a vulnerable person.
- The trustees would be chargeable to CGT in respect of those gains were it not for the application of *FA 2005, Ch 4*.
- The trustees are resident in the UK during any part of the tax year.
- The trustees make a claim for special treatment in the tax year.

If these conditions are fulfilled, the trustees and beneficiary are treated as if the chargeable gains had arisen to the latter, and he self-assesses accordingly. Thus, assuming the beneficiary had no other capital gains the trustees would get the benefit of the full capital gains tax exemption (for 2016/17 £11,100) rather than the maximum reduced allowance for trusts (for 2016/17 £5,550); if a beneficiary has capital gains tax losses these would also be taken into account to reduce the tax charge on the trust. The beneficiary can then reclaim the tax back from the trustees (see HMRC Trusts, Settlements and Estates Manual TSEM3415).

The special treatment does not apply in the tax year the beneficiary dies.

PROTECTED GIFTS WITHOUT TRUSTS

Pensions for grandchildren

12.20 Notwithstanding the rules for age 18-to-25 trusts, many taxpayers who wish to provide for young members of the family will insist on a late vesting age and will not wish the fund to be subject to the complications that are set out in **Chapter 8**.

One possibility is opened up by the liberalisation of the pensions regime. Quite simply, assuming that no other pension provision has been made for the grandchild, the grandparent can set aside limited contributions to a pension policy for a grandchild, knowing that the fund cannot be touched for very many years. The paperwork with many of the recognised investment houses and investment trusts is simple and the fees moderate. Pensions (of moderate size) are favoured by the government and, although there is no recovery of tax on dividend income within the fund, freedom from repayable income tax and from capital gains tax will combine to help the fund to grow. If the premiums are, as would be likely, paid on a regular basis it may be possible for the grandparents (or their executors) to claim relief for all of the gifts under *s 21*.

Pensions for young children

12.21 Generally, apart from the Child Trust Fund, Junior ISAs and NISAs described above, there is little scope for parents, rather than grandparents, to make tax-efficient provision for their children under the age of 18. The normal rules in the *Income Tax (Trading and Other Income) Act 2005, s 624* and following, especially *ITTOIA 2005, s 629*, prevent the arrangement from achieving any saving of income tax. For many years gains of trustees for children enjoyed the same low rate as individuals. The redefinition of 'settlor interested' for the purposes of CGT briefly had the effect of substituting the settlor's top tax rate. However *TCGA 1992, s 77* which imposed that rule, was no longer needed following the 18% rate of CGT and was repealed. The introduction of the 28% rate for all trusts has removed some of the attraction of trusts for young people.

However, parents, like grandparents, may within overall limits contribute to pension policies for children, which fall outside the trust regime and achieve useful long-term savings. Care should be taken not to try to take this too far, by using 'family pension pots' to try to slide assets down the generations free of IHT: that possibility has been foreseen by the legislation. Given the uncertainty that must now affect existing Child Trust Fund investments, many may prefer pensions as the vehicle for saving for children.

Qualifying non-UK pension scheme (QNUPS)

12.22 On 15 February 2010 the *Inheritance Tax (Qualifying Non-UK Pension Schemes) Regulations 2010 (SI 2010/51)* came into force, which enable UK domiciled non-resident individuals to save for retirement outside the UK IHT net by transferring their pension into a new type of trust known as Qualifying non-UK Pension Schemes (QNUPS). The regulation applies from 6 April 2006.

While QNUPS do not benefit from the annual allowance for pension contributions of £40,000 (2014/15), they might be attractive to individuals who are not resident in the UK or who are exceeding their annual allowance.

This is a complex area and specialist advice needs to be sought.

Options

12.23 This is a contentious area and one that a general practitioner should not enter without specialist advice. The clear intent of the government, when introducing *FA 2006*, was to deprive the benefit of gift relief as a PET to anything other than an outright gift. However, many taxpayers find it very difficult to bring themselves to make outright gifts, for a variety of reasons. Where the donor wishes to retain some benefit from the gift, such as the income, the result is clear. It is a gift with reservation within *FA 1986, s 102* and following. It is thus ineffective as a means of saving IHT.

12.24 More subtly, a donor may not wish actually to receive any benefit himself from the thing given away, but may wish to restrict the dispositive powers of the donee. This could apply either to shares in a family company of which the donor was still an active working director or to land, part of the family farm and still farmed by the donor. Many taxpayers who have worked hard to assemble capital are reluctant to risk its dissipation by their children, whether through the financial inexperience or waywardness, financial or marital, of the donees.

12.25 One structure that may be imagined is that of a gift which, sooner or later, is followed by the grant by the donee of an option to the donor that would allow the donor to repurchase the asset either at its market value or at some predetermined value if certain circumstances were to arise. There is probably little abuse where the option can be exercised only at full market value, because the donee exchanges the original subject matter of the gift for full value and no economic benefit passes back to the donor. The situation is more difficult where the option price is determined at the outset or where it becomes clear from a course of dealing between the parties that the donor would never have made the original gift unless the donee had already agreed in principle to enter into the option.

Given the very wide interpretation of the expression 'to the entire exclusion of the donor and of any benefit to him by contract or otherwise' as set out in RI55, it is likely that a 'gift plus option' arrangement might be challenged under *FA 1986, s 102*. Planners should also bear in mind the decision in the *Smith* case, noted in **Chapter 7**, on the issue of associated operations.

Family limited partnerships

12.26 For a time practitioners explored the idea of a partnership within the family in which younger members could enjoy a share but subject to carefully drawn limitations to ensure that they never actually got to enjoy the money unless and until their elders approved. It is fair to say that this structure is not for everyone. Chief among the problems has been investment, where the received wisdom is that the partner who manages the family money will need help from managers who are registered on the Financial Services Register. The cost of a dedicated adviser will put the arrangement out of the reach of most families and in any case reasonably wealthy families are often headed by an entrepreneur who would like to control the entity anyway. However, over time it may become possible to devise a form of partnership that does actually work and can be created and run at moderate cost.

Problems can arise in relation to IHT. Partnerships are regarded as opaque rather than transparent, with the partners holding a 'chose in action' in the partnership share. Shares in a holding company will not qualify for BPR when held in a partnership even though they would if held personally.

A further problem may arise on the death of a partner, as the underlying partnership share will not qualify for the CGT uplift on death is *TCGA 1992, s 62*.

TRADITIONAL PROTECTED GIFTS

Existing interest in possession trusts and the TSI facility

12.27 Following the enactment of *FA 2006*, trustees should have reviewed the interests of beneficiaries, identifying those interests that were interests in possession on 21 March 2006 and retaining the old IHT treatment where that was beneficial. Trustees should also have considered the possibility of replacing existing interests in possession with Transitional Serial Interests as described at **7.27** and in the example of Marian and her surrender of the life interest.

The facility expired on 5 October 2008, although a limited TSI facility still exists in respect of spouses and civil partners, and in respect of life insurance contracts (*IHTA 1984, ss 49D, 49E*).

A&M settlements as part of the relevant property regime

12.28 For many trustees, the main issue will now be extraction of value from the trust with the benefit of holdover relief from CGT. Care needs to be taken, especially if the trustees hold property.

Policy trusts

12.29 These were examined in **Chapter 7**. *Section 46A* deals only with life interest policy trusts that already existed on 22 March 2006, by and large preserving their status. Trustees of policies, perhaps more than those holding any other property, tend to take a relaxed view of their duties. They may not even know that they are appointed or that the policy is a trust with requirements as to compliance like any other. It is therefore possible that such trustees may have taken no action at all following the enactment of *FA 2006* and in particular will not have tried to vary the existing rights under the policies. In many cases, the best advice may have been to 'leave well alone'. As was noted at **7.41**, where the existing trusts are on an A&M basis it will have been important, as for any other 'ex-A&M trust', to see who the beneficiaries were and whether the trust should have been varied so as to accelerate vesting age. In one sense, it is still not too late to take action; such trusts have only recently entered the relevant property regime and the IHT charge on exit will not yet be significant, though the incidental costs of release may be.

There is one major conceptual difficulty for clients taking out policies and writing them in trust. Where the premiums are paid on a regular basis the donor may seek exemption under *s 19* or *s 21* (but not under *s 20* which refers to outright gifts only). An exempt transfer is not a chargeable one. It follows that the gift of a policy written in trust will often be outside the complications of **Chapter 8**. Previously, it was important to take care not to breach the limits described at **6.4** for reporting lifetime transfers, but the higher limits under the Regulations described in **Chapter 6** largely remove this worry.

Focus

- If the life insurance is intended to fund a potential IHT liability, awareness is needed of the new restrictions introduced by *FA 2013*.
- There has been no limit on the amount of premiums that may be paid into such 'qualifying policies'.
- A premium cap of £3,600 per year applies since April 2013, although policies which were in force then are excluded.

Discounted gift schemes

12.30 These arrangements became more popular after *FA 2006*. A capital redemption bond is put in trust. It leaves the estate of the settlor. There is an immediate discount, calculated by reference to the liability to make repayments, according to the sex, age and health, etc of the settlor. Withdrawals of 5% may be taken. The balance of the investment is a chargeable transfer for IHT. There are two separate interests, thus avoiding reservation of benefit; the settlor has no access to the balance of the investment. The key issue is the value of what is given away.

HMRC have considered discounted gift schemes; see the technical note posted to their website dated 1 May 2007. For a clear insight into the way that HMRC view such schemes, see IHTM20401 to IHTM20635, which contain not only a description of the schemes but also a 'checklist' of schemes in common use. It is considered that the taking out of the plan and the making of the gift are linked, as was found by the Special Commissioner in the similar, but slightly different scheme employed in *Smith v Revenue and Customs Commissioners* [2008] STC 1649.

The issue was fully explored in *HMRC v Bower and another (Executors of Bower Deceased)* [2009] STC 510. The deceased took out a life annuity in 2002, being then 90. She paid £73,000. The policy was issued to trustees of a settlement that she had created. She reserved rights to an annuity of 5%. She died within five months. That being within three years of the gift of the balance of the rights under the policy, there was a chargeable transfer of the amount of the gift. It was agreed that the gift was £73,000 less the value of the retained rights; but HMRC considered the value of the rights was negligible: £250, so the gift was of £72,750.

This contrasted with the insurance certificate, valuing the rights at £7,800, so the executors appealed to the Special Commissioner, who valued them at £4,200. That figure was arrived at by discounting the figure of £7,800 by one-third and by a further £1,000 for legal costs. HMRC appealed successfully to the High Court, which held that the Commissioner, in the absence of evidence, had gone too far in deciding the value.

Thus where the settlor is, by age or for any other reason uninsurable at the date of gift, the value of the retained rights will be nominal and virtually all the bond will be the gift. That will be true, see below, whenever the settlor is 90 or over. The May 2007 note explains the HMRC attitude to joint settlements and the apportionment of any discount. In the past, valuation was seldom necessary but that has changed now that the settlement is a chargeable transfer. The old procedure of lumping both discounts together is no longer appropriate. Instead, the discount must be calculated for each settlor in turn. In HMRC Brief 65/08, dated 31 December 2008, it was announced that the valuation rate of interest for discounted gift schemes, ie the discount rate (which the Commissioner had not felt able to use in *Bower*) would be reduced from 6.75% to 5.25% pa with effect from 1 February 2009. In HMRC Brief 21/09, issued after the High Court ruling in *Bower*, HMRC understandably reaffirmed their view of the valuation basis where the settlor is uninsurable or is (actually or for underwriting purposes) 90 or over at the transaction date. Only a nominal value will be attributed to the retained rights. Nothing in the legislation allows any withdrawals actually taken between the date of the gift and the death to be taken into account and set against the sum invested in the scheme.

The *Bower* case was confirmed in the recent First-tier Tribunal case of *Watkins and Harvey v HMRC* [2011] UKFTT 745 (TC).

Flexible reversion trusts

12.31 There is a constant desire among donors, which the life assurance industry tries to satisfy, to eat one's cake and still have it; to make an effective gift but to retain some 'comeback' if circumstances change. One such structure is the 'flexible reversion trust'. It is actually a settlement of a string of single premium endowment policies, but for clarity imagine a consignment of several cases of wine the contents of which will mature individually in successive years. The settlement of them, say for grandchildren, is a chargeable transfer, so best limited to the available nil rate band. The settlor retains the right, at maturity, to the proceeds (if he is still alive) but this is not treated by HMRC as the reservation of a benefit; nor is any payment to the settlor of those proceeds subject to an exit charge.

The trustees have wide powers, including the power to give one of the policies *before* maturity to beneficiaries or the power to defer maturity. As (it is hoped) the policy increases in value with time, that increase belongs to the trust, not the settlor. Although this is an insurance scheme, it is not limited to investment in life policies, so could admit some flexibility, though doubtless not actually into wine. It appears to have achieved a successful 'shearing' of the right to receive the maturity proceeds, not given away, from all the other rights under the policies: something possible with an insurance product but much harder to achieve with any other asset.

Lifetime gifts into trusts since FA 2006

12.32 Trusts, except disabled persons' trusts, set up by life transfers after 22 March 2006 are relevant property trusts and their creation is a chargeable transfer, unless exempt. This will probably have two effects. The taxpayer of substantial means may in the past have been willing to delay making gifts on the basis that a large gift made into an interest in possession trust or an A&M trust would have been potentially exempt and, if he survived it by seven years, substantial value could be transferred whilst retaining safeguards over the capital.

12.33 *FA 2006* has curtailed that facility. Transferors will probably not wish to pay IHT on the establishing of lifetime trusts and will not want the complications of grossing up. Many will therefore limit their generosity to settlements that are within the nil rate band. This will lend urgency to the situation because seven years must elapse after the making of a nil rate band discretionary trust before another one can be made that will not be 'tainted' by the existence of the prior trust, leading to the complications that are described in **Chapter 8**.

12.34 The second effect of the rule that virtually all new lifetime trusts are chargeable will be that, below a certain level, many taxpayers will decide that the complexities of a discretionary trust are simply not worthwhile even though the burden of IHT on a nil rate band trust for the first ten years is nil and, as has been seen in **Chapter 8**, the burden of tax on quite a substantial trust is only moderate. It is therefore likely that fewer small trusts will be set up because their administrative costs will be unacceptable.

Chapter 13

Wills and estate planning

SIGNPOSTS

- **EU Succession Regulation** – Increased mobility means that testators will have assets in other EU states. Although the UK has not opted into the Regulation, the rules may still affect the treatment of the testator's estate (see **13.1–13.2**).
- **Nil rate band discretionary trusts** – For many years it was common to include such trusts for IHT saving. Following the introduction of the transferable nil rate band the emphasis has shifted and asset protection often is the main objective of setting up such trusts (see **13.3–13.12**).
- **The residence nil rate band** – An additional nil rate band, the residence nil rate band (RNRB), will be available from 6 April 2017, when a residence is 'closely inherited'. This will impact will drafting (see **13.13**).
- **Wills leaving estate to surviving spouse** – This can be done either by an outright absolute gift or by passing the estate into an IPDI for the surviving spouse (see **13.13–13.18**).
- **Trusts for bereaved minors** – These trusts escape ongoing IHT charges for as long as the interests vest absolutely at age 18 (see **13.19**).
- **18-to-25 trusts** – The maximum IHT costs of such arrangements are 4.2% of the value of the fund (see **13.20**).
- **BPR, APR and woodland relief** – Careful will drafting avoids wasting these reliefs, especially where they overlap with the spouse exemption (see **13.22–13.28**).
- **Exempt gifts on death** – These include gifts to charity and gifts of heritage property (see **13.29–13.37**).
- **Post-death variations and disclaimers** – *IHTA 1984, s 142* permits families and advisors to 're-structure' the beneficial interests under a will or in the event of intestacy put provisions akin to a will in place (see **13.29–13.52**).

EU SUCCESSION REGULATION NO 650/2012

Background

13.1 The Succession Regulation (SR) is important in relation to testators who have assets in other EU countries. The UK opted out of the SR, but it applies to all other states in the EU, except Ireland, who also opted out, and Denmark, who did not participate. The SR was adopted on 4 July 2012 and most of the underlying rules took effect from 17 August 2015. The SR is also known as 'Brussels IV'. Despite the fact that the UK opted out, practitioners need to understand the underlying rules, as it will affect the devolution of someone's estate with assets in another EU country.

The governing law

13.2 The general rule is that if a testator is domiciled in Scotland, his estate will be governed by Scots law, and any assets abroad are governed by the law of the country where the property is situated. In contrast the SR provides that the law of the country where the testator has his 'habitual residence' shall apply. Article 22 of the SR states that alternatively a testator can choose the law of their nationality – this will replace 'habitual residence'. As the UK has not signed up to the Regulation, the SR provides that member states will still accept renvoi (the process by which a court adopts the rules of a foreign jurisdiction with respect to any conflict of laws that arises) from testators who are habitually resident in Scotland, England or Wales, unless such testators have made a choice of law to apply to their estate.

Example 13.1—UK national with holiday home in France

Simon is a UK national and is habitually resident in Scotland, but he has a holiday home in France.

If no choice of law has been made in his will, Scots law will apply to his moveable and immovable property in the UK, while France will accept renvoi and French law will apply to his French property. If, on the other hand, his will states that the Scots law shall apply to his entire estate, the French property will pass according to Scots law.

If Simon is habitually resident in France, and assuming he kept his UK nationality, he can also make a declaration for Scots law to apply.

> **Focus**
>
> - The SR does not determine which tax law applies and it therefore is important to ascertain the tax consequences of the chosen jurisdiction. For example, in Germany each beneficiary has the equivalent of a nil rate band, which depends on whether they are related to the testator, and if so how closely they are related.
> - It is important to take tax advice in the country where the asset is situated or which the testator elects to apply.

THE NIL RATE BAND

Nil rate band discretionary trusts

13.3 It was for many years common for the public to avoid straightforward mirror wills by which spouses (or civil partners) left everything to each other with remainder to children. Before the introduction of the right to transfer the nil rate band, such simple wills were tax-inefficient because they failed to use the nil rate band of the first of the spouses or partners to die. Instead a more complicated structure was used, seldom fully understood by those implementing it. This was inefficient in a different way, imposing significant extra work on taxpayers, on the one hand; and on HMRC, because of the multiplicity of forms to be processed that yielded little or no tax (unless the taxpayer committed some procedural error, which it was the tiresome duty of HMRC to spot and to penalise). All this became largely unnecessary by virtue of *FA 2008, s 10* and *Sch 4*, which are fully discussed in the next chapter.

While the introduction of the transferable nil rate band might have been the end of nil rate band discretionary trusts, they are still useful in certain circumstances. For example if advising a widow or widower who has remarried, a nil rate band discretionary trust can be used to protect the transferable nil rate band of a predeceased spouse, which would otherwise be wasted.

If nil rate band trusts are being incorporated into wills for clients who own property it is essential to check how the title to the property is held to see if the title contains a survivorship destination and if this should be removed (see *Chadda and Others (Tobin's Executors) v RCC* [2014] UKFTT 1061 (TC)).

The old 'debt' or 'charge' schemes

13.4 The solution commonly devised before the transferable nil rate band was a gift of the nil rate band to trustees coupled with a provision that that gift need not be satisfied by immediate payment, but might be satisfied either (and there were significant differences of approach here):

- by taking a charge over other assets in the estate; or
- by accepting a promise of payment from the surviving spouse or civil partner.

The difficulty was that few families really understood the structure (for examples in related fields, see *Wolff v Wolff and Wolff* [2004] STC 1633, in which the claimants were forced to apply to the court to set aside a reversionary lease scheme on the grounds that they had made a mistake as to the legal effect of the arrangement. See also *Bhatt v Bhatt and others* [2009] EWHC 734 (Ch), as to the difficulties for 'ordinary' people in engaging in tax planning). To work well, the scheme needed the executors to take certain action at certain times: many cases are now coming to light where this was not done, or was skimped.

The effect of *Finance Act 1986, s 103* ('Treatment of certain debts and incumbrances') on the scheme was even less well understood. It was litigated in *Phizackerley v IRC* [2007] SpC 00591, where the Special Commissioner had to decide whether deduction of the liability under the scheme was prevented by *FA 1986, s 103*. He noted that *s 103* prevents the deduction of the debt where, and to the extent that, the consideration given for the debt or incumbrance consists of 'property derived from the Deceased' and held that:

- On the face of it, the half share in the house in issue was indeed derived from the deceased. It was the subject matter of a disposition made by the deceased.
- The debt incurred by the deceased in favour of the trustees of the nil rate band was not deductible.

The Special Commissioner dismissed the taxpayer's appeal.

Is the debt or charge scheme any use, now?

13.5 The decision in *Phizackerley* did not totally invalidate the debt or charge scheme. The structure should not be entered into where the family would benefit more from the provisions of a transferable nil rate band, as will usually be the case. It will fail if the parties behave as if the nil rate band fund was always, and would remain, at the disposal of the surviving spouse. The surviving spouse must understand that the value comprised in the discretionary trust *is not his/her money*. There must always be the risk, from the point of view of the surviving spouse, that the trustees could at any time call in the loan.

Where, in relation to an existing scheme, the surviving spouse later decides to 'trade down' in property terms, the trustees must consider calling in their debt, and should encourage the surviving spouse to use his or her own resources to purchase and refurnish the replacement property. They may give assurances that the fund will not be dissipated, but should not compromise their discretion. This may also help to shield the family fund from the burden of nursing home fees. The surviving spouse should come to the trustees for help only when those resources are used up.

Note that if *s 103* had originally been a problem that was obviated by the imposition of a charge before assent to the surviving spouse, the sale of that property and the purchase of a new one with some help from the trustees throws the surviving spouse back into the *Phizackerley* situation: another reason to favour the use of an IPDI instead. Alternatively, the discretionary trustees could, instead of making a loan, join in as purchasers. Provided that two years had elapsed from the death, to prevent any relating back to the death, the trustees could then give the surviving spouse a formal right to occupy the share of the house that they had bought. It would not be aggregable with the free estate on the second death, but main residence relief would be secured.

It is prudent to review existing wills in light of the case of *Loring v Woodland Trust* [2013] EWHC 4400 Ch which is a useful decision on the interpretation of a nil rate band sum following the introduction of the transferable nil rate band. Here the testatrix made a will in 2001 leaving a nil rate band legacy with the residue passing to charity. The issue was whether the value of the nil rate band legacy was enhanced by the testator's husband's transferable nil rate band by a predeceased spouse ie a total of £650,000 rather than £325,000. As this depends on the wording of the will, practitioners are advised to review any nil rate band legacy clauses and compare them with HMRC's guidance at IHTM43065 to ascertain the value of a nil rate band legacy, as this may have unintended consequences on the value of the residue.

Avoiding *Phizackerley*: proof of contribution to the house by the spouse

13.6 Where it is for any reason appropriate to retain a pre-*FA 2008* form of will establishing a nil rate band discretionary trust, and *Phizackerley* issues arise, it must be increasingly common that, at some time during a marriage, particularly in the early years, both husband and wife will earn and pool those earnings. Most spouses will be able to claim, that they have made a contribution to the cost of the house and that the purchase of the house in joint names does not lead to the automatic conclusion that '*the funds must have been provided by the Deceased*'. The facts of *Phizackerley* can be distinguished where families can show that:

- both husband and wife worked at various times during the marriage;

- both directly or indirectly contributed to the cost of one home after another; and
- the family home that is in their joint ownership at the time of the death of the first of them to die is truly owned by them equally.

A serious issue to address is that *Finance Act 1986, s 103* contains no time limit. The debt which the executors seek to deduct from the estate of the second spouse to die is (see *s 103(1)*):

> 'subject to abatement to an extent proportionate to the value of any of the consideration for the debt or encumbrance which consisted of
>
> (a) property derived from the deceased; or
>
> (b) consideration (not being property derived from the deceased) given by any person who was at any time entitled to, or amongst whose resources there was at any time included, any property derived from the deceased.'

It matters not how long ago the gift was made. It could still be caught.

How will all this be proved? Some executors will be reluctant to carry out an expensive enquiry into transactions long ago. Beware of breaching the duty of care in delivering accounts under *IHTA 1984, s 216*. If there is any clear link between the debt which is to be deducted from the estate of the surviving spouse and a gift made, however long ago, by that spouse to the first spouse to die, *Phizackerley* can apply. This case increases the burden on executors and their advisers, and the risk of a penalty for failure to make proper enquiries.

The effect of *Phizackerley* on existing wills

13.7 The enactment of *FA 2008* no doubt triggered the rewriting of many wills. Many may choose to create an IPDI and achieve a transferable nil rate band. Subject to that, where there has been no gift of an interest in the house (which will usually be the relevant asset), it may not be necessary to change anything purely in the light of the decision in *Phizackerley*. If there has ever been a substantial gift, existing structures should be reviewed. The problem arises only where the donor spouse is the second to die: so in the common case of value transferred in lifetime by husband to wife, where she survives him, there is no problem.

Focus

- Nil rate band discretionary trusts are still useful in cases where asset protection is important, or where a widow/widower has remarried and the transferable nil rate band of the predeceased spouse would otherwise be wasted.

- Such trusts enable trustees to benefit a number of beneficiaries if and when they need funds. They offer greater flexibility than IPDIs.
- However, the disadvantage of the 45% income tax rate (2016/17) applicable to discretionary trusts and the administrative burden need to be considered carefully.

Procedural difficulties with existing structures

13.8 For the pre-*FA 2008* structures that remain, there may be difficulties of execution. Where, for example, the will has not been properly drawn and infant beneficiaries have interests in residue there can be difficulty in correcting the errors. Where there is a gift of the nil rate band, but no corresponding provision that that gift may be satisfied by an IOU it is not possible, by simple deed of variation, to put matters right. Any deed of variation, to be effective, must alter the *dispositions* of the estate of the testator, so the inclusion of the desired clauses must effectively ride on the back of another variation.

Even supposing the paperwork all to be correct, further difficulties arise both as to the intention of the parties and execution of the structure. The problem with intention is that, if the surviving spouse from the outset refuses to acknowledge that the debt is inevitably repayable and if the trustees go along with that, there is effectively a 'sham' because the parties have rejected the thinking behind the scheme. However, if the family are 'stuck' with an old will, there might almost be an advantage in suggesting that 'we never really meant/understood it' to get out of an old debt/charge scheme and into a transferable nil rate band situation.

At a less acute level, there may be simply inaccuracies or lapses which cause the scheme to fail. On the eventual death of the second spouse or civil partner it may be impossible to prove that appropriate formalities were put in place to recognise the debt. There may be no evidence that the trustees ever at any time considered calling it in. The trustees must recognise the realities of what is happening. They are lending an amount equal to the value, in many parts of Scotland, of a three or four-bedroom detached house. Trustees would not normally lend that amount of money without taking security. Trustees must therefore consider whether or not to take security. If they fail to do so they should have a reason for their failure.

There is certainly a risk that people will fall between two stools: the old structure fails for want of proper execution but it has been partly effective to use the nil rate band so that it is not transferable. The difficulty for advisers is that the ongoing trust may be administered by the family who may not remember all the advice given when it was set up; or it may not be possible to show that such advice was given; and yet if the scheme fails at the second death people may be quick to claim that the original adviser was at fault.

Practical issues arising out of existing debt or charge scheme structures

Choice of trustees

13.9 The choice of trustees is important. They should not be subject to the control of the surviving spouse. It is therefore helpful, but by no means essential, for one of the trustees to be independent. The trustees should have due regard for the requirements of the arrangement and should meet at reasonable intervals to consider whether or not to call in the debt. If left indefinitely, it can become statute barred. As far as the surviving spouse is concerned, there must always be a *frisson* of uncertainty that the trustees could call in the debt. Certainly, if the surviving spouse decides to move house the original loan should be repaid in full and the surviving spouse should then approach the trustees to ask for a fresh loan of such amount as is needed to finance the new purchase.

Liquidity

13.10 The next issue is the extent to which liquidity in the estate of the first to die should have been applied towards satisfying the gift of the nil rate band. Although there is no case precisely in point, it lends reality to the whole structure if the executors apply available securities and other savings in part satisfaction of the nil rate band so that the debt or charge is only for such sum as cannot be satisfied from the available liquid assets. That may be unpopular with the surviving spouse.

Interest and index linking

13.11 Interest may, but need not, be charged on the debt. In many instances the charging of interest will be tax neutral. Receipt of interest by the trustees of the nil rate band will attract income tax at 45%, whilst reducing the estate of the surviving spouse and thus saving IHT at 40%. At that point, therefore, the exercise seems not to be worthwhile. If, however, there are many beneficiaries of the nil rate band who, perhaps because they are young, do not pay income tax, there will be a saving because after expenses the trustees can make distributions of income to the non-taxpaying beneficiaries who will recover some or all of the tax thus paid.

Occasionally, the nil rate band is index linked. On final resolution of matters it is certainly arguable that the extra money so received is essentially payment, by reference to time, for the use of money and is therefore interest receivable at the time of repayment of the loan, even though it is calculated by reference to inflation or a house price index. Others argue to the contrary: there is no decided case directly in point. HMRC have litigated arguing that the extra money received represents interest which is subject to income tax. The case settled and uncertainty therefore remains. Well-drawn wills allow the trustees to waive their rights as to index-linking or the charging of interest.

13.12 *Section 175A* (discharge of liabilities after death) will apply to old debt and charge schemes where the second spouse dies on or after 17 July 2013. The effect of this provision is that liabilities are only deductible in determining the value of an estate, if they are actually repaid out of an estate on or after death unless there is a real commercial reason for the liability to remain outstanding.

Therefore if the debt together with any interest is discharged on the second death, the full sum can be deducted as a liability from the estate. HMRC state that the interest received will have to be taxed by the trustees as income at the rate of 45%, however this is disputed by a number of professionals.

If the interest is waived, there is no income tax liability on the waived sum. However HMRC state, that there is unlikely to be any commercial purpose to the interest not being repaid, as, had the creditor been at arm's length, they would have wanted the interest repaid as well. If the interest is waived, it cannot be taken into account as a liability on the estate. See HMRC's guidance at IHTM28029.

THE RESIDENCE NIL RATE BAND

Background

13.13 The new residence nil rate band (RNRB), introduced by *F(No2) A 2015* with further legislation in *Finance Act 2016,* will insert nine new provisions (*ss 8D–8M*) into *IHTA 1984*. The RNRB will have a major impact on will drafting and many wills which include a NRB discretionary trust may need to be reviewed. While the legislation will come into effect for deaths after 6 April 2017, it applies in respect of disposals on or after 8 July 2015 where either the taxpayer downsizes, or where the property is sold or given away because the taxpayer moves into residential care.

Families are advised to review existing wills to ensure that maximum use of the NRB and RNRB can be made on second death.

The importance for will drafting is that the RNRB is only available to a transfer of a residential property interest to a direct descendant and it is not available if the residential property or a share in the residential property is left on a discretionary trust. In general the transfer to a direct descendant must be outright, but some transfers into trusts for direct descendants qualify. They include:

- transfers into immediate post-death interest trusts;
- transfers into disabled trusts; or
- transfers into 18–25 trusts and trusts for bereaved minors.

Following the introduction of the downsizing rules for the RNRB published in *FA 2016*, professional bodies have made representations to HMRC, as these rules do not cover situations where the property is held as a trust interest (either as IIP or IPDI) and the liferenter either wishes to downsize or the property is sold, when the liferenter goes into care. Unless amendments are made to the *FA 2016,* a disposal by trustees of a dwelling-house in which a person has an interest in possession is not a disposal which qualifies for the RNRB.

Focus

- A transfer into a discretionary trust does not qualify as the property must be held directly for 'lineal descendants'. If such a trust is encountered when dealing with someone's estate, *s 144* can be used to appoint to lineal descendants and thereby attract the RNRB.
- It is common for parents to leave their estates to their children in equal shares with substitution for grandchildren in the event that a child predeceased their parent. If this includes an age contingency, for example 'for such of my daughter's children that reach the age of 25', and the daughter predeceases, and the grandchildren have not reached the age of 25 when the grandparent dies, the trust for the grandchildren will not qualify for the purposes of the RNRB. Again, *s 144* can come to the rescue.

DEFERRAL OF TAX USING SPOUSE RELIEF

Background

13.14 In its most simple form, this planning is acceptable and allowed for by the legislation.

Example 13.2—Spouse relief: post-war nuclear family

John was born in 1922, Susan in 1925. They married when he was home on leave in 1950 and had two sons, born in 1951 and 1955. Returning to civilian life he became an engineer. She was a teacher. By 1985 they were both enjoying a happy retirement and spending time with their grandchildren when John's smoking finally caught up with him and it became clear that he would not live much longer. His will provided for legacies for his grandchildren but left the bulk of his estate to Susan.

She was widowed in 1992, then aged only 67 and in good health. On John's death she inherited from him free of IHT, sold the family home, traded down and made substantial gifts to her sons, hoping to live seven years so that the gifts would be free of tax. In the event Susan survived until 2016. The gifts made soon after John's death fell out of account and her nil rate band, together with John's, was available to Susan's executors.

The scheme of deferral of tax in the above example has worked substantially in the way that legislation intended, saving the family from an immediate IHT charge on the death of John. However, many circumstances arose prior to *FA 2006* where the relief was claimed in circumstances less acceptable to the government.

Example 13.3—Life interest for spouse: William's life

William was born in 1912. His first wife, Mary was born in 1915. They married in 1940 and had two children, one born later that year and another born in 1943. Mary died in 1955, leaving William to bring up the boys, then aged 15 and 12, just when his building business was reaching a very busy stage of its development. A family friend, Rachel, helped bring up the boys and William and Rachel had a daughter born in 1960. By 1985 the stresses of running a family business had taken their toll on William, who had become so difficult to live with that Rachel had left him.

Whilst on holiday he met and married Anja who was Norwegian. By now, the construction business had developed substantially into a property investment business and was run by the younger of William's sons with some help from his daughter. In fairness to his children William wanted to provide substantially for them rather than Anja, so he made a will leaving the nil rate sum equally between his children and giving the residue of his estate to Anja on life interest trusts but with a power for the trustees to revoke those trusts at any time, with the fee to his children.

William died in 2000. There was no IHT on his death, because by then Anja had acquired a UK domicile of choice, so the residue of the estate qualified for unrestricted spouse relief. Anja then however indicated that she would like to return home. That suited the trustees well, because they had never intended that she should enjoy an interest in possession in the whole of the substantial estate for very long. Shortly after Anja left the UK, the trustees terminated the life interest. It was anticipated that Anja would live at least seven years. The cost of insuring against the possibility of her death within that period was moderate and was paid by the trustees.

Counteraction of perceived abuse

13.15 The device described in the example of William above was specifically counteracted by *FA 1986, s 102ZA*. The success of the device, as noted in the example, rested on the fact that the continued enjoyment of trust property after termination of an interest in possession in it was not reservation out of a gift because the gift had not been made by the former liferenter. The government considered that the abuse was sufficiently serious that it should be brought to an end in two ways. As part of a general attack on trusts there was initially provision that denied spouse relief wherever there was an ongoing trust (except for minors) following the death of the spouse.

13.16 As was noted in **Chapter 7**, those proposals were in part withdrawn but the more specific provisions of *FA 1986, s 102ZA* remain. The operative section is *FA 1986, s 102ZA(2)*, which provides that, on the ending of an interest in possession, an individual is treated as if he had disposed by way of gift of property in which the interest in possession previously subsisted. That may be enough to bring the GWR code into play. The provision applies where:

- an individual enjoys an interest in possession in settled property; and
- that individual became entitled to the interest before 22 March 2006 or became entitled to the interest in possession after that date but the interest is an IPDI, a disabled persons' interest or a TSI.

In other words it is one of the remaining categories of interest in possession that still falls to be taxed under the 'old' rules and is not treated as a relevant property trust.

13.17 The property that is deemed by the section to be given is described as 'the no-longer-possessed property'. This is any property in which there was an interest in possession, except such part of the fund as the liferenter actually retains and in which he or she does still have an interest in possession. Thus, if the fund is £100,000 and the trustees terminate the interest in three-quarters of it, the no-longer-possessed property is £75,000 because the remainder is still subject to the interest in possession.

Consequential amendments to *FA 1986, s 102* apply where there has been a termination of a life interest, now treated as being by way of gift under *FA 1986, s 102ZA*, but the property remains in the settlement. The new provision treats the property that is the subject of the deemed gift as consisting of the property that remains in the settlement except insofar as the trust fund does not consist of any asset in which there was an interest in possession that has been terminated by the gift.

There is an anti-avoidance provision to provide that the property in the deemed gift includes derived property, even including property derived from a loan made by the former liferenter to the trustees. Accumulations of income are also treated as being derived from property. All of this operates to increase the size of the gift in respect of which an interest in possession may apply.

Example 13.4—Termination of interest: failure to revise a will

Alec, a widower aged 80, had two sons Brian, 45 and Charles 40 when he married Denise, a 72-year-old. He wanted to provide adequately for Denise, but substantially for Brian and Charles. He made a will leaving the nil rate band to Brian and Charles between them and residue on terminable interests in possession for Denise with the fee to Brian and Charles. His estate comprised a substantial house and investments not qualifying for reliefs. The plan had been to use Denise as a 'peg life' to get substantial value down to Brian and Charles free of inheritance tax.

Alec died on 1 February 2006 when the house in his name was worth £1.5 million and the residue of his estate after debts amounted to £3,275,000. The trust fund was therefore £4.5 million (ie the total net estate, less the nil rate band of £275,000). The trustees, then of course unaware of the impending terms of the Finance Bill 2006, terminated the interest in possession of Denise in the house but allowed her to go on living there. They also advanced £1 million of residue each to Brian and Charles.

Finance Act 1986, s 102ZA treats the termination of the interest in possession in the house as a gift by Denise. The house is still in the trust. The interest in possession for Denise came into existence before 22 March 2006. The GWR code therefore applies so that, in the event of the death of Denise, the value of the house will be taxed as part of her estate. There is however no reservation of benefit out of the £2 million released to Brian and Charles. Those transfers are treated as PETs by Denise in the normal way. As she has survived the PET by more than seven years those gifts will fall out of account.

The tax planning has therefore partially succeeded. The PETs to the sons have now fallen out of account. It had however been hoped that the structure would effectively take the house out of the IHT net by way of gift whilst allowing Denise to go on living there. That part of the tax planning was frustrated.

Later IHT charge on a 'wait and see' basis

13.18 The prevalence of second marriages and of children who are 'his, hers, and ours' has resulted in a proliferation of wills that attempt to do justice to the reasonable expectations of the constituent parts of a modern day family. Each party to a second marriage may bring family and assets and may wish to benefit existing family alongside the issue of the union.

As originally drafted, the amendments in the Finance Bill 2006 were very strict. Any ongoing trust interests were taxed in such a way that spouse relief could very easily be lost. As revised, *s 49A* allows greater flexibility. Thus, parties to a second marriage may wish to give each other an interest in possession in the residue of estate with discretionary trusts thereafter so that the fund can be used according to the needs of the various beneficiaries at the time.

As noted in **Chapter 7**, an IPDI exists where a will trust provides for the liferenter; and not for bereaved minors or for a disabled person; and the interest in possession exists continuously from the death. The termination of that interest in possession on the occasion where discretionary trusts arise is a chargeable transfer. The ongoing trusts are then taxed under the regime described in **Chapter 8**. If full flexibility is what the family want, they can have it, but at a price. All of this must also be considered in the light of the *FA 2008* provisions as to transferability of the nil rate band.

Focus

- 'Mirror' wills leaving the estate to the surviving spouse are much more common since the introduction of the transferable nil rate band.
- Such wills are suitable in 'straightforward' cases where the combined estate does not exceed £650,000 (ie two nil rate bands of £325,000 each).

Trusts for bereaved minors

13.19 Having reviewed the ongoing tax charges that would otherwise apply, many taxpayers may decide to 'grumble and give in'. If they provide that shares that pass to children or grandchildren vest absolutely at 18, including accumulations of income, they will achieve the simplest tax treatment that is now available and there will be no ongoing IHT trust charges.

For England and Wales following the enactment of the *Inheritance and Trustees Powers Act 2014, ss 31 and 32 Trustee Act 1925* were amended. Trustees now have the power to apply income and to accumulate surplus income during the minority of a beneficiary 'as the trustees may think fit' as with a well drafted Scottish discretionary trust (in England and Wales *s 32 Trustee Act 1925* has been amended, to remove the limit on advancements of one half of vested or presumptive entitlement for trusts created on or after 15 May 2014).

18-to-25 trusts

13.20 Many families will want the slightly greater flexibility of a vesting age of 25. The maximum IHT cost of that arrangement, over and above the IHT charge on death, will be 4.2% as described in **Chapter 8**. In fact, as noted in that section, the actual ongoing IHT charge may be less than that.

Unfortunately the recent Government consultation into the simplification of periodic inheritance tax charges proved to be inconclusive. It intends to hold a further consultation but has rejected calls to exclude 18-to-25 trusts, accumulation and maintenance trusts and interest-in-possession trusts from the *FA 2006's* relevant property regime, because tax revenues would be lost.

Early life interest trusts

13.21 One possibility that in appropriate circumstances may give testators what they want is the creation by will of an immediate life interest in favour of a young beneficiary. An IPDI is now less restricted than formerly following the changes to the draft of *IHTA 1984, s 49A*. There is therefore scope for a long life interest (all subsequent statutory references are to *IHTA 1984,* unless otherwise stated).

Example 13.5—Life interest for grandchildren: by-passing the next generation

Fred's three sons George, Henry and Ian are all married and doing quite well financially. The grandchildren are respectively John, 9, Ken, 7, Lucy, 8, Mary, 6, Nancy, 5 and Olive, 3 (and it seems that there will be no more). It is hoped that they will attend good schools and go on to further education. Fred is widowed and does not need to provide for his sons. His will therefore divides the residue of his estate into six shares, held respectively for each of his grandchildren for life with wide powers of advancement of capital to each liferenter (but not to any of the others) and with the fee to great-grandchildren.

None of the grandchildren are disabled. The provisions of *s 71A* do not apply because those rules apply to children as opposed to grandchildren, and in any event the grandchildren will not automatically become entitled to capital at age 18. 'Condition 3' of *s 49A* is therefore satisfied and each of the interests in possession is an IPDI. If the trustees advance capital to any of the grandchildren to help fund secondary or tertiary education that is neutral for IHT because each already has an interest in possession so there is no change in the estate of any of them.

If any of the grandchildren marries, spouse relief may become available to exempt a transfer that would otherwise become taxable on the termination of an interest in possession by an advance to the spouse or to the liferenter for the benefit of the spouse providing the deed allows for this. The structure gives Fred's family considerable flexibility for years to come.

BPR, APR AND WOODLANDS RELIEF

Placing the relievable property

13.22 Gifts by will to spouses and civil partners are still exempt in 'uncomplicated' structures notwithstanding *FA 2006*. There is therefore overlap of property relief and exemption. This is wasteful but may be unavoidable.

Example 13.6—APR and spouse exemption (I): simple farming situation

Cedric inherited the family farm years ago and on his death its 150 acres were worth £450,000 and the house itself £400,000. Savings built up, when farming was better, have been eroded but still stand at £200,000. His wife Mary owns some adjoining land worth £50,000 which has always been occupied with the farm and savings of £300,000. They have two daughters. Cedric's will leaves the house and land to Mary and the cash to the daughters.

On his death in November 2015 there is no IHT because the gifts to the daughters are within the nil rate band (then £325,000), and the gift to Mary is exempt.

On Mary's death in May 2016, her estate comprises the house, land totalling £500,000 and savings, now reduced to £285,000. The nil rate band available is approximately 138.46% of the current figure of £325,000 ie £450,000, because 38.46% of the band was unused on Cedric's death and is thus still available (it is actually the same amount as was unused because the nil rate band is frozen but the calculation is set out to illustrate the principle).

Although Mary's death occurs only shortly after that of Cedric, APR is allowed on the farming assets under the succession provisions of *s 120*. Applying the valuation principles of *Antrobus (No 2)* [2002] STC (SCD) 468, APR on the farmhouse is restricted (ie to 70% of £400,000), so £120,000 of the value is chargeable, but even when added to her cash savings of £285,000, the resulting inheritance for Mary's daughters is within the nil rate band. The result is that the daughters inherit entirely tax free.

Example 13.7—APR and spouse exemption (II): wastage of exemption and the scope for 'double dipping'

The facts are the same as in the previous example, only some of the figures are larger. The house is worth £600,000, Cedric's savings are £400,000 (note the value of Cedric's farm remains at £450,000), and Mary has her own farmland worth £50,000 as before but her savings amount to £475,000. If the will provisions are the same, there is an IHT charge (in 2015/16) on Cedric's death on the amount by which his cash gift to his daughters exceeds the nil rate band, (£400,000 – £325,000) ie 75,000 × 40%: £30,000. Mary's estate, on death soon after that of Cedric, is £1,575,000.

There are other problems. Farmland worth £450,000 belonging to Cedric has been enjoyed with a house valued at £600,000. Questions arise as to whether such a valuable property is indeed a farmhouse and whether, to a working farmer, the purchase of the landholding as a whole for £1,050,000 might represent 'an appalling investment in terms of yield' within the rule in *Higginson v CIR*. APR may be denied on the house on the basis that the entity as a whole is really 'a house with land' rather than a farm. Matters will be eased if Mary's own land is included, though it is of relatively little value and there may be little connection between it and the farmhouse, which could present a problem.

Assuming that that problem can be overcome, APR on the house will be restricted to £420,000 (70% of £600,000), leaving £180,000 in charge. The daughters therefore inherit the house, the land which should qualify entirely for APR and a further £475,000 of cash: a chargeable estate of £655,000 (the gift to them from their father's estate exhausted the nil rate band, so there is no transferable nil rate band). Value of £330,000 after Mary's nil rate band (£325,000 in 2016/17) is taxable at 40%, attracting IHT of £132,000.

Alternative structures to save tax by 'double dipping'

13.23 There may have been some wastage of relief in the above example. Nothing much could be done if Mary died within two years of Cedric but, if she had been in good health at the time of his death and had survived by two years or so, tax could have been saved by reordering his will. Cedric could have given his daughters the farmland, which it may be remembered was worth £450,000, and the nil rate band. That would have allowed them, on the rates in force when he died, to inherit value amounting to £775,000 tax free. Mary's estate would then comprise the farmhouse, her own land and cash of £550,000, being the £475,000 that she already had plus cash from Cedric's estate of (£400,000 less the nil rate band, leaving) £75,000.

Mary could have used part of the cash to buy the farmland from her daughters. Only if she lived two years from Cedric's death would APR again be available to her (because she would not be within *s 120*). On her death, assuming that she lived two years, her estate would comprise the farmhouse, the land and cash of £100,000 or as much of it as she still had left after two more years of farming. There would still be the argument as to whether the house was a farmhouse, but assuming that the executors were successful most of its value would be relieved, leaving (on the assumptions already made) £180,000 in charge. Mary's chargeable estate would therefore amount to £280,000.

The nil rate band (where there is no augmentation by transfer) is £325,000 for the time being. The daughters should have no tax to pay. However, as noted above, this arrangement works only where Mary lives long enough after the purchase of the relievable assets to qualify for APR in her own right under *s 117*. Depending on ages and other factors, many will hope that we may return to index-linking of the nil rate band, which would increase the eventual nil rate band available and preserve the freedom for the surviving spouse to control assets in the meantime.

Woodlands relief

13.24 Woodlands relief is available on death only. Calculation of the relief can be complicated and, where it is possible to show that there is commercial occupation of the woodlands, it may be simpler and more effective to claim BPR. There is, for example, provision for 50% reduction in value under *s 127*, but this is rare and the practitioner is referred to specialist books on the subject. One situation in which will planning can exploit woodlands relief is illustrated below.

Example 13.8—Woodlands relief: ownership of wood

Ralph owns very valuable woods. The trees are of a quality and age that are very attractive to the market. Even timber of lesser quality now sells well to those who can no longer afford to heat their homes with oil. Ralph is not in good health but has an impecunious sister, Freda, who might well outlive him. Ralph leaves the woodland to Freda, who does not have a substantial chargeable estate and who, having no family of her own, is likely by her will to leave all of her estate to Ralph's children.

On Ralph's death an election is made to leave the value of the timber out of account on the basis that it will be chargeable on any later disposal by Freda. If Freda does dispose of the timber that will trigger an IHT charge against which can be set her nil rate band, but if she retains the woodland until her own death the charge (at 0%) on that death will frank the IHT charge on Ralph's death. Death is not an 'associated operation'.

It may be assumed, as a rule of thumb, that timber grows annually by around 4%. That is an incentive only to fell it when the price is good: in times of surplus, one simply waits for a better price on a larger volume of stock.

13.25 The more normal situation will be one in which the beneficiary of woodland which is ripe for felling will want to draw the cash. In this case a different arrangement may be appropriate.

Example 13.9—Woodlands relief: no deferral of taxable event

Steve owned woodlands similar to those of Ralph and recently had the land clear-felled and replanted. He leaves the woodland by will to his grandson. On his death woodlands relief is not claimed. The value of the timber at that time is negligible because the trees are still young and the cost of looking after them is greater than any economic benefit from the landholding.

There is no point in making an election for woodlands relief because when the deferred tax comes to be payable, it is hoped not until many years later, the woodlands may have increased considerably in value.

Although there might be some merit in electing for woodlands relief so as to relieve the value on the transfer to the grandson, on balance it will be better if residue can carry the moderate tax cost.

The problems of *s 39A*

13.26 The interaction of exempt transfers with business and agricultural property relief is examined at **3.29**. An inexpertly drawn will can easily lead to the complications of tax that are described at **3.30** and **3.31**. There is a single transfer on death to both chargeable and exempt beneficiaries. BPR and APR will be wasted on an exempt beneficiary such as spouse, civil partner or charity. That delicacy, ie the BPR or APR in the case of the estate, should have been reserved for the children or other chargeable beneficiaries.

The computations required under *s 39A* are complicated and the reader is referred to specialist books on the topic. For the general practitioner the answer is simply to take care to avoid gifts of chargeable property that will trigger the rules as to grossing-up. If a chargeable specific gift is made of an asset that qualifies for relief, that will fix the availability of the relief.

Example 13.10—BPR and *s 39A*: a will that should be varied

Kenneth has made no chargeable transfers or PETs in the last seven years. His estate comprises:

Business property with 50% BPR	£650,000
Quoted shares	£370,000
House	£325,000

His existing will leaves the house and the business assets to his widow Linda and the investments to his daughter Melanie. The gifts to Melanie slightly exceed the current nil rate band, triggering a modest charge to IHT.

On present tax rates, his will should be varied in his lifetime or by a deed of variation after his death. Quite apart from considerations of transferable nil rate band, Melanie should receive the business assets and the remainder of the estate should go to Linda. After relief at 50% the chargeable transfer is just slightly less than it was before, giving a small IHT saving; but more to the point the actual value that has passed to Melanie is now nearly double what it would have been.

The nil rate band is still available on Linda's death and there will be an overall saving on the second death. As with the example of Mary above, the transfer of the business property direct to Melanie leaves open the possibility that Linda might use some of the liquidity to buy business property back from Melanie in the hope that Linda will live two years from the purchase. That will effectively use the BPR twice, if Linda lives two years from the purchase.

13.27 Some consideration must be given to the possibility of remarriage. That will affect IHT planning and may encourage the first spouse to die at least to use the nil rate band to protect any existing children from disinheritance. It is in such situations that the debt/charge scheme may still be attractive, or that a gift of the nil rate band to or in trust for the children will be wholly appropriate. After all, if the spouse does remarry there can be only one transferable nil rate band on eventual death, so perhaps best to use the elder spouse's nil rate band now.

Further complications

13.28 In family situations and in the drafting of wills it is easy for the practitioner to be distracted by the various considerations, as can be seen in the following extended example.

Example 13.11—Case study: will-drafting traps

Melissa and Wendy lived together but did not consider marrying or entering into a civil partnership. Melissa owned the house which, though modest, enjoyed a wide road frontage. Wendy was her companion. Melissa also held stocks and shares worth £400,000 including £100,000 worth as a minority holding in her cousin's unquoted trading company.

Melissa instructed her solicitor that in the event of her death she would want Wendy to be able to continue to live in the house for as long as she wanted and to have a 'cushion' of money to tide her over. That provision ought to be tax free. Apart from that, Melissa wanted her estate as far as possible to go in equal shares to three charities and two cousins.

The first consideration for the draftsman will be to avoid the problems of *Re Benham*. This is explained at **3.39**. However, there is a second issue, *s 39A*, to be addressed by the will. It would also be unwise simply to give Wendy the right to continue to live in the house for life and a legacy tax free of such sum (not exceeding a stated maximum) as the executors might think necessary for her care. The reasons are as follows:

- The first is the rule in *Judge (personal representatives of Walden deceased) v Revenue and Customs Comrs* [2005] SSCD 863 (SpC 506), referred to at **7.3** and **15.38** et seq. Practitioners may consider that the decision in that case could have gone either way, in the light of the general rule of HMRC as expressed in Statement of Practice 10/79. The fact that one ill-drawn will did not create an interest in possession in a residence does not mean that SP 10/79 will never be invoked in future. There is therefore a risk that provision tax free of Melissa's house for Wendy to occupy for the rest of her life creates an interest in possession and, depending on the value, that gift alone could exhaust the nil rate band, particularly if the wide frontage of the property concerned constitutes access to back land and has considerable value. Supposing therefore that provision of the home for Melissa exceeds the nil rate band, grossing-up will be necessary.
- The second problem follows from the first. The further provision of the 'cushion' tax free will also require grossing-up and, applying the principles of *s 39A*, that gift will be seen as coming from the rest of the estate, including the part represented by the value of the unquoted shares which qualify for 100% BPR.
- Finally, the lack of a specific gift of the shares causes some of the BPR on them to be wasted on the charitable beneficiaries of residue.

A better drawn will would make a specific gift of the shares to the chargeable beneficiaries, perhaps especially the cousin who actually runs the company. That would secure BPR in full.

If it is known from the outset that part of the garden has development value, the provision for Melissa should be restricted to the residence itself excluding the garden, so as to minimise the amount by which that chargeable gift exceeds the nil rate band. Great care should be taken in drafting the clause relating to the house so as to show that the right of Wendy to live there can be terminated at any time by the trustees so that she does not have an interest in possession.

An alternative would have been a lifetime gift by Melissa of a share in the house to Wendy, effectively giving Wendy a right of occupation by virtue of her share in the house. The retained share in the house could then have been given to the charities outright. They would not have been able to sell the share of the house until Wendy moved out; but they would not have received any benefit from the house until Wendy's death anyway. That arrangement would have given charitable exemption on the value of the retained share in the house.

Obviously in practice the testator's wishes should take priority and the most tax efficient distribution of assets may not be practical.

EXEMPT GIFTS ON DEATH

Charities

13.29 Practitioners are regularly lobbied by charities to encourage clients to give in their wills. In the light of *RSPCA v Sharp* [2011] STC 553 some will writers may be discouraged from leaving residue, or a share of it, to charities, for fear that the charity may in some way 'make trouble' for the family, as (in the view of the High Court judge ([2010] STC 975) happened there. That is an issue to discuss carefully with the testator.

The issue in *Cancer Research Campaign v Ernest Brown & Co (a firm)* [1997] STC 1425 concerned the failure of a lawyer to take advantage of the relief. The facts are important enough to quote in detail.

Mr Berry died on 11 December 1986 leaving the residue of his estate to his sister Phoebe. They owned a house jointly which passed to Phoebe by survivorship. The rest of his estate amounted to some £170,000 from which was paid legacies of £30,000. About five months after her brother's death Phoebe visited Mr Palfreyman, a legal executive and executor of her brother's will, to make her own will. By then no application had been made for an English grant of probate of the brother's will, but it was assumed that Mr Palfreyman knew how much Phoebe would inherit.

13.30 She left virtually all her estate to seven charities. Details of the interview are scant because Mr Palfreyman himself died before the case came to trial. There was no record of any discussion between Phoebe and Mr Palfreyman of the possibility of a deed of variation. It was therefore not possible to say whether Phoebe lived so modestly that she did not need the cash inheritance from her brother. Phoebe then died, having included Mr Palfreyman as an executor. Phoebe's will was not proved until June 1989; that of her brother not until October 1992. Phoebe's estate was thus swollen by the 'unnecessary' inheritance from her brother, which could have been diverted to the charities.

The charities were concerned that Phoebe, had she been so advised, could have varied her brother's will to provide direct benefit to the charities, taking advantage of *s 142*, with the result that IHT could have been saved. The last date on which an effective variation could have taken place was 10 December 1988, but at that time the charities did not even know of their entitlement. They only learned of it from the probate agents, Smee and Ford, on 23 June 1989, by which time it was too late. IHT on the brother's estate was about £203,000, but was not paid until 7 October 1992. The figure included substantial interest and penalties.

13.31 Held, the solicitors had no duty to advise Phoebe on the possibilities of saving IHT in relation to her estate; nor any duty to advise on tax mitigation when administering the estate of her brother. Further, there was no duty to communicate the tax-mitigation possibilities of a deed of variation to the residuary legatees. The solicitors were obliged to administer the estate properly, but were under no obligation to advise the charitable legatees of the potential legacy.

Practitioners may think, given the whole circumstances, including the long time that it took to administer the estates of Phoebe and of her brother, that the solicitors did well to escape liability. Certainly, in drafting wills and in administering estates the practitioner should always be aware of the interests of the charities and the possibilities of exemption.

13.32 Note the limitation on charitable relief in *s 23(2)*. There is no relief where the charitable disposition takes effect only on the termination of an interest or period after the transfer of value, or where it depends on a condition which is not satisfied within 12 months, or where it is defeasible.

Example 13.12—Gifts to charity: non-exempt charitable gifts

Samantha's will leaves £100,000 on trust for her brother Robert for life with the fee to the Children's Society. The gift is not exempt on the death of Samantha, but the fund will be exempt on Robert's death.

Finance Act 2012 introduced a reduced rate of IHT where 10% or more of a deceased's estate (after deducting IHT exemptions, reliefs and the nil rate band) is left to charity. HMRC published their guidance notes in April 2012 (IHTM4500). The legislation provides that the IHT rate of 40% will be reduced to 36% where death occurs on or after 6 April 2012 and more than 10% of the net estate is left to charity. It is clear that only large estates will be able to benefit from this reduced rate.

The legislation determines that a person's estate is made up of a number of components. As a first step it is necessary to identify the components of the estate, which are:

- The *survivorship component*, which includes all property comprised in the estate that pass by survivorship or under a special destination, or under anything corresponding to survivorship under the law of a country or territory outside the UK.
- The *settled property component* which includes all property comprised in the estate in which an interest in possession subsists and in which the deceased was beneficially entitled immediately before death.

- The *general component* which is made up of all other property comprised in the estate.

As a next step it is necessary to calculate the *donated amount* (which is the property attracting the charity exemption under *s 23(1)*, and the *baseline amount* which is gross value of assets in the components mentioned above after deducting liabilities, reliefs, exemptions and the available nil rate band (after taking into account any lifetime gifts).

Finally, it will be necessary to compare the *baseline amount* with the amount left to charity to see if the estate qualifies for the lower IHT rate.

An on-line calculator is provided by HMRC on their website to work out whether the estate qualifies for the reduced rate – see www.gov.uk/inheritance-tax-reduced-rate-calculator

Example 13.13—Gifts to charity: calculation of reduced rate

Fred's estate (before legacies) is worth £950,000. He once used to be wealthier, but due to years of ill health, unfortunately most of his assets had to be sold.

He lived with his spinster sister Frieda and they owned a property, which was valued at £250,000, which contained a survivorship destination in the title – *survivorship component*. Fred was a liferenter under a pre-2006 family settlement which on his death passes to his two nephews in equal shares – the value of the settlement at the date of death was £450,000 – *settled property component*. The *general component* is valued at £250,000. His will, which was drafted more than 10 years ago during more prosperous times, left a legacy of £100,000 to a cancer charity with the residue passing to Frieda absolutely.

Prior to the introduction of reduced IHT for estates in respect of charitable gifts, the IHT charged on Fred's death would have been £210,000 (ie £950,000 less the charitable legacy of £100,000, less Fred's nil rate band of £325,000 @ 40%).

Assuming Fred died after 6 April 2012, the executors now need to check whether the 36% IHT rate applies. The *donated amount* is £100,000. The *baseline amount* is £625,000. As the gift to charity exceeds the 10% threshold, the reduced rate of IHT of 36% will apply to Fred's estate. The executors will pay IHT of £189,000 ((£950,000 less the charitable legacy of £100,000, less Fred's nil rate band of £325,000) @ 36%). This represents a tax saving of £21,000.

Heritage relief

13.33 The relief is valuable but rare. For detailed analysis the reader is referred to specialist works on the subject. The gift of heritage property by will is unlikely of itself to take account of heritage relief except to the extent that property is transferred to a maintenance fund under *s 27*. Mainly, therefore, the way in which a will takes account of the existence of heritage relief will be in avoiding dispositions that force or encourage the sale of property in respect of which an undertaking has already been given, because such a forced sale would breach any undertaking that had already been given under *s 31* or earlier legislation in force.

It is a particular feature of heritage relief that property may have benefited many years ago from the relief at a time when capital taxation was much higher. Care must be taken not to trigger the clawback of relief that had been given on an earlier occasion. The difficulty for the owner of conditional exempt property is in knowing who is actually the 'relevant person' for the purposes of undertaking it at any time. This is because the rules work in such a way that the identity of the relevant person changes according to a retrospective test. There are three rules set out in *s 33(5)*, as follows:

Rule 1: Simple cases

13.34 Where there has been only one conditionally exempt transfer of the heritage property before the chargeable event, the relevant person is the one who made the transfer.

Rule 2: Two or more conditional transfers, one going back 30 years

13.35 In these cases it is necessary to consider the ownership of the property for the period of 30 years leading up to the chargeable event. Where the most recent transfer of that property was more than 30 years ago, the person who made that transfer is the relevant person. Where there have been several transfers, and one of them took place in the last 30 years, that transferor is the relevant person.

Rule 3: Two or more recent conditional transfers

13.36 Suppose that there have been two or more transfers in the last 30 years. HMRC may choose whichever of the transferors they please as the relevant person. The reason for this is to prevent avoidance of tax by channelling heritage property through those members of the family who have few other assets in the hope of ensuring that, where there is a chargeable event, the tax charged will be as low as possible.

These rules make life very difficult for executors and trustees. They may have to keep sums back in the administration of an estate against the possibility of clawback of tax on breach of undertaking. They will not necessarily know how much will be involved. Two cases on the subject may offer some guidance: *Bedford (Duke), Re, Russell v Bedford* [1960] 3 All ER 756 and *Re Scott* [1916] 2 Ch 268.

13.37 Claims to heritage relief must be made within two years of the date of transfer (see *s 30(3BA)*), 'or … such longer period as the board may allow'. HMRC have discretion to allow a longer time than two years and will consider a late claim on its merits. The difficulty for the practitioner is that the property that might be the subject of a claim might also by its very nature qualify for, say, APR, a protective claim should be made.

Provisions were introduced in *Finance Act 2016* to cover situations where the conditional exemption was granted prior to 1975 under the estate duty regime. HMRC now has the choice to charge either IHT or the higher estate duty rate when the charge crystallises. This will bring the legislation into line with lifetime transfers of heritage objects.

Legislation will be introduced to amend *Finance Act 1930, s 40(2)* to cover situations where the heritage object has been lost. IHT or estate duty will become chargeable unless the owner can convince HMRC that the loss was outside his control.

POLICY TRUSTS

13.38 These were discussed in **Chapter 7**. Apart from bare trusts, which give no flexibility as to choice of beneficiary or vesting age, trusts entered into after 22 March 2006 will generally be treated as discretionary. Their creation will be a chargeable transfer, though the value of a new policy under which regular premiums are paid is likely to be not merely within the nil rate band, but also within the annual exemption. The payment of further premiums on the policy is likely to be exempt under *s 21*. If the policy is a single premium bond, the transfer will usually be of its value at the time of gift. If substantial, that triggers the compliance issues discussed in **Chapter 6**.

The tax charge on such trusts therefore arises principally when, at the occasion of a ten-year anniversary, the policy value exceeds the nil rate band; or on an exit charge when the value of the fund exceeds that band. There is a valuation rule, see *s 167*, which can apply to a policy, but it is limited in scope. Usually, the value will be the market value rather than the total of premiums paid.

In the past, it was commonplace for a financial adviser quite correctly not only to sell a policy but to arrange for it to be written in trust. Given the complexity of the regime for taxing discretionary trusts financial advisers may be less keen to undertake the full explanation of trust documents and their tax consequences that is likely to be necessary in future. Each structure must be analysed for its efficacy: it seems that discounted gift trusts in particular may be less viable than they once were.

POST-DEATH VARIATIONS

13.39 *Section 142* permits families and their advisers to be 'wise after the event'. Subject to various safeguards it is possible to rewrite a will or to put in place provisions akin to a will where a person has died intestate. The document need not be a deed, only 'an instrument in writing'. It must be signed by anyone who would have benefited but for the changes brought about by the deed. A difficulty therefore arises if the beneficiaries of the will to be changed or under intestacy are minors.

The Chancellor announced a review of the use of deed of variations as part of the government's clampdown on tax avoidance in the 2015 Budget speech. Following representations from professional bodies, it was announced in the 2015 Autumn Statement that the Government has decided not to restrict the use of deeds of variations for the time being, but that they will closely monitor it.

Variations where there are minor beneficiaries

13.40 Two courses are open. The first is to apply to the court for an order permitting the variation to take place on the ground that it is in the interests of the infant beneficiaries. The simpler course, which is not objected to by HMRC, is to frame any variation in such a way that it does clearly benefit younger members of the family.

Example 13.14—Minor beneficiaries: no need for an application to the court

Ian, a widower, left his estate in four equal shares, one for each of his three sons and the last for his grandchildren equally per capita. One of the sons, Donald, does not need his inheritance and wishes his share to pass immediately to his children. There is no need for any of Donald's children to sign the resulting deed of variation. None of them gives anything up. There is no need for any application to the court.

Example 13.15—Minor beneficiaries: avoiding an application to the court

Michael, who was widowed and who remarried late in life, made a will that carves out the nil rate band to be held on discretionary trusts with residue to his widow for life with the fee in four shares, one to each of his sons and the fourth to his grandchildren equally per capita. The will does not contain the 'debt or charge' provisions and for family reasons it is now desired to incorporate them.

As was noted in **Chapter 3**, it is not possible simply to incorporate the requisite clauses by deed of variation. The parties therefore wish to enter into a deed that will comply with *s 142*. They agree to vary the terms of the will. The gift of residue is changed so that each son receives 20% only and the grandchildren receive 40% between them.

Although there will be no benefit to the grandchildren during the lifetime of their 'step-grandmother', it is nevertheless clear from the face of the deed that the grandchildren, who are themselves too young to sign the deed, are better off by virtue of the deed than they would have been under the will. It is therefore not necessary to seek the approval of the court to the variation.

Posthumous severance

13.41 *Section 142* permits a variation of the dispositions of the property comprised in the estate of the deceased 'whether affected by will, under the law relating to intestacy or otherwise'. The words 'or otherwise' have been taken to include dispositions that take effect by operation of law, such as survivorship to property held jointly. Accordingly, it is possible by deed of variation posthumously to evacuate the survivorship destination in any property (for IHT purposes, at least) so that the share belonging to the deceased can pass under the will as varied rather than direct to the other joint owner. This is often essential where it is proposed to put in place the debt or charge scheme by deed of variation.

'Only one bite at the cherry'

13.42 A disposition that has been varied by deed of variation may not be further varied: see *Russell v IRC* [1988] STC195. The issue was discussed in *Law Society's Gazette* 22 May 1985, noting that the Revenue had taken further advice on the interpretation of *s 142* and had indicated that:

- an election which is validly made is irrevocable;
- an instrument will not fall within *s 142* if it further redirects any item or any part of an item that has already been redirected under an earlier instrument; and
- to avoid any uncertainty, variations covering a number of items should ideally be made in one instrument.

There must be no consideration for entering into a deed of variation, see *s 142(3)*, other than consideration consisting of the making in respect of another of the dispositions of a variation or disclaimer to which that subsection applies.

Abuse

13.43 Deeds of variation, like so many other documents, are open to abuse.

Example 13.16—Deed of variation: trying it on

By his will Henry left his estate to his son Ian absolutely. By deed of variation Ian changed the will so that it provided for Joan, the wife of Henry and the mother of Ian.

Careful reading of the deed showed that Joan's address was different from Henry's. Enquiries revealed that they had been separated for many years and that Joan was amply provided for. Further enquiries and the threat of the exercise of a power to call for documents under *s 219A* elicited from Ian the admission, fully documented in the solicitor's papers, that it was understood from the outset that Joan would release anything that she inherited from her husband's estate to Ian by way of gift.

Whilst a transfer from Henry to Joan would have been sheltered by spouse relief, since nothing in *s 18* requires spouses or civil partners to be living together, relief under *s 142* is likely to be denied on the basis that Joan gave Ian consideration within *s 142(3)*.

This example is similar to the case of *Executor of Werner Lau Deceased v HMRC* [2009] WTLR 627 where a deed of variation was made in favour of the surviving spouse to allow for spouse exemption on the understanding that the surviving spouse would then make gifts to the children, which would be treated as potentially exempt transfers. HMRC successfully argued that the understanding between the parties amounted to consideration and the deed of variation was ineffective.

Finance Act 2012 changed the rules where there is a gift to charity by an instrument of variation. Unless the charity is informed of their benefit under the variation, *s 142* will not apply to the variation. A letter from the charity acknowledging the gift will be sufficient.

Disclaimers

13.44 A disclaimer has been described as a 'blunt instrument'. By *s 142(1)(b)* it has the effect of redirecting inheritance to another party though, apart from entering into the disclaimer in the first place, the original beneficiary has no control over the destination of the property disclaimed. Relief is not available under *s 142* in respect of a disclaimer if consideration has been given for it.

A disclaimer failed to achieve its purpose in *Lau (executor of Lau Deceased) v HMRC* [2009] SpC 740. The husband had left his son £665,000 free of IHT. There were other legacies to other children. Residue was left to his (second) wife. The son disclaimed his legacy; £3,800,000 was transferred to the widow; she transferred £1,000,000 to the son; correspondence showed that this was part of a plan to save IHT. HMRC refused to allow *s 142* to apply because of the direct link between the disclaimer and the later payment. It was held on appeal that the evidence showed a direct link. The evidence of the widow was 'utterly unpersuasive'. The appeal was dismissed.

Formalities of post-death variations

13.45 Since 31 July 2002, notice of any deed of variation need not now be given to HMRC, except where IHT is thereby increased, but relief will not be given by *s 142* unless the variation contains a statement, made by all the relevant persons, that they intend the relief to apply.

Statement of variation

13.46 The following will be enough:

> 'The parties to this variation intend that the provisions of section 142(2) [and where appropriate and section 62(6) Taxation of Chargeable Gains Act 1992] shall apply.'

The relevant persons are those making the instrument and, where extra taxes are payable by virtue of the variation, the personal representatives.

Footnote: the *Glowacki* case

13.47 A case which is special to its own facts is *Wells (Personal representatives of Glowacki deceased) v HMRC* [2008] STC (SCD) 188. A deed of variation was entered into which purported to deem a gift of a house to have been made immediately before death; but if the deed did not have the intended effect, the variation was to have no effect, giving the family a second chance of a variation by avoiding the *Russell* rule noted above.

HMRC determined that the effect of the deed was to set the benefit of the nil rate band against the value of the house in priority to the gift in the will of the nil rate band. The personal representatives appealed, arguing that *IHTA 1984, s 17(a)*, which provides that a qualifying deed of variation is not a transfer of value, had the effect of taking the house out of the estate before death, so £230,000 could pass under the gift of the nil rate band.

Held, *IHTA 1984, ss 4* and *17* did not work that way. *IHTA 1984, s 142* could not remove property from the estate to take it outside *s 4*. Any variation under *s 17* was of the dispositions on death only. The variation therefore failed. HMRC had decided the effect of the deed and had taxed accordingly. That was wrong: they should have decided whether *s 142* could be used in the way attempted; and should then have decided whether the deed remained in force as a result; which it did not, so part of the determination was quashed.

Alternative post-death relief: *ss 143* and *144*

13.48 There are two alternatives to the relief under *s 142*. By *s 143*, there is limited relief where the will sets out a wish that property be transferred by a legatee to other persons and the legatee does, within two years, carry out those wishes.

An attempt to push this rule to the limit was illustrated in the case of *Harding (executors of Loveday) v IRC* [1997] STC (SCD) 321. The will contained a discretionary trust for the widow and children. The executors appointed a fund to the widow. The Revenue argued that this was not an exempt transfer, being outside the terms of *s 144*. The executors appealed, wishing the appointment to be treated as a transfer under *s 143*. The Special Commissioner decided against the executors for three reasons: a legatee could include a trustee, but here the trustees were not legatees within *s 143*; an appointment of property was different from a transfer of it, so outside what *s 143* contemplated; and there was no evidence that the appointment was what the deceased had wanted, thus failing the requirement expressed in *s 143*.

In practice, a gift to a spouse that is quickly followed by an ongoing gift to a non-exempt beneficiary may well be challenged by HMRC.

A further form of relief applies under *s 144* to discretionary trusts established by a will. If trustees of a discretionary will trust exercise their discretion within two years of the death *s 144* applies so as to treat the release of funds or other transactions by the trustees as if they had been made by the testator.

13.49 However, the position is slightly more complicated than this summary might suggest, as the advisers found to their cost of *Frankland v IRC* [1997] STC 1450. Commonly, a will may establish a discretionary trust for the close family of the testator, including the surviving spouse. The idea is that, following the death and perhaps following establishment of reliefs such as APR and BPR, the executors will be able to decide on the relative needs of various members of the family and will be able to make appropriate provision. It was common in such situations, particularly where the surviving spouse was young and likely to live many years, to appoint funds to the surviving spouse in the hope that he or she could be used as a 'peg life'.

However, the mechanics of *s 144(1)(a)* refer to an event which, but for the relief, would trigger an IHT charge, being either the ten-year anniversary charge under *s 64* or the fixed rate under *s 79*; or which would be subject to an exit charge except for certain special reliefs. The effect was therefore that an appointment by the trustees which would not under any circumstances have triggered an exit or periodic charge did not fall within *s 144(1)*.

The proportionate charge, which is described in **Chapter 8**, does not apply during the first period of three months from the creation of settlement. As a result, an appointment made within the first three months of death does not benefit from relief under *s 144*. That, most unfortunately, had the result, in *Frankland v IRC* [1997] STC 1450, that an appointment that could otherwise have saved significant tax triggered a very substantial tax charge.

Legislation was included in *F(No2)A 2015* which in effect overrides *Frankland* in that, where an appointment is made within three months of date of death in favour of the deceased's surviving spouse or civil partner, it can be read into the will and spouse exemption under *s 18* will be given.

Other forms of post-death restructuring

13.50 Apart from deeds of variation the parties may feel that they want to reorganise beneficial interests under a will, as happened in *Executors of Patch deceased* [2007] SpC 600, where the deceased had left his estate to his wife for life with the fee to his children. The fund was mainly shares, and it was agreed that the widow should have one-third (represented by the house) and the children two-thirds. Under a deed of partition, not a deed of variation, the widow assigned her interest in the fund, other than the house, to the children.

They in return assigned their interest in the house to her. She agreed to pay them £25,000 each within 30 days and to pay more later.

Only five months later, the widow died, not in fact having made the payments. Her executors sent HMRC details of the deed and of the widow's estate. Tax was levied on the value of the house; but later HMRC sought to tax also the value of the trust fund that had passed to the children because the arrangement had effectively achieved a transfer of value, taxable under *s 52(1)*, which was within seven years of death. The executors appealed, on two grounds: there was no transfer of value, because the money had never been paid over, and they had made full disclosure anyway.

Not so, held the Special Commissioner. The assignments were not conditional on the payment. There was a division of the fund, which was a transfer. The value that was deemed to have left the estate of the widow under the partition should have been included in the account of the estate. Further, there had not been full disclosure: although the deed itself was disclosed, the executors had not included in the account the value of the lifetime transfer, so HMRC were entirely right to claim the tax.

'Mending' discretionary trusts after *FA 2006*

13.51 The effect of *FA 2006* is to treat certain will trusts as discretionary that would not previously have been so treated. Amendments have been made to *s 144* so that estates caught by *FA 2006* may escape the full IHT charging regime if distributions are made of trust funds into one of the asset holding vehicles that is still acceptable under the 'new' regime.

Where *s 144(2)* now applies, tax is not to be charged on the basis of the original discretionary trust. In each case in which *s 144(2)* is in point tax is charged as if the will had provided that the fund should be held, not on the terms of the will but on the terms of the varied disposition. Whereas *s 144(1)* previously could apply only to a discretionary trust it can now, by virtue of *s 144(1A)*, apply to a conventional discretionary trust and to an interest in possession that is neither an IPDI nor a disabled person's interest.

13.52 Where the necessary conditions are satisfied *s 144(4)* provides that tax is to be charged as if the will had provided for the property to be held as it will be held by virtue of the actions of the trustees described below. Where that happens, the fund escapes the discretionary trust charging regime.

The conditions for this are as follows:

- Death on or after 22 March 2006.
- Property in the estate of the deceased settled by will.

- Within two years of death (but before there has subsisted, in relation to the property, either an IPDI or a disabled persons interest), there is a trust event. The event concerned is one by which the property in the estate comes to be held on favoured trusts ie:
  - an IPDI; or
  - a BMT; or
  - an 18-to-25 trust.

Effectively, by this amendment to s 144, trustees will be able to bring will trusts into line with the regime now favoured by the UK government.

Chapter 14

Transferable nil rate bands

SIGNPOSTS

- **Scope** – The transferable nil rate band (TNRB) provisions broadly allow claims for the unused nil rate band of a deceased spouse or civil partner to be transferred to a surviving spouse or civil partner (who dies on or after 9 October 2007). The survivor's nil rate band can be increased by up to 100%, or one additional nil rate band (see **14.1–14.7**).
- **Claims** – The TNRB must be claimed within a permitted period, although HMRC may allow a longer claim period at its discretion in some cases (see **14.8–14.10**).
- **Reduction or clawback of TNRB** – The TNRB may be reduced or clawed back in certain specific circumstances, such as where a deferred IHT charge arises on woodlands, by reference to the deceased spouse's estate (see **14.11–14.20**).
- **Practical issues** – Records and documents should be kept to support claims for the TNRB on the death of the surviving spouse or civil partner (see **14.21–14.23**).
- **Planning and other issues** – Various considerations may arise in relation to the TNRB, such as whether to use the nil rate band on the first death instead (eg a legacy to a nil rate band discretionary trust); the position of cohabiting couples with TNRBs from previous marriages or civil partnerships; and care fees issues (see **14.24–14.41**).
- **Residence nil rate band** – Residence nil rate band is available on death from 6 April 2017 when a home is passed on death to lineal descendants of the deceased. Unused residence nil rate band is transferable to a spouse or civil partner in a similar way to the transferable nil rate band, subject to a successful claim being made (see **14.42–14.48**).

BACKGROUND

14.1 Estate planning for many married couples and civil partnerships was simplified following changes introduced in *Finance Act 2008*. The transferable nil rate band provisions broadly allow a claim for all or part of an unused nil rate band on the death of a spouse or civil partner to be transferred to a surviving spouse or civil partner (who dies on or after 9 October 2007) (*IHTA 1984, ss 8A–8C;* all references in this chapter are to *IHTA 1984,* unless otherwise stated). The rules apply in the same way whether the survivor leaves a will, or dies intestate.

The facility to make claims for the transfer of unused nil rate band remains very useful despite the nil rate band initially remaining frozen at its 2009/10 level of £325,000 for the tax years 2010/11 to 2014/15 inclusive (*FA 2010, s 8*). Furthermore, the effective freezing of the nil rate band at £325,000 was extended (by *FA 2014, Sch 25, para 2*) for the tax years 2015/16 to 2017/18 inclusive.

14.2 Prior to the introduction of the transferable nil rate band facility, it was generally important to ensure that the estates of spouses or civil partners were sufficient to utilise their available IHT thresholds (or 'nil rate bands') if possible, and that optimum use was made of the nil rate band on the first death. If each spouse or civil partner owned sufficient assets to constitute their nil rate bands, the estates of each individual could be sheltered from IHT up to an amount equal to the nil rate band multiplied by the 40% 'death rate'.

However, as indicated at **1.20**, there is a complete exemption (in *s 18*) for transfers between UK-domiciled spouses or civil partners during lifetime and on death. It should be noted that if the transferor spouse or civil partner is UK domiciled but the transferee is non-UK domiciled, the exemption is restricted to a cumulative upper limit. This limit remained unchanged for many years (ie £55,000 up to and including 2012/13 but was increased (in *FA 2013)* to the prevailing nil rate band at the time of the transfer (£325,000 for 2016/17), unless a valid election is made for the transferee spouse or civil partner to be treated as UK domiciled (in which case the upper limit does not apply, but the individual's worldwide estate is then generally liable to IHT in the same way as a UK domiciled individual).

Thus, if a deceased spouse or civil partner leaves their entire estate to the surviving spouse, then (unless the recipient spouse or civil partner is non-UK domiciled), the legacy will normally be wholly exempt from IHT. However, the estate of the survivor increases accordingly.

14.3 Prior to the *Finance Act 2008* changes, exempt legacies between spouses or civil partners often resulted in an IHT liability on the second death, and a higher IHT liability overall, due to the nil rate band on the first death not being utilised. Therefore IHT planning for married couples or civil partners typically involved ensuring that an amount up to the available nil rate band was left to non-exempt legatees (eg children), or (say) to a family discretionary trust in which the surviving spouse was included among the class of beneficiaries. This planning was relatively straightforward and simple to implement if each spouse or civil partner owned sufficient 'liquid' assets (eg cash, shares or other investments) to constitute their nil rate bands.

However, lifetime transfers between spouses or civil partners were often necessary to achieve this result on death. In some cases, the only asset of any substantial value would be an interest in the family home. This resulted in relatively complicated (and sometimes artificial) arrangements involving an interest in the family home to constitute the nil rate band, such as 'debt' or 'charge' schemes (see **Chapter 15**).

Transferable nil rate band claims cannot be made by cohabiting couples who are not legally married or civil partners (see *Executor of Holland deceased v IRC* [2003] SpC 350), or by family members who occupy the same property, such as siblings (see *Burden and another v United Kingdom* [2008] All ER (D) 391 (Apr)).

14.4 Whilst nil rate band legacies to chargeable (non-exempt) beneficiaries on the first spouse or civil partner to die will undoubtedly be less common or popular than before the introduction of the transferable nil rate band facility, there may be circumstances in which such legacies are necessary or preferred, such as in terms of making provision for offspring. In addition, aside from IHT considerations there may be other reasons why an interest in the home may be left on trust (eg due to concerns about remarriage). However, the transferable nil rate band facility has undoubtedly made IHT planning simpler for many spouses or civil partners, compared with the position prior to 9 October 2007.

HMRC's published guidance on the transferable nil rate band provisions is contained in the Inheritance Tax Manual at IHTM43000 onwards, and reference is made to some of this guidance below.

HMRC has also published an 'Inheritance Tax Toolkit' to assist tax agents and advisers in the preparation of IHT account form IHT400 (www.gov.uk/government/publications/hmrc-inheritance-tax-toolkit). The toolkit identifies various areas of risk for completing IHT400. The 'risk' in respect of the transferable nil rate band is 'If full details of any pre-deceased spouse or civil partner have not been obtained the transferable nil rate band may be overlooked or not applied correctly…' The toolkit goes on to suggest various ways to mitigate this risk. See **14.17** below.

The residence nil rate band is available on death from 6 April 2017 if an interest in the home passes to a lineal descendant (*ss 8D–8M*). This residence nil rate band may generally be transferred to a surviving spouse (or civil partner) to the extent that it remains unused on the first death, subject to a successful claim being made. For commentary on the residence nil rate band see **14.42–14.48** below and **Chapter 15**.

OUTLINE OF THE RULES

14.5 The transferable nil rate band legislation forms *ss 8A–8C*, with consequential changes to *ss 239, 242* and *272* (note – *FA 2008* also amended *s 151BA*, prior to its repeal in *FA 2011*, with effect for deaths occurring from 6 April 2011).

The provisions broadly allow claims for the transfer of a spouse's or civil partner's unused nil rate band to a surviving spouse or civil partner who dies on or after 9 October 2007. Therefore, if both spouses or civil partners died before 9 October 2007, it is not possible to take advantage of the transferable nil rate band facility.

The amount that can be transferred is based on a percentage of the deceased's nil rate band. That percentage (which cannot exceed 100) represents the nil rate band (or bands, where there was more than one former spouse or civil partner) not used on any previous occasion, taking into account lifetime transfers made within seven years before death, and is applied to the nil rate band in operation on the death of the surviving spouse (*s 8A*).

A claim to transfer unused nil rate band must be made by the survivor's personal representatives, within two years from the end of the month in which the survivor dies, or (if later) within three months of the personal representatives first acting as such. However, HMRC may allow a longer period at their discretion. In the absence of a claim by the personal representatives, a late claim may be made by any person liable to IHT on the survivor's death, subject to HMRC's agreement (*s 8B*).

There are potentially complicated rules for dealing with the transfer of the nil rate band and the calculation of IHT when certain IHT and capital transfer tax deferred charges (ie on heritage assets and woodlands) are triggered, where the deferred IHT is calculated by reference to the earlier deceased spouse (*s 8C*).

There are also rules to determine the amount of nil rate band to be applied in calculating IHT where a dependant who inherits an alternatively secured pension (ASP) fund dies or ceases to be a dependant (see **14.15**). However, following changes introduced in *FA 2011*, the IHT provisions relating to ASP funds (in *ss 151A–151E*) do not apply (subject to transitional provisions) with effect for deaths occurring from 6 April 2011.

CALCULATING THE UNUSED NIL RATE BAND

14.6

Focus

- The provisions allowing for the transfer of unused nil rate band between spouses and civil partners broadly apply if someone dies leaving a surviving spouse or civil partner, and there is some unused nil rate band on the deceased's death (*s 8A(1)*).
- It does not matter if the unused nil rate band arises because no assets were owned on death.
- Nor does it matter whether the first spouse or civil partner to die was actually or deemed domiciled in the UK; every person (UK domiciled or not) is potentially entitled to a nil rate band (see HMRC's example at IHTM43042).
- The rules for calculating the unused nil rate band involve a formula approach *(s 8A(2))*. However, in essence there is 'unused' nil rate band to the extent that the spouse or civil partner's chargeable estate on first death was less than their available nil rate band.

On the death of the surviving spouse or civil partner, their available nil rate band is increased by a percentage. The legislation provides a formula for calculating that percentage (*s 8A(4)*).

The terminology and formulae used in the legislation for the basic calculation of the transferable nil rate band is reproduced below, but is broadly the amount of the deceased's unused nil rate band, divided by the nil rate band upon the deceased spouse's or civil partner's death.

Unused nil rate band on death (s 8A(2)):

M > VT, where:

- M is the maximum amount that could be transferred by a chargeable transfer made on the person's death if it were to be wholly chargeable to tax at the rate of 0%; and
- VT is the value actually transferred by the chargeable transfer so made (or nil, if applicable).

The percentage increase in the survivor's nil rate band maximum (Note: this is subject to an overriding maximum of 100% (*s 8A(5)*), and to the 'clawback' rules (*s 8C*) in respect of heritage property and woodlands relief):

$$\left(\frac{E}{\text{NRBMD}}\right) \times 100$$

Where –

- E is the amount by which M is greater than VT in the case of the deceased person; and
- NRBMD is the nil rate band maximum at the time of the deceased person's death.

In HMRC's view, the percentage should be taken to four decimal places, if necessary (IHTM43020).

Example 14.1—Practical effect of a nil rate band transfer

Adam died on 31 March 2016. His chargeable death estate amounted to £145,000, and he had made no lifetime gifts. His wife Bertha died on 1 November 2016 with a chargeable estate of £400,000 and having made no lifetime gifts.

Adam's unused nil rate band available on Bertha's death is calculated as follows:

Unused nil rate band (M > VT) (*s 8A(2)*):

£325,000 (M, being the nil rate band maximum for 2015/16) – £145,000 (VT, being the chargeable death estate) = £180,000

Percentage increase

$$\left(\frac{E}{\text{NRBMD}}\right) \times 100$$

(*s 8A(3)*):

Where E is Adam's unused nil rate band, and NRBMD is the nil rate band on Adam's death:

$$\frac{£180,000}{£325,000} \times 100 = 55.3846\%$$

On Bertha's death, 55.3846% of unused nil rate band (£325,000 for 201617) in respect of Adam can be added to her own:

£325,000 × 55.3846% = £180,000

The combination of Adam's unused nil rate band (£180,000) and Bertha's nil rate band (£325,000) is sufficient to cover Bertha's chargeable estate of £400,000. No IHT is therefore payable on her death.

14.7 However, the amount of unused nil rate band that can be claimed on the survivor's death is subject to potential restrictions in the following circumstances:

- The estate of the earlier spouse or civil partner to die made a claim to transfer unused nil rate band from a previous deceased spouse or civil partner. The estate of the surviving spouse or civil partner may only claim a maximum of the nil rate band then in force (*s 8A(6)(a)*).
- There is also an overriding limit of one additional nil rate band (based on the rate applicable on the survivor's death) if, for example, the surviving spouse was married more than once, and his or her deceased spouses did not use up their nil rate bands on death. The survivor's estate can claim in respect of both previous spouses, but the nil rate band of the survivor's estate can only be increased by 100%, or one additional nil rate band (*s 8A(6)(b)*).
- As indicated at **14.5**, the nil rate band of the deceased spouse or civil partner may be subject to adjustment in respect of certain deferred charges (*s 8A(3)*) (see **14.11** below).

Example 14.2—Maximum claim

Colin and Delia had been married for many years, until Delia sadly died on 31 January 2003. By her will, Delia left £50,000 to their only daughter Joanne, with residue to Colin.

Colin subsequently found friendship and love in Elizabeth, and they were married in 2007. Elizabeth died on 1 May 2013, leaving £150,000 to her nieces and nephews, with residue to Colin.

Colin passed away on 31 March 2017, leaving a chargeable estate of £800,000 to Joanne.

Delia's unused nil rate band amounted to £200,000, ie £250,000 (the nil rate band maximum for 2002/03), less the chargeable legacy of £50,000. The percentage nil rate band unused was 80%.

Elizabeth's unused nil rate band amounted to £175,000, ie £325,000 (the nil rate band maximum for 2013/14), less chargeable legacies of £150,000. The percentage unused nil rate band was 53.8462%.

On Colin's death, the unused nil rate band percentage from his two marriages amounts to 133.8462% (ie 80% for Delia and 53.8462% for Elizabeth). However, the maximum percentage that can be claimed by Colin's estate is 100%. A claim is therefore made to add 100% of £325,000 (the nil rate band maximum for 2016/17) to Colin's own nil rate band of £325,000. The combined nil rate bands therefore amount to £650,000.

The IHT payable in respect of Colin's estate is as follows:

£800,000 – £650,000 = £150,000 × 40% = £60,000

TRANSFER CLAIMS

14.8 Transfers of unused nil rate band on the death of a spouse or civil partner must be claimed (*s 8A(3)*). The rules for such claims are in *s 8B*.

Focus

- In practice, the claim is made on Schedule IHT402 ('Claim to transfer unused nil rate band') by the personal representative of the surviving spouse or civil partner within a 'permitted period' (see below).
- If an excepted estate meets the conditions for a transferable nil rate band claim, the claim can be made by the personal representatives completing form IHT217 ('Claim to transfer unused nil rate band for excepted estates') and submitting it to the Sheriff Court (or Probate Registry in England) along with form C5 or form IHT205 ('Return of estate information') (see IHTM06025).
- The 'permitted period' is (see *s 8B(3)*) two years from the end of the month in which the survivor dies or, if later, three months from the date on which the personal representatives first act as such. If no claim has been made by the personal representatives, a claim can be made by any other person who is liable to IHT on the survivor's death.
- The legislation permits late claims at HMRC's discretion (*s 8B(1)(b)*).

HMRC may admit claims submitted late due to reasons beyond the claimant's control on a discretionary basis. Possible circumstances may include the following (see IHTM43009):

- if there is a dispute over the estate, which must be resolved before the personal representatives can be identified, and there is subsequently insufficient time (beyond the extended 'permitted period' of three months mentioned above) for the recently identified personal representatives to make a claim;
- unforeseen postal disruptions resulting in the loss or delay of a claim;
- the loss of records supporting a claim due to fire, flood or theft, where the records could not be replaced in time for a claim within the permitted period;
- serious illness of the claimant (or possibly a close relative or partner, depending on the circumstances);
- the death of a close relative or partner shortly before the end of the permitted period, where necessary steps had already been taken to make the claim on time;
- the claimant can show that they were not aware (and could not reasonably have been aware) of their entitlement to make a claim.

Schedule IHT402 is available via the gov.uk website (www.gov.uk/government/uploads/system/uploads/attachment_data/file/497793/IHT402.pdf), as is form IHT217 in relation to excepted estates (www.gov.uk/government/uploads/system/uploads/attachment_data/file/371956/iht217.pdf).

The nil rate band in force upon the spouse or civil partner's death can generally be found the gov.uk website (www.gov.uk/government/publications/rates-and-allowances-inheritance-tax-thresholds/inheritance-tax-thresholds). HMRC's tables list the nil rate band from 16 August 1914 onwards. The nil rate band from that date until 9 April 1946 was £100.

If the personal representatives of the deceased's estate do not make a claim to transfer unused nil rate band (eg if there is no need to take out a grant), any other person liable for tax on the survivor's death (eg the trustees of a settlement or the donee of a gift) may make a claim, but only when the initial period for claim by the personal representatives (in *s 8B(3)(a)*) has passed. In those cases, the claimant should use form IHT216 (IHTM43006) which is available via the gov.uk website (www.gov.uk/government/publications/inheritance-tax-claim-to-transfer-unused-inheritance-tax-nil-rate-band-iht216).

HMRC's IHT & Trusts Newsletter (August 2008) included the following criticism of claims by agents to transfer unused nil rate bands on behalf of their clients, which is worth noting:

> 'One disappointing feature since the introduction of these new provisions is the very high initial failure rate by agents to provide the supporting details we ask for. The IHT216 claim form lists the documents that we want to see

to support the claim for relief, and in only 20 per cent of cases submitted by agents are all the requested documents provided. This is in stark contrast to claims made by unrepresented taxpayers who manage to provide all the documents at the first time of asking.'

14.9 The failure to make a claim on an earlier death could have an unfortunate knock-on effect on the amount of nil rate band that may subsequently be claimed.

However, the legislation provides for some possible relief. For example, when a surviving spouse ('C') dies and C's personal representatives discover that no claim was made on the deceased spouse's ('B') death in respect of an earlier spouse's death ('A'), a claim is allowed in respect of A's death as well as B's death, if the original IHT position of A is unaffected (*s 8B(2)*).

Once a claim is made it can be withdrawn, but no later than one month after the end of the permitted claim period (*s 8B(4)*).

14.10

> **Focus**
>
> - Claims for the transfer of unused IHT nil rate bands between spouses and civil partners apply 'for the purposes of the charge to tax on the death of the survivor' (*s 8A(3)*).
> - A transfer could therefore reduce IHT on the survivor's free estate, together with any gifts with reservation of benefit property treated as being included in the estate, and the value of property subject to a qualifying interest in possession.
> - It can also reduce the additional tax on a chargeable lifetime transfer, and the tax on a failed PET.

However, surviving spouses or civil partners should not try to claim an extra nil rate band on a chargeable lifetime transfer, such as to a discretionary trust. The deceased's nil rate band is not available in that event, and an unexpected IHT liability could therefore arise.

Of course, should the surviving spouse or civil partner die within seven years, an extra nil rate band may then be available. However, the rules do not provide for the refund of any lifetime IHT paid, in which case the transferred nil rate band effectively provides relief at only 20%, as opposed to 40%.

Example 14.3—Lifetime transfers and the death estate

Ken died in May 2008, leaving his entire estate to his wife Susan. In June 2014, Susan added £200,000 to a discretionary trust for her adult children. She had originally established the trust in July 2009, by settling an investment property worth £200,000. She used her annual exemptions elsewhere each year.

Susan died in September 2016, leaving her estate of £400,000 to her children.

June 2014 – IHT on lifetime transfer to discretionary trust

The value transferred of £200,000, when added to the earlier chargeable transfer of £200,000, exceeded Susan's nil rate band for 2014/15 of £325,000 (note that it is not possible to add Ken's unused nil rate band for this lifetime transfer) by £75,000. The IHT liability is £75,000 × 20% = £15,000.

September 2016 – Susan's death

Susan's estate amounted to £400,000. Her remaining nil rate band, after taking into account the gift of £200,000 in June 2014 (Note: the earlier gift of £200,000 in July 2009 is not taken into account for the purpose of this calculation, as it was made more than seven years previously) is £125,000 (ie £325,000 less £200,000). A claim is made for Ken's unused nil rate band percentage of 100%, giving Susan's estate an additional nil rate band of £325,000.

The total nil rate band of £450,000 is sufficient to cover Susan's death estate, so no IHT is due. However, the lifetime IHT in June 2014 cannot be repaid.

CLAWBACK OF NIL RATE BAND

14.11 It may become necessary to consider the effect on the transferable nil rate band of an IHT charge in respect of heritage assets (*ss 32, 32A*) and woodlands (*s 126*), where relief was given on an earlier death.

This is because where property is granted conditional exemption or woodlands relief on the first death, IHT is generally due on the sale proceeds of the property, or its value when the undertaking was breached. As may be imagined, the availability of the nil rate band can affect that tax charge.

Section 8C takes account of this, by providing rules dealing with the interaction of the nil rate band and the calculation of IHT where a heritage or woodland deferred IHT or capital transfer tax charge applies.

The clawback provisions apply if there was unused nil rate band on the death of a spouse or civil partner, and after the person's death a deferred tax charge arises on heritage assets or woodlands, by reference to the deceased spouse's or civil partner's estate (*s 8C(1)*).

Clawback whilst surviving spouse still alive

14.12 If the event triggering the charge happens before the death of the surviving spouse, it becomes necessary to recalculate the available nil rate band. Broadly, the original transferable nil rate band percentage is calculated. A further calculation (under *s 8C(2))* quantifies the nil rate band used by the charge on disposal. The original percentage is then reduced to give the revised percentage of nil rate band available for transfer to the estate of the surviving spouse. To apply the legislation:

- First, find the nil rate band for the first spouse to die (defined as 'NRBMD' in *s 8A(4)*).
- Next, find the current nil rate band, ie that in force at the time of the event triggering the charge (defined by *s 8C(2)* as 'NRBME').
- Next, establish 'E': this is the excess of the nil rate band over the chargeable transfer at the first death: effectively the unused nil rate band.
- Finally (for this stage of the computation), calculate 'TA': this is the amount on which the clawback is charged.

Then apply the formula:

$$\left(\frac{\text{E}}{\text{NRBMD}} - \frac{\text{TA}}{\text{NRBME}}\right) \times 100$$

The result represents the percentage of the nil rate band in respect of which a claim may be made.

A worked example is included in the Inheritance Tax Manual (see IHTM43045).

Example 14.4—Heritage property

Edwina owned a painting by a well-known artist, which was the subject of an undertaking (under *s 30*) upon her death in January 2015. That undertaking was breached in November 2016 when the general public were no longer allowed reasonable access to the painting, triggering an IHT charge (under *s 32*). The painting was worth £200,000.

Edwina had made no chargeable lifetime transfers. In her will, she left £10,000 to her cleaner Mavis, and the residue of her estate (apart from the painting) to her husband Frederick.

Nil rate band, January 2015 (NRBMD):	£325,000
Nil rate band, November 2016 (NRBME):	£325,000
Unused nil rate band, January 2015 (applying the formula in *s 8A(2)* and *(4)*) (E):	£315,000

M = £325,000

VT = £10,000

E = (M – VT) = £315,000

TA: £200,000

Computation: $\left(\frac{£315{,}000}{£325{,}000} - \frac{£200{,}000}{£325{,}000}\right) \times 100$

(0.9692 – 0.6154) × 100 = 35.3800% of the nil rate band available for transfer to Frederick's estate on his death.

If there is more than one breach of undertaking, or where for example there are several woodland clawback charges, the nil rate band that may be transferred is reduced by the proportion of the nil rate band clawed back by all the deferred charges, ie by the aggregate of TA/NRBME in respect of each triggering event (*s 8C(3)*).

Clawback after the second death

14.13 If a deferred charge is triggered after the nil rate band has been transferred, *s 8C(4)* reduces the nil rate band of the first spouse to die. The mechanics of the adjustment are set out in *s 8C(5)*.

The nil rate band of the first to die of the spouses or civil partners is first adjusted by applying *Sch 2* (the uprating provisions that give the benefit of any reduction in the tax that applies because the nil rate band has been increased over time).

That uprated nil rate band is then potentially both increased and decreased. The increase can apply where the first spouse to die might himself have more than one nil rate band available, perhaps being a widower. The reduction is the amount of any increase in that band by virtue of the nil rate band transfer rules, to the extent that it kept the survivor's estate free of an IHT charge. A worked example is included in the Inheritance Tax Manual (see IHTM43046).

Example 14.5—Practical effect of a clawback

Jonathan was first married to Katherine, who left her estate to Jonathan when she died in May 2001. Katherine had not used any of her nil rate band.

In January 2007, Jonathan married Lucy.

On Jonathan's death in January 2015, he left Lucy his estate, apart from a legacy of £100,000 to his favourite nephew Percy. Jonathan's family's heritage asset was sold for £150,000 by Lucy's executors shortly after her death in October 2016, thereby triggering a clawback charge under *s 32*.

The nil rate band in May 2001 was £242,000. None of it was used by Katherine.

The nil rate band on Jonathan's death in January 2015 was £325,000. The total nil rate band available to his executor is (£325,000 – £100,000 = £225,000 + £325,000) = £550,000.

The nil rate band at Lucy's death in October 2016, and when the heritage asset was sold, is £325,000. The clawback charge is on £150,000. Jonathan's estate now has available an increased nil rate band of (£550,000 – £150,000): £400,000.

Any clawback charge following the death of the survivor (Lucy) under *s 8C(5)* would depend upon the extent (if any) to which the nil rate band transferred from Jonathan's estate was required to keep Lucy's estate free of IHT. If a claim to 'legitim' is made after a claim to transfer unused nil rate band following the death of the second parent, HMRC may adjust the claim in respect of the unused nil band accordingly (*s 147(10)*; see IHTM43041).

Unexhausted Alternatively Secured Pension funds

14.14 As indicated at **14.5** above, the IHT provisions relating to alternatively secured pension (ASP) funds (in *ss 151A–151E*) ceased to apply following legislation in *FA 2011*, which amended the pension rules (in *FA 2004, Pt 4*) relating to registered pension schemes applying to individuals reaching the age of 75. The changes broadly removed the effective requirement to buy an annuity by the age of 75. From 6 April 2011, IHT generally ceased to apply to drawdown pension funds remaining under a registered pension scheme, including where the individual died after reaching the age of 75.

Although the IHT rules affecting the transferable nil rate band were repealed with effect for deaths occurring from 6 April 2011, they still need to be considered in respect of deaths prior to that date.

The background to the rules is the IHT charge that arises (under *s 151B*) on that part of an ASP fund which has not been used in benefits for the fund member and his dependants. In broad terms, the unexhausted fund is treated as the 'top slice' of the member's estate for IHT purposes. *Section 151BA(5)* uprates the nil rate band that is to be applied. The provisions were modified in *FA 2008*, by the introduction of *ss 151BA(6), (7)*.

Once again, a formula first requires the taxpayer to establish certain values:

E (as before) is the unused excess nil rate band available; and

NRBM is the nil rate band in force when the member died.

The formula is:

$$100 - \left(\frac{E}{NRBM}\right) \times 100$$

This produces 'the used up percentage', ie the fraction by which the nil rate band otherwise available to the member is to be reduced.

Example 14.6—Pension funds and the clawback

Martha died in May 2010, when the nil rate band was £325,000. She made no lifetime gifts but left £75,000 to her sister and the rest of her estate, including her pension rights, to her husband Norman. He did not draw the entire pension. He had no dependants. The unexhausted portion of the pension fund, at his death on 2 February 2011, was £150,000.

For Martha's estate:

E = £250,000 (ie £325,000 – £75,000);

NRBM = £325,000; and

The 'used up percentage' is 100 – ((£250,000/£325,000) × 100), ie 100% – 76.9231% = 23.0769%.

This is the part of Martha's nil rate band that has been used.

A section of HMRC's Inheritance Tax Manual is devoted to the interaction with ASPs (IHTM43047 to IHTM43052), and a full worked example where the deceased's estate includes funds in an ASP is included at IHTM43048 to IHTM43050.

14.15 The position becomes more complicated where the pension fund is still not exhausted by the death of the second person benefiting from it. This follows from *s 151BA(8)–(12)*, which was also introduced in *Finance Act 2008*.

First, the situation is addressed where there has been an IHT charge on an ASP fund by reference to the first spouse or civil partner to die. This affects the person's nil rate band and restricts the amount available for transfer later: it is 'appropriately reduced' (under *s 151BA(9)*) where the chargeable event occurred after the death of the surviving spouse.

If, however, the surviving spouse is still alive when the chargeable event happens, tax is charged when the survivor dies by adjusting the member's transferable nil rate band using a formula (see *s 151BA(12)*), which compares the 'adjusted excess' with the 'adjusted nil rate band maximum', expressed as a percentage.

Where the charge arises after both spouses have died, each may have used part of his or her nil rate band, so there may be less available to meet the IHT charge under *s 151B* (see *s 151BA(9)*), as augmented by the definitions set out in *s 151BA(10)*).

Where the charge arises whilst the surviving spouse is still alive, the formula in *s 151BA(12)* applies. This restricts the nil rate band available later. AE, the adjusted excess, deducts from the maximum nil rate band the value transferred by chargeable transfers after calculating the taxable amount and after adjusting the nil rate band itself: ANRBM. ANRBM is the nil rate band, adjusted for ASP charges under *s 151B*.

HMRC's Inheritance Tax Manual includes worked examples of the calculations of the recapture charge where the surviving spouse dies and transferable nil rate band has been claimed before the recapture charge is triggered (see IHTM43052), and also where the spouse dies after the recapture charge (see IHTM43052).

IHT clearance certificates

14.16 A 'certificate of discharge' (or clearance certificate) confirms HMRC's satisfaction that all the IHT due in a particular case has been (or will be) paid (*s 239*).

Inevitably, there is always a risk that tax charges will be missed. However, the clearance certificate issued by HMRC will not guarantee freedom from IHT charges where the amount of the nil rate band that was transferred must be adjusted, such as by the clawback in respect of heritage property.

Section 239 is qualified accordingly (with effect from 9 October 2007), so that if too little IHT has been paid because of adjustment to the nil rate band, those persons who are accountable remain liable to pay the balance (*s 239(4)(aa)*).

Penalties

14.17 The penalty regime for inaccuracies in tax returns (in *FA 2007, Sch 24*) was extended for IHT purposes (by *FA 2008, Sch 40*) in respect of events and periods from 1 April 2009, where the filing date is 1 April 2010 or later (although if information or a document is produced under *s 256* ('Regulations about accounts, etc') from 1 April 2009, the tax period must begin on or after that date). It generally provides for tax-geared penalties of between 0% and 100%, broadly depending on a person's behaviour and the level of disclosure to HMRC.

Note that the penalty regime for offshore tax evasion (introduced by *FA 2010, Sch 10*), which provides for significantly higher penalties, does not apply for IHT purposes under the original offshore penalty provisions. However, the offshore penalty regime is extended by *FA 2015* to include IHT, from a date to be appointed by statutory instrument (*FA 2015, s 120(2)*). The penalties regime in connection with offshore asset moves (in *FA 2015, Sch 21*) also applies for IHT (and income tax and CGT) purposes, with effect in relation to 'relevant offshore asset moves' from 27 March 2015.

The circumstances in which a penalty could be imposed potentially includes (for example) an overstated claim for the transfer of unused nil rate band, resulting in an IHT underpayment. Penalties can be imposed on the person making the return, and on another person who deliberately supplies false information resulting in an incorrect return (or who withholds information with the same intention) (*FA 2007, Sch 24, paras 1–1A*).

As to compliance and penalties generally, see **Chapter 6**.

14.18 For periods prior to the introduction of the above penalty regime for inaccuracies for IHT purposes, the relevant penalty rules in respect of the provision of incorrect information are contained in *s 247(1)* and *(2)*.

A person liable for the tax who fraudulently or negligently supplies an incorrect account, information or document to HMRC is liable to a penalty (*s 247(1)*). The maximum penalty is 100% of the tax potentially lost (ie broadly the difference between the amount of tax correctly payable, and the amount of tax payable based on the incorrect return etc).

Penalties can be calculated in respect of the liability of someone other than the person in default (under *s 247(2)*) if incorrect information was supplied in connection with a claim to transfer unused nil rate band. This provision was introduced from 21 July 2008, to apply to an incorrect IHT return delivered in respect of the first death from that date (see IHTM43061).

The IHT legislation concerning incorrect information provided for a penalty of up to £3,000 where any person (eg an agent) assisted in or induced incorrect returns, information etc (*s 247(4)*). This provision was repealed with effect from 1 April 2013 (by *The Finance Act 2012, Schedule 38 (Tax Agents: Dishonest Conduct) (Appointed Day and Savings) Order 2013, SI 2013/279*), following the introduction of legislation dealing with tax agents who engage in dishonest conduct (*FA 2012, Sch 38*). Those provisions include powers for HMRC to issue agents who are considered to be dishonest with a 'conduct notice', to access the agent's working papers, and to impose a penalty of up to £50,000.

Personal representatives of the surviving spouse or civil partner must be mindful of the potential risk, and exercise due diligence when claiming unused nil rate band from an earlier death.

HMRC's IHT Toolkit includes a checklist item concerning 'Information gathering': 'Has it been identified whether the deceased had a spouse or civil partner who died before them and if so, have their details been obtained?' The Toolkit defines the transferable nil rate band as an area of risk, if full details of any predeceased spouse or civil partner have not been obtained, and advocates thorough research on their background. The Toolkit also highlights a number of 'common points often overlooked' in connection with claims to transfer unused nil rate band.

The IHT Toolkit is available via the HMRC website: www.gov.uk/government/publications/hmrc-inheritance-tax-toolkit.

Valuations

14.19 The 'value ascertained' capital gains tax rule in *TCGA 1992, s 274* ('Value determined for inheritance tax'), under which values ascertained for IHT purposes apply for capital gains tax purposes, was amended in *Finance Act 2008* as a consequence of the introduction of the transferable nil rate band, from 6 April 2008.

The effect is that an asset valuation for the purposes of calculating the amount of transferable nil rate band (as opposed to calculating the amount of any IHT on death) cannot be applied for CGT purposes as well.

DEATHS BEFORE 25 JULY 1986

14.20 IHT was introduced in 1986. However, the transferable nil rate band provisions are adapted in cases where an earlier spouse died before 25 July 1986, and the surviving spouse died on or after 9 October 2007. *Finance Act 2008* modified *s 8A* accordingly, so that the rules apply for capital transfer tax purposes where the spouse died between 1 January 1985 and 24 July 1986, or between 13 March 1975 and 31 December 1984, as appropriate (*FA 2008, Sch 4 para 10(2), (3)*).

Similarly, the transferable nil rate band provisions are adapted for estate duty purposes where the spouse died between 16 April 1969 and 12 March 1975, or before 16 April 1969, as appropriate (*FA 2008, Sch 4 para 10(4), (5)*).

Between 22 March 1972 and 12 November 1974, the spouse exemption was limited to £15,000, and it was therefore possible that the estate may have been liable to estate duty. Prior to 22 March 1972. there was no spouse exemption at all. Thus if property was left to a spouse, an estate duty charge could have arisen. If the estate was large enough for duty to be paid, the equivalent of the nil rate band would have been exhausted, so that there would be nothing left to transfer.

Example 14.7—Elderly testatrix

Sarah is now nearly 90. She has savings and investments worth £600,000, and is looked after by her son Thomas in his home. Sarah married Frank in 1960 but he died in November 1971 intestate. Frank's personal estate, which passed to Sarah, was worth £2,500 at a time when the estate duty tax-free band was £12,500.

There was no spouse exemption in November 1971: the relief (limited to £15,000) was not introduced until 22 March 1972. That limitation was lifted from 13 November 1974. Sarah's inheritance of the share of the house therefore used 20% of the then equivalent of the nil rate band, so 80% was unused and is still available for transfer.

Against Sarah's estate of £600,000 her executors may set 180% of the current nil rate band, ie £585,000, leaving £15,000 to suffer an IHT charge at 40% of £6,000.

The 'clawback' provisions dealing with the interaction of the transferable nil rate band and IHT or capital transfer tax charges in respect of heritage relief and woodland relief (see **14.11**) are also adapted accordingly, where the surviving spouse died on or after 9 October 2007 and the earlier spouse died between 13 March 1975 and 24 July 1986 (ie between 1 January 1985 and 24 July 1986, or between 7 April 1976 and 31 December 1984, or between 13 March 1975 and 6 April 1976), so that the clawback rules in *s 8C* apply to the appropriate capital transfer tax legislation (*FA 2008, Sch 4 para 11*).

As to ascertaining the nil rate band for earlier years, see **14.8** above.

PRACTICAL ISSUES

Record keeping

14.21 The transferability of unused nil rate band comes at an administrative cost in terms of keeping records and documents. Some discipline will be required on the part of surviving spouses or civil partners and their personal representatives, in terms of obtaining, keeping and maintaining records in respect of the earlier spouse or civil partner to die and their estate.

Practical issues may arise in terms of the valuation of assets and the availability of IHT reliefs. For example, HMRC's present policy seems to be not to check claims for 100% business property relief (BPR) or agricultural property relief (APR) where there is no immediate IHT liability, such as where personal representatives claim relief on an individual's death and no IHT liability would arise on the death regardless of the availability of BPR or APR, due to the deceased's available nil rate band.

However, such an issue will be relevant in determining the unused nil rate band available to the surviving spouse or civil partner. This may result in HMRC testing the availability of BPR or APR following the second death.

Focus

One important self-help procedure will be for widows, widowers and surviving civil partners to make and keep a record of the extent to which their late spouses or civil partners had used the nil rate band.

The case of Sarah at **Example 14.7** shows that it may be difficult to produce values many years later.

IHT practitioners should also encourage their clients to keep good records.

The Law Society of Scotland was unsuccessful in requesting that HMRC acknowledge in the context of the Transferable Nil Rate Band that taxpayers should be under no obligation to provide evidence more than 10 years prior to the announcement of Transferable Nil Rate Band (9 October 2007). Many practitioners will not hold records or files older than 10 years which creates difficulties in providing the information.

A simple form, along the lines of **Example 14.8**, might be placed with the survivor's will.

Example 14.8—Record of use of the nil rate band for IHT purposes

The following sample record is designed to establish how much of the nil rate band was used by a former spouse. In it, the terms 'married' and 'widowed' include being a member of a registered civil partnership and still being such a member when the civil partner died.

Part 1: Your relationship to the deceased person(s)

1 Have you been married?

2 If so, how many times?

3 Did your marriage end only on the death of your spouse?

4 If so, state the date your spouse died.

5 If you have been widowed more than once, state the date that each spouse died.

Part 2: Details of transfers and of the nil rate band available

6 If you know it, state the amount of the nil rate band when your spouse died (or when each spouse died).

7 Do you have a copy of the will that your spouse made (if applicable)?

8 Was that will, if any, varied within two years of death? If so, do you have a copy?

9 Did your spouse leave all his or her estate to you?

10 If not, state the value given by your late spouse to others, and specify if any was left exempt (for example, to charity).

11 Did your spouse make gifts to others in the seven years before death?

12 If so, state the amount given and to whom (again noting any gifts that were exempt for any reason).

Documents to support a claim

14.22 In addition to keeping a record of material events, the deceased spouse's or civil partner's personal representatives should provide certain documents in support of their claim to transfer the available unused nil rate band, when submitting form IHT400 on the death of the surviving spouse or civil partner.

Schedule IHT402 ('Claim to transfer unused nil rate band') (www.gov.uk/government/uploads/system/uploads/attachment_data/file/497793/IHT402.pdf) sets out the photocopied documents which must accompany the claim:

- copy of the grant of Confirmation to the estate of the spouse or civil partner (or, if no grant has been taken out, a copy of the death certificate);
- if the spouse or civil partner left a will, a copy of it;
- if a deed of variation or other similar document was executed to change the people who inherited the estate of the spouse or civil partner, a copy of it.

In addition, the personal representatives of the deceased spouse or civil partner should typically keep the following information in a safe place, or provide it for the survivor to keep in a safe place, to help establish the unused nil rate band available on their death:

- a copy of the HMRC return (form IHT400 or IHT205, forms C1 or C5);
- a copy of the deceased's will (if any);
- a copy of the marriage certificate;
- a copy of any documents (eg a deed of variation) executed after the death of the first spouse or civil partner, that changes who benefits from their estate;
- any valuation(s) of assets that pass under will or intestacy other than to the surviving spouse or civil partner; and/or
- any evidence to support the availability of relief (such as APR or BPR) where the relievable assets pass to someone other than to the surviving spouse or civil partner.

In the case of jointly owned assets, and in certain other cases (eg assets of the deceased's 'estate' interests in possession, lifetime gifts within seven years before death and 'gift with reservation' (GWR) assets), surviving spouses or civil partners (or their personal representatives) will need to obtain whatever relevant information and documentation is available in support of nil rate band claims (eg details of the assets concerned, and any evidence of their values).

14.23 Particularly in cases where the earlier spouse or civil partner died some time ago, there may be gaps in the information and documentation available. The survivor may have been unaware of the importance of keeping them, or documents may have been lost, stolen or accidentally destroyed.

HMRC have previously pointed out that certain documents are obtainable from public records bodies (eg copies of wills, grants of confirmation from the Scottish Court Service, or copies of death or marriage (or civil partnership) certificates from the General Register Office for Scotland (website addresses for which are listed on page 4 of form IHT402)). The documents do not need to be originals, or official copies; certified copies will suffice (HMRC IHT & Trusts Newsletter, April 2008).

In addition, HMRC indicate that provisional claims to transfer any unused nil rate band may be allowed if the personal representatives are having difficulty obtaining all the documents and the time limit for making the claim (see **14.8**) is approaching (IHTM43006).

However, the full details to make a claim may still be incomplete (eg such as assets subject to the GWR rules, as mentioned above). In those circumstances, the survivor's personal representatives will need to complete the claim to the best of their knowledge and ability, attaching whatever documents are available, and explaining to HMRC the reason for any omission.

It will clearly be preferable if personal representatives of the earlier spouse or civil partner can undertake the preparatory work for a possible future claim on the survivor's death, such as by packaging together the required information and documents and passing them to the survivor.

The Law Society of Scotland has approached HMRC for guidance on the length of time prior to the second death that records should have been retained. It has also been queried whether HMRC would be prepared to publish a statement acknowledging that records relating to deaths which occurred on or before 9 October 1997 (practitioners are obliged to hold files for 10 years) may well not be available, and that their genuine absence should not prejudice claims for use of unused nil rate band unless there is contrary evidence.

PLANNING ISSUES

Should the nil rate band be used on the first death?

14.24 As mentioned earlier in this chapter, the facility (introduced in *Finance Act 2008*) to allow for claims to transfer the unused nil rate band were backdated to cases where the surviving spouse or civil partner died on or after 9 October 2007.

IHT was once charged on an ascending scale, which encouraged the equalisation of estates between husband and wife. However, since 15 March 1988 the position has been simpler. After the nil rate band (£325,000 in 2015/16) has been used, there is only one single rate of 40% on death (half of that, 20%, for lifetime chargeable transfers), although a lower IHT rate of 36% applies to a deceased person's estate in certain circumstances involving charitable legacies (*Sch 1A*).

Thus, as a general rule, there is no advantage for IHT purposes in equalising estates as between husband and wife or civil partners. Following the introduction of the transferable nil rate band facility, it is no longer necessary for the nil rate band to be used on the death of the first spouse or civil partner, due to the possibility of transferring the unused proportion of a nil rate band to the estate of the surviving spouse or civil partner.

The residence nil rate band (from 6 April 2017) is similarly transferable in appropriate circumstances (see **14.42–14.48**).

14.25 The thinking behind utilising the nil rate band on the first death was to leave it to chargeable beneficiaries. However, many testators really wanted the primary benefit to go to the surviving spouse or civil partner, so the trustees of a discretionary nil rate band trust were encouraged to regard the surviving spouse as the primary beneficiary.

The deceased spouse or civil partner would typically leave a sum equivalent to the upper limit of the nil rate band upon a discretionary trust so that the surviving spouse could have the benefit of the fund and at the same time the nil rate band could be utilised and not wasted. Distributions could be made in favour of the surviving spouse in case of need; and if they were of capital any exit charge under the discretionary trust regime in the first ten years would be by reference to the testator's nil rate band.

Much of that thinking was rendered obsolete by the introduction of the transferable nil rate band facility. In most cases, the emphasis is on *not* using the nil rate band on the first death, in the hope that the transferable band will be larger on the second death, when it will really be needed.

However, some individuals may prefer to 'bank' the nil rate band, rather than rely on its availability on the survivor's death. In addition, there are still certain circumstances where a will should contain a nil rate band trust (see **14.28**).

14.26 Particular care should be taken over '28-day' survivorship clauses, especially where the deceased spouse has most of the estate and the surviving spouse has very little. This is because the effect of not passing value to the spouse could be to pass (chargeable) value to the next generation on the first death that exceeded the nil rate band which, had it been channelled through the estate of the (short) surviving spouse, might have benefited from that survivor's unused nil rate band. Do the sums before drafting the will.

In cases where the order of death of spouses (or civil partners) cannot be ascertained (for example in an accident) there is a legal presumption under the *Succession (Scotland) Act 2016, s 9* that where two people die simultaneously, neither is presumed to have survived the other, provided the rule in *s 10* of the Act does not apply. *Section 10* covers situations where property will pass to a person depending on the order of death but that property does not form part of either person's estate (for example a life policy). This situation was not covered by the *Succession (Scotland) Act 1964 Act*. The new rules therefore provide that in situations such as this, the property is to be divided equally between the estates of those persons unless there is express provision to the contrary.

If a Will contains a conditional survivorship period and if there is insufficient evidence to suggest that the beneficiary survived for that period of time, the new rules in the *Succession (Scotland) Act 2016* provide that the beneficiary should be treated as having failed to survive where there is insufficient evidence to prove otherwise.

14.27 If it is appropriate to use the nil rate band, it is worth noting that the threshold can be expected to increase annually (*s 8*). This increase was historically by reference to the retail prices index (RPI). However, following changes introduced in *FA 2012*, the consumer prices index (CPI) replaces the RPI as the default indexation assumption, albeit that automatic indexation using the CPI will not take effect for IHT purposes until 2018/19 at the earliest (see below). Automatic indexation may be overridden if the UK Parliament so determines.

As mentioned at **14.1**, the nil rate band was initially frozen at £325,000 for the tax years 2011/12 to 2014/15 inclusive (*FA 2010, s 8(3)*). The freezing of the nil rate band at £325,000 was extended (by *FA 2014, Sch 25, para 2*) for tax years up to and including 2017/18. In practice, the testator's will is often drafted to ensure that the gift matches the ceiling of the nil rate band when he dies.

The gift in the will should therefore be of an amount equivalent to the upper limit of the IHT nil rate band in force at the time of the testator's death under *Sch 1*, as amended in accordance with the indexation provisions of *s 8*, if applicable. Such a formula, while most useful for cash gifts, cannot of course operate in the same straightforward way in the case of specific legacies of assets, particularly where business or agricultural reliefs are involved and changes in values may occur.

14.28 For those taxpayers who had previously considered IHT planning in respect of their wills, such as the inclusion of a nil rate band discretionary trust on the first death, there are several arguments for doing nothing at all.

For example, discretionary will trusts can still be helpful in the following cases:

- where there is property qualifying for business or agricultural property relief (ie to 'bank' the relief, in the event of any future reduction or withdrawal of it). Where business or agricultural property relief at 100% is available, the value of the gift on top of the nil rate band is unlimited; relief at 50% effectively doubles the nil rate band, ie the nil rate band can cover a transfer of £650,000 in 2016/17 (in either case, a trust would not really be a 'nil rate band trust' in the normal sense of the term); or
- to shelter property from care fees; or
- for asset protection purposes, such as in the event of a future marriage breakdown; or
- if an asset is likely to appreciate in value faster than the nil rate band; or
- in cases where both individuals have been married before, and up to four nil rate bands are therefore available (see **14.32**).

In some cases, if a discretionary will trust is no longer considered to be desirable, it may be possible to reverse its effects for IHT purposes. This can be achieved during lifetime through a codicil to revoke the nil rate band transfer, or possibly following death by means of a deed of appointment, as illustrated in the example below.

Example 14.9—Appointment from nil rate band trust

Oliver and Patricia, who have been married for many years, made wills in 2007 that incorporate nil rate band discretionary trusts.

There is scope (under *s 144*) for the trustees of a discretionary trust to appoint funds or assets to beneficiaries within two years of the death. A distribution from the discretionary trust generally takes effect as if it had been a gift under the terms of the will and not a distribution from the trust. Therefore, there is no need to change the will.

If the will of the *surviving* spouse is drafted in common form, the provision as to the nil rate band will not apply because it has been excluded where the surviving spouse is not married at the date of death. In this scenario, therefore, all that is needed is a deed of appointment by the trustees of the nil rate band set up by the will of the first spouse to die.

Note: where the testator's death occurred before 10 December 2014, to avoid the difficulty that arose in *Frankland v IRC* [1997] STC 1450 (see **15.50**), the trustees would not normally take any action until three months elapsed from the date of death. On the death of the first to die of husband and wife, the trustees would therefore simply wait three months and appoint the whole of the nil rate band to the surviving spouse. There was no need to wait three months if the effect of the deed of appointment was to create an 'immediate post-death interest' (see **9.9**) – only if the interest created was an absolute one.

However, the above '*Frankland* trap' was resolved (in *F(No 2)A 2015*) by a change in legislation (see *s 144(1)(b)* as amended). The provision (in *s 65(4)*) that prevents an IHT charge arising in the first three months after a settlement commences (or within a ten-year anniversary) does not apply to appointments out of property settled by will where the testator's death occurs from 10 December 2014. This amendment therefore broadly allows a distribution from the trust made within three months of death in favour of the surviving spouse to be read back into the will, such that the spouse exemption (in *s 18*) will generally be available.

14.29 However, family conflict or indolence can delay the application for a grant of Confirmation. Things can get left. If one of the executors is a professional person, he will probably be negligent if he fails to do what is right for the family in terms of IHT. If the executors are all family members and if they miss the various deadlines, they could be worse off than if they had simpler wills.

14.30 The family home, and the use of an interest in the family home to constitute the nil rate band, are discussed in **Chapter 15**.

'Debt' or 'charge' arrangements (see **15.52**) are relatively complicated and difficult for taxpayers to understand. In addition, where there is an *FA 1986, s 103* problem, as illustrated by the *Phizackerley* case (see **15.53**) it can be difficult for professional advisers to explain the scheme to clients. Many people may have been slightly uncomfortable with the complexity of wills containing nil rate band discretionary trusts and they may feel much happier with simple new wills even though that will involve paying a new fee to have them prepared.

If both spouses or civil partners died before 9 October 2007, it will not be possible to make use of the transferable nil rate band provisions. Similarly, if one spouse or civil partner died some time ago, it may be too late to take advantage of the rules.

Example 14.10—Nil rate band discretionary trust: too late for action

Quentin died in 2012, leaving a widow, Rose. Quentin's will had a nil rate band discretionary trust. In this situation, nothing can (or should) be done.

By putting in place a nil rate band discretionary trust, Quentin has used his nil rate band.

Due to the time which has elapsed since his death, it is too late to make any changes relying on the 'two-year rule' in *s 144*. It is also too late to consider a deed of variation because, to be effective, it also had to be made within two years of death to claim relief under *s 142*.

Therefore, the only nil rate band available to Rose in the above example (unless she remarries and survives her second husband) is the single nil rate band. It would be totally wrong for the family to assume that 'we don't need that scheme now' and to appoint all the funds in the discretionary trust to the widow. That would just increase her estate without giving her back her late husband's nil rate band.

If a spouse or civil partner died recently, perhaps with a pre-9 October 2007 will in place, it may be possible in some cases to re-assess earlier estate planning with hindsight.

Example 14.11—Discretionary will trust: estate planning updated

Stanley made a will including a nil rate band discretionary trust for the benefit of his close family, with residue to his wife Tracy. The main asset was their house, worth £700,000, which was held by them as tenants in common in equal shares. Stanley had savings of £200,000. He died on 30 September 2014, having made no chargeable lifetime gifts.

Tracy and her daughter Ursula agreed that Tracy would sell the family home and move to a less expensive property closer to Ursula. The house would now sell for £800,000. Stanley's nil rate band of £325,000 was to be satisfied with his savings of £200,000, plus a further £125,000 from the house sale.

Tracy subsequently realised that she would not need any of the nil rate band, and preferred that, following the house sale, all of the money be released to Ursula. The family met with their adviser in March 2016 to consider whether to take advantage of the transferable nil rate band provisions (which had been introduced after Stanley's will was drafted). They decided that since they were still within two years of Stanley's death, they should effectively rewrite his will so that all Stanley's estate went to Tracy. That way, the whole of Stanley's nil rate band would be available on Tracy's death.

Any assets that were to be transferred to Ursula would not now be from the discretionary trust, but would be treated as a gift by Tracy. If Tracy lived seven years, those gifts would fall out of account. Apart from that, if the will was varied, the sale of the house could be treated as made by Tracy, and the whole of the gain would be tax free. They decided that it would be worthwhile effectively rewriting Stanley's will so that his nil rate band was unused on his death. Care would be needed to ensure that subsequent gifts by Tracy did not amount to consideration for the deed of variation.

Earlier marriages or civil partnerships

14.31 The starting point in a claim to transfer unused nil rate band is that the spouses (or civil partners) were married to each other at the time of the earlier death. It does not matter if, for example, the surviving spouse later remarried (although the surviving spouse's personal representatives can only claim one extra nil rate band) and was subsequently divorced.

If the surviving spouse remarries and dies before their new spouse, the unused nil rate band of the earlier spouse to die from the first marriage may be claimed by the survivor's personal representatives. The surviving spouse from the later marriage may subsequently be able to claim unused nil rate band from the remarried spouse if appropriate, subject to the overriding maximum of 100% of the nil rate band applicable on the last survivor's death.

If an individual has survived more than one marriage or civil partnership, his personal representatives may be able to claim additional nil rate band from more than one estate, subject to the aforementioned maximum. A separate claim form is required in respect of each estate. It is important to remember that unused nil rate band is not available for chargeable lifetime transfers by the survivor, although it may be available when calculating the IHT position in the event of the survivor's death within seven years of making that transfer.

Remarried spouses or civil partners who have already accrued an extra nil rate band from an earlier marriage or civil partnership should consider chargeable legacies (eg a discretionary trust) in their wills, as opposed to leaving everything to their later spouse. The former course of action could result in three nil rate bands being utilised upon the last surviving spouse's death (ie the nil rate bands of the deceased spouse from the earlier marriage, the remarried spouse and the last surviving spouse). The latter course of action could result in the complete loss of the nil rate band from the earlier marriage.

Cohabiting couples

14.32 In certain circumstances, up to four nil rate bands may be available. This could happen if, for example, a cohabiting couple who had each been married before left their respective estates to chargeable legatees such as adult children (or to the survivor), in order to utilise both their own nil rate band and the transferred nil rate band of their deceased spouse.

However, following marriage their overall IHT position could dramatically worsen.

Example 14.12—Multiple nil rate band: the effect of marrying

Vera, widowed with one daughter, had inherited from her husband all his modest estate. Her house was now worth £550,000. She had also accumulated investments worth £75,000.

William was retired. He had also inherited all of his late wife's estate and intended to leave his entire estate worth £600,000 to their son and daughter.

Vera and William decided to set up home together, living in Vera's house and letting out William's house. They consulted a tax adviser about getting married and leaving their estates to each other. Their adviser pointed out that leaving their estates to each other would not only result in the nil rate band of either William or Vera being wasted on the first death, but also the unused nil rate band of the spouse from their first marriage.

Marrying each other may well create a further unused nil rate band on the first of William or Vera to die, but it could not be transferred to the survivor, whose maximum nil rate entitlement had already been reached. The deceased spouse's additional nil rate band entitlement from their first marriage could not be transferred either.

However, if Vera and William did marry in the above example, consideration could be given to including a legacy to chargeable beneficiaries (eg to adult children, or to a discretionary will trust) on the first death, sufficient to use the deceased's nil rate band plus the transferred nil rate band from that person's first marriage.

The residence nil rate band (for deaths from 6 April 2017) will also need to be considered, where appropriate (see **3.42**).

Business or agricultural property

14.33 As discussed elsewhere in this chapter, discretionary trusts are a relatively common feature of wills drafted before the introduction of the transferable nil rate band, as they represented a possible means of using the nil rate band of the first spouse or civil partner to die.

A discretionary will trust may still be a useful vehicle to hold assets that are within the nil rate band, if their value is wholly or partly reduced for IHT purposes by business or agricultural property reliefs. Alternatively, a legacy of assets qualifying for 100% business or agricultural property to non-exempt beneficiaries on the first death should similarly result in the deceased's unused nil rate band being available for later transfer.

The effect of those reliefs is very important. Where relief is at 100% the benefit on top of the nil rate band is unlimited. With relief at 50%, for 2015/16 the nil rate band can cover a transfer of £650,000.

As a general principle, because of this multiplying effect, business and agricultural property should be given to chargeable parties rather than to the surviving spouse, to prevent it being wasted.

Example 14.13—'Doubling up' BPR

Yogi's will left all his assets attracting relief from IHT at 100% to a discretionary trust for the benefit of his children, and the residue of his estate to his wife Zoe. They had both always taken a keen interest in the family company's business. At the date of Yogi's death, all his shares attracted 100% business property relief (BPR). The shares were worth £800,000.

Zoe received those parts of the estate that did not qualify for any relief, together with substantial cash from insurance policies.

Zoe used some of the cash to buy the shares from the trustees. That gave the trustees far more, in real terms, than the nil rate band, so effectively the children could benefit from more than Yogi could have given in simple cash terms.

If Zoe lives two years from her purchase of the shares, BPR will again be available. Meanwhile, there is control over the children's future inheritance.

In the case of a partially exempt estate (ie because the spouse or civil partner exemption in *s 18* applies) a specific gift should be made of the business or agricultural property itself. It is not sufficient merely to create a specific pecuniary legacy payable out of the business or agricultural property. In the latter situation, relief is denied on the value of the pecuniary legacy and therefore (at least in part) lost (*s 39A(6)*).

Care fees considerations

14.34 Many couples are more concerned about the likely burden of care fees than about IHT. Care fee considerations are outside the scope of this book. However, in very broad terms a discretionary trust, properly run, is expensive (eg compliance procedures such as anti-money laundering rules in the UK have become more detailed and complex) but can shelter from care fees the estate of the first spouse, who is often cared for by the spouse who survives, but who thereafter also needs care.

Alternatively, a simple 'immediate post-death interest' settlement would protect the capital, and might be cheaper to run.

OTHER ISSUES

14.35 The estate duty surviving spouse exemption (*Sch 6, para* 2) was unaffected by the introduction of the transferable nil rate band facility. Taxpayers should generally do nothing to disturb that very useful structure, which confers freedom from both IHT and capital gains tax.

14.36 An 'immediate post-death' interest (see **Chapter 7**) in favour of the surviving spouse or civil partner may be a suitable option if, for example, asset protection is a concern. Such a legacy is subject to the spouse or civil partner exemption, resulting in the deceased's unused nil rate band being available on the survivor's death.

14.37 Practitioners should note the effect of *s 143* ('Compliance with testator's request') (see **13.48**) and take care to avoid accidental use of the 'first' nil rate band where, for example, the surviving spouse transfers inherited investment assets to family members shortly after the first death.

14.38 As indicated at **14.28** above, a nil rate band relevant property trust may still be considered desirable for various reasons, despite the facility to transfer unused nil rate band. However, some care is required in respect of wills drafted before the introduction of the transferable nil rate band provisions, and also when drafting new wills that incorporate such trusts of the nil rate band.

For example, if the will of a surviving spouse or civil partner leaves a sum 'that is equal to an amount that will not give rise to an IHT charge' on a relevant property trust, in HMRC's view that amount will include nil rate band that has been transferred. The effect when calculating an exit charge before the first ten-year anniversary of the trust is that if the historic value of the fund is greater than the single nil rate band that applies when the property leaves the trust, there will be a positive rate of tax under *s 68(1)*, and an IHT liability arises on the exit (IHTM43065).

The inclusion of the transferred nil rate band from the first death with the survivor's own nil rate band legacy could also adversely affect charities, eg if the surviving spouse wished to leave a nil rate band legacy to family members, with the residuary estate after the nil rate band legacy to be left to a charity. Problems can arise if legacies to charities are not carefully worded (see *RSPCA v Sharp and others* [2010] EWCA Civ 1474 and *The Woodland Trust v Loring* [2014] EWCA Civ 1314).

14.39 Potential difficulties can be prevented such as by limiting the nil rate band legacy on the survivor's death by reference to the nil rate band in force at the date of death, rather than by reference to, say, 'such an amount that does not give rise to an IHT charge'.

In HMRC's view, the following wording of legacies will only transfer a single nil rate band (IHTM43065):

- 'To my trustees such sum as I could leave immediately before my death without IHT becoming payable'
- 'I give free of tax to my trustees an amount equal to the upper limit of the nil per cent rate band in the table of rates in Schedule 1'
- 'To my trustees an amount equal to the nil rate band in force at my death'

14.40 In *Loring v Woodland Trust* [2013] EWHC 4400 (Ch), the deceased died on 1 September 2011. Her will included the following nil rate band clause, with residue being left to charity:

> 'My trustees shall set aside out of my residuary estate assets or cash of an aggregate value equal to such sum as is at the date of my death the amount of my unused nil rate band for Inheritance Tax and to hold the same for such of the following as shall survive me…'

The net value of the deceased's estate was £680,805. She survived her husband, and her personal representatives claimed her husband's transferable nil rate band in full. The question arose whether the effect of the above clause was to pass £325,000 or £650,000 to the beneficiaries under that clause, who were members of the deceased's family. The residuary legacy to charity was therefore either £355,805 or £30,805.

The High Court ([2013] EWHC 4400 (Ch)) concluded that the clause should be construed to mean that the legacy to the family members amounted to

£650,000, being the amount of the enhanced nil rate band. The Court of Appeal subsequently considered that the High Court was correct in its interpretation of the above clause. It was held that the implicit purpose of the will was to give as much as possible to the deceased's family without incurring IHT, and to give the rest to charity. The High Court's decision was upheld, and the charity's appeal was dismissed.

The High Court referred to HMRC's guidance at IHTM43065 in its judgment. The clause was considered to be similar to the following specimen clause in HMRC's guidance at IHTM43065, which HMRC state will allow the 'uprated' nil rate band to be transferred:

> 'I give free of tax to my trustees such sum as at my death equals the maximum amount which could be given to them by this Will without inheritance tax becoming payable in respect of my estate'

The Court of Appeal was referred to a number of specimen clauses drafted by HMRC, together with comments by HMRC on which of those clauses were effective to pass unused nil rate band, and which were not. The HMRC guidance to which the Court was referred was probably IHTM43065. However, the Court of Appeal commented that it did not find the exercise helpful.

The *Woodland Trust* case illustrates the importance of clear drafting in wills, such as in terms of interpreting the extent of legacies by reference to the nil rate band.

14.41 For precedents in cases where the first to die intends to direct some portion of his nil rate band to persons other than his surviving spouse or civil partner, see the latest edition of *Parker's Will Precedents* by Richard Dew and Kevin Shannon (Bloomsbury Professional).

RESIDENCE NIL RATE BAND

Background

14.42 The Residence IHT nil rate band is available broadly where a home is passed to a lineal descendant of the deceased on death from 6 April 2017 (*ss 8D–8M*).

The maximum amount of the residence nil rate band (or 'residential enhancement') increases in stages, from £100,000 in 2017/18 to £175,000 in 2020/21 (*s 8D*).

14.43 However, this extra nil rate band is subject to a tapered withdrawal for estates valued at more than £2 million (for 2017/18 and later years).

The rate of withdrawal is broadly £1 for every £2 that the value of the person's estate exceeds the taper threshold.

Transferable residence nil rate band

> **Focus**
>
> To the extent that there is unused residence nil rate band, a claim is available to transfer the unused element (ie expressed as a percentage) to a surviving spouse or (civil partner). This brought forward allowance may be claimed on the death of the surviving spouse on or after 6 April 2017.

14.44 Residence nil rate band will be unused if, immediately before death, the estate of the earlier spouse to die did not include a 'qualifying residential interest' as defined. Alternatively, the spouse's estate might include an interest in the home that was not inherited by lineal descendants.

The overriding maximum residence nil rate band available for transfer is 100%, or one additional residence nil rate band. This potential restriction may apply if (for example) a surviving spouse was widowed on more than one occasion, and each earlier spouse's residence nil rate band was wholly or partly unused on death.

On the death of the earlier spouse before 6 April 2017, the amount treated for the above purposes as being available to transfer (and also the residential enhancement) is treated as being £100,000, subject to any taper relief if the value of the spouse's estate exceeded £2 million (*s 8G*).

14.45 Unused residence nil rate band must be claimed.

The claim must be made within certain prescribed time limits, depending on the circumstances. However, there is scope for HMRC to allow a longer claim period at its discretion in some cases (see *s 8L*).

14.46 There are potentially complex rules dealing with cases where a residence left to lineal descendants qualifies for conditional exemption, including where the exemption ceases to apply and IHT becomes chargeable (under *ss 32* or *32A*), and the effect of conditional exemption on the transfer of residence nil rate band (*s 8M*).

14.47 A combination of transferable nil rate band and unused residence nil rate band results in a maximum effective IHT threshold of £1 million on the surviving spouse's death, although this amount cannot be achieved until 2020/21 at the earliest, when the residence nil rate band increases to £175,000 (ie a nil rate band of £325,000 and residence nil rate band of £175,000 transferred following the earlier spouse's death, plus the same amounts available on the surviving spouse's death).

14.48 It should be noted that the residence nil rate band may not be available on every death, such as if the property is held in a discretionary trust; the residence nil rate band is not available to trustees.

The residence nil rate band provisions are extended (by legislation in *Finance Act 2016*) to allow the allowance to be enhanced, broadly for those who have downsized to a lower value residence, or have ceased to own their home, broadly where other assets of an equivalent value (up to the maximum available residence nil rate band) are left to direct descendants. The downsizing provisions are to apply for deaths from 6 April 2017 and for downsizing moves or disposals from 8 July 2015.

For detailed commentary on the residence nil rate band, including the transfer of unused residence nil rate band, see **Chapter 15** ('The family home and residence nil rate band') at **15.59–15.73**.

Chapter 15

The family home and the residence nil rate band

SIGNPOSTS

- **The family home** – This is most significant and valuable asset in the estates of many individuals. Various non-IHT measures affecting residential property have been introduced in recent years. Those measures have had the general effect of discouraging IHT planning involving the family home. Furthermore, the Government announced in summer Budget 2015 that it intended introducing legislation from April 2017 to ensure that IHT is payable on all UK residential property owned by non-UK domiciliaries, including property held indirectly through an offshore structure (see **15.1–15.15**).
- **Planning arrangements involving the family home** – A number of IHT schemes and arrangements have evolved over the years. Some of these were subsequently blocked by IHT anti-avoidance legislation, while others are affected by the 'pre-owned assets' income tax regime (see **15.10).**
- **Ownership** – The family home is sometimes owned by one spouse (or civil partner), or more commonly by both with a survivorship destination in the title or as tenants in common. Different IHT considerations apply to each. The spouses or civil partners may evacuate the special destination by written deed (see **15.16–15.17**).
- **Lifetime planning** – IHT planning arrangements involving the family home which are sometimes used include equity release arrangements or borrowing against the property to release funds to make gifts. Gifting the family home (or a share of it) can cause potential difficulties, such as under the 'gifts with reservation' anti-avoidance provisions (see **15.18–15.30**).
- **Will planning** – Spouses (or civil partners) who own the family home as tenants in common should make provision for their share of the property in their will. A non-exempt legacy of such a share (eg to adult children, or a discretionary trust) was a popular means of utilising the nil rate band of the first spouse to die. However, this

approach has been less common since the transferable nil rate band facility was introduced (see **15.31–15.58**).

- **Residence nil rate band** – The residence nil rate band will be available for deaths from 6 April 2017 if a qualifying residential interest is passed on death to lineal descendants (eg a child or grandchild). The maximum allowance is £100,000 in 2017/18, increasing in stages to £175,000 in 2020/21. However, the maximum nil rate band is subject to tapered withdrawal if the value of the deceased's estate exceeds £2 million. The residence nil rate band is in addition to the standard nil rate band of £325,000 mentioned above. As with the standard nil rate band, unused residence nil rate band is transferable to a surviving spouse or civil partner, subject to a successful claim being made. The benefit of the residence nil rate band was extended (in *Finance Act 2016*) in certain circumstances involving 'downsizing' on or after 8 July 2015, in relation to deaths from 6 April 2017 (see **15.61–15.75**).

THE FAMILY HOME

Introduction

15.1 The family home (a term used in this chapter to include a property owned and occupied by spouses, or civil partners) is probably the most significant asset in the estates of most individuals, and often the most valuable in monetary terms. Escalating property prices over a number of years resulted in the value of an increasing number of family homes exceeding the IHT nil rate band, which did not rise in step with property prices.

This chapter considers some IHT planning ideas involving the family home. It must be remembered that transactions undertaken to save IHT must be considered 'in the round' taking into account any legal implications, as well as the possible implications for other taxes and/or possibly means-tested state benefits.

Care will be needed if a valuation of the property is necessary. As to valuation issues generally, see **Chapter 4**.

IHT planning involving the family home will be considered unnecessary or less desirable for many individuals following the introduction of the residence nil rate band (*ss 8D–8M*) where a home is inherited on death by lineal descendants of the deceased on or after 6 April 2017 (see **15.55–15.69**). However, IHT planning in this area may still need to be considered in some cases, particularly in relation to high-value estates and/or if there are no lineal descendants.

15.2 A number of tax measures affecting residential property have been introduced in recent years.

Land and Buildings Transaction Tax

Land and Buildings Transaction Tax (LBTT) replaced UK Stamp Duty Land Tax (SDLT) in Scotland from 1 April 2015. *The Land and Buildings Transaction Tax (Scotland) Act 2013* sets out the LBTT due on purchases of property. *Section 24* provides for the calculation of LBTT and *s 59(1)* sets out what counts as residential property. Unlike Stamp Duty Land Tax the LBTT rates are progressive and the rates are as follows:

Purchase price	LBTT rate
Up to £145,000	0%
Above £145,000 to £250,000	2%
Above £250,000 to £325,000	5%
Above £325,000 to £750,000	10%
Over £750,000	12%

Additional Dwelling Supplement

Additional Dwelling Supplement (ADS) is a new LBTT supplement charged at 3% of purchases of additional residential properties in Scotland (such as buy-to-let properties and second homes) of £40,000 or more. The *Land and Buildings Transaction Tax (Amendment) (Scotland) Act 2016* came into force on 1 April 2016. It is significant for Inheritance Tax Planning considerations as testators will need to consider the impact on bequeathing property (such as a share of a holiday home) to beneficiaries who then subsequently purchase another property (such as a grown-up child purchasing their first home) who will be subject to ADS on their purchase of this second property.

Annual tax on enveloped dwellings

Finance Act 2013 introduced an annual tax on enveloped dwellings (ATED), ie an annual charge on residential properties worth more than £2 million that are owned by 'non-natural persons' (NNPs) (ie certain companies, partnerships with company members and collective investment schemes), subject to a limited range of reliefs (eg for property rental businesses, property developers, etc) (*FA 2013, Pt 3*). The ATED takes effect in relation to properties under the ownership of an NNP on or after 1 April 2013. The threshold of £2 million was progressively reduced to £500,000 in *FA 2014*.

From 1 April 2015, an annual charge of £7,000 applies for properties within a new band with a value greater than £1 million but not more than £2 million. From 1 April 2016, an annual charge of £3,500 now applies to properties within an additional band with a value greater than £500,000 but not more than £1 million (*FA 2014, s110*).

In addition, *FA 2015* increased the annual ATED charges for properties valued at more than £2 million, over and above the normal consumer prices index increase (eg an ATED charge of £23,350 for properties valued at more than £2 million but not more than £5 million). The increased charges were introduced with effect from the chargeable period beginning on 1 April 2015.

Capital gains

Legislation introduced in *Finance Act 2013* extended the capital gains tax (CGT) regime to gains on disposals by NNPs of UK residential property or interests in such property from 6 April 2013, where the consideration exceeds £2 million (reduced proportionately if the NNP owns or disposes of only part of the property). The charge applies to both resident and non-resident NNPs, and affects those companies or collective schemes within the scope of the ATED (*TCGA 1992, ss 2B-2F, Sch 4ZZA*). A CGT charge of 28% is imposed. However, gains accruing before 6 April 2013 remain outside the scope of the CGT charge.

Provisions in *Finance Act 2015* extended the ATED-related CGT charge for properties worth more than £1 million but not more than £2 million in relation to disposals occurring in the tax year 2015/16, and further extended the charge for properties worth more than £500,000 and not more than £1 million for disposals from 6 April 2016.

A change introduced in *FA 2014* reduced (subject to certain limited exceptions) the private residence relief final ownership period exemption for CGT purposes from 36 months to 18 months, in relation to disposals from 6 April 2014.

Further provisions in *FA 2015* extended the scope of CGT to include gains on the disposal of UK residential property interests by non-UK resident persons (or by individuals in the overseas part of a split year) from 6 April 2015. A restriction in private residence relief was also introduced in *FA 2015* for properties located in a territory in which the individual is not tax resident, broadly where the person does not meet a 90-day test for time spent in the property over the year (*TCGA 1992, s 222C*).

The rates of CGT were generally reduced by changes introduced in *Finance Act 2016* with effect from 6 April 2016. The basic rate of CGT was reduced to 10% (from 18%), and the higher rate was reduced to 20% (from 28%), on most gains made by individuals, trustees and personal representatives. However, gains on the disposal of interests in residential properties that do not qualify for private residence relief (and also gains arising in respect of carried interest), remain subject to the 18% and 28% rates. ATED-related gains also remain subject to the 28% rate.

15.3 The above measures have had the general effect of discouraging IHT planning involving the family home.

If a non-UK domiciled individual holds a UK property, it will generally be chargeable to IHT on his death (unless, for example, the property passed to his spouse). An IHT planning consideration for such individuals has therefore traditionally involved an offshore company holding the UK property, where the company's shares are held by the non-UK domiciled individual, perhaps via an offshore trust (such that the shares are excluded property, and outside the scope of IHT). Despite the potential implications for other taxes and duties in relation to residential properties, the benefit of UK residential property being excluded from IHT might have seemed worthwhile for some non-UK domiciled individuals.

However, the Government announced in summer Budget 2015 that it intended introducing legislation from April 2017 to ensure that IHT is payable on all UK residential property owned by non-UK domiciliaries, including property held indirectly through an offshore structure.

Duty of care in connection with tax

15.4 The disposal of a property interest involves issues of both tax and non-tax law. Professional advisers must consider their duty of care to clients (and other people affected by the transactions).

A warning for tax advisers on this note was provided in *Hurlingham Estates Ltd v Wilde & Partners* [1997] STC 627. In that case, it was held that a professional (a reasonably competent conveyancer and commercial lawyer) owed a duty to his client to advise on the tax implications of the transaction unless his retainer was limited, or unless it was apparent that advice was not needed by the client.

Apart from the direct duty to a client just described, an adviser may owe a duty of care to other people affected by the transaction. In *White v Jones* [1995] 2 AC 207, the House of Lords held that solicitors owed a duty of care to the intended beneficiary of a testator: in assuming responsibility to the client, the solicitor also became responsible to the intended beneficiary. The court wanted to do practical justice in a situation where the only person who might have a valid claim (the testator) would have suffered no loss and the only person who suffered a loss (the disappointed beneficiary) would have no claim.

15.5 The principle in *White v Jones* can apply even to lifetime transactions. In *Hughes v Richards (t/a Colin Richards & Co)* [2004] EWCA Civ 266, two parents and their children sued the accountant to the parents in respect of tax and investment advice that failed to produce the promised benefits. The accountant said that the children were not his clients and he owed them no duty of care. He therefore wanted to strike out their claim, but the Court of Appeal refused. The court did have some doubt as to whether the children were owed a duty of care, but that was based on the fact that, at that point, the parents were still alive and could therefore sue for the same loss.

15.6 Although there may be a duty of care, the client or third parties will not succeed unless the particular loss suffered falls within the duties of the adviser. In *Cancer Research Campaign v Ernest Brown & Co (a firm)* [1997] STC 1425, a solicitor was sued in connection with the administration of an estate. Tax could have been saved if the solicitor had recommended a deed of variation, but the solicitor successfully claimed that he was instructed merely to draw up a will in accordance with what the deceased wanted (which he had done) and that it was not within his instructions to advise the testatrix on how best to minimise tax for the advantage of (charitable) beneficiaries.

Professional negligence issues also potentially apply to a firm's directors and employees. Employed professional staff may perhaps believe that they are not at risk, on the basis that they are not principals or partners. However, an employee can be sued jointly or severally with the employer by the client. In *Merrett v Babb* [2001] EWCA Civ 214, Mr Babb was a surveyor and valuer, who was employed as branch manager for a firm of surveyors and valuers. Mr Babb prepared and signed a valuation report on behalf of his firm, following instructions by a building society in respect of a mortgage application. The principal of the firm of surveyors and valuers which employed Mr Babb was subsequently made bankrupt, and the firm ceased business. The firm's professional insurance was cancelled without run-off cover. The court held that the valuation report had failed adequately to report on cracks in the building, and that the failure to recommend further investigation was negligent. However, it is perhaps worth noting that the appellant in this case signed the original valuation report in his personal capacity, and therefore assumed personal responsibility for it.

15.7 In *Vinton and others v Fladgate Fielder and another* [2010] EWHC 904 (Ch), a family sued their advisers in respect of a flawed IHT planning scheme, described at **11.9**. They sued as the personal representatives of Mrs Dugan-Chapman; as the prospective executors; and as the residuary beneficiaries under her will. They wanted to recover the tax lost (which ran into hundreds of thousands of pounds) and the costs of the unsuccessful tax appeal (which themselves amounted to £106,394).

The lawyers argued that they had been engaged only to deal with a capital-raising project for the family company, not to advise on tax; and that their liability was to the deceased, not to her estate, nor to her personal representatives, nor to the beneficiaries.

The court considered the decisions in *Carr Glyn v Frearsons* [1999] Ch 326, *Daniels v Thompson* [2004] EWCA Civ 307 and *Richards v Hughes* [2004] EWCA Civ 266. It held that in so far as the claims lay in contract, there was a serious claim on which to adjudicate. It was clear that tax was a significant consideration in the proposed transaction on which advice was sought. In so far as the claims lay in tort, ie relied on allegations of negligence, it was inappropriate to strike them out: the claims were not fanciful.

15.8 It is generally important to ensure that the scope of any tax advice to be provided by a professional adviser is fully and clearly set out in an engagement letter or retainer. In *Swain Mason and others v Mills & Reeve (A Firm)* [2012] EWCA Civ 498, the claimants were executors of their late father's estate. The deceased (Mr Swain) was the shareholder of a company which was the subject of a management buyout (MBO). Mr Swain had a history of ill-health, and he sadly died during a heart procedure. The proceeds from the sale of the deceased's shares became liable to IHT, whereas if he had died while still owning the shares, no IHT liability would have arisen due to business property relief. A claim of professional negligence was made against the defendant firm, on the basis that the advice given was deficient, and that had the correct advice been given, completion of the MBO would have been deferred until after the heart procedure. However, the claim was dismissed. The court held (*inter alia*) that the defendant firm's retainer did not extend to advising the shareholders how the MBO fitted into their personal financial and tax planning positions. There had been no breach of duty.

15.9 A problem for an adviser is the level of expertise that he holds himself out as having and the extent to which, in his agreement with his client, he is able to limit his liability. It begins to look as if any family member who is disadvantaged by bad tax advice, even if not given to him direct but to a third party, may have a claim against the adviser. The terms and scope of an engagement letter can be an important protection for professional advisers, provided that its terms are not exceeded.

In *Mehjoo v Harben Barker (a firm) and another* [2014] EWCA Civ 358, the Court of Appeal held that an accountancy firm had not been in breach of duty by not pointing out that a client might be non-UK domiciled and by not recommending that the client should seek tax advice from a 'non-dom specialist' in respect of a disposal of shares. However, firms lacking the necessary knowledge or expertise in a particular area to undertake appropriate planning on the client's behalf should limit the scope of their work in engagement letters, and as indicated above should be careful not to stray beyond the scope of their engagement.

Planning arrangements involving the family home

15.10 The consideration of other taxes when undertaking IHT planning involving the family home (and generally) was emphasised by the introduction of the 'pre-owned asset' (POA) income tax charge from 6 April 2005 (see **Chapter 16**), which is primarily aimed at what the government apparently regarded as unacceptable IHT avoidance.

A detailed consideration of those IHT avoidance schemes which apparently provoked the POA regime is outside the scope of this chapter. However, the main types of scheme used in the past involving the family home are briefly summarised below.

A section of guidance on the POA income tax charge is included in HMRC's Inheritance Tax Manual (IHTM44000–IHTM44116), replacing and expanding upon the guidance which had previously featured on HMRC's website.

Reversionary lease schemes

15.11 The intention of 'reversionary lease schemes' is broadly to allow the home owner to make a gift of an interest in the property to reduce his IHT estate, whilst continuing to occupy and without being subject to the 'gifts with reservation' (GWR) anti-avoidance rules (see **Chapter 5**).

This once popular planning arrangement typically involved the donor retaining the property, but granting a deferred long lease as a gift, under which the right of the lessee to occupy is deferred (eg for 20 years).

The scheme was generally considered to be effective before 9 March 1999, although the position became less certain following legislative changes from that date. As mentioned at **5.13**, HMRC's guidance indicates (at IHTM14360) that reversionary lease schemes effected from 9 March 1999 are not caught by the GWR provisions in *FA 1986, s 102A* if the freehold interest was acquired more than seven years before the gift, as long as the lease contains no covenants of benefit.

In addition, HMRC guidance on reversionary lease schemes in the context of the POA income tax charge (at IHTM44102) confirms that where the freehold interest was acquired more than seven years before the gift, the continued occupation by the donor is not a 'significant' right (in view of *FA 1986, s 102A(5)*), so the GWR rules cannot apply and a POA charge arises instead.

HMRC's guidance at IHTM44102 also states that reversionary lease schemes established before 9 March 1999 succeed in avoiding the GWR provisions, so long as the lease does not contain any terms that are currently beneficial to the donor (eg covenants by the lessee to (say) maintain the property), and that the donor will consequently be subject to the POA charge (under *FA 2004, Sch 15, para 3(2)*). The HMRC guidance adds that the GWR provisions may apply if the lease contains terms currently beneficial to the donor, irrespective of when the freehold interest was acquired.

15.12 However, in *Buzzoni and others v Revenue & Customs* [2013] EWCA Civ 1684 (see **5.5**), the Court allowed an appeal against decisions by the First-tier Tribunal and Upper Tribunal that the deceased taxpayer had reserved a benefit (within *FA 1986, s 102(1)(b)*) in granting an sublease of her London flat to a trust in 1997. The sublease was subject to covenants. The covenants in the sublease mirrored the covenants in the headlease. On appeal, the Court held that the donor's benefit from the covenants made no difference to the lessees' enjoyment of the sublease. The imposition of duplicate obligations on the property did not add to the obligations already borne.

15.13 By contrast, in *Hood v Revenue & Customs* [2016] UKFTT 59 (TC), the lifetime grant by the deceased of a reversionary sub-lease of property in London to her sons out of a head lease interest was held to be a gift with reservation of benefit (by virtue of *FA 1986, s 102(1)(b)*). The facts were similar to the *Buzzoni* case, though not identical. The First-tier Tribunal noted in particular that, in contrast to the position in *Buzzoni*, the sub-lessees gave no direct covenants to the head lessor (ie the only positive covenants from the sub-lessees were those given in the sub-lease in favour of the deceased as sub-lessor). Furthermore, unlike the position in *Buzzoni*, the sub-lessees were under no obligation to the head lessor with respect to those covenants (see **5.5**).

Those reversionary lease schemes which are considered to be effective for IHT purposes are nevertheless subject to a potential income tax liability (from 2005/06) under the POA regime (*FA 2004, Sch 15, paras 3(2), (4)*), unless the donor elects out of the income tax charge and into the GWR rules for IHT purposes.

Lease 'carve-out' schemes

15.14 Lease carve-out arrangements were highlighted in *Ingram (Executors of Lady Ingram's Estate) v IRC* [1997] STC 1234 (see **5.11**), in which a carve-out scheme in relation to the late Lady Ingram's main residence and its transfer subject to leases was upheld by the House of Lords.

'*Ingram* schemes' involving lease carve outs were generally blocked from 9 March 1999 by changes to the GWR rules (*FA 1986, s 102A*), but as with reversionary leases, carve-out schemes before that date appear to be effective for IHT purposes. However, like reversionary lease schemes, pre-9 March

1999 Ingram schemes are also subject to an income tax charge under the POA rules (see IHTM44100), unless an election is made to the contrary.

Ingram schemes could still operate over 14 years. The GWR rules concerning interests in land (see **5.12**) state that a right or interest over land is not 'significant' for GWR purposes if it was granted or acquired before the seven-year period ending with the date of the gift (*FA 1986, s 102A(5)*). This exception could therefore apply if there was a gap of at least seven years between the creation of the lease and the gift of the freehold reversion. The gift to another individual would still be a PET, which would require the donor to survive a further seven years after making it. However, HMRC apparently consider that *Ingram* schemes effected from 9 March 1999 are still caught by the GWR rules if the lease is not at a full rent (IHTM14360).

Ingram schemes caught by the GWR rules are not subject to a POA income tax charge. However, those schemes not subject to the GWR rules (eg effective schemes entered into before 9 March 1999) are not excluded from a POA charge, and therefore such arrangements are subject to those income tax rules.

'*Eversden* schemes'

15.15 In *IRC v Eversden (exors of Greenstock, decd)* [2003] EWCA Civ 668, [2003] STC 822, the Court of Appeal upheld the effectiveness against the GWR rules of an arrangement whereby property was initially placed into an interest in possession trust for the spouse, followed by a discretionary trust in which the beneficiaries included the settlor and spouse. Accordingly, changes to the GWR rules were introduced in 2003 to block '*Eversden* schemes' (*FA 1986, 102(5A)*), affecting settlements created from 20 June 2003 (see **5.9**).

For schemes involving the family home, a POA income tax charge is excluded for so long as the spouse or civil partner continues to have a beneficial entitlement to an interest in possession in the trust (*FA 2004, Sch 15, para 10(1)(c)*). However, this exclusion is unlikely to apply in practice, because the initial interest in possession of the property is normally terminated during the life of the spouse or civil partner.

Eversden schemes of the family home effected before 20 June 2003 are considered to be potentially subject to income tax under the POA rules if the spouse's life interest comes to an end during their lifetime, whereas if the spouse's life interest continues until their death, the transaction is excluded from POA under *FA 2004, Sch 15, para 10(1)(c)* (IHTM44101). For a spouse whose life interest ends on or after 18 March 2006, an IHT charge may arise on death if he or she still benefits from the property, as the termination is treated as a gift under *FA 1986, s 102ZA*.

Schemes effected from 20 June 2003 are subject to the GWR rules in respect of the property, and therefore fall outside a POA charge. Furthermore, as mentioned the spouse may be subject to a separate GWR charge if the interest in possession terminates during their lifetime.

'Lifetime debt' or 'double trust' arrangements ('IOU schemes')

15.16

Example 15.1—'IOU scheme'

There are different names and variants of debt and trust arrangements ('IOU' or 'double trust' schemes), which were more popular prior to the introduction of stamp duty land tax (SDLT) from 1 December 2003. However, an example of a typical scheme would be one in which an individual (Jake) sold his house for £1 million in February 2006, to a trust in which he has a life interest (Trust 1). Note that the transaction would be liable to SDLT.

The trustees gave Jake an IOU for the purchase price, which Jake gifted to a second trust for the benefit of his adult children (Trust 2). He remains in occupation of the property. The outstanding debt owed to Trust 2 reduces the value of the house in Trust 1 in Jake's estate for IHT purposes.

HMRC seem to have taken particular exception to IOU schemes, and have adopted an increasingly harder line with them. HMRC had not previously accepted that all types of double trust arrangements achieved their desired IHT objective. In particular, if the loan to Trust 2 is repayable on demand, HMRC's view is that there is a GWR until the trustees call in the loan (note: the GWR is considered to be in the loan, as opposed to the house).

If the terms of the loan provide that the debt is only repayable after the death of the liferenter (ie Jake), HMRC initially appeared to accept that such schemes were not caught by the GWR rules in respect of the loan. However, HMRC's guidance was amended in October 2010 to the effect that loans repayable after the liferenter's death are caught under the GWR provisions (in addition to loans repayable on demand, which were previously considered to be caught). HMRC subsequently confirmed (in their Trusts & Estates Newsletter, December 2011) that their POA guidance had been updated to explain that HMRC's view is now that none of the home loan or double trust schemes succeed in mitigating IHT in the way intended.

HMRC's guidance on their website was updated in November 2011, but was subsequently replaced in March 2012 as part of a new POA section of its IHT Manual. This states that where the terms of the loan are that the debt is only repayable after the death of the liferenter, the settlor still obtains a benefit that is referable to the gift. HMRC therefore consider that a GWR charge applies to the loan. In addition, HMRC consider that a POA charge arises in respect of the house, on the basis that it is the asset previously owned by the individual (IHTM44105).

In addition to the above approach to the GWR provisions, HMRC's guidance advances the following arguments to negate the intended consequences of IOU schemes (IHTM44106):

> 'The first is that the provisions of *FA 1986 s 103* apply to disallow the deduction of the loan against the trust in which the individual retained a life interest. The sale of the property to the first trust is a disposition and since, in the majority of cases, the trustees had no means with which to pay for the property, the steps they took to fund their purchase created the debt which (through the trustees equitable lien) is an encumbrance against the property. The consideration for the debt was property derived from the deceased and *FA 1986 s 103* applies to abate the loan.'
>
> 'Secondly, having regard to the purpose and effect of home loan schemes, the steps taken are a pre-ordained series of transactions, and following the line of authority that is founded on *W T Ramsay v IRC* [1981] 1 AER 865, the individual steps should be treated as a single transaction comprising a number of elements which when taken together have the effect that the vendor has made a 'gift' of the property concerned for the purposes of *FA1986 s 102* and has continued to live there. So reservation of benefit arises in the property.'

The effectiveness (or otherwise) of home loan or double trust schemes is likely to be determined through litigation, although no cases have been reported at the time of writing. If there is a GWR in the property, a POA charge will not arise in respect of it. In that case, HMRC have previously stated that any POA income tax paid (ie on the basis that no such GWR applied) will be repaid with interest upon a claim being made, irrespective of the time limits for repayment that might otherwise apply (http://webarchive.nationalarchives.gov.uk/20140109143644/http://www.hmrc.gov.uk/poa/poa-guidance6.htm).

To assist executors and trustees in the administration of estates, HMRC stated that they would provide estimates of the tax that might be payable if HMRC succeed in future litigation. This would allow executors and trustees to make payments on account to HMRC to mitigate potential interest charges or to make an appropriate provision out of funds held (HMRC Trusts & Estates Newsletter, August 2012).

15.17 In the above example, the value of Jake's life interest forms part of his estate for IHT purposes (note that this IHT treatment does not generally apply to interests in possession created from 22 March 2006: see **Chapter 7**), less the outstanding debt owed to the trustees of the children's trust. If the scheme is effective for IHT purposes and the GWR rules do not apply in respect of the property, a POA income tax liability potentially arises on the basis that the debt is an 'excluded liability' (*FA 2004, Sch 15, paras 11(6),(7)*), unless Jake elects out of POA and into IHT.

HMRC's guidance includes an example of a POA charge in the context of a home loan scheme, where the debt (plus accrued interest) is treated as an excluded liability (IHTM44051).

The *Charge to Income Tax by Reference to Enjoyment of Property Previously Owned Regulations 2005, SI 2005/724* provide relief from a double IHT charge for taxpayers who elect into the GWR regime after making lifetime double trust home loan arrangements, where the individual dies after 5 April 2005 and within seven years of gifting the loan (*reg 6*).

Some taxpayers may decide to unravel their double trust home loan arrangements, and possibly consider other forms of IHT planning instead. The *Inheritance Tax (Double Charges Relief) Regulations 2005, SI 2005/3441* provide relief from the double IHT charge that may arise for taxpayers in such circumstances, ie where the loan is written off, waived or released (so that the value of the house forms part of their estate again) and the individual dies after 5 April 2005 and within seven years of gifting the loan (*reg 3*).

Ownership

15.18

> **Focus**
>
> The property may be owned in an individual's sole name (eg husband, wife or civil partner), or in survivorship, or as tenants in common.
>
> - *Survivorship* – On the death of a joint owner, the survivor takes the entire interest absolutely by operation of law due to the special destination/survivorship clause in the title deeds.
> - *Tenants in common* – By contrast, ownership as 'tenants in common' gives each owner a separate (typically equal) share of the property, which can be left by will or disposed of during lifetime. This is frequently found to be the most satisfactory form of ownership from both an IHT planning and a practical point of view.

If the property is held by spouses or civil partners in survivorship and the parties wish to evacuate the survivorship destination so that they become tenants in common instead, this can be done by a written deed or a further disposition.

15.19 If the notice is done by disposition it should be registered in the Land Register for Scotland or recorded in the Register of Sasines.

LIFETIME PLANNING

Equity release

15.20 A straightforward form of lifetime IHT planning involves releasing equity in the property, as opposed to making a direct gift of an interest in the property. The following possibilities could be considered.

Mortgage or loan

15.21 A loan or mortgage secured on the property will generally reduce its net value for IHT purposes, subject to certain restrictions (see below). The funds borrowed could be gifted to non-exempt beneficiaries such as adult children (ie a PET) or into trust from which the settlor is excluded as a beneficiary (the latter normally being a chargeable lifetime transfer since 22 March 2006).

Such planning should be best suited to individuals whose life expectancy is restricted by old age or infirmity, as a commercial loan or mortgage will bear interest. However, the donor would normally need to survive at least seven years for the gifted proceeds to escape IHT consequences on death. Decreasing term assurance could be considered to cover any IHT liability (with the donees paying the premiums).

Prior to changes introduced in *FA 2013*, if life expectancy was more than two years but less than seven years, consideration could be given to investing the loan proceeds in (for example) shares eligible for 100% business property relief (see **Chapter 11**), such as in the property owner's unquoted trading company, or in trading companies listed on the Alternative Investment Market (AIM) (albeit that commercially by their nature such investments are often high risk).

However, *FA 2013* introduced legislation which broadly provides that a liability used to acquire, maintain or enhance certain 'relievable property' (ie business property, agricultural property or woodlands relief property) reduces the value of that property, before business property relief (or agricultural property relief, or woodlands relief) is applied (*s 162B*). To that extent, the benefit of those reliefs is effectively lost.

Similarly, legislation introduced in *FA 2013* potentially restricts a deduction for a liability such as a loan or mortgage secured on a property, to the extent that the proceeds are used to acquire, maintain or enhance 'excluded property' (see **Chapter 9**). This general rule is subject to certain limited exceptions, such as where the excluded property has been sold and replaced by non-excluded property, or the liability exceeds the value of the excluded property, and certain conditions are satisfied (*s 162A*).

A foreign currency bank account balance (within *s 157*) is left out of account on the death of a person who is not domiciled and not resident in the UK. Those funds are not excluded property as such. However, provisions introduced in *FA 2014* treat foreign currency accounts in UK banks in a similar way as excluded property for the purposes of restricting the deduction of liabilities (*s 162AA*).

Furthermore, a deduction from the value of a person's estate for liabilities unpaid on death is subject to certain conditions and possible restrictions in *s 175A* (see **3.13**), as introduced in *FA 2013*. This anti-avoidance provision could particularly affect non-commercial loans, such as from friends or family members, which are unpaid following death.

'Downsizing'

15.22 Selling the family home and moving to a smaller, less expensive house represents an alternative form of equity release.

The surplus funds generated could be dealt with as outlined at **15.19** above. Note that the proceeds from trading down could be invested in business property (or other relievable property) without the restriction in respect of liabilities to finance such property (in *s 162B*) applying as mentioned in the previous paragraph, where any loan or mortgage had already been repaid.

Similarly, the restriction in respect of excluded property (in *s 162A*) does not apply if there was no remaining liability upon trading down, and the surplus proceeds are used to acquire excluded property.

Although often unpopular with clients, the equity release arrangement has side benefits:

- It may reduce imbalance in asset allocation: far too many families have too much capital tied up in the family home, so its sale can release liquidity that enhances the lifestyle of the elderly.
- A smaller property may be cheaper to run, increasing disposable income and releasing further freedom to save tax by gifts out of income under *s 21*.

- Tax is payable in hard cash, albeit by instalments where property is concerned. The reallocation of resources to increase liquidity can make the estate much easier to administer after the death.

Provisions allowing residence nil rate band (see **15.55**) that would otherwise be lost as a result of downsizing to remain available in certain circumstances were included in *Finance Act 2016* (see **15.69**).

Commercial sale

15.23 The house owner may wish to sell the whole of the property or an interest in it, so as to enhance his standard of living. A commercial sale is not a transfer of value for IHT purposes if it can be shown that there was no intention to confer a gratuitous benefit on any person, and *either* that it was an arm's-length transaction between unconnected persons, or that the transaction was on arm's-length terms (*IHTA 1984, s 10*).

Particularly in the case of sales between family members, independent property valuations should be obtained by both parties, to rebut any presumption by HMRC that gratuitous benefit has been conferred.

Similarly, for POA income tax purposes, the disposal of land (or chattels) is an 'excluded transaction' if it is a disposal by an individual of his whole interest in the property 'except for any right expressly reserved by him over the property either by an arm's-length transaction or by a transaction such as might be expected to be made at arm's length between unconnected persons' (*FA 2004, Sch 15, para 10(1)(a)*).

POA regulations also allow for partial arm's-length type equity releases in certain circumstances (the *Charge to Income Tax by Reference to Enjoyment of Property Previously Owned Regulations 2005, SI 2005/724, reg 5*). However, the scope of this exemption is restricted. It applies to transactions between unconnected persons. It also applies to any disposals between connected persons on arm's-length terms before 7 March 2005, or to disposals from that date if the consideration was not in money or readily convertible assets.

The latter exemption may assist in cases where an elderly or infirm parent gives an interest in their home to adult offspring in return for the provision of care in the property on an ongoing basis.

15.24 An alternative exclusion from the POA charge of possible relevance applies if the disposal was a disposition falling within *IHTA 1984, s 11* ('dispositions for maintenance of family'), such as a disposition in favour of a dependent relative for the reasonable provision of his care or maintenance. This is acknowledged in HMRC's guidance, albeit that it casts some doubt over the availability of the exclusion in such circumstances (IHTM44037):

> 'For the purposes of the contribution conditions relating to land and chattels, the contribution by a person to the acquisition of any property is an excluded transaction in relation to the chargeable person if it was a disposition that meets the conditions of IHTA84/S11, dispositions for maintenance of family (IHTM04171), FA04/Sch15/Para 10(2)(d).
>
> This provision is likely to be of limited application given that it is not easy to see how the contribution to the acquisition of a capital asset, such as land or chattels can be for the maintenance of the donee. However, the decision in *McKelvey v HMRC* [2008] UKSPC (SPC00694) was that exemption under IHTA84/S11 could apply, and any case where this exclusion is claimed should be referred to Technical.'

In *McKelvey (Personal Representative of McKelvey Deceased) v Revenue and Customs Commissioners)* [2008] SpC 694 the deceased (D) was a spinster who lived with her widowed mother (M), who was 85 years old, blind and in poor health. D was diagnosed with terminal cancer, and in 2003 gave away two houses that she owned to M. D died in 2005, and M died in 2007. HMRC sought to charge IHT on the value of D's gift of the houses to M of £169,000. D's executor appealed, on the grounds that the gifts were exempt transfers within *IHTA 1984, s 11(3)* as a disposition being a reasonable provision for the care and maintenance of a dependent relative. The executor contended that D gave the houses to M so that they could be sold to pay for nursing care.

The executor's appeal was allowed in part. The Special Commissioner held that it was reasonable for D to assume that M would need residential nursing care. The difficulty in this case was in determining what was 'reasonably required' for this purpose. The Commissioner concluded that 'reasonable provision at the time the transfers were made amounted in all to £140,500'. This amount qualified for exemption under *s 11*, with the balance of £28,500 being a chargeable transfer (*s 3A(4)*).

Gifting the family home

15.25 Lifetime planning involving the family home often includes gifting an interest in the property, or sometimes the property as a whole. Of course, such a gift is a disposal for CGT purposes at market value, although private residence relief will normally be available (*TCGA 1992, s 222*). It is possible that the donor(s) may wish to move out of the family home (eg into a residential nursing home or, for example, purchase a smaller property if they can afford to do so). For commentary on private residence relief, see *Capital Gains Tax 2016/17* (Bloomsbury Professional).

Where the family home (or an interest in it) is being gifted, the 'gifts with reservation' (GWR) anti-avoidance rules (see **Chapter 5**) must be safely navigated for IHT purposes.

The GWR provisions can apply (*inter alia*) if an individual makes a gift of property (from 18 March 1986) which is not enjoyed to the entire exclusion, or virtually the entire exclusion, of the donor (*FA 1986, s 102(1)(b)*).

As there is no definition of 'virtually the entire exclusion' in the IHT legislation, HMRC published guidance on their view of the expression in *Revenue Interpretation 55* (see **5.28**), which interprets it to include visits to stay at the house for certain limited periods, normal social visits, certain short-term stays (eg due to convalescence following medical treatment) and domestic visits (eg babysitting the donee's children).

Care should be taken to ensure that stays or visits to the house do not escalate beyond the *de minimis* limits and into a GWR charge. Examples given in *Revenue Interpretation 55* of situations in which those limits are exceeded include:

- a house in which the donor then stays most weekends, or for a month or more each year; and
- a house with a library in which the donor continues to keep his own books, or which the donor uses on a regular basis, for example because it is necessary for his work.

However, a GWR charge is avoided if the donor pays a market rent for any periods of occupation (eg a gift of the property to the children, followed by a leaseback at a full commercial rent throughout the period of occupation). An exception to the GWR rules applies if full consideration is paid in money or money's worth for occupying the land (*FA 1986, Sch 20, para 6(1)(a)*). Independent advice should be obtained, together with separate professional valuations to establish a full market rent.

Other tax issues may also need to be considered. For example, the payment of rent and/or a lease premium of a residential property has potential income tax implications for the recipient. In addition, the stamp duty land tax position of the lease must be considered. A subsequent sale of the property will also have capital gains tax implications in respect of any increase in value of the property.

Gifting a share of the home

Joint occupation

15.26 The gift of an 'undivided share of an interest in land' (from 9 March 1999) can give rise to a GWR charge (*FA 1986, s 102B(1)*; see **5.14**), subject to certain 'let-outs' considered below.

Example 15.2—Joint occupation: gift to family member

Freda, who is an elderly widowed parent, gifts a share in the house (say 50%) to her adult unmarried daughter, Gertrude. Both live together in the house until Freda's death.

What is the GWR position?

15.27 The basic principle is that the GWR rules apply to the gift of an undivided share in land, except in three cases:

- The donor does not occupy the land (*FA 1986, s 102B(3)(a)*). This would appear to allow a non-occupying donor to receive a share of rent and profit from the property without constituting a GWR; but it does not assist Freda in the above example.
- The donor's occupation is for full consideration in money or money's worth (*s 102B(3)(b)*). Whilst the parent's payment of rent to the daughter could reduce the eventual IHT liability on the parent's estate, it is often difficult to establish a market rent in these circumstances, and to ensure that the amount paid continues to reflect a market rent. In any event, the income tax implications for the daughter of receiving rental income are likely to make this option seem unattractive.
- Both donor and donee occupy the land, and the donor receives no benefit (other than a negligible one) provided by or at the expense of the donee in connection with the gift (*s 102B(4)*).

The third exception above appears to be based on a statement made by the Minister of State for the Treasury in 1986 (see below), although the above legislation did not take effect until 9 March 1999.

Hansard Statement

> 'It may be that my Hon. Friend's intention concerns the common case where someone gives away an individual share in land, typically a house, which is then occupied by all the joint owners including the donor. For example, elderly parents may make unconditional gifts of undivided shares in their house to their children and the parents and children occupy the property as their family home, each owner bearing his or her share of the running costs. In those circumstances, the parents' occupation or enjoyment of the part of the house that they have given away is in return for similar enjoyment of the children of the other part of the property. Thus the donors' occupation is for a full consideration.

> Accordingly, I assure my Hon. Friend that the gift with reservation rules will not be applied to an unconditional gift of an undivided share in land merely because the property is occupied by all the joint owners or tenants in common, including the donor.'

15.28 The scope of the 'shared occupation' rule in *FA 1986, s 102B(4)* is potentially wider than the example given in the Hansard statement indicates. For instance, the legislation deals with land in general, not necessarily the family home. In addition, the requirement that the donor must not receive any connected benefit (other than a negligible one) does not necessarily mean that household running costs must be shared proportionately. The donor may wish to continue paying all the running costs, or the 'lion's share' of them. Otherwise, the difficulty arises in establishing how much the donee can safely pay, without the donor falling foul of the GWR rules.

In the above, example, Freda gifted a 50% share of the house to her daughter. *FA 1986, s 102B* does not contain an express requirement to gift an equal share. The donor may therefore wish to consider giving away more than a 50% interest. However, HMRC could contend that if two individuals occupy a property jointly, the most that can be given away is 50%; the Inheritance Tax Manual at IHTM14332 (which provides a number of examples involving joint property) includes the following health warning:

> 'The joint property examples are on the basis that the joint owners take the property in equal shares. Refer any case in which the transferor takes less than an equal share to Technical Group.'

In cases where the interest given away is more than 50% (say 75%), it does not follow that the donee should pay 75% of the household running costs. To prevent the donor from receiving a possible benefit, any sharing of running costs should reflect their respective usage (eg water, gas and electricity), which may not be the same as their beneficial property ownership percentages. However, in practice it will probably be difficult to measure such usage: it would arguably be safer for the donor to continue paying all of the household running expenses.

The value of Freda's share of the house may be subject to a discount on her death of between 10–15%, subject to the Land Tribunal's agreement. The higher percentage potentially applies if the other co-owner continues to occupy the property (see **4.23**).

15.29 It should be noted that the above GWR exception applies while the property is occupied jointly. What would happen then if, for example, the daughter left home to get married? A GWR could be avoided by the mother paying a full market rent for her continued occupation in respect of her daughter's share.

It should be borne in mind that the above exception applies to the gift of an interest in land, not the whole.

For income tax purposes, there is an exemption from a POA charge in joint occupation circumstances in which *FA 1986, s 102B(4)* would apply (*FA 2004, Sch 15, para 11(5)(c)*).

Changes in circumstances

15.30 Consider the following example:

> **Example 15.3—Gift of house and change in circumstances: infirmity of donor**
>
> George gifted his house ('Blackacre') to his adult son Harold in April 2011, which Harold occupied as his home.
>
> In May 2016, George (who did not previously have any major health problems) suffered a serious heart attack, which left him needing constant care. After George's discharge from hospital, he had to move back to Blackacre where Harold looked after him, until George sadly died shortly afterwards.

15.31 There is a special relieving provision to prevent an unfortunate GWR charge arising following such an unexpected and sad change in circumstances. The donor's occupation of the gifted land is disregarded if (as in the above example) the donee is a relative of the donor or his spouse (or civil partner), and certain other conditions are satisfied (*FA 1986, s 102C(3)*; *Sch 20, para 6(1)(b)*); see **5.31**), ie:

- the occupation results from an unforeseen change in the donor's circumstances (ie the GWR exception would not apply in the above example if George had a long history of ill health, and he made the gift when it seemed likely that he would need looking after);
- the donor has become unable to maintain himself through old age, infirmity or otherwise; and
- the occupation represents reasonable provision by the donee for the donor's care and maintenance.

In the case of serious illness where the donor cannot maintain himself, HMRC accept that occupation represents reasonable provision for his care and maintenance (see the example at IHTM14342), although this exception would only be available until the donor sufficiently recovered.

For POA income tax purposes, there is also an exemption from charge if the above conditions are satisfied (*FA 2004, Sch 15, para 11(5)(d)*).

Statutory settlements

15.32 In some cases, a lifetime gift can result in a statutory settlement for IHT purposes, eg a leasehold interest for life for less than full consideration (*IHTA 1984, s 43(3)*). The same applies if property is 'held in trust for persons in succession or for any persons subject to a contingency' (*IHTA 1984, s 43(2)(a)*).

For example, the lifetime gift of a share in the family home between spouses or civil partners subject to provisions in their wills that the property may not be sold without the survivor's consent could result in HMRC arguing that there is an interest in possession of the deceased's interest if left to the children on the first death. See also **15.46** below, and *IRC v Lloyds Private Banking Ltd* [1998] STC 559 (at **15.49**) in particular.

In the *Trusts & Estates Newsletter* (April 2013), HMRC confirmed their view that the creation of a 'usufruct' (ie the right to the use and enjoyment of another's property) generally gives rise to a settlement under *s 43(2)*. The usufruct is treated as giving rise to an interest in possession in the property concerned.

WILL PLANNING

Will or intestacy?

Focus

- Spouses or civil partners who occupy the family home as tenants in common (see **15.16**) should make provision in their wills concerning their shares in the property.
- Property owned with a special destination in the title deeds passes by survivorship. Therefore, if the owners wish to leave their interests on death other than to each other, the survivorship should be evacuated during their lifetimes, and suitable provision made in their wills.

15.33 It may be possible for an instrument of variation to redirect property held in survivorship (assuming that those who would otherwise benefit agree), and also effectively to evacuate the destination for IHT purposes, if appropriate. The IHT provisions (*IHTA 1984, s 142*, 'Alteration of dispositions taking effect on death') apply to dispositions which are '… effected by will, under the law relating to intestacy, *or otherwise*' (emphasis added). The latter disposition would seem to cover property passing by survivorship, if the notice of variation so provides. This is a point that HMRC appear to accept (IHTM35092) (note all subsequent statutory references in this chapter are to *IHTA 1984*, unless otherwise stated).

The government announced at Budget 2015 that it would be reviewing the use of deeds of variation for tax purposes. However, it was subsequently confirmed in December 2015 that no new restrictions would be introduced on how deeds of variation can be used for tax purposes, although the government would continue to monitor their use. In any event, it would surely be easier, and would provide greater certainty, to deal with this issue in the wills of both spouses (or civil partners) during their lifetimes. The wills should be reviewed at regular intervals to ensure that they reflect current wishes, and to protect against unforeseen changes in circumstances.

Using the nil rate band

15.34 Prior to the transferable nil rate band changes introduced in *FA 2008*, it was important for married couples or civil partnerships to ensure that optimum use was made of the available IHT threshold (or 'nil rate band') on the first death (see **Chapter 13**). If a deceased spouse (or civil partner) leaves their entire estate to the surviving spouse, then (unless the recipient spouse is non-UK domiciled), the legacy will normally be wholly exempt from IHT (*s 18*). However, the estate of the survivor increases accordingly. This could result in a potentially higher IHT liability on the second death, and a higher IHT liability overall. If each spouse (or civil partner) owned sufficient assets to constitute their nil rate bands, a non-exempt legacy on the first death could have saved IHT of an amount up to the nil rate band multiplied by the 40% 'death rate'.

A common IHT planning technique before the *FA 2008* changes was therefore to ensure that an amount up to the available nil rate band was left to (say) adult children directly, or possibly by way of a 'nil rate band discretionary trust' in which the surviving spouse could be included among the class of beneficiaries. This planning was relatively straightforward and simple to implement if each spouse (or civil partner) owned sufficient 'liquid' assets to constitute their nil rate bands, such as cash, shares and securities. However, very often the only asset of any substantial value would be an interest in the family home.

Transferable nil rate bands

15.35 Estate planning for married couples or civil partnerships was simplified in many cases by the introduction of the transferable nil rate band facility from 9 October 2007 (*ss 8A–8C*). The provisions broadly allow claims for the transfer of a spouse's or civil partner's unused nil rate band to surviving spouses or civil partners (who die on or after 9 October 2007). The amount that can be transferred is based on the unused percentage of the deceased's nil rate band. That percentage is applied to the nil rate band in operation on the death of the survivor. See **Chapter 14** for further commentary.

From an IHT planning perspective, it is therefore no longer necessary for spouses and civil partners to utilise the nil rate band on the first death, such as by providing for the transfer of an interest in the family home to non-exempt beneficiaries (although if both spouses or civil partners died before 9 October 2007, it is not possible to take advantage of the transferable nil rate band).

The availability of the residence nil rate band where a home is passed on death to lineal descendants of the deceased from 6 April 2017 (see **15.55**) potentially enhances the attractiveness of such legacies. Alternatively, unused residence nil rate band may be transferred to the surviving spouse (or civil partner) in some cases. For example, if the family home (or an interest in it) passes to a surviving spouse it is possible to claim unused residence nil rate band brought forward from the earlier spouse to die, where the survivor leaves the family home to lineal descendants.

Whilst nil rate band legacies of interests in the family home to discretionary trusts or other chargeable beneficiaries on the first spouse or civil partner to die have probably been less prevalent since the introduction of the transferable nil rate band provisions, there may be circumstances in which such legacies are necessary or preferred, such as where the property occupants are, for example, unmarried or are siblings (see *Burden v United Kingdom* [2008] All ER (D) 391 (Apr)), or to make provision for offspring.

In addition, aside from IHT considerations there may be other reasons why an interest in the home may be left in trust (eg due to concerns about asset protection).

Ownership by first spouse (or civil partner) to die

15.36 Note: See **15.35** above and **Chapter 14** regarding the transferable nil rate band for spouses and civil partners.

The commentary below deals with situations in which it is not possible, or not preferred, to leave an outright legacy of the family home to the surviving spouse or civil partner on the first death for the purpose of claiming the deceased's unused nil rate band on the death of the surviving spouse or civil partner.

If one spouse or civil partner owns the entire family home and dies first, an interest in it could be left to a chargeable party (eg a daughter), whilst enabling the surviving spouse or civil partner to occupy by leaving another interest. Their respective shares may depend upon factors including the value of the family home, and the proportionate interest necessary to constitute the nil rate band (assuming that the deceased owned insufficient assets to do so otherwise).

For example, the surviving spouse or civil partner may receive (say) a 25% tenant in common share, with 75% to the daughter (the latter interest perhaps being worth up to the available nil rate band). The survivor would then be able to occupy the whole by virtue of their 25% interest as a tenant in common. There must be no restriction on the daughter occupying the house as co-owner, as this would give the survivor an interest in possession in the whole, with the result that the same overall IHT liability would arise as if the house had been given to them outright, unless the interest terminates more than seven years before the individual's death (ie the termination being a deemed PET). The survivor's occupation could be made informal (eg by way of a non-enforceable right to occupy).

However, legal issues arise, such as 'security of tenure'. Can the daughter (assuming that she lives elsewhere) be trusted not to sell her interest? Even if she can be trusted, her interest is not secure from creditors and others.

Alternatively, the will of the deceased spouse or civil partner may create a trust of the family home (see below).

Life interest trust

15.37 For life interests created before 22 March 2006, a beneficiary with an interest in possession in settled property is treated as owning the underlying trust assets. This treatment continues to apply to certain life interests created from that date, such as those created by will or on intestacy.

Subject to this and certain other exceptions (see **Chapter 7**), interests in possession created on or after 22 March 2006 are subject to the same IHT treatment as discretionary trusts (see **Chapter 8**).

If the first spouse or civil partner to die has already used the nil rate band (eg by making chargeable lifetime gifts) the deceased's will could establish a life interest trust of the whole home in favour of the survivor. From 22 March 2006, such an interest created by will (or under the laws of intestacy) is an 'immediate post-death interest' (*s 49A*), which qualifies for the spouse (or civil partner) exemption (*s 18*).

Alternatively, the deceased's will could establish a life interest in an appropriate share of the house to the surviving spouse, with the remaining interest to non-exempt beneficiaries (eg the children), in order to utilise the nil rate band, if available.

15.38 The trustees could subsequently decide to appoint a share of the life interest to (say) the children, the trust remaining subject to wide overriding powers of appointment. The survivor could remain in occupation, albeit on a non-exclusive basis, as the children must not be barred from occupying the home as well. On the survivor's death, the interest which falls to be taken into account for IHT purposes is the relevant proportion of the interest remaining (*s 50(5)*).

Consideration should be given to whether such an arrangement is appropriate where (for example) the family members who will eventually inherit the property are lineal descendants (eg children) and the residence nil rate band would be available following the survivor's death from 6 April 2017. However, if the survivor was beneficially entitled to an interest in possession, the property (or the relevant proportion of it) is 'inherited' for the purpose of the residence nil rate band which may therefore be available if lineal descendants become beneficially entitled to the property on the survivor's death (*s 8J(5)*).

There is thought to be no GWR if the survivor is a co-owner, and as such is legally entitled to occupy the whole. Prior to 22 March 2006 the termination of a life interest is not a disposal by way of gift for GWR purposes (*FA 1986, s 102(1)*). However, from that date, the lifetime termination of an interest in possession can be treated as a gift (*FA 1986, s 102ZA*). An IHT charge could therefore arise if an individual continues to derive a benefit from the property after it has been given away or the interest has been terminated. See **Chapter 13**.

What if the surviving spouse or civil partner is a trustee? HMRC generally accept that the appointment of a donor, spouse or civil partner as a trustee is not of itself a GWR. The spouse or civil partner holds the property in a fiduciary capacity only, and is required to deal with it in accordance with their fiduciary duties as a trustee. The same applies if the donor, spouse or civil partner is entitled to payment for their services as trustee, if the trust deed allows and provided the remuneration is not excessive (IHTM14394). Nevertheless, it may be considered safer if the survivor is not a trustee.

For capital gains tax purposes, private residence exemption should be available (eg if the property is sold during the survivor's lifetime) if he is 'entitled to occupy it under the terms of the settlement' (*TCGA 1992, s 225*).

It is important that the trust is properly administered and that the decisions of the trustees are made independently and in the best interests of the beneficiary, such as to reduce the possibility of a challenge by HMRC that the trust is a 'sham'. This point is discussed further at **15.58**. The same comment applies to trusts in general.

Discretionary trust

15.39 A discretionary trust is one in which the beneficiaries normally have no interest in possession of the settled property, because the discretionary nature of the trust means that they have no absolute entitlement to trust income or assets.

However, the trustees of a discretionary trust can exercise their powers under the trust deed in favour of a beneficiary in such a way that an interest in possession is created. The IHT treatment of such an interest in possession broadly depends on whether it is deemed to arise before 22 March 2006 or since that date, subject to certain exceptions (see **15.35** above).

Statement of Practice 10/79 and the Judge case

15.40 HMRC Statement of Practice 10/79 ('Power of trustees to allow a beneficiary to occupy a dwelling house') states that if the trust deed allows '... an exclusive or joint residence ... for a definite or indefinite period ... with the intention of providing a particular beneficiary with a permanent home, HMRC will normally regard the exercise of the power as creating an interest in possession'. In addition, a lease for life for less than full consideration is treated as an interest in possession (*s 43(3)*).

The correctness of SP 10/79 was called into question in *Judge (Personal representatives of Walden deceased) v Revenue and Customs Commissioners* [2005] SSCD 863, in which it was held that the beneficiary under a will trust had no right to occupy the property, but that the trustees had absolute discretion (not a duty) to allow her to occupy.

In the *Judge* case, Mr and Mrs Walden lived at 30 Perrymead Street in London. Mr Walden owned the property. He made a will. Clause 3 of that will, which dealt with the matrimonial home, included the following provision:

> 'AND I DECLARE my Trustees during the lifetime of my Wife to permit her to have the use and enjoyment of the said property for such period or periods as they shall in their absolute discretion think fit pending postponement of sale she paying the rates taxes and other outgoings and keeping the same in good repair and insured against fire to the full value thereof ... '

15.41 Mr Walden subsequently died. His personal representatives concluded that the effect of Clause 3 of Mr Walden's will was to give Mrs Walden an interest in possession in the property. The IHT account submitted to Capital Taxes (as it then was) for Mr Walden's estate was completed on that basis. A claim for the IHT spouse exemption was made on the value of Perrymead Street, which was shown as £625,000. This resulted in no IHT being paid on Mr Walden's estate, because his other estate assets were covered by the nil rate band.

Mrs Walden died a few years later. Her personal representatives submitted an IHT account to the Revenue's Capital Taxes Office, but the account did not mention the Perrymead Street property. This was presumably on the footing that Mr Walden's will established a discretionary trust, so that the property was not part of Mrs Walden's estate. The Revenue issued a determination on the basis that Mrs Walden had an interest in possession in the property, and the personal representatives appealed to the Special Commissioner.

The Special Commissioner said that a right of occupation can be an interest in possession. However, a proper construction of the will was crucial to the decision whether an interest in possession had been created. The Commissioner had to interpret Mr Walden's will. Where Clause 3 referred to 'for such period or periods as they shall in their absolute discretion think fit' the Commissioner considered that those words were clear and unambiguous. They gave Mrs Walden no right to occupy Perrymead Street, but gave the trustees an absolute discretion to allow Mrs Walden to occupy it. There was no duty to allow her to occupy the property. Therefore, Mrs Walden did not have an interest in possession. The personal representatives' appeal was allowed.

Points to note

15.42 It should be remembered that gifts to discretionary trusts are immediately chargeable transfers (and also that special treatment can apply to discretionary trusts created by will (*s 144*; see **Chapter 13**)).

In the *Judge* case, Mr Walden's will created a discretionary trust with an asset worth £625,000 at the time of his death, ie well in excess of the nil rate band at the time. However, no IHT was paid because the personal representatives assumed (incorrectly as it turned out) that Mrs Walden had an interest in possession in the house. The Special Commissioner's decision effectively meant that no IHT was payable on the property from Mrs Walden's estate, but was payable on Mr Walden's earlier death.

15.43 If an interest in the property is left outright to the surviving spouse (or civil partner) and the other interest is owned by a discretionary trust, there is an argument that the survivor should not be treated as having an interest in possession in it, on the basis that she is entitled to occupy by reason of the interest they own, ie as a tenant in common has a right to occupy the entire house (*Bull v Bull* [1955] 1 QB 234).

However, HMRC may challenge this analysis, particularly if the discretionary trust gives the survivor exclusive rights of occupation.

15.44 In England and Wales the *Trusts of Land and Appointment of Trustees Act 1996* provides for a trust of land, giving a statutory right of occupation of the family home to the surviving spouse or civil partner. The provisions confer on any 'beneficiary who is beneficially entitled to an interest in possession in land subject to a trust of land' a right of occupation if certain conditions are satisfied (*TLATA 1996, s 12*).

That right is not absolute – note the term 'interest in possession' does not necessarily confer the same meaning as for IHT purposes, although HMRC may contend that it does – and is subject to restriction (*TLATA 1996, s 13*). However, the trustees cannot exercise their powers to exclude or restrict occupation by a person who is in occupation of land from continuing to do so, unless consent is given or the approval of the court is obtained (*TLATA 1996, s 13(7)*).

Note that *TLATA 1996* does not extend to Scotland (*TLATA 1996, s 27(3)*).

15.45 In the case of a surviving tenant in common in England and Wales, some doubt has been expressed whether (s)he obtains an interest in possession in the whole property on the other's death. This is because *TLATA 1996, s 12* only gives rights of occupation to trust beneficiaries if the property (as opposed to a share in it) is held in trust (*TLATA 1996, s 22(1)*). Does *TLATA 1996, s 13(7)* effectively give the survivor a right to possess the whole property? Or is any right to occupy non-exclusive, so that the trustees may require a proportionate rent to be paid (indicating that there is not an interest in possession in the whole)?

If a half-share in the property was settled under the deceased's will, it is arguably possible to interpret *s 22(1)* as meaning that the trust beneficiaries have no right under *s 12*, so that *s 13* does not need to be considered. This would therefore seem to give the surviving spouse or partner the immediate right to possession. However, the position is not free from doubt, and ideally requires litigation to clarify the matter, or at least some guidance on HMRC's view.

The application of *TLATA 1996* (*ss 12, 22*) also raises questions over the availability of only or main residence relief for the trustees under *TCGA 1992, s 225* on a disposal of their interest in the family home, on the basis that the surviving spouse has no right of occupation as a beneficiary, and in addition occupied the property by reason of their rights as joint beneficial owner, rather than under the terms of the settlement as required for CGT relief purposes.

However, in Appendix 5 of *Drafting Trusts and Will Trusts: A Modern Approach* (12th Edition, Sweet & Maxwell) by James Kessler QC and Leon Sartin, the authors express the view that if the testator's interest in the property is appropriated to a nil rate band discretionary trust two years or more after the testator's death (ie to avoid the surviving spouse acquiring an 'immediate post-death interest', which would form part of the individual's estate) and the surviving spouse (who is not a disabled person for IHT purposes on the testator's death) is subsequently given an interest in possession in the trust's share, only or main residence relief should be available to the trustees when the property is eventually sold. The beneficiary would have an interest in possession in the trust's share of land (as required by *TLATA 1996, s 12*), and the relief in *TCGA 1992, s 225* does not require that the beneficiary is *only* entitled to occupy it by virtue of an entitlement under the settlement. The latter point is accepted in HMRC's guidance on co-owned property (at CG65407).

The arrangement described above is a simpler and potentially more convenient alternative way of dealing with a nil rate band trust than the 'debt' or 'charge' arrangements described at **15.54** below.

15.46 Consideration needs to be given to Statement of Practice 10/79 (see **15.38** above), which indicates that if the trustees have powers to allow the creation of an exclusive occupation and that power is exercised with the intention of providing a particular beneficiary with a permanent home, HMRC will normally regard the exercise of that power as creating an interest in possession.

However, notwithstanding SP 10/79 and depending on the circumstances, it would seem (following the *Judge* case) that trustees of a discretionary trust could claim private residence relief for CGT purposes, without the beneficiary who occupies the property being considered to have an interest in possession for IHT purposes (see also **15.45** below).

HMRC provided guidance ('Schedule 20 – SP 10/79 and Transitional Serial Interests') on interests in possession and SP 10/79 in November 2007, in response to queries raised by STEP and CIOT. HMRC's response included the following salient points:

- The circumstances in which HMRC would *not* regard the trustees as having exercised their power to give a beneficiary an exclusive right of occupation (ie so as not to create an interest in possession) are 'rare', but might include instances where there was no evidence of (or significant doubt as to) the intentions of the trustees.
- An SP 10/79 interest in possession generally arises if there is evidence that the trustees have knowingly exercised their powers so as to give a beneficiary exclusive occupation of the property.

- If the trustees have intended to grant a beneficiary the right to occupy a specific, named property owned by the trust, the beneficiary's interest in possession would end when the property was sold.

15.47 A CGT advantage of leaving a share in the family home to trustees (as opposed to a direct legacy to a family member who does not live there) is the potential availability of private residence relief on a subsequent disposal of the property. The relief applies if, during the trustees' period of ownership, a beneficiary is 'a person entitled under the terms of the settlement' to occupy the property as their only or main residence, and does so occupy it (*TCGA 1992, s 225*).

The relief is available to trustees of both interest in possession and discretionary trusts (*Sansom v Peay* [1976] STC 494; see also CG65407).

Appointing an interest in possession

15.48 Prior to *FA 2006*, a potential pitfall in HMRC successfully contending that the surviving spouse or civil partner had an interest in possession within Statement of Practice 10/79 in respect of the property interest held by the trustees of the discretionary trust was that the survivor fell to be treated as beneficially entitled to that property interest, which would therefore form part of their estate for IHT purposes.

However, following *FA 2006*, it does not normally matter if HMRC successfully argue that SP 10/79 applies, or if the trustees appoint an actual interest in possession to the surviving spouse or civil partner, provided that the interest does not arise within two years of death (or the survivor is not a disabled person, as defined for IHT purposes).

The relevance of this two-year period is that the provisions dealing with discretionary will trusts (*s 144*; see **Chapter 13**) broadly allow appointments of trust assets within two years following death to be effectively read back into the will. An interest in possession to the surviving spouse or civil partner on death would therefore fall to be treated as an 'immediate post-death interest' (see **Chapter 7**), subject to the spouse or civil partner exemption, resulting in the potential wastage of the deceased's nil rate band (although the transferable nil rate band facility could possibly assist in that case).

To avoid this treatment, the safest course of action for the trustees to consider would therefore be to wait until at least two years have expired following the first death if practical, before appointing an interest in possession in the family home to the survivor.

Joint ownership (tenants in common)

15.49 If the family home is jointly owned as tenants in common, the deceased spouse or civil partner may, for example, leave a share to adult children, to make use of the available nil rate band, including (from 6 April 2017) the residence nil rate band. The surviving spouse or civil partner may continue to occupy by reason of their own beneficial share in the home.

Interest in possession for survivor

15.50 An interest in possession created by will in favour of the surviving spouse or civil partner is generally subject to the spouse IHT exemption (*s 18*).

If the nil rate band has already been used elsewhere, it may be that the deceased's estate is left on a 'flexible life interest trust' in which the trustees are given wide, overriding powers of appointment. Those powers may enable the trustees to appoint property in whole or part to the survivor absolutely, and/or to terminate the life interest in whole or part and appoint the property to other beneficiaries under the will (eg children or grandchildren). As to the IHT treatment of interest in possession trusts generally, see **Chapter 7**.

Following *FA 2006*, the lifetime termination of an interest in possession, after which the former interest holder continues to occupy 'the no-longer possessed property', can constitute a gift for GWR purposes (see **Chapter 13**).

Even without a formal interest in possession trust, as indicated the terms of the will can create an effective interest in possession for the deceased. Such an interest in possession could be caused inadvertently.

15.51 In *IRC v Lloyds Private Banking Ltd* [1998] STC 559, an interest in possession was held to exist where a wife left her share in the matrimonial home, by her will, upon the following terms:

'(1) While my husband remains alive and desires to reside in the property and keeps the same in good repair and insured comprehensively to its full value with Insurers approved by my Trustees and pays and indemnifies my Trustees against all rates, taxes and other outgoings in respect of the property my Trustee shall not make any objection to such residence and shall not disturb or restrict it in any way and shall not take any steps to enforce the trust for sale on which the property is held or to realise my share therein or to obtain any rent or profit from the property.

(2) On the death of my said Husband … I devise and bequeath the said property … to my Daughter … absolutely.'

The High Court considered that the above clause in the wife's will was a dispositive provision, which conferred on the husband a determinable life interest in the half-share in the property. This created a settlement (within the meaning of *s 43(2)*) by which an interest in possession had been conferred on the husband. Accordingly, on his death IHT was charged on the basis that his estate included an interest in the entire property. This decision has been applied in other cases (*Woodhall v IRC* [2000] STC (SCD) 558, and *Faulkner (Adams' Trustee) v IRC* [2001] SSCD 112 (SpC 278)).

However, contrast those cases with the decision in the *Judge* case (see **15.38** above), in which the Special Commissioner held that the surviving spouse did not have an interest in possession of a residence because the deceased spouse's trustees had absolute discretion as to whether to permit her to occupy the property for any period, notwithstanding that a sale of the property required the consent of the surviving spouse.

'Nil rate band' discretionary trusts

15.52 An alternative to such a legacy of the first spouse or civil partner to die (eg the husband) is to gift the nil rate band in his will for chargeable beneficiaries through the use of a 'nil rate band discretionary trust'. The residue of his estate (ie in particular the home) is left to the widow. Such trusts are discussed in greater detail in **Chapter 13**.

The main asset in many estates is the family home. There may be insufficient other assets of value in the estate to constitute the nil rate band in some cases. This may result in an interest in the family home being used instead. Alternatively, arrangements commonly known as 'debt and charge' schemes may be considered (see **15.54** below). A detailed comparison of the potential merits and disadvantages of each route are beyond the scope of this chapter.

As indicated in this chapter, the planned use of nil rate band discretionary trusts should be reviewed where appropriate, following the introduction of the residence nil rate band from 6 April 2017, in view of the potential loss of the residence nil rate band.

15.53 It must be remembered that nil rate band discretionary trusts of an interest in the family home involve both tax law and property law considerations. The latter is outside the scope of this book. However, property law and tax law principles may diverge.

'Debt' or 'charge' schemes

15.54 Following the introduction of the facility to transfer unused nil rate bands between spouses and civil partners from 9 October 2007, in most cases it will no longer be necessary (or desirable) for married couples or civil partners to utilise the nil rate band on the first death (eg by leaving an interest in the family home to non-exempt beneficiaries such as the trustees of a nil rate band discretionary trust).

Previously, if the home was the main asset in the estate, a relatively well-known IHT planning arrangement was for a nil rate band gift to be satisfied either by a *debt* or *charge* on the property in favour of the trustees of the nil rate band discretionary trust (see **Chapter 13**).

Such arrangements may still be a feature of many wills drafted before 9 October 2007 in particular, in which the will of the deceased spouse or civil partner may give the trustees the power to make loans or to charge over the house, and on favourable terms (say) for the widow (eg an interest-free loan, capital payments deferred). However, the debt should preferably be repayable on demand to the trustees, to reduce the possibility of an argument by HMRC that the survivor has an interest in possession.

The charge should generally be a deduction from the widow's estate on her death, with her ownership allowing for continued occupation of the house during lifetime. However, in the case of a debt arrangement, a deduction may be restricted or denied in the above scenario if the widow made lifetime gifts to the husband. A loan is not deductible from an estate to the extent that the loan was property derived from the deceased, ie the widow (*FA 1986, s 103(1)(a)*).

15.55 For example, suppose that a widower, who had previously owned the family home, made a lifetime gift of a half share to his wife. The wife subsequently died, and her will created a nil rate band discretionary trust. The husband receives his wife's interest in the family home, and incurs a debt to the trust. HMRC are likely to contend that the widower's debt is disallowable for IHT purposes under *FA 1986, s 103*.

These were broadly the facts in *Phizackerley (Personal representative of Phizackerley, deceased) v Revenue and Customs Commissioners* [2007] SpC 591, where HMRC's disallowance of an 'IOU' as a liability of the surviving spouse's estate was upheld by the Special Commissioner.

Such a challenge could be avoided by using charge arrangements instead, where the charge is made by the personal representatives. The home should be part of the residuary estate. This would allow the personal representatives to appropriate the home to the widow, subject to a charge. The identity of the personal representatives and the trustees of the discretionary will trust should not be identical (particularly as to the first named), and the surviving spouse or civil partner should preferably not be a personal representative.

15.56 The charge method may also avoid stamp duty land tax (SDLT). HMRC originally published guidance on stamp duty land tax and nil rate band discretionary trusts on their website. This information is now contained in their Stamp Duty Land Tax Manual (at SDLTM04045), which contrasts debt and charge arrangements and their SDLT consequences (see below).

> *HMRC guidance: Charge scheme – SDLT liability*
>
> 'Land is transferred to the surviving spouse or civil partner and the spouse or civil partner charges the property with payment of the amount of the pecuniary legacy. The nil-rate band discretionary trustees accept this charge in satisfaction of the pecuniary legacy.
>
> The charge is money's worth and so is chargeable consideration for SDLT purposes.'
>
> *HMRC guidance: Charge scheme – no SDLT liability*
>
> 'The personal representatives charge land with the payment of the pecuniary legacy. The personal representatives and nil-rate band discretionary trustees also agree that the trustees have no right to enforce payment of the amount of the legacy personally against the owner of the land for the time being. The nil-rate band discretionary trustees accept this charge in satisfaction of the legacy. The property is transferred to the surviving spouse or civil partner subject to the charge.
>
> There is no chargeable consideration for SDLT purpose provided that there is no change in the rights or liabilities of any person in relation to the debt secured by the charge.'

15.57 By contrast, HMRC's view is that SDLT (LBTT for Scotland) is payable if the surviving spouse or civil partner (or the personal representatives) creates the debt – as it is then arguable that the land is transferred for consideration, ie the 'promise' to pay (see below).

> *HMRC guidance: Debt scheme – SDLT liability*
>
> 'The nil-rate band discretionary trustees accept the surviving spouse's or civil partner's promise to pay in satisfaction of the pecuniary legacy and in consideration of that promise land is transferred to the surviving spouse or civil partner.
>
> The promise to pay is chargeable consideration for SDLT purposes.'
>
> 'The nil-rate band discretionary trustees accept the personal representatives' promise to pay in satisfaction of the pecuniary legacy and land is transferred to the surviving spouse or civil partner in consideration of the spouse accepting liability for the promise.
>
> The acceptance of liability for the promise is chargeable consideration for SDLT purposes. The amount of chargeable consideration is the amount promised, not exceeding the market value of the land transferred.'

15.58 LBTT replaced SDLT in Scotland from 1 April 2015. A detailed discussion of LBTT and SDLT is outside the scope of this book. However, in Appendix 3 of *Drafting Trusts and Will Trusts: a Modern Approach* (12th Edition, Sweet & Maxwell by James Kessler QC and Leon Sartin), the authors have advanced the view that an SDLT liability should not normally arise on debt schemes. This is broadly on the footing that the execution of the survivor's undertaking to pay the debt does not involve the acquisition of a 'chargeable interest'.

Further, there is considered to be no SDLT on the assent of the land interest to the survivor, as an SDLT charge arises on 'chargeable consideration' (as defined in *FA 2003, Sch 4, para 1*), and the survivor's undertaking is not 'consideration' for acquiring the land. Whilst an SDLT charge arises in the above examples if the transfer is in fact in consideration of the spouse's promise to pay the nil rate band sum, the undertaking and assent do not need to be structured in this way.

Nevertheless, the charge route may be considered preferable to the debt route, on the basis that comfort is given in HMRC's confirmation that no SDLT charge arises if the documentation is in accordance with the wording of their statement above.

Some debt schemes are drafted on the basis that the spouse undertakes to pay the trustees an 'indexed-linked nil-rate sum', eg a nil rate sum increased by the retail price index. Charge schemes may be drafted on the basis that executors charge property with payment of the index-linked nil rate sum. The question arises whether the trustees are chargeable to tax on the indexation element when that amount is paid. It is understood that HMRC consider that such a tax charge arises. The authors of the above book (in Appendix 4) advance the view that there is no tax on the payment of the indexed-linked sum, and the benefit of a debt or charge is not a deeply discounted security for income tax purposes, or a debt on a security for CGT purposes.

However, a drafter unfamiliar with the tax rules could inadvertently create a debt on which interest accrues (liable to income tax if the interest is paid), or a deeply discounted security (liable to income tax on disposal), or a debt on a security (liable to CGT on disposal). Care and an understanding of the tax issues involved are therefore important.

15.59 For pre-owned assets income tax purposes, HMRC accept that no charge arises in respect of nil rate band discretionary trusts of a debt. HMRC's guidance on pre-owned assets in the context of debts and charge schemes includes the following example (IHTM44107):

> 'Jack and Jill own their home in equal shares as tenants in common. Under his Will, Jack leaves property not exceeding the nil-rate band for Inheritance

Tax to a discretionary trust, of which Jill is one of the potential beneficiaries. The remainder of his estate passes to Jill absolutely. Following Jack's death, his executors transferred his half share of the property to Jill and, in return, she executed a loan agreement equivalent to the value of the half-share. No Inheritance Tax is payable on Jack's death and when Jill dies, her estate is reduced by the debt and she also has her nil rate band to set against the couple's assets.

The POA charge does not apply here. As Jill did not own her husband's share at the relevant time and did not dispose of it, the disposal conditions (IHTM44004) in FA04/Sch15/Para3(2) are not met. If she did not provide Jack with any of the consideration given by him for the purchase of his half share the contribution condition (IHTM44005) in FA04/Sch15/Para3(3) will not apply either.

Even if she had provided him with some or all of the consideration the condition will still not apply as it would have been an excluded transaction (IHTM44032) under FA04/Sch15/Para10(2)(a). Had this been the case, however, the debt would not be allowable as a deduction on Jill's death by virtue of FA86/S103.'

Warning: 'sham' trusts

15.60

> **Focus**
>
> It is important that the trustees of nil rate band discretionary trusts (and trustees in general) act and properly perform their duties as such. Care should be taken to protect against accusations of a 'sham'.

It is not sufficient just to have a well-drafted trust deed. The trustees must be active rather than passive, and be seen to consider and (if appropriate) exercise their discretions and not just leave the survivor in indefinite, favourable occupation of the property. The trustees should meet regularly (eg twice a year) and carefully minute their decisions (eg whether to take a charge as opposed to a debt, as to the charging of interest, whether repayment of the loan should be requested etc).

If the trustees merely 'sit on their hands' the whole arrangement can be challenged by HMRC, or it may be argued that the widow has an interest in possession in the trust property.

RESIDENCE NIL RATE BAND

Introduction

15.61 Chargeable transfers within the seven-year period ending with the date of the latest chargeable transfer are cumulated for the purposes of determining the IHT rate. Where chargeable lifetime transfers and the individual's death estate do not exceed the IHT threshold or 'nil rate band', there is no IHT liability.

In addition, the transferable nil rate band provisions broadly allow claims for unused nil rate band of a deceased spouse or civil partner to be transferred to a surviving spouse or civil partner (who dies on or after 9 October 2007), thus potentially increasing the survivor's nil rate band by up to 100%, or one additional nil rate band.

15.62

> **Focus**
>
> Residence nil rate band (or 'extra nil rate band') is also available in relation to deaths on or after 6 April 2017, where a qualifying residential interest is passed on death to a lineal descendant of the deceased (*ss 8D–8M*).
>
> The residence nil rate band is in addition to the IHT threshold (or standard nil rate band), and any transferred nil rate band upon the earlier death of the deceased's spouse or civil partner.

The unused residence nil rate band is broadly transferable to a spouse or civil partner upon a claim being made, subject to an overriding maximum amount (see **15.63**).

The residence nil rate band is subject to tapered withdrawal for estates valued at more than £2 million on death.

15.63 The maximum amount of the residence nil rate band (or the 'residential enhancement', as the legislation describes it) for 2017/18 to 2020/21 is as follows (*s 8D(5)(a)*):

Example 15.4—The 'residence nil rate band'

Tax year	Residential enhancement
	£
2017/18	100,000
2018/19	125,000
2019/20	150,000
2020/21	175,000

The maximum amount of the residence nil rate band (and the taper threshold – see **15.65** below) is subject to indexation increases by reference to the CPI, unless Parliament determines otherwise, in a similar way to the IHT threshold. The relevant amounts for each year are to be specified in regulations. However, there is to be no such increase until 2021/22 at the earliest.

15.64 The residence nil rate band applies for the purposes of calculating the amount of IHT on a person's death (under *s 4*) on or after 6 April 2017. It is not available to trusts, although a beneficiary can 'inherit' the property for residence nil rate band purposes in some cases (see **15.70**).

The legislation sets out certain terms and abbreviations (in *s 8D(5)*) used for the purposes of determining the residence nil rate band available:

- TT is the 'taper threshold' (see **15.65**) at the person's death;
- E is the value of the person's estate immediately before the person's death; and
- VT is the value (if any) transferred by a *chargeable* transfer on the person's death.

The deceased's residence nil rate band (if greater than nil) broadly results in IHT being charged at a rate of 0% on the portion of VT falling within it; any remainder of VT is charged at the IHT rates on death (*s 8D(3)*).

Tapered withdrawal

Focus

The residence nil rate band is subject to a taper threshold, which reduces the nil rate band available according to the value of the deceased's estate (ie assets less liabilities, before reliefs or exemptions, if applicable).

15.65 This 'taper threshold' is set at £2 million for 2017/18 and subsequent tax years. It is subject to indexation increases (to be specified in regulations) by reference to the CPI unless Parliament determines otherwise, but is fixed at £2 million until 2021/22 at the earliest.

The person's residence nil rate band allowance is adjusted using a formula set out in the legislation (*s 8D(5)(g)*), which withdraws the 'default allowance' (see below) by £1 for every £2 that the value of the estate exceeds the taper threshold:

$$\text{Default allowance} - \left(\frac{E - TT}{2}\right)$$

where:

- 'default allowance' is the total of the residence nil rate band at the person's death, plus any 'brought forward allowance' (ie unused residence nil rate band transferred on an earlier death of a spouse or civil partner) (see **15.64** below);
- E (see **15.58**) is the value of the person's estate immediately before death (ie before any reliefs and exemptions); and
- TT is the taper threshold.

The result of the formula is described in the legislation as the 'adjusted allowance'.

Example 15.5—Tapered residence nil rate band

Arthur and Belinda jointly own their matrimonial home equally as tenants in common.

Arthur dies on 1 June 2017. His estate is worth £2.1 million. In his will, Arthur leaves his interest in the home, which is valued at £450,000, to his son Colin. The rest of his estate is left to Belinda.

Arthur's residence nil rate band is £100,000 (for 2017/18). His 'adjusted allowance' is:

$$\pounds 100{,}000 - \left(\frac{\pounds 2{,}100{,}000 - \pounds 2{,}000{,}000}{2}\right)$$

$$= \underline{\pounds 50{,}000}$$

In calculating the IHT on Arthur's estate, a residence nil rate band of £50,000 may be deducted from the value of his estate in respect of the property interest of £450,000, in addition to the main nil rate band of £325,000 (for 2017/18), if available.

15.66 Thus for 2020/21, the residence nil rate band will be reduced to nil if the person's estate value is £2,350,000 or higher. This assumes that no residence nil rate band (£175,000 for 2020/21) has been brought forward (ie transferred) following the earlier death of a spouse or civil partner.

Where it appears that the taper threshold might be exceeded on death, consideration might be given to the making of lifetime gifts to reduce the value of the estate accordingly in appropriate circumstances.

Eligibility and amount

15.67 The residence nil rate band applies if a person's estate includes a 'qualifying residential interest' (see **15.69** below), and all or part of that interest is left to one or more lineal descendants (ie it is 'closely inherited' – see **15.70** below). The value attributable to the qualifying residential interest is after the deduction of liabilities (*s 162(2)*, eg a mortgage or loan secured on the property) and any agricultural property relief and business property relief.

For estates not exceeding the taper threshold, if the value of the residence that passes to direct descendants is less than the 'default allowance' (ie the person's residence nil rate band, plus any amount transferred on the earlier death of a spouse or civil partner), the residence nil rate band is limited to the value of the residence; any unused residence nil rate band is available for transfer to a spouse (or civil partner) (*s 8E(2)*).

Example 15.6—Interest in home passing to a direct descendant

John and Karen jointly own their matrimonial home as tenants in common.

John died on 31 August 2020. His interest in the property was worth £125,000, and the rest of his estate was worth £500,000. In his will, John leaves the property interest to his adult daughter, Lisa.

The percentage of John's property interest that is 'closely inherited' (see **15.70**) is 100%.

The maximum residence nil rate band for 2020/21 is £175,000. However, John's residence nil rate is restricted to his interest in the residence (ie £125,000).

The unused element is available to transfer to Karen, expressed as the unused proportion of the residence nil rate band of 28.5714% (ie £50,000/£175,000) × 100).

If the value of the residence passing to direct descendants is greater than or equal to the person's default allowance, the residence nil rate band available is the default allowance, so none of the residence nil rate band is transferable to the spouse (*s 8E(3)*).

For estates above the taper threshold, if the value of the residence passing to direct descendants is less than the 'adjusted allowance' after taper relief has been applied (see **15.59** above), the residence nil rate band is limited to the value of that residence; any unused residence nil rate band is available for transfer to the spouse (*s 8E(4)*). If the value of the residence passing to direct descendants is greater than or equal to the person's adjusted allowance, the residence nil rate band available is the adjusted allowance, so none of the residence nil rate band is transferable to the spouse (*s 8E(5)*).

However, if the value of the residence exceeds the value of the estate (ie after deducting liabilities), the residence nil rate band is instead restricted to the value of the chargeable estate, and any unused excess is available for transfer to a spouse (*s 8E(7)*).

15.68 If the deceased's estate does not include a 'qualifying residential interest' (see **15.70** below), or if it does include such an interest but none of it is closely inherited, the person's residence nil rate band is nil. However, the residence nil rate band that has not been used is available for transfer to a spouse (*s 8F*).

Thus a surviving spouse who is the sole owner of the matrimonial home may still be able to claim the deceased spouse's unused residence nil rate band (see **15.71**).

Qualifying residences, etc

15.69 The legislation sets out the meaning of 'qualifying residential interest' and also 'qualifying former residential interest' and 'residential property interest', in the context of the residence nil rate band, including for downsizing purposes (*s 8H*, as amended by *FA 2016*).

A residential property interest is broadly an interest in a dwelling house that was the deceased's residence when it was part of their estate. There is no requirement that the property was occupied as a residence throughout the entire period of ownership. Where the person's death estate includes only one residence, that residence will be the qualifying residential interest. If the person's estate includes more than one residence, the deceased's personal representatives may nominate one of them, and that residence will be treated as the qualifying residential interest.

A dwelling house for these purposes includes land that is occupied and used as its garden or grounds, but excludes any trees or underwood in relation to which a woodlands election is made (under *s 125*) in relation to the person's death.

If a person lives in 'job-related' accommodation (ie within *TCGA 1992, s 222(8A)–(8D)*) and owns a house that they intend occupying as a residence in due course, that house is treated as if the person occupied it as such.

The deceased may have had more than one interest in a former residence (eg outright ownership in 50% of the residence, and a life interest in the other 50%). If the person made a lifetime disposal of one or more interests in a nominated former residence on the same day (on or after 8 July 2015), that interest (or those interests) will be a qualifying former residential interest(s) for the purposes of any downsizing addition (*s 8H(4B)*). If the person disposed of an interest (or interests) in a nominated former residence on different days, the personal representatives can nominate only one of those days, and the interest (or interests) disposed of on that day will be qualifying one(s) for the purposes of any downsizing addition (*s 8H(4C)*).

If an interest in a residence has been gifted but the donor continues to benefit from it within the gifts with reservation provisions (*FA 1986, s 102*), the gift does not count as a disposal for the purposes of determining the qualifying residential interest and downsizing addition. However, if the reservation subsequently ceases (eg upon moving out of the property) such that there is a deemed potentially exempt transfer (under *FA 1986, s 102(4)*), the donor is treated as making a disposal of the residential property interest (*s 8H(4D)*).

The above provisions in respect of former residential property interests were introduced (in *FA 2016*) with the downsizing legislation for residence nil rate band purposes (see **15.76–15.83**).

15.70 Further legislation (*s 8HA*) introduced in *FA 2016* deals with former residences held in interest in possession trusts, for the purposes of determining whether a person's residence held in such a trust may be considered as a qualifying former residential interest for downsizing purposes (in *s 8H(4A)–(4C)*: see above). It applies broadly where the person is beneficially entitled to an interest in possession in settled property (see below) which holds an interest in a residence.

If the trustees dispose of the residence but the beneficiary has an interest in possession in the trust property, the disposal is treated as being made by the beneficiary (under *s 49(1)*) for downsizing purposes, if that interest in possession is one to which the beneficiary became beneficially entitled before 22 March 2006 (and *s 71A* does not apply to the settled property), or if the beneficiary became beneficially entitled to the interest in possession on or after that date and the interest is an immediate post-death interest, disabled person's interest, transitional serial interest, or falls within *s 5(1B)*.

Similarly, if the beneficiary disposes of an interest in possession, or the beneficiary's interest in possession ends during their lifetime, and the trust property includes a residence, the beneficiary is treated as having made a disposal of the residence, if that interest in possession falls within one of the above categories (*s 8HA(3)–(6)*).

For commentary on the downsizing provisions for residence nil rate band purposes, see **15.76–15.83**.

'Inherited' and 'closely inherited'

15.71 The legislation also defines when property in a deceased person's estate ('D') is 'inherited' by another person ('B') for the purposes of the residence nil rate band (*s 8J*).

B inherits a property if it is transferred to B under D's will, or under the intestacy rules or otherwise as a result of D's death. The term 'or otherwise' in the legislation seemingly has a deliberately wide meaning, to potentially include a disposition by survivorship, or under an instrument of variation (*s 142*) or a distribution of the property out of a discretionary will trust to a lineal descendant beneficiary within two years of death (within *s 144*).

However, the meaning of 'inherits' is such that it does not generally apply to settled property, unless B becomes entitled to an immediate post-death interest or disabled persons interest, or unless the property becomes settled on trusts to which *s 71A* (ie trusts for bereaved minors) or *s 71D* applies (ie age 18 to 25 trusts) and is for B's benefit (*s 8J(4)*).

If the property was settled property in which D was beneficially entitled to an interest in possession immediately before death, B inherits the property if he becomes beneficially entitled to it on D's death (*s 8J(5)*).

Where the property is treated as forming part of D's estate immediately before death as a result of the gifts with reservation provisions (*FA 1986, s 102(3)*) applying to the gift, B inherits the property if he or she was the recipient of D's gift (*s 8J(6)*).

Something is 'closely inherited' for the above purposes if it is inherited by the person's child, grandchild or other lineal descendant. The definition extends to the spouse or civil partner of the deceased's lineal descendant. It also includes such a spouse (or civil partner) where the lineal descendant died (no later than the deceased), if they did not re-marry in the subsequent period ending with the deceased's death.

The meaning of closely inherited is extended to include stepchildren. Furthermore, an adopted person may be treated as a child of a natural parent or an adoptive parent. A person who was fostered at any time is treated (at that and all subsequent times) as the foster parent's child. Where a guardian or special guardian (both as defined) has been appointed for a person under 18 years old, that person is subsequently treated as a child of the guardian or special guardian. The direct descendants of someone treated as a child of another person for these purposes are also to be treated as direct descendants of that other person (*s 8K*).

Transferable allowance

15.72 As indicated at **15.65** above, a person's 'default allowance' is the total of the residence nil rate band (ie 'residential enhancement') in force at the person's death, plus any brought forward allowance.

'Brought forward allowance' (or transferable residence nil rate band) is available from what the legislation describes as a 'related person' (*s 8G(2)*). This is broadly the earlier spouse (or civil partner) to die. The parties must have been spouses immediately before the earlier death, so the nil rate band will not be transferable if the spouses were divorced (unless they subsequently remarried each other).

> **Focus**
>
> There are detailed rules for calculating the amount of residence nil rate band available for transfer (*s 8G(3)*).
>
> In broad terms, the calculation involves identifying unused residence nil rate band available from a deceased spouse, expressed as a percentage (ie of the residence nil rate band at the spouse's death). The percentage is aggregated if appropriate (eg if the surviving spouse was married twice, and both of the deceased spouses had unused residence nil rate band), subject to an overriding maximum of 100%, or one additional residence nil rate band.

However, no amount can be transferred unless a claim is made (see **15.74** below).

15.73 The much-publicised announcement by the government upon the introduction of the residence nil rate band was that this meant an effective IHT threshold of £1 million per married couple (or civil partnership). However, it should be noted that this threshold cannot be achieved until 2020/21.

The above £1 million threshold assumes that the spouses (or civil partners) each have a full standard nil rate band of £325,000 and residence nil rate band of £175,000 available, and that the nil rate bands are transferred on the first death to the surviving spouse.

Example 15.7—Effective IHT threshold of £1 million

David and his wife Eve jointly own their matrimonial home equally as tenants in common.

David dies on 1 December 2017. He made no lifetime gifts in the previous seven years. David's death estate comprised an interest in the home worth £275,000, bank and building society account balances of £100,000 and investment properties worth £300,000. David leaves his entire estate to Eve in his will.

Eve dies on 30 November 2020. Eve had made no lifetime gifts in the previous seven years. Eve's death estate is worth £1.6 million. It comprises the home (now worth £700,000), bank and building society balances of £250,000 and investment properties worth £650,000. Eve's entire estate passes to her adult daughter, Frances.

Eve's executors claim David's transferable nil rate band and residence nil rate band. The unused percentage of both nil rate bands was 100%. A claim is therefore made to add 100% of £325,000 (ie the nil rate band maximum for 2020/21) and 100% of £175,000 (ie the residence nil rate band maximum for 2020/21) to Eve's own nil rate bands. The combined nil rate bands therefore amount to (£650,000 + £350,000 =) £1 million.

The IHT payable in respect of Eve's estate is as follows:

		£	£
	Family home	700,000	
Less:	Residence nil rate band	(350,000)	350,000
	Other assets		900,000
			1,250,000

		£	£
Less:	Nil rate band		(650,000)
			600,000
	IHT £600,000 × 40%		240,000

> **Focus**
>
> If the death of the earlier spouse occurred before 6 April 2017, the survivor's residence nil rate band is increased without regard to whether the spouse qualified for the residence nil rate band when (s)he died. The standard amount available to transfer for the above purposes (and also the residence nil rate band) is treated as being £100,000.
>
> However, if the net value of the earlier spouse's death estate exceeds the £2 million taper threshold (see **15.59** above), their residence nil rate band available for transfer is subject to a reduction by tapering, ie it is reduced by £1 for every £2 that the estate value exceeds the £2 million threshold (*s 8G(4), (5)*).

Claims for the transferable residence nil rate band

> **Focus**
>
> The transferable residence nil rate band must be claimed (*s 8L*). The claim may be made by the deceased's personal representatives within a permitted period. Alternatively, a claim may be made by any other person liable to IHT on the person's death within such later period as HMRC may allow.

15.74 The 'permitted period' is two years from the end of the month in which the deceased died, or if later three months from the date when the personal representatives start to act. HMRC may allow a longer period at its discretion. A claim made within the normal time limits may be withdrawn no later than one month after whichever of those time limits applies (*s 8L(1)–(3)*).

The claim provisions also deal with situations involving a series of deaths where a claim was not made on the earlier death of a person ('P' in the legislation) to transfer any unused residence nil rate band, which would have affected the IHT liability on the later death of another person ('A'), but not P or anyone else.

A claim may be made by A's personal representatives for unused residence nil rate band in respect of P's estate within an allowed period. Alternatively, a claim may be made by any other person liable to IHT on A's death within such later period as HMRC may allow.

The 'allowed period' is two years from the end of the month in which A died, or if later three months from the date when the personal representatives start to act. A longer period may be allowed by HMRC at its discretion. A claim made within the normal time limits may be withdrawn no later than one month after the end of the relevant time limit *(s 8L(4)–(7))*.

Conditional exemption

15.75 In some cases, a residence may form part of an estate, where some or all assets of the estate are conditionally exempt from IHT. The conditionally exempt assets could include a qualifying residential interest. The residence nil rate band provisions are adapted accordingly to deal with such cases (*s 8M*). The provisions in *s 8M* were amended (in *FA 2016*) to take into account circumstances involving downsizing (see **15.70**).

For deaths from 6 April 2017, to the extent that a qualifying residential interest is conditionally exempt, it is not eligible for the residence nil rate band. The conditional exemption provisions for residence nil rate band purposes apply when at least some of the qualifying residential interest is closely inherited by direct descendants. The legislation applies a formula approach (see *s 8M(2A)*) to calculate the proportion of the conditionally exempt qualifying residential interest which is not eligible for the residence nil rate band.

If the whole of the qualifying residential interest is conditionally exempt (ie none of it qualifies for the residence nil rate band) and there is no entitlement to the downsizing addition (ie none of the assets in the estate are closely inherited), all of the unused residence nil rate band is carried forward. If some or all of the assets are closely inherited, and there is entitlement to a downsizing addition, the residence nil rate band is equal to the downsizing addition, and any unused amount is available to carry forward (*s 8M(2B), (2C)*).

If only part of the qualifying residential interest is conditionally exempt, the residence nil rate band is restricted to the proportion which is closely inherited, and also to the percentage which is not conditionally exempt (*s 8M(2D), (2E)*).

Where assets other than the qualifying residential interest are conditionally exempt, and the deceased is entitled to a downsizing addition (ie assets are closely inherited), and the downsizing addition is more than the value of non-conditionally exempt other assets (ie 'Y' in the legislation), the downsizing addition applies to any non-conditionally exempt assets first, and is not reduced (under *s 8M(2G)*) if it is equal to or less than Y (*s 8M(2F)*).

The downsizing addition is subject to a reduction for assets other than the qualifying residential interest which are conditionally exempt (see *s 8M(2G), (2H)*).

Where conditional exemption ceases to apply and IHT becomes chargeable (under *s 32* or *s 32A*) on a chargeable event related to the residence (and, following *Finance Act 2016*, any other assets in the estate – see below) (ie if the conditional exemption undertakings are not kept, or if the beneficial owner dies, or on disposal), the relevant provisions (in *s 8M(3)*) allow the residence nil rate band and any downsizing addition to be taken into account in the calculation of the IHT charge (under *s 33*), broadly by reversing any reduction in the downsizing addition, and by enabling the residence nil rate band to be recalculated.

The provisions in *s 8M(3)*, which are in point when conditional exemption ceases to apply following a chargeable event and a tax charge arises, were extended in *Finance Act 2016* to ensure that the residence nil rate band and any downsizing addition applies when conditional exemption ceases in respect of the qualifying residential interest and any other assets in the estate.

The deceased's (D's) surviving spouse or civil partner (P) may have died before the chargeable event resulting from conditional exemption ceasing to apply. If the IHT charge arises after P's death and any residence nil rate band was previously transferred from D to P, the residence nil rate band available in the calculation of the IHT charge is reduced by the amount transferred to P (*s 8M(5)*).

If the IHT charge arises before P's death, the amount of residence nil rate band available for transfer to P is recalculated using a 'recapture percentage' by means of a formula (in *s 8M(6)*), to take account of any residence nil rate band used in the IHT charge when the conditional exemption ceased to apply. The calculation is adjusted accordingly if there has been more than one chargeable event (*s 8M(7)*).

The above provisions in *s 8M(5)–(7)* were extended (in *Finance Act 2016*) to conditionally exempt assets other than the qualifying residential interest.

DOWNSIZING AND THE RESIDENCE NIL RATE BAND

Introduction

15.76 Following the introduction of the residence nil rate band provisions (in *F(No 2)A 2015*), the benefit of the residence nil rate band was extended (in *FA 2016*) in certain circumstances involving 'downsizing' on or after 8 July 2015, in relation to deaths from 6 April 2017.

The broad effect of these provisions is that the residence nil rate band, including the part that would otherwise be lost on the deceased's death (from 6 April 2017) as a result of downsizing (on or after 8 July 2015) generally remains available, provided the less valuable qualifying residential interest held on death and assets worth up to the 'lost' residence nil rate band are closely inherited by direct descendants etc (see **15.65**).

The same applies if the deceased sold their only qualifying residential interest and the sale proceeds have been left to direct descendants; or if the deceased otherwise ceased to own the residence and other assets worth up to an equivalent value have been left to direct descendants.

Less valuable residence in death estate

15.77 The downsizing provisions dealing with 'low value' interests in the home apply broadly where a person has downsized from a more valuable residence and there is a less valuable residence left in the estate on death.

Where certain conditions (A to F in the legislation) are all met, there is entitlement to a 'downsizing addition' (ie an increased amount of residence nil rate band). Those conditions are broadly as outlined below (see *s 8FA*):

- Condition A has two alternative requirements. The first is that there is a residence in the estate on death which qualifies for the residence nil rate band (ie a 'qualifying residential interest') but the full amount is not due because the value of the residence (or the proportion which is 'closely inherited' by direct descendants; see **16.65**) is below the maximum residence nil rate band available for that person. Condition A only tests whether there is scope for any downsizing addition (ie it does not give effect to it), so *s 8E(6), (7)* and any entitlement to the downsizing addition are ignored for these purposes.

  The alternative requirement is that there is a residence in the estate on death but none of it is closely inherited and the value of the residence is less than the maximum residence nil rate band available for that person.
- Condition B is that the value transferred by the chargeable transfer on death (VT) is more than the value of the residence (ie the person's 'qualifying residential interest').
- Condition C is that there is a 'qualifying former residential interest' (see *ss 8H(4A)–(4F), 8HA*), ie broadly the person previously had a residence which could have qualified for the residence nil rate band.
- Condition D is that the value of the qualifying former residential interest is more than the chargeable value of the residence in the estate on death.

- Condition E is that at least some of the 'remainder' (ie other assets in the estate immediately before death, other than the qualifying residential interest) is closely inherited.
- Condition F is that a claim is made for the downsizing addition, in accordance with the provisions in *s 8L(1)–(3)* (see **15.68**).

If the conditions are satisfied, the downsizing addition equals the lost residence nil rate band (ie the 'lost relievable amount'; see *s 8FE*) resulting from the downsizing move. However, the additional amount is limited to the value of other assets (or proportion of that value) which is closely inherited (*s 8FA(8)*). Furthermore, there is a potential reduction in certain cases involving conditional exemption (see *s 8M(2G)*).

No residence in death estate

15.78 The downsizing provisions also deal with circumstances where a person has ceased to own a residence, so that there is no residence in the estate on death. A downsizing addition is available if certain conditions (G to K in the legislation) are all satisfied. Those conditions are broadly as outlined below (see *s 8FB*):

- Condition G is that there is no residential property interest in the person's estate on death.
- Condition H is that the value transferred by the chargeable transfer on death (VT) is greater than nil.
- Condition I is that the person previously had a qualifying former residential interest (see **15.70**).
- Condition J is that at least some of the other assets in the estate are closely inherited (see **15.64**).
- Condition K is that a claim is made for the downsizing addition (see **15.68**).

If the conditions are satisfied, the downsizing addition equals the lost residence nil rate band (ie the 'lost relievable amount'; see *s 8FE*) as a result of disposing of the residence. However, the additional amount is limited to the value of the other assets (or proportion of that value) which are closely inherited (*s 8FB(7)*). There is also a potential reduction in certain cases involving conditional exemption (see *s 8M(2G)*).

The 'downsizing addition'

15.79 The effect of the downsizing addition depends on whether or not an interest in the home is left to direct descendants.

If there is an entitlement to a downsizing addition because a person has downsized and the residence in their estate (or a part of it) is left to direct descendants, the downsizing addition is added to the residence nil rate band that would otherwise be due (see *s 8E*), to arrive at the total residence nil rate band for the estate (*s 8FC*).

15.80 If no residence is left to direct descendants, the effect of the downsizing addition (ie where entitlement arises because either a person has downsized but none of the residence has been inherited by direct descendants, or has disposed of a residence so that it cannot be inherited by direct descendants) is given by *s 8FD*. Section *8F* ('Residence nil rate amount: no interest in home goes to descendants etc') does not apply, such that the downsizing addition is available even if no part of the residence is inherited by direct descendants.

The residence nil rate band in these circumstances is equal to the downsizing addition *s 8FD(3)*).

If the downsizing addition equals the residence nil rate band plus any transferred residence nil rate band (ie the 'default allowance' where the value of the estate is below the taper threshold, or 'adjusted allowance' if it is above the taper threshold), no amount is available to carry forward, as the downsizing addition is fully used and nothing is available to be transferred to a spouse or civil partner's estate.

If the value of the estate is equal to or below the taper threshold and the downsizing addition is less than the residence nil rate band plus any transferred residence nil rate band (ie the default allowance), the difference between the downsizing addition and the default allowance is available to be carried forward to a spouse or civil partner's estate.

If the value of the estate is above the taper threshold and the downsizing addition is less than the residence nil rate band plus any transferred residence nil rate band (the adjusted allowance), the difference between the downsizing addition and the adjusted allowance is available to be carried forward to a spouse or civil partner's estate (*s 8FD(4)–(6)*).

The lost relievable amount

15.81 The calculation of the 'lost relievable amount' as a result of downsizing where a less valuable residence is left in the death estate (under *s 8FA(8)*; see **15.71**), or as a result of disposal where there is no residence in the estate on death (under *s 8FB(7)*; see **15.72**), is dealt with in accordance with *s 8FE*.

The value of a person's qualifying former residential interest is the open market value of the residence (or interest in it) upon completion of the disposal.

A person's 'former allowance' comprises the following (*s 8FE(3)*):

(a) the available residence nil rate band at the time of disposal of the qualifying former residential interest;

(b) any brought forward allowance (ie transferred residence nil rate band) that would have been due if the person had died at the time of disposal; and

(c) the difference (if any) between the brought forward allowance which would have been due at the time of disposal and the actual brought forward allowance at the time of the person's death.

For the purposes of (b) above, there are provisions for calculating the brought forward allowance that would have been due had the person died at the time of disposal of the former residence (*s 8FE(4)*). In addition, for the purpose of (c) above, the calculation of the brought forward allowance where the estate on death exceeds the taper threshold involves several steps (see *s 8FE(5)*). The calculation broadly reduces the brought forward allowance by reference to the taper reduction. Furthermore, if completion of the disposal of the residence occurs before 6 April 2017, for the purposes of (a) and (b) above the residence nil rate band is treated as £100,000, and there is no brought forward allowance (*s 8FE6)*).

The calculation of the lost residence nil rate band as a result of downsizing to a less valuable residence (ie the 'lost relievable amount' in *s 8FA*) involves a multi-step process (see *s 8FE(9)*). Step one broadly calculates the percentage of the residence nil rate band that was 'lost' at the time of the disposal. Step two calculates the percentage of the residence nil rate band on death that is used up by the residence on death. Step three calculates the difference between those two percentages. Step four multiplies the person's allowance on death by the percentage calculated in step three to determine the lost relievable amount.

Example 15.8—Downsizing to a less expensive residence

George (who is divorced) downsized in May 2020 from a home worth £250,000 to a home worth £140,000. He sadly died in September 2020. The residence nil rate band is calculated as follows:

Step 1 – Percentage of lost residence nil rate band at the time of disposal:

$$\frac{£250{,}000}{£175{,}000} \times 100\% = 142.8571\%$$

However, the above percentage is restricted to 100%.

Step 2 – Percentage of residence nil rate band on death used up by the residence on death:

$$\frac{\pounds140{,}000}{\pounds175{,}000} \times 100\% = 80\%$$

Step 3 – Subtract the percentage in *Step 2* from the percentage in *Step 1*:

100% – 80% = 20%

Step 4 – Lost relievable amount:

£175,000 × 20% = £35,000

George has potentially lost 20% of the full residence nil rate band of £175,000 (in 2020/21), which would otherwise have been available. However, the full residence nil rate band may still be available on George's death in September 2020 if he left the home (still worth £140,000) plus £35,000 of other estate assets to his adult daughter Harriet. This residence nil rate band is in addition to George's standard nil rate band of £325,000 (for 2020/21), if available.

15.82 The calculation of the lost relievable amount resulting from the disposal of the residence (in *s 8FB*) similarly involves a multi-step process (see *8FE(10)*). Step one broadly calculates the percentage of the residence nil rate band that was 'lost' at the time of the disposal. Step 2 involves multiplying the person's allowance on death by that percentage, to determine the lost relievable amount.

Example 15.9—No residential interest at death

Harriet (a widow) sold her home for £300,000 in May 2020, and moved into nursing care. She sadly died in March 2021, following a short illness. Her estate on death was valued at less than £2 million.

The residence nil rate band is calculated as follows:

Step 1 – Percentage of lost residence nil rate band at the time of disposal

Harriet's 'former allowance' (see *s 8FE(3)*) is the residence nil rate band at the time of disposal of the qualifying former residential interest (£175,000)

plus the transferred residence nil rate band that would have been due if Harriet's husband had died at the time of disposal (£175,000), ie £350,000.

$$\frac{£300{,}000}{£350{,}000} \times 100\% = 85.7142\%$$

Step 2 – Lost relievable amount £350,000 × 85.7142% = £300,000

In her will, Harriet left £500,000 to her only child, Irene. Harriet's executors may therefore claim a residence nil rate band of £300,000.

Other points

15.83 The downsizing provisions can apply in some circumstances where an individual had more than one interest in a former residence, or the former residence was held in certain types of interest in possession trust, or if an individual gave away a residential property interest but continued to live in it and subsequently moved out, following changes introduced in *FA 2016* (see **15.70–15.72**).

As indicated above, a claim must be made for the downsizing addition, where applicable. The deceased's personal representatives can nominate only one disposal of a residence (or an interest in it) on or after 8 July 2015 (and before the person's death) to qualify for the downsizing addition.

There could be any number of downsizing moves between 8 July 2015 and the individual's death. A practical issue to address will therefore be the retention of adequate records to support a claim for the enhanced element of the residence nil rate band following several such moves from the above date.

As to the application of the residence nil rate band provisions concerning conditional exemption in circumstances involving downsizing, see **15.75.**

Chapter 16

Pre-owned assets

SIGNPOSTS

- **POAT on land, chattels and intangible property** – The scope of the POAT legislation can be very wide as illustrated in various examples (see **16.3–16.11**).
- **POAT 'plugged' a loop hole in the GWR legislation** (see **Chapter 5**) – The provisions can trace through cash (see **16.13**).
- **Calculation of POAT on land, chattels and intangible property** – A complex formula is applied to calculate the charge (see **16.14–16.17**).
- **Excluded transactions** – A number of transactions in relation to land and chattels are excluded. Excluded transactions have no application to intangible property (see **16.18**).
- **Exemptions** – There are a number of exemptions from POAT arising on land, chattels and intangible property (see **16.19–16.26**).
- **Opting out of POAT** – Procedural issues (see **16.27–16.28**).
- **Remedial action in relation to existing arrangements** – A tax analysis of unscrambling an arrangement which is subject to POAT (see **16.29**).

INTRODUCTION

16.1 The *Finance Act 2004* (*s 84* and *Sch 15*) introduced a charge to tax which draws on a combination of income tax and inheritance tax rules.

Ever since the introduction of the gift with reservation (GWR) rules in 1986 (see **Chapter 5**), tax advisers have been devising schemes by which individuals could make gifts of property without being caught by the reservation of benefit rules, while at the same time continuing to enjoy the property given away. The pre-owned assets (POAT) legislation has primarily targeted artificial inheritance tax avoidance schemes, as outlined below, but some more 'innocent' arrangements are also now caught. The schemes (see **5.10**ff for an illustration of the various schemes) initially targeted are as follows:

- Lease carve-out schemes (*Ingram* schemes) following the case *of Ingram (Executors of Lady Ingram's Estate) v IRC* [2000] 1 AC 293.
- Settlements on interest in possession trusts (*Eversden* schemes) following the case of *IRC v Eversden (executors of Greenstock, decd)* [2003] EWCA Civ 668, [2003] STC 822.
- Reversionary lease schemes.
- 'Double trust' or 'Lifetime debt' schemes.

Focus

- HMRC stated that they are challenging home loan and double trust schemes and now contends that none of the schemes work.
- HMRC now considers that any home loans scheme fails to mitigate IHT. However a test case was settled in favour of the taxpayer as HMRC accepted that the taxpayer had acted in reliance on the Guidance at the time.
- HMRC now states that 'Where there has been an enquiry into the POA charge and HMRC has accepted that the charge applies, either in the figures returned or after adjustment, HMRC may not revisit the position on death'.
- If there has been no such POAT enquiry, HMRC have indicated that the scheme was ineffective.
- HMRC advises executors to contact them if an estate involves a home loan arrangement. HMRC will provide a figure for executors to make payment on account for a potential IHT liability.

It is very rare indeed to see entries on personal tax returns relating to the tax, suggesting that:

- people have unscrambled offensive transactions; or
- the values involved are covered by the *de minimis* rules; or
- most likely people do not realise that the transactions that were entered into offend the rules; or
- the transactions entered into did not achieve their tax objective and were caught by the gift with reservation rules.

Perhaps it is too early to assess the impact of the POAT rules, which will be seen more clearly when taxpayers die who in their lifetimes have tried to circumvent the GWR rules.

However it seems to be clear that any arrangement which circumvents the GWR rules is likely to be challenged by HMRC.

16.2 The pre-owned asset tax is not a charge to inheritance tax. The regime imposes an income tax charge on the use of capital based on:

- the benefit an individual enjoys from the occupation of land or the possession or use of chattels which they once owned, or which they assisted other persons to acquire; and
- their deemed power to enjoy intangible property in certain settlor-interested settlements.

The pre-owned asset tax can be charged on the use of:

- land;
- chattels; and
- intangible assets.

The legislation provides that certain transactions are excluded (see **16.18** below) and there are a number of exemptions (see **16.19**ff below). It also gives the option to elect out of the pre-owned assets charge arising (as discussed in **16.27**ff below). All references in this chapter are to *FA 2004*, unless otherwise stated.

HMRC, on their website provide useful guidance on how the pre-owned asset charge is assessed.

THE PRE-OWNED ASSETS CHARGE ON LAND

16.3 A charge to income tax may arise when an individual:

- occupies any land, whether alone or together with other persons; and
- either the 'disposal condition' or the 'contribution condition' is met in respect of that land (*Sch 15, para 3(1)*).

Unfortunately, the term 'occupation' is not defined within the legislation. HMRC's Technical Guidance provides the following, rather vague, explanation (see IHTM44003):

> 'The meaning of the word "occupies" should be taken quite widely. It goes wider than the chargeable person being physically present at the property

concerned. Case law suggests that the word "occupy" requires some element of control. So a visitor may not be in occupation (even someone who stays for an extended period of time due to illness) but someone who has a key and can freely enter and leave premises as they please is more likely to be in occupation; even if they are absent for significant periods. It does not mean the place you reside which implies a greater level of permanence so a lower threshold is required to satisfy the occupation condition.'

Each case is likely to be decided on the facts and the particular circumstances relating to it. However, in line with HMRC's Interpretation of inheritance tax and gifts with reservation (RI 55 (November 1993)) – the list of examples which excludes the pre-owned assets charge on a *de minimis* basis can be found in **5.28**.

16.4 Examples of more significant use of the property which may bring the chargeable person within the scope of *Sch 15, para 3* are as follows:

- a house in which the chargeable person stays most weekends or for more than a month each year;
- a second home or holiday home which the chargeable person and the owner both then use on an occasional basis;
- a house with a library in which the chargeable person continues to keep their own books, or which they use on a regular basis, for example because it is necessary for their work.

An exemption from a pre-owned assets charge may apply if the property in question is treated for inheritance tax purposes as being subject to the gift with reservation rules (see **16.21**).

16.5 In addition to the 'occupation' condition, the 'disposal condition' or the 'contribution condition' has to be satisfied for the pre-owned asset charge to apply.

The 'disposal condition' (in *para 3(2)*) in relation to any land is that:

- at any time after 17 March 1986 the individual owned an interest in the relevant land; or
- in other property, the proceeds of the disposal of which were (directly or indirectly) applied by another person towards the acquisition of an interest in the relevant land; and
- the individual has disposed of all, or part of, his interest in the relevant land or the other property, otherwise than by an excluded transaction (see **16.18** below).

16.6 The 'contribution condition' (in *para 3(3)*) in relation to any land is that:

- at any time after 17 March 1986 the individual has directly or indirectly provided, otherwise than by an excluded transaction, any of the consideration given by another person for the acquisition of:
  - an interest in the relevant land; or
  - an interest in any other property the proceeds of the disposal of which were (directly or indirectly) applied by another person towards the acquisition of an interest in the relevant land.

HMRC confirm in IHTM44005 that the contribution condition is not met where a lender resides in property purchased by another with money loaned to him by the lender (even if the loan was interest free), as the outstanding debt remains part of the lender's estate for IHT.

Whether the pre-owned asset charge applies can best be illustrated by a number of examples. Some of the examples below, while prima facie being caught by the charge, may escape a charge to income tax due to one of the exemptions listed at **16.19**ff below.

Example 16.1—No POAT charge: father moves in with donee son

Mr Jones gifts one of his three properties to his son. After later having been widowed, Mr Jones moves in to live with his son. While the disposal condition is met, Mr Jones is likely to escape a charge to income tax as (by virtue of *para 11(5)(a)*) the property will be subject to a gift of reservation for inheritance tax purposes. For exemptions, see **16.19**ff; see also **Example 16.15**.

Example 16.2—POAT and IHT: sale at an undervalue

Mrs Smith required funds to renovate her property. She considered a number of commercial options but then decided to sell a half-share in the property to her son for £100,000. The market value of the half-share is £300,000. Mrs Smith continues to live in the house.

The disposal condition is met and Mrs Smith may face an income tax charge on the £100,000 cash. However, as she will have reserved a benefit in two-thirds of the half share, she is likely to escape a charge to income tax on that share, as it will be subject to the gift with reservation rules.

Example 16.3—Link with property broken

Mrs Williams owned a number of investments which she gave to her daughter, who subsequently sold them and used the proceeds to extend her existing house, adding a 'granny flat' in which Mrs Williams now lives.

Neither the disposal condition nor the contribution condition is satisfied, because the proceeds of the sale of the shares were applied by the daughter in improving her existing property and not in acquiring an interest in land.

Example 16.4—Contribution condition: funding of residence

In 2010, Mr Smith gifts his son £300,000, which in 2015 he uses the funds to buy a house where Mr Smith now lives with him.

The contribution condition is met and Mr Smith may face an income tax charge. The gifts with reservation rules do not apply, as they do not trace through gifts of cash (see **16.12**).

Example 16.5—Contribution condition: change of circumstances

Mr White decided to move to Spain and after he sold his property in Scotland, he gave his daughter £200,000. She used this money to purchase a property. Mr White now finds that the heat in Spain in summer is too much for his health and he therefore stays with his daughter for three months of each year.

The contribution condition is met during each period of occupation and it will be a question of fact whether he will be seen to be in occupation during the remaining nine months. If, for example, he has a room set aside for him for the rest of the year, he will be seen as in occupation for the whole year and Mr White's occupation may be subject to income tax.

THE PRE-OWNED ASSETS CHARGE ON CHATTELS

16.7 The pre-owned assets charge on chattels (*Sch 15, para* 6) is similar to that on land. Therefore, a charge to income tax may arise on an individual where:

- the individual is in 'possession' of, or has the 'use' of, a chattel, whether alone or together with other persons; and
- either the 'disposal condition' or the 'contribution condition' is met in respect of the chattel.

16.8 The terms 'possession' and 'use' are not defined in *FA 2004* and HMRC's Technical Guidance is vague (see IHTM44006):

> 'Very limited or occasional use of the chattel in question will not incur an income tax charge under this schedule.'

In line with the GWR legislation the example of a car used to give occasional lifts (ie less than three times a month) to the chargeable person will not be liable to the charge. But if the chargeable person is taken to work every day in the car it is likely an income tax charge will be incurred.

16.9 The expression 'chattel' is defined for the purpose of *Sch 15* (at *para 1*) and includes any tangible movable property other than money.

The 'disposal condition' (in *para 6(2)*) in relation to any chattels is that:

- at any time after 17 March 1986 the individual owned the chattel; or
- any other property, the proceeds of the disposal of which were (directly or indirectly) applied by another person towards the acquisition of the chattel; and
- the individual has disposed of all, or part of, the chattel or the other property, otherwise than by an excluded transaction (see **16.18** below).

16.10 The 'contribution condition' (in *para 6(3)*) in relation to any chattel is that at any time after 17 March 1986 the individual has directly or indirectly provided, otherwise than by an excluded transaction, any of the consideration given by another person for the acquisition of:

- the chattel; or
- an interest in any other property the proceeds of the disposal of which were (directly or indirectly) applied by another person towards the acquisition of the chattel.

16.11 Some of the examples below, while prima facie being caught by the charge, may escape a charge to income tax due to one of the exemptions listed at **16.19**ff below.

Example 16.6—Exemption from charge: retained painting

Mr Smith gives a valuable painting to his daughter, but he keeps the painting hanging on display in his own house for safekeeping and to meet insurance requirements.

The disposal condition is met, but (by virtue of *para 11(5)(a)*) Mr Smith is likely to escape an income tax charge, as the gift is subject to the gift with reservation rules.

Example 16.7—Possession of chattels: costly storage arrangements

Mrs Jones gifted a flat to her son. He sold it in 2006 for £500,000. He purchased another flat for £350,000 and with the remaining £150,000 he purchased several pieces of art. The son is now working abroad and let his flat. All his possessions are in storage apart from the valuable paintings, which are temporarily displayed in his mother's house. As the mother is 'enjoying' the chattels, she may now face an income tax charge. The gift with reservation rules do not apply.

Example 16.8—Contribution condition: shared campervan

Mr Williams gave his daughter cash of £100,000, which, in 2007, she used towards the purchase price of a £50,000 motor home. Mr Williams borrows the motor home for long holidays.

The contribution condition is met during each period of its use and Mr Williams may face an income tax charge.

PRE-OWNED ASSETS CHARGE ON INTANGIBLE PROPERTY COMPRISED IN SETTLOR-INTERESTED SETTLEMENTS

16.12 The pre-owned assets charge on intangible property (*Sch 15, para* 8) is drafted in different terms from the charges on land and chattels.

The charge arises, when all the following elements exist:

- a person has settled any property (not necessarily intangible property); and
- the terms of the settlement, as they affect any property comprised in the settlement, are such that any income arising from the property would be treated by virtue of *ITTOIA 2005, s 624* as settlor-interested; and
- such income would be so treated even if *ITTOIA 2005, s 625(1)* ('Settlor's retained interest') did not include any reference to the spouse/ civil partner of the settlor; and
- that property includes any intangible property which is or represents property which the chargeable person settled, or added to the settlement, after 17 March 1986.

For the pre-owned assets charge on intangible property to apply, it is only necessary that the above elements exist. There is no need for the individual to benefit from the intangible property in question, and no need for that intangible property to produce any actual income.

A charge under *para 8* is not triggered where *ITTOIA 2005, s 624* only applies because the settlor's spouse rather than the settlor has retained an interest within *s 625*. However if, for example, the settlor sets up a trust where his wife receives the income but he can benefit if she dies, an income tax charge may potentially apply subject to any relevant exemptions.

The expression 'intangible property' is defined for the purposes of *Sch 15* (at *para 1*) as meaning any property other than chattels or interests in land. Therefore most investments are caught, and it also includes money. The pre-owned assets charge on intangible property does not apply to any land or chattels included in a settlement.

The intangible charge does not apply to intangibles which are owned by a company which is in turn owned by a trust. However the shares of the underlying company are caught by the POAT charge.

None of the 'excluded transactions' provisions (see **16.18**) apply in relation to intangible property, but all of the exemptions (see **16.19**ff) potentially apply.

SCOPE OF THE PRE-OWNED ASSETS LEGISLATION

16.13 The pre-owned assets legislation is drafted in much wider terms than the gift with reservation (GWR) rules (see **Chapter 5**). For example, for inheritance tax purposes, an absolute gift of cash is not subject to the GWR rules. In contrast, for pre-owned assets purposes, tracing through cash is permissible when determining whether proceeds on disposal have been applied or consideration has been provided in respect of land or chattels, for a period of up to seven years (*Sch 15, para 10(2)(c)*).

The use of the expression 'directly or indirectly' in the contribution condition extends the scope of this provision to cover circumstances where an individual routes a gift indirectly through a third party. However, it is considered that a contribution can only be traced through a third party where that party is obliged, or expected to pass this gift on.

Example 16.9—Cash gift: no trace of the money

A grandfather gifts £300,000 to each of his two sons. One of the sons is well off and decides to pass his share to his daughter, who subsequently buys a property with these funds. The grandfather, who in the interim was widowed, moves into the property with his granddaughter.

Although the gift of £300,000 was used in purchasing the property, the grandfather is likely to escape a charge to income tax. However, if there was an agreement or understanding between the grandfather and his son, that he would pass the gift of money on to his daughter, the contribution condition is likely to be met and the grandfather may face a charge to tax.

CALCULATION OF TAX CHARGE IN RELATION TO LAND

16.14 In relation to land, income tax will be charged on the 'rental value' less the amount of certain allowable payments made by the taxpayer in respect of their occupation of the relevant land. The 'appropriate rental value' is based on a hypothetical letting from year to year where the tenant undertakes to pay all taxes, rates and charges usually paid by a tenant, and the landlord undertakes to pay for repairs, insurance and any other necessary maintenance. Where the taxpayer occupies the property for less than a year, the rental value is applied pro rata and the income tax charge is adjusted accordingly.

HMRC's Technical Guidance does not indicate whether (and, if so, how) the appropriate rental value may be reduced to reflect any limitations or restrictions on the taxpayer's occupation of the land. For example, where the relevant land is a holiday home that is available for occupation by the taxpayer and by other persons and occasional use is made of it by the taxpayer and by others, it is unclear what adjustments can be made to the appropriate rental value to reflect any periods of non-use or shared use by the taxpayer.

The 'appropriate rental value' is defined as such proportion of the rental value (R) as is found by the following formula (*Sch 15, para 4*):

$$R \times \frac{DV}{V}$$

R is the rental value of the relevant land for the taxable period;

V is the value of the relevant land at the valuation date; and

DV can assume a variety of different values, as follows:

- where the disposal condition is met and the taxpayer owned an interest in the relevant land, DV is the value at the valuation date of the interest in the relevant land disposed of by the taxpayer; or
- where the disposal condition is met and the taxpayer owned an interest in replaced property, DV is such part of the value of the relevant land at the valuation date as can reasonably be attributed to the property originally disposed of by the taxpayer;
- where the contribution condition is met, DV is such part of the value of the relevant land at the valuation date as can reasonably be attributed to the consideration provided by the taxpayer.

In calculating the chargeable amount, certain payments made in respect of the occupation of the land may be deducted. These are payments which, in pursuance of any legal obligation, are made by the taxpayer to the owner of the land in respect of the occupation by the chargeable person.

Example 16.10—Calculation of POAT on land: moving in with daughter

Mr Jones gifts his daughter £500,000 to purchase a property. He subsequently moves in and now lives there with his daughter. He has use of the whole house. He pays his daughter £50 per week to cover expenses. The contribution condition has been met and (subject to any exclusions or exemptions, which are discussed below) the question now arises how to assess the 'appropriate rental value'. The value of the house is £600,000. The rental value is £18,000. The payments made by Mr Jones do not qualify for deduction as they are not made in relation to rental payments and also are not made under a legal obligation.

If Mr Jones had paid the £50 each week as rental payments following a legal obligation, they would be deductible from the rental value.

Mr Jones will pay income tax on £18,000 at his marginal tax rate. Therefore, if he is a 40% taxpayer, the pre-owned asset charge will cost him £7,200 per annum.

In contrast, if the house had included a self-contained annexe and he only occasionally visited the main house, eg for Sunday lunch, the income tax charge would have been assessed on the 'appropriate rental value' of the annexe rather than the whole house.

CALCULATION OF TAX CHARGE IN RELATION TO CHATTELS

16.15 In relation to chattels, income tax will be charged on the 'appropriate amount' less the amount of certain allowable payments made by the taxpayer in respect of his possession or use of the chattel.

In contrast to the pre-owned assets charge on land, which is based on rental value, the charge on a chattel is based on the notional amount of interest that would be payable for the taxable period if interest were payable at the 'prescribed rate' on an amount equal to the value of the chattel at the valuation date. Therefore, the fact that the donor is paying a market rent for the use of the chattel, does not necessarily prevent a charge to income tax.

The 'prescribed rate' of interest is set by regulations and is equal to 'the official rate of interest' as defined for the purposes of taxable benefits on taxable cheap loans (see the *Charge to Income Tax by Reference to Enjoyment of Property Previously Owned Regulations, SI 2005/724, reg 3*). The official rate of interest is defined by *ITEPA 2003, s 181*. On 1 March 2009 it decreased from 6.25% to 4.75%, with a further decrease to 4% from 6 April 2010. For 2012/13 the rate remained at 4%, and reduced to 3% for 2015/16 and 2016/17.

The 'appropriate amount' is found by multiplying the prescribed interest (N) for the taxable period by the fraction as follows (*Sch 15, para 7*):

$$N \times \frac{DV}{V}$$

N is the notional interest for the taxable period, at the prescribed rate, on the value of the chattel at the valuation date;

V is the value of the chattel at the valuation date; and

DV can assume a variety of different values, as follows:

- where the disposal condition is met and the taxpayer owned an interest in the chattel, DV is the value at the valuation date of the interest in the chattel disposed of by the taxpayer; or
- where the disposal condition is met and the taxpayer owned an interest in replaced property, DV is such part of the value of the chattel at the valuation date as can reasonably be attributed to the property originally disposed of by the taxpayer;
- where the contribution condition is met, DV is such part of the value of the chattel at the valuation date as can reasonably be attributed to the consideration provided by the taxpayer.

In calculating the chargeable amount, certain payments made in respect of the possession or use of the chattel may be deducted. These are payments which, in pursuance of any legal obligation, are made by the taxpayer to the owner of the chattel in respect of the possession or use of the chattel by the chargeable person (*Sch 15, para 7(1)*).

Example 16.11—Calculation of POAT on chattels: gift and leaseback

The following example is contained in HMRC's guidance notes IHTM 44018.

Hermione gives away a sculpture subject to a lease over it in her favour. The POA charge first applies to Hermione on 6 April 2005 when open market value of the sculpture is £600,000 and the value subject to the lease is £400,000. The official rate is 5%, so the value for N is £30,000. The appropriate amount is therefore

30,000 × (400,000 ÷ 600,000) = £20,000.

This will be the amount subject to the POA charge for Hermione in tax year 2005/06. The values for the sculpture will remain the same in the next four tax years, although the amount subject to the POA charge will vary in line with changes to the official rate; so for tax year 2009/10, the POA charge will be £19,000. The valuation process will need to be repeated again on 6 April 2010 to establish the capital values to use for the next five tax years.

If Hermione had been paying a rent of £5,000 for the use of the sculpture, the amount subject to the POA charge would be reduced for 2005/06 to £15,000.

CALCULATION OF TAX CHARGE IN RELATION TO INTANGIBLE PROPERTY

16.16 In relation to intangible property, the 'chargeable amount' is broadly as follows (*Sch 15, para 9*):

N minus T

Where:

N Is the 'prescribed interest'

T Is the 'tax allowance'

The 'prescribed interest' is the amount of interest that would be payable for the taxable period if interest were payable at the prescribed rate on an amount equal to the value of the relevant property at the valuation date. The 'prescribed rate' is set by regulations and is equal to 'the official rate of interest' as defined for the purposes of taxable benefits on taxable cheap loans, and was reduced to 3% from 6 April 2015.

The 'tax allowance' is the amount of any income tax or capital gains tax payable by the taxpayer in respect of the taxable period by virtue of any of a number of specified provisions, so far as the tax is attributable to the relevant property. The provisions in question are *ITTOIA 2005, ss 461, 624*, *ITA 2007, ss 720–730*, and *TCGA 1992, ss 77* (although this section was repealed from 2008/09), *86*.

In contrast to the computation of the pre-owned assets charges relating to land and chattels, there is no provision for the deduction of any allowable payments made by the taxpayer in respect of his enjoyment or potential enjoyment of the intangible property.

Example 16.12—Calculation of POAT on intangibles

The following example is contained in HMRC's guidance notes IHTM44025, but amended to reflect current tax rates

Andrew is the UK resident and domiciled settlor of a non-resident settlor interested settlement. The settled property does not form part of his estate nor has he reserved a benefit in the settled property. The settlement comprises 'intangible' property of cash and shares with a value of £1,500,000 at the valuation date.

In the tax year 2016/17 the trustees receive income of £20,000 which is chargeable to income tax on the trustees, but Andrew also will need to report this income under *ITTOIA 2005, s 624*. A further £150,000 capital gains on the sale of shares are realised which are deemed to be Andrew's gains by virtue of *TCGA 1992, s 86*.

Income tax of £9,000 (£20,000 × 45%) and CGT of £30,000 (£150,000 × 20%) becomes payable. As Andrew is a higher rate taxpayer, he can reclaim some of the tax paid by the trustees (5%) ie the difference between 40% and 45% tax rate – hence £1,000. This sum will have to be repaid to the trustees. The tax allowance (T) against the potential charge under *FA 2004, Sch 15, para 8* is therefore £38,000. (£30,000 + (£9,000 – £1,000)).

The chargeable amount (N) is 3% (the prescribed rate from 6 April 2015) × £1,500,000 = £45,000, so the tax charge under *FA 2004, Sch 15, para 8* will be £7,000 (£45,000 less £38,000).

VALUATION PROBLEMS

16.17 For the purposes of the pre-owned asset charge, the value of any property is broadly the price which the property might reasonably be expected to fetch if sold in the open market at that time (*Sch 15, para 15*); this reflects the 'market value' provision for inheritance tax purposes (*IHTA 1984, s 160*).

In relation to any land, chattel or intangible property, the 'valuation date' is prescribed by regulations (*Charge to Income Tax by Reference to Enjoyment of Property Previously Owned Regulations, SI 2005/724*) and is 6 April in the relevant year of assessment or, if later, the first day of the 'taxable period'. The regulations dispense with annual valuations but instead require a new valuation on the 'five-year anniversary' of the previous valuation.

A new valuation may be required when the value of the retained benefit is reduced, for example, because the taxpayer moved into a smaller property.

The second fifth anniversary of the implementation of POAT charge passed on 6 April 2015, therefore taxpayers who have been subject to POAT will need to obtain relevant capital or rental values as of 6 April 2015. If any adjustments to the payment of income tax need to be made, the deadline will be 31 January 2017.

EXCLUDED TRANSACTIONS

16.18 The concept of excluded transactions has no application to intangible property. The provisions only serve to exclude certain transactions in relation to land and chattels from the income tax charge.

Schedule 15, para 10 includes different provisions for the 'disposal' condition and 'contribution' condition in relation to interest in possession trusts for the spouse/civil partner, as outlined below:

- Disposals of entire interests to unconnected third parties at arm's length are excluded transactions.
- Disposals of entire interests to connected parties at arm's length are excluded transactions, if the transaction is such as might be expected at arm's length between unconnected parties.
- An inter-spouse/civil partner disposal remains an excluded transaction in relation to the original donor, even if it is followed by an onward disposal to a third party.
- A disposal by virtue of which the property became settled property in which his spouse/civil partner or former spouse/civil partner is beneficially entitled to an interest in possession, and that interest in possession has not come to an end *except* on the death of the spouse/civil partner or former spouse/civil partner. In relation to the disposal condition, it is stipulated that the disposal has to be a gift, while under the contribution condition it is only required that the property become settled on acquisition.
- A disposition falling within the inheritance tax exemption available in respect of dispositions for the maintenance of family members (*IHTA 1984, s 11*).
- The provision by a person of consideration for another's acquisition of land or chattels is an excluded transaction if it constituted an outright gift of money by the individual to the other person and was made at least seven years before the earliest date on which either the individual occupies the land or, in the case of chattels, the individual is in possession of, or has the use of the chattel.
- It is an outright gift to an individual and is wholly exempt by virtue of either the inheritance tax annual exemption (*s 19*) or the inheritance tax small gifts exemption (*s 20*).

Note that there is no exclusion from the pre-owned assets regime for gifts that are exempt from inheritance tax under the provisions relating to normal expenditure gifts out of income, or gifts in consideration of marriage.

Example 16.13—Equity release: daughter moves in

In 2011 Mr Miller sold a half-share of his property to his daughter Alice at full market value. This is not a transfer of value for inheritance tax purposes. The transaction however is a disposal under *para 3(2)*, but does not qualify as an excluded transaction under *para 10*. According to HMRC guidance Mr Miller's occupation of the half-share would be subject to an income tax charge if the appropriate rental value exceeds the *de minimis* limit.

If he had sold all his interest, the transaction would have been excluded from the pre-owned asset charge. However, see below regarding the full consideration exemption in **16.23** and reference to the gift with reservation exemption following *FA 1986, s 102B(4)* (see **16.22**).

As to the equity release exemption and its limitations, see **16.24**.

Example 16.14—Excluded transaction: gift of cash

In 2004, Mrs Smith gave her daughter £500,000, which the daughter uses to purchase a property. In 2014, the mother moves into the property.

As Mrs Smith's commencement of her occupation occurred more than seven years after the gift was made, this will be an excluded transaction (*para 10(2)(c)*).

EXEMPTIONS

16.19 There are a number of exemptions (in *Sch 15, paras 11, 12* and *13*) from the pre-owned assets charge otherwise arising on land, chattels or intangible property:

- exemption for property that is in the taxpayer's estate for inheritance tax purposes;
- exemption for property that is deemed to be in the taxpayer's estate under the gift with reservation of benefit (GWR) provisions;
- property that escapes the GWR provisions by virtue of certain specified inheritance tax exemptions or reliefs;
- property covered by certain equity release arrangements defined in regulations; and
- certain *de minimis* amounts.

Exemption for property in the taxpayer's estate

16.20 There is no pre-owned assets charge on land, chattels or intangible property where the taxpayer's estate for inheritance tax purposes includes the following (*Sch 15, para 11(1)*):

- the relevant property; or
- other property which derives its value from the relevant property and whose value, so far as attributable to the relevant property, is not substantially less than the relevant property.

This exemption recognises that the pre-owned assets charge should not penalise taxpayers in respect of their enjoyment of property that is still included in their estate for inheritance tax purposes.

Exemption where the gift with reservation rules apply

16.21 There is no pre-owned assets charge on land, chattels or intangible property where the 'gift with reservation' (GWR) provisions apply for IHT (see *Sch 15, para 11(5)*), or would apply but for certain specified provisions, to:

- the relevant property; or
- other property which derives its value from the relevant property and whose value, so far as attributable to the relevant property, is not substantially less than the relevant property.

This exemption for property that falls within the GWR provisions is fundamental to the concept of the pre-owned assets charge, and recognises that the charge should not penalise taxpayers in respect of their enjoyment of property that is still deemed to be included in their estate under the GWR provisions, or would be deemed to be so included but for certain specific inheritance tax exemptions.

16.22 See **Chapter 5** for discussion on when property is subject to the GWR rules. The GWR exemption from the pre-owned assets charge extends to property subject to the GWR rules, and property that would have been subject to the GWR rules but for certain specified provisions contained in *Sch 15, para 11(5)*:

- Any of the exemptions in *FA 1986, s 102(5)(d)–(i)*, which cover certain cases where disposal by way of gift is an exempt transfer for inheritance tax purposes. This includes gifts to charities, gifts to political parties, gifts to housing associations, gifts for national purposes, maintenance funds for historic buildings and employee trusts (see **Chapter 9**).
- *FA 1986, s 102B(4)*, which deals with gifts with reservation (share of interest in land). This relief from inheritance tax was introduced with

effect from 9 March 1999; it applies where an individual disposes by way of gift of an undivided share of an interest in land, which is then occupied by donor and donee without the donor receiving any benefit, other than a negligible one, provided by or at the expense of the donee for some reason connected with the gift.

- *FA 1986, s 102C(3)* provides that in applying *FA 1986, ss 102A* and 102*B*, no account is to be taken of a donor's occupation of land in circumstances where that occupation would be disregarded in accordance with *FA 1986, Sch 20, para 6(1)(b)*. It allows occupation by the donor to be disregarded where:
  - it arises from an unforeseen change in circumstances; and
  - it arises when the donor has become unable to maintain himself through old age, infirmity or otherwise; and
  - it represents reasonable provision by the donee for the care and maintenance of the donor; and
  - the donee is a relative of the donor or his spouse/civil partner.

Example 16.15—POAT exemption: illness intervening (see Example 16.1)

Mr Jones gives his son £300,000 to purchase a property. After having been widowed, Mr Jones moves in to live with his son. The contribution condition is met and Mr Jones may face a charge to income tax.

Assuming Mr Jones moves in because he became unable to maintain himself through age or infirmity and the occupation represents reasonable provision by his son for his father's care and maintenance, Mr Jones will escape a charge to income tax, as well as an inheritance tax charge under the GWR rules. This is provided by *Sch 15, para 11(5)(d)* and *FA 1986, s 102C(3)*.

Exemption – Foreign element

16.23 The pre-owned asset charge does not apply in relation to any person for any year of assessment during which he or she is not resident in the UK for the purposes of income tax (*Sch 15, para 12*).

Where a person is resident, but not domiciled, in the UK the pre-owned asset charge does not apply to him unless the land, chattel or intangible property in respect of which the charge arises is situated in the UK.

The deemed domicile rules of *s 267* (see **Chapter 1**) have seemingly been imported for the purposes of the income tax charge on pre-owned assets. Whilst not specifically stated in the legislation, a person is regarded as domiciled in the UK if he or she would be treated as such under *IHTA 1984*.

Under *IHTA 1984, s 48*, settled property that is not situated in the UK is excluded from a charge to IHT if the settlor was non-UK domiciled when the settlement was made. Holdings in authorised unit trusts and open-ended investment companies (OEICs) are also excluded from IHT despite being situated in the UK.

However POAT still applies to holdings in authorised unit trusts and OEICs situated in the UK. The settlor, despite being non-UK domiciled and the settlement being an excluded settlement under *s 48*, therefore is subject to an income charge on the value of any such holdings unless he or she makes an election for IHT to opt into the gift with reservation rules.

Example 16.16—Not UK resident

See **Example 16.4** – Mr Smith has been paying POAT since moving into the property. However in March 2015 he decides to move to Spain and the property is let. As Mr Smith is not resident in the UK for tax purposes during 2016/17, he will not be liable to the POAT charge. He will be subject to POAT during 2015/16 though.

Example 16.17—Not UK domiciled

Boris a wealthy Bulgarian is resident in the UK, but is non-UK domiciled. He owns a property in France, which he uses for extended periods during spring and summer. The property is owned by an offshore company.

As a non-UK domiciled person Boris will escape POAT on the property. The scenario will have to be revisited when Boris becomes deemed domiciled for IHT during 2016/17.

Focus

- An election treats the property as being subject to a gift with reservation (see **16.27**).
- However as the gift with reservation rules have no application to excluded property settlements, the settlor will escape any IHT liabilities.

Equity release exemption

16.24 Following concerns whether equity release schemes were affected by the pre-owned asset charge, the Treasury used its power to confer further exemptions by regulations (*Charge to Income Tax by Reference to Enjoyment of Property Previously Owned Regulations, SI 2005/724*).

Under this exemption, the pre-owned assets charging provisions on land and chattels do not apply to a person in relation to a disposal of *part* of an interest in any property if:

- the disposal was by a transaction made at arm's length with a person not connected with him; or
- the disposal was by a transaction such as might be expected to be made at arm's length between persons not connected with each other and the disposal was for a consideration not in money or in the form of readily convertible assets; or
- the disposal was made before 7 March 2005 (*SI 2005/724, reg 5*).

Note that this exemption applies to transactions between unconnected persons. It also applies to any disposals on arm's-length terms before 7 March 2005, or disposals from that date in the limited circumstances described above. Sadly, despite representations, the treatment for unconnected parties is not extended to similar transactions within the family, even if on full commercial terms.

De minimis exemption

16.25 An individual will not be chargeable to pre-owned assets in a year of assessment if the aggregate of the amounts specified below in respect of that year do not exceed £5,000 (*Sch 15, para 13*). Those amounts are:

- the appropriate rental value in relation to land (see **16.14** above);
- the appropriate amount in relation to chattels (see **16.15** above); and
- the chargeable amount in relation to intangible assets (see **16.16** above).

> **Focus**
>
> - Note that the amounts to be included in respect of land and chattels are not the chargeable amounts;
> - Instead, they are the sums arrived at before deducting any eligible payments made in respect of occupation, possession or use. A person therefore cannot avoid the tax charge by paying an annual rent to bring him below the £5,000 limit.

16.26 The *de minimis* exemption is available to each individual, and therefore applies independently to husband and wife. When the pre-owned assets provisions were introduced, the then Paymaster General, Dawn Primarolo, explained the effect of the exemption as follows:

> 'With regard to the £5,000 … I would call it a cliff edge effect: essentially, if the value is £5,001, taxation would be paid on the whole £5,001, not just on the £1 excess.'

Example 16.18—*De minimis* exemption: over the limit

Alice gave her daughter £500,000, which she used towards the purchase of a property and towards the purchase of a painting that is displayed in her property. Alice now lives in the property with her daughter, and pays her £50 per week as rent under a legal agreement. The contribution condition applies in respect of the relevant land and the chattel. The appropriate rental value of the land amounts to £5,000, and the appropriate amount in respect of the painting amounts to £1,000.

The aggregate of the amounts is £6,000 which exceeds the *de minimis* exemption of £5,000, therefore Alice must pay the pre-owned assets tax charge. The fact that she pays an annual rent of £2,600 will not help her to bring herself within the *de minimis* exception.

'OPTING OUT' OF THE PRE-OWNED ASSETS CHARGE

16.27 An individual taxpayer facing the pre-owned asset charge has a right to elect that *Sch 15* shall not apply to him during the 'initial year' and subsequent years of assessment by reference to that property or any other property for which it has been substituted (*Sch 15, paras 21–23*).

The opt-out election treats the property as though it were subject to a reservation under the gift with reservation rules, even though there had been no gift. The opt-out provisions dispense with the requirement for there to have been a gift; an election simply invokes the GWR rules as though there had been a gift.

An election to opt out of the pre-owned assets charge in respect of land, chattels, or intangible property, must be made in the prescribed manner. The election must be made on form IHT500. The relevant filing date for the 'opt-out' is 31 January in the year of assessment immediately following the 'initial year' when the pre-owned asset charge arises. The *Finance Act 2007* relaxed this deadline, so that (from 21 March 2007) elections can be accepted at HMRC's discretion that would otherwise be late (*Sch 15, para 23(3)*, as amended).

HMRC will accept a late election in certain circumstances. Examples of what they may accept as 'reasonable' excuses are:

- the election is lost or delayed in the post;
- loss of the chargeable person's financial records or relevant papers;
- serious illness;
- bereavement.

16.28 The pre-owned assets legislation, as originally enacted, created a possibility that, where a valid opt-out election is made and the taxpayer dies within the next seven years, there might be two inheritance tax charges on the same underlying asset value. The government recognised this as a particular risk for taxpayers using 'double trust' schemes, and the regulations introduced a new relief from inheritance tax in such circumstances. The relief ensures that tax is due on only one of these components, whichever gives the larger tax liability (the *Inheritance Tax (Double Charges) Regulations 2005 SI 2005/3441*: see HMRC's Technical Guidance at IHTM44061.

Whether or not to opt out of the pre-owned assets regime in respect of particular property will depend upon the facts in each case, in particular the financial position and life expectancy of the taxpayer. If the taxpayer is elderly with a relatively low life expectancy, he may decide to pay the pre-owned assets charge rather than elect for a full 40% inheritance tax charge on death.

REMEDIAL ACTION IN RELATION TO EXISTING ARRANGEMENTS

16.29 It is unlikely that clients, who have taken appropriate advice, will enter into new arrangements that fall foul of the POAT rules. Any who were caught by those rules in relation to existing structures should long since have taken advice and, if appropriate, remedial action to avoid payment of the pre-owned asset charge. The available options depend on the clients' circumstances and the type of scheme they entered into, but in essence they are as follows:

- Pay the pre-owned asset charge. This will depend upon a number of factors including the age and life expectancy of the chargeable person and any potential inheritance tax, capital gains tax and income tax charges which may become payable when opting for one of the alternatives.
- Pay rent in respect of the occupation of the land or the use of the chattel. As such rent payments have to be paid out of taxed income and are likely also to be taxed in the hands of the recipient, this option may not be very attractive.

- Opt into the gift of reservation legislation, which will make the previous arrangement ineffective for IHT planning, while at the same time, the property will continue to be subject to capital gains tax in the hands of the donee, as there will no uplift in the value of the asset on the donor's death.
- Unwind the arrangements and pass the property or chattel back to the donor. The taxation consequences (including IHT, CGT and in some cases stamp duty land tax) may be prohibitive and each case requires careful consideration. As the donee (whether this may be an individual or in many cases trustees) has to consent to the 'unravelling', this alternative may not be feasible.
- End the benefit, ie cease occupation of the property in question or enjoyment of the chattel. Especially in relation to property this often is not practical as the donor may not have sufficient funds to purchase alternative accommodation.

One feature that may work in favour of the taxpayer is stability in the value of property, both in terms of capital and rental value. Many schemes relating to the family home that were later caught by the POAT were sold to families of moderate wealth. The schemes were often short-term in nature, being entered into by elderly home owners, so might run their course before the quinquennial review of the value of occupation. The review was mentioned at **16.17** and is required by the *Charge to Income Tax by Reference to Enjoyment of Property Previously Owned Regulations 2005, SI 2005/724, reg 4*. Often the value of occupation initially fell below £10,000 and was therefore potentially covered by the *de minimis* charge, if there were two estate owners.

Example 16.19—Property subject to the 'Ingram' scheme

Mr Moore entered into an *Ingram* scheme in January 1999. The value of the property was £500,000. Mr Moore retained a lease in his favour, valued at £200,000 in January 1999 and the property (valued at £275,000) was passed into an accumulation and maintenance trust for the benefit of his grandchildren.

House prices increased in the interim and, on 6 April 2015 (this is the second five-year anniversary since introduction of POAT – see **6.17**), the value of the property was £450,000; the lease interest also was valued at £450,000. The market value of the property interest in possession (ie assuming that it is not subject to the lease carve-out) is £1 million.

The market rent is £1,000 per week (£52,000 per annum).

Mr Moore has a number of options. Mr Moore's financial and personal circumstances have to be considered carefully. For example, if his life expectancy is low, it may be preferable to pay the pre-owned asset charge rather than choosing one of the alternatives. His options were as follows:

1 *Pay the income tax charge*

As Mr Moore retained the leasehold the appropriate rental value is calculated as follows:

$$\text{Market rent} \times \frac{\text{Value of freehold as of 6 April 2015}}{\text{Value of freehold (without leasehold)}}$$

$$£52{,}000 \times \frac{£450{,}000}{£1{,}000{,}000} = £23{,}400$$

As Mr Moore is a 40% taxpayer, he will suffer an annual income tax charge of £9,360.

The lease will remain in Mr Moore's estate for IHT and on his death his estate will face an IHT charge of £180,000 (£450,000 @ 40%), assuming that his nil rate band has been used elsewhere.

If the trustees, after Mr Moore's death, decide to sell the property, they will incur a substantial charge to CGT, as the base cost is only £275,000 and the property over time will increase in value with the diminishing term of the lease.

2 *Pay a market rent to the trustees of the A&M settlement*

The payment of the market rent has to be made subject to a legal obligation and will cost Mr Moore £52,000 per annum. At that level, from 6 April 2015 the trustees of the A&M settlement will have to pay tax of £23,400 (£52,000 @ 45%) (for earlier tax years, the tax charge would depend on the trust tax rate).

Alternatively, the rent could be paid to the trustees following a deed of covenant which would avoid a charge to income tax payable by the trustees under *ITTOIA 2005, s 727.*

The IHT and CGT considerations outlined in option 1 will also have to be considered.

This option has to be considered carefully, as Mr Moore may not have sufficient funds to continue paying rent until his death or until he moves out of the property.

3 *Elect for the property to be charged to IHT*

Mr Moore could opt into the reservation of benefit rules and elect to have the property charged to IHT as an asset of his estate. Assuming that the nil rate band has been exhausted, an IHT charge of £400,000 (£1,000,000 @ 40%) will arise on his death.

In addition to the IHT charge, the trustees of the A&M settlement will suffer a charge to CGT if they decide to sell the property after Mr Moore's death (see option 1 above).

Mr Moore is outside the time limit for an election. In practice, HMRC have discretion (from 21 March 2007) to consider any election that should have been made (by 31 January 2007) to see whether there may be a reasonable excuse for the delay (see **16.27** above).

4 *Unscramble the scheme*

If the trustees of the A&M settlement agree to unscramble the scheme, they will face a substantial charge to CGT when the property passes back to Mr Moore.

The property then will form part of his estate for IHT with a potential charge of £400,000 (£1,000,000 @ 40%).

5 *End the benefit*

Mr Moore could consider moving out of the property, but this will only be a viable option if he has sufficient funds to purchase or rent another property. Any rent received on the property will have to be taxed and, for CGT and IHT considerations, the problems outlined in option 1 remain.

Index

[all references are to paragraph number]

S